I0056260

μC/TCP-IP™

The Embedded Protocol Stack

Christian Légaré

Weston, FL 33326

Micrium Press
1290 Weston Road, Suite 306
Weston, FL 33326
USA
www.Micrium.com

For bulk orders, please contact Micrium Press at: +1 954 217 2036

ISBN: 978-1-935772-06-4
100-uC-TCPIP-Renesas-RX62N-001

To my loving and caring wife, Nicole, our two daughters, Julie Maude and Valérie Michèle and our two grand children, Florence Sara and Olivier Alek. I have always encouraged them to follow their passion, I thank them for their support and comprehension for allowing me to follow mine.

Table of Contents

Part I: μC/TCP-IP: The Embedded Protocol Stack

Part II: µC/TCP-IP and the Renesas YRDKRX62N

Foreword to µC/TCP-IP by Rich Nass

Transmission Control Protocol/Internet Protocol, or more commonly known as TCP/IP. Designers take it for granted and end users have never heard of it, nor do they realize the vital role it plays in their lives. But it's the foundation of every networked device. More specifically, the Internet protocol suite is the set of communications protocols that implement the protocol stack on which the Internet and most commercial networks run. The two protocols within the TCP/IP protocol suite were also the first two networking protocols defined. Most historians will tell you that they were originally developed by the Department of Defense (DoD) in the mid 1970s.

If you follow the correct steps to implement the TCP/IP protocols, you can get past this stage of the design without any holdups. But make one wrong turn, and you could find yourself in some pretty muddy water.

There are lots of places where you can learn the ins and outs of the TCP/IP protocol. One good place is the Embedded Systems Conference (ESC). It was at an ESC quite a few years ago that I first met Christian Legare. Preceding the conference where we met, before I was involved with ESC, Christian raved about how popular his TCP/IP class was.

I decided to check it out Christian's class for myself, and truth be told, he was right, and for good reason. He held the attention of better than 50 engineers for the better part of a day. Not only that, I learned something myself. I fashioned myself as somewhat of a newbie before taking Christian's Embedding TCP/IP class, and was fairly astounded that Christian could teach the class at the differing levels of his students, almost simultaneously. Whether you were a newbie like me, or an expert like some of the other students, Christian held everyone's attention and made sure that every question was asked, answered, and understood.

I was quite pleased to see that Christian has taken a similar approach with this book. In fact, when I first saw the chapters and figures in the book, it all looked vaguely familiar. There is a definite correlation between how Christian teaches his popular class and how he has organized this book. To that I say, "Nice job." If you have a winning formula, stick with it.

It doesn't make a difference whether you're a seasoned pro (or at least think you're a pro), or you're a newbie like I was back when I first met Christian. The book starts off with the basics, explaining what TCP/IP is, why it's important, and why you need to understand it. It goes though the various elements of the protocol in a step-by-step process.

While the book explains the theory behind TCP/IP, that's not it's most useful feature—far from it. Where this book separates itself from similar books is in its ability to explain very complex concepts in a very simple manner.

In the first portion of the book, you'll learn about things like Ethernet technology and device drivers, IP connectivity, client and server architectures, and system network performance. The second portion goes into detail on a commercial product, µC/TCP-IP, which is Micrium's specific version of TCP/IP. It explains the technology through a host of sample applications.

Thank you Christian, for allowing me to precede your simple guide to embedded TCP/IP implementation. And to the readers, I hope you enjoy this book as much as I have.

Rich Nass, Director of Content/Media, EE Times Group

Preface

There are many sources that explain the TCP/IP protocol stack and how TCP/IP protocols work. These sources typically explain the protocol structure and interrelations. On occasion, authors actually provide code on the protocol stack implementation, however, these examples generally target systems with plenty of resources, which is not the case with resource-scarce embedded systems.

Semiconductor manufacturers generally produce microprocessors and microcontrollers for the embedded industry with a ROM/RAM ratio of 8:1 and, in some cases, 4:1. These systems are far from the heavyweight systems capable of running Unix, Linux or Windows since they often have access to kilobytes of code/data space as opposed to the megabytes available in larger environments.

Embedded systems often have real-time requirements that larger operating systems were not designed for. So, when used in an embedded system, a TCP/IP stack must certainly follow TCP/IP specifications, but with a watchful eye towards the resource constraints of the end product. Micrium kept these issues in mind when developing µC/TCP-IP for use in embedded systems. The µC/TCP-IP stack adheres to the same philosophy used for µC/OS-II and µC/OS-III as it pertains to the high quality of its code, its documentation, and ease of use.

It's no wonder that readers of the µC/OS-II and µC/OS-III books have been requesting an equivalent for TCP/IP.

WHAT IS DIFFERENT ABOUT THIS BOOK?

Early on, Micrium defined a set of coding standards, naming conventions and coding rules that allowed us to produce code that is clean, easy to read and maintain. These apply to all products developed at Micrium, and we thus believe that µC/TCP-IP contains the cleanest TCP/IP stack source code in the industry.

µC/TCP-IP is available in library format so you can experiment with a companion evaluation board (see Part II of this book). The full source code is provided to µC/TCP-IP licensees. With the Micrium source code, it is possible to obtain a basic understanding of how this series of complex data communications protocols work.

In this book, we take a practical approach to show you how a TCP/IP stack can be embedded in a product. The book provides multiple examples using µC/TCP-IP when specific topics are covered. Numerous illustrations are provided to help you understand the different concepts covered, as a diagram can often best represent the complexity of a network stack.

WHAT IS µC/TCP-IP?

Micrium was incorporated in 1999 to continue the development and provide support for µC/OS-II and now µC/OS-III, the Real-Time Kernel. The first version of the kernel was released in 1992. Since then, the company has received an ever-increasing number of requests for a TCP/IP stack.

In 2002, Micrium evaluated the TCP/IP stacks that were available to the embedded community. Unfortunately, we couldn't find anything that would properly complement µC/OS-II, concluding that Micrium would need to create a TCP/IP stack from the ground up. This was a huge undertaking and has taken us well over 15 man-years to develop.

The purpose of this huge undertaking was to create the best TCP/IP stack available for embedded applications. µC/TCP-IP is not an academic exercise but a world-class product which is currently used in applications worldwide.

Micrium's µC/TCP-IP assumes the use of a Real-Time Kernel, because a TCP/IP stack is highly event driven. Using a single-threaded environment would not properly satisfy most of the requirements found in resource-limited embedded systems that require TCP/IP. µC/TCP-IP was written in such a way that it would be fairly easy to adapt µC/TCP-IP to just nearly any Real-Time Kernel. Specifically, a file called **`net_os.c`** encapsulates the Application Programming Interface (API) calls allowing it to work equally well with µC/OS-II, µC/OS-III or other kernels.

µC/TCP-IP requires a driver for the network interface to be used in the system. Micrium provides drivers for the most popular Ethernet controllers. However, it is fairly easy to write a network interface controller driver for µC/TCP-IP if one is not available. More information on developing drivers is covered in Chapter 14, "Network Device Drivers" on page 299.

µC/TCP-IP works best on 32-bit CPUs but may be used with high end 16-bit processors, as long as they have sufficient resources.

The footprint of µC/TCP-IP is relatively small considering that it completely implements the essential RFCs (Request For Commnent, the protocol specifications) and supports private and public networks.

WHO IS THE INTENDED AUDIENCE?

Micrium's mission is to provide the best quality software to the embedded community. The use of commercial and industrial grade off-the-shelf software has proven to reduce a project development schedule by an average of three months.

Embedded software or hardware engineers developing a product and looking at using TCP/IP, will find the information they require to configure a TCP/IP stack for connectivity only and/or for performance.

µC/TCP-IP and µC/OS-III are also available as linkable object libraries to be used with the companion evaluation board available with this book.

You will need to contact Micrium to license µC/TCP-IP if you intend on using it in a commercial product. In other words, µC/TCP-IP is a licensed software. It is *not* free.

Students and teachers, however, can use the libraries and the evaluation board for academic purposes.

The embedded software version numbers used for this book are:

μC/TCP-IP	TCP-IP protocol stack	V2.10
μC/DHCPc	DHCP Client	V2.06
μC/HTTPs	HTTP Server	V1.91
μC/OS-III	Real-Time kernel	V3.01.2
μC/CPU	CPU abstraction layer	V1.31
μC/LIB	C library	V1.25

The required linkable libraries to run the examples presented in this book are downloaded from a webpage specifically dedicated to this book. This information is provided in Part II.

For licensed customers that have access to the complete μC/TCP-IP source code, it is always better to get the latest code version. If you are not currently under maintenance, please contact Micrium for update information.

ACKNOWLEDGEMENTS

First and foremost, I'd like to thank my loving and caring wife Nicole for her unconditional support, encouragement, understanding and patience. This book was a major project, and I could not have done it without her.

I also want to thank my long-term friend, colleague and partner, Jean J. Labrosse for his support and direction during this undertaking. Jean's feedback and comments improved this work immensely. It is truly a better result because of his efforts. Jean wrote a few books and often told me how exhausting such a task could be. I only have one thing to answer Jean: Now I know what you mean!

It is also very important to note that a good portion of this book builds on many chapters from the μC/TCP-IP user manual. This user manual was written by Jean J. Labrosse and the engineers who developed μC/TCP-IP. The TCP/IP team also played a huge role in reviewing the book to make sure that all the technical details were accurate.

I want to extend a special thank you to:

- Ian T Johns
- Fabiano Kovalski
- Samuel Richard
- Eric Shufro

A very special thanks to Carolyn Mathas who has done an awesome job editing and reviewing this huge project. Your patience and tenacity are greatly appreciated.

I would also like to thank the many fine people at Micrium who have tested the code, reviewed and formatted the book. In alphabetic order:

- Alexandre Portelance Autotte
- Jim Royal
- Freddy Torres

ABOUT THE AUTHOR

Christian Legare has a Master's degree in Electrical Engineering from the University of Sherbrooke, Quebec, Canada. In his 22 years in the telecom industry, he was involved as an executive in large organizations and start-ups, mainly in engineering and R&D. He was recently in charge of an Internet Protocol (IP) certification program at the International Institute of Telecom (IIT) in Montreal, Canada as their IP systems expert. Mr. Legare joined Micrium, as Vice-President in 2002, where he supervises the development of embedded communication modules, including TCP/IP. His substantial corporate and technical expertise further accelerated the company's rapid growth.

Chapter 1

Introduction

The chapters in this book cover the theory of TCP/IP as applied to embedded systems. The topics include:

- TCP/IP technology
- How TCP/IP is applied to embedded systems via the Micrium µC/TCP-IP protocol stack
- The architecture and design of the µC/TCP-IP stack

There are many elements to consider when employing TCP/IP source code in a product design. Many of the following chapters provide the required information to use Micrium µC/TCP-IP.

HOW THE BOOK IS ORGANIZED

This book consists of two parts. Part I describes TCP/IP and its embedded implementation by Micrium, µC/TCP-IP. It is not tied to any specific CPU or network architecture. Here, you will learn about TCP/IP through µC/TCP-IP. Specifically, Ethernet technology and device drivers, IP connectivity, Client and Server architecture, system network performance, how to use µC/TCP-IP's API, how to configure µC/TCP-IP, and how to port µC/TCP-IP network driver to different network interfaces, are all topics covered.

Part II (beginning on page 797) of this book delivers to the reader the experience of µC/TCP-IP through the use of world-class tools and step-by-step instruction. Ready-to-run µC/TCP-IP projects are provided and explained. The application examples use the evaluation board which is advertised with this book. The tools are all downloadable from the Micrium website for the code and networking tools as explained in Part II.

CONVENTIONS

There are a number of conventions in this book. First, notice that when a specific element in a figure is referenced, the element has a number next to it in parenthesis or in a circle. A description of this element follows the figure and in this case, the letter 'F' followed by the figure number, and then the number in parenthesis. For example, F3-4(2) indicates that this description refers to Figure 3-4 and the element (2) in that figure. This convention also applies to listings (starts with an 'L') and tables (starts with a 'T').

At Micrium, we pride ourselves in having the cleanest code in the industry. Examples of this are seen in this book. Jean Labrosse created and published a coding standard in 1992 that was published in the original µC/OS book. This standard has evolved over the years, but the spirit of the standard has been maintained throughout. The Micrium coding standard is available for download from the Micrium website, www.Micrium.com

One of the conventions used is that all functions, variables, macros and **`#define`** constants are prefixed by **`Net`** (which stands for Network) followed by the acronym of the module (e.g., **`Buf`**), and then the operation performed by the function. For example **`NetBuf_Get()`** indicates that the function belongs to the TCP/IP stack (µC/TCP-IP), that it is part of the Buffer Management services, and specifically that the function performs a **`Get`** operation. This allows all related functions to be grouped together in the reference manual, and makes those services intuitive to use.

CHAPTER CONTENTS

Figure 1-1 shows the layout and flow of Part I of the book. This diagram should be useful to understand the relationship between chapters. The first column on the left indicates chapters that should be read in order to understand µC/TCP-IP's structure. The second column relates to chapters that will help port µC/TCP-IP to different network interfaces. The third column shows chapters that are related to additional services provided by µC/TCP-IP and how to obtain valuable run-time and compile-time statistics from µC/TCP-IP. This is especially useful if developing a stack awareness plug-in for a debugger, or using µC/Probe. The top of the fourth column explains the µC/TCP-IP Application Programming Interface and configuration manuals. The middle of column four is a chapter with all the tips and tricks on configuring µC/TCP-IP. Finally, the bottom of the last column contains the Bibliography and the Licensing policy.

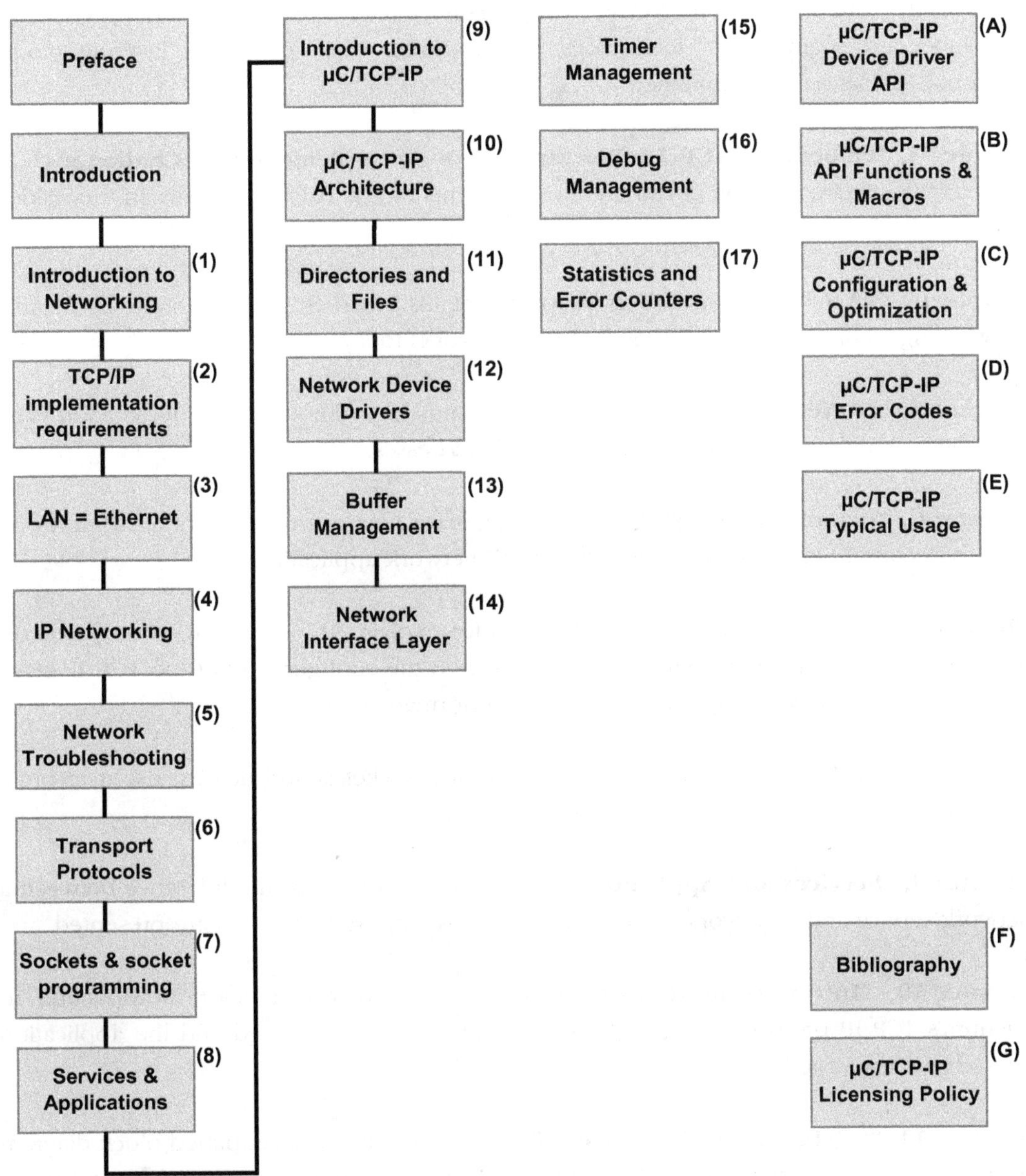
Preface
Introduction
Introduction to Networking
(1)
TCP/IP implementation requirements
(2)
LAN = Ethernet
(3)
IP Networking
(4)
Network Troubleshooting
(5)
Transport Protocols
(6)
Sockets & socket programming
(7)
Services & Applications
(8)
Introduction to µC/TCP-IP
(9)
µC/TCP-IP Architecture
(10)
Directories and Files
(11)
Network Device Drivers
(12)
Buffer Management
(13)
Network Interface Layer
(14)
Timer Management
(15)
Debug Management
(16)
Statistics and Error Counters
(17)
µC/TCP-IP Device Driver API
(A)
µC/TCP-IP API Functions & Macros
(B)
µC/TCP-IP Configuration & Optimization
(C)
µC/TCP-IP Error Codes
(D)
µC/TCP-IP Typical Usage
(E)
Bibliography
(F)
µC/TCP-IP Licensing Policy
(G)

Figure 1-1 **h µC/TCP-IP Book Layout**

Chapter 2, "Introduction to Networking". This chapter explains networking concepts for embedded engineers. IP technology is introduced. The networking layering model concept is presented and explained.

Chapter 3, "Embedding TCP/IP: Working Through Implementation Challenges". In this chapter, understand the constraints for implementing a TCP/IP stack in an embedded system.

Chapter 4, "LAN = Ethernet". This chapter explains Ethernet, the ubiquitous Local Area Networking technology in use in most of our networks today.

Chapter 5, "IP Networking". This chapter explains IP technology, mainly IP addressing and how to configure a network interface for IP addresses.

Chapter 6, "Troubleshooting". In this chapter, learn how to troubleshoot an IP network, how to decode IP packets and how to test an IP network applications.

Chapter 7, "Transport Protocols". This chapter explains the most important protocols used in IP technology. A special attention is given to the configuration of the TCP/IP stack to optimize the embedded system networking performance.

Chapter 8, "Sockets". In this chapter, learn what a socket is and how to use it to build your application.

Chapter 9, "Services and Applications". This chapter explains the difference between a network service and a network application. The most important services are presented.

Chapter 10, "Introduction to µC/TCP-IP". This chapter is a short introduction to Micrium's TCP/IP protocol stack, µC/TCP-IP. Its attributes are covered and the application add-ons are also listed.

Chapter 11, "µC/TCP-IP Architecture". This chapter contains a simplified block diagram of the various different µC/TCP-IP modules and their relationships. The relationships are then explained.

Chapter 12, "Directories and Files". This chapter explains the directory structure and files needed to build a µC/TCP-IP-based application. Learn about the files that are needed, where they should be placed, which module does what, and more.

Chapter 13, "Getting Started with µC/TCP-IP". In this chapter, learn how to properly initialize and start a µC/TCP-IP based application for users that have access to the source code.

Chapter 14, "Network Device Drivers". This chapter explains how to write a device driver for µC/TCP-IP. The configuration structure of the driver is presented.

Chapter 15, "Buffer Management". This chapter is an introduction to one of the most important aspects of a TCP/IP stack, the configuration and management of network buffers.

Chapter 16, "Network Interface Layer". This chapter describes how network interfaces are configured and added to the system.

Chapter 18, "Timer Management". This chapter covers the definition and usage of timers used to keep track of various network-related timeouts. Some protocols like TCP extensively use timers.

Chapter 19, "Debug Management". This chapter contains debug constants and functions that may be used by applications to determine network RAM usage, check run-time network resource usage, or check network error or fault conditions.

Chapter 20, "Statistics and Error Counters". This chapter presents how µC/TCP-IP maintains counters and statistics for a variety of expected, unexpected, and/or error conditions. The chapter also explain how to enable/disable these counters and statistics.

Appendix A, "µC/TCP-IP Device Driver APIs". This appendix provides a reference to the µC/TCP-IP Device Driver API. Each of the user-accessible services re presented in alphabetical order.

Appendix B, "µC/TCP-IP API Reference". This appendix provides a reference to the µC/TCP-IP application programming interfaces (APIs) to functions or macros.

Appendix C, "µC/TCP-IP Configuration and Optimization". In this appendix, learn the µC/TCP-IP `#defines` found in an application's `net_cfg.h` and `app_cfg.h` files. These `#defines` allow configuration at compile time and allow the ROM and RAM footprints of µC/TCP-IP to be adjusted based the application requirements.

Appendix D, "µC/TCP-IP Error Codes". This appendix provides a brief explanation of µC/TCP-IP error codes defined in `net_err.h`.

Appendix E, "µC/TCP-IP Typical Usage". This appendix provides a brief explanation of µC/TCP-IP error codes defined in `net_err.h`.

Appendix F, "Bibliography".

Appendix G, "µC/TCP-IP Licensing Policy" on page 795.

Chapter

2

Introduction to Networking

Networking is a new concept for many embedded engineers. The goal of this book, therefore, is to provide a bridge that spans from basic concepts to how to add networking functionality to an embedded design. This chapter provides a quick introduction to networking protocols and then moves rapidly to a discussion on TCP/IP over Ethernet, today's preferred network technology combo with the widest usage in terms of the number of devices and applications.

Adding connectivity to an embedded system is now increasingly common, and networking options are numerous. While networking platforms include wireless (Bluetooth, ZigBee, 3G Cellular, Wi-Fi, etc…) and wired (TCP/IP over Ethernet, CAN, Modbus, Profinet, etc…), the networking technology that has revolutionized communications is the Internet Protocol (IP).

2-1 NETWORKING

The foundation of communications that we use on a daily basis is the Public Switched Telephone Network (PSTN), a global collection of interconnected public telephone networks. This circuit-switched network was the long standing fixed-line analog telephone system of the past. Today, analog has mostly given way to digital and the network includes both fixed-line telephones and mobile devices.

With PSTN, network resources are dedicated for the duration of the service, typically the length of a phone call. The same can be said for all real-time services such as voice and video. In a real-time service the data transmitted is inherently time sensitive.

In the following diagrams, elements composing the network between two connected devices are often represented as a cloud. Clouds are shown in subsequent diagrams throughout this book.

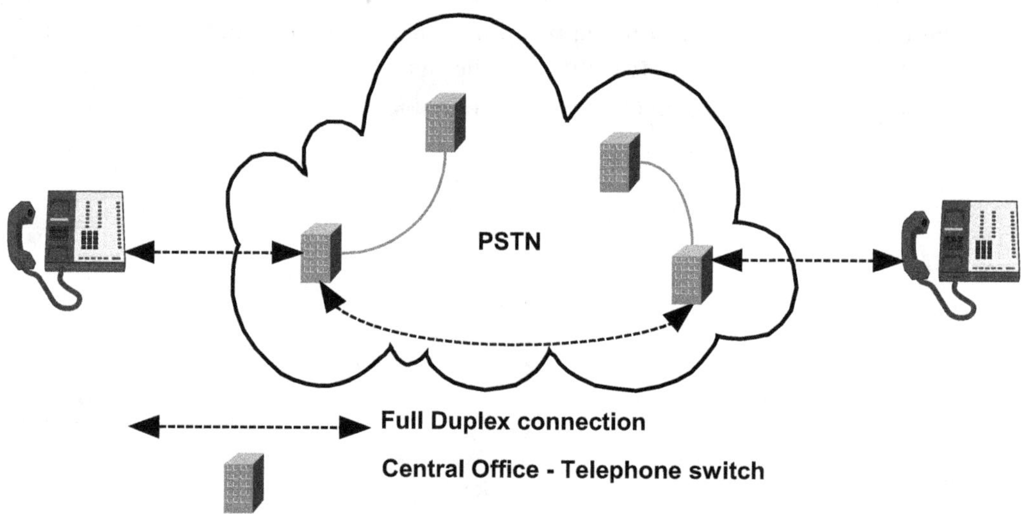

Figure 2-1 **Public Switched Telephone Network (PSTN)**

Figure 2-1 represents a circuit-switched network such as the PSTN. In such a network, elements represented by telephone switches allocate network links between a source and destination, in both directions (full duplex), for the duration of the service. Once the circuit is established, switches do not intervene until it is time to dismantle the circuit (one of the parties hangs up). In this situation, the switches are aware of the connection, however the terminals are not.

With data services, when data is transferred, data is chopped into small entities called packets. Network resources are used only when a packet is transferred between a source and destination. This leads to improved network asset utilization as the same equipment can be used to forward packets between different sources and destinations. A permanent connection is not required since the transfer is not time sensitive. if we receive an e-mail a fraction of a second late, nobody will complain!

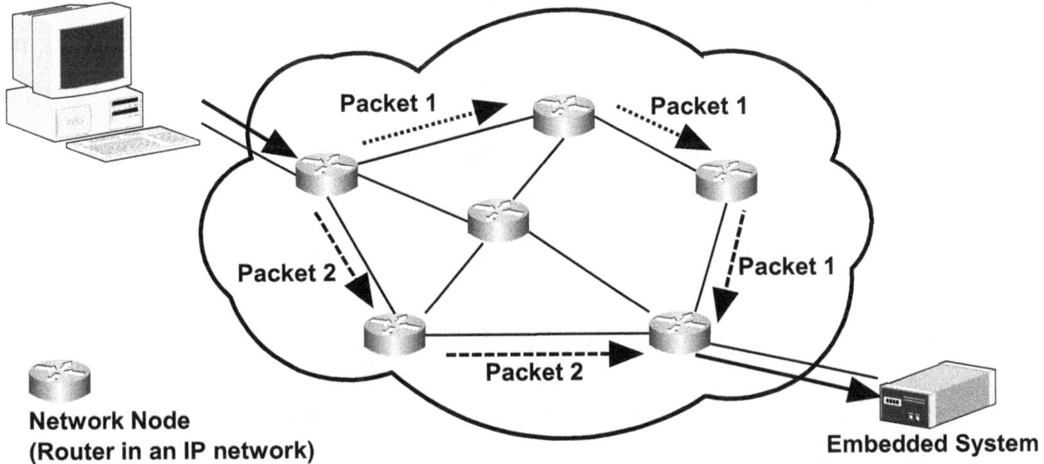

Figure 2-2 **Packet Switched Network**

Figure 2-2 represents a packet-switched network wherein terminals are the extremities of the network connections and are referred to as either hosts or devices. The network elements forwarding packets from the source to a destination are called nodes. Packets are forwarded on a node-to-node basis, one hop at a time, a hop being the path segment between two nodes. Each packet is processed by each node on the path between the source and the destination. In an IP network nodes are called routers.

IP networks are not limited to use by computers (PCs) and mainframes. In fact, increasingly more networks are formed with embedded systems: factory floor automation, household and office devices including heating systems, ovens, washing machines, fridges, drink dispensers, security alarms, Personal Digital Video Recorder, intelligent set-top-boxes, audio equipment, and more. In fact, it is easy to imagine that your refrigerator, washing machine, dryer or toaster will be Internet enabled in the not so distant future.

In Figure 2-2, packets travel in one direction, from the PC workstation to the embedded system. In a full-duplex exchange, two paths are used and processing is performed in both directions. The same processing is required for packets travelling from the embedded system to a PC workstation. An important aspect of packet switching is that packets may take different paths from a source to a destination. In this example, it is possible for packet #2 to arrive before packet #1.

In a packet-switched network, nodes are very busy since the same processing is required for every packet transmitted from the source to the destination. However, the nodes are not aware of the connection, only the terminals (hosts and devices) are.

Modern networks extensively use packet switching technology. The main characteristics of a packet-switching network include:

- Networks transfer packets using store-and-forward
- Packets have a maximum length
- Long messages are broken into multiple packets (i.e., fragmentation)
- Source and destination addresses are stored in every packet

Packet Switching technology uses packet switches (computers) and digital transmission lines. It features no per-call connections. The network resources are shared by all communications. It also uses a store-and-forward mechanism referred to as routing in IP technology.

Store-and Forward:

- Stores each arriving packet
- Reads the destination address in the packet
- Consults a routing table to determine the next hop
- Forwards the packet

At the end of the 1990's, for the first time, data service bandwidth began to exceed real-time services bandwidth. This trend created a dilemma for telecom operators. They were forced to decide whether to make capital expenditures on PSTN equipment to provide both real-time and data services when the latter represented the majority of the traffic. If not, how could they monetize their investment on the data-service side?

Today, most networking-related capital expenditure is spent on equipment supporting data services. Two technologies receiving the majority of this investment are Ethernet and Internet Protocol (IP), which are increasingly evident in embedded systems. This investment ensures that, in the near future, our phone services will run exclusively on Voice over IP (VoIP) and our television over IP networks (IPTV). Voice, video and all real-time services with time-sensitive data will depend upon IP technology.

The Internet Protocol is rapidly becoming the ubiquitous network technology. The related protocol stack used by a myriad of devices is called a *TCP/IP stack*.

2-2 WHAT IS A TCP/IP STACK?

The *Internet Protocol suite* (also referred to as network protocol suite) is the set of communication protocols upon which the Internet and most commercial networks run. Also called *TCP/IP stack*, it is named after two of the most important protocols that comprise it: the Transmission Control Protocol (TCP) and Internet Protocol (IP). While they are important networking protocols, they are certainly not the only ones.

2-3 THE OSI SEVEN-LAYER MODEL

The Internet Protocol suite can be viewed as a set of layers. Each layer solves a set of requirements involving the transmission of data, and provides a well-defined service to upper-layer protocols by implementing services provided by lower layers.

Upper-layer protocols are logically closer to the user and deal with abstract data while lower-layer protocols translate data into a form that can be physically transmitted. Each layer acts as a "black box" containing predefined inputs, outputs, and internal processes.

For clarity regarding layers, we define:

Layer: A grouping of related communications functions

- Each layer provides services to the layers above
- Layering introduces modularity and simplifies design and modification

Protocol: Rules governing how entities in a layer collaborate to deliver desired services

- There may be several protocols in each layer

Application: That which is accessed by the end user to perform a function. The application layer is built on top of a "stack" of protocols.

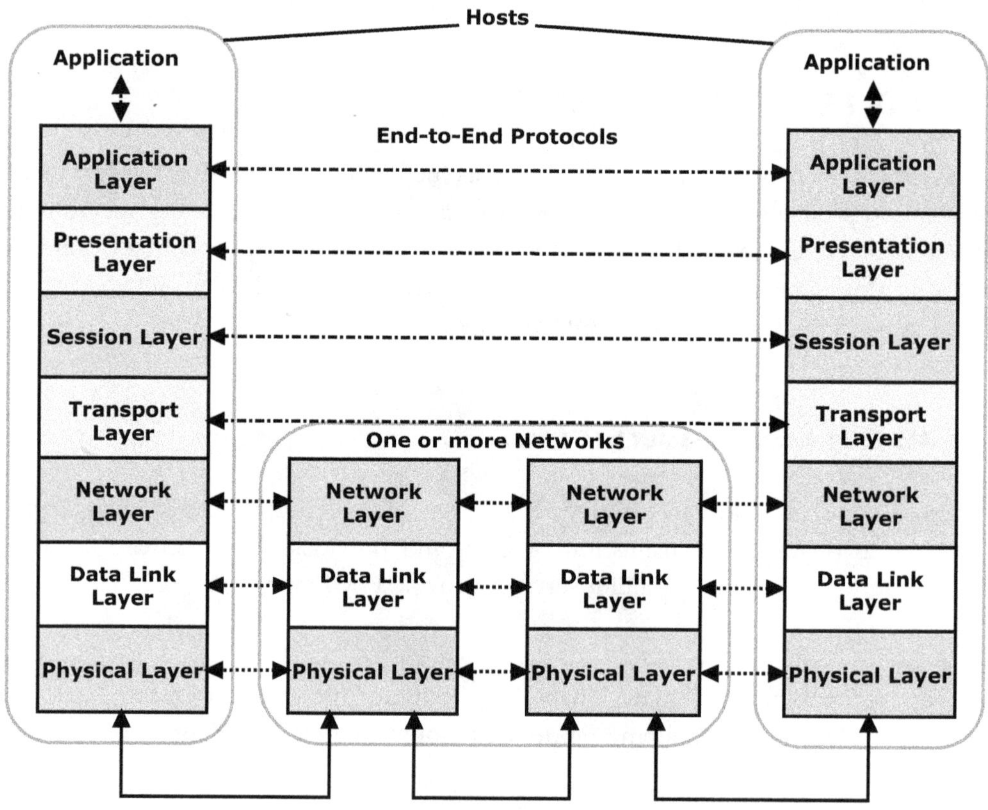

Figure 2-3 **OSI Seven-Layer Model**

The International Organization for Standardization (ISO) developed an Open Systems Interconnection (OSI) seven-layer model in 1977. In Figure 2-3, OSI Reference Model, two major components exist: an abstract model of networking, and a set of specific protocols. Hosts are separate devices connected on the same or different network, anywhere in the world. There is no notion of "distance" in the diagram. Information travels vertically in each host from top to bottom for the transmitting host and from bottom to top for the receiving host. The OSI model provides a fixed set of seven layers that can be roughly compared to the IP suite.

Conceptually, two instances at one layer are connected by a horizontal protocol connection on that layer. For example, a layer that provides data integrity supplies the mechanism needed by applications above it, while it calls the next lower layer to send and receive packets that make up the communication. This is represented by the dotted line "End-to-End Protocol."

In IP technology we group the last three layers (Session, Presentation and Application) into a single layer, and refer to this newly created single layer as the Application layer. This layer provides to various programs a means to access interconnectivity functions on lower layers, facilitating data exchange.

The Session layer controls the dialogues (sessions) between computers and establishes, manages, and terminates connections between local and remote applications. Sessions were predominant in the past with mainframe and minicomputers. However, with the arrival of IP networking, this protocol has been replaced with a new connection mechanism between the application and the TCP/IP stack. Refer to the discussion on sockets in Chapter 8, on page 205.

The Presentation layer orchestrates the handling of the data exchanged including translation, encryption, and compression, as well as data format functions. Today, there is global acceptance of the ASCII character set transferred in bytes, and such new global encoding standards as HTML or XML, simplify the Presentation layer. This layer is the main interface for the user(s) to interact first with the application and ultimately the network.

Strictly speaking, while Session and Presentation layers exist in the TCP/IP stack, they are less often used other than older protocols. For example at the Presentation Layer we find:

- Multipurpose Internet Mail Extensions (MIME) for e-mail encoding (see the section "Simple Mail Transfer Protocol (SMTP)" on page 238).
- eXternal Data Representation (XDR)
- Secure Socket Layer (SSL)
- Transport Layer Secure (TLS)

And, at the Session Layer, we find:

- Named Pipes
- Network Basic Input/Output System (NetBIOS)
- Session Announcement Protocol (SAP)

Examples of application layer protocols include Telnet, File Transfer Protocol (FTP), Simple Mail Transfer Protocol (SMTP), and Hypertext Transfer Protocol (HTTP).

2-4 APPLYING THE OSI MODEL TO TCP/IP

When working with TCP/IP, the model is simplified to four layers plus the physical layer as shown in Figure 2-4. This figure depicts the encapsulation process with protocol overhead down to Ethernet, and the proper naming for each encapsulation level throughout the layers.

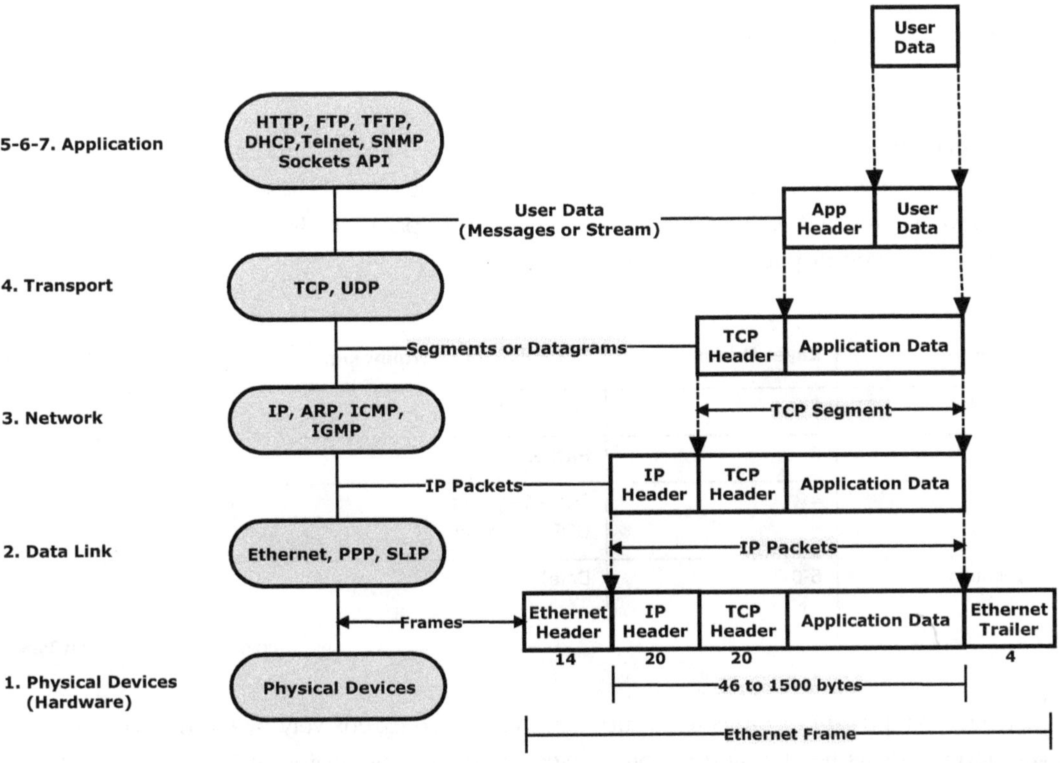

Figure 2-4 **TCP/IP Layered Model**

Ethernet is the ubiquitous Data Link layer, and will therefore be used in all of the examples provided in this book.

Protocols require that select control information be inserted into headers and trailers. Using packet-switching technology, data generated by the application is passed to the transport layer and is encapsulated with the addition of a header to the application payload, and so on, for every layer in the model.

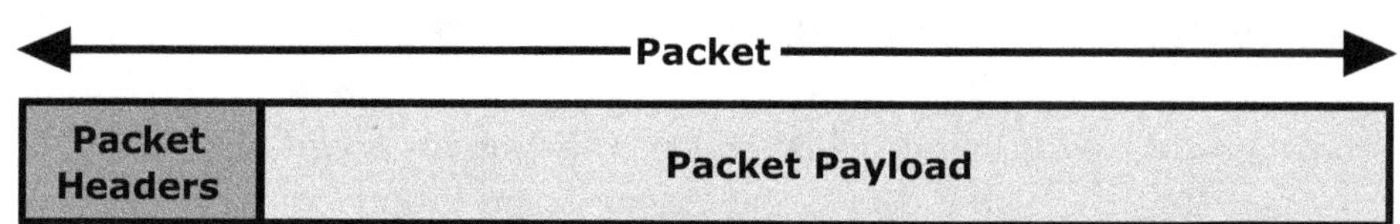

Figure 2-5 **Packet Encapsulation**

Figure 2-5 demonstrates the encapsulation mechanism when data travels from one layer to the next layer.

As information travels up and down the stack, data is encapsulated and de-capsulated in various structures (adding or removing a specific header). These structures are often referred to as packets (TCP packet, IP packet, Ethernet packet). However, there is a specific term for every type of packaging or encapsulation:

Layer Name	Layer Number	Encapsulation terminology
Data Link	2	Frame (Ethernet)
Network	3	Packet
Transport	4	TCP - Segment UDP - Datagram
Application	5-6-7	Data

Table 2-1 **Encapsulation Types**

The packet-wrapping mechanism described above is used extensively by the IP protocol suite. Every layer adds its header, and in some cases, trailer. The wrapping of information with this overhead information creates new data types (datagrams, segments, packets, frames).

Specifications for the TCP/IP protocol stack are managed by the Internet Engineering Task Force (IETF), an open standards organization. The IETF describes methods, behaviors, research, or innovations applicable to TCP/IP and Internet Protocol suite in Request for Comments (RFCs). A complete list of RFCs is available at http://www.faqs.org/rfcs/.

Micrium's µC/TCP-IP design follows the specifications contained in the RFCs.

```
/*
*********************************************************************************************
*                   NetARP_CfgCacheTimeout()
*
* Description : Configure ARP cache timeout from ARP Cache List.
*
* Argument(s) : timeout_sec   Desired value for ARP cache timeout (in seconds).
*
* Return(s)   : DEF_OK,  ARP cache timeout configured.
*
*               DEF_FAIL, otherwise.
*
* Caller(s)   : Net_InitDflt(),
*               Application.
*
*               This function is a network protocol suite application interface (API)
*               function & MAY becalled by application function(s).
*
* Note(s)     : (1) RFC #1122, Section 2.3.2.1 states that "an implementation of the
*               Address Resolution Protocol (ARP) ... MUST provide a mechanism to
*               flush out-of-date cache entries. If this mechanism involves a
*               timeout, it SHOULD be possible to configure the timeout value".
*
*               (2) Timeout in seconds converted to 'NET_TMR_TICK' ticks in order to
*               pre-compute initial timeout value in 'NET_TMR_TICK' ticks.
*
*               (3) 'NetARP_CacheTimeout' variables MUST ALWAYS be accessed exclusively
*               in critical sections.
*********************************************************************************************
*/
```

Listing 2-1 **RFC Reference in µC/TCP-IP Function Heading**

Every relevant RFC is implemented to the functionality provided by µC/TCP-IP. When an RFC section or the complete RFC is implemented, a note similar to Note (1) in Listing 2-1 is created. Listing 2-1 is an example from the µC/TCP-IP ARP module (`net_arp.c`).

RFCs for current IP technology are very stable. Work on newer standards continues to progress, especially involving issues of security.

When the IP protocol suite was developed, an important technical assumption was made. At the end of the 1970's, electrical transmission susceptible to electromagnetic interference was predominant, and fiber optics was only operating in R&D labs. Therefore, based on using electrical transmission systems, Layer-2 protocols were extremely complex given the amount of error checking and error corrections that needed to be performed.

The assumption made by IP designers was that the transmission network over which IP would operate would be reliable. They were correct when IP became the network protocol driving the global public Internet and later corporate networks, fiber optics were well deployed. Today, as a result, Layer-2 protocols are less complex.

In the IP protocol suite, data error detection and correction, other than simple Cyclic Redundancy Check (CRC), is the responsibility of protocols higher than Layer 2, specifically those at Layer 4 (see Chapter 7, "Transport Protocols" on page 165).

Now, however, with the rapid market penetration rate of new wireless technologies, the Layer 2 reliability assumption is no longer valid. Wireless transmission systems are highly susceptible to interference, resulting in higher bit-error rates. The IP protocol suite, especially Layer-2 protocols, must address this issue. There are a number of recommendations and improvements to the standard TCP/IP stack. For example, RFC 2018, selective acknowledgments improve performance when multiple packets are lost from one window of data (see Chapter 7, "Transport Protocols" on page 165 and other RFCs).

It seems that nearly every protocol ending in "P" is part of the IP protocol suite (a slight exaggeration, but not far from the truth). Let's look at many of these protocols as we climb from the bottom of the stack (Layer 1), the Physical layer, toward the top of the stack (Layers 5-6-7), the Application layer.

2-5 THE STARTING POINT

General literature on TCP/IP programming or usage typically explains how the stack works and how the protocol layers operate by taking the reader from the application or user data, and moving down to the physical layer. The programmer's point of view, from the application to the network interface, always assumes that the hardware is known and stable. For a programmer, that may be the case, but for an embedded engineer, the first challenge is to get the physical layer to work.

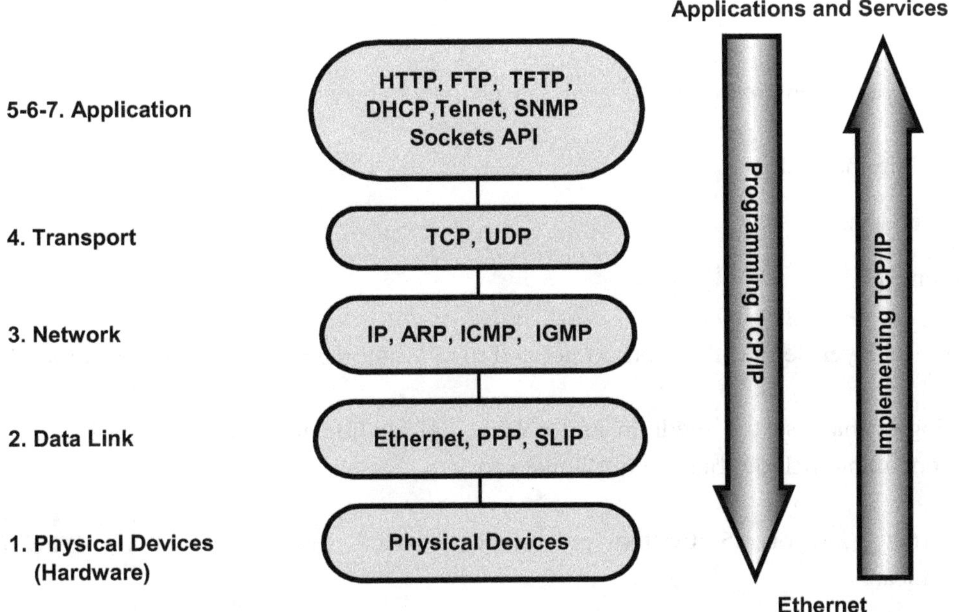

Figure 2-6 **The Starting Point**

When embedding a TCP/IP stack, the embedded engineer begins with the physical layer, since most of the time, the hardware represents a new design. First, the designer must define the Local Area Network (LAN) technology to be used. Then, the Network Interface Card (NIC) or Data Link Controller (DLC) driver must be implemented and tested.

Only when frames are transmitted and received properly by the embedded device can the embedded engineer begin to move up the stack and finally test that the data can be transmitted and received by applications. Since this book follows the point of view of the embedded engineer, the TCP/IP stack is presented from the bottom up taking an implementation point of view instead of the traditional programming top-down approach.

2-6 LAYER 1 - PHYSICAL

The Physical layer handles the transmission of bits over physical circuits. It is best described by its mechanical physical parameters, and includes such elements as:

- Cable
- Connectors
- Plugs
- Pins

And, its bit-processing techniques:

- Signaling method
- Voltage levels
- Bit times

The Physical layer defines the method needed to activate, maintain, and deactivate the link.

Technologies that use the medium and specify the method for clocking, synchronization and bit encoding include, but are not limited to:

- Ethernet: Category 5 twisted pair cable, coaxial, fiber (defined by IEEE 802 specifications)
- Wireless: frequency, modulation (Bluetooth radio, Wi-Fi IEEE 802.11, etc.)
- Digital subscriber loop (DSL) provided by the telephone operator to transport high-speed Internet on the phone line between the Central Office and the customer. This equipment is vendor specific.
- Coaxial cable (cable modem) provided by the cable operator to transport high-speed internet on the coaxial cable between the network head and the customer.

The physical layer is the hardware you can hold in your hands, the network interface card, or Data-Link controller on a board. Anything located above this layer is software.

2-7 LAYER 2 - DATA LINK

The Data-Link layer handles the packaging of bits into frames and their transmission or reception over physical circuits. It is at this layer that most error detection and correction is performed.

This layer supports various transmission protocols, including:

- Asynchronous Transfer Mode (ATM)
- Frame Relay
- Ethernet
- Token Ring

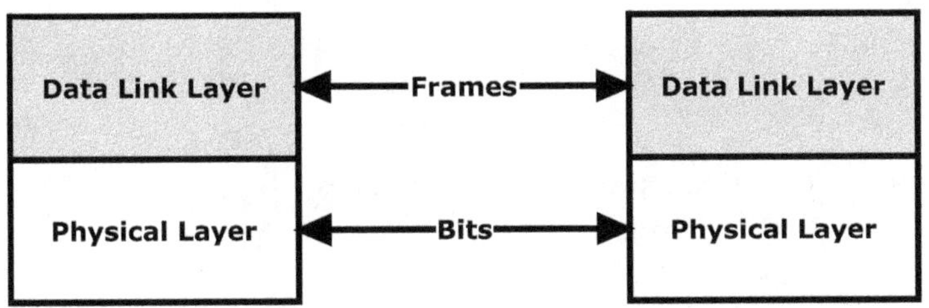

Figure 2-7 **Data Link**

The first task of the embedded engineer is to develop and test the software that drives the NIC (the network driver) used in the Data-Link Layer in Figure 2-7 (see Chapter 16, "Network Interface Layer" on page 343 and Chapter 14, "Network Device Drivers" on page 299).

Although a few technologies exist at this layer, Ethernet, as a Layer-2 protocol eclipses all others.

Over 95 percent of all data traffic originates and terminates on Ethernet ports according to Infonetics Research, an international market research firm specializing in data networking and telecom. Rarely has a technology proved to be so simple, flexible, cost-effective, and pervasive.

For embedded systems, Ethernet is also the most preferred Layer-2 technology (see Chapter 4, "LAN = Ethernet" on page 83). The following section on Ethernet provides a short introduction.

2-7-1 ETHERNET

Given the prevalence of Ethernet technology, there is an almost incestuous relationship between IP and Ethernet. Ethernet's meteoric rise is based on the fact that Ethernet:

- Is a simple yet robust technology
- Is a non-proprietary open standard
- Is cost effective per host
- Is well understood
- Has a range of speeds
  - 10, 100, 1000 Mbps (Megabits per second), 24 Gbps (Gigabits per second) and more...
- Runs on copper, coax, fiber, and wireless interfaces

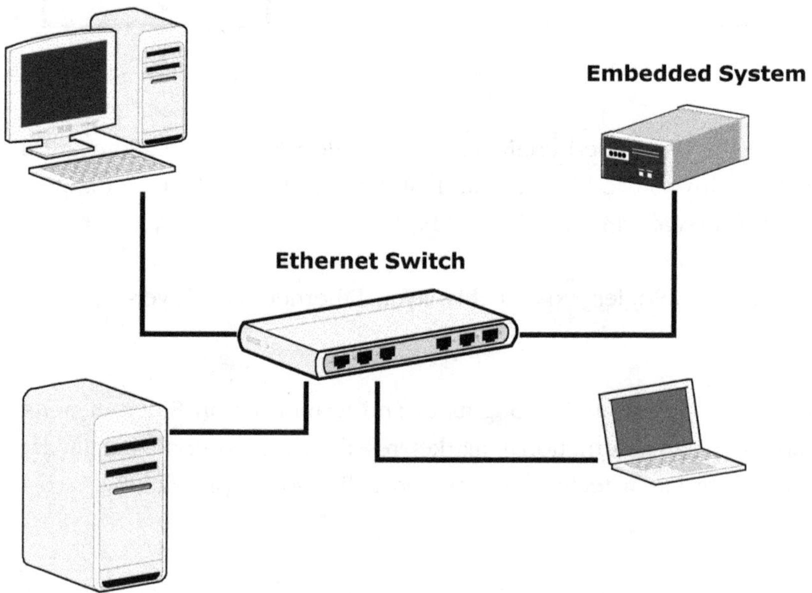

Figure 2-8 **Ethernet**

Figure 2-8 provides an example of an Ethernet-based network. The Network Interface Card (NIC) connects hosts to a Local Area Network (LAN). Each Ethernet-based NIC has a globally unique address over a "flat" address space. Given that LANs usually have a small geographic footprint, they use higher data-transfer rates than do Wide Area Networks (WANs). Ethernet and other Layer-2 protocols facilitate developers to build LANs.

Frames of data are transmitted into the physical layer medium (copper, coax, fiber, and radio interfaces). NICs listen on this physical medium for frames with unique LAN addresses, known as Media Access Control (MAC) addresses (more on this in Chapter 4, "LAN = Ethernet" on page 83).

Although the structure of data handled by Ethernet NICs is called a frame, Ethernet is a packet-switching technology. Copper wire is the predominant physical layer used by Ethernet in local areas. Its inherent star topology, as shown in Figure 2-8 and its low cost implementation are the primary reasons for Ethernet's success as a preferred LAN technology.

In the last few years, Ethernet has also emerged as a viable alternative in metro networks and Wide Area Networks (WANs) due to the rapid deployment of full-duplex, fiber optic Gigabit Ethernet technology during the now infamous techno bubble in the late 1990's. The success of the 802.11 standard (Wi-Fi) has also propelled Ethernet to predominant LAN technology status for wireless networks, as it uses and extends the Ethernet interface between Layer 3 and Layer 2.

The IEEE 802.3 standard defines Ethernet. Twisted pair Ethernet is used in the LAN, and fiber optic Ethernet is mainly used in WAN, giving rise to Ethernet as the most widespread wired networking technology. Since the end of the 1980's, Ethernet has replaced such competing LAN standards as Token Ring, Fiber Distributed Data Interface (FDDI), and Attached Resource Computer NETwork (ARCNET). In recent years, Wi-Fi has become prevalent in home and small office networks and augments Ethernet's presence. WiMAX (IEEE 802.16) will also contribute to Ethernet domination. It is used for wireless networking in much the same way as Wi-Fi but it can provide broadband wireless access up to 30 miles (50 km) for fixed stations, and 3 - 10 miles (5 - 15 km) for mobile stations.

2-8 LAYER 3 - NETWORK

To expand the reach of our hosts, internetworking protocols are necessary to enable communication between different computers attached to diverse local area networks.

Internet: a network of networks (in other words, between the networks: Inter Net)

The public Internet is a familiar example. A private network of networks is referred to as an Intranet.

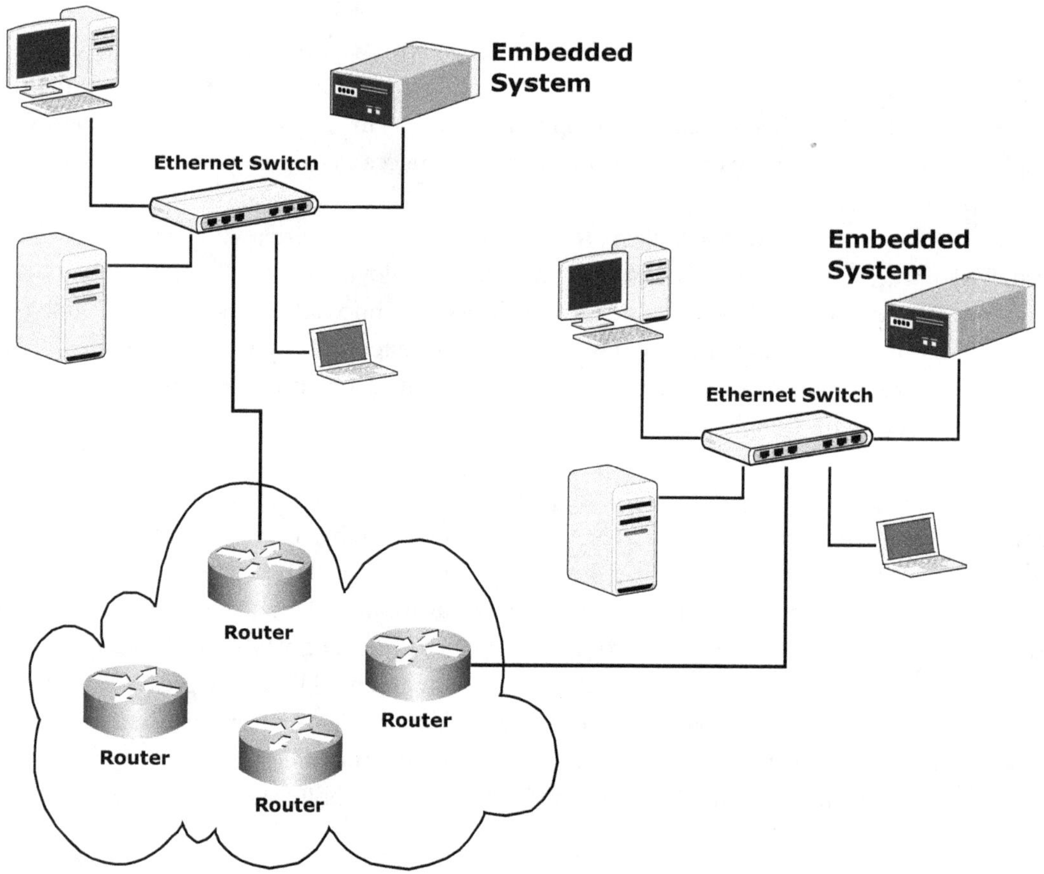

Figure 2-9 **Local Area Networking**

When it is advantageous to link together multiple LANs, Layer 3 protocols and equipment (routers) are brought into play (see Figure 2-9). Three LANs are linked together with a cloud where the Layer 3 nodes (routers), used to forward frames between the LANs, are located. The Layer 2 device, the Ethernet switch, is connected to the Layer 3 router, to participate in the larger network. The Network layer handles the packaging of frames into packets and their routing from one piece of equipment to another. It transfers packets across multiple links and/or multiple networks. What is not represented in Figure 2-9 are network connections between the nodes in the cloud.

Collectively, the nodes execute routing algorithms to determine paths across the network. Layer 3 is the unifying layer bringing together various Layer 2 technologies. Even if all of the hosts access these networks using different Layer 2 technologies, they all have a common protocol. In an IP network, this is represented by the IP packet and the well-known IP address which is used by the routing algorithm. See Chapter 5, "IP Networking" on page 111, for a complete definition of IP addresses.

We already know that a device such as an embedded system requires a MAC address to participate in the LAN. Now, we also see that in a network of networks using IP technology, each device also needs an IP address. Other configuration requirements will be covered in depth in Chapter 5, "IP Networking" on page 111.

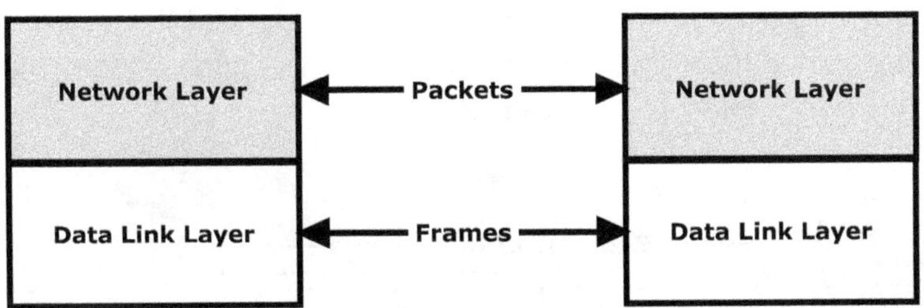

Figure 2-10 **Layer 3 – Network**

The links depicted in Figure 2-10 are not direct links, but instead represent that the information carried between the two hosts on the network is made up of structure that is relevant only to certain layers of the TCP/IP stack. The information contained in the packets encapsulated in the frames, is processed by the Network layer. When transmitting a packet, the Network layer takes the information received from the layer above and builds the packet with relevant Layer 3 information (an IP address and other data making up the Layer 3 header). The Network layer, upon receiving a packet, must examine its content and decide what do to with it. The most plausible action is to send it to the layer above.

2-9 LAYER 4 – TRANSPORT

The Transport layer ensures the reliability of point-to-point data communications. It transfers data end-to-end from a process in one device to a process in another device.

In IP technology, we have two protocols at this layer:

TRANSMISSION CONTROL PROTOCOL (TCP)

- A reliable stream transfer providing:
  - Error recovery
  - Flow control
  - Packet sequencing

USER DATAGRAM PROTOCOL (UDP)

- A quick-and-simple single-block transfer

At this stage of implementation, the embedded system engineer must evaluate which or if both of these protocols will be required for the type of embedded application at hand. Assistance to help answer these questions can be found in Chapter 7, on page 165, which describes transport layer protocols in greater detail.

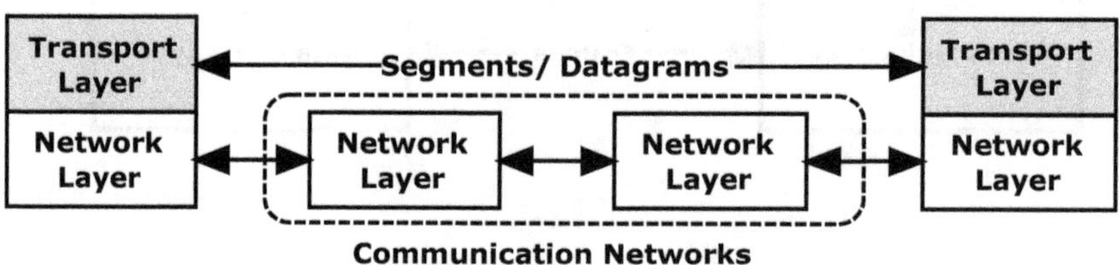

Figure 2-11 **Layers 3 and 4**

Figure 2-11 above shows that at the Network layer, the packet may have gone through different nodes between the source and destination. The information contained in the packet may be a TCP segment or a UDP datagram. The information contained in these segments or datagrams is only relevant to the transport layer.

2-10 LAYERS 5-6-7 - THE APPLICATION

It is at the Application layer that an embedded engineer implements the system's main functions. An application is the software that interfaces with the TCP/IP stack and contains either a basic network service such as file transfer, e-mail or a custom application. Chapter 9, "Services and Applications" on page 221 provides a more detailed explanation of the applications and services that can be used as add-on modules to the TCP/IP stack.

To develop a customer application, the embedded engineer must understand the interface between the application and the TCP/IP stack. This interface is referred to as the socket interface and it allows the developer to open a socket, to send data using the socket, to receive data on the socket, and so on. To use the interface and its Application Programming Interface (API), refer to Chapter 8, "Sockets" on page 205, and Chapter 17, "Socket Programming" on page 355 which contain additional information on how a socket interface works.

Micrium also provides a test application for a TCP/IP stack called µC/IPerf. This application, delivered in source code, provides examples on how to write applications using TCP/IP. Part II of this book provides many sample applications that can be customized for use.

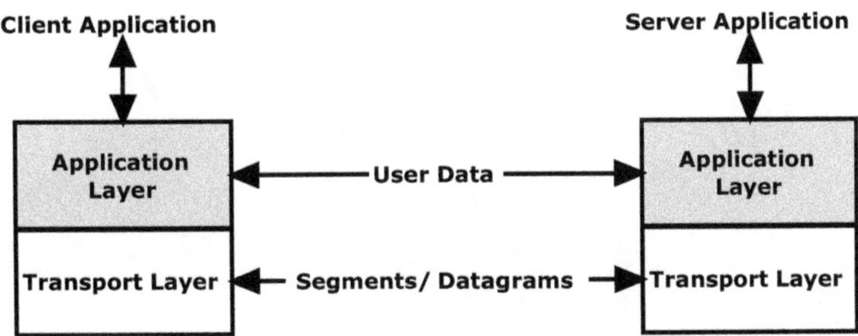

Figure 2-12 **Application Layer and Layer 4**

The interface between the Application layer and the Transport layer is often the demarcation point of the TCP/IP stack as shown in Figure 2-12. The junction of the Application Layer (5-6-7) and Layer 4 is the location of the socket interface previously discussed. The application can be a standard application such as FTP or HTTP and/or an embedded system-specific application that you would develop. As previously explained, user data going from the source host to the destination host must travel across many layers and over one or many network links.

From the concepts introduced so far, it can be deduced that the challenges for the embedded engineer reside in the driver for the Data Link Layer and in the application, assuming the project is using a commercial off the-shelf TCP/IP stack.

In fact, depending on Data Link Layer hardware, a driver is required. If the embedded engineer is lucky, the TCP/IP stack vendor already has a driver for this hardware. Otherwise, it must be developed and tested. This can be a challenge depending on the complexity of the hardware and the level of integration required with the TCP/IP stack.

The second challenge is the application itself. What does the product do? Mastering socket programming and being sufficiently knowledgeable to test the application for all possible eventualities are two important skills a developer must possess.

2-11 SUMMARY

Figure 2-13 below summarizes the concepts discussed so far.

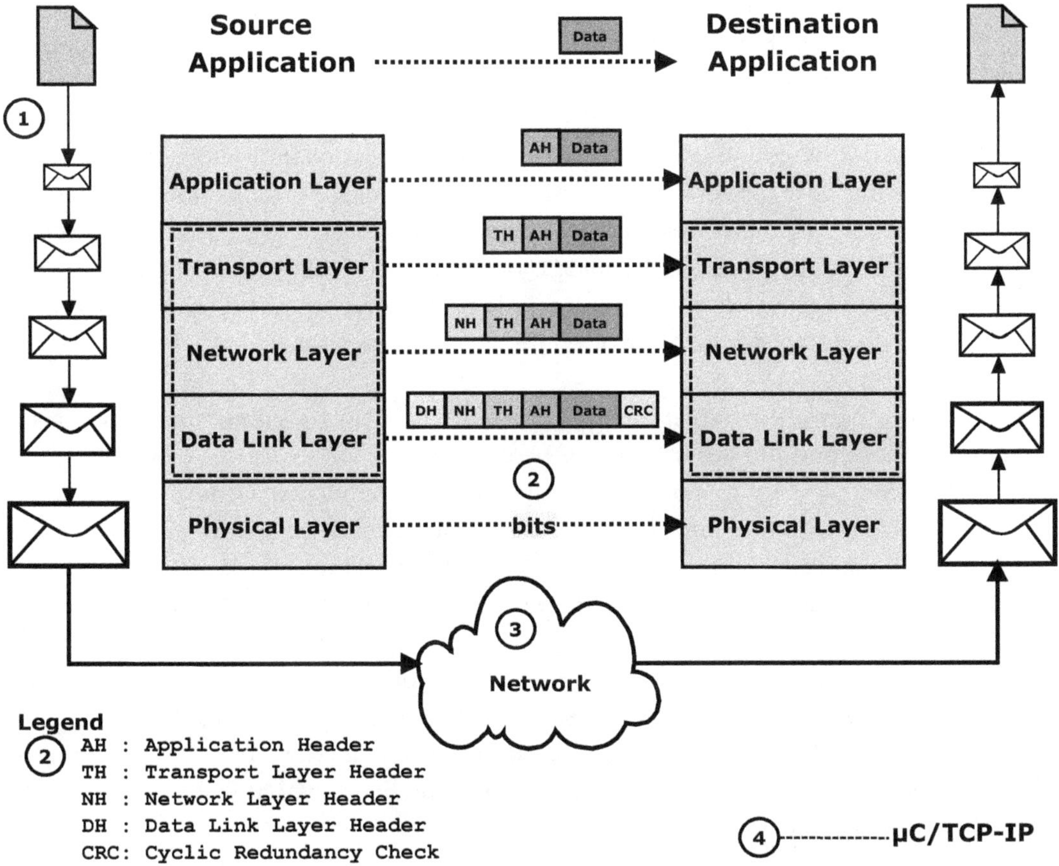

Figure 2-13 **TCP/IP process**

F2-13(1) Data traveling through the stack from the user application down to the physical medium is encapsulated at every layer by a series of protocols. This is represented by the envelope icon, and the envelope is getting larger as user data travels toward the network interface at the physical layer. This payload inflation is referred to as protocol overhead. The overhead is a non-negligible quantity and can affect system performance, especially if user data is relatively small. The following chapters provide the size of each header so that the overhead ratio to user data payload can be calculated to estimate effective system performance.

As far as the user application is concerned, it sends data and the same data is retrieved at the other end. The application is blissfully unaware that the data went through layers and network nodes.

F2-13(2) Each protocol adds its own header that contains control information required by this layer/protocol to perform its task. The use of protocol overhead is only relevant for the corresponding layer in the connected host. This is represented by the dotted lines in the middle of this diagram. These lines are not effective physical connections but represent logical interactions between corresponding layers in the two hosts involved in the communication.

F2-13(3) The network is represented as a cloud. The network connection between the source and the destination can be as simple as a LAN if both hosts are on the same LAN, or as complex as the Internet if the two hosts are in different locations (anywhere in the world). Device configuration will vary depending on the reach required. Chapter 5, "IP Networking" on page 111 provides a broader discussion of these various network configurations.

F2-13(4) The dotted line around the Transport, Network and Data Link Layers represents the software that encompasses μC/TCP-IP (or any other TCP/IP stack). The Physical Layer is the hardware used in the system. This means that when using μC/TCP-IP to develop an embedded system, the only part that is missing is the Application.

The chapters that follow provide greater detail for several important IP protocols, pointing out the advantages and possible challenges to using each in an embedded system.

Chapter

3

Embedding TCP/IP: Working Through Implementation Challenges

Before using a TCP/IP stack in an embedded product, it is important to acknowledge and understand the reasons to do so. Obviously, the product is to be connected to an IP network. We can say the embedded system in this case requires *connectivity*. An embedded system might be called on to exchange large amounts of data over a reliable connection. In this case, we can say that the embedded system demands *performance*.

Most embedded system resources are extremely limited when compared to the resources available on a desktop or laptop PC. Product manufacturers must create products at the lowest cost possible to offer them at the best possible price to their customers, yet work within the constraints of RAM, CPU speed, and peripheral hardware performance inherent in hardware platforms used for embedded design. With limited hardware resources, how can an embedded designer meet system design requirements? They begin by asking and answering a fundamental question:

Do you need a TCP/IP stack...

- to connect to an IP network without any minimum performance requirement?

  or

- to connect to an IP network and obtain high throughput?

The answer to this question has a major impact on hardware choices that ultimately drive product cost. These hardware choices include CPU performance, NIC interface type, and RAM availability.

Connectivity, throughput and bandwidth are concepts that shape the configuration system hardware and software parameters. Let's look at an overview of each:

BANDWIDTH

As a best practice, the performance of an Ethernet connection should be measured in Megabits per second (Mbps). This allows us to easily compare system performance with respect to the Ethernet link's maximum bandwidth.

Currently, Ethernet over twisted pair is the preferred physical medium. The available bandwidth of the link is normally 10 Mbps, 100 Mbps or 1 Gbps. These numbers are used as the reference for the efficiency of an Ethernet NIC. For example, if we have an Ethernet NIC with a 100 Mbps link, we already know that our embedded system maximum bandwidth is 100 Mbps. However, there are a number of limiting factors in embedded systems that do not allow them to reach what we call the Ethernet line speed, in this case 100 Mbps. Such factors include duplex mismatch, TCP/IP stack performance based on CPU speed, RAM available for buffers, DMA vs. non-DMA Ethernet driver design, performance related to clock and peripheral power management, and the use of a true zero-copy architecture. These embedded system bandwidth-limiting factors are included in this and subsequent chapters.

CONNECTIVITY

Connectivity in this context is the exchange of information without any performance constraints. Many embedded systems requiring connectivity only may work optimally with hardware and software that provide a low-bandwidth TCP/IP connection.

For example, if an embedded system is sending or receiving a few hundreds bytes every second (let's say of sensor data), then the constraints on the system are fairly relaxed. It means that the CPU may be clocked at a lower speed. It may also mean that if the NIC is Ethernet, it can be a 10 Mpbs instead of a 100-Mbps interface and the RAM requirement is reduced since there is less data flowing in the system.

THROUGHPUT

A system that needs throughput can be one that transmits or receives streamed video, for example. Streamed video transmission can be anything from a few megabits per second (Mbps) to many Mbps depending on the signal quality and the compression rate used. This type of application requires an embedded system with sufficient resources to achieve higher bandwidth than a "connectivity-only" system. Constraints on the NIC, CPU and RAM availability are clearly higher. For the CPU and NIC, these issues are hardware dependent, but for RAM usage, the constraints are related to software and the requirements of the application.

The transport protocols at Layer 4, have a greater influence on RAM usage. It is at this layer, for example, that flow control, or how much data is in transit in the network between the hosts, is implemented. The basic premise of flow control is that the more data in transit, more RAM is required by the system to handle the data volume. Details on how these protocols work and their impact on RAM usage are located in Chapter 7, "Transport Protocols" on page 165.

Achieving high throughput in a system requires greater resources. The question becomes, how much? Each element influencing performance must be analyzed separately.

3-1 CPU

There is an inherent asymmetry in a TCP/IP stack whereby it is simpler to transmit than to receive. Substantially more processing is involved in receiving a packet as opposed to transmitting one, which is why embedded system transmit speeds are typically faster. We therefore say that most embedded targets are slow consumers.

Let's look at a personal computer by way of an example. On a PC, the CPU is clocked at approximately 3 GHz and has access to gigabytes of memory. These high-powered computers invariably have an Ethernet NIC with its own processor and dedicated memory (often megabytes worth). However, even with all of these resources, we sometimes question our machine's network performance!

Now, imagine an embedded system with a 32-bit processor clocked at 70MHz and containing a mere 64 Kilobytes of RAM which must be allocated to duties apart from networking. The Ethernet controller is capable of 100 Mbps. However, it is unrealistic to ask even a 70-MHz processor with only 64 Kbytes of RAM to be able to achieve this performance level. Standard Ethernet link bandwidths are 10, 100 Mbps and 1 Gbps and semiconductor manufacturers integrate these Ethernet controllers into their microcontrollers. The CPU may not be able to fill this link to its maximum capacity, however efficient the software.

Even when the Ethernet controller used in the system is designed to operate at 10 Mbps, 100 Mbps, or 1 Gbps, it's unlikely that the system will achieve that performance. A high-performance PC as described above will have no trouble transmitting Ethernet frames at bandwidths approaching the Ethernet line speed. However, if an embedded system is connected to such a PC, it is very possible that the embedded system will not be able to keep up with the high data rates and therefore some of the frames will be lost (dropped).

Performance is not only limited by the embedded system's CPU, but also by the limited amount of RAM available to receive packets. In the embedded system, packets are stored in buffers (called network buffers) that are processed by the CPU. A network buffer contains one Ethernet frame plus control information concerning that frame. The maximum Ethernet frame payload is 1500 bytes and therefore additional RAM is required for each network buffer. On our PC, in comparison, there is sufficient RAM to configure hundreds (possibly even thousands) of network buffers, yet this is typically not the case for an embedded target. Certain protocols will have difficulty performing their duties when the system has few buffers. Packets generated by a fast producer and received by the target will consume most or all the TCP/IP stack network buffers and, as a result, packets will be dropped. This point will be explained in greater detail when we look at Transport protocols.

Hardware features such as Direct Memory Access (DMA) and CPU speed may improve this situation. The faster the target can receive and process the packets, the faster the network buffers are freed. No matter how quickly data comes in or goes out, the CPU still must process every single byte.

3-2 ETHERNET CONTROLLER INTERFACE

Other important factors influencing the performance of an embedded system include the system's ability to receive Ethernet frames in network buffers to be later processed by upper protocol layers, and to place data into network buffers for transmission. The predominant method for moving Ethernet frames between the Ethernet controller and the system's main memory are via software (using functions such as **memcopy()** which copies every byte from one location to another), or via Direct Memory Access (DMA).

With **memcopy()**, the CPU must copy every byte from one memory location to another. As a result, it is the slower of the two methods. **memcopy()** is always slower than DMA, even when writing the **memcopy()** function in highly optimized assembly language. If the only solution is to create an optimized **memcopy()**, in µC/TCP-IP, this function is located in the µC/LIB module.

DMA support for the Ethernet controller is a means to improve packet processing. It is easy to understand that, when frames are transferred quickly to and from the TCP/IP stack, network performance improves. Rapid transfer also relieves the CPU from the transfer task, allowing the CPU to perform additional protocol processing. The most common CPU to Ethernet Controller configurations are shown in Figure 3-1.

Moving Ethernet frames between an Ethernet controller and network buffers often depends upon specific Ethernet controller and microprocessor/microcontroller capabilities.

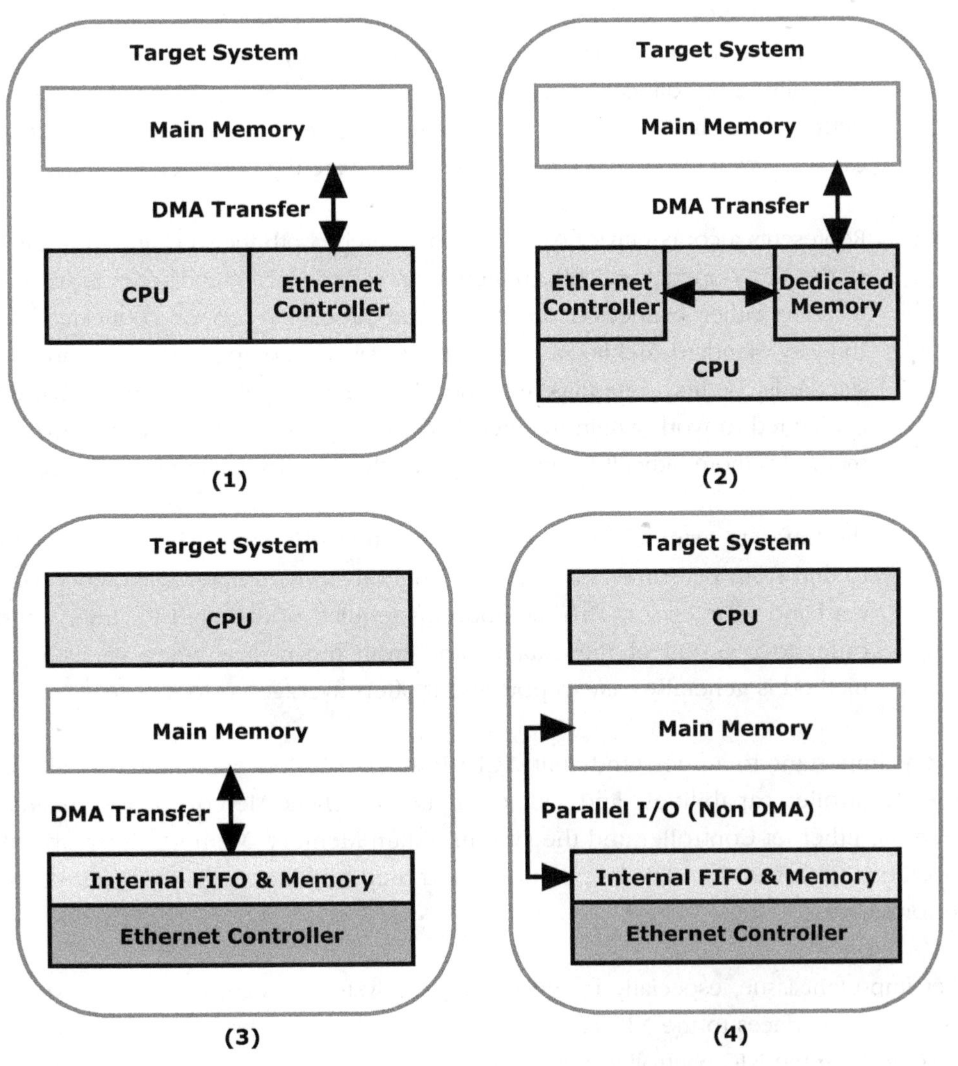

Figure 3-1 **Ethernet Controller Interface**

F3-1(1) Illustrates a CPU with an integrated Media Access Controller (MAC). When a frame is received by the MAC, a DMA transfer from the MAC's internal buffer is initiated by the MAC into main memory. This method often enables shortened development time and excellent performance.

F3-1(2) Represents a CPU with an integrated MAC, but with dedicated memory. When a frame is received, the MAC initiates a DMA transfer into this dedicated memory. Most configurations of type 2 allow for transmission from main memory while reserving dedicated memory for either receive or transmit operations. Both the MAC and the CPU read and write from dedicated memory, and so the TCP/IP stack can process frames directly from dedicated memory. Porting to this architecture is generally not difficult and it provides excellent performance. However, performance may be limited by the size of the dedicated memory; especially in cases where transmit and receive operations share the dedicated memory space.

F3-1(3) Represents a cooperative DMA solution whereby both the CPU and MAC take part in the DMA operation. This configuration is generally found on external devices that are either connected directly to the processor bus or connected via the Industry Standard Architecture (ISA) or Peripheral Component Interconnect (PCI) standards. Method 3 requires that the CPU contain a DMA peripheral that can be configured to work within the architectural limitations of the external device. This method is more difficult to port, but generally offers excellent performance.

F3-1(4) Illustrates an external device attached via the CPU's external bus. Data is moved to and from main memory and the external device's internal memory via CPU read and write cycles. This method thus requires additional CPU intervention in order to copy all of the data to and from the device when necessary. This method is generally easy to port and it offers average performance.

It is very important to understand that TCP/IP stack vendors may not use all of the Ethernet Controller capabilities, and will often implement a Memory Copy mechanism between the Ethernet Controller and the system's Main Memory. Memory Copy operations are substantially slower than DMA operations, and therefore have a major negative impact on performance.

Another important issue, especially for an embedded system design, is how the NIC driver (i.e., software) interfaces to the NIC controller. Certain TCP/IP stacks accomplish the task via polling (checking the NIC controller in a loop to see what needs to be done). This is not the best technique for an embedded system since every CPU cycle counts. The best interface mechanism is to use interrupts and have the NIC controller raise an interrupt when CPU attention is required. The µC/TCP-IP Driver Architecture is interrupt-driven. Driver development and porting are described in Chapter 14, "Network Device Drivers" on page 299.

3-2-1 ZERO COPY

TCP/IP stack vendors may qualify their stack as a zero-copy stack. A true zero-copy architecture refers to data in the memory buffers at every layer instead of moving the data between layers. Zero copy enables the network interface card to transfer data directly to or from TCP/IP stack network buffers. The availability of zero copy greatly increases application performance. It is easy to see that using a CPU that is capable of complex operations just to make copies of data is a waste of resources and time.

Techniques for implementing zero-copy capabilities include the use of DMA-based copying and memory mapping through a Memory Management Unit (MMU). These features require specific hardware support, not always present in microprocessors or microcontrollers used in embedded systems, and they often involve memory alignment requirements.

Use care when selecting a Commercial Off-the-Shelf (COTS) TCP/IP stack. Vendors may use the zero-copy qualifier for stacks that do not copy data between layers within the stack, but perform `memcopy()` between the stack and the Ethernet controller. Optimum performance can only be achieved if zero copy is used down to the Data Link Layer. Micrium's µC/TCP-IP is an example of a zero copy stack from the Data Link layer to the Transport layer. The interface between the Transport layer and the Application layer in µC/TCP-IP is currently not a zero copy interface.

3-2-2 CHECK-SUM

Another element which combines the CPU and data moves and which is frequently used in the stack is the checksum mechanism. Providing checksum assembly routines, replacing the C equivalent functions is another optimization strategy that is effective.

3-2-3 FOOTPRINT

As we are discovering, the IP protocol family is composed of several protocols. However, when developing an embedded system, ask yourself if you need them all. The answer is, probably not.

Another important question is: Is it possible to remove certain unused protocols from the stack? If the TCP/IP stack is well written, it should be possible to exclude protocols that are not required. Because an embedded system is often used in a private network, the embedded developer may decide not to implement protocols that are required on the public Internet. At this point, understanding each protocol's capabilities, as you will see in subsequent chapters, will help in deciding if that protocol is required for the application.

For any of the protocols listed below, if the feature is not required by the system, we may want to remove it from the target's build (assuming that this is allowed by the TCP/IP stack architecture). The figures provided are only an estimate based on µC/TCP-IP. Other TCP/IP stacks may have different footprints depending on how closely they follow RFCs and how many of the specification's features are actually included in each module.

The following are candidate protocols that can be removed from a TCP/IP stack if allowed by the stack software architecture:

Protocol	**Why it can be removed from the TCP/IP stack**	**Footprint**
IGMP	Protocol allows the host to use multicasting.	1.6KB
ICMP	Protocol is used for error control and error messaging. If the system is used in a closed, private network, it may not be required.	3.3KB
IP Fragmentation	Used to reassemble IP packets travelling across networks of different Maximum Transmission Unit (MTU) size. If the system is used on networks with the same MTU, it is typically not required.	2.0KB
TCP Congestion Control	On a private network where bandwidth is known and sufficient, this TCP feature may not be required.	10.0KB
TCP Keep-alive	According to RFC 1122, TCP Keep-alive is an optional feature of the protocol and, if included, must default to off. If the system has no need to check for dead peers or prevent disconnection due to network inactivity, the feature can be removed.	1.5KB
TCP	If the system does not send substantial amounts of data and you can afford to do sequencing and data acknowledgment in the top application, the system may be happy with UDP and you can eliminate TCP. See Chapter 7, "Transport Protocols" on page 165 for more details.	35KB

Table 3-1 **Protocols that can be 'compiled out' of µC/TCP-IP**

The footprints (code size) for the protocols are approximations and can thus vary from one TCP/IP stack to another. Some of these protocols are not part of µC/TCP-IP and therefore show that a TCP/IP stack can work without them. Current µC/TCP-IP limitations include:

No IP Transmit Fragmentation	RFC #791, Section 3.2 and RFC #1122, Section 3.3.5
No IP Forwarding/Routing	RFC #1122, Sections 3.3.1, 3.3.4, 3.3.5
IP Security Options	RFC #1108
No Current PING Utility (Transmission of ICMP Echo Request)	RFC #1574, Section 3.1 Current µC/TCP-IP ICMP implementation replies with ICMP Echo Reply to ICMP Echo Request.
ICMP Address Mask Agent/Server	RFC #1122, Section 3.2.2.9
No TCP Keep Alives	RFC #1122, Section 4.2.3.6
TCP Security and Precedence	RFC #793, Section 3.6
TCP Urgent Data	RFC #793, Section 3.7

Table 3-2 **µC/TCP-IP limitations**

Without introducing all of the µC/TCP-IP modules and data structures, the following sections provide an estimate of the µC/TCP-IP code and data footprint. The complete list of files required to build µC/TCP-IP is provided in Chapter 12, "Directories and Files" on page 263.

3-2-4 µC/TCP-IP CODE FOOTPRINT

Memory footprints were obtained by compiling the code on a popular 32-bit CPU architecture. Compiler optimization was set to maximum optimization for size or speed as indicated. µC/TCP-IP options are set for most disabled or all enabled. The numbers are provided as orders of magnitude for design purposes.

The table excludes NIC, PHY, ISR and BSP layers since these are NIC and board specific.

µC/TCP-IP Protocols Layers	All Options Enabled		All Options Disabled	
	Compiler Optimized for Speed (Kbytes)	Compiler Optimized for Size (Kbytes)	Compiler Optimized for Speed (Kbytes)	Compiler Optimized for Size (Kbytes)
IF	9.3	7.3	4.2	3.9
ARP	4.3	3.8	3.3	2.6
IP	10.1	9.0	6.4	6.0
ICMP	3.3	3.0	1.7	1.7
UDP	1.9	1.9	0.4	0.4
TCP	42.7	24.4	30.2	17.3
Sockets	23.5	13.8	2.0	1.7
BSD	0.7	0.6	0.7	0.6
Utils	1.5	0.9	1.1	0.6
OS	6.3	4.7	3.4	3.1
µC/LIB V1.31	3.5	3.2	2.9	2.6
µC/CPU V1.25	0.6	0.5	0.6	0.5
µC/TCP-IP Total:	107.7	73.0	56.9	41.0

Table 3-3 **µC/TCP-IP Code Footprint**

To see additional information regarding options, refer to Chapter 19, "Debug Management" on page 379, Chapter 20, "Statistics and Error Counters" on page 381, and Appendix C, "µC/TCP-IP Configuration and Optimization" on page 723.

3-2-5 µC/TCP-IP ADD-ON OPTIONS CODE FOOTPRINT

As seen in Layers 5-6-7 – The Application, services and standard application software modules found at the Application layer can be used in the product design to provide certain functionalities. Such application modules are offered as options for µC/TCP-IP. Although an in-depth discussion of memory footprint is outside the scope of this book, the memory footprint for the optional modules is included below for planning purposes. Chapter 9, "Services and Applications" on page 221 describes what some of these applications and services do and how they do it.

The footprints below were obtained by compiling the code on a popular 32-bit CPU architecture. The numbers are provided as orders of magnitude for design purposes.

µC/TCP-IP Add-on Options	**Compiler Optimized for Size (Kbytes)**	**Compiler Optimized for Speed (Kbytes)**
µC/DHCPc	5.1	5.4
µC/DNSc	0.9	1.0
µC/FTPc	2.8	2.9
µC/FTPs	4.5	4.5
µC/HTTPs	2.6	2.7
µC/POP3c	1.8	2.8
µC/SMTPc	2.0	2.1
µC/SNTPc	0.5	0.5
µC/TELNETs	2.0	2.1
µC/TFTPc	1.2	1.3
µC/TFTPs	1.2	1.2

Table 3-4 **µC/TCP-IP Add-ons Code Footprint**

3-2-6 µC/TCP-IP DATA FOOTPRINT

Cutting protocols out of the code will reduce the code footprint with little impact on the data (i.e., RAM) footprint. The greatest impact on the data footprint is a result of the number of "objects" such as network buffers and connections, and most specifically from network buffers. See a detailed explanation on buffers and how to use them appropriately in Chapter 7, "Transport Protocols" on page 165 and in Chapter 15, "Buffer Management" on page 335.

Data usage estimates are provided to complement the code footprint discussion. There are multiple modules requiring data to operate as shown in Table 3-5. Many of the data sizes calculated in the following sub-sections assume 4-byte pointers. The data requirements for each of the objects must be added, as needed by the configuration of the TCP/IP stack. The configuration of the objects is represented in a formula for each. The equation variables all in upper case are **#define** configuration parameters found in Appendix C, "µC/TCP-IP Configuration and Optimization" on page 723. Calculation methods follow.

BUFFER REQUIREMENTS

µC/TCP-IP stores transmitted and received data in data structures known as network buffers. µC/TCP-IP's buffer management is designed with embedded system constraints in mind. The most important factor on the RAM footprint is the number of buffers. For this reason, three types of buffers are defined: large receive, large transmit and small transmit buffers.

The data space for EACH network interface's buffers is calculated as:

```
[(224(max) + Net IF's Cfg'd RxBufLargeSize) * Net IF's Cfg'd RxBufLargeNbr] +
[(224(max) + Net IF's Cfg'd TxBufLargeSize) * Net IF's Cfg'd TxBufLargeNbr] +
[(224(max) + Net IF's Cfg'd TxBufSmallSize) * Net IF's Cfg'd TxBufSmallNbr]
```

These calculations do not account for additional space that may be required for additional alignment requirements.

Also, the (minimum) recommended defaults for network buffer sizes:

```
RxBufLargeSize = 1518
TxBufLargeSize = 1594
TxBufSmallSize = 152
```

The data space for network buffer pools is calculated as:

384 * (NET_IF_CFG_NBR_IF + 1)

Where: NET_IF_CFG_NBR_IF is the (maximum) number of network interfaces configured.

NETWORK INTERFACE REQUIREMENTS

µC/TCP-IP supports multiple network interfaces if the hardware has multiple network controllers (see Chapter 16, "Network Interface Layer" on page 343). Network Interfaces are used to represent an abstract view of the device hardware and data path that connects the hardware to the higher layers of the network protocol stack. In order to communicate with hosts outside the local host, the application developer must add at least one network interface to the system. The data size for network interfaces is calculated as:

```
76(max) * NET_IF_CFG_NBR_IF
```

Where: NET_IF_CFG_NBR_IF is the (maximum) number of network interfaces configured.

TIMER REQUIREMENTS

µC/TCP-IP manages software timers used to keep track of various network-related timeouts. Each timer requires RAM. The data size for timers is calculated as:

```
28 * NET_TMR_CFG_NBR_TMR
```

Where: NET_TMR_CFG_NBR_TMR is the number of timers configured.

ADDRESS RESOLUTION PROTOCOL (ARP) CACHE REQUIREMENTS

ARP is a protocol used to cross-reference an Ethernet MAC address (see Chapter 4, "LAN = Ethernet" on page 83) and an IP address (see Chapter 5, "IP Networking" on page 111). These cross-references are stored in a table called the ARP cache. The number of entries in this table is configurable. The data size for the ARP cache is calculated as:

```
56 * NET_ARP_CFG_NBR_CACHE
```

Where: NET_ARP_CFG_NBR_CACHE is the number of ARP cache entries configured.

IP REQUIREMENTS

A network interface can have more than one IP address. The data size for IP address configuration is calculated as:

```
[(20 * NET_IP_CFG_IF_MAX_NBR_ADDRS) + 4] * (NET_IF_CFG_NBR_IF + 1)
```

Where: NET_IF_CFG_NBR_IF is the (maximum) number of network interfaces configured, NET_IP_CFG_IF_MAX_NBR_ADDRS is the (maximum) number of IP addresses configured per network interface.

ICMP REQUIREMENTS

Internet Control Message Protocol (ICMP) transmits ICMP source quench messages to other hosts when network resources are low. The number of entries depends on the number of different hosts. It is recommended to start with a value of 5. The data size for ICMP source quench is calculated as:

```
20 * NET_ICMP_CFG_TX_SRC_QUENCH_NBR
```

Where: NET_ICMP_CFG_TX_SRC_QUENCH_NBR is the number of ICMP transmit source quench entries configured, if enabled by NET_ICMP_CFG_TX_SRC_QUENCH_EN.

IGMP REQUIREMENTS

The Internet Group Management Protocol (IGMP) adds multicasting capability to the IP protocol stack (see Appendix B, "µC/TCP-IP API Reference" on page 433). The data size for IGMP host groups is calculated as:

```
32 * NET_IGMP_CFG_MAX_NBR_HOST_GRP
```

Where: NET_IGMP_CFG_MAX_NBR_HOST_GRP is the (maximum) number of IGMP host groups configured, if enabled by NET_IP_CFG_MULTICAST_SEL configured to NET_IP_MULTICAST_SEL_TX_RX.

CONNECTION REQUIREMENTS

A connection is a µC/TCP-IP structure containing information regarding the IP protocol parameters required to identify two hosts communicating with each other. A connection is a structure that is used for all Layer 4 protocols (UDP and TCP). The data size for connections is calculated as:

```
56 * NET_CONN_CFG_NBR_CONN
```

Where: NET_CONN_CFG_NBR_CONN is the number of connections (TCP or UDP) configured.

TCP REQUIREMENTS

In addition to the connection data structure defined previously, a TCP connection requires additional state information, transmit and receive queue information as well as time-out information to be stored in a specific TCP connection data structure.

The data size for the TCP connections is calculated as:

```
280 * NET_TCP_CFG_NBR_CONN
```

Where: NET_TCP_CFG_NBR_CONN is the number of TCP connections configured.

SOCKETS REQUIREMENTS

As seen in section Layers 5-6-7 – The Application, the interface between the application and the TCP/IP stack is defined as a socket interface. For each socket that the application wants to open and use, a socket structure exits that contains the information about that specific socket.

The data size for sockets is calculated as:

```
48 * NET_SOCK_CFG_NBR_SOCK
```

Where: NET_SOCK_CFG_NBR_SOCK is the number of sockets configured.

μC/TCP-IP INTERNAL DATA USAGE

This represents the amount of data space needed for μC/TCP-IP's internal data structures and variables, and varies from about 300 to 1900 bytes depending on the options configured.

	μC/TCP-IP	Number	Bytes per	Total
1	Small transmit buffers	20	152	3,040
2	Large transmit buffers	10	1,594	15,940
3	Large receive buffers	10	1,518	15,180
4	Network interfaces	1	76	76
5	Timers	30	28	840
6	IP addresses	2 + 1	24	72
7	ICMP source quench	20	1	20
8	IGMP groups	32	1	32
9	ARP cache	10	56	560
10	Connections	20	56	1,120
11	TCP connections	10	280	2,800
12	Sockets	10	48	480
13	μC/TCP-IP fixed data usage			1,900
	Total:			42,060

Table 3-5 **μC/TCP-IP Data Footprint**

Lines 1 to 8 in Table 3-5 provide data sizes that may vary as the number of each element is determined at configuration time. You could build a spreadsheet to reproduce the table above using the equations described above. Line 9 is the fixed internal data usage for μC/TCP-IP. With such a configuration, we see that the system total RAM usage exceeds 40 K.

3-2-7 μC/TCP-IP ADD-ON OPTIONS DATA FOOTPRINT

The RAM data usage for the μC/TCP-IP add-on options is provided for planning assistance. In the following table, we use the definition of the size of **CPU_STK** as being 4 bytes.

μC/TCP-IP ADD-ON OPTIONS	RAM Size (Kbytes)	Based on Note
μC/DHCPc	3.4	
μC/DNSc	8.8	DNSc_MAX_HOSTNAME_SIZE * DNSc_MAX_CACHED_HOSTNAMES Where: DNSc_MAX_HOSTNAME_SIZE is the maximum DNS name size in characters DNSc_MAX_CACHED_HOSTNAMES is the maximum number of cached DNS names configured.
μC/HTTPs	17.7	sizeof(CPU_STK) * HTTP_CFG_TASK_STK_SIZE Typical configuration: HTTP_CFG_TASK_STK_SIZE = 2048
μC/FTPs	27.1	sizeof(CPU_STK) * FTP_CFG_TASK_STK_SIZE Typical configuration: FTP_CFG_TASK_STK_SIZE = 512
μC/FTPc	0.1	sizeof(CPU_STK) * FTP_CFG_TASK_STK_SIZE Typical configuration: FTP_CFG_TASK_STK_SIZE = 512
μC/TFTPs	8.6	sizeof(CPU_STK) * TFTP_CFG_TASK_STK_SIZE Typical configuration: TFTP_CFG_TASK_STK_SIZE = 1024
μC/TFTPc	2.0	sizeof(OS_STK) * TFTP_CFG_TASK_STK_SIZE Typical configuration: TFTP_CFG_TASK_STK_SIZE = 1024
μC/SNTPc	N/A	
μC/SMTPc	1.0	104 bytes + 1024 bytes (DATA memory)
μC/POP3c	1.1	128 bytes + 1004 bytes (DATA memory)
μC/TELNETs	4.1	

Table 3-6 **μC/TCP-IP Add-ons RAM Usage**

3-2-8 SUMMARY

Several considerations are necessary when adding a TCP/IP stack to an embedded system. Most of these are performance related, including:

- The CPU's ability to process all of the packets to be transmitted or received
- The Ethernet Controller type has an impact on the driver
- The transfer method between the Ethernet Controller and the TCP/IP stack has an impact on performance
  - Byte copy from one location to another via the CPU
  - DMA transfer
- The Zero-Copy architecture of the TCP/IP stack has an impact on performance
- The code and data footprints:
  - Code footprint depends on what protocols are used and this depends on what the specific goal of the application.
  - A data footprint is largely affected by the number of network buffers required. Chapter 7, "Transport Protocols" on page 165 gives the means to evaluate the number of buffers a system should configure. Sample applications provided in Part II of this book and the µC/IPerf application found in Chapter 6, "Troubleshooting" on page 135, provide additional means to evaluate a system's performance based on its configuration.

Next, we will examine Ethernet in the first layer at the bottom of the reference model to discover its importance in the product design. Ethernet driver development and test represent challenges the embedded engineer must face. We will then move up through the layers on our way to the Application layer, finding additional obstacles to overcome in order to efficiently embed a TCP/IP stack into a product.

Chapter

4

LAN = Ethernet

With the widespread use of copper twisted pair and its star topology, Ethernet as a LAN technology offers the lowest computer or embedded target cost per node at a performance that enables a large number of applications.

Regardless of the speed (10/100/1000 Mbps) and medium (coaxial, twisted pair, fiber, radio frequencies) the following two aspects are always the same:

- Frame format
- Access method

Because these elements do not change for a specific physical medium, the interface to IP, the protocol in the layer above does not change either, which makes life a lot easier. Note that the discussion in this chapter is valid for wired Ethernet. Most of it can also be applied to Wi-Fi with minimal changes to an Ethernet frame header.

Wired Ethernet supports various speeds under the IEEE 802.3 Standard, as follows:

Speed	Standard
10 Mbps	IEEE 802.3
100 Mbps	IEEE 802.3u
1000 Mbps	IEEE 802.3z
10,000 Mbps	IEEE 802.3ae

Table 4-1 **Wired Ethernet Speeds and IEEE Standards**

4-1 TOPOLOGY

Ethernet was developed to address communication over a shared coaxial cable, as shown in Figure 4-1. The design of Ethernet had to take into account such challenges as collision detection on the coaxial cable, as it is possible for two hosts to transmit simultaneously.

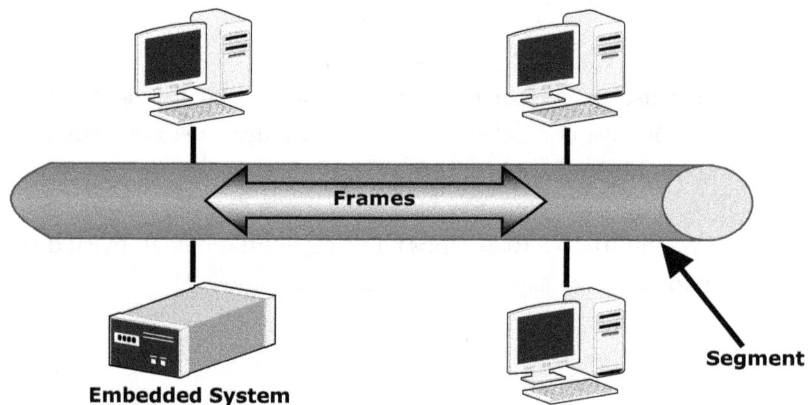

Figure 4-1 **First-Generation Ethernet - Coaxial Cable**

The sheer weight of coaxial cable made it impractical for use in high-rise buildings. Easy adaptation to telephony wiring with twisted pair cabling, hubs, and switches allows Ethernet to achieve point-to-point connectivity, and increase reliability. Twisted-pair wiring also lowers installation costs, enabling Ethernet to offer a cost per workstation that was unbeatable compared to competing technologies (i.e., ARCNET and Token Ring).

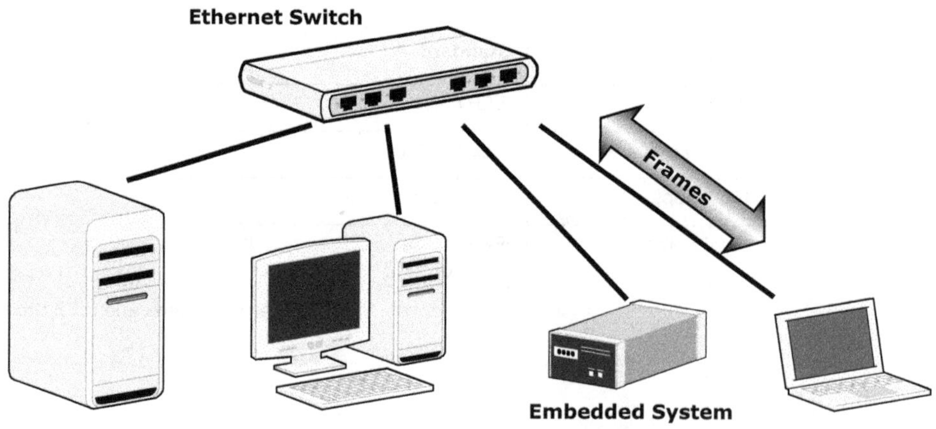

Figure 4-2 **Ethernet Today - Twisted Copper Pair and Switching**

Figure 4-2 shows an Ethernet network as we would connect it today. Between the original coaxial cable of the first generation Ethernet, and today's switch, Ethernet twisted pair cabling used hubs. A hub has the form factor of an Ethernet switch, but it acts as a coaxial cable. In a hub, all traffic from any RJ-45 port is visible on any other port, which is especially useful for troubleshooting. In that capacity, a Network protocol analyzer can be connected to any port on the hub and decode all of the traffic to and from any ports. This means that the hub is therefore the segment.

With today's Ethernet switch, each link to an RJ-45 is a segment, a concept called micro-segmentation. We will see in upcoming sections that certain traffic on an Ethernet network is undesirable. A switch allows for the removal of this traffic since the host connected to a port receives only the traffic destined to it, improving Ethernet network performance.

As with many other embedded technologies, hardware costs have constantly decreased over the past two decades. Given Ethernet's popularity, it is extremely common for a microcontroller to feature an integrated Ethernet Controller.

4-2 ETHERNET HARDWARE CONSIDERATIONS

Developing an Ethernet Driver is a fairly complex task. In addition to the Ethernet controller, often the developer must take into consideration on-chip clock and power peripheral management. If the developer is lucky, the semiconductor vendor may provide a Board Support Package (BSP) to tackle peripheral configurations. Pin multiplexing via general purpose I/O (GPIO) is required in some cases. Do not underestimate the complexity of this task.

4-3 ETHERNET CONTROLLER

In Chapter 2 we saw that there are a few Ethernet controller architectures to choose from when designing an embedded system. The main factor influencing choice is the location of the RAM used to hold received or transmitted frames.

For system design, you can use a specific chip for Ethernet or a microcontroller/ microprocessor with an integrated Ethernet controller. The Ethernet controller must cover the two bottom layers of the networking model: Data Link and Physical Layer (PHY).

IEEE-802.3 defines the Ethernet media access controller (MAC) which implements a Data Link layer. The latest MACs support operation at 10 Mbps, 100 Mbps and 1000 Mbps (1 Gbps).

The interface between the MAC and the PHY is typically implemented via the Media Independent Interface (MII), which consists of a data interface and a management interface between a MAC and a PHY (see Figure 4-3).

The PHY is the physical interface transceiver, implementing the Ethernet physical layer described in Chapter 1. IEEE 802.3 specifies several physical media standards. The most widely used are 10BASE-T, 100BASE-TX, and 1000BASE-T (Gigabit Ethernet), running at 10 Mbps, 100 Mbps and 1000 Mbps (1 Gbps), respectively.

The naming convention of 10BASE-T corresponds to the Ethernet physical media:

- The number in the name represents the maximum line speed in megabits per second (Mbps).
- BASE is the abbreviation for baseband. There is no frequency-division multiplexing (FDM) or other frequency shifting modulation in use; each signal (RX, TX) has full control of the wire.
- T stands for twisted pair cable. There may be more than one twisted pair standard at the same line speed. In this case, a letter or digit is added following the T. For example, 100BASE-TX.

Typically, integrated PHY on a microcontroller use the 10/100 PHY Ethernet implementation and incorporate separate 10BASE-T (10 Mbps) and 100BASE-TX (100 Mbps) interfaces. Most recently, 1-Gbps Ethernet became available in some MACs.

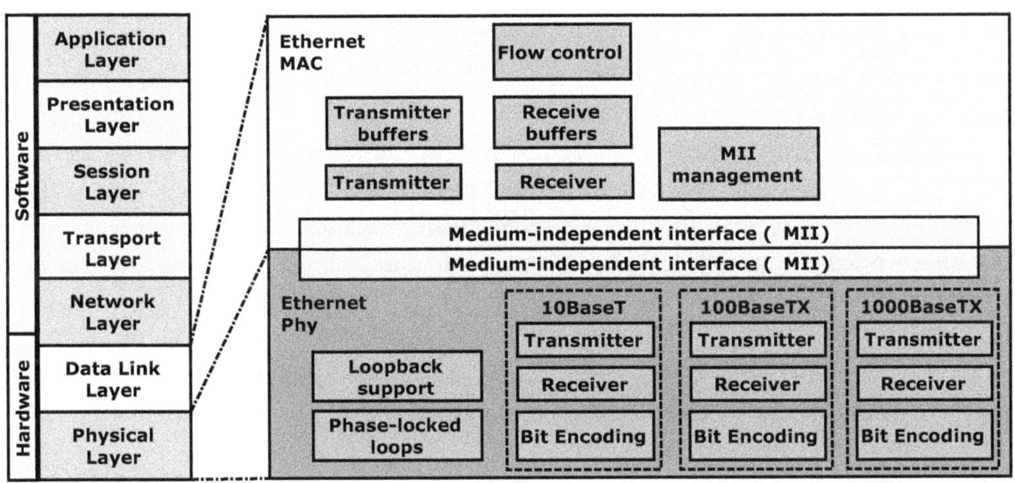

Figure 4-3 **10/100/1000 Ethernet MAC and PHY**

Many semiconductor vendors do not implement the PHY and MAC on the same chip since the PHY incorporates a significant amount of analog hardware. In comparison, the MAC is typically a purely digital component, and it is easier to integrate the MAC with current chip technologies. Adding the PHY adds analog signal circuits and increases the chip footprint and production costs. Semiconductor vendors sometimes leave the PHY off-chip. However, thanks to recent chip technology advances, the MAC and PHY can be effectively integrated on the same chip.

The typical PHY implementation still requires such components as an RJ-45 female jack and a local area network magnetic isolation module to protect the PHY from electrical abuse. To save space on the printed circuit board, it is possible to find dedicated Ethernet RJ-45 jacks that integrate analog components.

Single-chip Ethernet microcontrollers are popular in the embedded industry as the microcontrollers incorporating the Ethernet MAC and PHY on a single chip eliminate most external components. This reduces the overall pin count, chip footprint, and can also lower power consumption, especially if power-down mode management is available.

With the MII management interface, upper layers of the TCP/IP stack can monitor and control the PHY, for example, it can monitor the link status. Let's see how this is accomplished.

4-3-1 AUTO-NEGOTIATION

As Ethernet evolved, hubs gave way to switches, electronics improved, and the Ethernet link advanced from half duplex (alternative transmission and reception) to full duplex (simultaneous transmission and reception). Given that Ethernet offers various transmission rates (such as 10 Mbps, 100 Mbps and 1000 Mbps) and different duplex modes, a method is therefore necessary so that two Ethernet interfaces communicate together using different transmission rates (note that an Ethernet switch port is defined as an Ethernet interface). This method is called auto-negotiation, and is a feature offered in the majority of PHY interfaces used today.

For Ethernet to work with diverse link capabilities, every Ethernet device capable of multiple transmission rates uses auto-negotiation to declare its possible modes of operation.

The two devices (host and/or switch port) involved select the best possible mode of operation that can be shared by both. Higher speed (1000 Mbps) is preferred over lower speed (10 or 100 Mbps), and full duplex is preferable over half duplex at the same speed.

If one host of the two cannot perform auto-negotiation and the second one can, the host that is capable of auto-negotiation has the means to determine the speed of the facing host and set its configuration to match. This method does not, however, detect the presence of full-duplex mode. In this case, half duplex is assumed, which may create a problem called "duplex mismatch." This issue arises when one host operates in full duplex while the corresponding host operates in half duplex.

It is always a good idea to keep auto-negotiation configured, as Ethernet link capabilities are controlled via auto-negotiation.

If you believe that the PHY driver is not negotiating the link speed and duplex properly, use an oscilloscope to verify the signals on the link.

The mechanism used by auto-negotiation to communicate between two Ethernet devices is similar to the mechanism used by a 10BASE-T host to connect to another device. It uses pulses transmitted when the devices are not exchanging data.

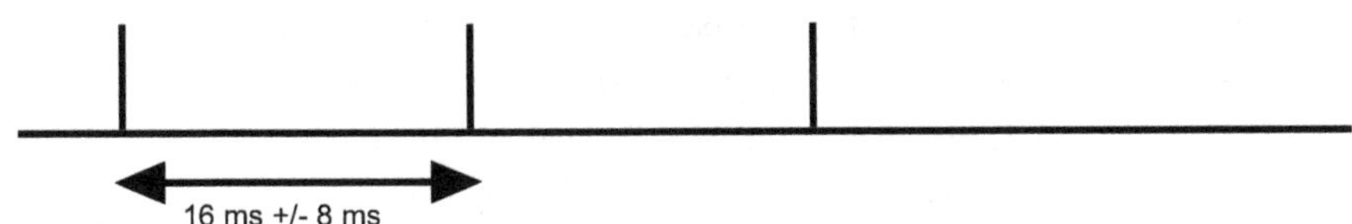

Figure 4-4 **10BASE-T Normal Link Pulses (NLP)**

Figure 4-4 shows that the pulses are unipolar positive-only electrical pulses of 100 ns duration, generated at intervals of 16 ms (with a tolerance of 8 ms). These pulses are called link integrity test (LIT) pulses in 10BASE-T terminology, and are referred to as normal link pulses (NLP) in the auto-negotiation specification. This is usually the signal that is used to light the LED on certain RJ-45 connectors.

When a frame or two consecutive LIT pulses are received, the host will detect a valid link status. The failure of a link or a host is detected by the other host if a frame or pulses are not received for 50 to 150 ms.

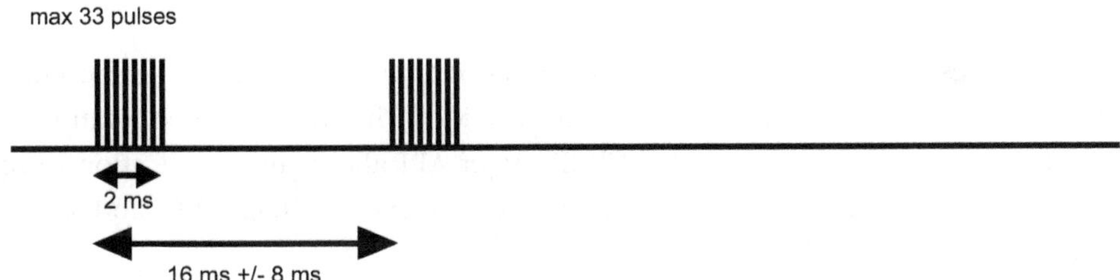

Figure 4-5 **Auto-negotiation Fast-Link Pulses (FLP)**

In Figure 4-5, auto-negotiation borrows from the pulse mechanism. The difference is that the pulse sequence is at most 33 pulses and is called a fast-link pulse (FLP) burst.

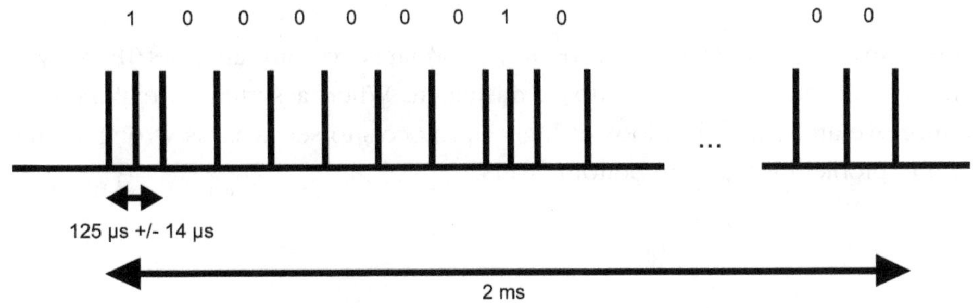

Figure 4-6 **Link code word (a 16-bit word) encoded in a fast link pulse burst**

Figure 4-6 pictures FLP made up of 17 pulses, 125 µs apart. An intermediate pulse can be inserted between each set of two pulses in the stream of the 17 pulses. The presence of a pulse represents a logical 1,and the absence a logical 0. These intermediate pulses number 16 and are called a link code word (LCW). The 17 pulses are always present and are used as a clock, while the 16 pulses represent the actual information transmitted.

The embedded software engineer can debug the PHY driver by looking at the PHY controller registers via the MII interface and make sure the values in these registers match the pulses on the link.

Figure 4-7 **Link status as represented in Microsoft Windows**

Figure 4-7 indicates how Ethernet PHYs and corresponding drivers can make the link status available to the stack and the stack to the application. This is how an operating system provides information on link status. µC/TCP-IP driver API allows the application to receive the link status (see Chapter 14, "Network Device Drivers" on page 299 and Chapter A, "µC/TCP-IP Device Driver APIs" on page 385).

The non-recognition of the FLP also can create duplex mismatch. For a 10BASE-T device, an FLP does not make an NLP. This means that when a 10BASE-T host communicates with a host at a higher speed, the 10BASE-T host detects a link failure and switches to half-duplex mode while the higher-speed host will be in full-duplex mode. The next section describes what happens in this case.

There are many possible causes for poor performance on an Ethernet/IP network. As mentioned earlier, one of them is duplex mismatch. When a system is experiencing bad performance, we are tempted to look at higher protocols to see what is wrong. Sometimes, however, the problem is with the bottom layers.

4-3-2 DUPLEX MISMATCH

When two Ethernet devices are configured in two different duplex modes, a *duplex mismatch* results. A host operation in half duplex is not expecting to receive a frame when it is transmitted. However, because the connecting host is in full duplex, frames can be transmitted to the half duplex host. The receiving host senses these frames as late collisions interpreted as a hard error rather than a normal Ethernet Carrier Sense Multiple Access/Collision Detection (CSMA/CD) collision, and will not attempt to resend the frame. At the same time, the full-duplex host does not detect a collision and thus does not resend the frame. The other host would have discarded the frame since it was corrupted by the collision. Also, the full duplex host will report frame check sequence (FCS) errors because it is not expecting incoming frames to be truncated by collision detection.

These collisions and frame errors disrupt the flow of communication. Some protocols in the Application layer or the Transport layer manage flow control and make sure packets not completed are retransmitted. This is explained in more detail when we cover Transport Protocols.

It is recommended that you avoid using older Ethernet hubs with new switches as duplex mismatch can be expected. Any duplex mismatch degrades link performance. The network runs, but at a much lower bandwidth. Never force one end of a connection to full duplex while the other end is set to auto-negotiation. Retransmission slows down data exchange. This is acceptable for a link with low traffic (connectivity needs only), but will be a real problem for a link with high-bandwidth requirements (node with throughput requirement).

Auto-negotiation in PHY driver
To avoid duplex mismatch that can be a cause for performance degradation in the Ethernet network, it is recommended that you always keep the PHY driver auto-negotiation feature enabled.

4-4 ETHERNET 802.3 FRAME STRUCTURE

4-4-1 802.3 FRAME FORMAT

This is the Ethernet frame as standardized by IEEE 802.3.

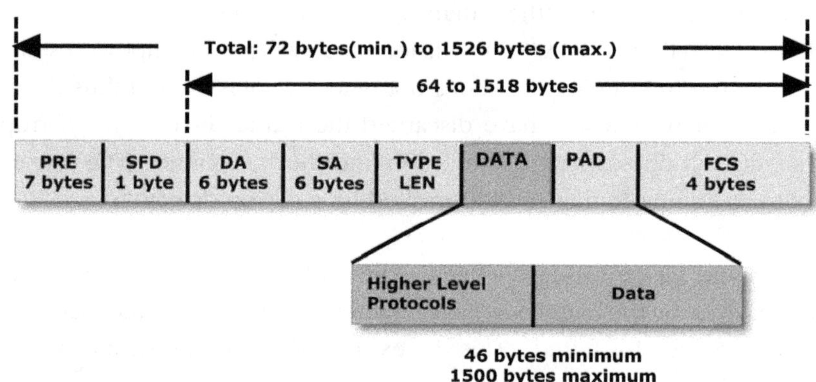

Figure 4-8 **802.3 Frame Format**

Acronym	Description
PRE	Preamble
SFD	Start Frame Delimiter
DA	Destination Address
SA	Source Address
TYPE/LEN	Length
Higher Level Protocols	Protocol code being carried in this frame
DATA	....
PAD	Padding
FCS	Frame Check Sequence

Table 4-2 **Ethernet Frame fields**

RFC 1010 EtherType (2 bytes)

0X0800	IP
0x0806	ARP

Table 4-3 **EtherTypes**

There are more protocol numbers in RFC 1010 than the two listed above. For practicality, these are the two most widely used in the type of networks we work with today.

The figure above is labeled 802.3 Frame Format, but it describes what is referred to as the Ethernet II frame or the so-called DIX (after Digital, Intel and Xerox). It is the most common frame format used and is directly used by IP.

Other Ethernet frame formats include:

- Novell's non-standard variation of IEEE 802.3
- IEEE 802.2 LLC frame
- IEEE 802.2 LLC/SNAP frame

With 802.3 format and the three formats listed above, depending on the types of hosts connected on the network, it is possible that on networks where the embedded system is installed there may be additional Ethernet frame formats.

A Virtual LAN (VLAN) is a network of hosts that communicate as if they were connected to the same LAN, regardless of their physical location. Ethernet frames may optionally contain an IEEE 802.1Q tag to identify what VLAN it belongs to and its IEEE 802.1p priority (class of service). The IEEE 802.3ac specification defines this encapsulation and increases the maximum frame by 4 bytes from 1518 to 1522 bytes.

This quality of service field is used by the Ethernet switches to process certain frames in priority, for example, for such real-time services as voice or video versus data. The TCP/IP stack and the Ethernet switch must be able to process 802.1Q tag and 801.1p priority if VLAN support and quality of service is required in the dedicated network.

With the evolution of Ethernet, it became necessary to eventually unify the formats. The convention is that values of the TYPE/LEN field between 64 and 1522 indicate the use of the 802.3 Ethernet format with a length field, while values of 1536 decimal (0x0600 hexadecimal) and greater indicate the use of the Ethernet II frame format with an EtherType sub-protocol identifier (see Table 4-3 above or RFC 1010). This convention allows software to determine whether a frame is an Ethernet II frame or an IEEE 802.3 frame, enabling the coexistence of both standards.

Using a Network Protocol Analyzer as explained in Chapter 6, "Troubleshooting" on page 135, it is possible to capture Ethernet frames on the network. Diagrams will often refer to frame and packet structures as decoded by the Network Protocol Analyzer. Figure 4-8, 802.3 Frame Format, is a good example. When decoding an Ethernet frame, the Network Protocol Analyzer presents the structure of the frame.

Important fields for the software are the Destination Address (DA), the Source Address (SA), the type/length of the frame (TYPE/LEN) and the payload (DATA). The Frame Check Sequence (FCS) determines the validity of the frame. If the frame is invalid, the Ethernet controller discards it.

The combination of the DA, SA and TYPE field are referred as the MAC header.

Preamble and the Start Frame Delimiter are used for clocking and synchronization. The Ethernet controller strips these out and will only transfer the remaining frame to a buffer beginning with the Destination Address and ending with the Frame Check Sequence.

Given that Ethernet was initially developed for a shared medium, Ethernet controllers transmit 12 bytes of idle characters after each frame so that interfaces detect collisions created by frames transmitted from other interfaces on the same network. For 10 Mbps interfaces this takes 9600 ns, for 100 Mbps interfaces 960 ns, and for 1 Gbps interfaces 96 ns.

4-5 MAC ADDRESS

As indicated earlier, frames of data are transmitted into the physical layer medium (copper, coax, fiber, and radio interfaces). NICs listen over the physical medium for frames with a unique LAN address called the Media Access Control (MAC) address.

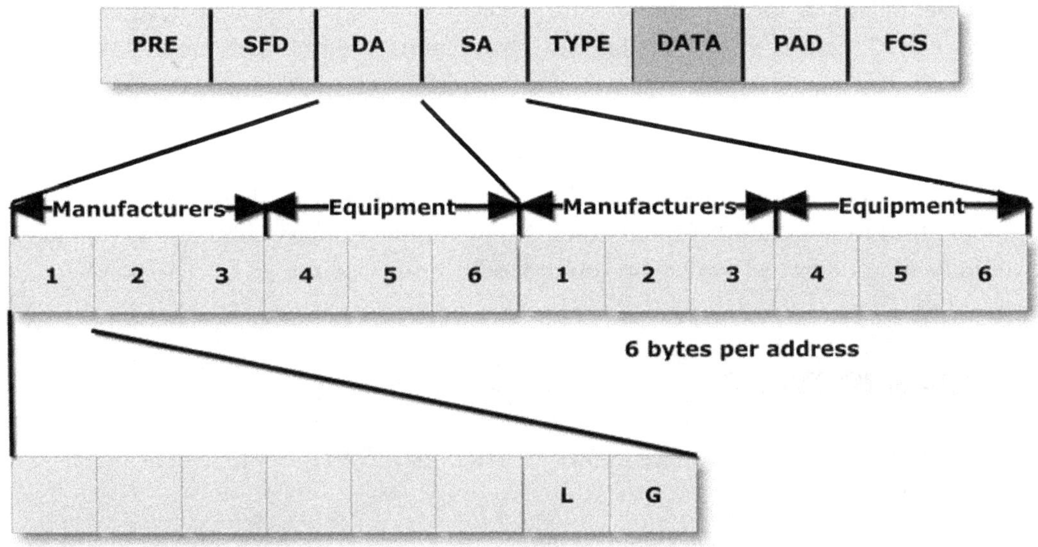

Figure 4-9 **MAC Address**

Figure 4-9 Illustrates MAC addresses, Destination (DA) and Source (SA) in an Ethernet Frame. It also shows that an Ethernet MAC address is made of 6 bytes (48 bits). The first three bytes are the manufacturer ID. The last three bytes represent the serial number for the manufacturer. The MAC address is represented with each byte in hexadecimal notation separated by either a colon (:) or a hyphen (-), or a semicolon which is more common, for example: 00:00:0C:12:DE:7F. This is also referred as a universally administered individual address as per the L and G bits in Figure 4-9.

The manufacturer ID is assigned by the IEEE and is called an Organizationally Unique Identifier (OUI). The IEEE OUI Registry at http://standards.ieee.org/regauth/oui/oui.txt contains OUI that are registered. ID 00:00:0C in the previous example belongs to Cisco.

Each NIC is required to have a globally unique MAC address which is typically burned or programmed into the NIC, yet can also be overwritten via software configuration. When this happens, a locally administered address can be used. Universally administered and locally administered addresses are distinguished by setting the second least significant bit of the most significant byte of the address as depicted in Figure 4-9. The bit is 0 in all OUIs.

As its name states, a locally administered address is assigned to a host by a network administrator. Generally, however, the use of the universally administered MAC address provided by the manufacturer removes this management requirement on the network administrator.

Whichever method is used, attention should be paid to the MAC address assigned to a NIC as it could lead to duplicate MAC addresses. No two hosts can have the same MAC address. It would be akin to having two houses on the same street with the same civic number.

4-6 TRAFFIC TYPES

Network interfaces are usually programmed to listen for three types of messages that:

- are sent to their specific address
- qualify as a multicast for the specific interface
- are broadcast to all NICs

There are three types of addressing:

1. Unicast: A transmission to a single interface.
2. Multicast: A transmission to a group of interfaces on the network.
3. Broadcast: A transmission to all interfaces on the network.

Figure 4-9 shows that if the least significant bit of the most significant byte of the MAC address is set to a 0, the packet is meant to reach only one receiving NIC. This is called unicast.

If the least significant bit of the most significant byte is set to a 1, the packet is meant to be sent only once but will reach several NICs. This is called multicast.

All other messages are filtered out by the interface software, unless it is programmed to operate in promiscuous mode (this is a pass-through mode that allows the driver to pass all frames decoded to an application such as a network protocol analyzer (see section 6-2-2 "Wireshark" on page 152) to perform network sniffing.

All of the above-mentioned address types are used by Ethernet; however, IP also uses the same type of addressing. The scope is evidently different as IP operates on a different layer than Ethernet.

UNICAST

Unicast is a type of frame used to send information from one host to another host when there is only one source and one destination. Unicast is the predominant form of transmission on LANs and within the Internet. You are probably quite familiar with such standard unicast applications as HTTP, SMTP, FTP, and TELNET.

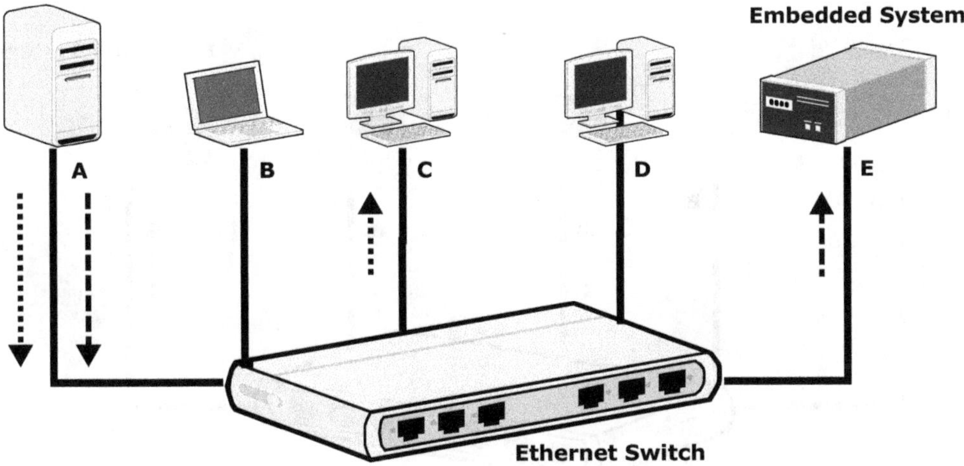

Figure 4-10 **Unicast: (host to host)**

In Figure 4-10, the dotted line represents a Unicast frame from A to C and the dashed line a Unicast frame from A to E.

BROADCAST

Broadcast is used to transmit information from one host to all other hosts. In this case there is just one source, but the information is sent to all connected destinations. Broadcast transmission is supported on Ethernet and may be used to send the same message to all computers on the LAN.

Broadcasting is very useful for such protocols as:

- Address Resolution Protocol (ARP) on IP when looking for the MAC address of a neighboring station.
- Dynamic Host Configuration Protocol (DHCP) on IP when a station is booting and is requesting an IP address from a DHCP server.
- Routing table updates. Broadcasts sent by routers with routing table updates to other routers.

The Ethernet broadcast destination address in hexadecimal is FF:FF:FF:FF:FF:FF.

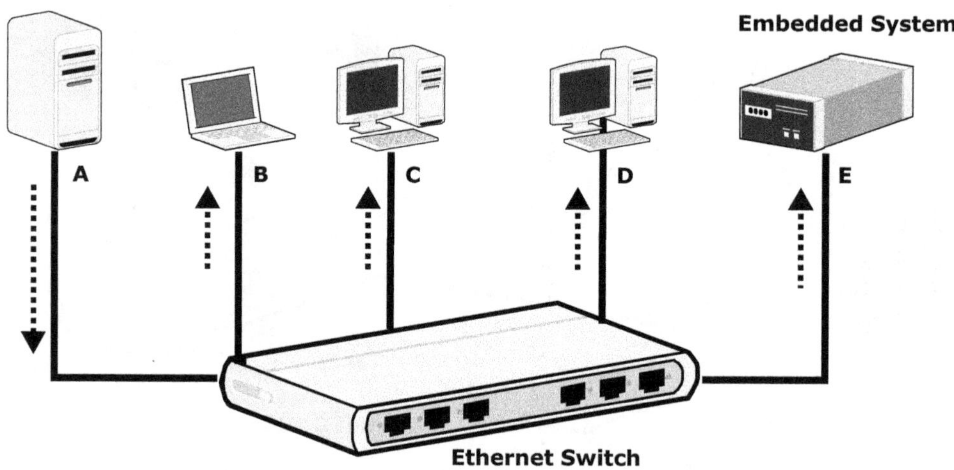

Figure 4-11 **Broadcast (one host to all hosts)**

The dotted line in Figure 4-11 is a Broadcast message from A to all other Ethernet interfaces on the LAN.

With coaxial-cable technology (shared medium), and a growing number of workstations per network, broadcast may create an undesired volume of traffic. Twisted pair physical layer and daisy-chained Ethernet switches often configured in a loop for redundancy purposes will create a broadcast storm (i.e., the broadcast message will circle forever in the loop). This is why Ethernet switches implement micro-segmentation and spanning-tree protocols. The spanning tree protocol allows Ethernet switches to determine where to break the loop to avoid a broadcast storm. It uses a Multicast address type.

MULTICAST

Multicast addressing is used to transmit data from one or more hosts to a set of other hosts. There is possibly one or multiple sources, and the information is distributed to a set of destinations. LANs using hubs/repeaters inherently support multicast since all packets reach all network interfaces connected to the LAN.

Multicasting delivers the same packet simultaneously to a group of hosts. For example, a video server application that uses multicast transmits networked TV channels. Simultaneous delivery of high-quality video to a large number of stations will exhaust the capability of even a high-bandwidth network with a powerful server. This can be a major scalability issue for applications that require sustained bandwidth. One way to optimize bandwidth usage for larger groups of clients is the use of multicast networking.

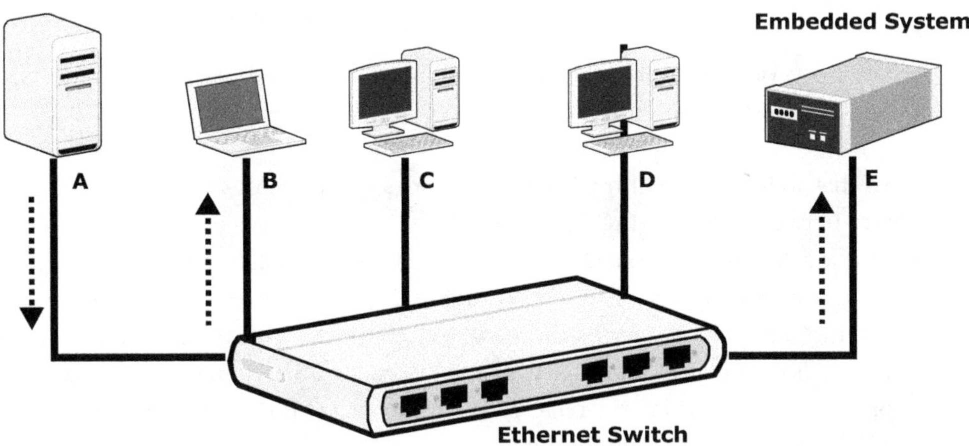

Figure 4-12 **Multicast: (from one host to a group)**

In Figure 4-12, the dotted line represents a Multicast message from A to a group of host, in this case B and E.

The Internet Assigned Numbers Authority (IANA) allocates Ethernet addresses from 01:00:5E:00:00:00 through 01:00:5E:7F:FF:FF for multicasting. This means there are 23 bits available for the multicast group ID plus reserved groups as the spanning tree group address used by Ethernet switches. The spanning tree group address is 01-80-C2-00-00-01.

4-7 ADDRESS RESOLUTION PROTOCOL (ARP)

In our discussion of Ethernet, we specified that as a Data-Link layer protocol, Ethernet employs a MAC address to identify each NIC. We also saw at the Network layer that for internetworking, we need a network address (in our case, an IP address). The IP address definition and structure is covered in the next chapter, but it is interesting to note that an IP address consists of 32 bits while a MAC address consists of 48 bits. So, the next logical question might be: "How are these addresses related to one another?"

The relationship/translation between the Data-Link address and the IP address is required so that data can follow a path between layers and this cross-reference is accomplished via the Address Resolution Protocol (ARP).

In some IP technology descriptions, ARP is placed at Layer 2 while others place it at Layer 3. In reality, we can say that ARP is a layer 2.5 protocol, as it interfaces between Network addresses and Data-Link addresses.

ARP is used by hosts on a network to find MAC addresses of neighbors when the hosts want to connect to a neighbor using an IP address.

In the figures that follow, we will track an ARP process. The result of the ARP process is a cross-reference between IP and MAC addresses. These cross-references are stored in an ARP cache, which is a data structure found in the TCP/IP stack. Each station on a network has its own ARP cache, the size of which can be configured to customize its RAM footprint. You need to know the number of stations the host will connect to on the network, since one entry per connection will be created in the ARP cache. See Appendix C, "µC/TCP-IP Configuration and Optimization" on page 723, for the µC/TCP-IP configuration parameter relating to the number of ARP cache entries.

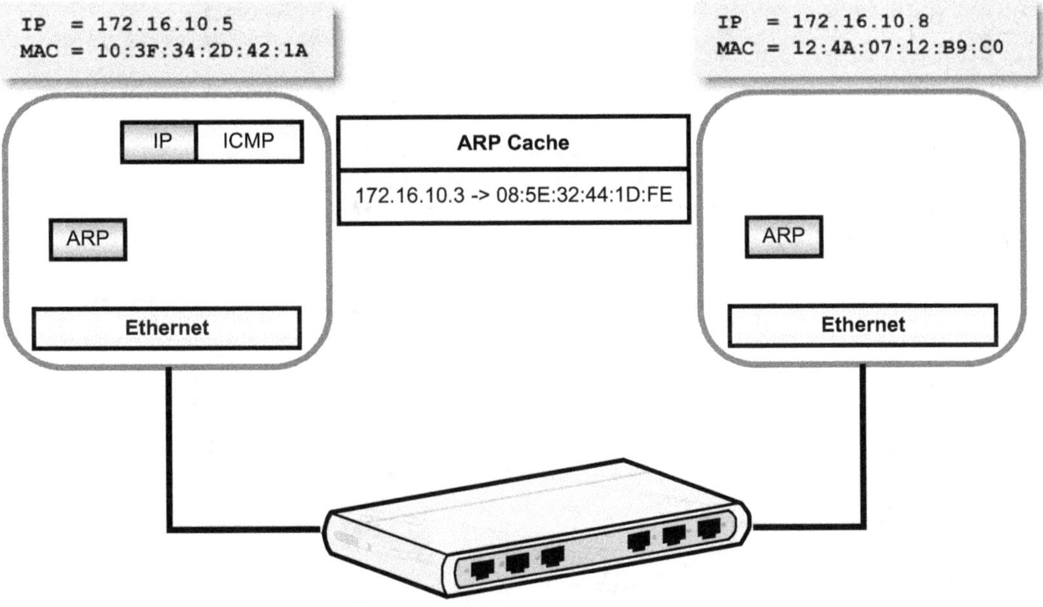

Figure 4-13 **ARP - Step 1**

Figure 4-13 represents the network for our example. The station on the left with IP address 172.16.10.5 sends a ping request (ICMP) to station on the right with IP address 172.16.10.8.

The ICMP module of the TCP/IP stack sends the command to the IP module of the stack.

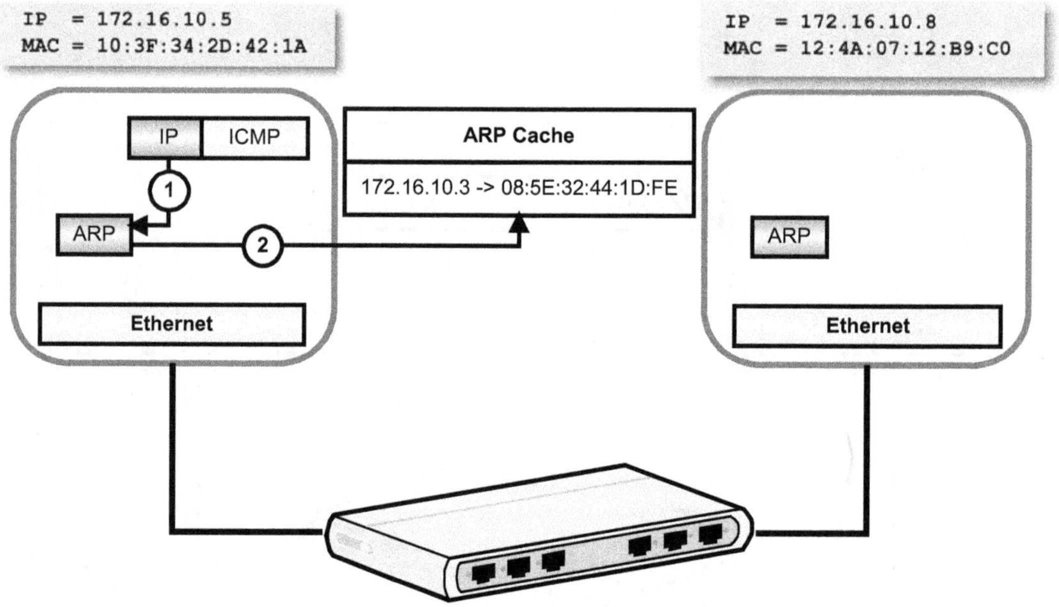

Figure 4-14 **ARP - Step 2**

F4-14(1) The IP module asks the ARP module to supply it with the MAC address (Layer 2).

F4-14(2) The ARP module consults its ARP cache (a table containing known IP to MAC addresses). The desired IP address is not in the table.

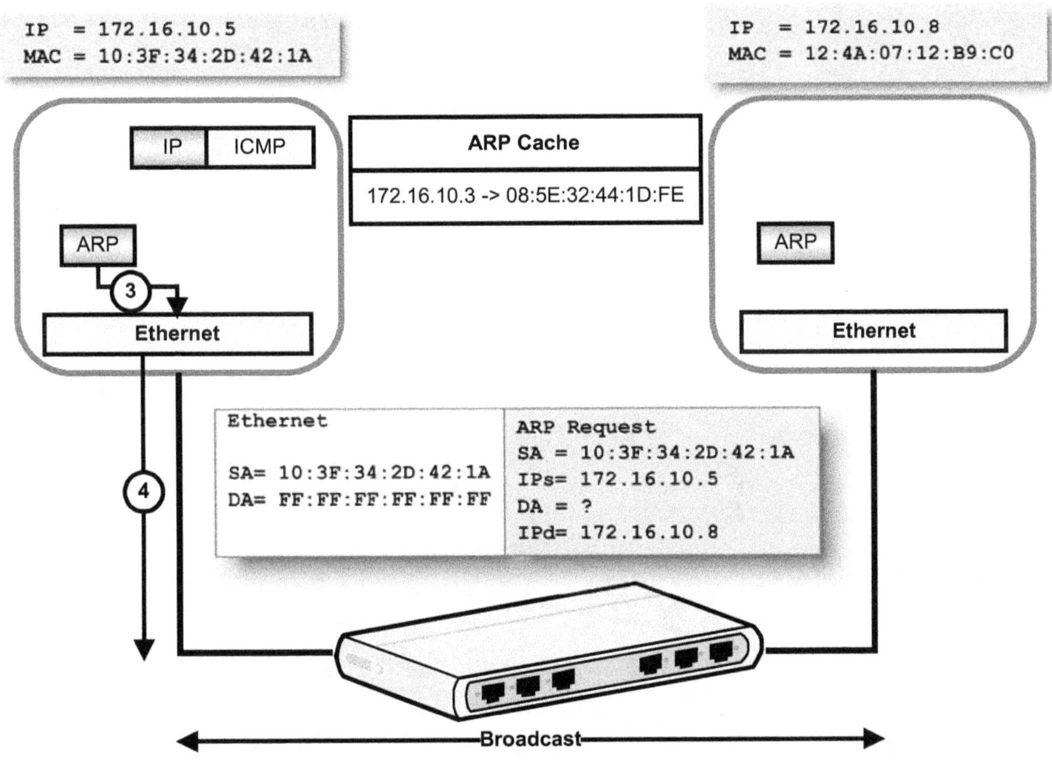

Figure 4-15 **ARP - Step 3**

F4-15(3) The ARP module sends an «ARP request» packet to the Ethernet module.

F4-15(4) The Ethernet module sends it to everyone («broadcast»). The Ethernet destination address (DA) in the ARP request packet is the Ethernet broadcast address. The source address (SA) is the MAC address of the host generating the request. The complete content of the ARP request is provided in the following section.

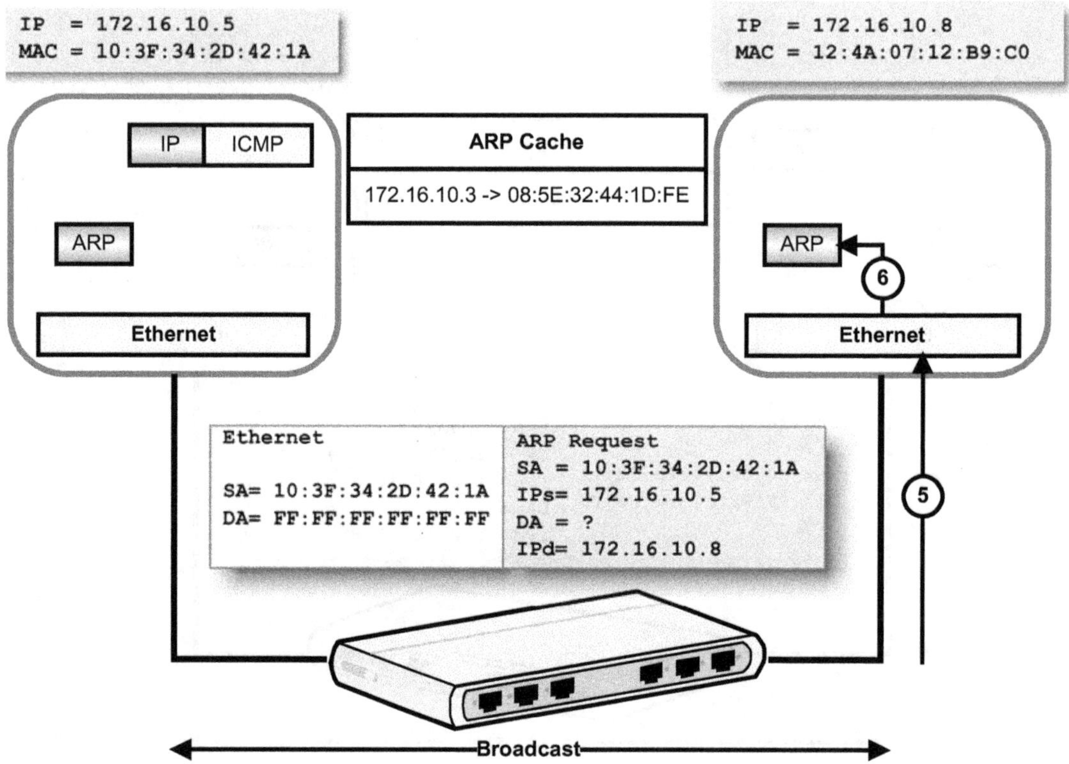

Figure 4-16 **ARP - Step 4**

F4-16(5) All stations on this network receive and decode the Ethernet broadcast frame.

F4-16(6) The ARP request is sent to the ARP module. Only station 172.16.10.8 realizes that it is an «ARP request» for itself.

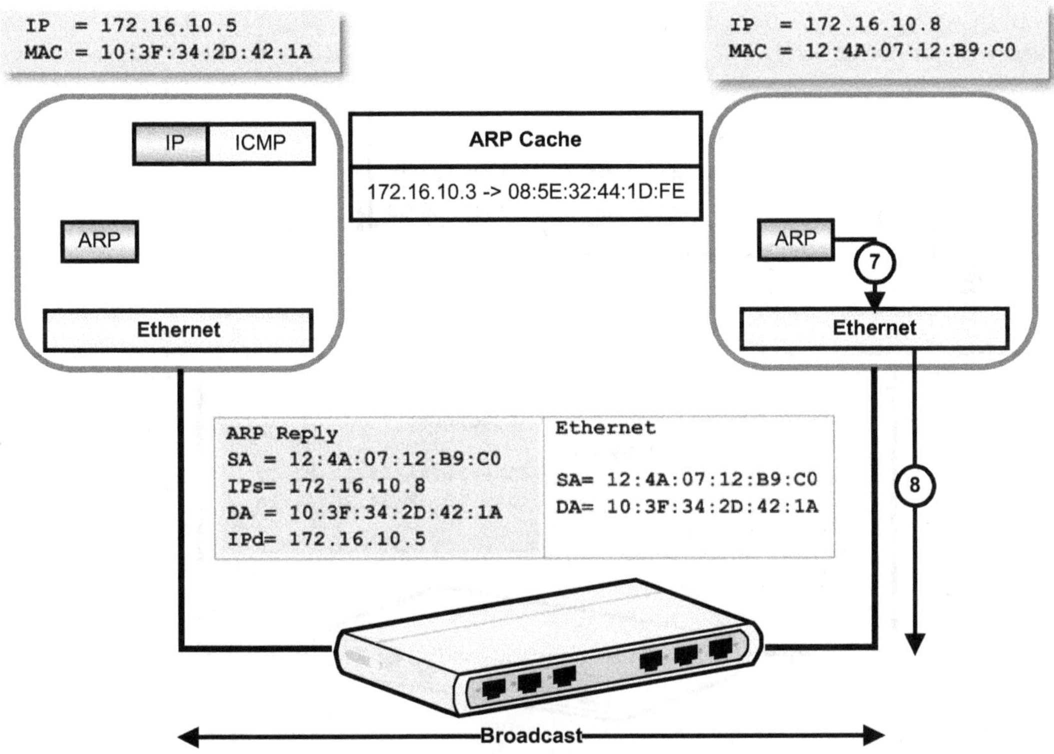

Figure 4-17 **ARP - Step 5**

F4-17(7) The ARP module in station 172.16.10.8 acknowledges the request and replies back with an answer («ARP reply») to the Ethernet module.

F4-17(8) The response is sent in an Ethernet frame to the station with the IP address 172.16.10.5. The Ethernet destination address is known because it is the source address that was part of the ARP Request. The Ethernet source address is the MAC address of station 172.16.10.8

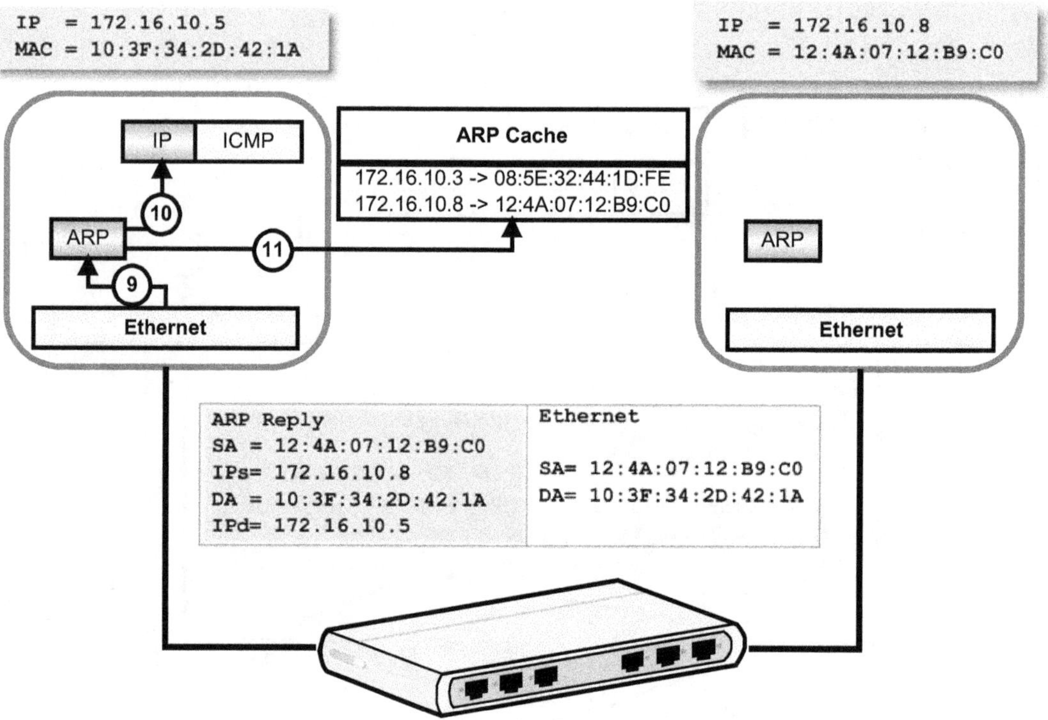

Figure 4-18 **ARP - Step 6**

F4-18(9) The Ethernet module of the station with the MAC address corresponding to the destination address in the Ethernet frame passes the reply to the ARP module.

F4-18(10) The ARP module forwards the missing information to the IP module that requested it initially.

F4-18(11) The ARP module also stores the information in the ARP cache.

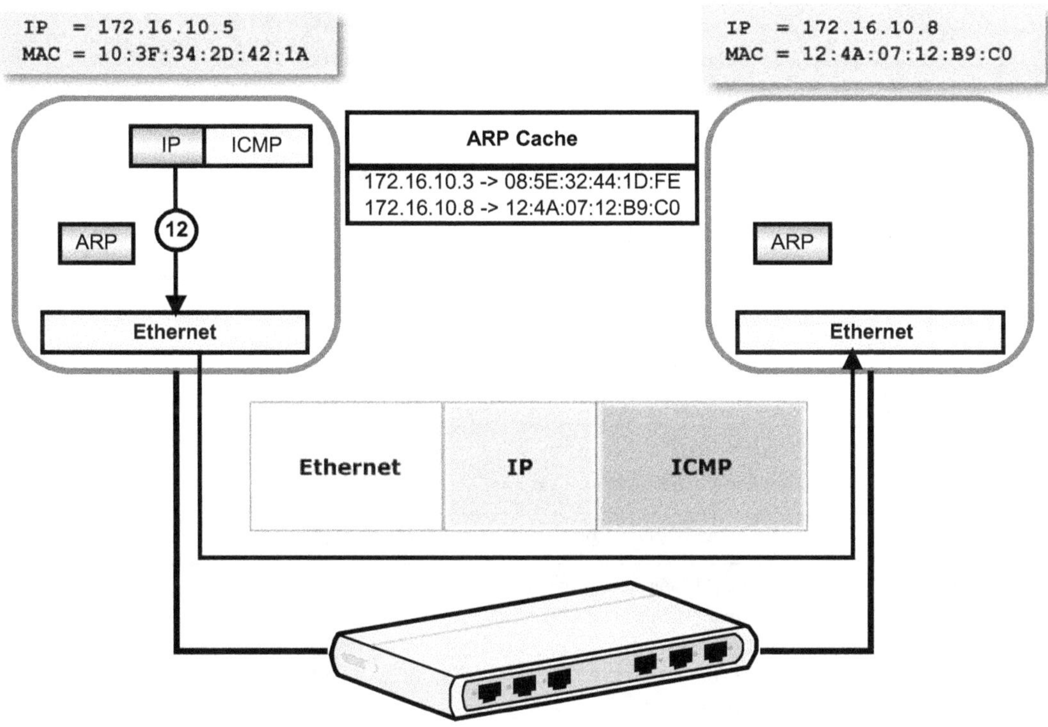

Figure 4-19 **ARP - Step 7**

F4-19(12) The IP module now sends the initial ICMP message to the station with the IP address of 172.16.10.8 because it now knows its Ethernet address, 12:4A:07:12:B9:C0.

4-8 ARP PACKET

When a host sends a packet to another host on the LAN for the first time, the first message seen on the network will be an ARP request. The ARP header is found at the beginning of each ARP packet. The header contains fields of fixed length, and each field has a specific role to play. Figure 4-20 provides the definition of this protocol header. This representation will be use throughout this book for all protocol headers. A Network Protocol Analyzer, explained in Chapter 6, “Troubleshooting” on page 135, allows you to examine ARP requests.

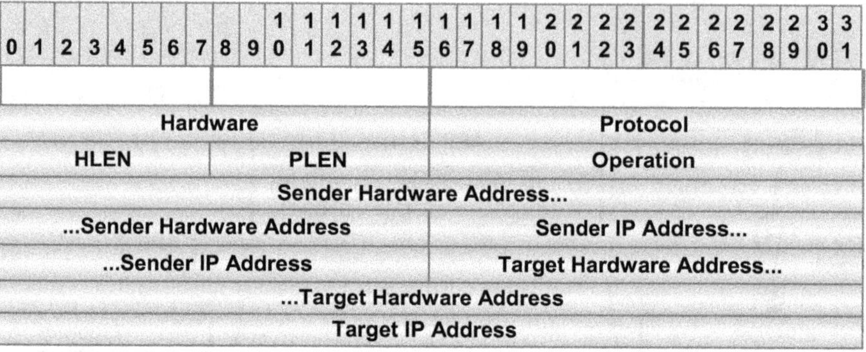

0 1 2 3 4 5 6 7 8 9 10 11 12 13 14 15 16 17 18 19 20 21 22 23 24 25 26 27 28 29 30 31
Hardware
Protocol
HLEN
PLEN
Operation
Sender Hardware Address...
...Sender Hardware Address
Sender IP Address...
...Sender IP Address
Target Hardware Address...
...Target Hardware Address
Target IP Address

Figure 4-20 **ARP Header**

HLen	Length of the physical address in bytes, Ethernet = 6
PLen	Length of the protocol address in bytes, IP = 4
Operation	The possible values for the Operation field are: 1.ARP request 2.ARP reply 3.RARP request 4.RARP reply
Hardware	Specifies the type of hardware address (1 specifies Ethernet)
Protocol	Represents the type of protocol addressing used (IP = 0x0800)
Sender Hardware	Physical address of the sender
Target Hardware	Target hardware address (normally FF:FF:FF:FF:FF:FF)
Sender IP	IP address of the sender
Target IP	IP address of target

Table 4-4 **ARP Header Fields**

A Network Protocol Analyzer decodes the Ethernet frame and presents the frame content. In the case of ARP messages, this figure will help understand the information decoded.

4-9 SUMMARY

Ethernet is the most popular technology to use for a LAN. The driver is made of two modules: the MAC driver and the PHY driver.

MII is a simple standard for the PHY layer as this standard is very well implemented and supported by most hardware vendors. Micrium, for example, provides a generic PHY driver that can easily be adapted to most MIIs.

Getting the hardware up and running is a challenge based on the complexity of various peripherals. Ethernet controllers that are integrated inside microcontrollers are complicated to use as there are multiple configurations to take care of such as those involving clock, power and general purpose I/O pins.

When testing an Ethernet driver, the first test should be to validate that the PHY layer negotiates the link speed and duplex properly. Once this is done, the developer is ready to send a first packet to the embedded system. This is usually done using the PING utility. (see Chapter 6, “Troubleshooting” on page 135). When the Ethernet and PHY are configured properly, the first packet on the network will be an ARP request followed by an ARP reply. In this case, the ARP request will be issued from the host sending the PING and the ARP reply will come from the embedded target.

The next chapter looks deeper into the subject of IP networking and protocol possibilities.

Chapter

5

IP Networking

With one or more protocols at every layer of the protocol stack, we often refer to Internet Protocol (IP) technology as the sum of all protocols. Strictly speaking, however, IP is the protocol used at the Network Layer.

For the embedded system developer, when employing IP technology in an embedded system, there is not much to actually do concerning the IP layer itself. What is important to know is how it works so that it can be used efficiently; configuring the TCP/IP stack actually requires minimal effort.

5-1 PROTOCOL FAMILY

The TCP/IP protocol stack is comprised of more than TCP and IP. Figure 5-1 shows that the TCP/IP stack represents a family of protocols (not all are included in this figure). The stack receives its name from the prevalent use of the TCP and IP protocols for the majority of data exchanges between two network devices.

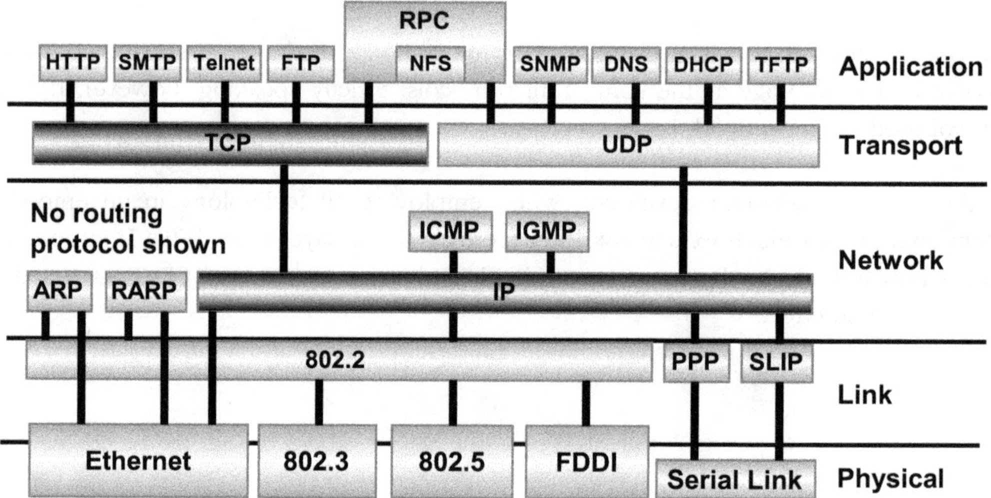

Figure 5-1 **IP Family of Protocols**

Figure 5-1 also introduces many new acronyms, and indicates which protocols are supported by Micrium's µC/TCP-IP. The important protocols used in embedded designs are covered in this book.

Protocol	Description	Micrium offer
HTTP	Hyper Text Transfer Protocol, the main web protocol	µC/HTTPs
SMTP	Simple Message Transport Protocol, used to send e-mails	µC/SMTPc
Telnet	Protocol used to provide a bidirectional interactive ASCII-based communications	µC/Telnet
FTP	File Transfer Protocol, used to exchange files	µC/FTPc and µC/FTPs

Protocol	Description	Micrium offer
RPC	Remote Procedure Call, uses Inter-Process Communication methods to create the illusion that the processes exchanging them are running in the same address space	Not Available
NFS	Network File System, file system developed by Sun Microsystems, Inc. a client/server system	Not Available
DNS	Domain Name Service, translates fully qualified domain names such as "www.mysite.com" into an IP address	µC/DNSc
DHCP	Dynamic Host Configuration Protocol, a network application protocol used by devices (DHCP clients) to obtain configuration information, primarily an IP address, subnet mask and default gateway, for operation in an IP network.	µC/DHCPc
SNMP	Simple Network Management Protocol, a set of standards for network management, including an application layer protocol, a database schema, and a set of data objects used to monitor network-attached devices.	Not available
TFTP	Trivial File Transfer Protocol, a simple file-transfer protocol, such as FTP using UDP as the transport layer.	µC/TFTPc and µC/TFTPs
TCP	Transport Control Protocol, the most widely-used transport layer protocol, developed for the Internet to guarantee the transmission of error-free data from one network device to another.	Part of µC/TCP-IP
UDP	User Datagram Protocol, the other transport layer protocol, which has no error recovery features, and is mostly used to send streamed material over the Internet.	Part of µC/TCP-IP
ARP	Address Resolution Protocol, a protocol used to map IP addresses to MAC addresses.	Part of µC/TCP-IP
RARP	Reverse Address Resolution Protocol, a protocol used by a host computer to obtain its IP address when it has its MAC address. DHCP is the current preferred method to obtain an IP address.	Not available
ICMP	Internet Control Message Protocol resides at the Network layer and is used to perform network troubleshooting and problem location.	Part of µC/TCP-IP
IGMP	Internet Group Management Protocol is used to manage the membership of IP multicast groups. IGMP is used by IP hosts and adjacent multicast routers to establish multicast group memberships.	Part of µC/TCP-IP
IP	Internet Protocol is arguably the world's single most popular network protocol	Part of µC/TCP-IP
Routing	Multiple routing protocols can be used at the IP layer.	Not available

Protocol	Description	Micrium offer
PPP	Point-To-Point Protocol, used for the transmission of IP packets over serial lines. It is faster and more reliable than SLIP because it supports functions that SLIP does not, such as error detection, dynamic assignment of IP addresses and data compression.	Not available
SLIP	Serial Line Internet Protocol is used for connection to the Internet via a dial-up connection.	Not available
FDDI	Fiber Distributed Data Interface provides a standard for data transmission in a local area network that provides a transmission range of up to 200 kilometers (124 miles). Although FDDI topology is a token ring network, it does not use the IEEE 802.5 token ring protocol as its basis;	Not available
802.2	IEEE 802.2 is the IEEE 802 standard defining Logical Link Control (LLC), which is the upper portion of the data link layer of the OSI Model.	Part of the Ethernet driver
802.3	IEEE 802.3 is a collection of IEEE standards defining the physical layer, and the media access control (MAC) sub layer of the data link layer, of wired Ethernet.	Part of the Ethernet driver
802.5	IEEE 802.5 is a collection of IEEE standards defining token ring local area network (LAN) technology. It resides at the data link layer (DLL) of the OSI model.	Not available

Table 5-1 **Short List of IP Family Protocols**

So far in this book, we've explained certain elements of a TCP/IP stack. When analyzing a network it is not surprising to open an Ethernet frame and find that the Ethernet payload is composed of an IP packet (EtherType 0x8000). Figure 5-2 shows how an IP packet is constructed. In this example, we see a Version 4 IP packet (IPv4), which is currently the Internet Protocol used in most private and public networks.

There are certain limitations in IPv4, the most important is the shortage of IP addresses for devices that can be connected globally. A new version of IP was developed at the end of the 1990's called IP Version 6 (IPv6) but is not yet widely deployed. This book, therefore, describes IPv4 since most embedded systems are devices operating in private networks that run on this protocol.

As we discussed in Chapter 1, data is encapsulated by different layers of the TCP/IP stack. As we move along the stack from the bottom to the top, every header will be described using the format shown in Figure 5-2.

The packet diagrams will become useful when analyzing network traffic using a Network Protocol Analyzer.

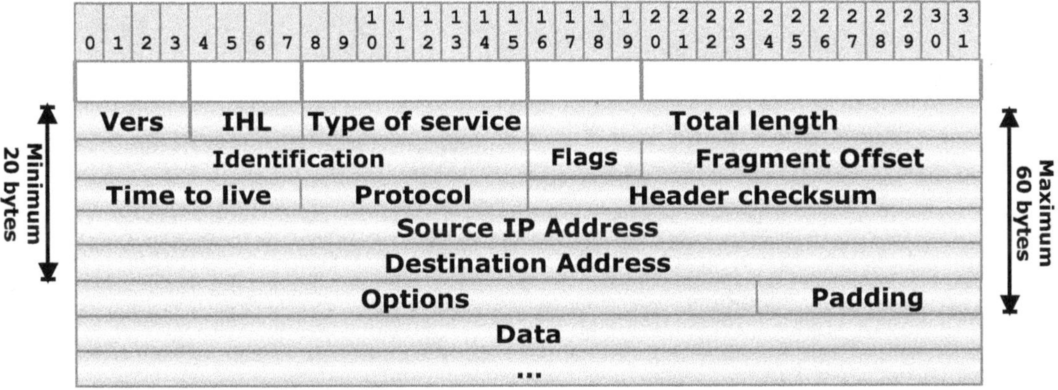

Figure 5-2 **IP version 4 Header and Packet**

5-2 INTERNET PROTOCOL (IP)

Every node on an IP network implements IP. Nodes in charge of forwarding IP packets are referred to as *routers*. Routers or gateways interconnect different networks, acting as the IP equivalent of a telephone switch.

Host computers or embedded systems prepare IP packets and transmit them over their attached network(s) using network-specific protocols (Data-Link protocols). Routers forward IP packets across networks.

IP is a best-effort protocol, since it does not provide for retransmission when the packet does not reach its final destination. Retransmission is left to protocols in the layers above IP.

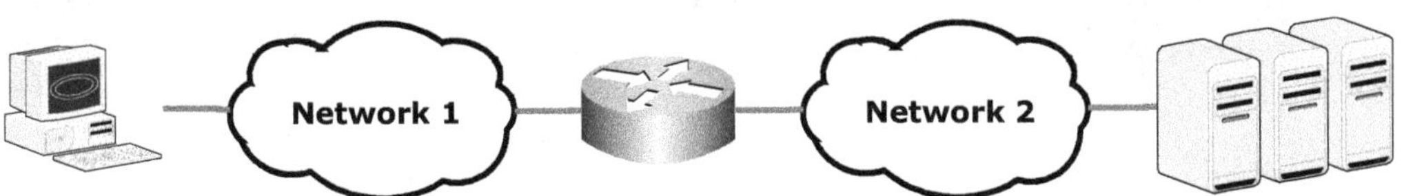

Figure 5-3 **IP Forwarding**

Figure 5-3 shows the path of IP forwarding or routing. It is the process of moving IP packets from a host on one network to a host on a different network.

IP does not offer:

- Connections or logical circuits
- Data-error checking
- Flow control
- Datagram acknowledgements
- Retransmission of lost packets

IP's main goal, instead, is to direct packets in the networks. From the limitations listed above, it is clear that additional protocols are required to guarantee data accuracy and delivery.

A TCP/IP stack can include routing protocols. For example, a host running Microsoft Windows or Linux featuring more than one network interface may act as a router. However, a TCP/IP stack can have multiple network interfaces without necessarily performing routing. µC/TCP-IP is an example of such a stack as it does not provide routing function but can receive and transmit on more than one interface. An example using such an implementation is a gateway, a device that acts as a bridge between two networks. In this case, one interface may be in an administration network and another in a production network, with the gateway providing a level of protection and isolation between the two.

The configuration of the TCP/IP stack needs a minimum of three parameters per network interface. We already know about the MAC address. A network interface also needs an IP address. In the next sections, we'll describe how the IP address is constructed. This information will bring us to the need for the third and last parameter required to configure a network interface, the subnet mask.

5-3 ADDRESSING AND ROUTING

5-3-1 IP ADDRESS

In a network, the IP address and subnet mask are automatically provided by the network (see section 9-1-1 "Dynamic Host Configuration Protocol (DHCP)" on page 222) or configured manually by the network administrator. Even if the parameters are not chosen by the system developer it is important to understand their purpose and how to use them.

IP addresses are composed of 32 bits. An IP address is typically represented with the decimal value of 4 bytes separated by a dot (.), and is referred to as the Dotted Decimal Notation. The address is used to identify the source or destination host.

- Addresses are hierarchical: Net ID + Host ID (e.g., 114.35.56.130)

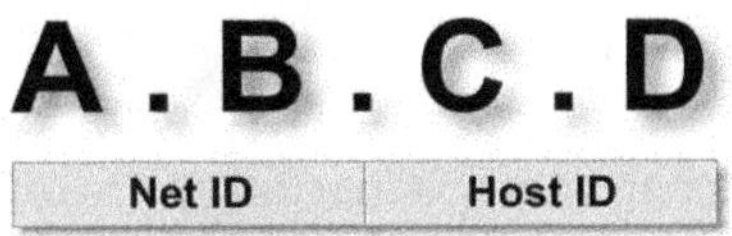

Figure 5-4 **IP Address**

Figure 5-4 is the graphical representation of the NetID + HostID concept. A, B, C and D are four bytes making up the IP address. IP packets are routed (forwarded) according to the Net ID. Routers automatically compute routing tables using a distributed algorithm called a routing protocol, located at the network layer.

Although IP addresses are hierarchical within their own structure, the distribution of these addresses on the surface of the Earth is not. The rapid growth of the Internet created situations where a NetID in one continent will have the preceding or following NetID in another continent. This means that the routing tables in the router must contain all the NetIDs since NetIDs may not be geographically grouped.

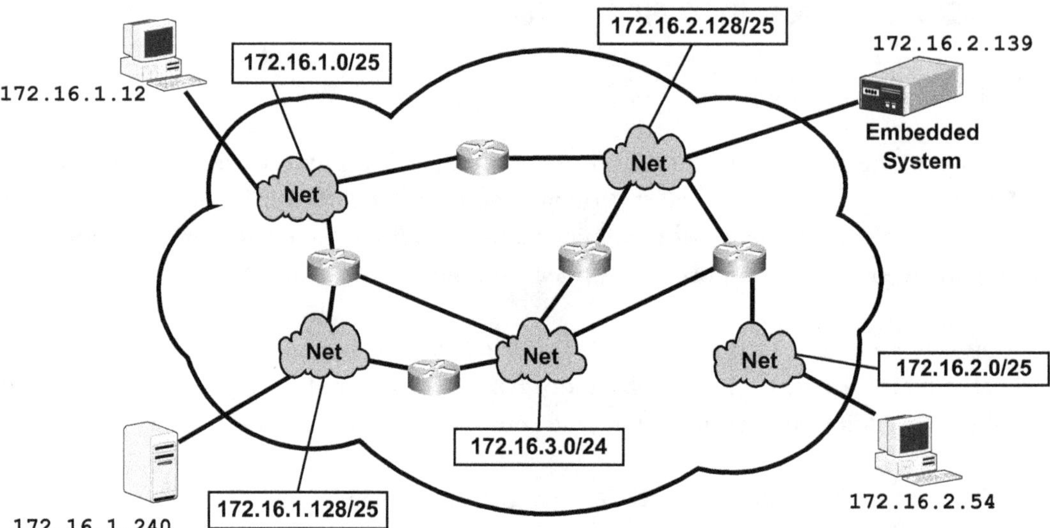

Figure 5-5 **Network of Networks**

In Figure 5-5, multiple networks are interconnected via many routers. Each router contains all of the network addresses within a routing table. The routing table identifies the interface number in order to reach the desired network.

With the current state of private and public IP networks, it is not required to have a discussion on classfull and classless networks. What is important to know now is that IP networks can be of various sizes. Network size is determined by another IP parameter, the subnet mask.

5-4 SUBNET MASK

A subnet mask is also a 32-bit element and is comprised of two sections. The first section consists of all bits set to "1" and identifies the NetID. The second section of the subnet mask consists of all bits set to "0" and identifies the HostID. The change from "1" to "0" is the limit, or frontier between the NetID and the HostID. The subnet mask is used to define network size: the larger the NetID (number of ones), the smaller the number of HostIDs available on that network.

With the rapid growth of IP networks, it became necessary to create smaller or sub-networks out of larger networks to reuse a good part of the addressing space. Today these are called classless networks.

The subnet mask is used to determine the exact values of the NetID and HostID. This also means that the frontier between NetID and HostID is not fixed to 8, 16 or 24 bits, but can be virtually anywhere within the 32-bit area.

Subnet Mask	Number Of Addresses
255.255.255.252	4
255.255.255.248	8
255.255.255.240	16
255.255.255.224	32
255.255.255.192	64
255.255.255.128	128
255.255.255.0	256
255.255.254.0	512
255.255.252.0	1024
255.255.248.0	2048
255.255.240.0	4096
255.255.224.0	8192
255.255.192.0	16384
255.255.128.0	32768
255.252.0.0	65536
255.254.0.0	131072
...	...

Table 5-2 **Variable Subnet Mask**

Table 5-2 is a quick reference to determine how many addresses can be defined in a network based on the subnet maks value. When not comfortable with binary artithmetics, software tools exist to calculate subnet mask and the number of addresses available in a network. Search for IP calculator or IPCALC on the internet.

5

5-5 RESERVED ADDRESSES

It is important to now note that there are restrictions for certain combinations of addresses. In fact, the following rules must be respected when the addressing plan is first developed.

In any network address range, two addresses cannot be assigned to hosts:

1 The lowest address in the range is used to define the network and is called the Network Address.

2 The highest address in the range is used to define the IP broadcast address in the same range.

Here are a few examples:

Network	Subnet Mask	Network Address	Broadcast Address
10.0.0.0	255.0.0.0	10.0.0.0	10.255.255.255
130.10.0.0	255.255.0.0	130.10.0.0	130.10.255.255
198.16.1.0	255.255.255.0	198.16.1.0	198.16.1.255
10.0.0.0	255.255.255.0	10.0.0.0	10.0.0.255
172.16.0.0	255.255.255.128	172.16.0.0	172.16.0.127
192.168.1.4	255.25.255.252	192.168.1.4	192.168.1.7

Table 5-3 **IP Addresses and Subnet Mask Examples**

The smallest network that can be defined is a network with a subnet mask of 255.255.255.252. In this type of network, there are four addresses. Two are used for devices and the remaining two are the network address and broadcast address. This network represents a point-to-point network, for example between two routers.

5-5-1 ADDITIONAL RESERVED ADDRESSES

THE 0.0.0.0 ADDRESS

The 0.0.0.0 address is used by routers to define a default route, used when no other route matches the NetID of a packet being forwarded.

THE 127.X.X.X NETWORK

When 127 appears in the first byte of the network address, it represents a network that is reserved for management functions and, more specifically, to execute loop backs (127.X.X.X). It is an address that is assigned to the TCP/IP stack itself. Any address in the 127.X.X.X range can be used as the loopback address, except for 127.0.0.0 and also 127.255.255.255. We are all familiar with the 127.0.0.1 address.

5-6 ADDRESSING TYPES

5-6-1 UNICAST ADDRESS

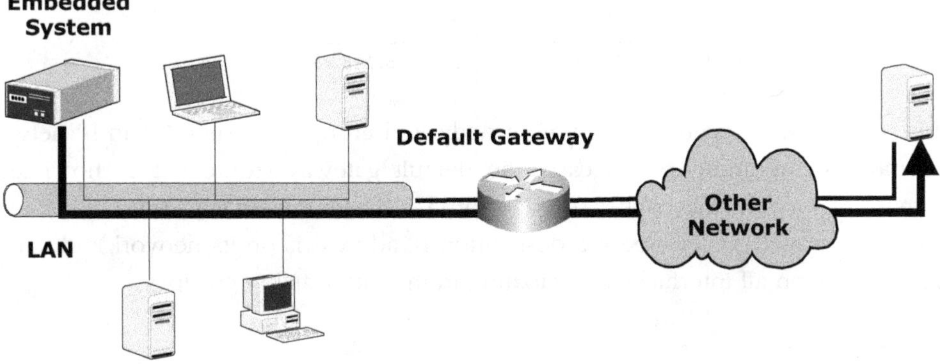

Figure 5-6 **IP Unicast Address**

Source Address	192.168. 2. 63
Source Subnet Mask	255.255.255. 0
Destination Address	207.122. 46.142

Figure 5-6 illustrates a host communicating with another host over an IP network using a unicast address. The embedded system is a host with IP address 192.168.2.63, and is attempting to reach a host with an IP address of 207.122.46.142.

5-6-2 MULTICAST ADDRESS

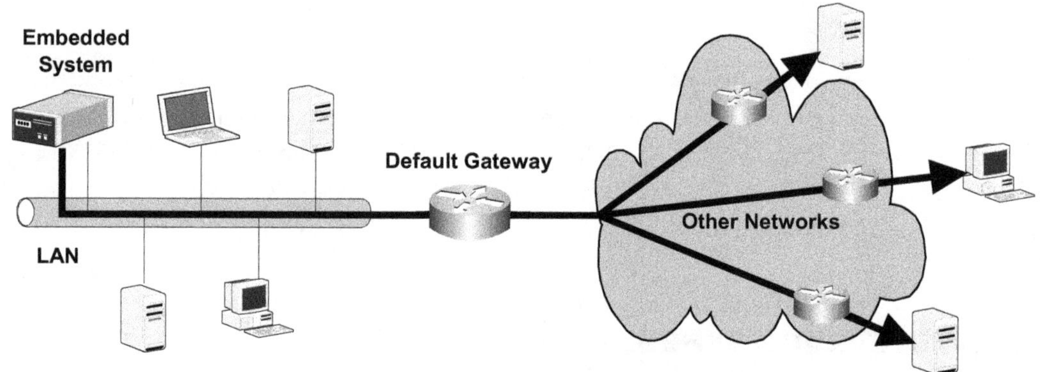

Figure 5-7 **IP Multicast Address**

Source Address	192.168. 2. 63
Destination Address	224. 65.143. 96

In Figure 5-7, a host communicating with a dedicated group of hosts over an IP network is using a multicast address. In this case, the default gateway (router) does not need the subnet mask to forward the packet (see section 5-7 "Default Gateway" on page 124 for an explanation on how to determine if a destination IP address is on its network). Multicasting forwards packets on all interfaces participating in the multicasting group.

5-6-3 BROADCAST ADDRESS

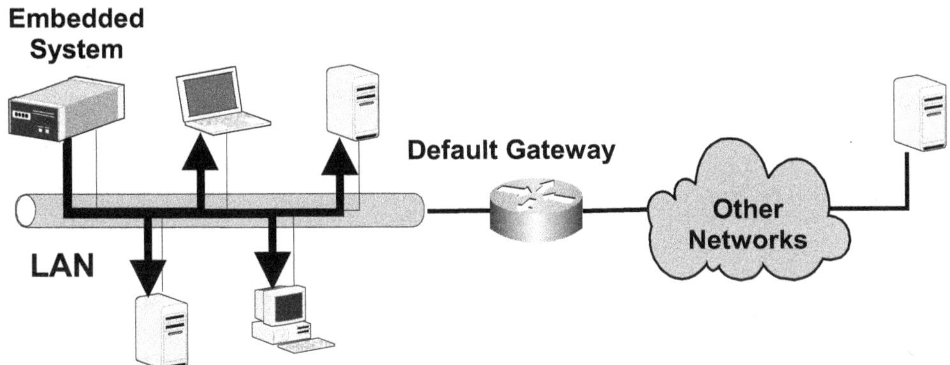

Figure 5-8 **IP Broadcast Address**

Source Address	192.168. 2. 63
Destination Address	192.168. 2. 255

In Figure 5-8, a host communicating with all the hosts on its IP network is using a broadcast address, Remember that the broadcast address is the highest address in an IP network. In this case the subnet mask is not required as the host converts the IP broadcast address into an Ethernet broadcast address to transmit the packet on the network.

On an IP network, a router will not forward broadcast messages, as these messages are dedicated to a specific network, not all networks. In certain cases, however, a router will be configured to forward certain types of IP broadcast packets. For example, proxy ARP is a method to forward ARP requests and replies in case we want to extend the network size between adjunct networks.

5-7 DEFAULT GATEWAY

We saw earlier how a host on a LAN communicates to neighbors on the same LAN using a physical address (MAC address in the case of an Ethernet LAN). What happens when a host wants to communicate with a host on a different network?

First, the origin host needs to know whether the receiving host is on the same network. The only information the origin host knows about the destination host is its IP address.

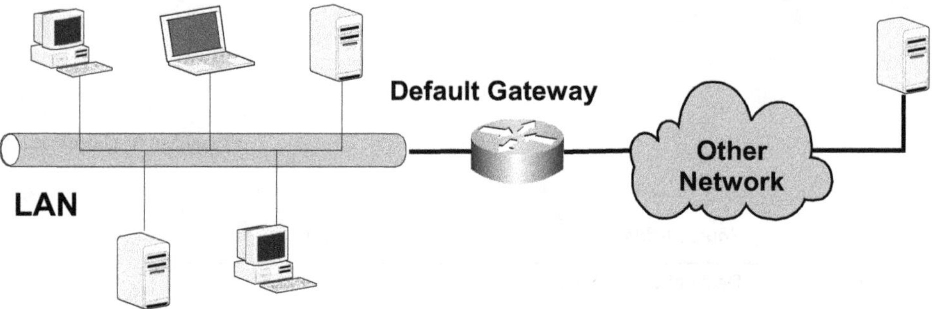

Figure 5-9 **Default Gateway**

Source Address	192.168. 2. 63
Source Host Subnet Mask	255.255.255. 0
Default Gateway	192.168. 2. 1
Destination Address	207. 65.143. 96

Figure 5-9 above indicates where the default gateway is located relative to the hosts in our network and to outside networks. Let's build an example. Figure 5-10 outlines the steps necessary to use the default gateway to forward packets outside of our network.

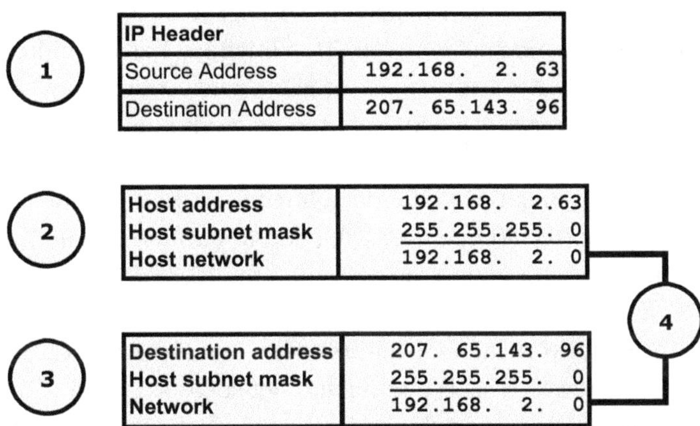

Figure 5-10 **Determining where to send an IP packet**

F5-10(1) The IP header of the packet being sent between the source host and the destination host contains the IP address of the source host and the IP address of the destination host.

F5-10(2) The IP layer of the TCP/IP stack calculates the network address of the source host. The TCP/IP stack applies the subnet mask of its network interface to the source IP address. The result of this logical AND operation is a network address, the host network address.

F5-10(3) The TCP/IP stack determines if the destination host is on the same network. To achieve this, the sending host applies the subnet mask of its network to the IP address of the destination host. The result of this logical AND operation is a network address.

F5-10(4) The question now is: Are these two network address identical? If the answer is:

YES, send the packet over the LAN using the physical address (MAC address) of the destination host.

NO, the result is not the network to which the source host is connected. The source host then needs to find a device that can forward this information. This device is the default gateway, or the router connected to this LAN.

In our example, the answer is No.

Is my default gateway on my network? YES. The default gateway is a router that has one interface in our network. This interface has an address that is part of our network. Remember that the default gateway address is one of the four mandatory parameters to configure per network interface.

The host now sends the information to the default gateway. Because the default gateway is also a host on this network, the source host will need to find the default gateway's physical address before transmitting information, using ARP in the case of Ethernet.

As a standard practice, network administrators often use the first available address in a network for the default gateway. This is a good and not-so-good practice. It is good because in this way it is possible to easily find the address of the default gateway for that network. However, it is also not the best action, since hackers also can find their way more easily into the network. To confuse hackers, use any address in the network address range other than the first available address. This is not a problem if a DHCP server is used (see Chapter 9, "Services and Applications" on page 221).

5-8 IP CONFIGURATION

A host needs four mandatory parameters for each NIC collaborating on a network (see Figure 5-11):

- A physical address (Ethernet MAC address)
- An IP address
- A subnet mask
- A default gateway IP address

There are two ways to configure these parameters in the system. They can be configured statically (hard-coded) or dynamically.

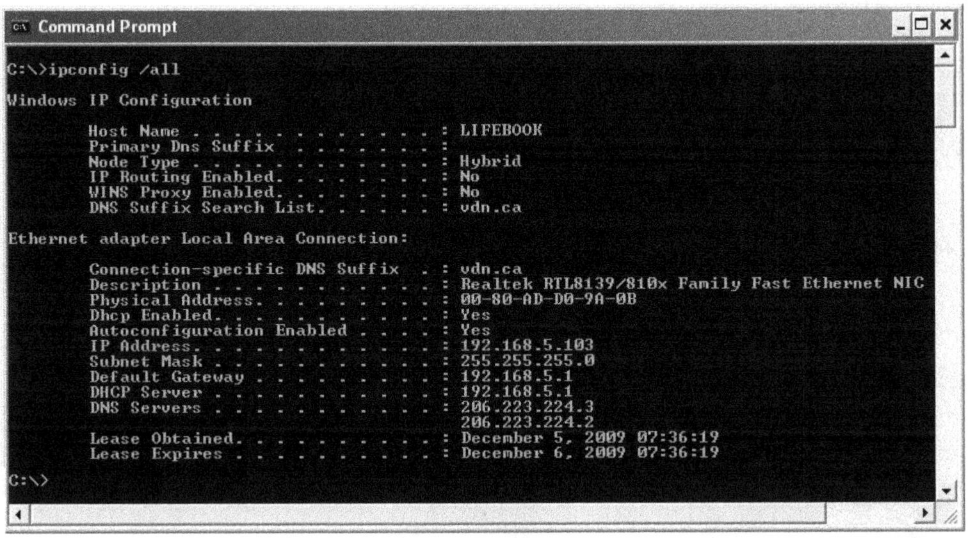

```
Command Prompt

C:\>ipconfig /all

Windows IP Configuration

        Host Name . . . . . . . . . . . . : LIFEBOOK
        Primary Dns Suffix  . . . . . . . :
        Node Type . . . . . . . . . . . . : Hybrid
        IP Routing Enabled. . . . . . . . : No
        WINS Proxy Enabled. . . . . . . . : No
        DNS Suffix Search List. . . . . . : vdn.ca

Ethernet adapter Local Area Connection:

        Connection-specific DNS Suffix  . : vdn.ca
        Description . . . . . . . . . . . : Realtek RTL8139/810x Family Fast Ethernet NIC
        Physical Address. . . . . . . . . : 00-80-AD-D0-9A-0B
        Dhcp Enabled. . . . . . . . . . . : Yes
        Autoconfiguration Enabled . . . . : Yes
        IP Address. . . . . . . . . . . . : 192.168.5.103
        Subnet Mask . . . . . . . . . . . : 255.255.255.0
        Default Gateway . . . . . . . . . : 192.168.5.1
        DHCP Server . . . . . . . . . . . : 192.168.5.1
        DNS Servers . . . . . . . . . . . : 206.223.224.3
                                            206.223.224.2
        Lease Obtained. . . . . . . . . . : December 5, 2009 07:36:19
        Lease Expires . . . . . . . . . . : December 6, 2009 07:36:19

C:\>
```

Figure 5-11 **IP Configuration**

Figure 5-11 is an example of the result of an IP configuration on a Microsoft Windows host. This configuration is a dynamic configuration as you can see from the additional DHCP server address and lease data in the list of parameters. The result of this configuration was obtained using the command: `ipconfig /all`. On a Linux host, the Terminal Window command is similar. It is `ifconfig`.

Static parameter configuration requires the knowledge of the value of these parameters and the use of certain µC/TCP-IP API functions.

```
NET_IP_ADDR    ip;
NET_IP_ADDR    msk;
NET_IP_ADDR    gateway;
CPU_BOOLEAN    cfg_success;
NET_ERR        err_net;
ip          = NetASCII_Str_to_IP((CPU_CHAR *)"192.168.0.65",  &err_net);  (1)
msk         = NetASCII_Str_to_IP((CPU_CHAR *)"255.255.255.0", &err_net);  (2)
gateway     = NetASCII_Str_to_IP((CPU_CHAR *)"192.168.0.1",   &err_net);  (3)
cfg_success = NetIP_CfgAddrAdd(if_nbr, ip, msk, gateway,  &err_net);      (4)
```

Listing 5-1 **Static IP Configuration**

L5-1(1) Hard-coded IP address.

L5-1(2) Hard-coded Subnet Mask.

L5-1(3) Hard-coded Default Gateway IP address.

L5-1(4) Configures the IP address, the Subnet Mask and the Default Gateway IP address.

Please refer to Appendix B, “µC/TCP-IP API Reference” on page 433, for the description of the functions in Listing 5-1.

Dynamic IP configuration is covered in Chapter 9, “Services and Applications” on page 221.

5-9 PRIVATE ADDRESSES

As IP networks evolved, the number of IP addresses became increasingly scarce. The address space of IP Version 4 is limited to approximately four billion device addresses, which is woefully inadequate to support all of the devices connected to global networks.

One way to stretch IP address availability is define private addresses and reuse them as often as possible. These private addresses include:

```
10.0.0.0/8
172.16.0.0/16 to 172.31.0.0/16
192.168.0.0/24 to 192.168.255.0/24
```

These addresses can only be used on private networks and not on the public Internet. We probably all know at least one example of a private address. The router (wired or wireless) we use at home behind our cable or DSL modem uses private addresses for home hosts.

Another group of IP addresses is also reserved in case there is no automatic IP assignment mechanism like DHCP. RFC 3927 defines the 169.254.0.0/16 range of addresses, but the first and last /24 subnet (256 addresses each) in this block are excluded from use and are reserved. This technique is also described in Chapter 9, "Services and Applications" on page 221,

The vast majority of embedded systems connected to an IP network use private addresses. When a network is built to serve a specific purpose, it does not need to be connected to the public Internet. Therefore, it makes sense to use a private addressing scheme.

However, when a host on a private network must access another host on the public network, we need to convert the private address into a public address. In our home example above, this is performed by the home gateway/router and is called Network Address Translation (NAT). Similarly in a private network where an embedded system is located, the network default gateway provides that capability for the embedded system to reach the public network.

NETWORK ADDRESS TRANSLATION - NAT

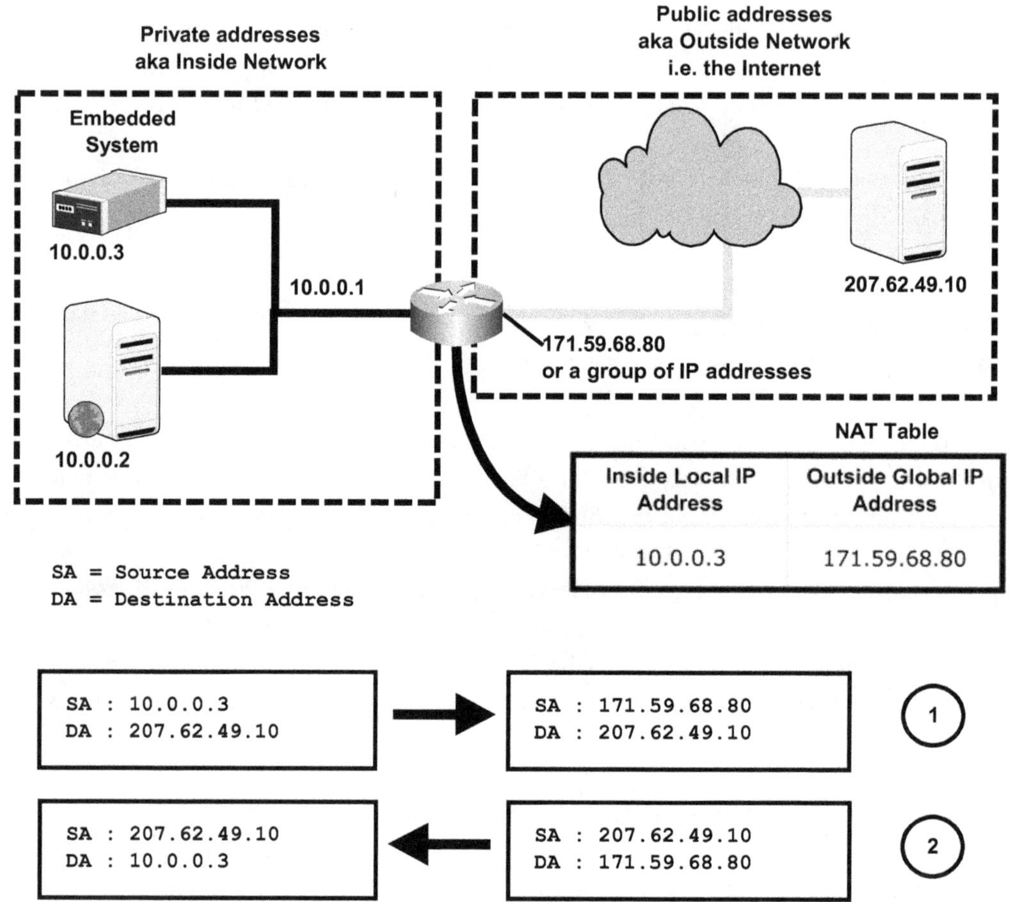

Figure 5-12 **Network Address Translation**

In Figure 5-12 above, a 10.0.0.0 private network is assigned to the network on the left. The router in the figure is the default gateway for this network. This gateway has two network interfaces: one facing the network on the left (the private network) and one facing the network on the right (the public network). We often refer to the private network as the inside network and the public network as the outside network.

F5-12(1) In this simple case, the embedded system with IP address 10.0.0.3 on the private network wants to connect with a host at 207.62.49.10 on the Internet. The embedded system private address is translated into the public address associated with the gateway public interface of 171.59.68.80. The public address is provided by the Internet Service Provider (ISP) when the private network initially requested to connect to the Internet. In this case, the ISP provided one IP address with the contract. It is also possible to be assigned a block of IP addresses from the ISP. The cross-reference between the private address and the public address is stored in a table in the gateway. The packet sent by the embedded system now travels on the public network since all addresses are public. In this example, only one connection can be established between the private network and the Internet. One solution to access more than one connection is to have a block of public addresses. In this way, there can be as many connections as there are public addresses available, however this is a waste of IP addresses. Another method is to use one of the Transport Layer protocol fields called a port. (see section 7-3-1 "Port Address Translation (PAT)" on page 171, for more information).

F5-12(2) When the host on the public network answers the query from the host in the private network system with IP translated to 171.59.68.80, it answers this message the same way it would answer another host request on the Internet. When the reply reaches the gateway, the gateway translates the destination address from 171.59.68.80 to 10.10.10.3 using the translation table it created on the initial outgoing packet. This works as long as the communication is established from the private network out.

Another scenario is for a host on the public network to connect to a host on the private network. In this case, the concept of nail-down public addresses must be introduced. It is possible to configure a public IP address to be always connected to a private address as in the following figure:

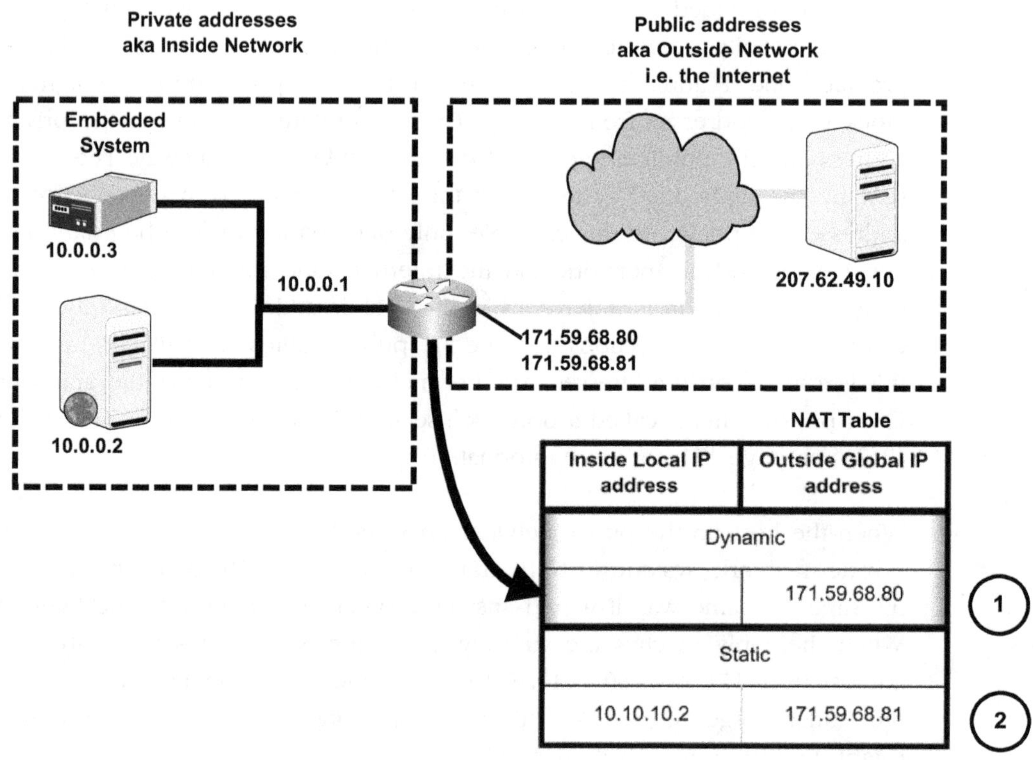

Figure 5-13 **Static Public IP Address**

F5-13(1) The Dynamic portion of the NAT table configuration in the router/gateway is similar to the previous example. It is used for private hosts that want to access public hosts.

F5-13(2) The Static portion of the NAT table configuration in the gateway ensures that a private host can always be reached from the public network. In the example, the Web server at IP address 10.10.10.3 is associated with the public IP address 171.59.69.81. The public network identifies the Web server at IP address 171.59.69.81. As long as the gateway translates 10.10.10.3 to 171.59.69.81 and vice-versa, this server will appear as any other server on the Internet. If an embedded system in this example at IP address 10.10.10.2 is offering an HTTP service, it may also be made accessible from the Internet using the exact same process. An additional Static Public IP address is required for this host.

5-10 SUMMARY

The IP address, subnet mask and default gateway do not directly translate to the design of the embedded system. However, it is important to know where they come from, how they are structured, which one to use and, once selected, how to configure it.

These parameters are always provided by the network administrator and are not selected randomly. The connected host must collaborate with other hosts and nodes in the network. Once these parameters are known, they need to be configured either statically or dynamically following the methods described in 5-8.

Chapter

6

Troubleshooting

As we move up through the TCP/IP protocol stack, we'll stay at the Network layer for one more chapter. Why? Because it is at this layer that we also find a very important protocol used in the troubleshooting of IP networks.

6-1 NETWORK TROUBLESHOOTING

When a connection between two hosts is broken, it is very common for the user to attempt to reach the destination host knowing that there is a problem. Unfortunately, the problem may be located anywhere between the source host and the destination host, and the culprit is usually a failed node or link. To troubleshoot this problem, a reasonable approach is to first verify the closest links and nodes. When we are sure that the problem does not lie at this location, we move towards the destination host.

When we detect a communication problem between two hosts, the initial step is to validate that the TCP/IP stack in the source host is operational. This can be done by using the PING utility, and "pinging" the source host local host address: 127.0.0.1.

The second step is to validate that the network interface on the source host is in good working order. To achieve this on the source host, ping the IP address associated with this network interface.

The third step is to ping the IP address of the default gateway associated to the LAN to which the source host is connected.

Finally, we can ping all of the nodes on the path between the source host and destination host. The second section of this chapter demonstrates the use of another tool called "Trace Route," which will assist in identifying these nodes.

To recap, the sequence used to find the location of a problem on an IP network:

1 Ping the local host TCP/IP stack (127.0.0.1)

2 Ping the network interface(s)

3 Ping the default gateway

4 Ping nodes on the path between the source and destination

At this stage, it is important to understand that communications on an IP network is typically bidirectional. The path from source to destination may work, but we also have to make sure that the return path is also operational. As we learned earlier, IP is not a connection-oriented protocol. The source host and destination host are not aware of a connection between the two devices. Unlike the PSTN where a physical connection exists, with IP, a packet forwarding network, there are two paths: one from A to B and one from B to A.

The troubleshooting process therefore, must at times be able to be applied in both directions to find the cause of the network problem.

In addition to the PING Utility, let's look at the Internet Control Message Protocol (ICMP), which is used by this troubleshooting tool and others.

6-1-1 INTERNET CONTROL MESSAGE PROTOCOL (ICMP)

While the IP protocol does not guarantee datagram delivery, it does provide a means of sending alerts and diagnostic messages by way of the ICMP protocol. Such errors typically occur in intermediary routers and systems when a datagram cannot, for whatever reason, be forwarded.

There are two types of ICMP messages:

- error messages
- request/response messages

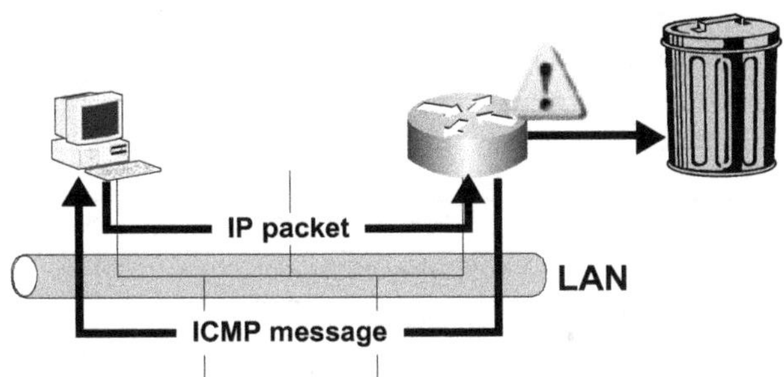

Figure 6-1 **Internet Control Message Protocol (ICMP)**

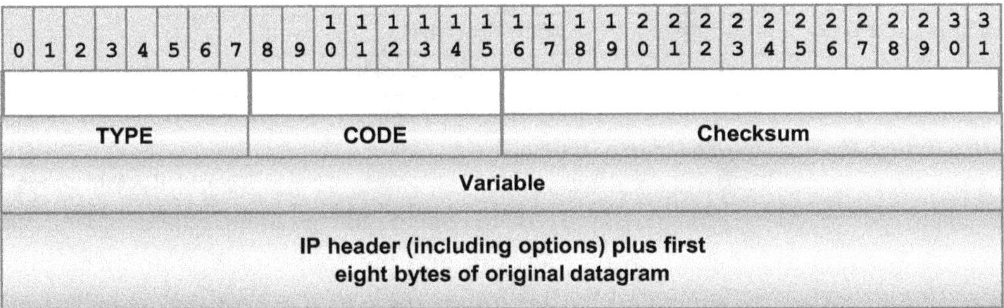

Figure 6-2 **ICMP Message Structure**

Given that the ICMP message is carried in an IP packet, the IP PROTOCOL field in the IP header is equal to 1. The ICMP message structure is as follows:

- The TYPE field is the first byte of the ICMP message. This field's value determines the contents of the rest of the data field. (see Table 6-1 for a list of TYPE-possible values).
- The CODE field depends directly on the TYPE field.
- The CHECKSUM field is the 16-bit 1's complement of the 1's complement sum of the ICMP message.

ICMP Message Type #	Function
0	Echo reply
3	Destination unreachable
4	Source quench

ICMP Message Type #	Function
5	Redirect
8	Echo request
9	Router advertisement
10	Router solicitation
11	Time exceed
12	Parameter problem
13	Timestamp request
14	Timestamp reply
15	Information request
16	Information reply
17	Address mask request
18	Address mask reply

Table 6-1 **ICMP Message Types**

When a datagram is transmitted on the network and the router detects an error, an error message (ICMP packet) is generated by the router back to the host that initially sent the datagram. Fields from the datagram that created the error are used in the ICMP ERROR message and include:

- IP header (20 bytes)
- IP options (0-40 bytes)
- First (8) bytes of the IP packet data field (8 bytes)

The first eight (8) bytes of the data field include port numbers in the case of upper-layer TCP and UDP protocols. These ports indicate the application to which the datagram belongs, information which is very useful for troubleshooting.

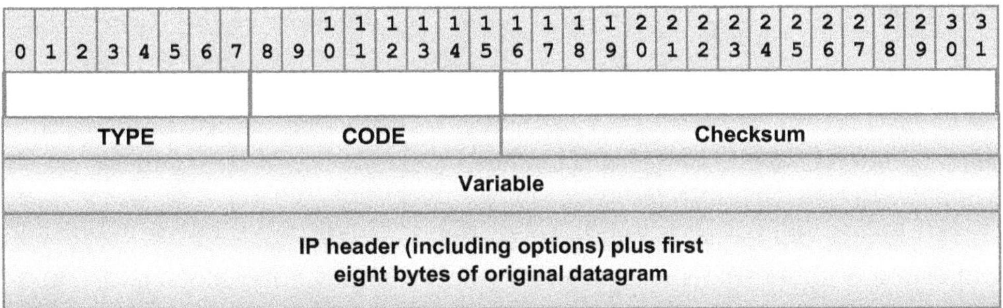

Figure 6-3 **ICMP Error Message Structure**

The next section is dedicated to troubleshooting tools. PING, as we have seen, is one of them. PING uses a form of ICMP messages, echo request and echo reply. Echo requests use type 8 and echo replies use type 0.

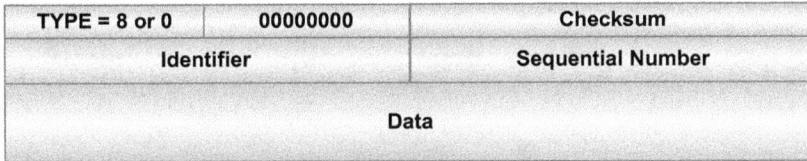

TYPE = 8 or 0	00000000	Checksum
Identifier		Sequential Number
Data		

TYPE	8 = Echo Request 0 = Echo Reply
Identifier	An arbitrary number for linking a request with a reply
Sequential Number	A counter set to 0 and incremented after a reply is received
Data	This field is used as a payload so that the Echo Reply can have something to send back. It is often the alphabet and is 32-bytes long.

Figure 6-4 **Echo Request, Echo Reply**

In the IP toolbox, there are a few tools that rely on ICMP and are quite useful. These tools are:

- PING
- Trace Route

6-1-2 PING

The PING utility relies on the ICMP Echo Request and Echo Reply messages. As previously indicated, PING is used when we want to know if a node is operational, or to locate a fault on the path between source and destination hosts.

Here is an example of PING:

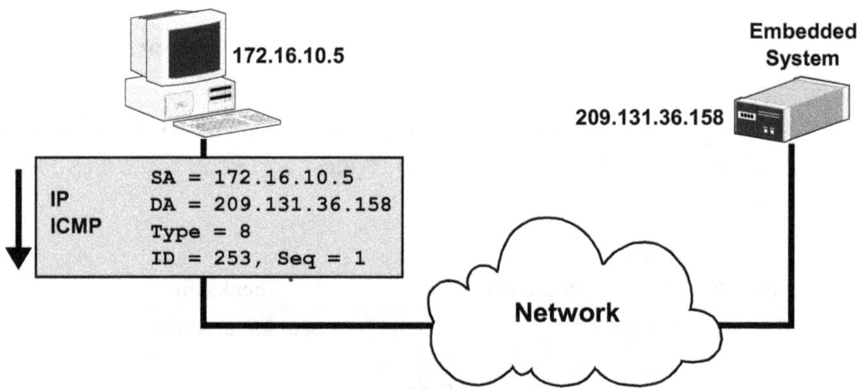

Figure 6-5 **Echo Request**

In Figure 6-5 above, PING is used on a host with IP address 172.16.10.5. On a Windows PC, open a command prompt window and use the PING command. The format of the command is: `ping [Destination IP address or URL]`. Linux also has a PING utility that is launched from a terminal window.

If the destination IP address is known, or the name of the host you want to "PING," for example www.thecompany.com," either can be used. However, the operating system, Windows in this case, uses the Domain Name Service (DNS) to translate the name into an IP address (see Chapter 9, "Services and Applications" on page 221 for more detail).

Figure 6-6 **Ping Command in a Command Prompt Window**

In our example the host with IP address 172.16.10.5 is "pinging" the embedded system with IP address 209.131.36.158 (see Figure 6-7). The host of origin, (172.16.10.5) and the destination host (209.131.36.158) are not on the same network. In most tests, it is probable that the two hosts will be on the same network. It does not make any difference other than the reply to the PING command will have a longer RTT should the hosts be further apart.

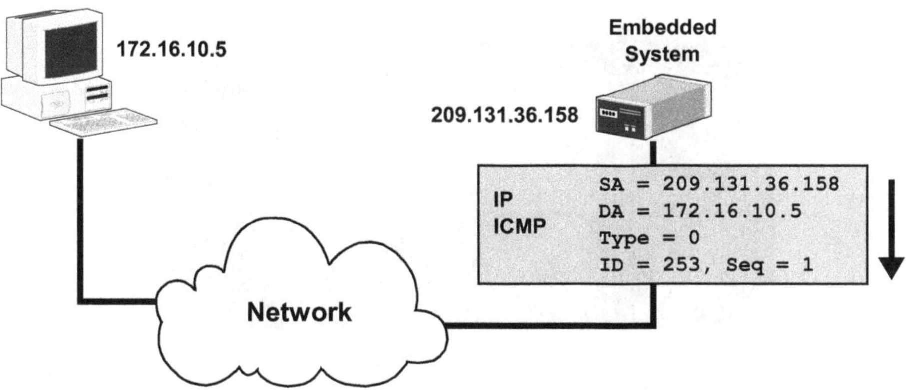

Figure 6-7 **Echo Reply**

The reply from the embedded system is shown in Figure 6-7.

Both Windows and Linux PING implementations send four echo request messages at one second intervals.

```
Command Prompt

C:\>ping 209.131.36.158

Pinging 209.131.36.158 with 32 bytes of data:

Reply from 209.131.36.158: bytes=32 time=107ms TTL=128
Reply from 209.131.36.158: bytes=32 time=92ms TTL=128
Reply from 209.131.36.158: bytes=32 time=92ms TTL=128
Reply from 209.131.36.158: bytes=32 time=93ms TTL=128

Ping statistics for 209.131.36.158:
    Packets: Sent = 4, Received = 4, Lost = 0 (0% loss),
Approximate round trip times in milli-seconds:
    Minimum = 92ms, Maximum = 107ms, Average = 96ms

C:\>_
```

Figure 6-8 **PING Execution**

The PING utility has multiple options. To get a list of the options, simply type "ping" without any arguments.

The most interesting of the options include:

- `-t` to send a Echo Request every second until the program is stopped
- `-l` to send more than the default 32-byte standard Echo Request payload.

```
Command Prompt

C:\>ping

Usage: ping [-t] [-a] [-n count] [-l size] [-f] [-i TTL] [-v TOS]
            [-r count] [-s count] [[-j host-list] | [-k host-list]]
            [-w timeout] target_name

Options:
    -t             Ping the specified host until stopped.
                   To see statistics and continue - type Control-Break;
                   To stop - type Control-C.
    -a             Resolve addresses to hostnames.
    -n count       Number of echo requests to send.
    -l size        Send buffer size.
    -f             Set Don't Fragment flag in packet.
    -i TTL         Time To Live.
    -v TOS         Type Of Service.
    -r count       Record route for count hops.
    -s count       Timestamp for count hops.
    -j host-list   Loose source route along host-list.
    -k host-list   Strict source route along host-list.
    -w timeout     Timeout in milliseconds to wait for each reply.

C:\>_
```

Figure 6-9 **PING Options**

The PING utility features a small default 32-byte payload. This option can be changed by issuing the '`–l`' argument in the command. Changing the payload, the delay, and the number of echo requests, creates an inexpensive traffic generator. However, it only tests Data Link and Network layers. In many cases, if you can ping your target, you have a good chance of having the rest of the TCP/IP stack on the target working. Arriving at this point is the most difficult part of implementing TCP/IP in an embedded system.

There are other third-party command-prompt tools that can be used for this purpose. One of them is the well-known fast PING (FPING) from www.kwakkelflap.com/downloads.html.

What is specifically important to understand is that the current version of µC/TCP-IP can reply to ICMP Echo Request, but does not initiate ICMP Echo Request messages. This means that an embedded system running µC/TCP-IP can reply to a PING command but can not initiate a PING command. In the troubleshooting scenario above, the host issuing the PING command must be a host other than the embedded system running µC/TCP-IP.

6-1-3 TRACE ROUTE

Another useful network troubleshooting tool is Trace Route ("tracert" in the command prompt). This utility uses the Time-To-Live (TTL) field of the IP packet header to retrieve the IP address of every router on the path between the source and destination. When a router processes a packet it decrements the IP packet header TTL field by 1. Initially the TTL field was designed to calculate the amount of time a packet was spent on a router, hence its name "Time-To-Live." As this example suggests, the final implementation of the TTL field is more of a hop count between the source and destination. TTL is decremented by one and when its value reaches zero, the router discards the packet and sends an error message to the host that initiated the packet. The error code of the ICMP message sent back to the source host is Type 11 (Time Exceeded).

Let's see how this works.

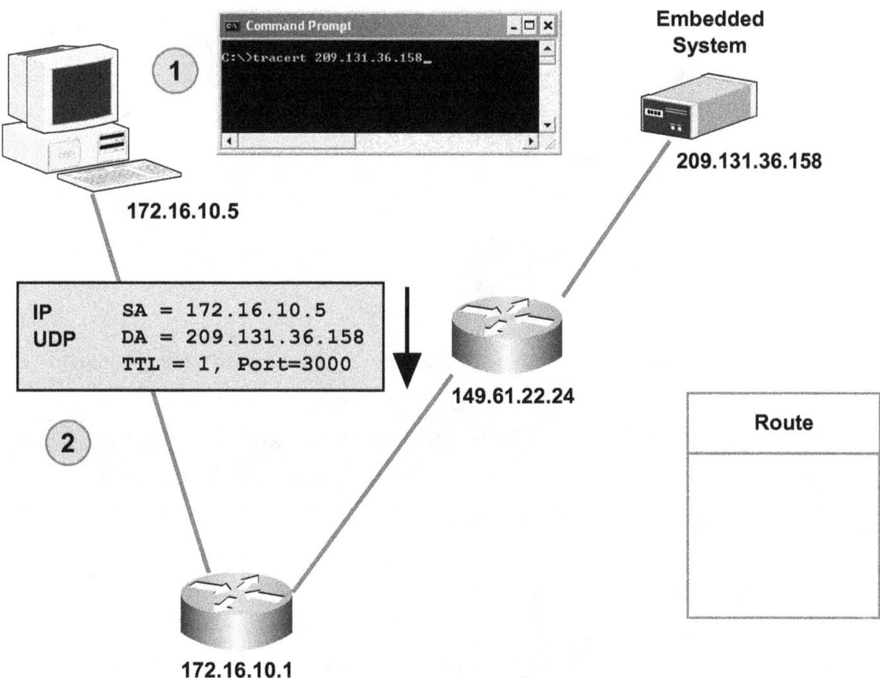

Figure 6-10 **Source Host Sends a Packet to Destination Host with TTL=1**

F6-10(1) Host 172.16.10.5 issues a "TRACERT" command using 207.42.13.61 as the destination IP address.

F6-10(2) This creates a UDP datagram to be sent to the destination address and the IP packet carrying this UDP datagram sees a TTL set to 1. In this example, the port number used is 3000, however this number is arbitrary.

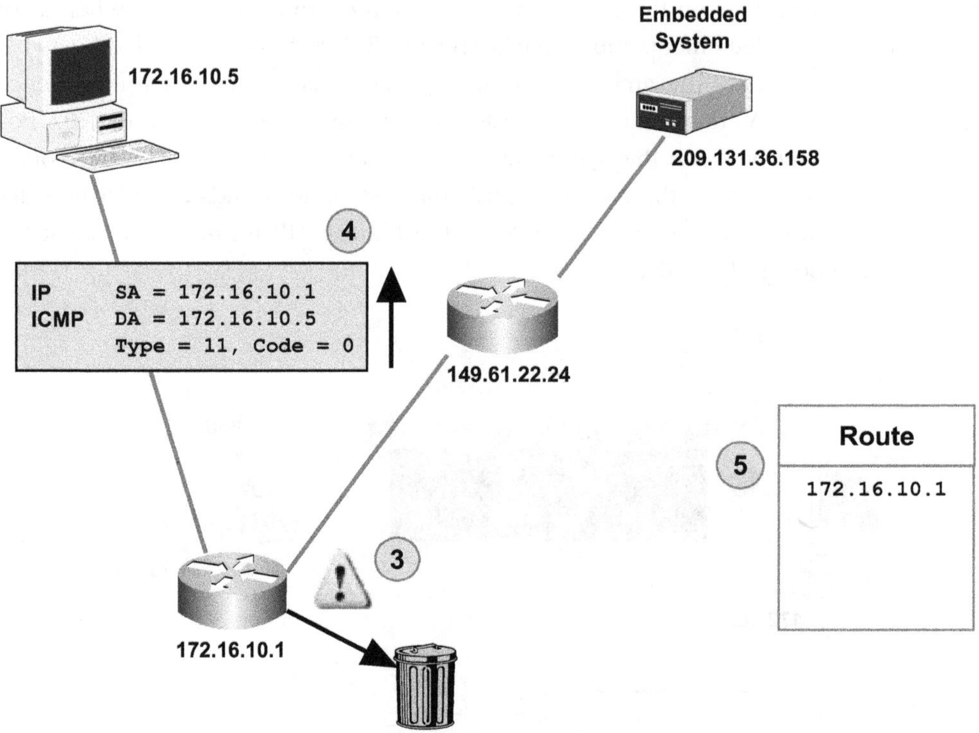

Figure 6-11 **The first node discards the packet because the "Time-To-Live" expires.**

F6-11(3) The first node on the path between the source and the destination receives the packet and decrements the TTL field. Because the TTL was 1, it is now zero representing an error condition.

F6-11(4) An ICMP Type 11 error message is sent back to the source host.

F6-11(5) Because the ICMP message is from the node that detected the error, the source address of this node is used as the IP source address for the error message. The source host therefore learns the IP address of the first node on the path to the destination host.

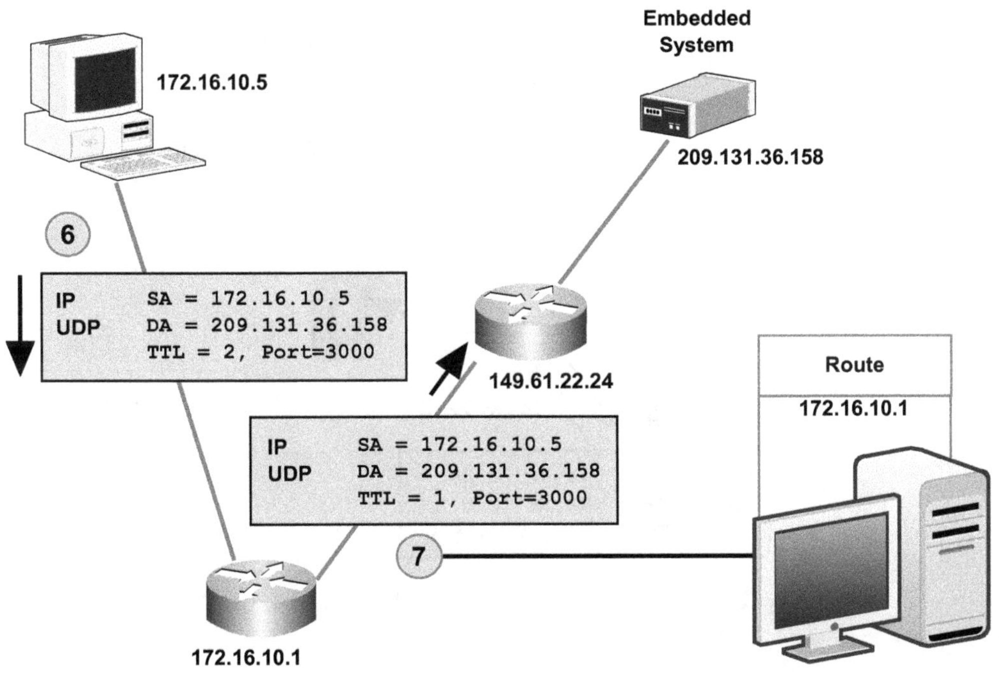

Figure 6-12 **Source Host sends a packet to Destination Host with TTL=2**

F6-12(6) The TRACERT received the reply to the first message with TTL equal to one. The application continues. The next step is to send the same initial packet, but this time with a TTL equal to 2.

F6-12(7) The packet processed by the first node on the path from the source to the destination will decrement the TTL from 2 to 1. The packet is then forwarded on its path to the destination.

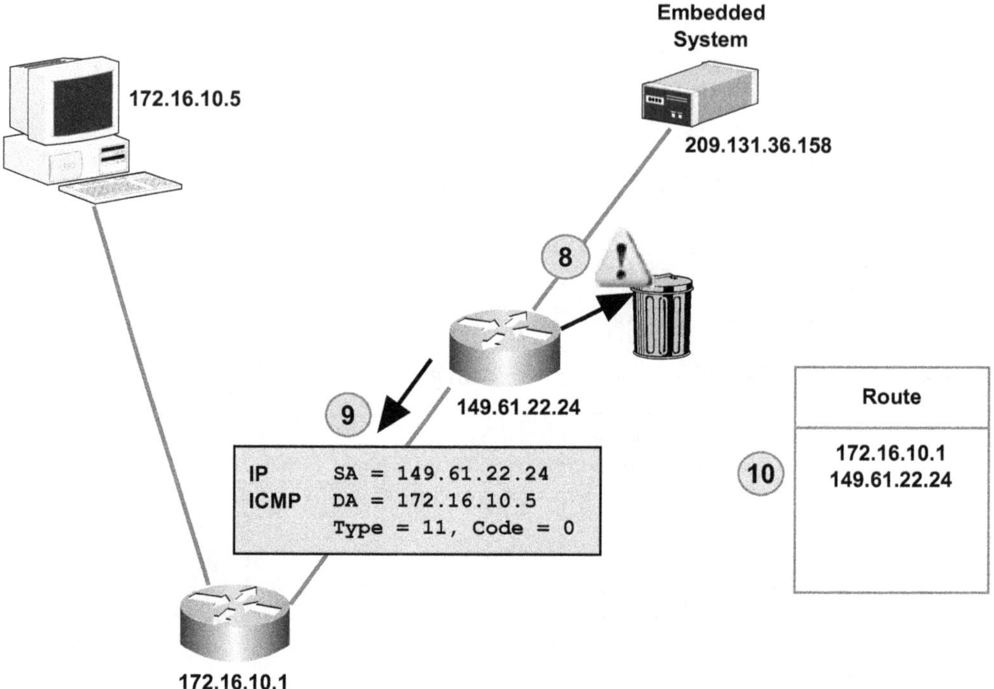

Figure 6-13 **The second node discard the packet since the "Time-To-Live" expires.**

F6-13(8) The second node on the path from the source to the destination decrements the TLL from 1 to 0 and thus discards the packet.

F6-13(9) An ICMP Type 11 error message is sent to the source host. Because the ICMP message is from the node that detected the error, the source address of this node is used as the IP source address for the error message.

F6-13(10) The source host therefore learns the IP address of the second node on the path to the destination host.

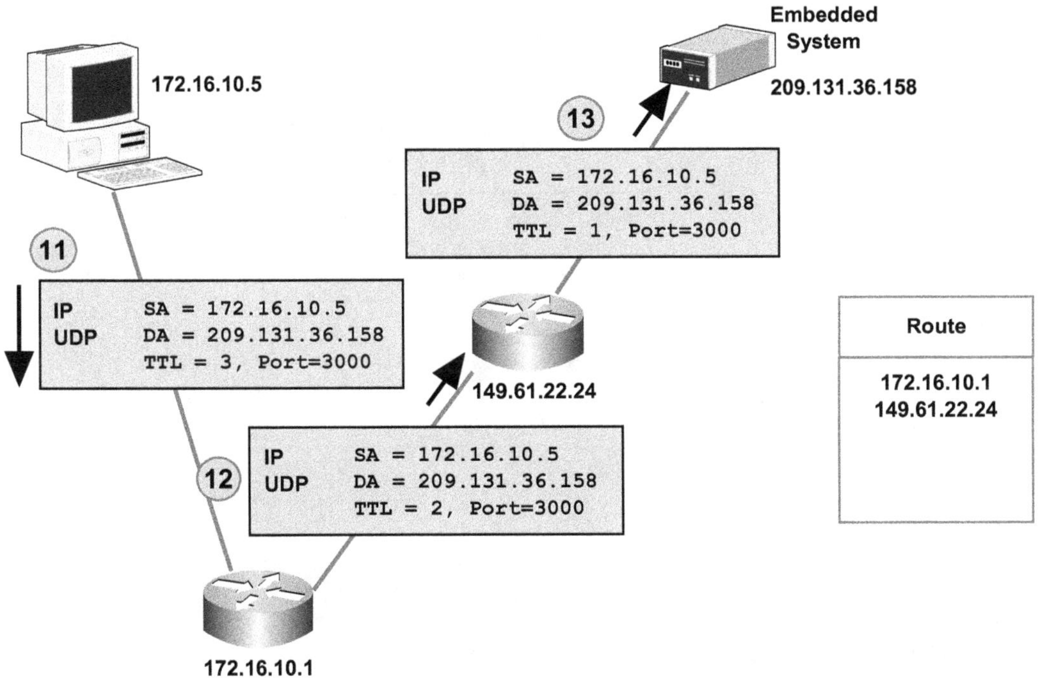

Figure 6-14 **Source Host sends a packet to Destination Host with TTL=3**

F6-14(11) The TRACERT has received two replies so far. The application continues and the same initial packet is sent, but this time with a TTL equal to 3.

F6-14(12) The packet processed by the first node on the path from the source to the destination decrements the TTL to 2 and forwards the packet on its path to the destination.

F6-14(13) The second node also decrements the TTL of the packet it receives down to 1. The packet is forwarded on its path to the destination.

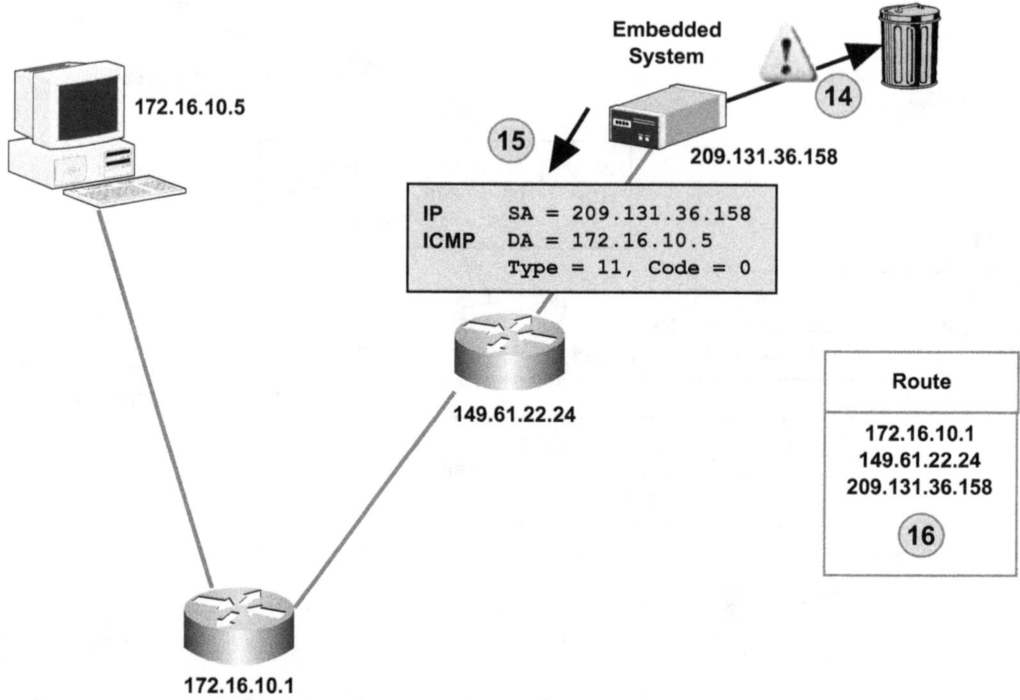

Figure 6-15 **The fourth node discards the packet since the "Time-To-Live" expires.**

F6-15(14) The third node on the path from the source to the destination decrements the TLL. It is now zero.

F6-15(15) An ICMP Type 11 error message is sent to the source host. Because the ICMP message is from the node that detected the error, the source address of this node is used as the IP source address for the error message.

F6-15(16) The source host therefore learns the IP address of the third node on the path to the destination host. Because this address is the one that was used when the TRACERT utility was launched, the final destination is reached. The list of IP addresses for the nodes on the path between the source and the destination is now known.

This process can be applied to as many nodes as exist between the source and destination. The default option of the TRACERT command probes thirty nodes and then stops. If there are more than thirty nodes on the path being analyzed, the default option must be changed using the –h parameter. To display the TRACERT parameters, enter TRACERT without any parameter.

As we learned in Chapter 1, there are no dedicated circuits. It is quite possible that multiple IP packets exchanged between a source and destination take different routes. It is also possible to imagine that issuing the TRACE ROUTE command multiple times could produce different results. However, this is not the case. Current networks are stable enough and have sufficient resources to produce the same result every time.

However, if the TRACERT command fails to reach the final destination, a hint about the location of the network problem we are looking for is provided. This is likely the location of the problem.

Here is an example of the "tracert" command:

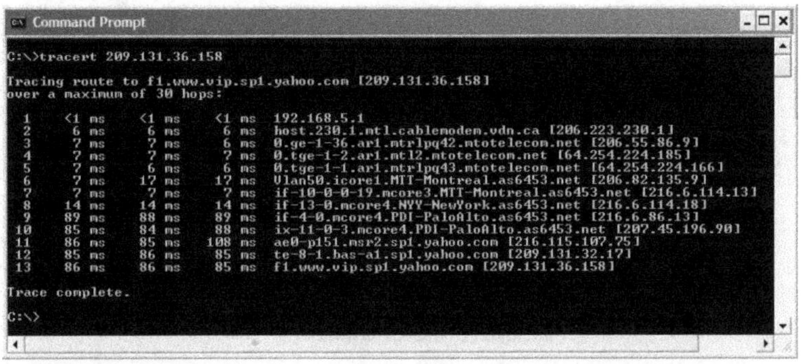

```
Command Prompt
C:\>tracert 209.131.36.158

Tracing route to f1.www.vip.sp1.yahoo.com [209.131.36.158]
over a maximum of 30 hops:

  1    <1 ms    <1 ms    <1 ms  192.168.5.1
  2     6 ms     6 ms     6 ms  host.230.1.mtl.cablemodem.vdn.ca [206.223.230.1]
  3     7 ms     7 ms     6 ms  0.ge-1-36.ar1.mtrlpq42.mtotelecom.net [206.55.86.9]
  4     7 ms     7 ms     7 ms  0.tge-1-2.ar1.mtl2.mtotelecom.net [64.254.224.185]
  5     7 ms     6 ms     6 ms  0.tge-1-1.ar1.mtrlpq43.mtotelecom.net [64.254.224.166]
  6     7 ms    17 ms    17 ms  Vlan50.icore1.MTT-Montreal.as6453.net [206.82.135.9]
  7     7 ms     7 ms     7 ms  if-10-0-0-19.mcore3.MTT-Montreal.as6453.net [216.6.114.13]
  8    14 ms    14 ms    14 ms  if-13-0.mcore4.NYY-NewYork.as6453.net [216.6.114.18]
  9    89 ms    88 ms    89 ms  if-4-0.mcore4.PDI-PaloAlto.as6453.net [216.6.86.13]
 10    85 ms    84 ms    88 ms  ix-11-0-3.mcore4.PDI-PaloAlto.as6453.net [207.45.196.90]
 11    86 ms    85 ms   108 ms  ae0-p151.msr2.sp1.yahoo.com [216.115.107.75]
 12    85 ms    86 ms    85 ms  te-8-1.bas-a1.sp1.yahoo.com [209.131.32.17]
 13    86 ms    86 ms    85 ms  f1.www.vip.sp1.yahoo.com [209.131.36.158]

Trace complete.

C:\>
```

Figure 6-16 **TRACERT Execution**

There is also a graphical version of this tool called Visual TraceRoute. Search the Internet for "Visual TraceRoute," and have fun seeing geographically where all routers are located!

6-2 PROTOCOLS AND APPLICATION ANALYSIS TOOLS

The network troubleshooting tools in the first sections of this chapter are very useful to understand the workings of the network. As an embedded developer, your challenges are likely not with the network but with an ability to test to see if the system is operational. The following sections cover tools that are useful to validate TCP/IP protocol stack behavior and to test system TCP/IP performance.

6-2-1 NETWORK PROTOCOL ANALYZER

A network protocol analyzer (also known as a packet analyzer or sniffer) is software or hardware that can intercept and log traffic passing over a network. As data streams flow across the network, a network protocol analyzer captures each packet, and decodes and analyzes its content according to the appropriate RFC.

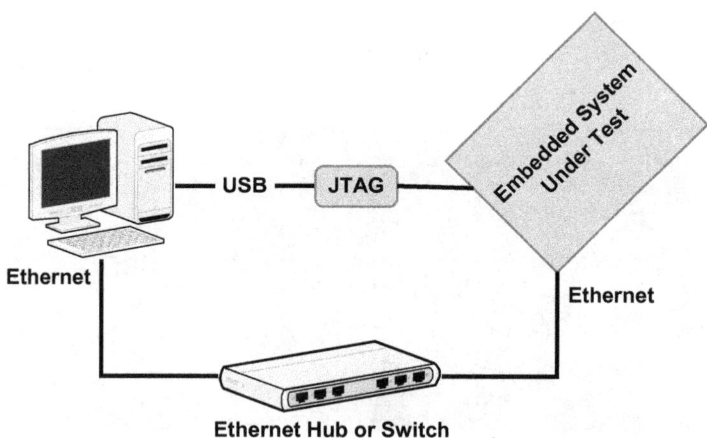

Figure 6-17 **Network Protocol Analyzer Setup**

In order to work, a network protocol analyzer must be able to capture Ethernet frames on the network. To do so, the setup requires an Ethernet hub or an Ethernet switch (see Figure 6-17).

Let's look at the various elements involved in the process. Given a hub, for example, a network protocol analyzer can connect to any port since the hub repeats all traffic from every port. In this case, the challenge is to filter the frame capture or frame display with network protocol analyzer options as the network protocol analyzer captures all network traffic, which may be more than what is needed.

An Ethernet switch is designed to reduce the traffic by micro-segmenting traffic on every port, and keeping only the traffic to and from the host connected on a specific port. To be able to monitor the traffic to and from a port on a switch, the network protocol analyzer must be connected to that port. If it is not possible to connect the network protocol analyzer to the port where the traffic needs to be monitored, a more sophisticated Ethernet switch must be used. These Ethernet switches allow the mirroring of the traffic of the port where traffic needs to be monitored to a free port where the network protocol analyzer is connected for the capture.

In the setup in Figure 6-17, the network protocol analyzer is software running in the PC. It captures all traffic to and from the PC. In this case, the PC is used for many purposes, one of them is to test the TCP/IP stack of the embedded system under test. The other use for the PC is also to load the code via a JTAG interface (or other debug interface) to test to the embedded system. The development tool chain runs on the PC and binary code is downloaded to the embedded system under test. This way, the embedded developer can also use the debugger and single step through the code as the PC tests the TCP/IP stack.

To capture traffic other than unicast traffic sent to the host running the network protocol analyzer software, multicast traffic, and broadcast traffic, the network protocol analyzer must put the NIC into "promiscuous" mode. However, not all network protocol analyzers support this. On wireless LANs, even if the adapter is in promiscuous mode, packets that are not meant for Wi-Fi services for which the NIC is configured will be ignored. To see these packets, the NIC must be in monitor mode.

For our development objectives, we want to use the network protocol analyzer to:

- Debug network protocol implementations
- Analyze network problems
- Debug client/server applications
- Capture and report network statistics
- Monitor network usage

There are multiple commercial network protocol analyzers. Micrium engineers typically use Wireshark, a free network protocol analyzer.

Wireshark uses **p**acket **cap**ture (**pcap**) and consists of an API for capturing network traffic. Unix-like systems implement pcap in the libpcap library, while Windows uses a port of libpcap known as WinPcap to configure the NIC in promiscuous mode to capture packets. Wireshark runs on Microsoft Windows and on various Unix-like operating systems including Linux, Mac OS X, BSD, and Solaris. Wireshark is released under the terms of the GNU General Public License.

6-2-2 WIRESHARK

Wireshark will be used for many of the examples provided in Part II of this book.

Wireshark, previously called Ethereal, was developed by Gerald Combs as a tool to capture and analyze packets. Today there are more than 500 contributing authors while Mr. Combs continues to maintain the overall code and releases of new versions.

Wireshark is similar to the Unix utility "tcpdump", however Wireshark features a graphical front-end, and additional data sorting and filtering options. To download and install Wireshark on a Microsoft Windows host, the WinPcap utility is installed by the installer tool. This utility enables NIC(s) to be placed in promiscuous mode so that the Wireshark software captures all Ethernet frames travelling on the Ethernet interface selected for frame capture.

WIRESHARK QUICKSTART

While Wireshark documentation is excellent, it is a very sophisticated tool with many features and options. To help the embedded developer, here are a few hints to get started quickly.

First download and install Wireshark on the PC host to be used. Wireshark is a network protocol analyzer that provides decoding for the largest number of protocols. By default all protocols are selected. To help reduce what will be captured and displayed in the Wireshark decoding window, we recommend limiting the protocols that can be decoded to only the ones that will be used for the purposes of this book.

To launch Wireshark, from the main window, select Analyze -> Enabled Protocols.

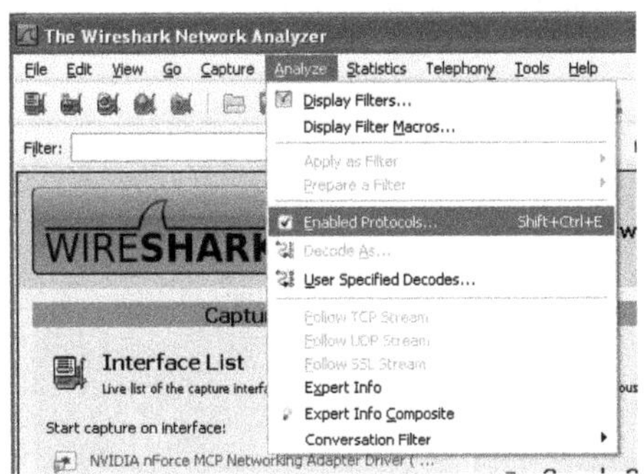

Figure 6-18 **Wireshark – Analyze, Enabled Protocols**

From this selection, the following pop-up window is displayed:

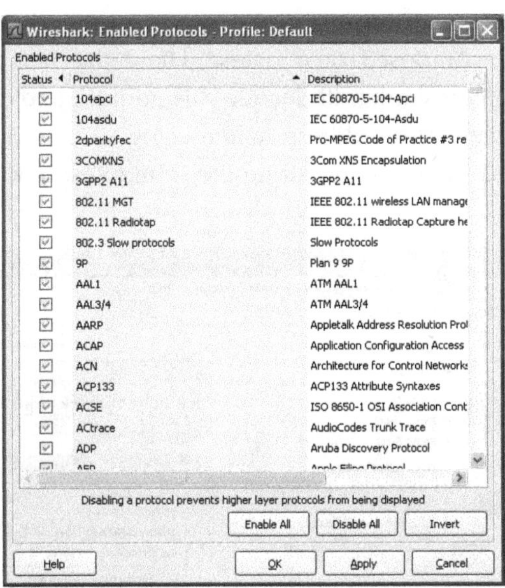

Figure 6-19 **Wireshark – Analyze, Enabled Protocols**

The protocols of interest for this book are:

- ARP
- IP
- ICMP
- TCP
- UDP

Even with these protocols, a substantial amount of data will be captured since many higher-level protocols rely on this list. When troubleshooting a HTTP service, HTTP must also be selected in the list of enabled protocols.

Before we select the interface to begin capture, there is one additional suggestion. As the Ethernet MAC address is composed of 6 bytes, where the first three bytes identify the manufacturer. By default, Wireshark will decode this address and present the manufacturer name instead of the complete MAC address. When using Wireshark for the first time, it may be confusing, therefore we suggest configuring the Name Resolution option.

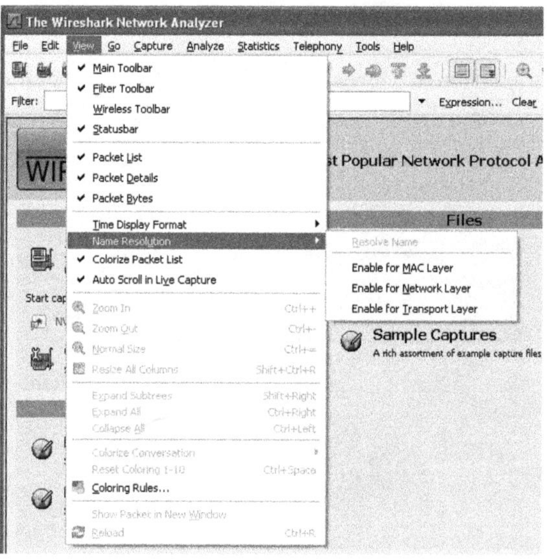

Figure 6-20 **Wireshark – Name Resolution**

From the main window drop-down menu, select View -> Name Resolution.

Name resolution can be configured for the following:

- MAC Layer (Data-Link, Ethernet in our case)
- Network Layer (IP)
- Transport Layer (TCP and UDP)

If you are new to protocol decoding, it is better to see the fields and their values rather than names. Therefore, display complete addresses and port numbers, and not aliases.

Next, configure the capture and/or display filters. The capture filter allows for a reduction in the size of the capture file by only saving the traffic of interest.

On the Wireshark main window, select Capture -> Capture Filters.

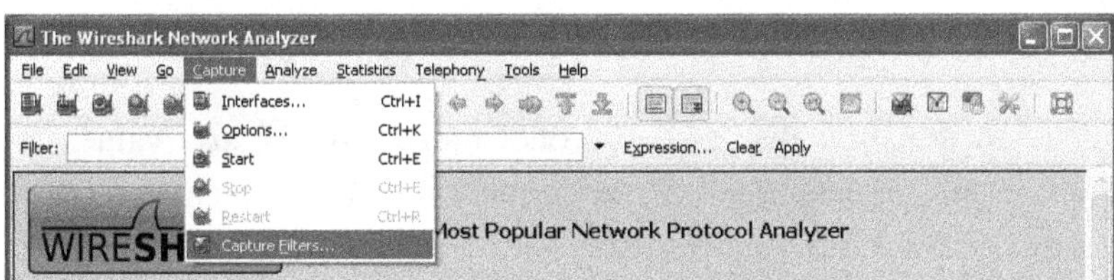

Figure 6-21 **Wireshark – Capture Filters**

This pop-up window is displayed:

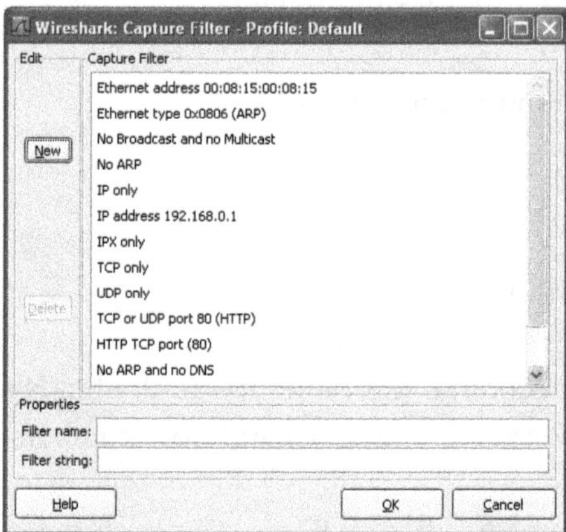

Figure 6-22 **Wireshark – Capture Filters Edition**

On the Wireshark main window toolbar, select Edit Capture Filter. Only one capture filter can be applied per capture. The capture filter is applied on the Interface Capture Options window as seen below.

A capture filter is an equation that uses protocol names, fields, and values to achieve the desired result. For an explanation on the equation syntax, please refer to Wireshark documentation or use the Help button in the bottom left corner of this window.

Capture filters allow for the reduction of the size of the capture file, but capturing everything may be required in certain cases. Capturing all the traffic on a link on a network can yield a substantial amount of data. Finding the frames of interest in a sea of frames is often difficult. However, once the data is captured, it can be displayed using different display filters to see only what is of interest.

From the main window drop-down menu, select Analyze -> Display Filters.

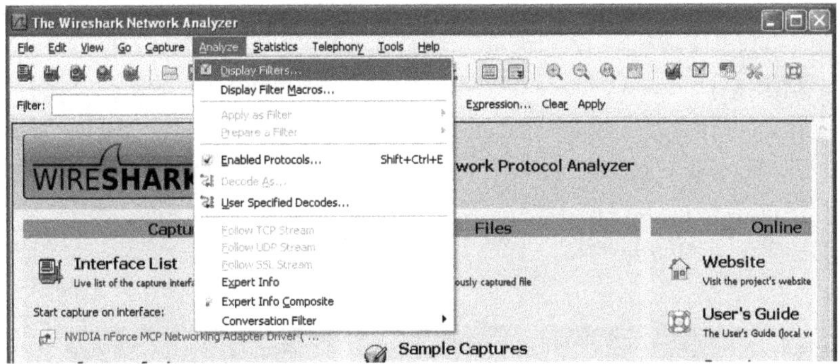

Figure 6-23 **Wireshark – Display Filters**

This pop-up window is displayed:

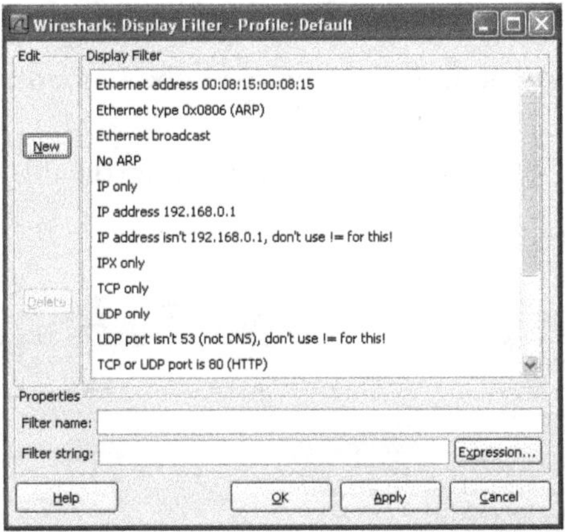

Figure 6-24 **Wireshark – Display Filters Edition**

The rules to create and edit a display filter are not the same as those used for a capture filter. Refer to the Wireshark documentation or use the Help button at the bottom left of the window.

Now, let's set the interface to be used for capturing the network traffic.

From the main window drop-down menu, select Capture -> Interfaces.

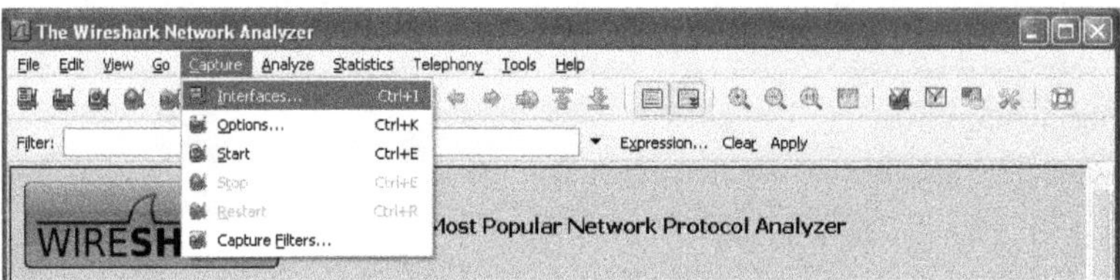

Figure 6-25 **Wireshark – Capture Interface**

This pop-up window is displayed.

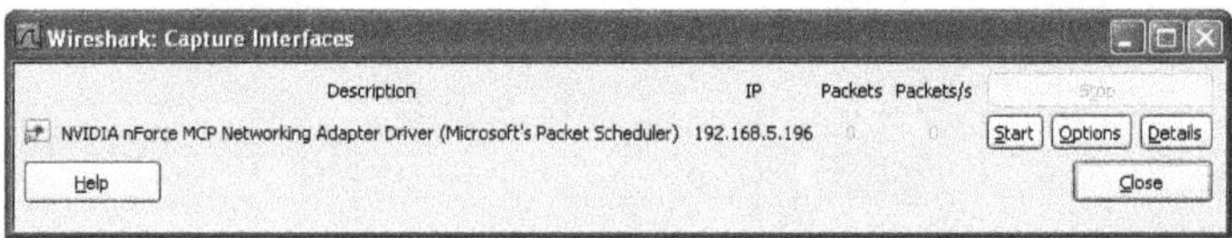

Figure 6-26 **Wireshark – Capture Interfaces**

Select the computer NIC used to connect to the network to be analyzed. Remember this is the interface that will capture the traffic to and from the embedded system.

If the name resolution is not set, do it here by clicking on the Options button associated with the interface selected.

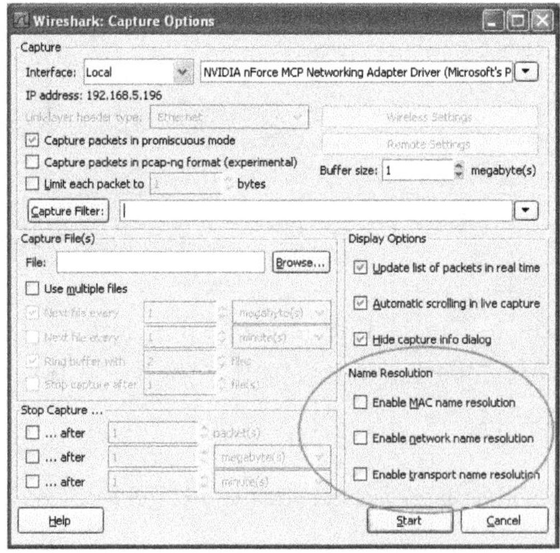

Figure 6-27 **Wireshark – Name Resolution**

Click the Start button to begin the capture. Without setting options, clicking the Start button associated to an interface of interest in the interface selection window also begins frame capturing.

The following figure provides a capture sample:

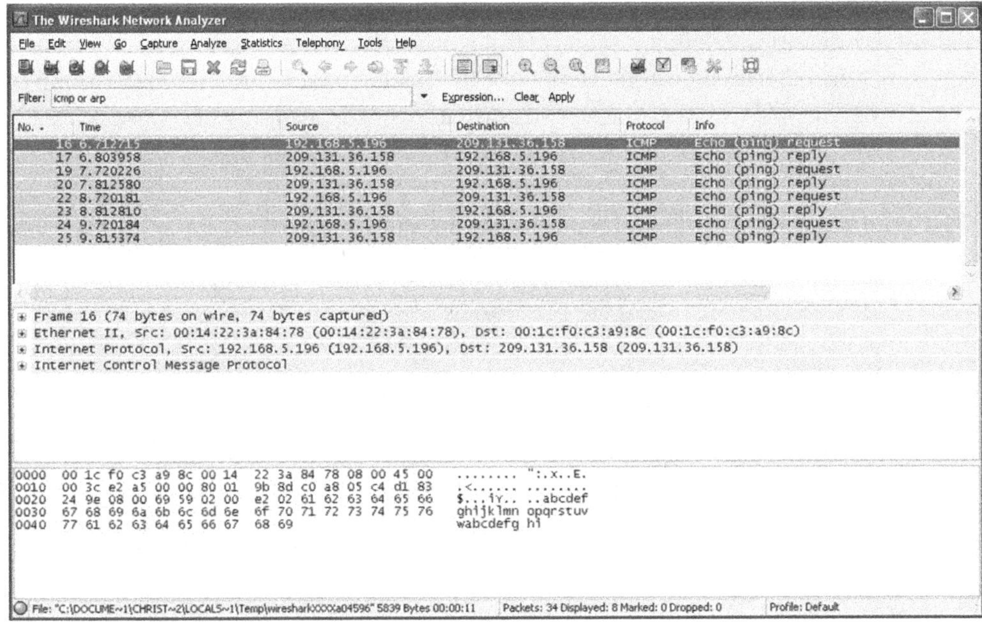

Figure 6-28 **Wireshark – Capture**

The capture shown in Figure 6-28 is a PING test from a host on a private network to a host on the Internet at IP address 209.131.36.158. For this example, the display filter is set to view ICMP traffic only. Even if what is being captured and stored are Ethernet frames, Wireshark refers to every record as a packet. The Wireshark capture window offers three different views of the captured "packets:"

- Packet List
- Packet Details
- Packet Bytes

The Packet list is a summary of all packets captured during the test. By default, the first packet in the list is selected. Click on any packet in the list to make it the selected packet.

Packet Details and Packet Bytes are the decoded representation of the selected packet. Packet Details is a view the can be expanded by clicking on the + expansion icons, which is a view of the encapsulation process introduced in Chapter 1.

The Packet Bytes view is often not required when analyzing a network or application problem. It is a hexadecimal and ASCII view of the packet, similar to a memory dump view. A Packet Bytes view is useful if packet construction is suspected. TCP/IP stacks are very stable software components, which mean that we can turn off this view.

From the main window drop-down menu, select View -> Packet Bytes.

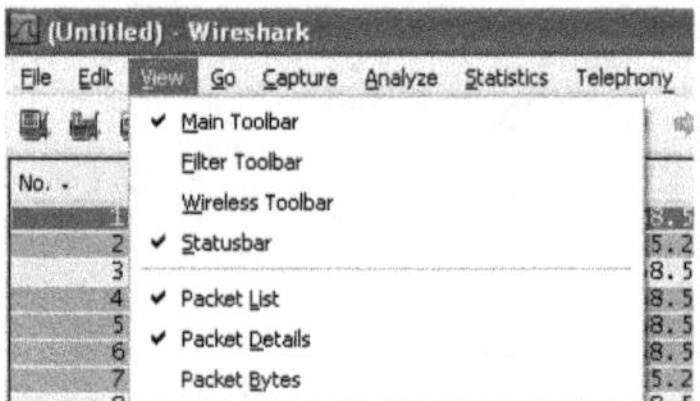

Figure 6-29 **Wireshark – Packet Bytes**

Wireshark has many more features and options including its ability to save the capture to files. In this way, when analyzing a situation, it is possible to share a problem with colleagues.

Wireshark captures are used extensively in Part II.

6-2-3 µC/IPerf

IPerf was developed by The National Laboratory for Applied Network Research (NLANR) as a means to measure maximum TCP and UDP bandwidth performance. The source code can be found on Sourceforge: http://iperf.sourceforge.net/. IPerf is open source software written in C++ that runs on various platforms including Linux, Unix and Windows. Micrium ported IPerf source code to µC/TCP-IP and created a module in C called µC/IPerf, which can be downloaded with all code and tools for this book at: http://www.micrium.com/page/downloads/uc-tcp-ip_files

IPerf is a standardized tool that can be used on any network, and outputs standardized performance measurements. It can also be used as an unbiased benchmarking tool for comparison of wired and wireless networking equipment and technologies. As the source code is available, the measurement methodology can be analyzed by anyone.

With IPerf, you can create TCP and UDP data streams and measure the throughput of a network for these streams. IPerf reports bandwidth, delay jitter, and datagram loss, and allows you to set various parameters to tune a network. IPerf has client and server functionality. Because Micrium provides the µC/IPerf source code, it is also an excellent example of how to write a client and/or server application for µC/TCP-IP. The IPerf test engine can measure the throughput between two hosts, either uni-directionally or bi-directionally. When used for testing UDP capacity, IPerf allows you to specify datagram size, and provides results for datagram throughput and packet loss. When used for testing TCP capacity, IPerf measures the throughput of the payload.

In a typical test setup with two hosts, one is the embedded system under test (see Figure 6-30). The second host is ideally a PC. A command line version of IPerf is available for PCs running Linux, Unix and Windows. There is also a graphical user interface (GUI) front end called Jperf available on sourceforge: http://iperf.sourceforge.net/. It is definitely fun to use.

The examples shown in this book use a Jperf variant called KPerf. There is no official site for KPerf and there are just a few links to download it. Micrium uses KPerf because of its ease of use. Download KPerf from the Micrium site at: www.micrium.com/page/downloads/uc-tcp-ip_files.

KPerf was originally created by the same IPerf and Jperf authors, but the source code and executables do not seem to be maintained. If you want the source code for the PC host in the test setup, Jperf is more advantageous.

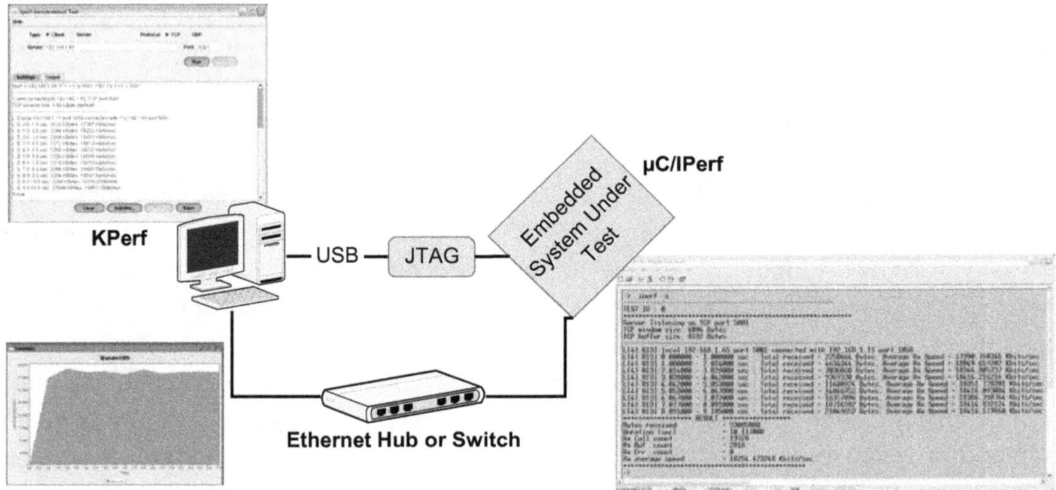

Figure 6-30 **IPerf Setup**

The µC/IPerf setup is reproduced in Figure 6-30. In this case, the Ethernet hub or switch can be replaced with a cross-over cable, an Ethernet cable where the TX wires and the RX wires are crossed so that two Ethernet devices have a face-to-face connection without the use of a hub or switch. This type of cable is very useful for troubleshooting, but must be identified carefully as using it with certain Ethernet switches may not work. More recent computer NICs and Ethernet switches detect the TX and RX wires. This is called AutoSense. With this equipment any Ethernet cable type can be used.

Typically, an IPerf report contains a time-stamped output of the amount of data transferred and the throughput measured. IPerf uses 1024*1024 for megabytes and 1000*1000 for megabits.

Here is an example of an IPerf test where the PC is configured as a client and the embedded system under test as a server.

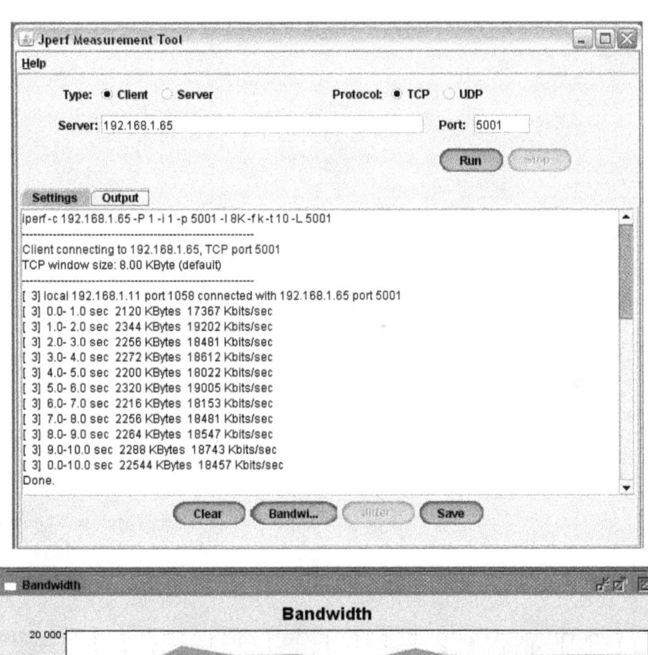

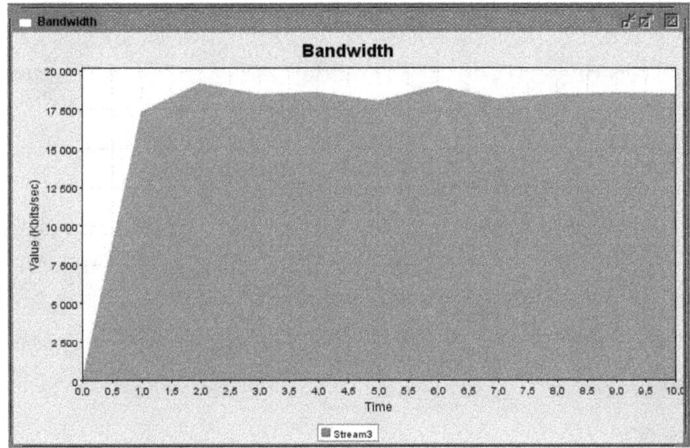

Figure 6-31 **KPerf on PC in Client mode**

6

```
-> iperf -s
-------------------------------------------------------------
TEST ID : 0
*****************************************************************
Server listening on TCP port 5001
TCP window size: 4096 Bytes
TCP buffer size: 8192 Bytes
-----------------------------------------------------------------
L[4] R[3] local 192.168.1.65 port 5001 connected with 192.168.1.11 port 1058
L[4] R[3] 0.000000 - 1.000000 sec : Total received = 2258664 Bytes, Average Rx Speed = 17390.760346 Kbits/sec
L[4] R[3] 1.000000 - 2.014000 sec : Total received = 4634344 Bytes, Average Rx Speed = 18049.659202 Kbits/sec
L[4] R[3] 2.014000 - 3.028000 sec : Total received = 7036060 Bytes, Average Rx Speed = 18346.805737 Kbits/sec
L[4] R[3] 3.028000 - 4.042000 sec : Total received = 9369320 Bytes, Average Rx Speed = 18416.216216 Kbits/sec
L[4] R[3] 4.042000 - 5.053000 sec : Total received = 11680924 Bytes, Average Rx Speed = 18351.728201 Kbits/sec
L[4] R[3] 5.053000 - 6.067000 sec : Total received = 14046952 Bytes, Average Rx Speed = 18416.093084 Kbits/sec
L[4] R[3] 6.067000 - 7.077000 sec : Total received = 16357096 Bytes, Average Rx Speed = 18386.398764 Kbits/sec
L[4] R[3] 7.077000 - 8.091000 sec : Total received = 18716392 Bytes, Average Rx Speed = 18414.832124 Kbits/sec
L[4] R[3] 8.091000 - 9.105000 sec : Total received = 21049652 Bytes, Average Rx Speed = 18416.119860 Kbits/sec
***************** RESULT *****************
Bytes received          = 23085080
Duration (sec)          = 10.117000
Rx Call count           = 19728
Rx Buf  count           = 2818
Rx Err  count           = 0
Rx average speed        = 18254.423248 Kbits/sec
*************************************************
->
```

Figure 6-32 **µC/IPerf on Embedded System Under Test in Server mode**

In the Figure 6-30 setup, all possible network configurations can be tested: TCP or UDP tests in client-to-server or server-to-client mode, using different parameters settings. If necessary, refer to the IPerf or µC/IPerf user manuals.

µC/IPerf testing samples are used extensively in Part II of this book to test UDP and TCP configurations and to demonstrate concepts introduced so far, especially in the area of performance.

6-3 SUMMARY

A TCP/IP stack is a complex embedded software component and using TCP/IP can also be complicated.

In this chapter, we introduced the following network troubleshooting tools: PING, TRACEROUTE, Wireshark and IPerf. Many other network traffic analysis tools and load generators exist. It's unlikely that you will need more than the concepts presented so far when developing your TCP/IP-based embedded system.

Chapter

7

Transport Protocols

Since we already know that Internet Protocol (IP) does not check data integrity, it is necessary to use protocols that have complementary characteristics to ensure that the data not only arrives at its intended destination, but is in good shape when it does. The protocols most often used with IP are Transmission Control Protocol (TCP) and User Datagram Protocol (UDP), both of which check data integrity. Although TCP and UDP have similar data-carrying capabilities, they have specific differences and characteristics that dictate their use.

7-1 TRANSPORT LAYER PROTOCOLS

The following table represents a comparison between TCP and UDP:

	TCP	**UDP**
Service	Connection oriented	Connectionless
Data verification	Yes	Yes
Rejection of erroneous segments/datagrams	Yes	Yes
Sequence control	Yes	No
Retransmission of erroneous and lost segments	Yes	No
Reliability	High	Low
Delay generated	High	Low
Total throughput	Lower	Higher

Table 7-1 **TCP vs. UDP at the protocol level**

Data verification is the data integrity checking capability for both protocols. If a TCP segment or UDP datagram is received and data corruption is detected, the segment or datagram is rejected.

Given that with packet networks such as IP, packets may take different paths depending on network conditions, it is possible for packets transmitted to reach their final destination out of order. With TCP, segments received out of order are re-sequenced so that the data is received in the order it was originally transmitted.

TCP also implements a flow-control mechanism which ensures that all packets transmitted are received at a pace that is based on available resources, even if the process takes longer to achieve. Flow control also prevents segments from being discarded because the receiver does not have the resources to receive it. This is why TCP is considered a high-reliability protocol in comparison to UDP. The flow-control mechanism is not part of the UDP protocol. Instead, UDP has a fire-and-forget strategy and it is also known as a best-effort protocol. TCP's reliability has a corresponding expense. All of the processing required with TCP to ensure the reliable delivery of data adds transmission delay between the source and destination. This is why in Table 7-2 it is noted that TCP has a lower total throughput than UDP.

TCP and UDP can also be differentiated by the type of applications that use them:

Protocol	Service Type	Examples
TCP	Reliable stream transfer	Non time-sensitive data transfer: File transfer, web pages (an embedded system running a web server), e-mail...
UDP	Quick-and-simple single-block transfer	Network services with short queries and short answers: DHCP and DNS Time Sensitive data that can cope with a minimal packet loss: Voice, video, repetitive sensor data

Table 7-2 **TCP vs. UDP at the Application Level**

TCP's inherent characteristics make it an appropriate protocol for transporting non real-time (data) traffic, which does not tolerate errors. The TCP Specifics section that follows this chapter provides an in-depth look at these characteristics.

Examples of standard protocols or network services that use TCP include:

- File Transfer Protocol (FTP)
- Hyper Text Transfer Protocol (HTTP)
- Simple Mail Transfer Protocol (SMTP)

For an embedded system, any information exchange requiring a guarantee of delivery to the recipient benefits from TCP. A configuration application for a numerical milling machine is an example.

Delays generated by TCP's reliability have consequences on the quality of the transmission of real-time traffic, such as voice or video. Moreover, since several types of real-time traffic tolerate a certain error rate, the use of the UDP protocol is more appropriate. When the message generated by the application is short, the risk of error decreases.

Examples of standard protocols or network services that use UDP include:

- Domain Name Service (DNS)
- Dynamic Host Configuration Protocol (DHCP)
- Trivial File Transfer Protocol (TFTP)

An embedded system that tolerates errors in data transmission may benefit from UDP. In fact, Micrium has many customers that use a UDP/IP configuration only. A system that collects sensor data at periodic intervals and transfers it to control a recording station is an example. If the system can suffer the infrequent loss of a report, UDP may be the best protocol option.

7-2 CLIENT/SERVER ARCHITECTURE

A very important application design feature used on IP networks is the client/server architecture, as it separates functions between service requesters (clients) and service providers (servers).

A client is a host application that executes a single task. This task is for the host alone and is not shared with any other hosts on the network. When a client requests content or a service function from a server, servers are listening to connection requests initiated by clients. Since a server shares its resources with clients, the server can execute one or more tasks.

Such familiar networked functions as email, web access, and database access, are based on the client-server model. For example, a web browser is a client application running on a host that accesses information at any web server in the world.

The client-server model is the architecture of most IP-based applications including HTTP, SMTP, Telnet, DHCP and DNS. Client software sends requests to one or many servers. The servers accept requests, process them, and return the requested information to the client.

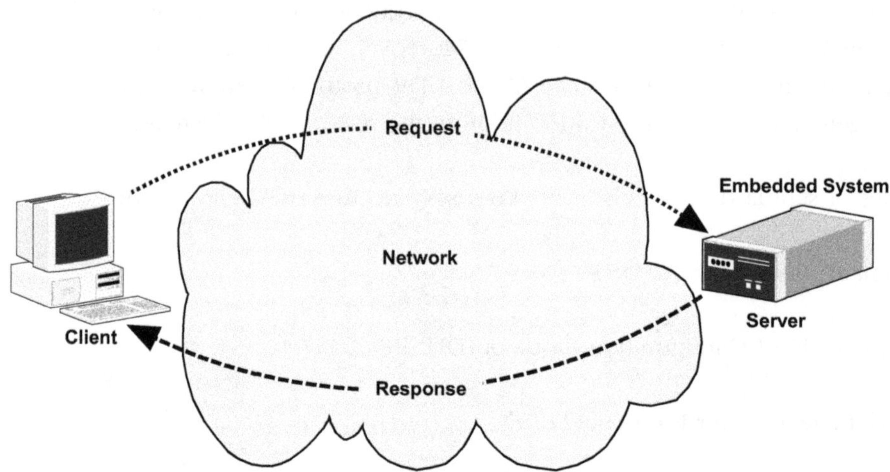

Figure 7-1 **Client/Server Architecture**

In Figure 7-1 above, note that the embedded system can also be the Client.

To implement a client/server architecture, a connection is established between the client and the server. This is where transport layer protocols come into play.

7-3 PORTS

UDP and TCP share common fields in their respective headers, two being port numbers. A port is a logical entity that allows UDP and TCP to associate a segment (datagram) with a specific application. This is how IP addresses are reused with multiple applications, or multiple instances of the same application on a single client or server Host.

The next chapter addresses socket concepts and demonstrates how a port number is used to differentiate between applications running on the same host.

For the source host, the destination port indicates to which logical entity the datagram must be sent. In a client-server environment, the destination port at the client's station normally takes on a value that is predetermined by the Internet Assigned Numbers Authority (IANA) depending on the application that is solicited. These destination ports are also identified as well-known ports and are defined in RFC 1700.

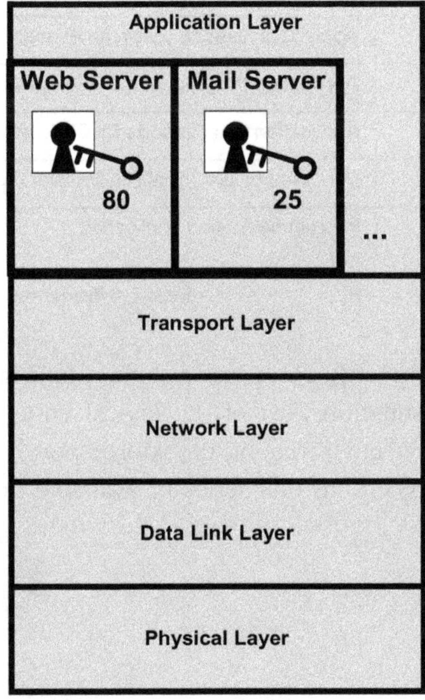

Figure 7-2 **Server application port number use**

Figure 7-2, shows two very popular services: A web server that replies to requests on port number 80 and a SMTP mail server that replies to requests on port 25.

Although UDP offers connectionless service, the station must be able to determine the application to which the information contained in the datagram will be sent. The UDP port contains this information.

Table 7-3 shows predetermined values of port numbers based on popular applications as per RFC 1700:

Port	Transport	Application	Description
20	TCP	FTP-Data	Port used by the FTP application for data transfer.
21	TCP	FTP-Control	Port used by the FTP application to transport control fields.
23	TCP	Telnet	Application providing remote access.
25	TCP	SMTP	E-mail application.
53	UDP	DNS	Application used to obtain an IP address based on a domain name.
67	UDP	BOOTPS	Application that supports DHCP (server port).
68	UDP	BOOTPC	Application that supports DHCP (client port).
69	UDP	TFTP	Port used by the Trivial File Transfer Protocol (TFTP)
80	TCP,UDP	HTTP	Internet navigation application.

Table 7-3 **Transport Layer Port Number Definitions**

For the source host, the source port keeps a trace of the application where the datagram originated, and informs the destination host of the logical entity where it must send the reply. Generally, in a client-server environment, the source port at the client's station takes on a value between 1024 and 65535. In this series of available ports, several are reserved but not allocated by the IANA.

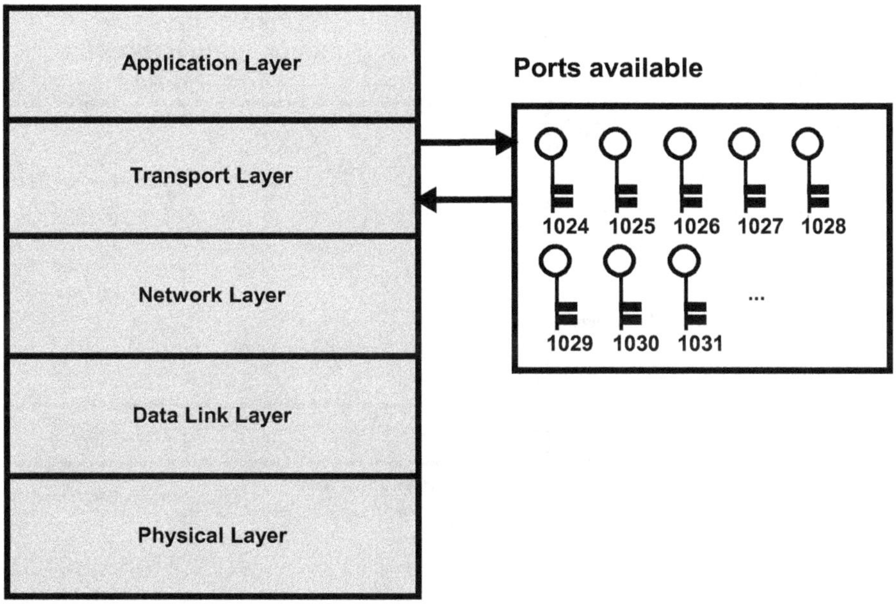

Figure 7-3 **Client Application Port Number Use**

Figure 7-3 shows a client using available socket numbers. The client port can take any number from 1024 to 65535. Computers and embedded systems both use this approach.

The accepted notation used to represent an IP address and port number is to specify the IP address in dotted decimal notation followed by a colon and then the port number. For example: 10.2.43.234:1589.

7-3-1 PORT ADDRESS TRANSLATION (PAT)

Network address translation (NAT) was introduced previously in Chapter 4. It is important to note here that there is a NAT variant called Port Address Translation (PAT) that uses port numbers to reduce the number of public IP addresses required to connect hosts on a private network to hosts on the Internet. Port numbers can be utilized to reuse a single public IP address to allow a private network to access the Internet (see Figure 7-4). This graphic is typical of the mechanism used by our earlier example of gateways in homes that access the Internet.

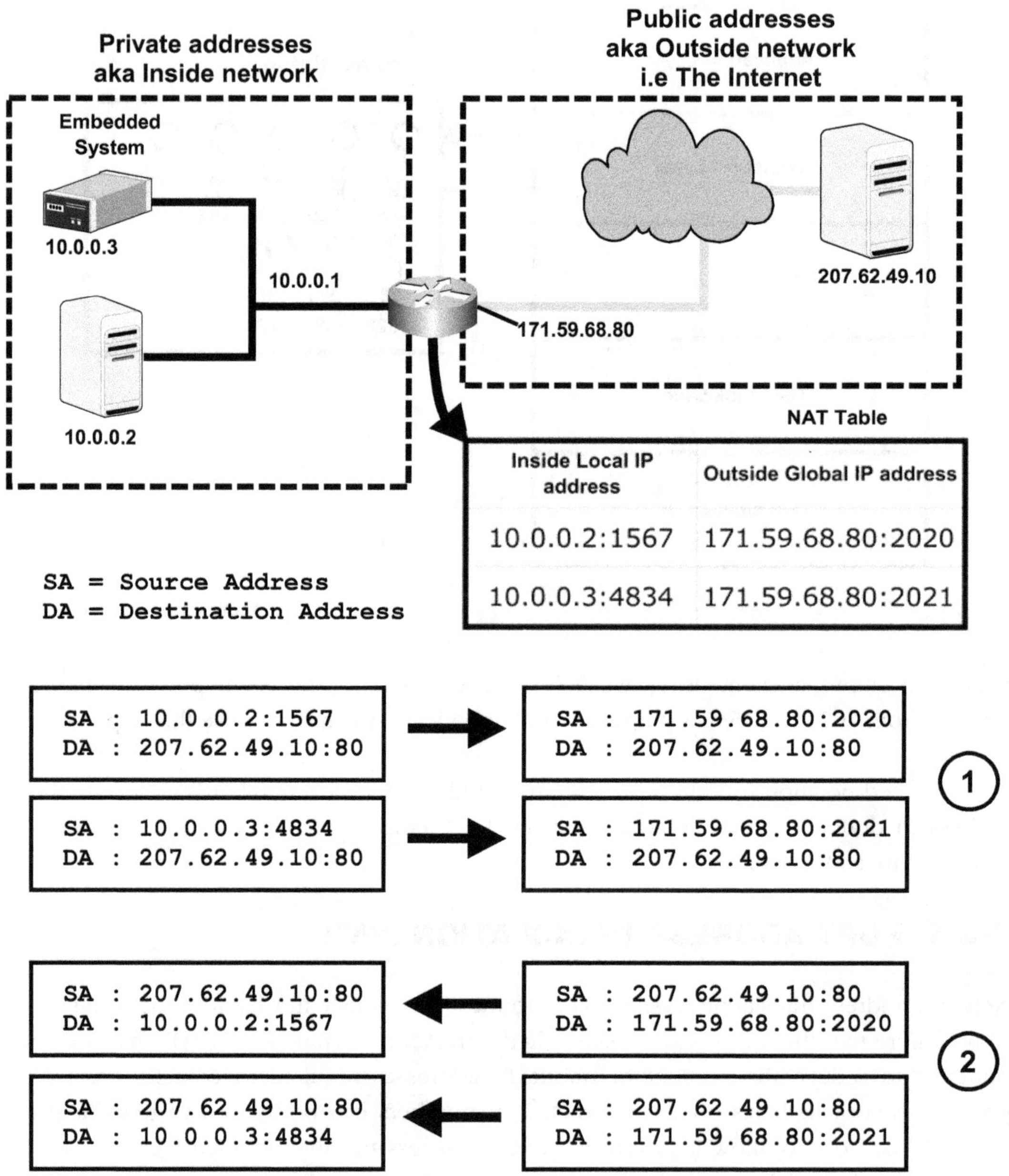

Private addresses
aka Inside network

Embedded
System

10.0.0.3

10.0.0.1

10.0.0.2

Public addresses
aka Outside network
i.e The Internet

207.62.49.10

171.59.68.80

NAT Table

Inside Local IP address	Outside Global IP address
10.0.0.2:1567	171.59.68.80:2020
10.0.0.3:4834	171.59.68.80:2021

SA = Source Address
DA = Destination Address

SA : 10.0.0.2:1567
DA : 207.62.49.10:80
→
SA : 171.59.68.80:2020
DA : 207.62.49.10:80

SA : 10.0.0.3:4834
DA : 207.62.49.10:80
→
SA : 171.59.68.80:2021
DA : 207.62.49.10:80

1

SA : 207.62.49.10:80
DA : 10.0.0.2:1567
←
SA : 207.62.49.10:80
DA : 171.59.68.80:2020

SA : 207.62.49.10:80
DA : 10.0.0.3:4834
←
SA : 207.62.49.10:80
DA : 171.59.68.80:2021

2

Figure 7-4 **Port Address Translation**

Figure 7-4 shows a 10.0.0.0 private network assigned to the network on the left. The router in the Figure is the default gateway for this network. The gateway has two network interfaces: one facing the network on the left, the private network; and one facing the network on the right, the public network.

F7-4(1) In this simple case, embedded systems with IP address 10.0.0.2 and 10.0.0.3 on the private network want to connect with a host at 207.62.49.10 on the Internet. The embedded system's private address and source port number (10.0.0.2:1567) is translated into the public address associated with the gateway's public interface of 171.59.68.80 plus a port number (2020). Similarly, the PC's private address and source port number (10.0.0.3:4834) is translated into the public address associated with the gateway's public interface of 171.59.68.80 plus a port number (2021). The Internet Service Provider (ISP) assigns the public address when the private network is registered. When the private network is running, all connection requests from the private network to the Internet will be granted.

The cross-reference between the private addresses and the public addresses is stored in a table in the gateway. The packets sent by the embedded system and PC can now travel on the public network since all addresses are public. In this example, we see that multiple connections are established between the private network and the Internet, reusing a single public address, yet having multiple source port numbers.

F7-4(2) When the host on the public network answers the query from the host in the private network system with IP translated to 171.59.68.80, it answers the message the same way it would answer another host request on the Internet. When the reply reaches the gateway, it translates the destination address from 171.59.68.80 and associated port number to the correct private address and associated port number using the translation table it created on the initial outgoing packet. This works as long as the communication is established from the private network out.

The same discussion can be made regarding the use of static public addresses to access hosts on the private network from hosts on the public network, as shown in the NAT section in the previous chapter. This process (NAT or PAT) happens in the gateway. When troubleshooting from a private network to a public network or vice-versa, take this process into consideration.

7-4 UDP

UDP is a communication protocol at Layer 4, the Transport Layer. It is often believed that UDP is a deprecated protocol because all of the Internet services used on a daily basis including web browsing and e-mail use TCP. This, however, is not the case. As previously stated, there are many services and applications that rely solely on UDP. UDP provides limited services when information is exchanged between two stations on the network; yet it is often all that is required.

When two hosts exchange information using UDP, there is no information regarding the status of the connection between them. Host A knows that it is sending or receiving data from Host B, and vice-versa, but that's all. The UDP layer in both hosts does not know if all of the data was transmitted and received properly. This means that the application layer above UDP in Hosts A and B must implement the necessary mechanisms to guarantee the delivery of data, if necessary. Remember, UDP is a best-effort, connectionless protocol.

UDP encapsulation provides checksum on the payload to detect accidental errors. When the UDP datagram is received, UDP checks for data validity. If validated, UDP will move the data to the application. If the data is invalid, however, the datagram is discarded without additional warning.

<table>
<tr><td>0</td><td>1</td><td>2</td><td>3</td><td>4</td><td>5</td><td>6</td><td>7</td><td>8</td><td>9</td><td>10</td><td>11</td><td>12</td><td>13</td><td>14</td><td>15</td><td>16</td><td>17</td><td>18</td><td>19</td><td>20</td><td>21</td><td>22</td><td>23</td><td>24</td><td>25</td><td>26</td><td>27</td><td>28</td><td>29</td><td>30</td><td>31</td></tr>
<tr><td colspan="16"></td><td colspan="16"></td></tr>
<tr><td colspan="16">Source Port</td><td colspan="16">Destination Port</td></tr>
<tr><td colspan="16">Datagram Length</td><td colspan="16">Data Checksum</td></tr>
<tr><td colspan="32">Data</td></tr>
<tr><td colspan="32">...</td></tr>
</table>

Figure 7-5 **UDP Header Fields**

The UDP header format is given in Figure 7-5. This information will be useful when decoding UDP datagrams with a network protocol analyzer as presented in Chapter 6, "Troubleshooting" on page 135.

Because UDP is a simple protocol without control mechanisms, it executes quickly, however datagrams may be lost for many reasons such as network congestion or lack of resources in the receiving host. This can well be the case on an embedded target as typically, embedded targets have scarce resources, especially RAM for buffers.

In a normal application, UDP is used in a system where the exchange of information between the client and server is accomplished with short client requests generating short server replies. Examples of this include DHCP and DNS, which both use UDP.

When a host using DHCP is powered up, it sends a DHCP request as a broadcast message looking for a DHCP server, and asks for an IP address. This is a short request since not many bytes are required to build such a request. Similarly, the reply from the server is fairly short, containing the information required to use the IP address assigned to it by the Server.

Another example is the use of DNS to obtain an IP address associated with a fully qualified domain name or URL. The request is a short question: "What is the IP address of this site?" The answer is also short: "Here's the IP address!"

From here, it is possible to imagine the use of UDP in many industrial-control applications where the amount and therefore duration of data to be transferred is relatively small. Another criteria is that the transfers occur at a reasonable periodic rate easily accommodated by the embedded target hardware. Another requirement is for the system to cope with missing packets discarded somewhere in the network.

If a system meets these requirements, the system TCP/IP stack may not need to implement TCP. The TCP module has a substantially larger code footprint than UDP (see section 3-2-3 "Footprint" on page 71). If UDP alone is used, the total system footprint is substantially smaller, which is an excellent situation for most embedded systems.

Given that UDP is a fairly light protocol, UDP transmission from the target to any other host can maximize throughput performance between the two devices. On many embedded targets, it is quite possible for the target to be a slower consumer, especially if the producer is a PC. UDP transmission from a host PC to an embedded target can flood the network interface. Depending on the processor speed and the number of buffers available, only a certain percentage of the traffic is received by the embedded target. The system designer in this case must consider whether or not the loss of any UDP datagram is critical.

Performance Impact on UDP

When the UDP producer is faster than the UDP consumer, there are potentially limiting factors to performance optimization:

1 The capacity of the Ethernet driver to receive all frames destined to its address.

2 The capacity for the TCP/IP stack and its associated Ethernet driver to move the Ethernet frames into network buffers.

3 In case the CPU cannot process all of the Ethernet frames, the capacity for the stack to have sufficient buffers so that they are kept in a queue for later processing. Of course, this is valid only if this is a transmission burst and not a sustained transmission.

An example of such a design decision is the use of UDP to transport such time-sensitive information as voice or video content. In this case, the timely delivery of the information is more important than the guaranteed delivery of the information.

When control mechanisms are added in a system to guarantee information delivery, it is quite possible that certain data packets will be delayed. Delaying information in a voice conversation or a video stream is not a good idea. This is the cause of clicking sounds, choppiness and delays experienced in early Voice over IP (VoIP) systems. UDP can help. Because UDP is a lighter protocol, it reduces the overhead required to process data. This does not mean that the system will not lose data. The system designer must consider whether or not the application can live with the loss of a few data packets. The new coders/decoders (codecs) in VoIP system do exactly that.

Part II of this book contains a sample project showing how to experiment with this behavior in an evaluation board. It is using the µC/IPerf application previously introduced in Chapter 6, “Troubleshooting” on page 135.

7-5 TCP SPECIFICS

Unlike IP and UDP, which are connectionless protocols, TCP is connection-oriented. This means that this protocol connection requirement involves the following three steps:

- Establishing a connection
- Transferring information
- Closing the connection.

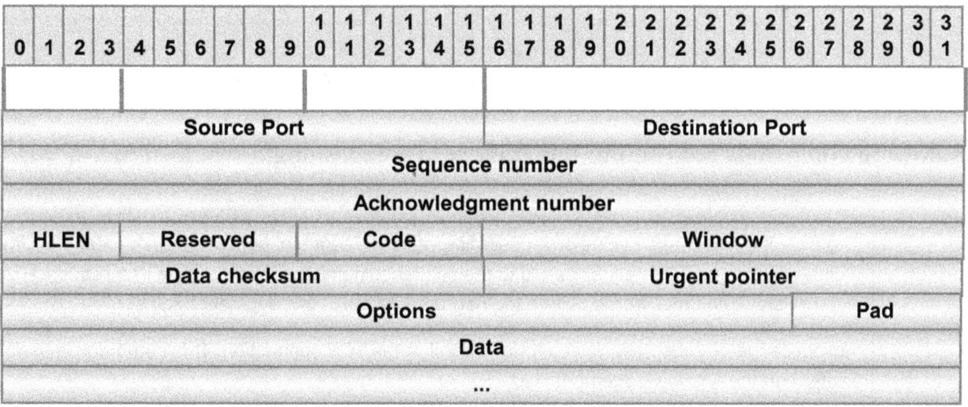

Figure 7-6 **TCP Header Fields**

Figure 7-6 shows s TCP header. It is a useful reference when decoding TCP segments with a network protocol analyzer.

The term "connection oriented" means that both hosts involved in a TCP communication are aware of each other. TCP is not one connection but two connections: one from A to B and one from B to A. The establishment of the full-duplex connection is accomplished using the TCP header "Code" field as shown in Figure 7-6. This field defines the function of the segment or a transmission characteristic.

Each of the six code-field bits corresponds to a command. When the value of a bit is set at 1, the command is active. The six commands in the Code field are:

- URG: Urgent
- ACK: Acknowledge
- PSH: Push
- RST: Reset
- SYN: Synchronize
- FIN: Finalize

The following commands are used in the context of establishing a connection:

URG	Urgent— if the field has a value of 1, it identifies that this segment contains urgent data. The Urgent Pointer field in the TCP header points to the sequence number of the last byte in a sequence of urgent data or, in other words, where the non-urgent data in this segment begins.
ACK	Acknowledge — code used to accept and confirm the TCP connection. This command is used jointly with the Acknowledgement field.
PSH	Push — if the field has a value of 1, the PSH command forces the receiver's TCP protocol to immediately transmit the data to the application without waiting for other segments.
RST	Reset — code used to abruptly interrupt a TCP connection without using the FIN or the ACK commands). This code is used under abnormal transmission conditions. Such browsers as Internet Explorer use it to close a connection without going through the normal closing sequence.
SYN	Synchronize — code used to request the establishment of a connection by defining the first sequence numbers used by the source and by the destination. The first number in the sequence is called the Initial Sequence Number (ISN).
FIN	Finalize — code used to ask the receiver to terminate the TCP connection.

Table 7-4 **TCP Code (6 bits)**

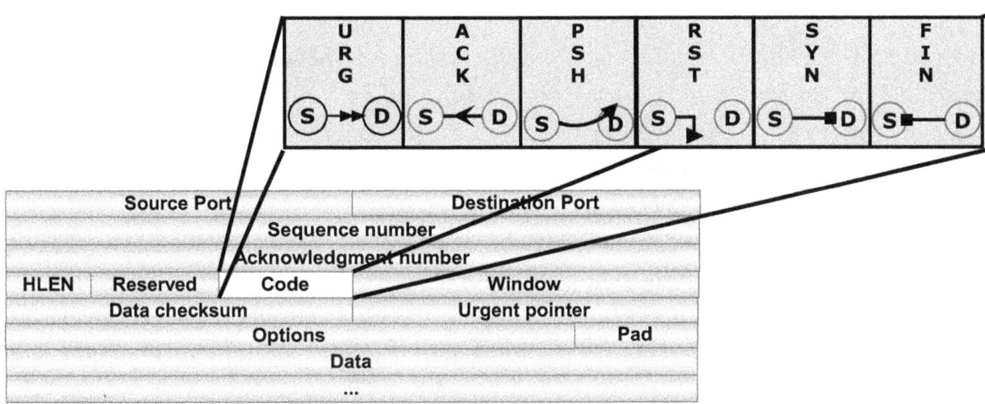

Figure 7-7 **TCP Code (6 bits)**

The six Code bits listed in Table 7-4 and depicted in Figure 7-7 are used in the following connection establishment mechanism.

7-6 TCP CONNECTION PHASES

The basis of the connection mechanism in TCP is called the three-way handshake.

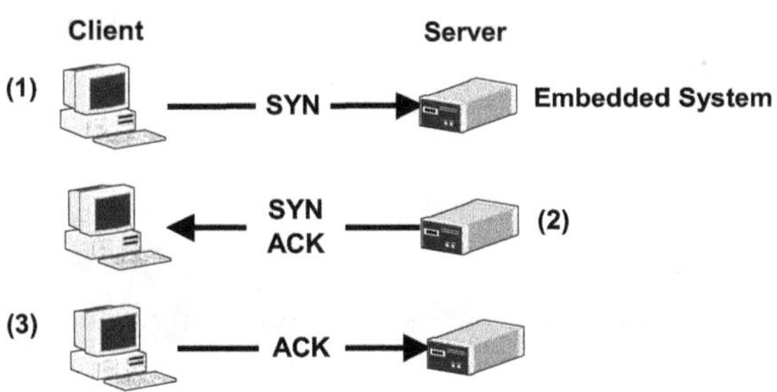

Figure 7-8 **The Three-Way Handshake**

F7-8(1) The client sends a SYN command to open a connection from the client to the server.

F7-8(2) The server answers the request for a connection with an ACK command and in the same message also asks to open a connection from the server to the client with a SYN command.

F7-8(3) The client confirms the connection with an ACK command.

Two connections are established: one from the client to the server and one from the server to the client. Normally, four messages would have been necessary, two per connection. Because the server acknowledges the connection request from the client and in the same message also requests to establish a connection to the client, this saves one message in the process. Three messages are used instead of four resulting in the three-way handshake.

Once the client and the server are aware of the connection, data can be exchanged between the two. For each packet transmitted from the client to the server, the server will acknowledge its reception and vice-versa. The PUSH code used when sending data tells the TCP stack to send this data to the application immediately. Data may also be sent without the PUSH bit. In this case data is accumulated in the receiving stack and, depending on the stack coding, is sent immediately or at a later time.

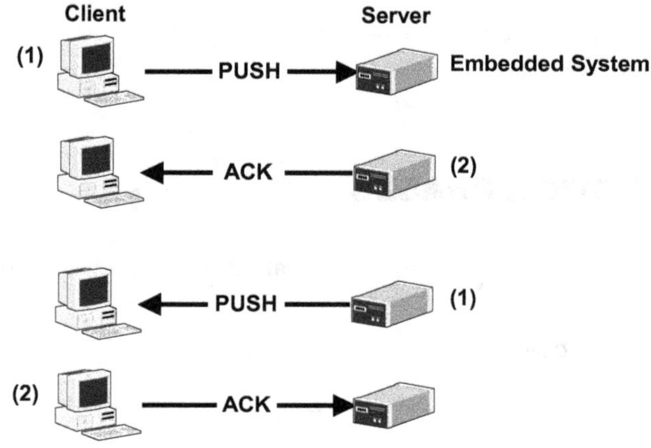

Figure 7-9 **Information Transfer**

F7-9(1) The PUSH command forces the receiving station to send data to the application.

F7-9(2) All TCP data received is acknowledged with the ACK command in the following packet transmitted in the opposite direction.

Upon completion of the data transfer, the two connections will be closed by the client and the server. In this case, the FIN command is used.

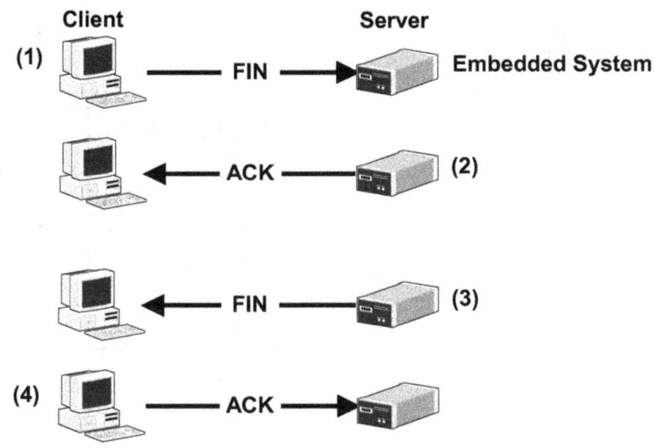

Figure 7-10 **Disconnection**

F7-10(1) Graceful connection termination is accomplished via the FIN command.

F7-10(2) The FIN command is also acknowledged with an ACK command.

It is possible to close only one connection of the two. For example, when the client requests a substantial amount of data from the server, the client can close its connection to the server, but the connection from the server to the client will be up until the server completes the data transfer to the client. This mechanism is called a half-close connection. When the server closes the connection steps (3) and (4) of Figure 7-10 above are executed.

7-7 TCP SEQUENCES THE DATA

When we write a letter that is several pages long, we write a sequence number on each page: 1-of-4, 2-of-4, etc. In a similar manner, TCP enters a sequence number into its header that allows for different segments to be put in order at reception.

Figure 7-11 represents the location of the sequence number in the TCP header. The sequence number is a 32-bit field. The initial sequence number in the first TCP segment used to establish connection is a random number selected by TCP. µC/TCP-IP takes care of this for you. The embedded developer does not need to be concerned about the randomness of this field. The sequence number is relative, it is not absolute. From this point, the sequence number is used as a relative pointer to the TCP payload carried by the TCP segment.

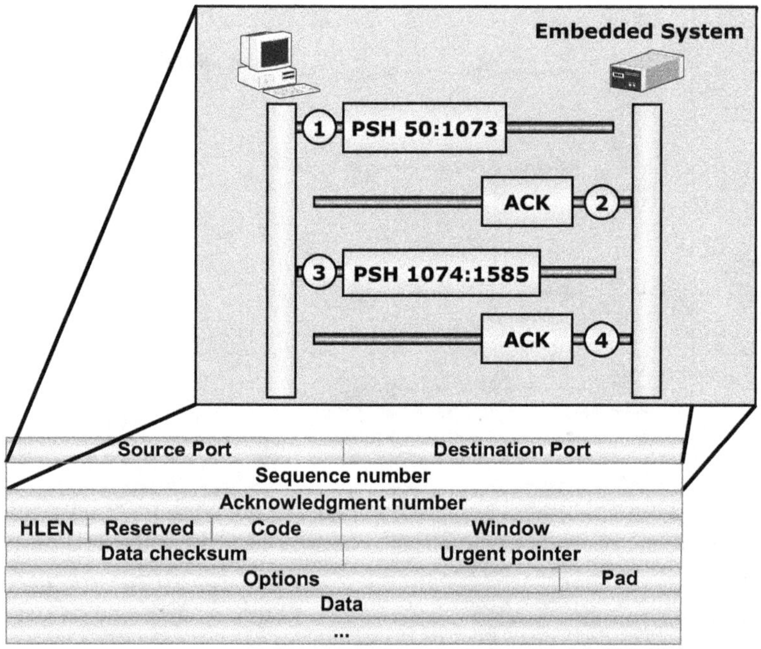

Figure 7-11 **Sequence Number (32 bits)**

F7-11(1) The sequence number is 50. The segment is carrying 1024 bytes, which means that if the first byte carried by the segment is a byte with index 50, then the last byte has index 1073. The next sequence number is therefore the previous sequence number plus the segment size in bytes (50 + 1024 = 1074).

F7-11(2) Once the segment is acknowledged, the next segment is ready.

F7-11(3) 512 bytes are transmitted. The sequence number now starts at 1074 which makes the pointer to the last byte carried at 1585.

F7-11(4) This segment is also acknowledged.

If segments are received out of order, TCP re-orders them. This is a function that is taken for granted today. For example, Simple Mail Transfer Protocol (SMTP) relies on TCP and ensures that the text and attachments in an e-mail are received in order. Similarly, Hyper Text Transfer Protocol (HTTP), which also relies on TCP, ensures that the multimedia content on a web page is placed in the proper location. If that didn't happen, it would not be TCP's error.

7-8 TCP ACKNOWLEDGES THE DATA

The sequence number is also used to check the delivery of data by way of an acknowledgement number based on the sequence number.

When a TCP segment is transmitted by the source host, and received by the destination host, the destination host acknowledges the receipt of the segment. To perform this task, the destination host uses the value of the segment number to create the acknowledgment number that it will use in its next exchange with the corresponding host. As the sequence number is viewed as a pointer to data payload bytes, the acknowledgement number is the value of the pointer to the next byte the destination host expects to receive.

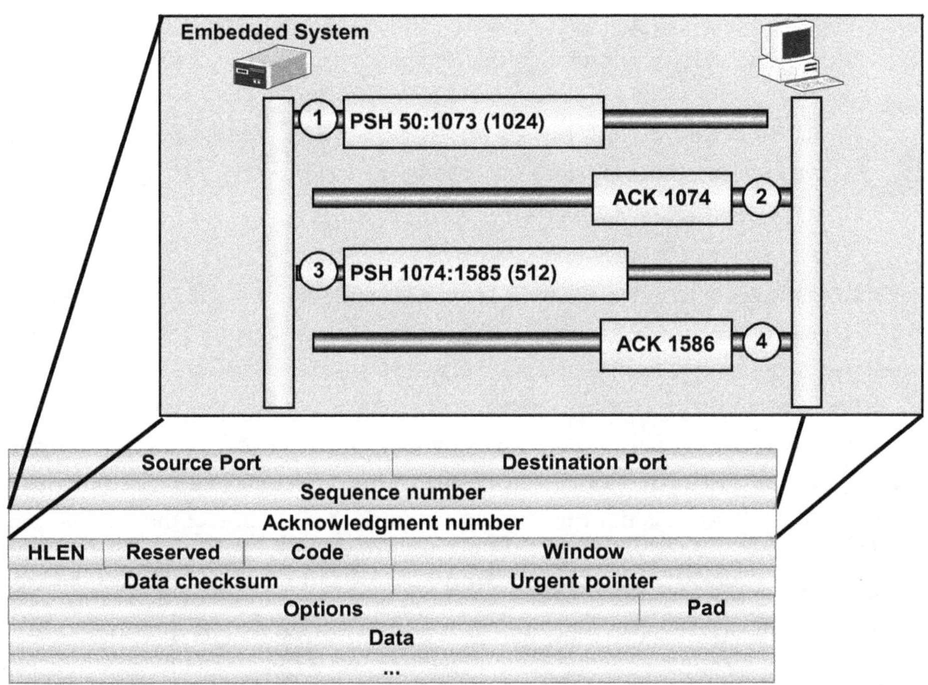

Figure 7-12 **Acknowledgement Number (32 bits)**

The acknowledgement number is related to the sequence number. The same example as in Figure 7-12 is used here, but the ACK number is included in steps (2) and (4).

F7-12(1) The source host sends 1024 bytes with a sequence number of 50

F7-12(2) The acknowledgment number is 1074, the pointer to the next byte that follows the byte with index 1073 just received

F7-12(3) The source host sends 512 bytes with a sequence number of 1074

F7-12(4) The acknowledgment number is 1586

Acknowledgements use Buffers

When a TCP segment is received, an acknowledgement must be transmitted. If the system is also sending data, an acknowledgement can piggyback on a TCP segment. Otherwise, an empty segment must be generated to acknowledge the TCP segment received.

If the system is low on resources because all of the buffers are used for reception, this presents a problem as buffers are not available to acknowledge data received.

TCP/IP stacks, such as Micrium's µC/TCP-IP, implement delayed acknowledgment as per RFC 1122. Delayed acknowledgement allows for the receiving station to send an acknowledgment for every two segments received instead of for each single segment received. When a system is receiving a stream of data, this technique relieves the receiving task from performing additional processing, making better use of buffers. It is important to know that when you use a network protocol analyzer, you may notice this behavior and believe that the TCP/IP stack is not performing properly. This is in fact the desired behavior.

Another interesting point regarding sequence numbers and acknowledgement numbers is that in the three-way handshake mechanism, the acknowledgement number used in the ACK message to the SYN message is the sequence number of the SYN message plus one (also shown in Figure 7-12). The receiver is telling the sender to send the next byte. The next TCP segment from the sender will use the value of the acknowledgement number as its sequence number.

7-9 TCP GUARANTEES DELIVERY

When segments are not delivered, or are erroneous, TCP uses a mechanism that enables the source host to retransmit. TCP uses the sequence number, acknowledgement number, and timers to guarantee data delivery. After a certain amount of time, when the TCP layer in a transmitting host is not receiving an acknowledgment for one of the segments transmitted, it will retransmit the segment. This is the first attempt at retransmitting a lost or corrupted segment. Special timers are involved in this mechanism.

7-9-1 ROUND-TRIP TIME (RTT)

Round-Trip Time (RTT) is the time that passes between the sending of a TCP segment (SYN or PSH), and the receipt of its acknowledgment (ACK). The RTT is recalculated over the duration of the connection and varies according to network congestion.

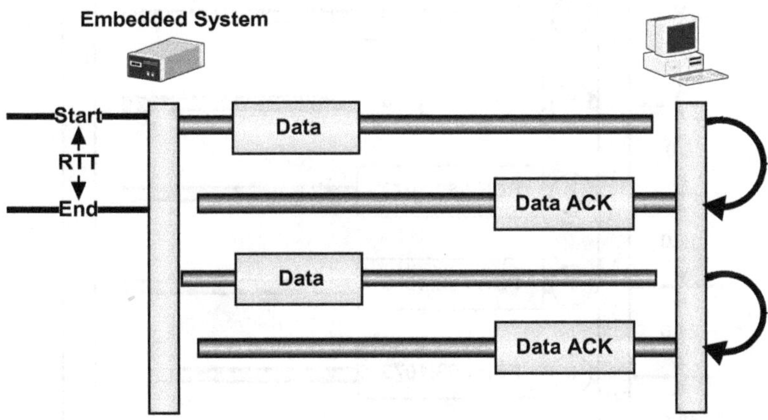

Figure 7-13 **RTT**

Figure 7-13 demonstrates how RTT is measured.

RTT is used to calculate an important timeout used for the retransmission of missing or corrupted segments called the Retransmission Time-Out (RTO). RTO is a function of RTT and has a fixed initial value as implemented in µC/TCP-IP.

When TCP does not receive an acknowledgement message within the RTO limit, the transmitting host retransmits the segment. The RTO is doubled and re-initialized. Each time it expires, the transmitting host retransmits the segment until a maximum of 96 seconds is reached. If an acknowledgement is still not received, the transmitting host closes/resets the connection.

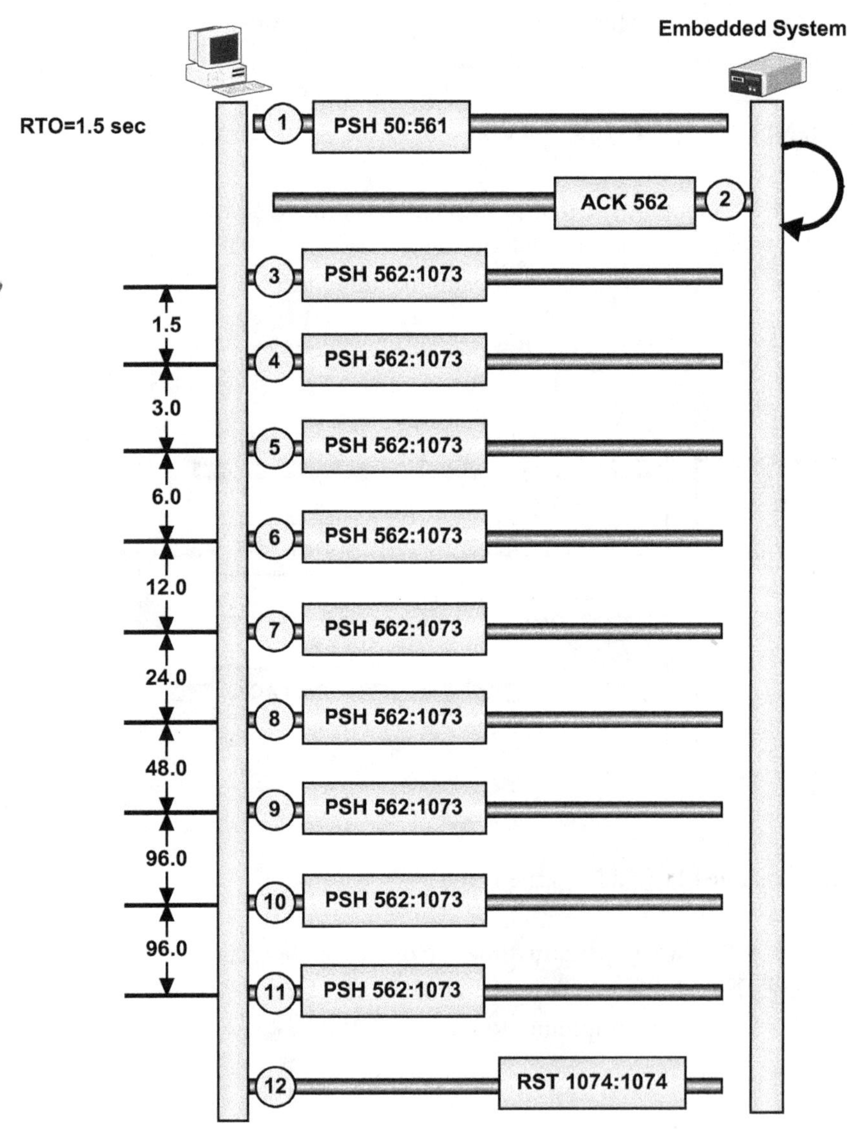

Figure 7-14 **RTO (Retransmission Time Out) Example**

In the RTO example in Figure 7-14, the initial Retransmission Time-out is set to 1.5 seconds.

F7-14(1) A TCP segment with 512 bytes is transmitted.

F7-14(2) The segment is acknowledged

F7-14(3) A second segment with 512 bytes is transmitted.

F7-14(4) Because the second segment is not acknowledged within the RTO, it is retransmitted and the RTO is doubled to 3 seconds.

F7-14(5) Because the segment is not acknowledged within the RTO, it is retransmitted and the RTO is doubled to 6 seconds.

F7-14(6) Because the segment is not acknowledged within the RTO, it is retransmitted and the RTO is doubled to 12 seconds.

F7-14(7) Because the segment is not acknowledged within the RTO, it is retransmitted and the RTO is doubled to 24 seconds.

F7-14(8) Because the segment is not acknowledged within the RTO, it is retransmitted and the RTO is doubled to 48 seconds.

F7-14(9) Because the segment is not acknowledged within the RTO, it is retransmitted and the RTO is doubled to 96 seconds.

F7-14(10) Because the segment is not acknowledged within the RTO, it is retransmitted and the RTO is kept at 96 seconds.

F7-14(11) Because the segment is not acknowledged within the RTO, it is retransmitted one last time.

F7-14(12) The transmitter quits and resets the connection.

The idea is clear after a few steps, but the complete process is required to explain how it ends. When the RTO reaches 96 seconds, TCP resets (RST) the connection.

Retransmission Impact on Memory

Retransmission has an important performance impact. To be able to retransmit a segment, the TCP stack must put aside the segment it is transmitting until it receives an acknowledgment. This means that the network buffer(s) remain unavailable until acknowledgment takes place. In an embedded system with limited RAM, this limits system performance.

Sequence number, acknowledge number, and Retransmission Time-Out are TCP header fields and timers used to guarantee delivery. In networks, it is possible for packets to become corrupt or lost. When this happens, and TCP is used, packets will be retransmitted. An application would therefore use TCP when data delivery is more important than its time sensitivity. This is why e-mails, file transfers, and all web services all make use of TCP.

7-10 TCP FLOW CONTROL (CONGESTION CONTROL)

A very important TCP feature is its flow control. With additional features it also becomes a congestion control.

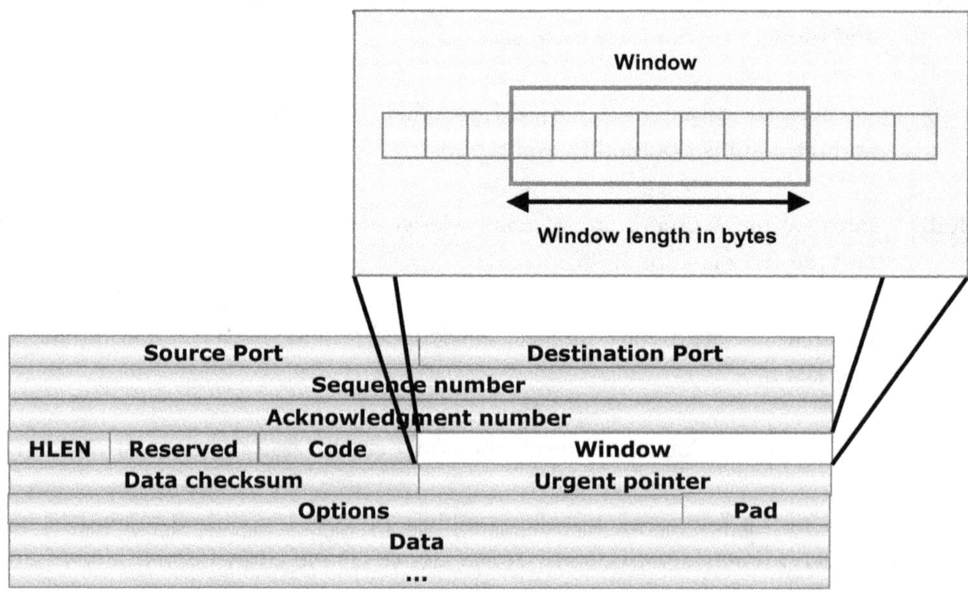

Figure 7-15 **Window (16 bits)**

TCP features a receive window and a transmit window. Figure 7-15 indicates where the window field is located in the TCP header. This field is the TCP receive window size and the field is used to advertise the window size to a corresponding host.

The window field is transmitted to the connected host to advise how many bytes may be transmitted without overflowing the receive buffers. TCP/IP stacks such as µC/TCP-IP allow you to configure the initial value of the receive window. To see how to calculate the size of this parameter (which is important to achieve optimum performance), see section 7-11 "Optimizing TCP Performance" on page 195.

As data is received, the window value is decremented by the number of bytes received. When the receiving target processes the data received, the window value is incremented by the number of bytes processed. In this way, the transmitting TCP host knows if it still can transmit.

If the window size field value is too small, the transmitting host must wait before it can transmit, as it has reached its transmission limit. In the extreme case, the transmitting host will have to wait after each transmitted TCP segment to receive a response before sending the next segment. Having to wait slows throughput considerably. On the other hand, if the window size field is made too large, the transmitting host may transmit many segments and possibly overload the receiving host. The window size field provides flow control. Because it is used by both hosts in the connection, both TCP modules use it to regulate the rate of transmission.

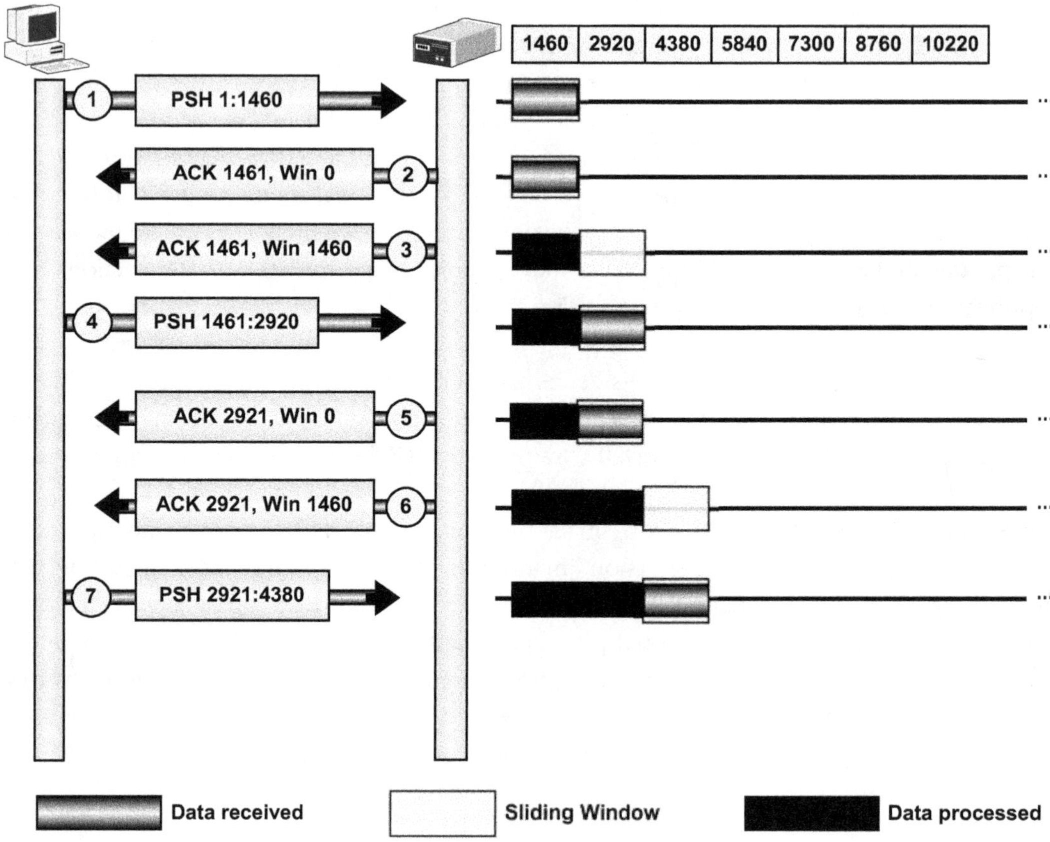

1460 2920 4380 5840 7300 8760 10220

1 PSH 1:1460

ACK 1461, Win 0 2

ACK 1461, Win 1460 3

4 PSH 1461:2920

ACK 2921, Win 0 5

ACK 2921, Win 1460 6

7 PSH 2921:4380

Data received

Sliding Window

Data processed

Figure 7-16 **TCP Receive Window Usage**

The TCP Window usage example shown in Figure 7-16 assumes a TCP receive window size of 1460 bytes. This value was selected to immediately show the operation of the windowing mechanism since the first packet received will fill the TCP receive window. For illustration, it was also chosen to use relative sequence and acknowledge numbers. In other words, the first byte sent in the first packet has the sequence number 1.

The example indicates how the TCP receive window size changes as data is received and processed and why it is referred to as the TCP sliding window.

F7-16(1) A TCP segment with 1460 bytes is transmitted. The receive window is decreased to 0.

F7-16(2) The first segment is acknowledged. The receive window (currently 0) is sent to the transmitting host. This is a Zero-Window message. The transmitting host now knows that it must stop transmitting.

F7-16(3) The network buffer used to receive the first segment is now free. The receive window size is increased to 1460 and this is communicated to the transmitting host. This is a Window Update message. The transmitting host now knows that it can resume transmission up to 1460 bytes.

F7-16(4) A TCP segment with 200 bytes is transmitted. The receive window is decreased to 1260.

F7-16(5) It is assumed here that the embedded target is busy and cannot process and acknowledge the segment. A Window Update message is sent with the value of the current receive window, which is now 1260.

F7-16(6) A TCP segment with 1260 bytes is transmitted. The receive window is decreased to 0.

F7-16(7) The second and third segments are acknowledged. The receive window is decreased to 0.

F7-16(8) Network buffers that were used to receive the second and third segments are freed. The receive window is increased to 1460 and this is communicated to the transmitting host.

F7-16(9) A TCP segment with 1460 bytes is transmitted. The receive window is decreased to 0, and so on...

From the example above, it can be extrapolated that this is not an optimal configuration for performance, however on an embedded system with little RAM, it is a configuration that allows TCP to be functional. There are many possible scenarios with this configuration. For example in Step 5 and 6, it is assumed that the receive window size is 1460 and more than one buffer is receiving packets. If using a single receive buffer, the segment transmitted at step 6 would be rejected. Another possibility is for the 200-byte segments to be acknowledged before transmitting the 1260-byte segment. When analyzing the capture of a network protocol analyzer, all of these possible scenarios must be considered.

It is recommended to make the TCP receive window a multiple of the Maximum Segment Size (MSS), scaled appropriately as per RFC 1323.

The name "maximum segment size" is in fact a bit misleading. The value actually refers to the maximum amount of data that a segment can hold but it does not include TCP headers. The actual maximum segment size may be larger by 20 for a regular TCP header, or even larger if the segment includes TCP options.

The TCP maximum segment size specifies the maximum number of bytes in the TCP segment's data field, regardless of any other factors that influence segment size. With Ethernet as the preferred Data Link Layer technology, the data carrying capacity is 1500 bytes. The MSS for TCP in this case is 1460, which comes from taking the minimum Ethernet maximum transmission unit (MTU) of 1500 and subtracting 20 bytes each for IP and TCP header. For most computer users, MSS is set automatically by the operating system. This is also the case with µC/TCP-IP. When using µC/TCP-IP, the MTU is defined by the device driver (see Chapter 14, "Network Device Drivers" on page 299).

SECTION 6-x shows how to calculate an optimal TCP receive window size and how to configure it in µC/TCP-IP.

7-10-1 NAGLE'S ALGORITHM

It is not efficient for an application to repeatedly transmit small packets (for example, 1 byte) because every packet has a 40 byte header (20 bytes for TCP, 20 bytes for IP), which represents substantial overhead. Telnet sessions often produce this situation where most keystrokes generate a single byte that is transmitted immediately. Over slow links, the situation is worse. Many of these small packets may be in transit at the same time, potentially leading to a congestion problem (TCP is not able to ACK packets leading to connections reset). It is referred as the "small packet problem" or "tinygram." This problem is addressed by RFC 896 which describes the Nagle's algorithm.

Nagle's algorithm works by grouping small outgoing TCP segments together, and sending them all at once. Specifically, as long as there is an already transmitted packet not yet acknowledged, the transmitter keeps buffering the output until a full packet is ready and can be transmitted.

In section 7-8 "TCP Acknowledges the Data" on page 183, it is noted that µC/TCP-IP implements delayed acknowledgment. This means that every second packet is acknowledged instead of every packet, to ease the load on the network and protocols.

Nagle's algorithm does not operate well in the presence of delayed acknowledgement. It may prevent an embedded system implementing a real-time application from performing as expected. Any application that needs to send a small quantity of data and expects an immediate answer will not react appropriately because the algorithm's goal is to increase throughput at the expense of network delay (latency). Nagle's algorithm in the transmitting host groups data and will not release a second segment until it has received an acknowledgment for the first.

With delayed acknowledgement, an acknowledgement is not transmitted by the receiving host until two segments are received, or after 200ms of reception of a first segment that is not followed by a second one. When a system uses both Nagle and delayed acknowledgement, an application that performs two successive transmissions and wants to receive data may suffer a delay of up to 500 milliseconds. This delay is the sum of Nagle's waiting for its data to be acknowledged and the 200 ms timer used by the delayed acknowledgment on single segment transmission.

Here is another example where the combination of these two mechanisms may result in poor system performance. If the sum of data to be transmitted fits into an even number of full TCP segments plus a small last segment, all will work fine. The TCP segments will all be acknowledged (automatic ACKs on even segment numbers by the delayed acknowledgment mechanism). The last segment will be released by the Nagle's algorithm since everything was acknowledged and this last segment will be acknowledged by the receiving application, completing the transaction.

However, if the sum of data to transmit ends up being an odd number of full TCP segments, plus a small last segment, the last full segment will suffer a 200 ms delay since it is alone. Nagle's algorithm will wait for this ACK to release the last small segment that completes the transaction. On a high-bandwidth link, all of the data could be transmitted in a few milliseconds. Adding a 200 ms delay greatly degrades performance. In numbers, if 1 Megabyte is transmitted in 500 ms with the system bandwidth, the throughput is 16 Mbps. Applying the additional delay due to the Nagle/Delay acknowledge problem, the throughput falls to 11.43 Mbps.

For real-time data transmission and systems with low bandwidth, disabling the Nagle's algorithm may be desirable. The system design may not allow for delays introduced by the solution to reduce the tinygram problem. The system may be designed to use small packet transmissions only. In practice it is not recommended to disable the Nagle's algorithm. As suggested by Mr. Nagle himself, it is preferable for the application to buffer the data before transmission and avoid sending small segments. If that is not possible, the only solution is to disable the Nagle's algorithm.

BSD sockets (see section "Sockets" on page 205) use the **TCP_NODELAY** option to disable Nagle's algorithm. µC/TCP-IP implements the Nagle algorithm, however the µC/TCP-IP BSD and proprietary socket APIs do not currently implement the **TCP_NODELAY** option.

7-10-2 SILLY WINDOW SYNDROME

There is another issue with the TCP windowing mechanism. It is called the silly window syndrome, and it occurs when the TCP receive window is almost full. The silly window syndrome may create a tinygram problem.

As seen in the windowing mechanism, the TCP receive window will decrease when segments are received and will not be increased until the receiver has processed the data. On an embedded system with few resources, this could easily happen, leading to the silly window syndrome. As the TCP receive window size decreases and is advertised to the sender, the sender will send smaller and smaller segments to meet this requirement. The TCP receive window size is getting small enough to become "silly." Smaller segments transmitted will create Nagle's problem described above.

The solution to the silly window syndrome is described in RFC # 812, Section 4 for transmit and receive. Additionally, RFC #1122, Section 4.2.3.3 adds information about the reception and RFC #1122, Section 4.2.3.4 about transmission. The solution is to wait until the TCP receive window can be increased by the size of at least one full TCP segment (MSS as defined in a previous section). This way the TCP receive window will probably decrease to a small number (or even zero), which the transmitting host will not be able to use until the TCP receive window is restored to at least one full TCP segment. This solution is implemented in µC/TCP-IP.

7-11 OPTIMIZING TCP PERFORMANCE

The performance of data transfer is related to Ethernet controller driver performance and the CPU clock speed as described in Chapter 2. The concept of performance related to the availability of network buffers has also been discussed. Optimizing TCP performance is directly related to the number of buffers available and how they are used. In this section, the most important relation of buffers to performance is the TCP receive window size.

Research on TCP performance resulted in the definition of the Bandwidth-Delay Product (BDP) concept. BDP is an equation that determines the amount of data that can be in transit within the network. It is the product of the available bandwidth of the network interface and network latency.

The available bandwidth of the network interface is fairly simple to calculate, especially with standard Ethernet interfaces at 10, 100 or 1000 Megabits per second. As presented in Chapter 2, we now know that on a typical embedded system, it is quite possible that the system cannot sink or source data at line speeds. A method to evaluate Ethernet controller performance is provided in Part II of this book. µC/IPerf (introduced in Chapter 6, "Troubleshooting" on page 135) can be used to reach this goal.

The latency is the RTT as seen in the previous section. The best way to estimate the round trip time is to use PING from one host to the other and use the response times returned by PING as shown in section 6-1-2 "PING" on page 140.

```
BDP (bytes) = total_available_bandwidth (KBytes/sec) * round_trip_time (ms)
```

The notion here is that Kilobytes multiplied by milliseconds leads to bytes which is the unit of measurement for the BDP. Moreover, the BDP is a very important concept and it is also directly related to the TCP Receive Window Size value which is also expressed in bytes. The TCP Receive Window Size is one of the most important factors in fine tuning TCP. It is the parameter that determines how much data can be transferred before the transmitting host waits for acknowledgement. It is in essence bound by the BDP.

If the BDP (or TCP receive window) is lower than the product of the latency and available bandwidth, the system will not be able to fill the connection at its capacity since the client cannot send acknowledgements back fast enough. A transmission cannot exceed the TCP receive window latency value, therefore the TCP receive window must be large enough to fit the maximum available bandwidth multiplied by the maximum anticipated delay. In other words, there should be enough packets in transit in the network to make sure the TCP module will have enough packets to process due to the longer latency.

The resulting BDP is a measure of an approximation of the TCP receive window value.

Let's assume that the **total_available_bandwidth** is 5 Mbps and that our embedded system is operating on a private network where all of the hosts are located closely, and the RTT to any device is approximately 20 milliseconds.

The BDP in this case is:

```
BDP = 5 Megabits/second * 20 milliseconds
    = 625 kilobytes     * 20 milliseconds
    = 12500 bytes
```

As suggested, the TCP receive window size should be a multiple of the MSS. In our Ethernet-based system, with the MSS at 1460:

```
TCP Receive Window = RoundUp(BDP/1460)    * 1460
                   = RoundUp(12500/1460) * 1460
                   = 9          * 1460
                   = 13140
```

The configuration for the TCP Receive Window from the example above requires nine (9) network buffers. This does not mean that your system needs nine (9) buffers. The system also requires a few network buffers for the data it must transmit. Even if the system does not have data to transmit, it must have network buffers to send ACK messages for TCP segments received. So, more than nine receive buffers need to be configured. As a rule of thumb, adding three to four additional buffers is adequate. In this case, it is close to 50%.

The previous example assumes a private network with all of the nodes in the same local network--not distributed geographically. When a system has to communicate over the public Internet, RTT is substantially larger. Let's take the same system bandwidth of 5 Mbps but with a RTT of 300 ms. In this case, the BDP is:

```
BDP = 5 Mbps       * 300 milliseconds
    = 625 Kbytes   * 300 milliseconds
    = 187500 bytes
```

And, the TCP receive window size:

```
TCP Receive Window = RoundUp(187500/1460) * 1460
                   = 129                  * 1460
                   = 188340
```

It is not far fetched to imagine that an embedded system with limited RAM will not be able to meet the required configuration. This does not mean the system will not work. This only means that system performance will not be optimal. TCP guarantees delivery. However, if there are insufficient buffers, the connection can be extremely slow because of the flow-control effect or because of the large number of retransmissions required.

Part II of this book provides sample code to evaluate system performance based on hardware performance and memory availability.

With µC/TCP-IP the receive window size is configured with a **#define** in the **net_cfg.h** file (see Chapter 12, "Directories and Files" on page 263, and also, Appendix C, "µC/TCP-IP Configuration and Optimization" on page 723).

```
#define NET_TCP_CFG_RX_WIN_SIZE_OCTET          13140
#define NET_TCP_CFG_TX_WIN_SIZE_OCTET          13140
```

Listing 7-1 **TCP Receive and Transmit Window Sizes**

It is a general practice to set the TCP transmit window size and the TCP receive window size to the same value as they are both based on the same BDP calculation and must be configured and negotiated by both ends of the connection. However, as shown in the TCP header, only the receive window size is communicated to the peer.

TCP Window Sizes

A poor configuration for the TCP Receive Window size is for it to be larger than the number of receive buffers available. In this case, the transmitter believes it could still send data while the receiver is out of resources for processing. This configuration would result in a substantial number of dropped packets creating unnecessary retransmission and drastically slowing down the connection.

Never configure the TCP receive window size to be larger than the number of configured receive buffers.

Use the bandwidth delay product to estimate the right value for TCP window sizes.

7-11-1 MULTIPLE CONNECTIONS

The discussion in the previous section is valid for the whole system. If the system has a single active TCP connection, all bandwidth and network buffers are used by this TCP connection. If the system has more than one connection, the bandwidth must be shared between all active TCP connections.

Depending on the reasons you are embedding TCP/IP into a product, a system performance assessment is something that must be either calculated if the system parameters are known in advance, or validated with hardware and simulation code. This is covered in Part II of this book.

7-11-2 PERSIST TIMER

With the TCP receive window size, the receiver performs flow control by specifying the amount of data it is willing to accept from the sender.

When the TCP receive window size goes to 0, the sender stops sending data. It is possible for ACKs not to be reliably transmitted, and if ACKs are lost, the receiver will wait to receive data and the sender will wait to receive the TCP window update. This may create a deadlock which can be prevented if the sender uses a persist timer that enables it to query the receiver periodically to find out if the window size has been increased. These segments from the sender are called window probes. They are sent as long as needed – with no timeout.

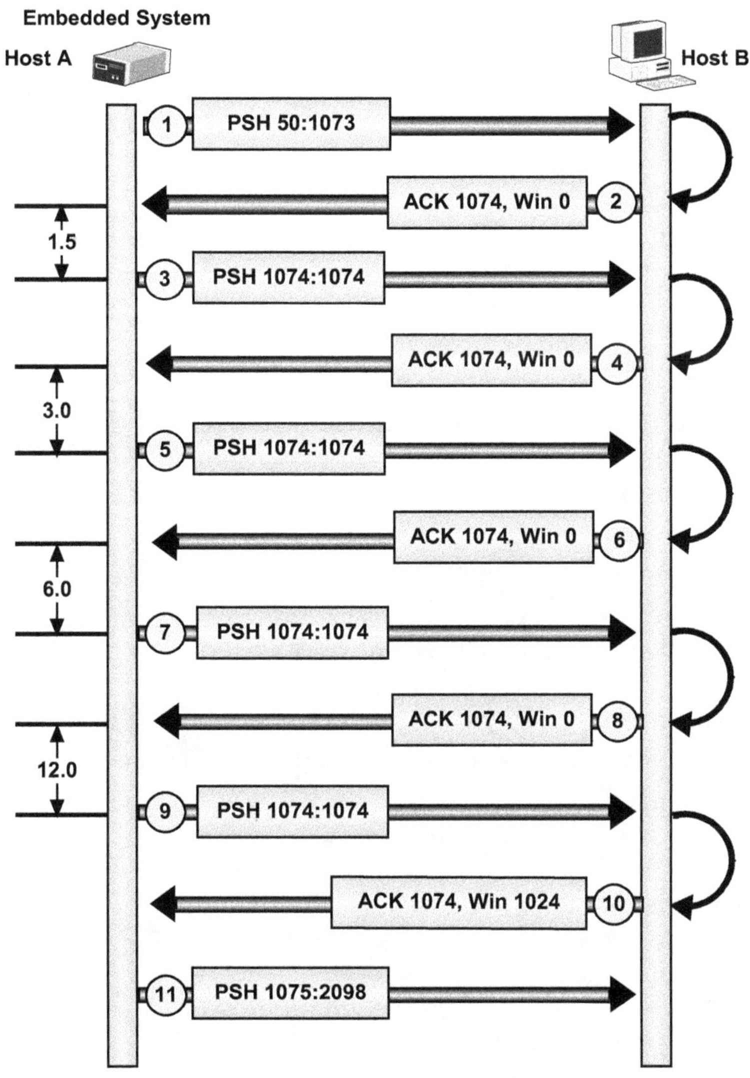

Figure 7-17 **Example of Persist Timer Usage**

F7-17(1) A TCP segment with 1024 bytes is transmitted.

F7-17(2) The receiving host acknowledges the segment, but also advertises that its TCP receive window is full (Window = 0).

F7-17(3) After the first Persist Timer time-out, Host A sends a window probe segment.

F7-17(4) Host B sends a window update, but it is still 0.

F7-17(5) After the second Persist Timer time-out, Host A sends a window probe segment.

F7-17(6) Host B sends a window update, but it is still 0.

F7-17(7) After the third Persist Timer time-out, Host A sends a window probe segment.

F7-17(8) Host B sends a window update, but it is still 0.

F7-17(9) After the fourth Persist Timer time-out, Host A sends a window probe segment.

F7-17(10) Host B processed packets and has freed space in its TCP receive window.

F7-17(11) Host A can now transmit more data.

The normal TCP exponential back off is used to calculate the persist timer as shown in Figure 7-17.

- The first timeout is calculated as 1.5 sec for a typical LAN connection
- This is multiplied by 2 for a second timeout value of 3 sec
- A multiplier of 4 gives a value of 6 (4 x 1.5)
- Then 8 results in 12 (8 x 1.5)
- And so on... (exponentially)

However, the Persist Timer is always bounded between 5 and 60 seconds.

7-11-3 KEEPALIVE

Keepalive is the maximum period of time between two activities on a TCP connection. Many TCP/IP stacks have the maximum period of inactivity set at two hours. The timer is restarted every time an activity occurs on the connection.

The keepalive concept is very simple. When the keepalive timer reaches zero, the host sends a keepalive probe, which is a packet with no data and the ACK code bit turned on. It acts as a duplicate ACK that is allowed by the TCP/IP specifications. The remote endpoint will not object to the reception of an empty packet, as TCP is a stream-oriented protocol. On the other hand, the transmitting host will receive a reply from the remote host (which doesn't need to support keepalive at all, just TCP/IP), with no data and the ACK set.

If the transmitting host receives a reply to the keepalive probe, we conclude that the connection is still up and running. The user application is totally unaware of this process.

Two main usages for keepalive include:

- Checking for dead peers
- Preventing disconnection due to network inactivity

Keepalive is useful since, if other peers lose their connection (for example by rebooting), the TCP/IP stack on the host of interest will notice that the connection is broken, even if there is no active traffic. If keepalive probes are not replied to by the peer host, it can be assumed that the connection is not valid and corrective action can be initiated.

Keepalive is really used to have an idle connection up forever. TCP keepalive is not a mandatory requirement and Micrium did not implement this feature in µC/TCP-IP. But µC/TCP-IP replies to keepalive messages if implemented by the other host.

7

7-12 SUMMARY

For the embedded developer, the transport layer and data link layer are probably the two most important layers. If a system needs to achieve sustained performance, the majority of the parameters to fine tune it are found in the network device driver and transport layer.

This chapter covered transport protocols. Two protocols at the transport layer are very useful and have different goals. Here is a summary of the protocol pros and cons.

With TCP, the analysis and transmission of its parameters generate certain delays, and add data processing overhead, which makes it better suited to non-real-time (data) traffic requiring error-free transmission. When the embedded system needs to guarantee data delivery, TCP is the best solution, yet it comes at a price. TCP code is larger and TCP requires a substantial amount of RAM to properly perform its duties. If the system requires performance and reliable data delivery, it must allocate plenty of RAM for the TCP/IP stack.

TCP handles:

- reliable delivery
- retransmissions of lost packet
- re-ordering
- flow control

UDP can and will be used if:

- TCP congestion avoidance and flow control measures are unsuitable for the embedded application
- The application can cope with some data loss
- More control of the data transported over the network is required
- The application is delay/jitter sensitive (audio, video)
- Delays introduced by TCP ACK are unacceptable

- Maximizing throughput (UDP uses less resources and can achieve better performance. See the Sample Applications in Part II of this book)

- Minimize code and data footprint (see section 3-2-3 “Footprint” on page 71)

Many embedded systems have resource constraints (mainly CPU processing speed and RAM availability) and thus, these systems often use a UDP/IP-only stack instead of a full blown TCP/IP stack.

Chapter 8

Sockets

The client-server architecture is a familiar concept. Simply, servers contain information and resources, and clients request access to them. The Web and e-mails are examples of client-server architectures. Web servers receive requests from browsers (Internet Explorer, Firefox, Safari, etc.) and e-mail servers receive requests from such mail client as Outlook and Eudora.

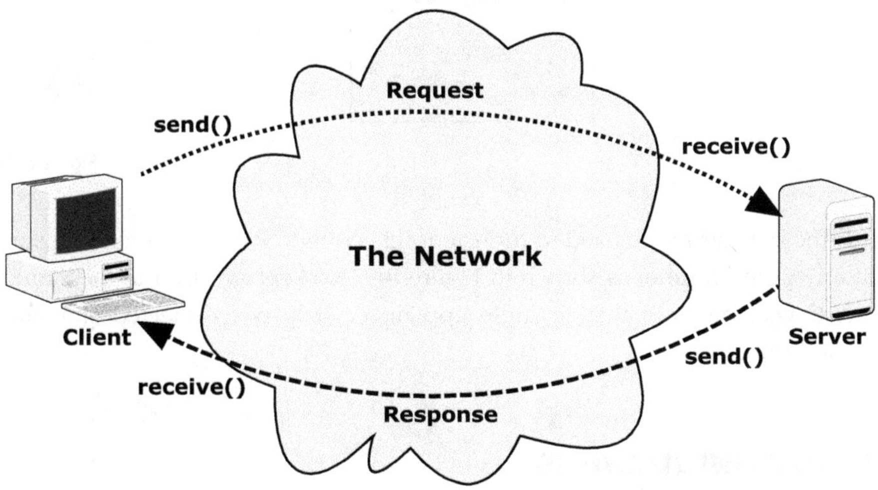

Figure 8-1 **Client and Server**

In contrast with the client-server approach is a peer-to-peer architecture whereby communication between hosts occurs at the same level, with each host offering the same capabilities to each another. Examples of a peer-to-peer approach include applications such as Skype and BitTorrent.

In both client-server and peer-to-peer architectures one host must take the initiative and contact a second host. Within IP technology, applications interface with the TCP/IP stack via socket function calls. The use of Transport Layer port numbers makes it possible for one host to establish multiple data exchanges with another host.

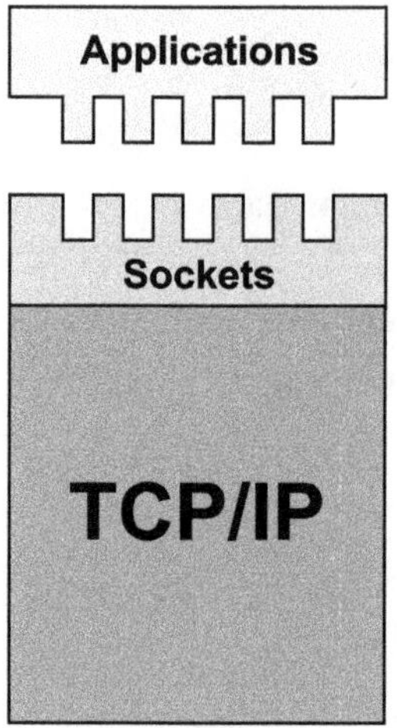

Figure 8-2 **Sockets**

The socket is the data structure used to represent this connection. More than one socket can be active at any point in time, as shown in Figure 8-2. Sockets are used in the same way as household A/C wall plugs in that multiple appliances may be connected simultaneously, throughout the house.

8-1 SOCKET UNIQUENESS

Imagine if several hosts transmit a segment to a given port on a server (P80 for a Web server). The server needs a way to identify each connection so that replies are sent to the correct client. On the client side, source port numbers are dynamically assigned by a TCP/IP stack, from 1024 to 65535. To differentiate between clients, the TCP/IP stack associates port numbers and IP addresses from the source and destination. This data grouping, or association (IP addresses and port numbers) is a "socket."

Therefore, the socket contains the following association:

Socket	=	Source IP address	+	Source port
	+	Destination IP address	+	Destination port

It is common to use nomenclature to identify the IP address and port number as follows:

AAA.BBB.CCC.DDD:1234

where 'AAA.BBB.CCC.DDD' is the IP address in dotted decimal notation and '1234' is the port number. This nomenclature is used in a web browser's address bar to establish a connection to a specific IP address and port number.

A connection using this notation is illustrated in Figure 8-3. Specifically, the host on the left 172.16.10.5:1468 (local host) connects to 172.16.10.8:23 (remote host) on the right.

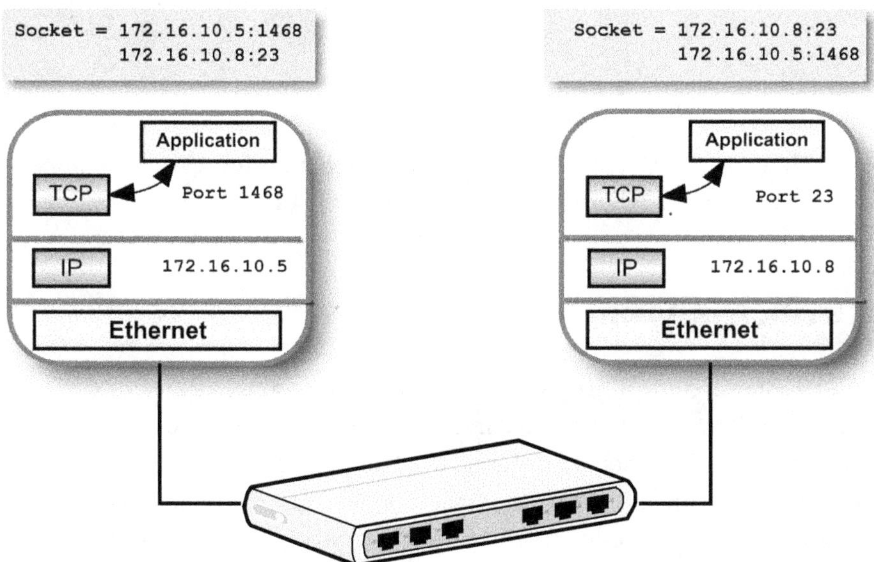

Figure 8-3 **Sockets: Source IP address + Port Number + Destination IP address + Port Number**

The Source IP address, the Source Port number, the Destination IP address and the Destination Port create a unique identifier for the connection. A server, therefore may have multiple connections from the same client yet differentiate them. As long as one of these four fields is different, the connection identifier is different.

In µC/TCP-IP, both the Source and Destination address and port information are stored in a data structure called `NET_CONN` as `AddrLocal` and `AddrRemote` fields. These two fields contain concatenated address/port information for the local address used by the product that embeds the stack and the remote address accessed by the product.

The use of 'Local' vs. 'Remote' addresses as either the source or destination address depends on when they are used to receive or transmit.

For Receive:

- Local = Destination
- Remote = Source

For Transmit:

- Local = Source
- Remote = Destination

Internally, to identify sockets, µC/TCP-IP uses an index so that each socket is identified by a unique socket ID from 0 to N-1 whereby N is the number of sockets created.

8-2 SOCKET INTERFACE

An application can interface to µC/TCP-IP using one of two network socket interfaces as shown in Figure 8-4. Although both socket interfaces are available, BSD socket interface function calls are converted to their equivalent µC/TCP-IP socket interface function calls. µC/TCP-IP socket interface functions feature greater versatility than their BSD counterparts as they return meaningful error codes to callers instead of just 0 or -1. µC/TCP-IP socket interface functions are also reentrant making them more useful to embedded applications.

A description of all µC/TCP-IP socket error codes is found in section D-7 "IP Error Codes" on page 756 and fatal socket error codes are described in section 17-7-1 "Fatal Socket Error Codes" on page 374.

Micrium layer 7 applications typically use µC/TCP-IP socket interface functions. However, if the system design requires off-the-shelf TCP/IP components that are not provided by Micrium, BSD socket interface functions are typically used. In this case, the BSD socket Application Programming Interface (API) is enabled via the **NET_BSD_CFG_API_EN** configuration constant found in **net_cfg.h** (see section C-17-1 on page 747).

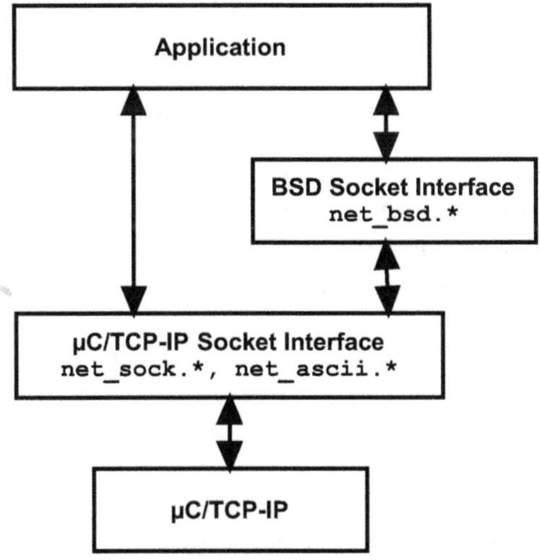

Figure 8-4 **Application relationship to µC/TCP-IP Network Socket Interface**

8-3 SOCKET API

Let's look at socket programming concepts and socket API function calls. A complete list of the µC/TCP-IP socket API functions may be found in Appendix B, "µC/TCP-IP API Reference" on page 433.

BSD socket API	µC/TCP-IP socket API	API description
socket()	NetSock_Open()	Appendix B on page 650
bind()	NetSock_Bind()	Appendix B on page 585
listen()	NetSock_Listen()	Appendix B on page 648
accept()	NetSock_Accept()	Appendix B on page 583
connect()	NetSock_Connect()	Appendix B on page 634
send()	NetSock_TxData()	Appendix B on page 662

BSD socket API	µC/TCP-IP socket API	API description
sendto()	NetSock_TxDataTo()	Appendix B on page 662
recv()	NetSock_RxData()	Appendix B on page 655
recvfrom()	NetSock_RxDataFrom()	Appendix B on page 655
select()	NetSock_Sel()	Appendix B on page 659
close	NetSock_Close()	Appendix B on page 632

Table 8-1 **BSD and µC/TCP-IP proprietary socket API**

Table 8-1 contains examples from the BSD and µC/TCP-IP API lists. The BSD socket interface is used in the following examples as it is the most widely known. Note that Micrium applications use the µC/TCP-IP proprietary socket interface as it provides enhanced error management.

8-3-1 socket()

Before communicating with a remote host, it is necessary to create an empty socket. This is done by calling the **socket()** function which returns a socket descriptor. At this point, the socket is useless until it is assigned a local IP Port. This descriptor is used in subsequent socket API function calls. µC/TCP-IP maintains a "pool" of sockets and the **socket()** call allocates one of the available sockets from this pool to the **socket()** caller.

8-3-2 bind()

The **bind()** function is used to assign a local IP address and port number to a socket. When the port number is assigned, it can not be reused by another socket, allowing for a fixed port to be used as the connection point by the remote host. Standard applications have pre-determined port numbers (FTP, HTTP, SMTP) that must be assigned to socket(s) used for the application so that clients can reach the server.

8-3-3 listen()

Server applications that use TCP, must set a socket to be a listener. As a connection-oriented protocol, TCP requires a connection; however UDP, as a connectionless protocol, does not. Using **listen()** allows an application to receive incoming connection requests. The listen socket contains the IP address and port number of the server, yet it is not aware of a client.A new listen socket will be created when a connection is established and remain open for the lifetime of the server.

8-3-4 accept()

The `accept()` function spawns a new socket. The listen socket used to receive a connection request remains open and a new socket is created that contains the IP address and port number of both client and server. This allows a server to have multiple connections with clients.

8-3-5 connect()

The `connect()` function is the client equivalent of the `listen()` and `accept()` functions used by server applications. `Connect()` allows a client application to open a connection with a server.

8-3-6 send() and sendto()

The `send()` function is used to transmit data through a TCP-based socket, while the `sendto()` function transmits data through a UDP-based socket.

8-3-7 recv() and recvfrom()

The `recv()` function receives data from a TCP-based socket while the `recvfrom()` function receives data through a UDP-based socket.

8-3-8 select()

`Select()` provides the power to monitor several sockets simultaneously. In fact, `select()` indicates which sockets are ready for reading and writing, or which sockets have raised exceptions.

`Select()` allows you to specify a timeout period in case there is no activity on the desired sockets. If `select()` times outwit returns with an appropriate error code.

8-3-9 close()

The **close()** function ends a connection and frees the socket to return to the "pool" of available sockets. Note that **close()** will send any remaining buffered data before closing the connection.

8-4 BLOCKING VERSUS NON-BLOCKING SOCKETS

One of the issues a developer faces with sockets is the difference between blocking and non-blocking sockets. When socket operations are performed, the operation may not be able to complete immediately and the function may not be able to return to the application program. For example, a **recv()** on a socket cannot complete until data is sent by the remote host. If there is no data waiting to be received, the socket function call waits until data is received on this socket. The same is true for the **send()**, **connect()** and other socket function calls. The connection blocks until the operation is completed. When the socket waits, it is called a "blocking" socket.

The second case is called a non-blocking socket, and requires that the application recognize an error condition and handle the situation appropriately. Programs that use non-blocking sockets typically use one of two methods when sending and receiving data. In the first method, called polling, a program periodically attempts to read or write data from the socket (typically using a timer). The second, and preferred method, is to use asynchronous notification. This means that the program is notified whenever a socket event takes place, and in turn responds to that event. For example, if the remote program writes data to the socket, a "read event" is generated so that the program knows it can read the data from the socket at that point.

It is also possible for the socket to return immediately with an error condition. The error condition in the previous **recv()** case is -1 (**NET_ERR_RX** if the µC/TCP-IP proprietary socket interface is used). When using non-blocking sockets in the application, it is important to check the return value from every **recv()** and **send()** operation (assuming a TCP connection). It is possible that the application cannot send or receive all of the data. It is not unusual to develop an application, test it, and find that when used in a different environment, it does not perform in the same way. Always checking the return values of these socket operations ensures that the application will work correctly, regardless of the bandwidth of the connection or configuration of the TCP/IP stack and network.

Be aware that making non-blocking **send()** or **recv()** calls from a high-priority task may cause low-priority tasks to starve. This is especially true if the **send()** or **recv()** functions are called in a tight loop and there is no data to send or none to receive. In fact, if the internal µC/TCP-IP tasks are configured as low-priority tasks, µC/TCP-IP will not have a chance to run and perform its duties. This type of polling is a sign of poor design. In comparison, the use of **select()** creates a more elegant solution.

With µC/TCP-IP, sockets can be configured in "blocking" or "non-blocking" mode using the configuration switches described in section C-15 "Network Socket Configuration" on page 740.

8-5 SOCKET APPLICATIONS

There are two types of sockets: Datagram sockets and Stream sockets. The following sections describing how these sockets work.

8-5-1 DATAGRAM SOCKET (UDP SOCKET)

Datagram sockets use the User Datagram Protocol (UDP). Data received is error-free and may be out of sequence as explained in Chapter 7, "Transport Protocols" on page 165. With datagram sockets, there is no need to maintain an open connection and the protocol is therefore called 'connectionless'. The application simply prepares data to be sent. The TCP/IP stack appends a UDP header containing destination information and sends the packet out. No connection is needed. Datagram sockets are generally used either when TCP is unavailable, or when a few dropped packets here and there is of no consequence. When a short query requires a short reply and if the reply is not received, it is acceptable to re-send the query. Sample applications include: TFTP, BOOTP(DHCP), DNS, multi-player games, and streaming audio and video conferencing.

TFTP and similar programs add their own protocol on top of UDP. For example, for each packet sent with TFTP, the recipient must send back an acknowledgement packet that says, "I got it!" ("ACK"). If the sender of the original packet receives no reply within a timeout period, it retransmits the packet until it finally receives an ACK. This acknowledgment procedure is very important when implementing reliable datagram socket applications. However, it is the responsibility of the application and not the UDP to implement these acknowledgements. For time-sensitive applications such as voice or games that can cope with dropped packets, or perhaps that can cleverly compensate for them, it is the perfect protocol.

Figure 8-5 shows a typical UDP client-server application and the BSD socket functions typically used. Figure 8-6 is the same diagram with µC/TCP-IP proprietary socket functions.

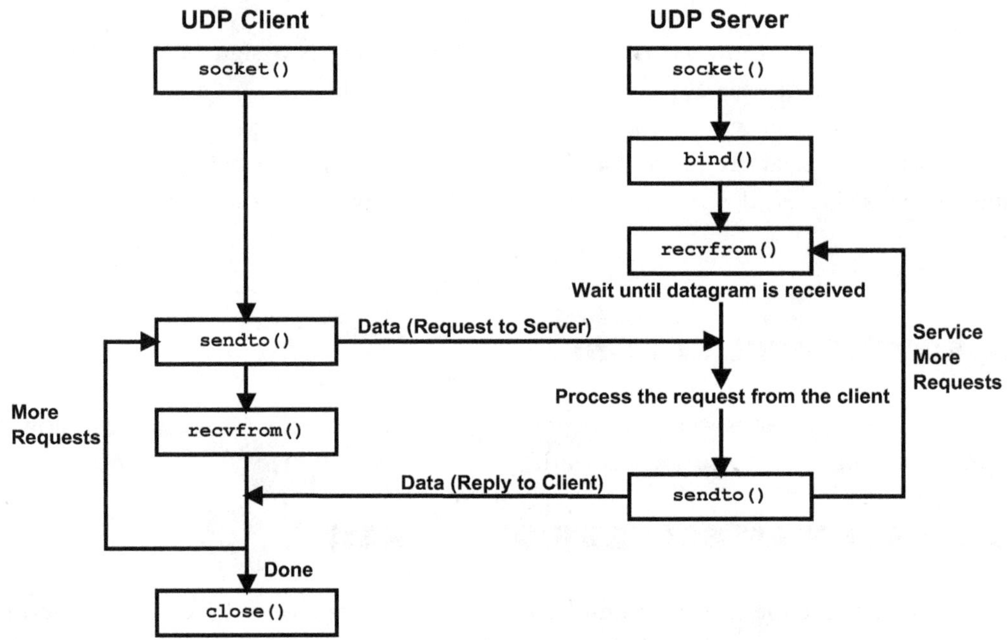

Figure 8-5 **BSD Socket calls used in a typical UDP client-server application**

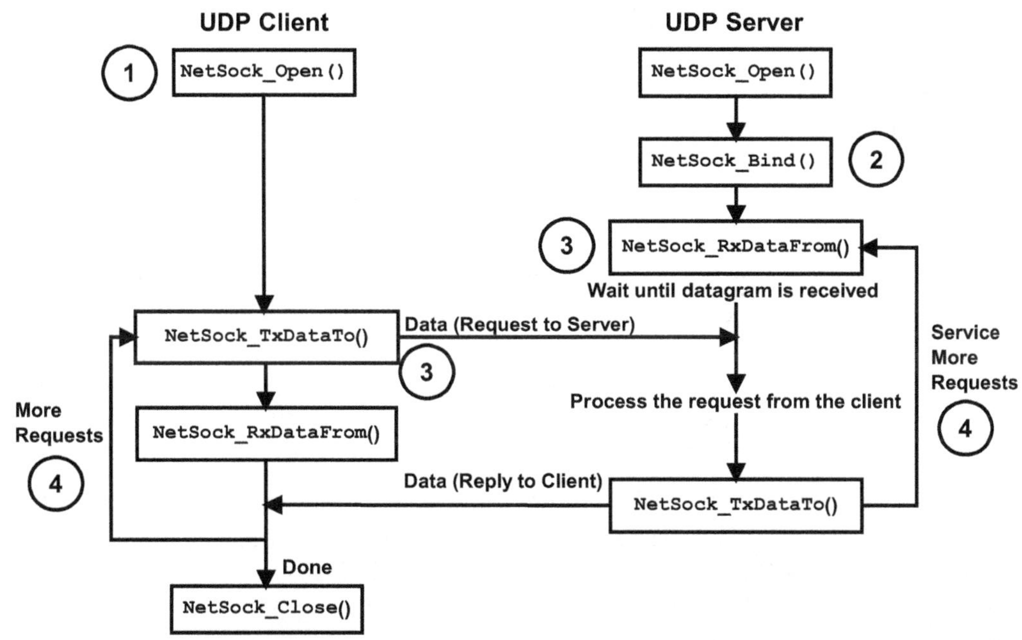

Figure 8-6 **μC/TCP-IP Socket calls used in a typical UDP client-server application**

F8-6(1) The first step in establishing a UDP communication between two hosts is to open sockets on both hosts.

F8-6(2) The server binds the IP address and port number to be used to receive data from the client

F8-6(3) UDP clients do not establish (dedicated) connections with UDP servers. Instead, UDP clients send request datagrams to UDP servers by specifying the socket number of the server. A UDP server waits until data arrives from a client, at which time the server processes the client's request, and responds.

F8-6(4) The UDP server waits for new client requests. Since UDP clients/servers do not establish dedicated connections, each request from each UDP client to the same UDP server is handled independently as there is no state or connection information preserved between requests.

8-5-2 STREAM SOCKET (TCP SOCKET)

Stream sockets are reliable two-way connected communication streams using the Transmission Control Protocol (TCP). Data is received sequentially and error-free. There is a "notion" of a connection. HTTP, FTP, SMTP and Telnet are examples of protocols that use stream sockets.

TCP handles the reliable delivery of data, the retransmissions of lost packets, and the re-ordering of packets and flow control. This additional processing adds overhead to the communication channel. TCP is it best suited for non-real-time (data) traffic requiring error-free transmission, yet extra overhead and the larger size of the TCP code module is the price to pay.

The use of sequence number, acknowledge number and window size in the TCP header guar a tee the delivery of data using a segment acknowledgement mechanism coupled with a retransmission capability.

TCP performance optimization is accomplished by carefully configuring the number of buffers in transmission and reception. In reception, buffers are defined in the Network Device Driver and up into the stack. For transmission, application buffers and network buffers are also required to be of similar number and size for data to flow efficiently from the application down the stack to the network interface. The optimization of the number of buffers can be calculated using the Bandwidth-Delay Product (see Chapter 6).

TCP requires a substantial amount of RAM to properly perform its duties. With the acknowledgment mechanism, TCP will not release a buffer until it has been acknowledged by its peer. While this buffer is in stand-by, it cannot be used for additional transmission or reception. If the system design dictates performance and reliable data delivery, allocate sufficient RAM for the TCP/IP stack.

Figure 8-7 indicates a typical TCP client-server application and the BSD socket functions used. Figure 8-8 is the same diagram with µC/TCP-IP proprietary socket functions.

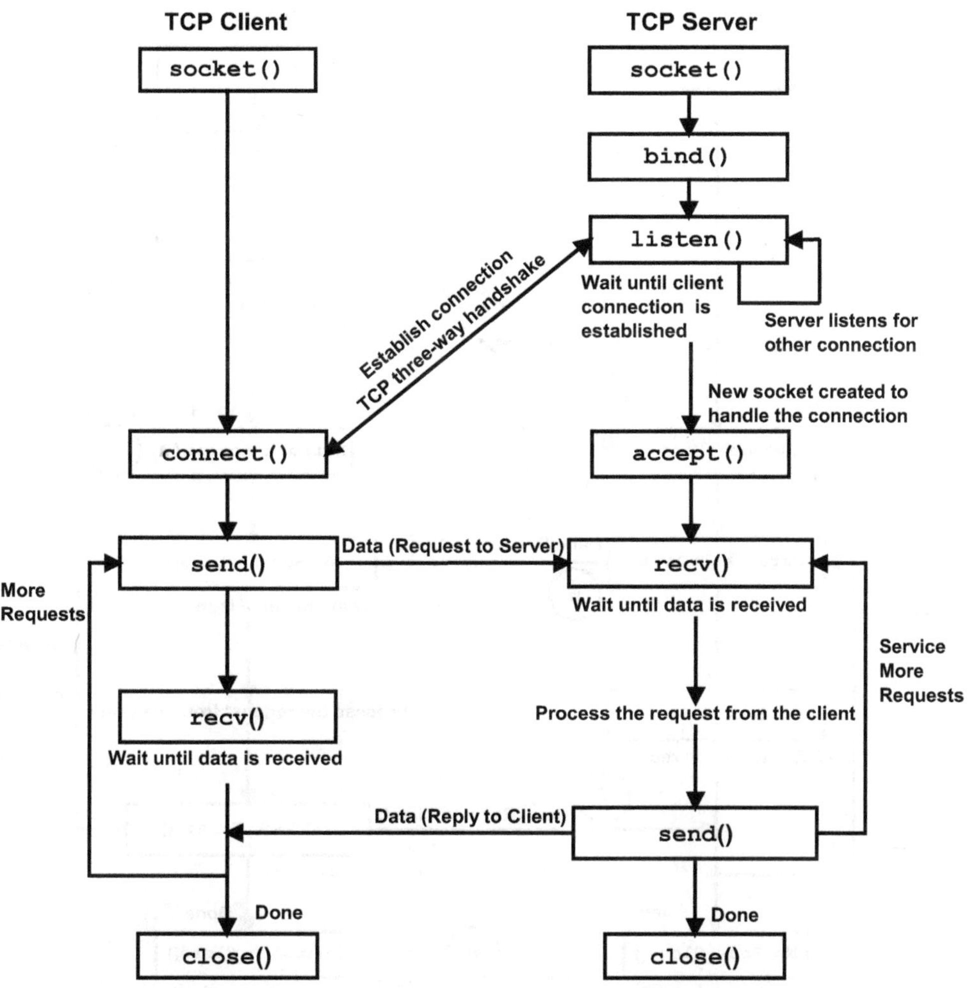

Figure 8-7 **BSD Socket calls used in a typical TCP client-server application**

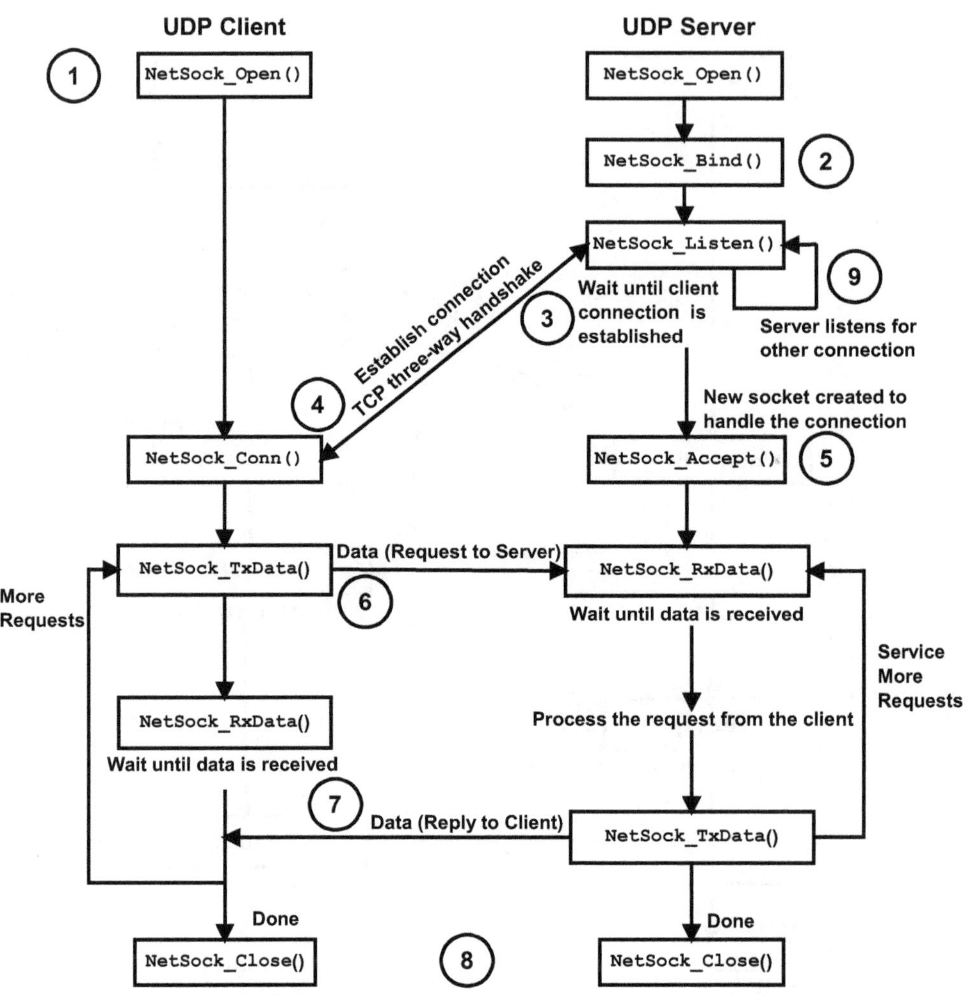

Figure 8-8 **µC/TCP-IP Socket calls used in a typical TCP client-server application**

F8-8(1) The first step in establishing TCP communication between two hosts is to open the sockets on both hosts.

F8-8(2) The server binds the server IP address and port number to be used to receive the connection request from the client.

F8-8(3) The server waits until a client connection is established using the listen() function call.

F8-8(4) When the server is ready to receive a connection request it allows clients to connect to the server.

F8-8(5) The server accepts a connection request from the client. A new socket is created to handle the connection.

F8-8(6) TCP client sends a request to the server

F8-8(7) The server replies back to the client (if necessary).

F8-8(8) This continues until either the client or the server closes the dedicated client-server connection.

F8-8(9) When handling multiple and simultaneous client-server connections, the TCP server is still available for new client-server connections.

For socket programming information please refer to Chapter 17, "Socket Programming" on page 355. This chapter provides code samples to write UDP and TCP clients and servers. Part II of the book contains sample projects with source code examples.

Chapter 9

Services and Applications

When an IP network is deployed, certain basic services are implemented for the hosts that connect to the network. These services are programs that run at the application layer in servers. There is a basic difference, however, between a service and an application.

A service implements a protocol that is useful to the hosts and engines powering every IP networked device. Two services most often used by embedded systems are the Dynamic Host Configuration Protocol (DHCP) and the Domain Name System (DNS). Additional services also exist such as the Network Information System (NIS), a client-server directory service protocol for distributing system configuration data including user and host names, or the Lightweight Directory Access Protocol (LDAP), an application protocol for querying and modifying directory services. These network services are usually deployed in corporate networks to manage a large number of users. For the scope of this book, we will look specifically at DHCP and DNS.

Any protocol "above" the TCP/IP stack is considered an *application protocol*. The use of these application protocols is valid for network services as described in the previous paragraph and for applications. In the case of the application, you can write your own application protocols, or you can augment the system by purchasing "standard" application-level protocols. There are many available with most TCP/IP stacks including File Transfer Protocol (FTP), web (HTTP), Telnet, Simple Mail Transport Protocol (SMTP), and more.

An application implements a protocol that is useful to the system application and not to the device. Basic TCP/IP protocols provided in a stack such as µC/TCP-IP may not be practical or sufficient for a typical embedded system. For instance, protocols such as FTP and SMTP may be required for the embedded system to transfer files or send e-mails.

9

9-1 NETWORK SERVICES

9-1-1 DYNAMIC HOST CONFIGURATION PROTOCOL (DHCP)

Since typical embedded systems operate in private networks, it is quite possible that the IP addressing scheme in these networks, is fixed or static. In this case, every device participating in the network receives its IP address and all other network-related parameters from the network administrator and they are hard-coded in the device. This method of parameter assignment is referred to as static addressing, and it provides added security. While no device can be part of a network without the network administrator's knowledge, all servers can be configured to accept requests from specific device IP addresses that correspond to the list of valid devices.

Dynamic addressing, in comparison, was developed as a means to reuse IP addresses in IP networks, especially because of the limited number of IP addresses available. An example is a device often used by home networks. High-speed service delivered by an Internet Service Provider (ISP) is performed by a DSL or cable modem. This modem includes an Ethernet switch and a DHCP server, or another device is connected between the modem and computers on the home network. This additional device often serves such multiple functions as an Ethernet switch, a DHCP server, a router, and a firewall. This is what is shown in Figure 9-1

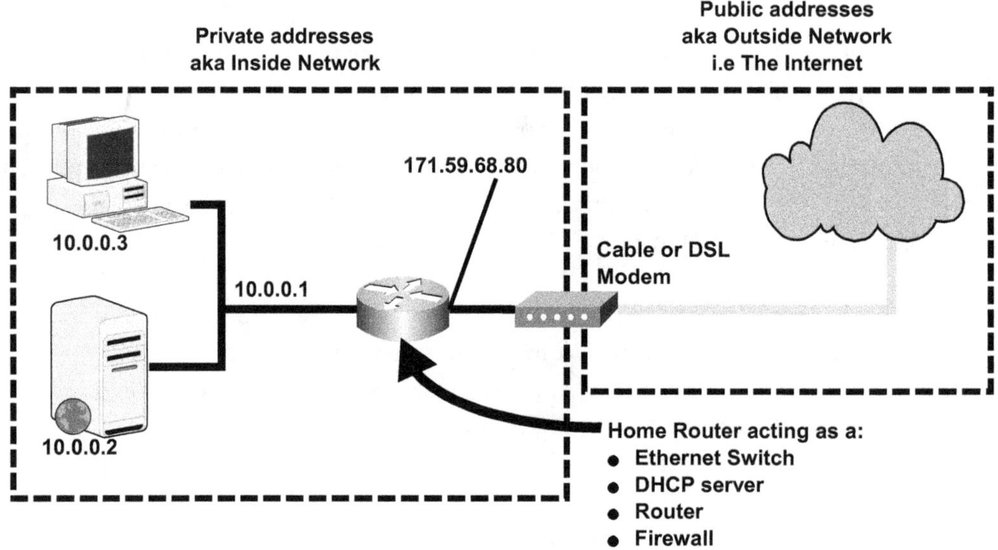

Figure 9-1 **Home Router acting as a DHCP server**

Upon power up, a device running a DHCP client simply sends a request to any DHCP server to obtain an IP address (and other parameters). The DHCP server(s) maintain a "pool" of available IP addresses and assigns a unique IP address to requesting client(s). The DHCP protocol between clients and servers simplifies the work of the network administrator.

DHCP use UDP as the transport protocol. The DHCP server listens for incoming requests on UDP port 67 and sends out offers on UDP port 68 as shown in Figure 9-2 and Figure 9-3.

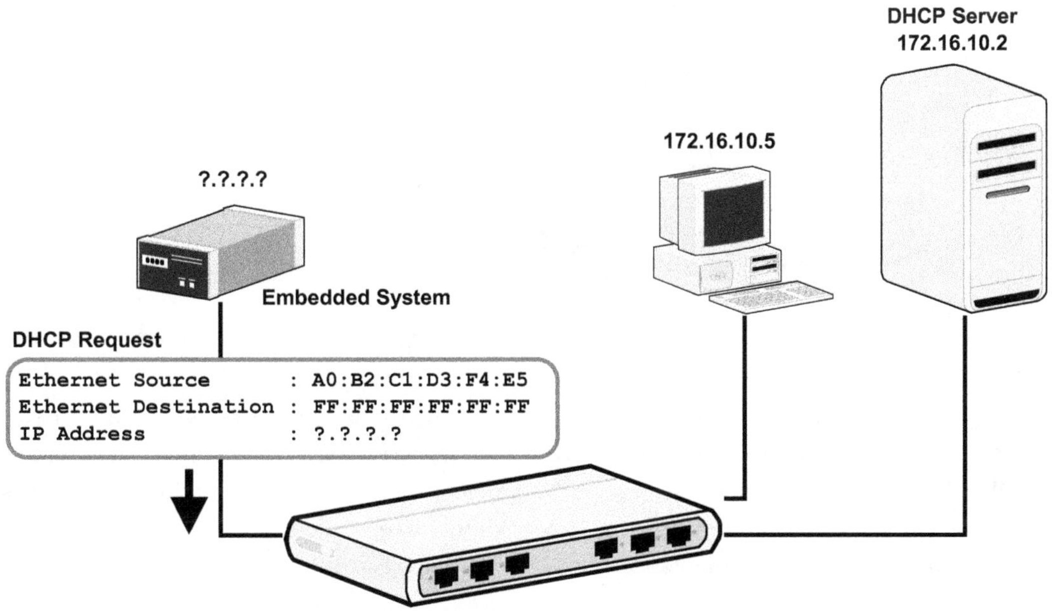

Figure 9-2 **DHCP Request**

DHCP requests are usually transmitted by a device when booting up since that host does not have an IP address and it requires one. The DHCP request message is a broadcast message (Ethernet destination address is FF:FF:FF:FF:FF:FF) since the host does not know anything about the network it is connected to and must obtain that information.

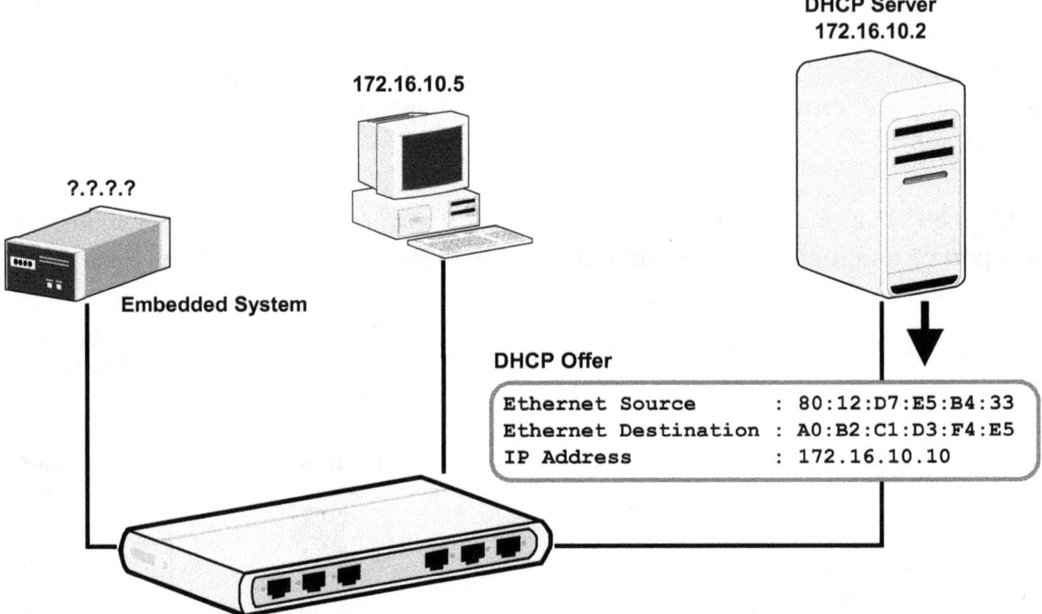

Figure 9-3 **DHCP Offer**

With typical DHCP server implementations, any DHCP server on the network will answer the host DHCP request. Once this offer is received, the host sends an acknowledgement to the DHCP server that the offer is accepted, The DHCP server reserves the address and does not assign it to any other hosts. Again, please note that this is a typical DHCP implementation. Other implementations could work differently.

The IP address and other network parameters required for the host to operate on the network are not assigned permanently. Instead, DHCP uses a leasing principle. After a predefined time-out period, the host must again request for the IP address. The DHCP server refreshes the lease allowing the host to continue using the already assigned address for another time-out period.

There may be more than one DHCP server on a network and the host may receive one offer per DHCP server. Usually, a DHCP client accepts the first offer received and will reject subsequent offers.

If the host disconnects from the network and then reconnects and the IP address previously assigned is still available, the host receives the same address. This is the typical behavior of most DHCP servers. However, it is possible that other DHCP implementations do not reassign previously assigned parameters.

The mandatory parameters the DHCP server provides are:

- The IP address
- The subnet mask

The default gateway IP address is not mandatory but is generally included when the host needs to access networks outside of the local network.

The DHCP client is an application invoked by the Application Layer although it impacts the Network Layer. Examples in Part II of this book demonstrate DHCP usage.

There is alternative to obtaining an IP address on single private network referred to as the dynamic configuration of link-local addresses, sometimes called by MIcrosoft and other vendors:

- Automatic Private IP Addressing (APIPA)
- AutoNet
- AutoIP

When a TCP/IP stack in a host requires an IP address using DHCP, and there is no DHCP server present or the DHCP server is not responding, the DHCP client can invoke APIPA.

The Internet Assigned Numbers Authority (IANA) reserves private IP addresses in the range of 169.254.0.0 to 169.254.255.255 for APIPA or written differently, the network reserved is 169.254.0.0/16.

If a DHCP server does not reply, the host selects an IP address within this range and sends a message to this address to see if it is in use. If it receives a reply, the address is in use and another address is selected. This process is repeated until an address is found to be available.

After the network adapter is assigned an IP address with APIPA, the host can communicate with any other hosts on the local network also configured by APIPA, or ones that have a static IP address manually set in the 169.254.X.X sub-network with a subnet mask of 255.255.0.0. This is particularly useful for embedded systems where the manual management of IP configuration is not desired or possible.

Whether using DHCP or APIPA, the embedded device must have a way to display the IP address or make it available to other hosts in order for these other hosts to establish communication with the embedded device. If the device is the one to establish the connection, then advertising the IP address is not required.

9-1-2 DOMAIN NAME SYSTEM (DNS)

When communicating with other hosts on the public Internet, it is possible that the only information known regarding these hosts is their 'Fully Qualified Domain Name' (FQDN). For example, it is easier to refer to web servers by their name, i.e., the Web server at Micrium is www.micrium.com.

The DNS is used to establish an association between a system name and its IP address. It is a protocol with two parts:

- Client: Resolver
- Server: Name server

DNS uses UDP or TCP as transport protocols to deliver its service on port 53.

The structure of DNS is very similar to the file structures that we find in our existing computers. It is possible, but not recommended, to have up to 127 levels.

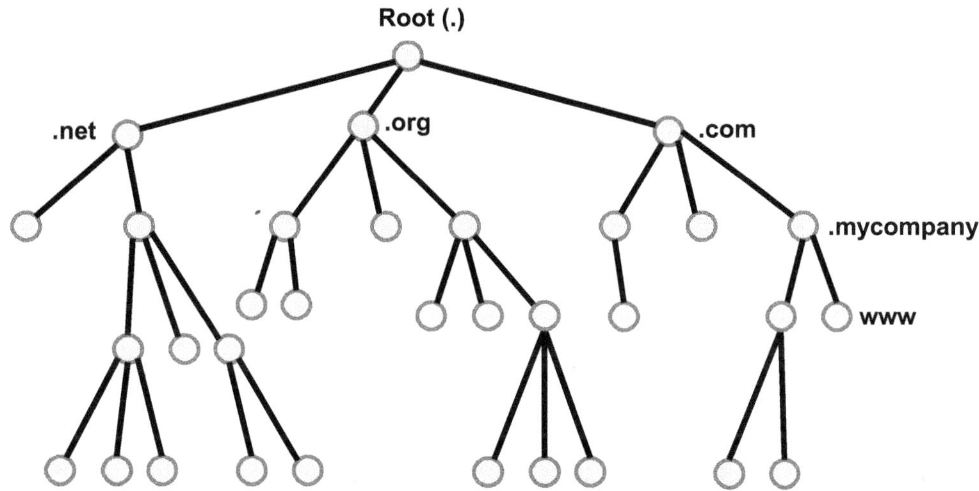

Figure 9-4 **DNS Structure**

Figure 9-4 shows the DNS database, which is depicted as an inverted tree. Each element/node of the tree has a label of up to 63 characters that identifies it relative to its parent. Note that not all nodes at each level are represented. This is only a sample of the DNS structure.

The root, in comparison, uses a reserved label, i.e., « nil character » or « ». The levels are separated from each other by periods « **.** » The label of each child belonging to a given parent must be unique.

WWW.MYCOMPANY.COM

Service name	Domain name

Figure 9-5 **Syntax of Domain Names**

As shown in Figure 9-5, a FQDN is read from right to left. To the extreme right of the domain defined after the **.com** is the root domain (an empty string). The root domain is also represented by a single dot (.), as shown in Figure 9-4. DNS software does not require that the terminating dot be included when attempting to translate a domain name to an IP address.

Reading from right to left, from the root, the **.com** domain is found, which contains the mycompany domain, and finally contains the web server (www). As you can now see, the service or subdomain is the last field. We are all familiar with the www.mycompany.com

model because web servers are hosts we access often. However, many other services can be available from a domain. For example:

- An FTP server: `ftp.mycompany.com`
- A mail server: `mail.mycompanny.com`

When it is required to translate names, an embedded system includes a DNS Client. This software module is also referred to as a DNS resolver or in the case of a DNS server, it is called a network service.

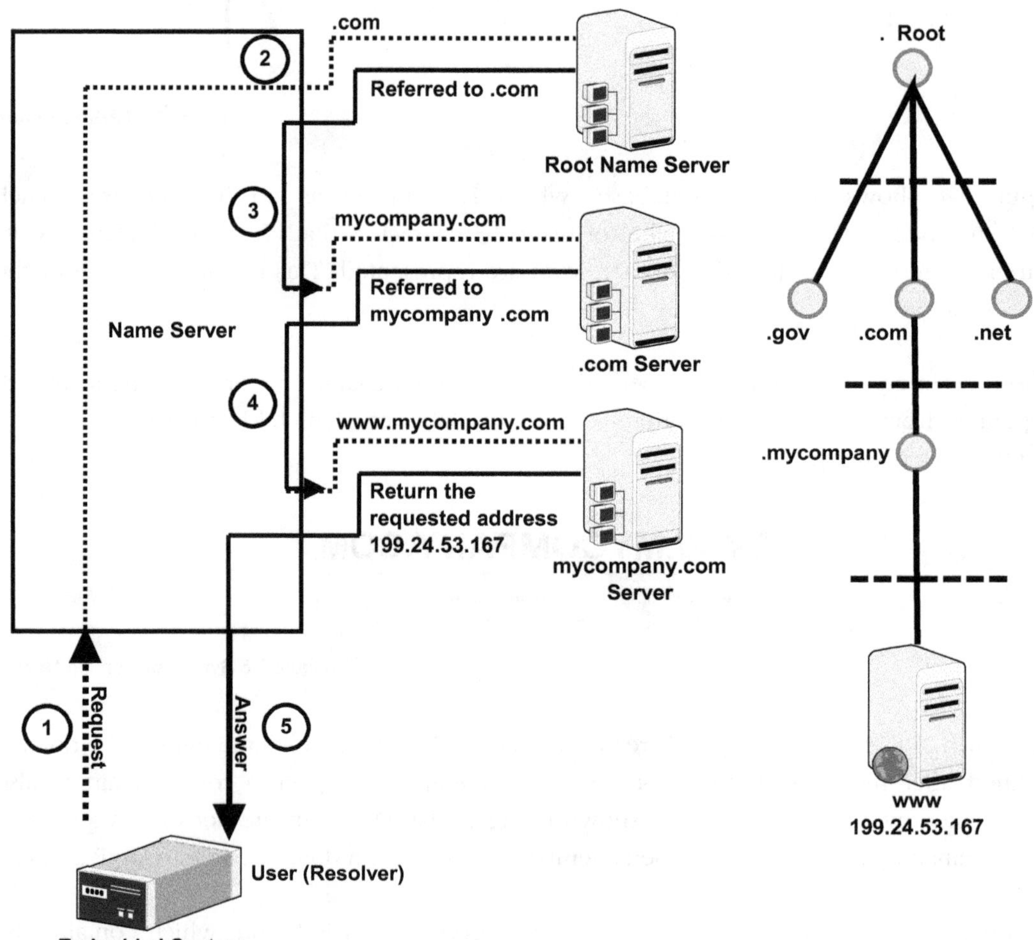

Figure 9-6 **Resolution Mechanism**

F9-6(1) The first step in converting a FQDN into an IP address is for the host to use its DNS Resolver to send a DNS request to the DNS server on its network, represented by the Name Server box.

F9-6(2) In this scenario, let's assume the DNS server does not know the answer to the request. The name server must send the request to one of thirteen 'well known' root name servers to find the answer. These thirteen root name servers implement the root name space domain for the Internet's Domain Name System. The root name servers are a critical part of the Internet as they are the first step in resolving human-readable host names into IP addresses. Normally the addresses of these root name servers are configured in the local name server.

The local DNS server (name server) begins its search by reading the FQDN from right to left and sends a request for each field, one at a time. It sends a request to one of the root name servers to find where the `.com` domain is located.

F9-6(3) The root name server replies with the address or addresses of the location of the.com domain. This information is stored in the local name server, which now asks the servers for the `.com` domain for the location of the `mycompany.com` domain.

F9-6(4) The root name server(s) for the `.com` replies with the address or addresses of where the mycompany.com domain is located. This information is stored in the local name server, which can now ask the `mycompany.com` domain name server for the location of the `www.mycompany.com` service.

F9-6(5) The root name server(s) for the `mycompany.com` replies with the address or addresses of where `www.mycompany.com` service is located. This information is stored in the local name server, which can now answer the request from the resolver with the IP address of the `www.mycompany.com` service.

DNS servers make use of a caching mechanism. Once a request is resolved, the cross-reference between the name and the IP address is kept in the cache so that the next time a DNS request for the same name is received, the server need not reprocess the complete request. This is also one of the reasons that, when a new IP address is assigned to a name, it can take up to 24 hours for the new IP address to propagate through the Internet.

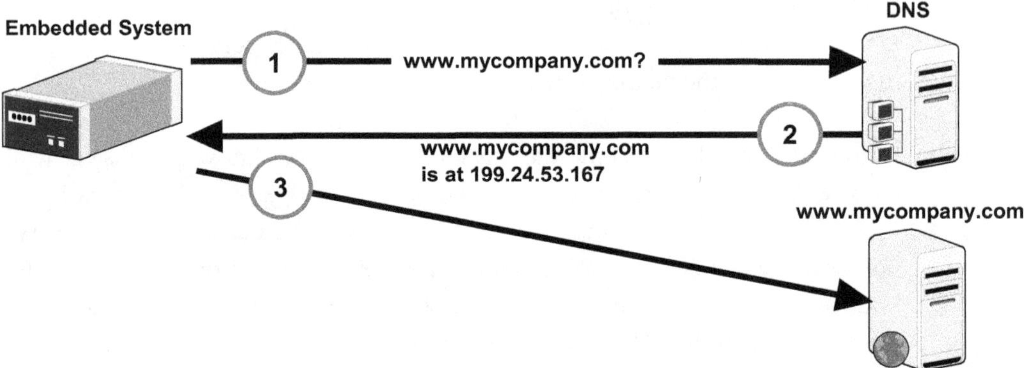

Figure 9-7 **DNS Client (Resolver)**

Figure 9-7 demonstrates the process once the local DNS server knows the IP address for the FQDN submitted to it.

9-2 APPLICATIONS

As previously stated, applications are code running above the TCP/IP stack, and are often referred to as Layer 7 applications. There are standard applications based on standard protocols that are defined by RFCs. These can be used as a software module in embedded systems.

In addition to standard applications, there are any number of user-written applications that are crucial to the embedded product as their code represents a particular field of expertise. Sample code demonstrating how to write a client application, or a server application, is provided in Chapter 19, "Socket programming" and in Part II of this book.

9-3 APPLICATION PERFORMANCE

Performance of the TCP/IP stack has been a constant consideration for this book. Chapter 6, for example, is dedicated to configuring TCP to get the most out of the stack depending on the hardware resources available, particularly RAM.

There is one additional item to consider in order to achieve optimum performance for the complete system. The socket interface between the application and the TCP/IP stack must be configured correctly. When attempting to attain maximum throughput, the most important options involve TCP Window sizes and the number of network device transmit and receive buffers. These are calculated according to the bandwidth-delay product (BDP - see Chapter 7, "Transport Protocols" on page 165). For the connection to achieve an acceptable performance, the flow of packets between the Network Device and TCP and vice-versa is dictated by this configuration.

The same is true between the application layer and the transport layer. Applications usually have their own set of buffers and the number and size of these buffers should match TCP Window sizes based on network buffers, to complete the optimization of a connection (socket). Given the application send and receive buffers and the TCP transmit and receive Windows, the closer their number and size, the more optimal the throughput on the embedded system.

With the BSD socket API, the configuration of the TCP transmit and receive window sizes is accomplished by setting socket send and receive buffer sizes. Most operating systems support separate per connection send and receive buffer limits that can be adjusted by the user application, or other mechanism, as long as they stay within the maximum memory limits of system hardware. These buffer sizes correspond to the **SO_SNDBUF** and **SO_RCVBUF** options of the BSD **setsockopt()** call.

µC/TCP-IP socket API implementation (BSD or proprietary) does not support the **SO_SNDBUF** and **SO_RCVBUF** socket options. With the Micrium application add-ons to µC/TCP-IP such as µC/HTTPs and others, application buffers are specified and configured in the application. This is where the configuration must be performed to optimize the connection throughput. The closer the send and receive buffers configuration for the application is to the TCP Window sizes the better the performance will be. An important performance improvement is to make sure that memory copies between the application buffers and the network buffers are aligned to/from application buffers to network buffers. This means to make sure that application data starts on memory addresses that are optimally-aligned for the memory copy from/to network socket buffers.

Very often, the bandwidth of a TCP connection is restricted by the configuration of transmitter and receiver buffer sizes, resulting in the connection not utilizing the available bandwidth of the links. Making the buffers as large as possible is the preferred approach, in the case of TCP, the size of the MSS (see Chapter 7, "Transport Protocols" on page 165). It is possible to test and validate the buffer and TCP Window sizes configuration. However, very few applications provide you with a way to configure buffer sizes. Network utilities such as **ttcp**, **netperf** and **iperf** allows you to the specify buffer sizes in the command line, and offer the possibility to disable the Nagle's algorithm, assuming you know or can determine what the optimal settings are. With µC/IPerf (see Chapter 6, "Troubleshooting" on page 135), it is possible to configure the buffer size however µC/TCP-IP does not currently have an option to disable the Nagle's algorithm. With µC/IPerf, it is possible to test and validate the buffer and TCP Window sizes configuration. Part II of this book contains UDP and TCP examples using µC/IPerf.

Hardware resources, particularly RAM, may limit the maximum values for certain configurable parameters. The default TCP transmit and receive window sizes can be for ALL connections, as is the case for µC/TCP-IP. While in some applications, that be sub-optimal and wasteful of system memory, in an embedded system, the concurrent number of connections is usually not high so that it is possible to work with default settings for all connections.

Application Performance

When attempting to attain maximum throughput, the most important options involve TCP window sizes and send/receive buffers.

It is crucial to configure the application send/receive buffers. The closer the send and receive buffers configuration for the application is to the TCP Window sizes the better the performance will be.

9-3-1 FILE TRANSFER

FILE TRANSFER PROTOCOL (FTP)

The three most used Internet applications are e-mail, web and FTP. FTP is the standard Internet file transfer protocol and is also one of the oldest application protocols. Its main design goal is to transfer files (computer programs and/or data). When FTP was created, there were many operating systems in use and each OS had its own file system in addition to its own character encoding. FTP was conceived to shield you from variations in file systems between different hosts. Today, FTP's main feature is to reliably and efficiently transfer data between hosts.

FTP is an application-layer protocol using TCP transport service. FTP utilizes separate control and data connections between client and server applications. FTP control uses TCP port 21 while FTP data uses TCP port 20. The use of two separate ports is called "out-of-band control." Dedicated connections are opened on different port numbers for control and data transfers.

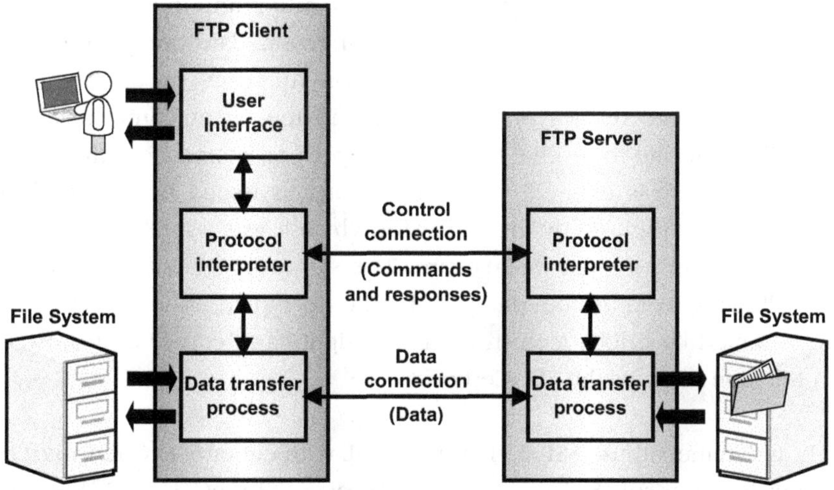

Figure 9-8 **File Transfer Protocol (FTP)**

Figure 9-8 shows two TCP connections used by FTP for control and data. A system that utilizes FTP also requires a file system, as shown.

The FTP client and server have different operating modes: active or passive. In each mode, the dynamic port number (another port number picked from the available pool) is used by the client or server to bind the source port of the connection to a different port based on a negotiated connection.

FTP can be used either with user-based password authentication or with anonymous (generic) user access. The latter allows a client to connect to a server without having an account with that given server. Some network administrators can force an anonymous user to enter an e-mail address that contains the domain (see section "Simple Mail Transfer Protocol (SMTP)" on page 238) as the password. With a DNS lookup, the FTP server retrieves the IP address of that e-mail server. By comparing the FTP connection request IP address and the e-mail domain IP address, it is possible to confirm the validity of the connection request as the two addresses should be in the same network.

FTP is an unsecure method of transferring files, as no encryption method is used. User names, passwords, FTP commands, and transferred files are exposed to the "middle man attack" using a network protocol analyzer (see the section "Troubleshooting" on page 135).

The Secure Socket Layer (SSL) is an industry standard that represents a solution to this problem. SSL is a layer between the application and socket layers. It is a session layer protocol that encrypts data flowing between the application and the TCP/IP stack, ensuring high-level security over an IP network. SSL is based on standard encryption methods using private and public keys provided by a Certification Authority by the issuance of a SSL Certificate. The certificate resides on the server and the client connecting to the server retrieves the SSL Certificate to receive the public key. Upon connection, the client checks to see if the SSL Certificate is expired, whether or not it is issued by a trusted Certification Authority, and if it is being used by the server for which it was issued. If any checks fail, the client will think the server is not SSL secure. The server matches the SSL Certificate to a private key, allowing data to be encrypted and decrypted. The secure connection is normally represented by a lock icon in the lower right-hand corner of a browser window. Clicking on the icon displays the SSL Certificate.

HTTP, SMTP, and Telnet all use SSL. FTP applies SSL with either SSH (the Unix/Linux Secure Shell) File Transfer Protocol (SFTP), or FTPS (FTP over SSL). µC/TCP-IP does not currently offer an SSL module, but third party modules are readily available.

TRIVIAL FILE TRANSFER PROTOCOL (TFTP)

The Trivial File Transfer Protocol (TFTP) is a similar, yet simplified, non-interoperable, and unauthenticated version of FTP. TFTP is implemented on top of UDP. The TFTP client initially sends a read/write request through port 69. Server and client then determine the port that they will use for the rest of the connections (dynamic port with FTP). The TFTP simple architecture is deliberate for easy implementation For an embedded system, it may very well be the right choice since this simplistic approach has many benefits over traditional FTP. For example, it can be:

- Used by flash-based devices to download firmware
- Used by any automated process when it is not possible to assign a user ID or password
- Used in applications where footprint is limited or resources constrained, allowing it to be implemented inexpensively.

NETWORK FILE SYSTEMS

Network file systems may also provide the necessary functionality to access files on remote hosts. The Network File System (NFS), Andrew File System (AFS), and the Common Internet File System (CIFS - also referred or decoded as Server Message Block (SMB) by a network protocol analyzer), provide this type of functionality.

9-3-2 HYPERTEXT TRANSFER PROTOCOL (HTTP)

Hypertext Transfer Protocol (HTTP) is used to exchange data in all types of formats (text, video, graphics and others) over the World Wide Web. This protocol uses TCP port 80 for sending and receiving data. The protocol works in client/server mode, and HTTP client is the familiar browser used by all.

The server side of HTTP is popular in the embedded industry. Implementing an HTTP server (a web server) in an embedded system allows users or applications to connect to the embedded device with a browser enabling information to be exchanged graphically. Users or applications receive data from the embedded system. Examples are the HTTP interfaces provided by home gateways and printers.

Not so long ago, connecting to configure an embedded system or to retrieve data from it was performed by way of either a console port using RS-232 or Telnet over a network connection. Both provide a terminal I/O interface and are text based. With HTTP, the user interface is more elaborate, using graphical elements, and is accessible from virtually anywhere as long as the embedded device has access to the Internet.

An HTTP server "serves" web pages, files requested by the browser and usually stored on a mass storage medium. A file system is typically required to retrieve these web pages. Some embedded HTTP servers such as Micrium's μC/HTTPs allow for web pages to be stored as part of the code. In this case, a file system is unnecessary, and a custom method is used to read and transfer information. Part II of this book shows an example of using HTTP with web pages stored as code.

HTTP provides the possibility of invoking other protocols. For example, file transfer using FTP can be initiated from a web page. This implies that an FTP client is active on the host that runs the browser. Similarly, an e-mail can be generated from a hyperlink on the page. This implies that a mail client is also running on the host running the browser.

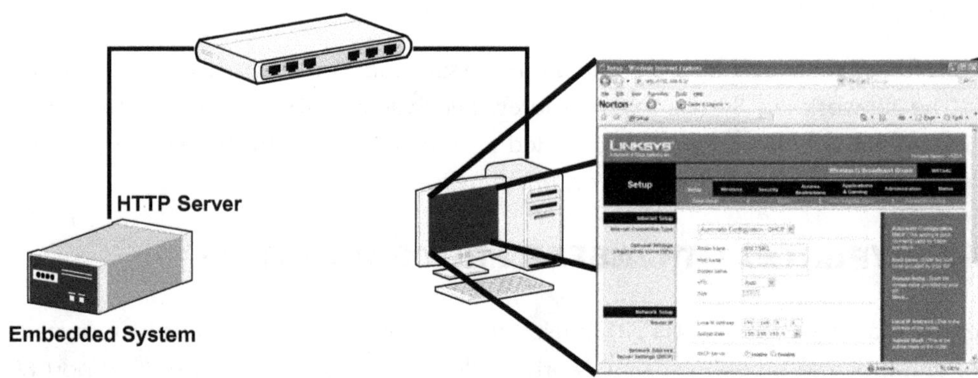

Figure 9-9 **HyperText Transfer Protocol (HTTP)**

Figure 9-9 represents a web page taken from a Linksys Wireless-G Broadband Router (i.e a Home gateway), and is an example of what an embedded system implementing an HTTP server can do.

HTTP is one of the easiest ways to access multimedia content such as music and videos.

A secure HTTP connection can be established using SSL and is referred to as an HTTPS connection which is particularly popular for financial transactions over the Internet, including e-commerce.

On certain embedded systems, the performance of an embedded HTTP server can largely be affected by the memory resources available to dictate the number of buffers and sockets. The current method used by browsers is to retrieve files from the HTTP server and open simultaneous parallel connections to download as many files as possible. This improves the perception of performance. This method is excellent on systems that have sufficient resources and bandwidth. On an embedded system, it may not be possible to operate many sockets in parallel due to the incapacity to allocate sufficient resources.

9-3-3 TELNET

Telnet is a standard protocol offered by most TCP/IP implementations. TCP Port 23 is used by the Telnet server to listen for incoming connection requests. Telnet is widely used to establish a connection between a host and a remote system, to manage the system from a distance. Telnet is very popular in the telecom market. Most telecommunications equipment today, such as routers and switches, supports the Telnet protocol.

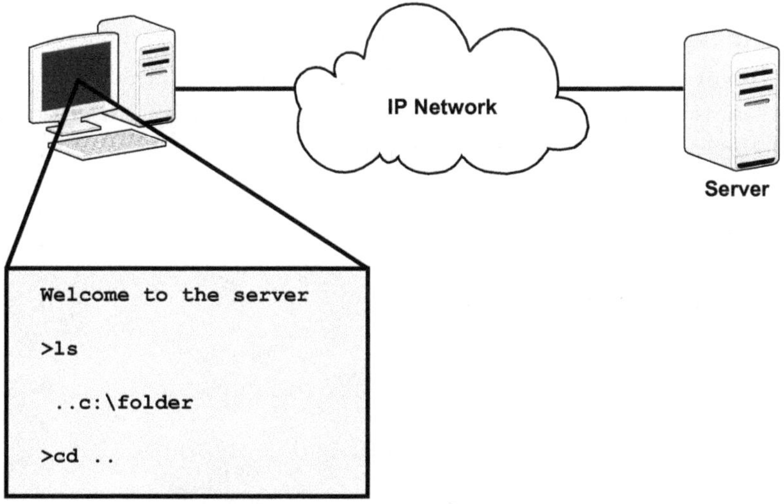

Figure 9-10 **Telnet example**

With Telnet, a virtual session allows the client to run applications via a command-line interface on the remote server in terminal mode (see Figure 9-10). In this case, the remote system may have a shell application allowing the host to issue commands and visualize execution results on the Telnet terminal window. Micrium offers µC/Shell for this purpose.

The two hosts involved in the telnet session begin by exchanging their capabilities (also referred to as options such as binary transmission, echo, reconnection, etc...). After the initial negotiation is complete, the hosts choose a common level to use between them.

Because Telnet uses clear text user name and password, its use has diminished in favor of SSH for secure remote access. Micrium offers µC/Telnet TCP/IP add-on modules.

9-3-4 E-MAIL

When designing an embedded system, messages are likely to be exchanged. It is possible that a proprietary messaging system can be developed, and in most cases this is the best solution. At times, sending e-mail instead of a proprietary message may be a clever alternative. For example, when the embedded system detects an alarm condition and needs to report it, sending an e-mail to an iPhone or Blackberry can be the best way to communicate the information.

Or conversely, to send information to an embedded system, sending an e-mail to the embedded system may be a simple way to implement such functionality. The e-mail may be automated and transmit from another device, or it can be sent by a user or administrator telling the embedded system to execute a function.

TCP/IP protocols dealing with e-mail include:

- Simple Mail Transport Protocol (SMTP)
- Sendmail
- Multipurpose Internet Mail Extensions (MIME)
- Post Office Protocol (POP)
- Internet Message Access Protocol (IMAP)

SIMPLE MAIL TRANSFER PROTOCOL (SMTP)

To send an e-mail, a connection is required to an IP network and access to a mail server that forwards the mail. The standard protocol used for sending Internet e-mail is called Simple Mail Transfer Protocol (SMTP). If a system's needs are limited to sending messages, only SMTP is required. However, to receive e-mails, the most popular service is the Post Office Protocol (POP) Version 3 or POP3.

SMTP uses TCP as the transport layer protocol and Port 25 is used by the STMP server to listen to incoming connections. An e-mail client sends an e-mail message to an SMTP server. The server looks at the e-mail address and forwards it to the recipient's mail server, where it's stored until the addressee retrieves it (see Figure 9-11).

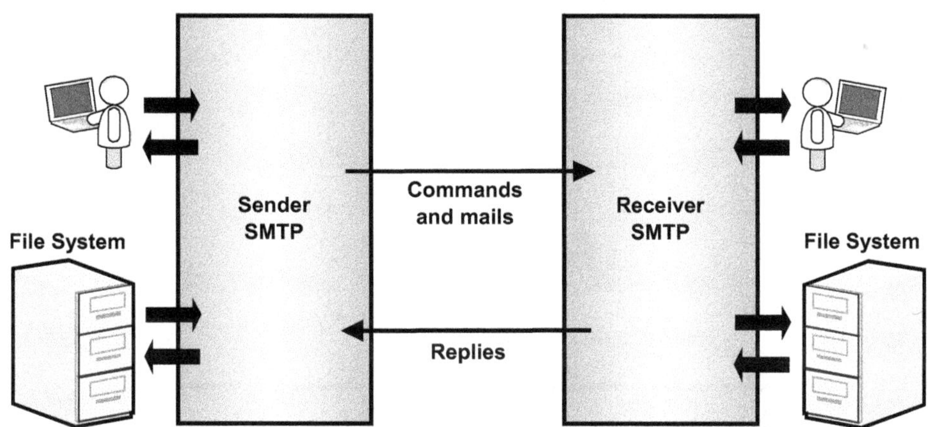

Figure 9-11 **SMTP**

All Internet service providers and major online services offer e-mail accounts (each having an address). The SMTP destination address, also known as the mailbox address, has this general form: User@Domain.

User	A unique user on the Domain
Domain	The domain name of the network to reach.

The e-mail address can also take several other forms, depending of whether the destination is on the same TCP/IP network, a user on a non-SMTP destination remote-host going through the mail gateway-host, or involving a relayed message.

SMTP is an end-to-end delivery system. An SMTP client contacts the destination host's SMTP server directly, on Port 25, to deliver the mail. DNS is invoked, as the domain is part of the e-mail address. The remote Domain Name Server must contain the address of the mail server. The SMTP client ensures that the mail is transmitted until it is successfully copied to the recipient's SMTP server. In this way, SMTP guarantees delivery of the message.

In SMTP, each message has:

- A header, or envelope defined by RFC 2822
- A mail header terminated by a null line (a line with nothing preceding the <CRLF> sequence).

- Content: Everything after the null (or blank) line is the message body, which is a sequence of lines containing ASCII characters (characters with a value less than 128 decimal). Content is optional.

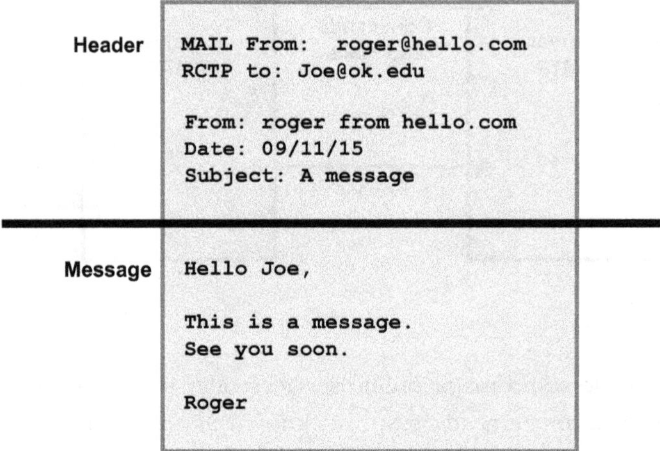

Header
MAIL From: roger@hello.com
RCTP to: Joe@ok.edu
From: roger from hello.com
Date: 09/11/15
Subject: A message
Message
Hello Joe,
This is a message.
See you soon.
Roger

Figure 9-12 **SMTP message**

SMTP is simple and light enough to be used on an embedded system when transmission of messages is required. Initially, e-mails were text messages only. Today, given Multipurpose Internet Mail Extension (MIME), and other encoding schemes, such as Base64 and UUencode, formatted documents (Word, PDF, etc.), photos (JPEG and other formats), audio and video files can now be attached to e-mail. An e-mail message containing an attachment has a MIME header in the message body. The encoding schemes used by MIME provide a means for non-text information to be encoded as text. This is how attachments can be carried by SMTP. However, it is important that the recipient has compatible software to open attachments.

MIME is also used by HTTP (www) as it requires data to be transmitted in text-based messages (HTML, DHTML, XML and others).

SENDMAIL

Sendmail is a command-line tool found on most large operating systems. It is a client/server application supporting multiple mail protocols. Sendmail is one of the oldest mail transfer agents on the Internet and is available as open source and with proprietary software packages.

POST OFFICE PROTOCOL (POP)

Post Office Protocol version 3 (POP3) is an e-mail protocol with both client and server functions. POP3 client establishes a TCP connection to the server, using Port 110 and supports basic functions (download and delete) for e-mail retrieval. For more advanced functions IMAP4 is suggested. When retrieving messages on an embedded system, POP3 is simpler and smaller to implement than IMAP4. Micrium currently offers µC/POP3.

INTERNET MESSAGE ACCESS PROTOCOL (IMAP4)

The Internet Message Access Protocol, version 4 (IMAP4) is an e-mail protocol with both client and server functions. As with POP, IMAP4 servers store user account messages to be retrieved upon client request. IMAP4 allows clients to have multiple remote mailboxes from which messages are retrieved. Message download criteria can be specified by IMAP4 clients. For example, a client may be configured to not transfer message bodies or not transfer large messages over slow links. IMAP4 always keeps messages on the server and copies are replicated to clients.

IMAP4 clients can make changes when connected or when disconnected. The changes will be applied when the client is reconnected. POP client must always be connected to make changes to the mailbox. Changes made on the IMAP4 client when disconnected, take effect on the server with automatic periodic re-synchronization of the client to the server. This is why implementing a POP3 client is a lot simpler than implementing an IMAP4 client. For embedded systems with limited resources, these are important considerations.

9-4 SUMMARY

On any IP network, there may exist several useful network services in addition to the ones introduced in this chapter. DHCP and DNS, however, remain the two main network services most often used by embedded systems.

On the application level, basic “standard” TCP/IP Application-Layer applications were discussed. Often, these “standard” applications may be complemented by a custom application. This embedded application is used to differentiate devices from the competition. User-written client or server applications leverage the TCP/IP stack.

Application buffer configuration is an important factor in performance considerations. When using a TCP protocol, make sure buffer configurations match TCP Window sizes. If a system uses UDP, allocate sufficient resources (i.e., buffers) to meet system requirements. These assumptions can be tested using the tools and sample applications provided in Part II of this book.

The following chapters explain Micrium's µC/TCP-IP for building efficient TCP/IP-based applications.

Chapter

10

Introduction to µC/TCP-IP

µC/TCP-IP is a compact, reliable, high-performance TCP/IP protocol stack. Built from the ground up with Micrium's unique combination of quality, scalability and reliability, µC/TCP-IP, the result of many man-years of development, enables the rapid configuration of required network options to minimize time to market.

The source code for µC/TCP-IP contains over 100,000 lines of the cleanest, most consistent ANSI C source code available in a TCP/IP stack implementation. C was chosen since C is the predominant language in the embedded industry. Over 50% of the code consists of comments and most global variables and all functions are described. References to RFC (Request For Comments) are included in the code where applicable.

10-1 PORTABLE

µC/TCP-IP is ideal for resource-constrained embedded applications. The code was designed for use with nearly any CPU, RTOS, and network device. Although µC/TCP-IP can work on some 8 and 16-bit processors, µC/TCP-IP is optimized for use with 32 or 64-bit CPUs.

10-2 SCALABLE

The memory footprint of µC/TCP-IP can be adjusted at compile time depending on the features required, and the desired level of run-time argument checking appropriate for the design at hand. SinceµC/TCP-IP is rich in its ability to provide statistics computation, unnecessary statistics computation can be disabled to further reduce the footprint.

10-3 CODING STANDARDS

Coding standards were established early in the design of μC/TCP-IP. They include:

- C coding style
- Naming convention for #define constants, macros, variables and functions
- Commenting
- Directory structure

These conventions make μC/TCP-IP the preferred TCP/IP stack implementation in the industry, and result in the ability to attain third party certification more easily as outlined in the next section.

10-4 MISRA C

The source code for μC/TCP-IP follows Motor Industry Software Reliability Association (MISRA) C Coding Standards. These standards were created by MISRA to improve the reliability and predictability of C programs in safety-critical automotive systems. Members of the MISRA consortium include such companies as Delco Electronics, Ford Motor Company, Jaguar Cars Ltd., Lotus Engineering, Lucas Electronics, Rolls-Royce, Rover Group Ltd., and universities dedicated to improving safety and reliability in automotive electronics. Full details of this standard can be obtained directly from the MISRA web site at: www.misra.org.uk.

10-5 SAFETY CRITICAL CERTIFICATION

µC/TCP-IP was designed from the ground up to be certifiable for use in avionics, medical devices, and other safety-critical products. Validated Software's Validation Suite™ for µC/TCP-IP will provide all of the documentation required to deliver µC/TCP-IP as a pre-certifiable software component for avionics RTCA DO-178B and EUROCAE ED-12B, medical FDA 510(k), IEC 61508 industrial control systems, and EN-50128 rail transportation and nuclear systems. The Validation Suite, available through Validated Software, will be immediately certifiable for DO-178B Level A, Class III medical devices, and SIL3/SIL4 IEC-certified systems. For more information, check out the µC/TCP-IP page on the Validated Software web site at: www.ValidatedSoftware.com.

If your product is not safety critical, however, the presence of certification should be viewed as proof that µC/TCP-IP is very robust and highly reliable.

10-6 RTOS

µC/TCP-IP assumes the presence of an RTOS, yet there are no assumptions as to which RTOS to use with µC/TCP-IP. The only requirements are that it:

- must be able to support multiple tasks
- must provide binary and counting semaphore management services
- must provide message queue services

µC/TCP-IP contains an encapsulation layer that allows for the use of almost any commercial or open source RTOS. Details regarding the RTOS are hidden from µC/TCP-IP. µC/TCP-IP includes the encapsulation layer for µC/OS-II and µC/OS-III real-time kernels.

10-7 NETWORK DEVICES

µC/TCP-IP may be configured with multiple-network devices and network (IP) addresses. Any device may be used as long as a driver with appropriate API and BSP software is provided. The API for a specific device (i.e., chip) is encapsulated in a couple of files and it is quite easy to adapt devices to µC/TCP-IP (see Chapter 20, "Statistics and Error Counters" on page 381).

Although Ethernet devices are supported today, Micrium is currently working on adding Point-to-Point Protocol (PPP) support to µC/TCP-IP.

10-8 µC/TCP-IP PROTOCOLS

µC/TCP-IP consists of the following protocols:

- Device drivers
- Network Interfaces (e.g., Ethernet, PPP (TBA), etc.)
- Address Resolution Protocol (ARP)
- Internet Protocol (IP)
- Internet Control Message Protocol (ICMP)
- Internet Group Management Protocol (IGMP)
- User Datagram Protocol (UDP)
- Transport Control Protocol (TCP)
- Sockets (Micrium and BSD v4)

10-9 APPLICATION PROTOCOLS

Micrium offers application layer protocols as add-ons to µC/TCP-IP. A list of these network services and applications includes:

- µC/DCHPc, DHCP Client
- µC/DNSc, DNS Client
- µC/HTTPs, HTTP Server (web server)
- µC/TFTPc, TFTP Client
- µC/TFTPs, TFTP Server
- µC/FTPc, FTP Client
- µC/FTPs, FTP Server
- µC/SMTPc, SMTP Client
- µC/POP3, POP3 Client
- µC/SNTPc, Network Time Protocol Client

Any well known application layer protocols following the BSD socket API standard can be used with µC/TCP-IP.

Chapter

11

μC/TCP-IP Architecture

μC/TCP-IP was written to be modular and easy to adapt to a variety of Central Processing Units (CPUs), Real-Time Operating Systems (RTOSs), network devices, and compilers. Figure 11-1 shows a simplified block diagram of μC/TCP-IP modules and their relationships.

Notice that all μC/TCP-IP files start with '**net_**'. This convention allows us to quickly identify which files belong to μC/TCP-IP. Also note that all functions and global variables start with '**Net**', and all macros and **#defines** start with '**net_**'.

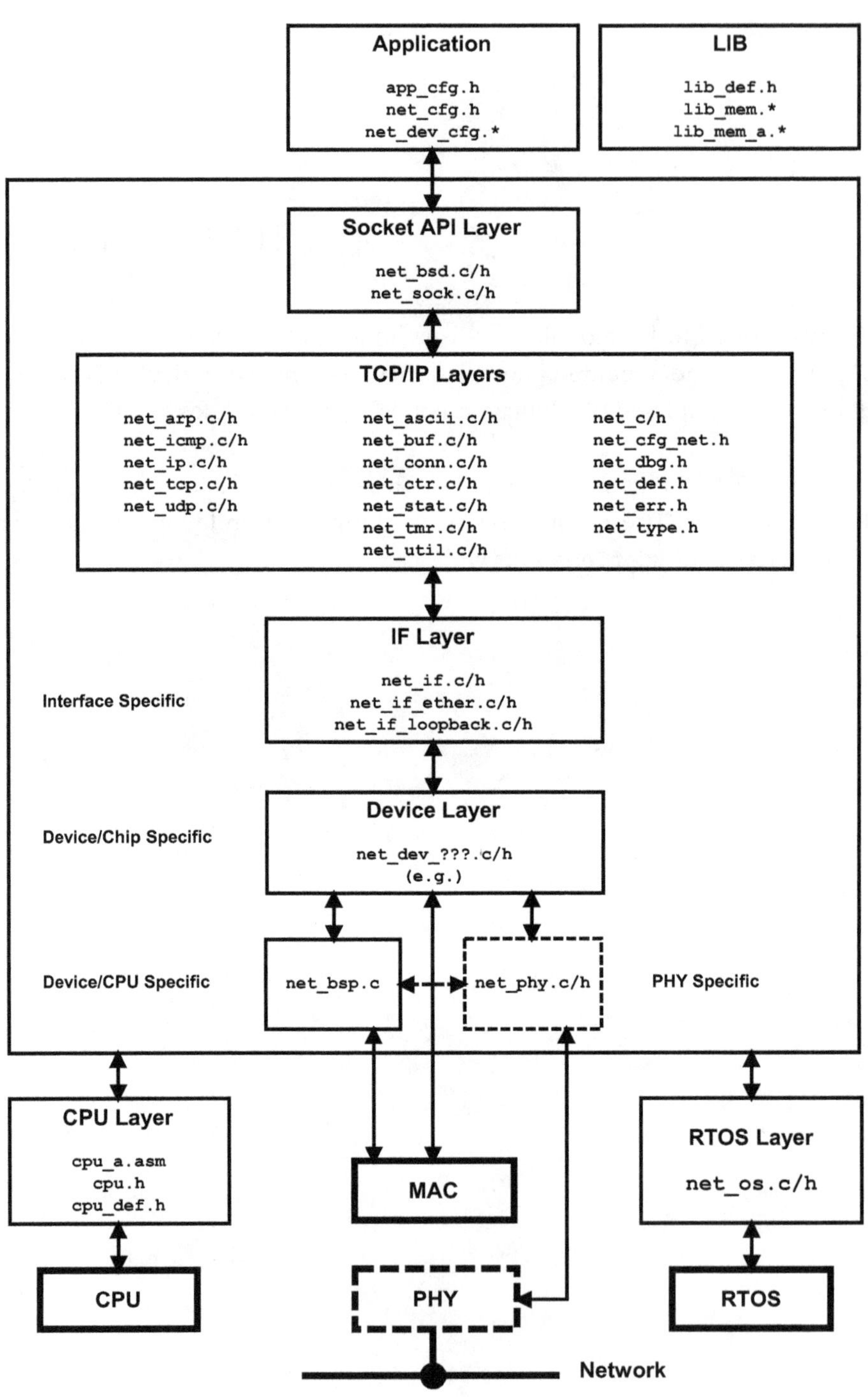

Figure 11-1 **Module Relationships**

11-1 µC/TCP-IP MODULE RELATIONSHIPS

11-1-1 APPLICATION

An application provides configuration information to µC/TCP-IP in the form of four C files: `app_cfg.h`, `net_cfg.h`, `net_dev_cfg.c` and `net_dev_cfg.h`.

`app_cfg.h` is an application-specific configuration file that *must* be present in the application. `app_cfg.h` contains **`#defines`** to specify the task priorities of each of the tasks within the application (including those of µC/TCP-IP), and the stack size for those tasks. Task priorities are placed in a file to make it easier to "see" task priorities for the entire application in one place.

Configuration data in `net_cfg.h` consists of specifying the number of timers to allocate to the stack, whether or not statistic counters will be maintained, the number of ARP cache entries, how UDP checksums are computed, and more. One of the most important configurations necessary is the size of the TCP Receive Window. In all, there are approximately 50 **`#define`** to set. However, most of the **`#define`** constants can be set to their recommended default value.

Finally, `net_dev_cfg.c` consists of device-specific configuration requirements such as the number of buffers allocated to a device, the MAC address for that device, and necessary physical layer device configuration including physical layer device bus address and link characteristics. Each µC/TCP-IP-compatible device requires that its configuration be specified within `net_dev_cfg.c`.

11-1-2 µC/LIB LIBRARIES

Given that µC/TCP-IP is designed for use in safety critical applications, all "standard" library functions such as **`strcpy()`**, **`memset()`**, *etc.* have been rewritten to conform to the same quality as the rest as the protocol stack.

11

11-1-3 BSD SOCKET API LAYER

The application interfaces to µC/TCP-IP uses the BSD socket Application Programming Interface (API). The software developer can either write their own TCP/IP applications using the BSD socket API or, purchase a number of off-the-shelf TCP/IP components (Telnet, Web server, FTP server, etc.),for use with the BSD socket interface. Note that the BSD socket layer is shown as a separate module but is actually part of µC/TCP-IP.

Alternatively, the software developer can use µC/TCP-IP's own socket interface functions (`net_sock.*`). `net_bsd.*` is a layer of software that converts BSD socket calls to µC/TCP-IP socket calls. Of course, a slight performance gain is achieved by interfacing directly to `net_sock.*` functions. Micrium network products use µC/TCP-IP socket interface functions.

11-1-4 TCP/IP LAYER

The TCP/IP layer contains most of the CPU, RTOS and compiler-independent code for µC/TCP-IP. There are three categories of files in this section:

1 TCP/IP protocol specific files include:

ARP (`net_arp.*`),
ICMP (`net_icmp.*`),
IGMP (`net_igmp.*`),
IP (`net_ip.*`),
TCP (`net_tcp.*`),
UDP (`net_udp.*`)

2 Support files are:

ASCII conversions (`net_ascii.*`),
Buffer management (`net_buf.*`),
TCP/UDP connection management (`net_conn.*`),
Counter management (`net_ctr.*`),
Statistics (`net_stat.*`),
Timer Management (`net_tmr.*`),
Other utilities (`net_util.*`).

3 Miscellaneous header files include:

Master µC/TCP-IP header file (**net.h**)
File containing error codes (**net_err.h**)
Miscellaneous µC/TCP-IP data types (**net_type.h**)
Miscellaneous definitions (**net_def.h**)
Debug (**net_dbg.h**)
Configuration definitions (**net_cfg_net.h**)

11-1-5 NETWORK INTERFACE (IF) LAYER

The IF Layer involves several types of network interfaces (Ethernet, Token Ring, etc.). However, the current version of µC/TCP-IP only supports Ethernet interfaces. The IF layer is split into two sub-layers.

net_if.* is the interface between higher Network Protocol Suite layers and the link layer protocols. This layer also provides network device management routines to the application.

net_if_*.* contains the link layer protocol specifics independent of the actual device (i.e., hardware). In the case of Ethernet, **net_if_ether.*** understands Ethernet frames, MAC addresses, frame de-multiplexing, and so on, but assumes nothing regarding actual Ethernet hardware.

11-1-6 NETWORK DEVICE DRIVER LAYER

As previously stated, µC/TCP-IP works with just nearly any network device. This layer handles the specifics of the hardware, e.g., how to initialize the device, how to enable and disable interrupts from the device, how to find the size of a received packet, how to read a packet out of the frame buffer, and how to write a packet to the device, etc.

In order for device drivers to have independent configuration for clock gating, interrupt controller, and general purpose I/O, an additional file, **net_bsp.c**, encapsulates such details.

net_bsp.c contains code for the configuration of clock gating to the device, an internal or external interrupt controller, necessary IO pins, as well as time delays, getting a time stamp from the environment, and so on. This file is assumed to reside in the user application.

11-1-7 NETWORK PHYSICAL (PHY) LAYER

Often, devices interface to external physical layer devices, which may need to be initialized and controlled. This layer is shown in Figure 11-1 asa “dotted” area indicating that it is not present with all devices. In fact, some devices have PHY control built-in. Micrium provides a generic PHY driver which controls most external (R)MII compliant Ethernet physical layer devices.

11-1-8 CPU LAYER

µC/TCP-IP can work with either an 8, 16, 32 or even 64-bit CPU, but it must have information about the CPU used. The CPU layer defines such information as the C data type corresponding to 16-bit and 32-bit variables, whether the CPU is little or big endian, and how interrupts are disabled and enabled on the CPU.

CPU-specific files are found in the **...\uC-CPU** directory and are used to adapt µC/TCP-IP to a different CPU, modify either the **cpu*.*** files or, create new ones based on the ones supplied in the uC-CPU directory. In general, it is much easier to modify existing files.

11-1-9 REAL-TIME OPERATING SYSTEM (RTOS) LAYER

µC/TCP-IP assumes the presence of an RTOS, but the RTOS layer allows µC/TCP-IP to be independent of a specific RTOS. µC/TCP-IP consists of three tasks. One task is responsible for handling packet reception, another task for asynchronous transmit buffer de-allocation, and the last task for managing timers. Depending on the configuration, a fourth task may be present to handle loopback operation.

As a minimum, the RTOS:

1 Must be able to create at least three tasks (a Receive Task, a Transmit De-allocation Task, and a Timer Task)

2 Provide semaphore management (or the equivalent) and the µC/TCP-IP needs to be able to create at least two semaphores for each socket and an additional four semaphores for internal use.

3 Provides timer management services

4 Port must also include support for pending on multiple OS objects if BSD socket `select()` is required.

µC/TCP-IP is provided with a µC/OS-II and µC/OS-III interface. If a different RTOS is used, the **net_os.*** for µC/OS-II or µC/OS-III can be used as templates to interface to the RTOS chosen.

11-2 TASK MODEL

The user application interfaces to µC/TCP-IP via a well known API called BSD sockets (or µC/TCP-IP's internal socket interface). The application can send and receive data to/from other hosts on the network via this interface.

The BSD socket API interfaces to internal structures and variables (i.e., data) that are maintained by µC/TCP-IP. A binary semaphore (the global lock in Figure 11-2) is used to guard access to this data to ensure exclusive access. In order to read or write to this data, a task needs to acquire the binary semaphore before it can access the data and release it when finished. Of course, the application tasks do not have to know anything about this semaphore nor the data since its use is encapsulated by functions within µC/TCP-IP.

Figure 11-2 shows a simplified task model of µC/TCP-IP along with application tasks.

11-2-1 µC/TCP-IP TASKS AND PRIORITIES

µC/TCP-IP defines three internal tasks: a Receive Task, a Transmit De-allocation Task, and a Timer Task. The Receive Task is responsible for processing received packets from all devices. The Transmit De-allocation Task frees transmit buffer resources when they are no longer required. The Timer Task is responsible for handling all timeouts related to TCP/IP protocols and network interface management.

When setting up task priorities, we generally recommend that tasks that use µC/TCP-IP's services be configured with higher priorities than µC/TCP-IP's internal tasks. However, application tasks that use µC/TCP-IP should voluntarily relinquish the CPU on a regular basis. For example, they can delay or suspend the tasks or wait on µC/TCP-IP services. This is to reduce starvation issues when an application task sends a substantial amount of data.

We recommend that you configure the Network Interface Transmit De-allocation Task with a higher priority than all application tasks that use µC/TCP-IP network services; but configure the Timer Task and Network Interface Receive Task with lower priorities than almost other application tasks.

See also section C-20-1 "Operating System Configuration" on page 749.

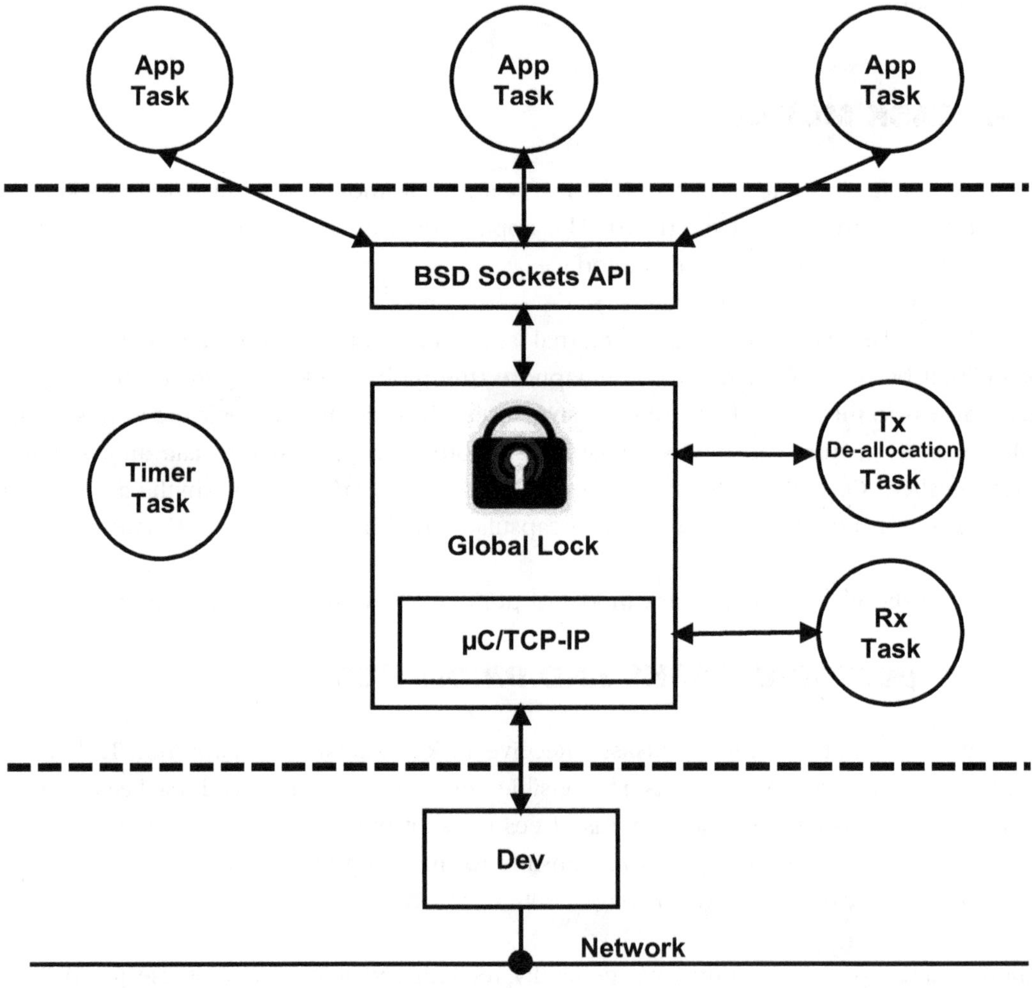

Figure 11-2 **µC/TCP-IP Task Model**

11-2-2 RECEIVING A PACKET

Figure 11-3 shows a simplified task model of µC/TCP-IP when packets are received from the device.

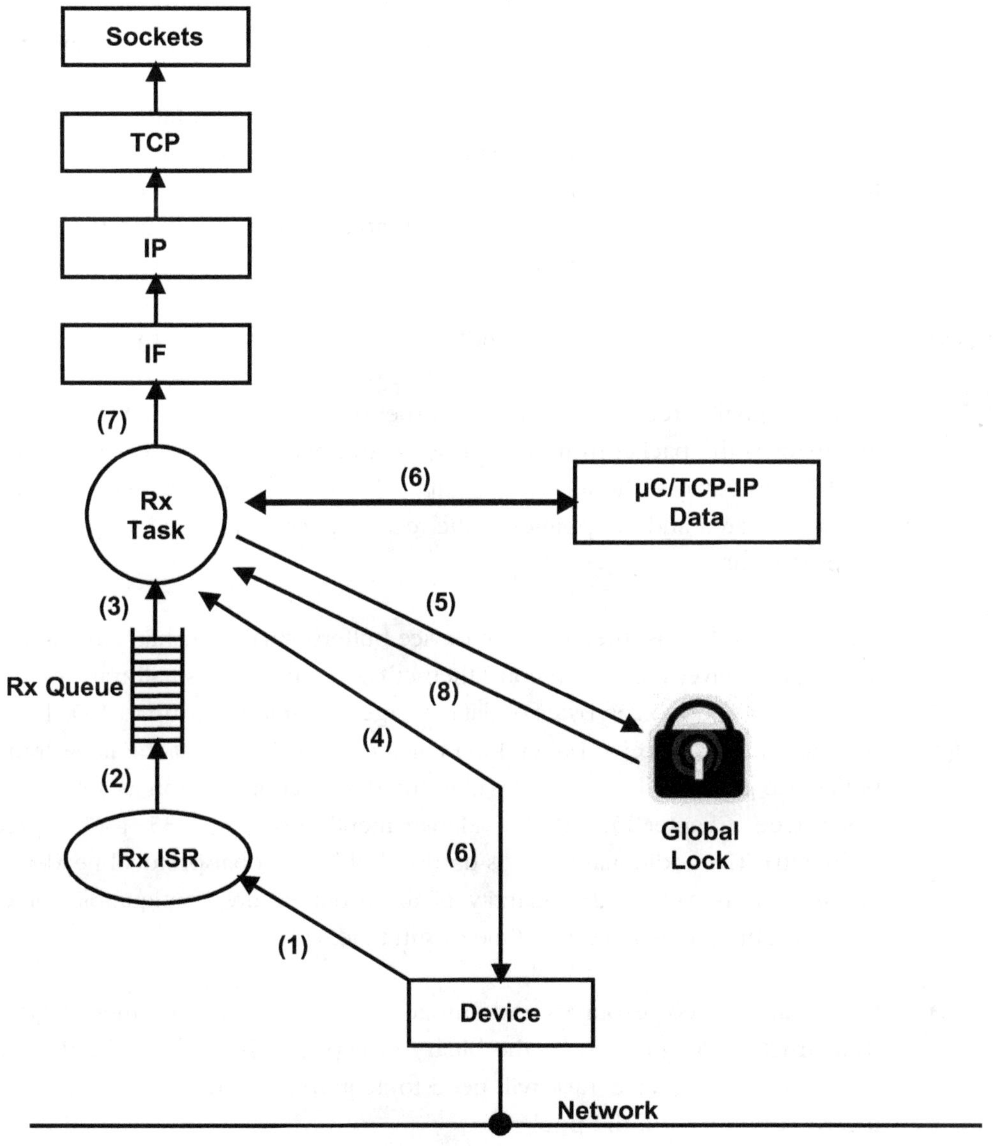

Figure 11-3 **µC/TCP-IP Receiving a Packet**

F11-3(1) A packet is sent on the network and the device recognizes its address as the destination for the packet. The device then generates an interrupt and the BSP global ISR handler is called for non-vectored interrupt controllers. Either the global ISR handler or the vectored interrupt controller calls the Net BSP device specific ISR handler, which in turn indirectly calls the device ISR handler using a predefined Net IF function call. The device ISR handler determines that the interrupt comes from a packet reception (as opposed to the completion of a transmission).

F11-3(2) Instead of processing the received packet directly from the ISR, it was decided to pass the responsibility to a task. The Rx ISR therefore simply "signals" the Receive Task by posting the interface number to the Receive Task queue. Note that further Rx interrupts are generally disabled while processing the interrupt within the device ISR handler.

F11-3(3) The Receive Task does nothing until a signal is received from the *Rx ISR*.

F11-3(4) When a signal is received from an Ethernet device, the Receive Task wakes up and extracts the packet from the hardware and places it in a receive buffer. For DMA based devices, the receive descriptor buffer pointer is updated to point to a new data area and the pointer to the receive packet is passed to higher layers for processing.

µC/TCP-IP maintains three types of device buffers: small transmit, large transmit, and large receive. For a common Ethernet configuration, a small transmit buffer typically holds up to 256 bytes of data, a large transmit buffer up to 1500 bytes of data, and a large receive buffer 1500 bytes of data. Note that the large transmit buffer size is generally specified within the device configuration as 1594 or 1614 bytes (see Chapter 15, "Buffer Management" on page 335 for a precise definition). The additional space is used to hold additional protocol header data. These sizes as well as the quantity of these buffers are configurable for each interface during either compile time or run time.

F11-3(5) Buffers are shared resources and any access to those or any other µC/TCP-IP data structures is guarded by the binary semaphore that guards the data. This means that the Receive Task will need to acquire the semaphore before it can receive a buffer from the pool.

F11-3(6) The Receive Task gets a buffer from the buffer pool. The packet is removed from the device and placed in the buffer for further processing. For DMA, the acquired buffer pointer replaces the descriptor buffer pointer that received the current frame. The pointer to the received frame is passed to higher layers for further processing.

F11-3(7) The Receive Task examines received data via the appropriate link layer protocol and determines whether the packet is destined for the ARP or IP layer, and passes the buffer to the appropriate layer for further processing. Note that the Receive Task brings the data all the way up to the application layer and therefore the appropriate µC/TCP-IP functions operate within the context of the Receive Task.

F11-3(8) When the packet is processed, the lock is released and the Receive Task waits for the next packet to be received.

11

11-2-3 TRANSMITTING A PACKET

Figure 11-4 shows a simplified task model of µC/TCP-IP when packets are transmitted through the device.

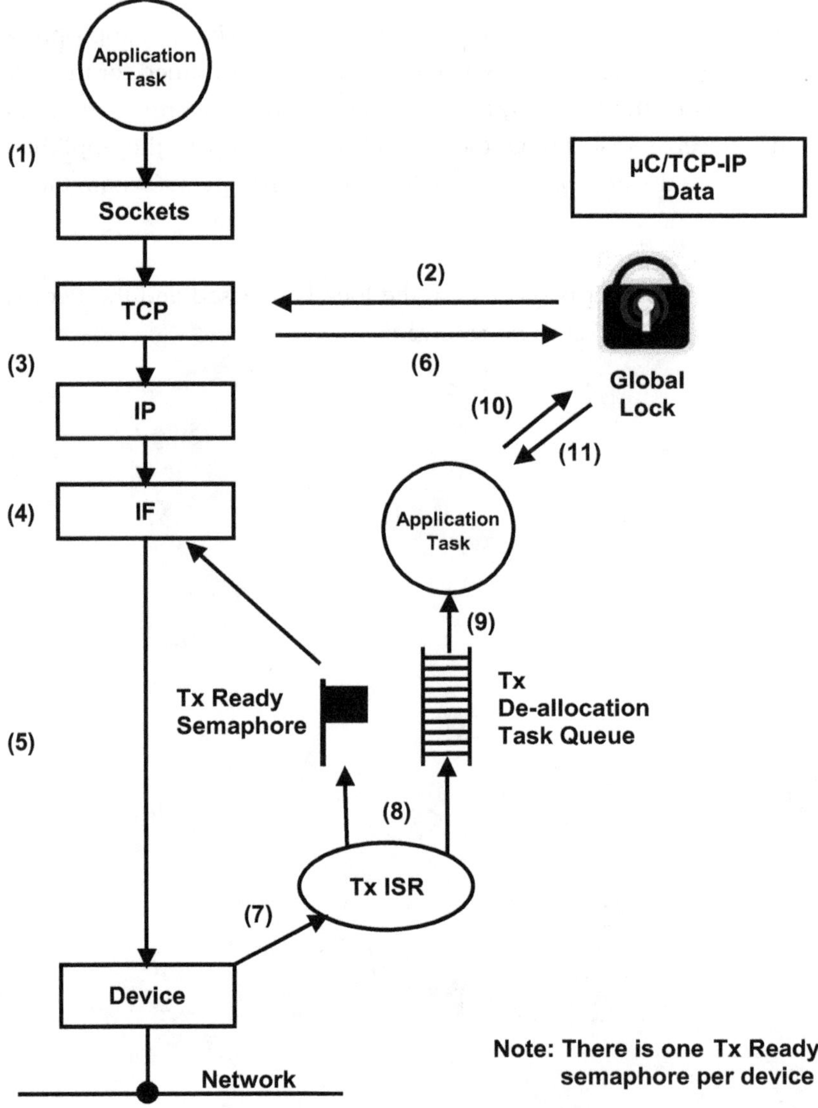

Figure 11-4 **µC/TCP-IP Sending a Packet**

F11-4(1) A task (assuming an application task) that wants to send data interfaces to µC/TCP-IP through the BSD socket API.

F11-4(2) A function within µC/TCP-IP acquires the binary semaphore (i.e., the global lock) in order to place the data to send into µC/TCP-IP's data structures.

F11-4(3) The appropriate µC/TCP-IP layer processes the data, preparing it for transmission.

F11-4(4) The task (via the IF layer) then waits on a counting semaphore, which is used to indicate that the transmitter in the device is available to send a packet. If the device is not able to send the packet, the task blocks until the semaphore is signaled by the device. Note that during device initialization, the semaphore is initialized with a value corresponding to the number of packets that can be sent at one time through the device. If the device has sufficient buffer space to be able to queue up four packets, then the counting semaphore is initialized with a count of 4. For DMA-based devices, the value of the semaphore is initialized to the number of available transmit descriptors.

F11-4(5) When the device is ready, the driver either copies the data to the device internal memory space or configures the DMA transmit descriptor. When the device is fully configured, the device driver issues a transmit command.

F11-4(6) After placing the packet into the device, the task releases the global data lock and continues execution.

F11-4(7) When the device finishes sending the data, the device generates an interrupt.

F11-4(8) The Tx ISR signals the Tx Available semaphore indicating that the device is able to send another packet. Additionally, the Tx ISR handler passes the address of the buffer that completed transmission to the Transmit De-allocation Task via a queue which is encapsulated by an OS port function call.

F11-4(9) The Transmit De-allocation Task wakes up when a device driver posts a transmit buffer address to its queue.

F11-4(10) The global data lock is acquired. If the global data lock is held by another task, the Transmit De-allocation Task must wait to acquire the global data lock. Since it is recommended that the Transmit De-allocation Task be configured as the highest priority µC/TCP-IP task, it will run following the release of the global data lock, assuming the queue has at least one entry present.

F11-4(11) The lock is released when transmit buffer de-allocation is finished. Further transmission and reception of additional data by application and µC/TCP-IP tasks may resume.

Chapter

12

Directories and Files

This chapter will discuss the modules available for µC/TCP-IP, and how they all fit together. A Windows®-based development platform is assumed. The directories and files make references to typical Windows-type directory structures. However, since µC/TCP-IP is available in source form, it can also be used with any ANSI-C compatible compiler/linker and any Operating System.

The names of the files are shown in upper case to make them stand out. However, file names are actually lower case.

12-1 BLOCK DIAGRAM

Figure 12-1 is a block diagram of the modules found in µC/TCP-IP and their relationship. Also included are the names of the files that are related to µC/TCP-IP

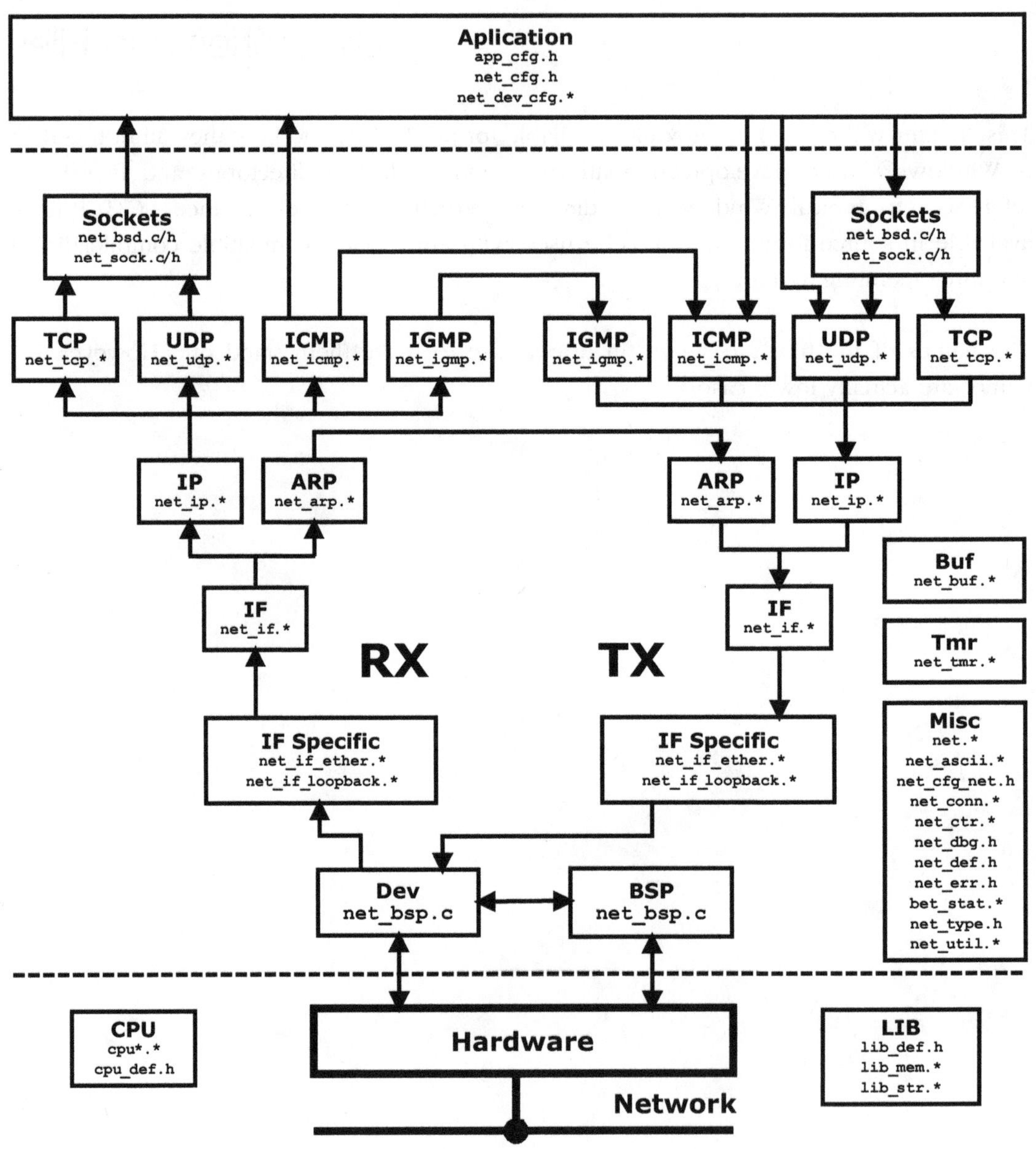

Figure 12-1 **µC/TCP-IP Block Diagram**

12-2 APPLICATION CODE

When Micrium provides example projects, they are placed in a directory structure shown below. Of course, a directory structure that suits a particular project/product can be used.

```
\Micrium
    \Software
        \EvalBoards
            \<manufacturer>
                \<board_name>
                    \<compiler>
                        \<project name>
                            \*.*
```

\Micrium
This is where we place all software components and projects provided by Micrium. This directory generally starts from the root directory of the computer.

\Software
This sub-directory contains all software components and projects.

\EvalBoards
This sub-directory contains all projects related to evaluation boards supported by Micrium.

\<manufacturer>
This is the name of the manufacturer of the evaluation board. The ‘<’ and ‘>’ are not part of the actual name.

\<board name>
This is the name of the evaluation board. A board from Micrium will typically be called `uC-Eval-xxxx` where `xxxx` represents the CPU or MCU used on the board. The ‘<’ and ‘>’ are not part of the actual name.

\<compiler>
This is the name of the compiler or compiler manufacturer used to build the code for the evaluation board. The ‘<’ and ‘>’ are not part of the actual name.

\<project name>

The name of the project that will be demonstrated. For example a simple µC/TCP-IP project might have a project name of '**OS-Ex1**'. The '**-Ex1**' represents a project containing only µC/OS-III. A project name of **OS-Probe-Ex1** contains µC/TCP-IP and µC/Probe. The '<' and '>' are not part of the actual name.

.

These are the source files for the project. Main files can optionally be called **APP*.***. This directory also contains configuration files **app_cfg.h**, **net_cfg.h**, **net_decv_cfg.h**, **net_dev_cfg.c**,**os_cfg.h**, **os_cfg_app.h** and other project-required source files.

includes.h is the application-specific master include header file. Almost all Micrium products require this file.

net_cfg.h is a configuration file used to configure such µC/TCP-IP parameters as the number of network timers, sockets, and connections created; default timeout values, and more. **net_cfg.h** *must* be included in the application as µC/TCP-IP requires this file. See Chapter 16, "Network Interface Layer" on page 343 for more information.

net_dev_cfg.c and **net_dev_cfg.h** are configuration files used to configure µC/TCP-IP interface parameters such as the number of transmit and receive buffers. See Chapter 14, "Network Device Drivers" on page 299 on interface configuration for more details.

os_cfg.h is a configuration file used to configure µC/OS-III parameters such as the maximum number of tasks, events, and objects; which µOS-III services are enabled (semaphores, mailboxes, queues); *etc.* **os_cfg.h**is a required file for any µC/OS-III application. See µC/OS-III documentation and books for further information.

app.c contains the application code for the Processor example project. As with most C programs, code execution starts at **main()** which is shown in Listing 13-1 on page 291. The application code starts µC/TCP-IP.

12-3 CPU

The directory shown below contains semiconductor manufacturer peripheral interface source files. Any directory structure that suits the project/product may be used.

```
\Micrium
    \Software
        \CPU
            \<manufacturer>
                \<architecture>
                    \*.*
```

\Micrium

The location of all software components and projects provided by Micrium.

\Software

This sub-directory contains all software components and projects.

\CPU

This sub-directory is always called CPU.

\<manufacturer>

Is the name of the semiconductor manufacturer providing the peripheral library. The **<** and **>** are not part of the actual name.

\<architecture>

The name of the specific library, generally associated with a CPU name or an architecture.

.

Indicates library source files. The semiconductor manufacturer names the files.

12-4 BOARD SUPPORT PACKAGE (BSP)

The Board Support Package (BSP) is generally found with the evaluation or target board, and it is specific to that board. In fact, when well written, the BSP should be used for multiple projects.

```
\Micrium
    \Software
        \EvalBoards
            \<manufacturer>
                \<board name>
                    \<compiler>
                        \BSP
                            \*.*
```

\Micrium
Contains all software components and projects provided by Micrium.

\Software
This sub-directory contains all software components and projects.

\EvalBoards
This sub-directory contains all projects related to evaluation boards.

\<manufacturer>
The name of the manufacturer of the evaluation board. The **<** and **>** are not part of the actual name.

\<board name>
The name of the evaluation board. A board from Micrium will typically be called **uC-Eval-xxxx** where **xxxx** is the name of the CPU or MCU used on the evaluation board. The **<** and **>** are not part of the actual name.

\<compiler>
The name of the compiler or compiler manufacturer used to build code for the evaluation board. The **<** and **>** are not part of the actual name.

\BSP
This directory is always called BSP.

.

The source files of the BSP. Typically all of the file names start with BSP. It is therefore normal to find **bsp.c** and **bsp.h** in this directory. BSP code should contain such functions as LED control functions, initialization of timers, interface to Ethernet controllers, and more.

BSP stands for Board Support Package and the 'services' the board provides are placed in such a file. In this case, **bsp.c** contains I/O, timer initialization code, LED control code, and more. The I/Os used on the board are initialized when **BSP_Init()** is called.

The concept of a BSP is to hide the hardware details from the application code. It is important that functions in a BSP reflect the function and do not make references to any CPU specifics. For example, the code to turn on an LED is called **LED_On()** and not **MCU_led()**. If **LED_On()** is used in the code, it can be easily ported to another processor (or board) by simply rewriting **LED_On()** to control the LEDs on a different board. The same is true for other services. Also notice that BSP functions are prefixed with the function's group. LED services start with **LED_**, timer services start with **Tmr_**, etc. In other words, BSP functions do not need to be prefixed by **BSP_**.

12-5 NETWORK BOARD SUPPORT PACKAGE (NET_BSP)

In addition to the general (BSP) there are specific network initialization and configuration requirements. This additional file is generally found with the evaluation or target board as it is specific to that board.

```
\Micrium
    \Software
        \EvalBoards
            \<manufacturer>
                \<board name>
                    \<compiler>
                        \BSP
                            \TCPIP-V2
                                \*.*
```

\Micrium
Contains all software components and projects provided by Micrium.

\Software
This sub-directory contains all software components and projects.

\EvalBoards
This sub-directory contains all projects related to evaluation boards.

\<manufacturer>
The name of the manufacturer of the evaluation board. The '<' and '>' are not part of the actual name.

\<board name>
The name of the evaluation board. A board from Micrium will typically be called `uC-Eval-xxxx` where `xxxx` is the name of the CPU or MCU used on the evaluation board. The '<' and '>' are not part of the actual name.

\<compiler>
The name of the compiler or compiler manufacturer used to build code for the evaluation board. The '<' and '>' are not part of the actual name.

\BSP
This directory is always called BSP.

\TCPIP-V2
This directory is always called TCPIP-V2 as it is the directory for the network related BSP files.

.
The `net_bsp.*` files contain hardware-dependent code specific to the network device(s) and other µC/TCP-IP functions. Specifically, these files may contain code to read data from and write data to network devices, handle hardware-level device interrupts, provide delay functions, and get time stamps, etc.

12-6 µC/OS-III, CPU INDEPENDENT SOURCE CODE

The files in these directories are available to µC/OS-III licensees (see Appendix X, "Licensing Policy").

```
\Micrium
    \Software
        \uCOS-III
            \Cfg\Template
            \Source
```

\Micrium
Contains all software components and projects provided by Micrium.

\Software
This sub-directory contains all software components and projects.

\uCOS-III
This is the main µC/OS-III directory.

\Cfg\Template
This directory contains examples of configuration files to copy to the project directory. These files can be modified to suit the needs of the application.

\Source
The directory contains the CPU-independent source code for µC/OS-III. All files in this directory should be included in the build (assuming the presence of the source code). Features that are not required will be compiled out based on the value of #define constants in os_cfg.h and os_cfg_app.h.

12-7 µC/OS-III, CPU SPECIFIC SOURCE CODE

The µC/OS-III port developer provides these files. See Chapter 17 in the µC/OS-III book.

```
\Micrium
    \Software
        \uCOS-III
            \Ports
                \<architecture>
                    \<compiler>
```


\Micrium
Contains all software components and projects provided by Micrium.

\Software
This sub-directory contains all software components and projects.

\uCOS-III
The main µC/OS-III directory.

\Ports
The location of port files for the CPU architecture(s) to be used.

\<architecture>
This is the name of the CPU architecture that µC/OS-III was ported to. The '<' and '>' are not part of the actual name.

\<compiler>
The name of the compiler or compiler manufacturer used to build code for the port. The **<** and **>** are not part of the actual name.

The files in this directory contain the µC/OS-III port, see Chapter 17 "Porting µC/OS-III" in the µC/OS-III book for details on the contents of these files.

12-8 µC/CPU, CPU SPECIFIC SOURCE CODE

µC/CPU consists of files that encapsulate common CPU-specific functionality and CPU and compiler-specific data types.

```
\Micrium
    \Software
        \uC-CPU
            \cpu_core.c
            \cpu_core.h
            \cpu_def.h
            \Cfg\Template
                \cpu_cfg.h
            \<architecture>
                \<compiler>
                    \cpu.h
                    \cpu_a.asm
                    \cpu_c.c
```

\Micrium
Contains all software components and projects provided by Micrium.

\Software
This sub-directory contains all software components and projects.

\uC-CPU
This is the main µC/CPU directory.

cpu_core.c contains C code that is common to all CPU architectures. Specifically, this file contains functions to measure the interrupt disable time of the CPU_CRITICAL_ENTER() and CPU_CRITICAL_EXIT() macros, a function that emulates a count leading zeros instruction and a few other functions.

cpu_core.h contains function prototypes for the functions provided in cpu_core.c and allocation of the variables used by the module to measure interrupt disable time.

cpu_def.h contains miscellaneous #define constants used by the µC/CPU module.

\Cfg\Template

This directory contains a configuration template file (**cpu_cfg.h**) that is required to be copied to the application directory to configure the µC/CPU module based on application requirements.

cpu_cfg.h determines whether to enable measurement of the interrupt disable time, whether the CPU implements a count leading zeros instruction in assembly language, or whether it will be emulated in C, and more.

\<architecture>

The name of the CPU architecture that µC/CPU was ported to. The '<' and '>' are not part of the actual name.

\<compiler>

The name of the compiler or compiler manufacturer used to build code for the µC/CPU port. The '<' and '>' are not part of the actual name.

The files in this directory contain the µC/CPU port, see Chapter 17 of the µC/OS-III book, "Porting µC/OS-III" for details on the contents of these files.

cpu.h contains type definitions to make µC/OS-III and other modules independent of the CPU and compiler word sizes. Specifically, one will find the declaration of the CPU_INT16U, CPU_INT32U, CPU_FP32 and many other data types. This file also specifies whether the CPU is a big or little endian machine, defines the CPU_STK data type used by µC/OS-III, defines the macros OS_CRITICAL_ENTER() and OS_CRITICAL_EXIT(), and contains function prototypes for functions specific to the CPU architecture, etc.

cpu_a.asm contains the assembly language functions to implement code to disable and enable CPU interrupts, count leading zeros (if the CPU supports that instruction), and other CPU specific functions that can only be written in assembly language. This file may also contain code to enable caches, and setup MPUs and MMU. The functions provided in this file are accessible from C.

cpu_c.c contains the C code of functions that are based on a specific CPU architecture but written in C for portability. As a general rule, if a function can be written in C then it should be, unless there is significant performance benefits available by writing it in assembly language.

12-9 μC/LIB, PORTABLE LIBRARY FUNCTIONS

μC/LIB consists of library functions meant to be highly portable and not tied to any specific compiler. This facilitates third-party certification of Micrium products. μC/OS-III does not use any μC/LIB functions, however the μC/CPU assumes the presence of **lib_def.h** for such definitions as: DEF_YES, DEF_NO, DEF_TRUE, DEF_FALSE, *etc.*

```
\Micrium
    \Software
        \uC-LIB
            \lib_ascii.c
            \lib_ascii.h
            \lib_def.h
            \lib_math.c
            \lib_math.h
            \lib_mem.c
            \lib_mem.h
            \lib_str.c
            \lib_str.h
            \Cfg\Template
                \lib_cfg.h
            \Ports
                \<architecture>
                    \<compiler>
                        \lib_mem_a.asm
```

\Micrium
Contains all software components and projects provided by Micrium.

\Software
This sub-directory contains all software components and projects.

\uC-LIB
This is the main μC/LIB directory.

\Cfg\Template
This directory contains a configuration template file (**lib_cfg.h**) that is required to be copied to the application directory to configure the µC/LIB module based on application requirements.

> **lib_cfg.h** determines whether to enable assembly language optimization (assuming there is an assembly language file for the processor, i.e., **lib_mem_a.asm**) and a few other **#defines**.

12

12-10 µC/TCP-IP NETWORK DEVICES

The files in these directories are

```
\Micrium
    \Software
        \uC-TCPIP-V2
            \Dev
                \Ether
                    \PHY
                        \Generic
                    \<Controller>
```

\Micrium
Contains all software components and projects provided by Micrium.

\Software
This sub-directory contains all software components and projects.

\uC-TCPIP-V2
This is the main directory for the µC/TCP-IP code. The name of the directory contains a version number to differentiate it from previous versions of the stack.

\Dev
This directory contains device drivers for different interfaces. Currently, µC/TCP-IP only supports one type of interface, Ethernet. µC/TCP-IP is tested with many types of Ethernet devices.

\Ether

Ethernet controller drivers are placed under the Ether sub-directory. Note that device drivers must also be called **net_dev_<controller>.***.

\PHY

This is the main directory for Ethernet Physical layer drivers.

\Generic

This is the directory for the Micrium provided generic PHY driver. Micrium's generic Ethernet PHY driver provides sufficient support for most (R)MII compliant Ethernet physical layer devices. A specific PHY driver may be developed in order to provide extended functionality such as link state interrupt support.

net_phy.h is the network physical layer header file.

net_phy.c provides the (R)MII interface port that is assumed to be part of the host Ethernet MAC. Therefore, (R)MII reads/writes *must* be performed through the network device API interface via calls to function pointers **Phy_RegRd()** and **Phy_RegWr()**.

\<controller>

The name of the Ethernet Controller or chip manufacturer used in the project. The '<' and '>' are not part of the actual name. This directory contains the network device driver for the Network Controller specified.

net_dev_<controller>.h is the header file for the network device driver.

net_dev_<controller>.c contains C code for the network device driver API.

12

12-11 µC/TCP-IP NETWORK INTERFACE

This directory contains interface-specific files. Currently, µC/TCP-IP only supports two type of interfaces, Ethernet and Loopback. The Ethernet interface-specific files are found in the following directories:

```
\Micrium
    \Software
        \uC-TCPIP-V2
            \IF
```

\Micrium
Contains all software components and projects provided by Micrium.

\Software
This sub-directory contains all software components and projects.

\uC-TCPIP-V2
This is the main µC/TCP-IP directory.

\IF
This is the main directory for network interfaces.

net_if.* presents a programming interface between higher µC/TCP-IP layers and the link layer protocols. These files also provide interface management routines to the application.

net_if_ether.* contains the Ethernet interface specifics. This file should not need to be modified.

net_if_loopback.* contains loopback interface specifics. This file should not need to be modified.

12-12 µC/TCP-IP NETWORK OS ABSTRACTION LAYER

This directory contains the RTOS abstraction layer which allows the use of µC/TCP-IP with nearly any commercial or in-house RTOS. The abstraction layer for the selected RTOS is placed in a sub-directory under OS as follows:

```
\Micrium
    \Software
        \uC-TCPIP-V2
            \OS
                \<rtos_name>
```

\Micrium
Contains all software components and projects provided by Micrium.

\Software
This sub-directory contains all software components and projects.

\uC-TCPIP-V2
This is the main µC/TCP-IP directory.

\OS
This is the main OS directory.

\<rtos_name>
This is the directory that contains the files to perform RTOS abstraction. Note that files for the selected RTOS abstraction layer must always be named **net_os.***.

µC/TCP-IP has been tested with µC/OS-II, µC/OS-III and the RTOS layer files for these RTOS are found in the following directories:

```
\Micrium\Software\uC-TCPIP-V2\OS\uCOS-II\net_os.*

\Micrium\Software\uC-TCPIP-V2\OS\uCOS-III\net_os.*
```

12-13 μC/TCP-IP NETWORK CPU SPECIFIC CODE

Some functions can be optimized in assembly to improve the performance of the network protocol stack. An easy candidate is the checksum function. It is used at multiple levels in the stack, and a checksum is generally coded as a long loop.


```
\Micrium
    \Software
        \uC-TCPIP-V2
            \Ports
                \<architecture>
                    \<compiler>
                        \net_util_a.asm
```

\Micrium
Contains all software components and projects provided by Micrium.

\Software
This sub-directory contains all software components and projects.

\uC-TCPIP-V2
This is the main μC/TCP-IP directory.

\Ports
This is the main directory for processor specific code.

\<architecture>
The name of the CPU architecture that was ported to. The '<' and '>' are not part of the actual name.

\<compiler>
The name of the compiler or compiler manufacturer used to build code for the optimized function(s). The '<' and '>' are not part of the actual name.

net_util_a.asm contains assembly code for the specific CPU architecture. All functions that can be optimized for the CPU architecture are located here.

12-14 μC/TCP-IP NETWORK CPU INDEPENDENT SOURCE CODE

This directory contains all the CPU and RTOS independent files for μC/TCP-IP. Nothing should be changed in this directory in order to use μC/TCP-IP.

```
\Micrium
    \Software
        \uC-TCPIP-V2
            \Source
```

\Micrium
Contains all software components and projects provided by Micrium.

\Software
This sub-directory contains all software components and projects.

\uC-TCPIP-V2
This is the main μC/TCP-IP directory.

\Source
This is the directory that contains all the CPU and RTOS independent source code files.

12-15 µC/TCP-IP NETWORK SECURITY MANAGER CPU INDEPENDENT SOURCE CODE

This directory contains all the CPU independent files for µC/TCP-IP Network Security Manager. Nothing should be changed in this directory in order to use µC/TCP-IP.

```
\Micrium
    \Software
        \uC-TCPIP-V2
            \Secure
                \<security_suite_name>
                    \OS
                        \<rtos_name>
```

\Micrium
Contains all software components and projects provided by Micrium.

\Software
This sub-directory contains all software components and projects.

\uC-TCPIP-V2
This is the main µC/TCP-IP directory.

\Secure
This is the directory that contains all the security suite independent source code files. These files must be included in the project even if no security suite is available or if the Network Security Manager is disabled.

\<security_suite_name>
This is the directory that contains the files to perform security suite abstraction. These files should only be included in the project if a security suite (i.e µC/SSL) is available and is to be used by the application.

\<rtos_name>
This is the directory that contains the RTOS dependent files of the security suite layer, if any. These files should only be included in the project if the a security suite (i.e µC/SSL) is available and is to be used by the application. It is possible that a security suite does not require an OS abstraction layer. Please refer to the security suite user's manual for more information.

µC/TCP-IP has been tested with µC/SSL, µC/OS-II and µC/OS-III. The security suite and RTOS files for this security suite are found in the following directories:

```
\Micrium\Software\uC-TCPIP-V2\Secure\uC-SSL\net_secure.*

\Micrium\Software\uC-TCPIP-V2\Secure\uC-SSL\OS\uCOS-II\net_secure_os.*
\Micrium\Software\uC-TCPIP-V2\Secure\uC-SSL\OS\uCOS-III\net_secure_os.*
```

12-16 SUMMARY

Below is a summary of all directories and files involved in a µC/TCP-IP-based project. The '**<-Cfg**' on the far right indicates that these files are typically copied into the application (i.e., project) directory and edited based on project requirements.

```
\Micrium
    \Software
        \EvalBoards
            \<manufacturer>
                \<board name>
                    \<compiler>
                        \<project name>
                            \app.c
                            \app.h
                            \other
                        \BSP
                            \bsp.c
                            \bsp.h
                            \others
                            \TCPIP-V2
                                \net_bsp.c
                                \net_bsp.h
```

```
\CPU
    \<manufacturer>
        \<architecture>
            \*.*
\uCOS-III
    \Cfg\Template
        \os_app_hooks.c
        \os_cfg.h                         <-Cfg
        \os_cfg_app.h                     <-Cfg
    \Source
        \os_cfg_app.c
        \os_core.c
        \os_dbg.c
        \os_flag.c
        \os_int.c
        \os_mem.c
        \os_msg.c
        \os_mutex.c
        \os_pend_multi.c
        \os_prio.c
        \os_q.c
        \os_sem.c
        \os_stat.c
        \os_task.c
        \os_tick.c
        \os_time.c
        \os_tmr.c
        \os_var.c
        \os.h
        \os_type.h                         <-Cfg
    \Ports
        \<architecture>
            \<compiler>
                \os_cpu.h
                \os_cpu_a.asm
                \os_cpu_c.c
```

```
\uC-CPU
    \cpu_core.c
    \cpu_core.h
    \cpu_def.h
    \Cfg\Template
        \cpu_cfg.h                          <-Cfg
    \<architecture>
        \<compiler>
            \cpu.h
            \cpu_a.asm
            \cpu_c.c
\uC-LIB
    \lib_ascii.c
    \lib_ascii.h
    \lib_def.h
    \lib_math.c
    \lib_math.h
    \lib_mem.c
    \lib_mem.h
    \lib_str.c
    \lib_str.h
    \Cfg\Template
        \lib_cfg.h                          <-Cfg
    \Ports
        \<architecture>
            \<compiler>
                \lib_mem_a.asm
\uC-TCPIP-V2
    \BSP
        Template
            \net_bsp.c                      <-Cfg
            \net_bsp.h                      <-Cfg
            OS
                \<rtos_name>
                    \net_bsp.c              <-Cfg
```

```
\CFG
    \Template
        \net_cfg.h                          <-Cfg
        \net_dev_cfg.c                      <-Cfg
        \net_dev_cfg.h                      <-Cfg
\Dev
    \Ether
        \<controller>
            \net_dev_<controller>.c
            \net_dev_<controller>.h
        \PHY
            \controller>
                \net_phy_<controller>.c
                \net_phy_<controller>.h
            \Generic
                \net_phy.c
                \net_phy.h
\IF
    \net_if.c
    \net_if.h
    \net_if_ether.c
    \net_if_ether.h
    \net_if_loopback.c
    \net_if_loopback.h
\OS
    \<template>
        \net_os.c                          <-Cfg
        \net_os.h                          <-Cfg
    \<rtos_name>
        \net_os.c
        \net_os.h
\Ports
    \<architecture>
        \<compiler>
            \net_util_a.asm
```

```
\Secure
    \net_secure_mgr.c
    \net_secure_mgr.h
    \<security_suite_name>
        \net_secure.c
        \NET_secure.h
        \OS
            \<rtos_name>
                \net_secure_os.c
                \net_secure_os.h
\Source
    \net.c
    \net.h
    \net_app.c
    \net_app.h
    \net_arp.c
    \net_arp.h
    \net_ascii.c
    \net_ascii.h
    \net.bsd.c
    \net.bsd.h
    \net.buf.c
    \net.buf.h
    \net.cfg_net.h
    \net.conn.c
    \net.conn.h
    \net.ctr.c
    \net.ctr.h
    \net.dbg.c
    \net.dbg.h
    \net.def.h
    \net.err.c
    \net.err.h
    \net.icmp.c
    \net.icmp.h
    \net.igmp.c
    \net.igmp.h
    \net.ip.c
```

\net.ip.h
\net.mgr.c
\net.mgr.h
\net.sock.c
\net.sock.h
\net.stat.c
\net.stat.h
\net.tcp.c
\net.tcp.h
\net.tmr.c
\net.tmr.h
\net.type.h
\net.udp.c
\net.udp.h
\net.util.c
\net.util.h

Chapter

13

Getting Started with μC/TCP-IP

As previously stated, the Directories and Files structure used herein assumes access to μC/TCP-IP source code. The samples and examples in Part II of this book, however, use μC/TCP-IP as a library. The project structure is therefore different.

μC/TCP-IP requires an RTOS and, for the purposes of this book, μC/OS-III has been chosen. First, because it is the latest kernel from Micrium, and second, because all the examples in this book were developed with the evaluation board that is available with the μC/OS-III book. This way there is no need for an additional evaluation board.

13-1 INSTALLING μC/TCP-IP

Distribution of μC/TCP-IP is performed through release files. The release archive files contain all of the source code and documentation for μC/TCP-IP. Additional support files such as those located within the CPU directory may or may not be required depending on the target hardware and development tools. Example startup code, if available, may be delivered upon request. Example code is located in the Evalboards directory when applicable.

Figure 13-1 **Directory tree for μC/TCP-IP**

13-2 µC/TCP-IP EXAMPLE PROJECT

The following example project is used to show the basic architecture of µC/TCP-IP and to build an empty application. The application also uses µC/OS-III as the RTOS. Figure 13-1 shows the project test setup. A Windows-based PC and the target system were connected to a 100 Mbps Ethernet switch or via an Ethernet cross-over cable. The PC's IP address is set to 10.10.10.111 and one of the target's addresses is configured to 10.10.10.64.

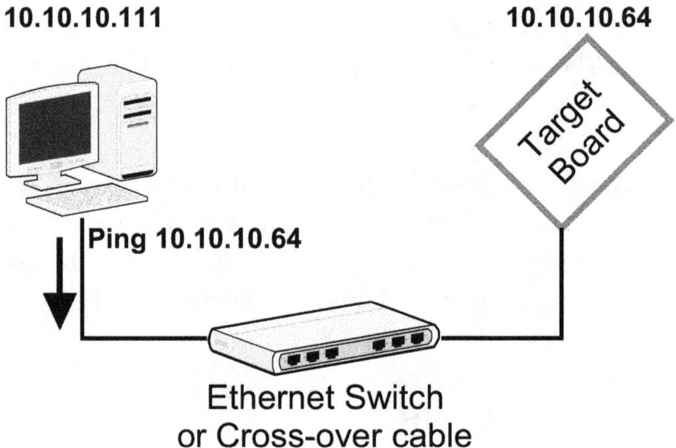

Figure 13-2 **Test setup**

This example contains enough code to be able to ping the board.The IP address of the board is forced to be 10.10.10.64. With a similar setup, the following command from a command-prompt is issued:

```
ping 10.10.10.64
```

Ping (on the PC) should reply back with the ping time to the target. µC/TCP-IP target projects connected to the test PC on the same Ethernet switch or Ethernet cross-over cable achieve ping times of less than 2 milliseconds.

The next sections show the directory tree of different components required to build a µC/TCP-IP example project.

13-3 APPLICATION CODE

File **app.c** contains the application code for the Processor example project. As with most C programs, code execution starts at **main()** which is shown in Listing 13-1. The application code starts µC/TCP-IP.

```
void  main (void)
{
    OS_ERR  err_os;

    BSP_IntDisAll();                                                            (1)

    OSInit(&err_os);                                                            (2)
    APP_TEST_FAULT(err_os, OS_ERR_NONE);

    OSTaskCreate((OS_TCB     *)&AppTaskStartTCB,                                (3)
                 (CPU_CHAR   *)"App Task Start",                                (4)
                 (OS_TASK_PTR ) AppTaskStart,                                   (5)
                 (void       *) 0,                                              (6)
                 (OS_PRIO     ) APP_OS_CFG_START_TASK_PRIO,                     (7)
                 (CPU_STK    *)&AppTaskStartStk[0],                             (8)
                 (CPU_STK_SIZE) APP_OS_CFG_START_TASK_STK_SIZE / 10u,           (9)
                 (CPU_STK_SIZE) APP_OS_CFG_START_TASK_STK_SIZE,                (10)
                 (OS_MSG_QTY  ) 0u,
                 (OS_TICK     ) 0u,
                 (void       *) 0,
                 (OS_OPT      ) (OS_OPT_TASK_STK_CHK | OS_OPT_TASK_STK_CLR),   (11)
                 (OS_ERR     *)&err_os);                                       (12)
    APP_TEST_FAULT(err_os, OS_ERR_NONE);

    OSStart(&err_os);                                                          (13)
    APP_TEST_FAULT(err_os, OS_ERR_NONE);
}
```

Listing 13-1 **Code execution starts at main()**

L13-1(1) Start **main()** by calling a BSP function that disables all interrupts. On most processors, interrupts are disabled at startup until explicitly enabled by application code. However, it is safer to turn off all peripheral interrupts during startup.

L13-1(2) Call **OSInit()**, which is responsible for initializing µC/OS-III internal variables and data structures, and also creates two (2) to five (5) internal tasks. At minimum, µC/OS-III creates the idle task (**OS_IdleTask()**), which executes when no other task is ready to run. µC/OS-III also creates the tick task, responsible for keeping track of time.

Depending on the value of **#define** constants, µC/OS-III will create the statistic task (**OS_StatTask()**), the timer task (**OS_TmrTask()**), and interrupt handler queue management task (**OS_IntQTask()**).

Most µC/OS-III's functions return an error code via a pointer to an **OS_ERR** variable, err in this case. If **OSInit()** was successful, **err** will be set to **OS_ERR_NONE**. If **OSInit()** encounters a problem during initialization, it will return immediately upon detecting the problem and set err accordingly. If this occurs, look up the error code value in **os.h**. All error codes start with **OS_ERR_**.

Note that **OSInit()** must be called before any other µC/OS-III function.

L13-1(3) Create a task by calling **OSTaskCreate()**. **OSTaskCreate()** requires 13 arguments. The first argument is the address of the **OS_TCB** that is declared for this task.

L13-1(4) **OSTaskCreate()** allows a name to be assigned to each of the tasks. µC/OS-III stores a pointer to the task name inside the **OS_TCB** of the task. There is no limit on the number of ASCII characters used for the name.

L13-1(5) The third argument is the address of the task code. A typical µC/OS-III task is implemented as an infinite loop as shown:

```
void  MyTask (void *p_arg)
{
    /* Do something with 'p_arg'.
    while (1) {
        /* Task body */
    }
}
```

The task receives an argument when at inception. The task resembles any C function that can be called by code. However, the code *must not* call **MyTask()**.

L13-1(6) The fourth argument of **OSTaskCreate()** is the argument that the task receives when it first begins. In other words, the **p_arg** of **MyTask()**. In the example a NULL pointer is passed, and thus **p_arg** for **AppTaskStart()** will be a NULL pointer.

The argument passed to the task can actually be any pointer. For example, you may pass a pointer to a data structure containing parameters for the task.

L13-1(7) The next argument to **OSTaskCreate()** is the priority of the task. The priority establishes the relative importance of this task with respect to other tasks in the application. A low-priority number indicates a high priority (or more important task). Set the priority of the task to any value between 1 and **OS_CFG_PRIO_MAX-2**, inclusively. Avoid using priority #0, and priority **OS_CFG_PRIO_MAX-1**, because these are reserved for µC/OS-III. **OS_CFG_PRIO_MAX** is a compile time configuration constant, which is declared in **os_cfg.h**.

L13-1(8) The sixth argument to **OSTaskCreate()** is the base address of the stack assigned to this task. The base address is always the lowest memory location of the stack.

L13-1(9) The next argument specifies the location of a "watermark" in the task's stack that can be used to determine the allowable stack growth of the task. In the code above, the value represents the amount of stack space (in **CPU_STK** elements) before the stack is empty. In other words, in the example, the limit is reached when 10% of the stack is left.

L13-1(10) The eighth argument to **OSTaskCreate()** specifies the size of the task's stack in number of **CPU_STK** elements (not bytes). For example, if allocating 1 Kbytes of stack space for a task and the **CPU_STK** is a 32-bit word, pass 256.

L13-1(11) The next three arguments are skipped as they are not relevant to the current discussion. The next argument to **OSTaskCreate()** specifies options. In this example, it is specified that the stack will be checked at run time (assuming the statistic task was enabled in **os_cfg.h**), and that the contents of the stack will be cleared when the task is created.

L13-1(12) The last argument of **OSTaskCreate()** is a pointer to a variable that will receive an error code. If **OSTaskCreate()** is successful, the error code will be **OS_ERR_NONE** otherwise, the value of the error code can be looked up in **os.h** (see **OS_ERR_xxxx**) to determine the problem with the call.

L13-1(13) The final step in **main()** is to call **OSStart()**, which starts the multitasking process. Specifically, µC/OS-III will select the highest-priority task that was created before calling **OSStart()**. The highest-priority task is always **OS_IntQTask()** if that task is enabled in **os_cfg.h** (through the **OS_CFG_ISR_POST_DEFERRED_EN** constant). If this is the case, **OS_IntQTask()** will perform some initialization of its own and then µC/OS-III will switch to the next most important task that was created.

A few important points are worth noting. You can create as many tasks as you want before calling **OSStart()**. However, it is recommended to only create one task as shown in the example. Notice that interrupts are not enabled. µC/OS-III and µC/OS-II always start a task with interrupts enabled. As soon as the first task executes, the interrupts are enabled. The first task is **AppTaskStart()** and its contents is examined in can Listing 13-2.

```
static  void  AppTaskStart (void *p_arg)                        (1)
{
    CPU_INT32U  cpu_clk_freq;
    CPU_INT32U  cnts;
    OS_ERR      err_os;

    (void)&p_arg;

    BSP_Init();                                                 (2)
    CPU_Init();                                                 (3)
    cpu_clk_freq = BSP_CPU_ClkFreq();                           (4)
    cnts = cpu_clk_freq / (CPU_INT32U)OSCfg_TickRate_Hz;
    OS_CPU_SysTickInit(cnts);

    Mem_Init();                                                 (5)
    AppInit_TCPIP(&net_err);                                    (6)

                                                                (7)
```

```
    BSP_LED_Off(0u);                                              (8)
    while (1) {                                                   (9)
        BSP_LED_Toggle(0u);                                      (10)
        OSTimeDlyHMSM((CPU_INT16U) 0u,                           (11)
                      (CPU_INT16U) 0u,
                      (CPU_INT16U) 0u,
                      (CPU_INT16U) 100u,
                      (OS_OPT     ) OS_OPT_TIME_HMSM_STRICT,
                      (OS_ERR    *)&err_os);
    }
}
```

Listing 13-2 **AppTaskStart**

L13-2(1) As previously mentioned, a task looks like any other C function. The argument **p_arg** is passed to **AppTaskStart()** by **OSTaskCreate()**.

L13-2(2) **BSP_Init()** is a BSP function responsible for initializing the hardware on an evaluation or target board. The evaluation board might have General Purpose Input Output (GPIO) lines that need to be configured, relays, and sensors, etc. This function is found in a file called **bsp.c**.

L13-2(3) **Cuprite()** initializes µC/CPU services. µC/CPU provides services to measure interrupt latency, receive time stamps, and provide emulation of the count leading zeros instruction if the processor used does not have that instruction.

L13-2(4) **BSP_CPU_ClkFreq()** determines the system tick reference frequency of this board. The number of system ticks per OS tick is calculated using **OSCfg_TickRate_Hz**, which is defined in **os_cfg_app.h.** Finally, **OS_CPU_SysTickInit()** sets up the µC/OS-III tick interrupt. For this, the function needs to initialize one of the hardware timers to interrupt the CPU at the **OSCfg_TickRate_Hz** rate calculated previously.

L13-2(5) **Mem_Init()** initializes the memory management module. µC/TCP-IP object creation uses this module. This function is part of µC/LIB. The memory module *must* be initialized by calling **Mem_Init()** *prior* to calling **Net_Init()**. It is recommended to initialize the memory module before calling **OSStart()**, or near the top of the startup task. The application developer must enable and configure the size of the µC/LIB memory heap available to the system. **LIB_MEM_CFG_HEAP_SIZE** should be defined from within **app_cfg.h** and set to match the application requirements.

L13-2(6) **AppInit_TCPIP()** initializes the TCP/IP stack and the initial parameters to configure it. See section E-1-6 "µC/TCP-IP Initialization" on page 766 for a description of **AppInit_TCPIP()**.

L13-2(7) If other IP applications are required this is where they are initialized

L13-2(8) **BSP_LED_Off()** is a function that will turn off all LEDs because the function is written so that a zero argument refers to all LEDs.

L13-2(9) Most µC/OS-III tasks will need to be written as an infinite loop.

L13-2(10) This BSP function toggles the state of the specified LED. Again, a zero indicates that all the LEDs should be toggled on the evaluation board. Simply change the zero to 1 causing LED #1 to toggle. Exactly which LED is LED #1? That depends on the BSP developer. Encapsulate access to LEDs through such functions as **BSP_LED_On()**, **BSP_LED_Off()** and **BSP_LED_Toggle()**. Also, LEDs are assigned logical values (1, 2, 3, etc.) instead of specifying a port and specific bit on each port.

L13-2(11) Finally, each task in the application must call one of the µC/OS-III functions that will cause the task to "wait for an event." The task can wait for time to expire (by calling **OSTimeDly()**, or **OSTimeDlyHMSM()**), or wait for a signal or a message from an ISR or another task.

AppTaskStart() calls the **AppInit_TCPIP()** to initialize and start the TCP/IP stack. This function is shown in:

```
static  void  AppInit_TCPIP (NET_ERR *perr)
{
    NET_IF_NBR    if_nbr;
    NET_IP_ADDR   ip;
    NET_IP_ADDR   msk;
    NET_IP_ADDR   gateway;
    NET_ERR       err_net;


    err_net = Net_Init();                                                (1)
    APP_TEST_FAULT(err_net, NET_ERR_NONE);

    if_nbr  = NetIF_Add((void     *)&NetIF_API_Ether,                    (2)
                        (void     *)&NetDev_API_<controller>,            (3)
                        (void     *)&NetDev_BSP_<controller>,            (4)
                        (void     *)&NetDev_Cfg_<controller>,            (5)
                        (void     *)&NetPhy_API_Generic,                 (6)
                        (void     *)&NetPhy_Cfg_<controller>,            (7)
                        (NET_ERR *)&err_net);                            (8)
    APP_TEST_FAULT(err_net, NET_ERR_NONE);

    NetIF_Start(if_nbr, perr);                                           (9)
    APP_TEST_FAULT(err_net, NET_IF_ERR_NONE);

    ip      = NetASCII_Str_to_IP((CPU_CHAR *)"10.10.1.65",              (10)
                                 (NET_ERR *)&err_net);
    msk     = NetASCII_Str_to_IP((CPU_CHAR *)"255.255.255.0",           (11)
                                 (NET_ERR *)&err_net);
    gateway = NetASCII_Str_to_IP((CPU_CHAR *)"10.10.1.1",               (12)
                                 (NET_ERR *)&err_net);

    NetIP_CfgAddrAdd(if_nbr, ip, msk, gateway, &err_net);               (13)
    APP_TEST_FAULT(err_net, NET_IP_ERR_NONE);

}
```

Listing 13-3 **AppInit_TCPIP()**

L13-3(1) `Net_Init()` is the Network Protocol stack initialization function.

L13-3(2) `NetIF_Add()` is a Network Interface function responsible for initializing a Network Device driver. The first parameter is the **`address of`** the Ethernet API function. `if_nbr` is the interface index number. The first interface is index number 1. If the loopback interface is configured it has interface index number 0.

L13-3(3) The second parameter is the address of the device API function.

L13-3(4) The third parameter is the address of the device BSP data structure.

L13-3(5) The third parameter is the address of the device configuration data structure.

L13-3(6) The fourth parameter is the address of the PHY API function

L13-3(7) The fifth and last parameter is the address of the PHY configuration data structure.

L13-3(8) The error code is used to validate the result of the function execution.

L13-3(9) `NetIF_Start()` makes the network interface ready to receive and transmit.

L13-3(10) Definition of the IP address to be used by the network interface. The `NetASCII_Str_to_IP()` converts the human readable address into a format required by the protocol stack. In this example the `10.10.1.65` address out of the 10.10.1.0 network with a subnet mask of `255.255.255.0` is used. To match different network, this address, the subnet mask and the default gateway IP address have to be customized.

L13-3(11) Definition of the subnet mask to be used by the network interface. The `NetASCII_Str_to_IP()` converts the human readable subnet mask into the format required by the protocol stack.

L13-3(12) Definition of the default gateway address to be used by the network interface. The `NetASCII_Str_to_IP()` converts the human readable default gateway address into the format required by the protocol stack.

L13-3(13) `NetIP_CfgAddrAdd()` configures the network parameters (IP address, subnet mask and default gateway IP address) required for the interface. More than one set of network parameters can be configured per interface. Lines from (10) to (13) can be repeated for as many network parameter sets as need to be configured for an interface.

Once the source code is built and loaded into the target, the target will respond to ICMP Echo (ping) requests.

Chapter

14

Network Device Drivers

μC/TCP-IP operates with a variety of network devices. Currently, μC/TCP-IP supports Ethernet type interface controllers, and will support serial, PPP, USB, and other popular interfaces in future releases.

There are many Ethernet controllers available on the market and each requires a driver to work with μC/TCP-IP. The amount of code needed to port a specific device to μC/TCP-IP greatly depends on device complexity.

If not already available, a driver can be developed as described in this book. However, it is recommended to modify an already existing device driver with the device's specific code following the Micrium coding convention for consistency. It is also possible to adapt drivers written for other TCP/IP stacks, especially if the driver is short and it is a matter of simply copying data to and from the device.

14-1 μC/TCP-IP DRIVER ARCHITECTURE

This section describes the hardware (device) driver architecture for μC/TCP-IP, including:

- Device Driver API Definition(s)
- Device Configuration
- Memory Allocation
- CPU and Board Support

Micrium provides sample configuration code free of charge; however, the sample code will likely require modification depending on the combination of processor, evaluation board, and Ethernet controller(s).

14-2 DEVICE DRIVER MODEL

μC/TCP-IP is designed to work with the several hardware memory configurations.

14-3 DEVICE DRIVER API FOR MAC

All device drivers must declare an instance of the appropriate device driver API structure as a global variable within the source code. The API structure is an ordered list of function pointers utilized by μC/TCP-IP when device hardware services are required.

A sample Ethernet interface API structure is shown below.

```
const  NET_DEV_API_ETHER  NetDev_API_<controler> = { NetDev_Init,                        (1)
                                                     NetDev_Start,                       (2)
                                                     NetDev_Stop,                        (3)
                                                     NetDev_Rx,                          (4)
                                                     NetDev_Tx,                          (5)
                                                     NetDev_AddrMulticastAdd,            (6)
                                                     NetDev_AddrMulticastRemove,         (7)
                                                     NetDev_ISR_Handler,                 (8)
                                                     NetDev_IO_Ctrl,                     (9)
                                                     NetDev_MII_Rd,                     (10)
                                                     NetDev_MII_Wr                      (11)
};
```

Listing 14-1 **Ethernet interface API**

Note: It is the device driver developers' responsibility to ensure that all of the functions listed within the API are properly implemented and that the order of the functions within the API structure is correct.

L14-1(1) Device initialization/add function pointer

L14-1(2) Device start function pointer

L14-1(3) Device stop function pointer

L14-1(4) Device Receive function pointer

L14-1(5) Device transmit function pointer

L14-1(6) Device multicast address add function pointer

L14-1(7) Device multicast address remove function pointer

L14-1(8) Device interrupt service routine (ISR) handler function pointer

L14-1(9) Device I/O control function pointer

L14-1(10) Physical layer (Phy) register read function pointer

L14-1(11) Physical layer (Phy) register write function pointer

Note: µC/TCP-IP device driver API function names may not be unique. Name clashes between device drivers are avoided by never globally prototyping device driver functions and ensuring that all references to functions within the driver are obtained by pointers within the API structure. The developer may arbitrarily name the functions within the source file so long as the API structure is properly declared. The user application should never need to call API functions by name. Unless special care is taken, calling device driver functions by name may lead to unpredictable results due to reentrancy.

14-4 DEVICE DRIVER API FOR PHY

Many Ethernet devices use external (R)MII compliant physical layers (PHYs) to attach themselves to the Ethernet wire. However, some MACs use embedded PHYs and do not have a MII compliant communication interface. In this case, it may acceptable to merge the PHY functionality with the MAC device driver, in which case a separate PHY API and configuration structure may not be required. In the event that an external (R)MII compliant device is attached to the MAC, the PHY driver must implement the PHY API as follows:


```
const NET_PHY_API_ETHER NetPHY_API_DeviceName = { NetPhy_Init,            (1)
                                                   NetPhy_EnDis,           (2)
                                                   NetPhy_LinkStateGet,    (3)
                                                   NetPhy_LinkStateSet,    (4)
                                                   0                       (5)
};
```

Listing 14-2 **PHY interface API**

L14-2(1) Phy initialization function pointer

L14-2(2) Phy enable/disable function pointer

L14-2(3) Phy link get status function pointer

L14-2(4) Phy link set status function pointer

L14-2(5) Phy interrupt service routine (ISR) handler function pointer

µC/TCP-IP provides code that is compatible with most (R)MII compliant PHYs. However, extended functionality, such as link state interrupts must be implemented on a per PHY basis. If additional functionality is required, it may be necessary to create an application specific PHY driver.

Note: It is the PHY driver developers' responsibility to ensure that all of the functions listed within the API are properly implemented and that the order of the functions within the API structure is correct. The **NetPhy_ISR_Handler** field is optional and may be populated as **(void *)0** if interrupt functionality is not required.

14-5 INTERRUPT HANDLING

Interrupt handling is accomplished using the following multi-level scheme.

1 Processor level interrupt handler

2 µC/TCP-IP BSP interrupt handler (Network BSP)

3 Device driver interrupt handler

During initialization, the device driver registers all necessary interrupt sources with the BSP interrupt management code. This may also be accomplished by plugging an interrupt vector table during compile time. Once the global interrupt vector sources are configured and an interrupt occurs, the system will call the first-level interrupt handler. The first-level handler then calls the network device's BSP handler which in turn calls `NetIF_ISR_Handler()` with the interface number and ISR type. The ISR type may be known if a dedicated interrupt vector is assigned to the source, or it may be de-multiplexed from the device driver by reading a register. If the interrupt type is unknown, then the BSP interrupt handler should call `NetIF_ISR_Handler()` with the appropriate interface number and `NET_IF_ISR_TYPE_UNKNOWN`.

The following ISR types have been defined from within µC/TCP-IP, however, additional type codes may be defined within each device's `net_dev.h`:

```
NET_DEV_ISR_TYPE_UNKNOWN
NET_DEV_ISR_TYPE_RX
NET_DEV_ISR_TYPE_RX_RUNT
NET_DEV_ISR_TYPE_RX_OVERRUN
NET_DEV_ISR_TYPE_TX_RDY
NET_DEV_ISR_TYPE_TX_COMPLETE
NET_DEV_ISR_TYPE_TX_COLLISION_LATE
NET_DEV_ISR_TYPE_TX_COLLISION_EXCESS
NET_DEV_ISR_TYPE_JABBER
NET_DEV_ISR_TYPE_BABBLE
NET_DEV_ISR_TYPE_TX_DONE
NET_DEV_ISR_TYPE_PHY
```

Depending on the architecture, there may be a network device BSP interrupt handler for each implemented device interrupt type (see also section 14-7-1 "Network Device BSP" on page 320 and section A-3-5 "NetDev_ISR_Handler()" on page 430). PHY interrupts should call **NetIF_ISR_Handler()** with a type code equal to **NET_DEV_ISR_TYPE_PHY**.

The device driver must call the network device BSP during initialization in order to configure any module clocks, GPIO, or external interrupt controllers that require configuration. Note: Network device BSP is processor- and device-specific and must be supplied by the application developer. See section 14-7 "Network BSP" on page 320 for more details.

14-5-1 NETDEV_ISR_HANDLER()

In general, the device interrupt handler must perform the following functions:

1 Determine which type of interrupt event occurred by switching on the ISR type argument or reading an interrupt status register if the event type is unknown.

2 If a receive event has occurred, the driver must post the interface number to the µC/TCP-IP Receive task by calling **NetOS_IF_RxTaskSignal()** for each new frame received.

3 If a transmit complete event has occurred, the driver must perform the following items for each transmitted packet.

   a Post the address of the data area that has completed transmission to the transmit buffer de-allocation task by calling **NetOS_IF_TxDeallocTaskPost()** with the pointer to the data area that has completed transmission.

   b Call **NetOS_Dev_TxRdySignal()** with the interface number that has just completed transmission.

4 Clear local interrupt flags.

External or CPU's integrated interrupt controllers should be cleared from within the network device's BSP-level ISR after **NetDev_ISR_Handler()** returns. Additionally, it is highly recommended that device driver ISR handlers be kept as short as possible to reduce the amount of interrupt latency in the system.

DEVICE RECEIVE INTERRUPT HANDLING

A device's receive interrupt signals µC/TCP IP for each packet received so that each receive is queued and later handled by µC/TCP IP's Network Interface Receive Task. Processing devices' received packets is deferred to the Network Interface Receive Task to keep device receive ISRs as short as possible and make the driver easier to write.

Figure 14-1 shows the relationship between a device's packet reception, its receive ISR handling, and µC/TCP IP's Network Interface Receive Task's reception of the device's packet.

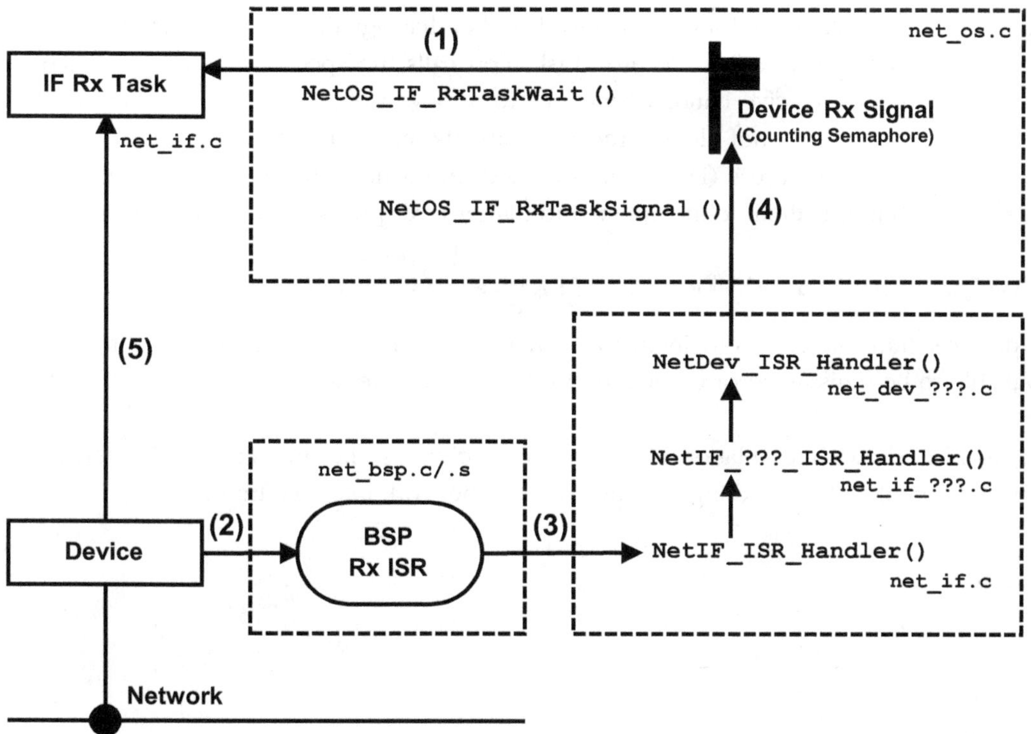

Figure 14-1 **Device receive interrupt and network receive signaling**

F14-1(1) The µC/TCP IP's Network Interface Receive Task calls `NetOS_IF_RxTaskWait()` to wait for device receive packets to arrive by waiting (ideally without timeout) for the **Device Rx Signal** to be signaled.

F14-1(2) When a device packet is received, the device generates a receive interrupt which calls the device's BSP-level ISR handler.

F14-1(3) The device's BSP-level ISR handler determines which network interface number the specific device's interrupt is signaling and then calls **NetIF_ISR_Handler()** to handle the device's receive interrupt.

F14-1(4) The specific network interface and device ISR handlers [e.g. **NetIF_Ether_ISR_Handler()** and **NetDev_ISR_Handler()**] call **NetOS_IF_RxTaskSignal()** to signal the **Device Rx Signal** for each received packet.

F14-1(5) µC/TCP IP's Network Interface Receive Task's call to **NetOS_IF_RxTaskWait()** is made ready for each received packet that signals the **Device Rx Signal**. The Network Interface Receive Task then calls the specific network interface and device receive handler functions to retrieve the packet from the device. If the packet was not already received directly into a network buffer [e.g., via direct memory access (DMA)], it is copied into a network buffer data. The network buffer is then de-multiplexed to higher-layer protocol(s) for further processing.

DEVICE TRANSMIT COMPLETE INTERRUPT HANDLING

A device's transmit complete interrupt signalsµC/TCP-IP that another transmit packet is available to be transmitted or be queued for transmit by the device.

Figure 14-2 shows the relationship between a device's transmit complete interrupt, its transmit complete ISR handling, and µC/TCP-IP's network interface transmit.

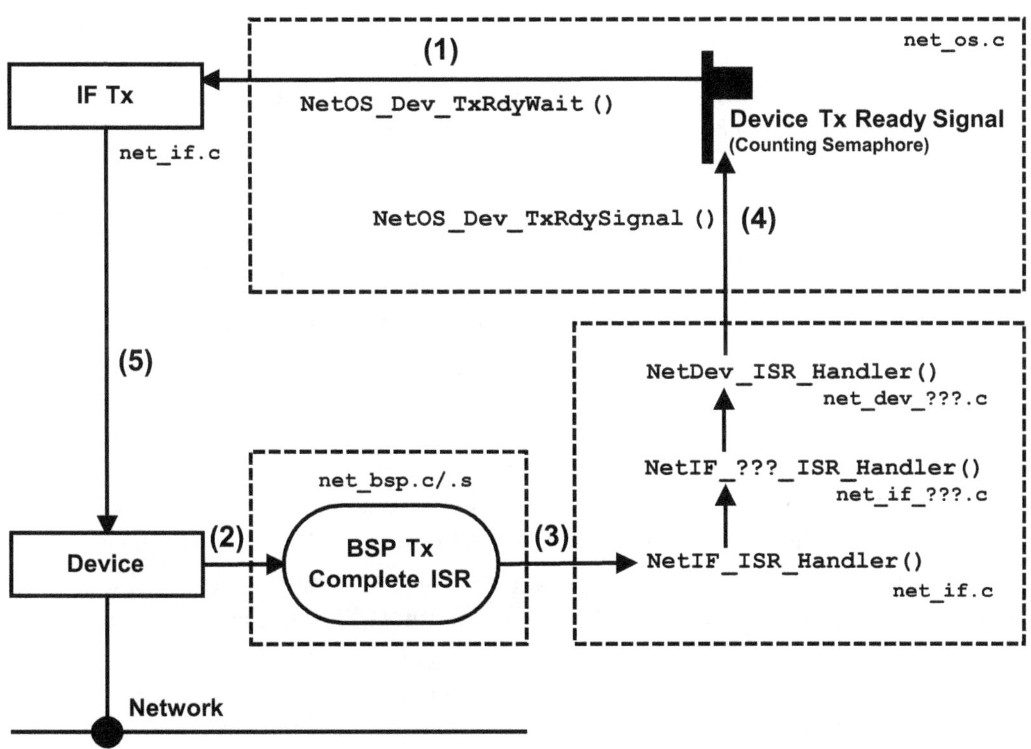

Figure 14-2 **Device transmit complete interrupt and transmit ready signal**

F14-2(1) The µC/TCP IP's Network Interface Transmit calls `NetOS_Dev_TxRdyWait()` to wait for a specific network interface's device to become ready and/or available to transmit a packet by waiting (with or without timeout) for the specific network interface's **Device Tx Ready Signal** to be signaled.

F14-2(2) When a device is ready and/or available to transmit a packet, the device generates a transmit complete interrupt which calls the device's BSP-level ISR handler.

F14-2(3) The device's BSP-level ISR handler determines which network interface number the specific device's interrupt is signaling and then calls `NetIF_ISR_Handler()` to handle the transmit complete interrupt.

F14-2(4) The specific network interface and device ISR handlers [for example, **NetIF_Ether_ISR_Handler()** and **NetDev_ISR_Handler()**] both call **NetOS_Dev_TxRdySignal()** to signal the **Device Tx Ready Signal** for each packet that is now available to transmit by the device.

F14-2(5) µC/TCP IP's Network Interface Transmit's call to **NetOS_Dev_TxRdyWait()** is made ready by each available device transmit complete that signals the Device **Tx Ready Signal**. The Network Interface Transmit then calls the specific network interface and device transmit handler functions to prepare the packet for transmission by the device.

14-5-2 NETPHY_ISR_HANDLER()

The PHY ISR handler is called though the network device BSP in a similar manner to that of the Device ISR handler. The network device BSP is used to initialize the host interrupt controller, clocks, and any necessary I/O pins that are required for configuring and recognizing PHY interrupt sources. When an interrupt occurs, the first level interrupt handler calls the network device BSP interrupt handler which in turn calls **NetIF_ISR_Handler()** with the interface number and interrupt type set to **NET_IF_ISR_TYPE_PHY**. The PHY ISR handler should execute the necessary instructions, clear the PHY interrupt flag and exit.

Note: Link state interrupts must call both the Ethernet device driver and Net IF in order to inform both layers of the current link status. This is performed by calling **pdev_api->IO_Ctrl()** with the option **NET_IF_IO_CTRL_LINK_STATE_UPDATE** as well as a pointer to a **NET_DEV_LINK_ETHER** structure containing the current link state speed and duplex. Additionally, the PHY device driver must call **NetIF_LinkStateSet()** with a pointer to the interface and a Boolean value set to either **NET_IF_LINK_DOWN** or **NET_IF_LINK_UP**.

Note: The Generic PHY driver provided with µC/TCP-IP does not support interrupts. PHY interrupt support requires use of the extended PHY registers which are PHY-specific. However, link state is polled periodically by µC/TCP-IP and you can configure the period during compile time.

14-6 INTERFACE / DEVICE / PHY CONFIGURATION

All µC/TCP-IP devices, including secondary devices such as Ethernet PHYs require that the application developer provide a configuration structure during compile time for each device.

All device configuration structures and declarations must be placed within developer provided files named **net_dev_cfg.c** and **net_dev_cfg.h**. Each configuration structure must be completely initialized in the specified order.

14-6-1 LOOPBACK CONFIGURATION

Listing 14-3 shows a sample configuration structure for the loopback interface.

```
const  NET_IF_CFG_LOOPBACK  NetIF_Cfg_Loopback = {

    NET_IF_MEM_TYPE_MAIN,                              (1)
    1518,                                              (2)
      10,                                              (3)
       4,                                              (4)
       0,                                              (5)

    NET_IF_MEM_TYPE_MAIN,                              (6)
    1594,                                              (7)
       5,                                              (8)
     134,                                              (9)
       5,                                             (10)
       4,                                             (11)
       0,                                             (12)

    0x00000000,                                       (13)
             0,                                       (14)

    NET_DEV_CFG_FLAG_NONE                             (15)
};
```

Listing 14-3 **Sample Loopback Interface Configuration.**

L14-3(1) Receive buffer pool type. This configuration setting controls the memory placement of the receive data buffers. Buffers may either be placed in main memory or in a dedicated, possibly higher speed, memory region (see L14-3(13)). This field should be set to one of the two macros:

```
NET_IF_MEM_TYPE_MAIN
NET_IF_MEM_TYPE_DEDICATED
```

L14-3(2) Receive buffer size. This field sets the size of the largest receivable packet and may be set to match the application's requirements.

Note: If packets are sent from a socket bound to a non local-host address, to the local host address, e.g., 127.0.0.1, then the receive buffer size must be configured to match the maximum transmit buffer size, or maximum expected data size, that could be generated from a socket bound to any other interface.

L14-3(3) Number of receive buffers. This setting controls the number of receive buffers that will be allocated to the loopback interface. This value *must* be set greater than or equal to one buffer if loopback is receiving *only* UDP. If TCP data is expected to be transferred across the loopback interface, then there *must* be a minimum of four receive buffers.

L14-3(4) Receive buffer alignment. This setting controls the alignment of the receive buffers in bytes. Some processor architectures do not allow multi-byte reads and writes across word boundaries and therefore may require buffer alignment. In general, it is probably best practice to align buffers to the data bus width of the processor which may improve performance. For example, a 32-bit processor may benefit from having buffers aligned on a 4-byte boundary.

L14-3(5) Receive buffer offset. The loopback interface receives packets starting at base index 0 in the network buffer data areas. This setting configures an offset from the base index of 0 to receive loopback packets. The default offset of 0 *should* be configured. However, if loopback receive packets are configured with an offset, the receive buffer size *must* also be adjusted by the additional number of offset bytes.

L14-3(6) Transmit buffer pool type. This configuration setting controls the memory placement of the transmit data buffers for the loopback interface. Buffers may either be placed in main memory or in a dedicated, possibly higher speed, memory region (see L14-3(13)). This field should be set to one of two macros:

```
NET_IF_MEM_TYPE_MAIN
NET_IF_MEM_TYPE_DEDICATED
```

L14-3(7) Large transmit buffer size. At the time of this writing, transmit fragmentation is *not* supported; therefore this field sets the size of the largest transmittable buffer for the loopback interface when the application sends from a socket that is bound to the local-host address.

L14-3(8) Number of large transmit buffers. This field controls the number of large transmit buffers allocated to the loopback interface. The developer may set this field to zero to make room for additional large transmit buffers, however, the number of large plus the number of small transmit buffers *must* be greater than or equal to one for UDP traffic and three for TCP traffic.

L14-3(9) Small transmit buffer size. For devices with a minimal amount of RAM, it is possible to allocate small transmit buffers as well as large transmit buffers. In general, we recommend 152 byte small transmit buffers, however, the developer may adjust this value according to the application requirements. This field has no effect if the number of small transmit buffers is configured to zero.

L14-3(10) Number of small transmit buffers. This field controls the number of small transmit buffers allocated to the device. The developer may set this field to zero to make room for additional large transmit buffers, however, the number of large plus the number of small transmit buffers *must* be greater than or equal to one for UDP traffic and three for TCP traffic.

L14-3(11) Transmit buffer alignment. This setting controls the alignment of the receive buffers in bytes. Some processor architectures do not allow multi-byte reads and writes across word boundaries and therefore may require buffer alignment. In general, it is probably best practice to align buffers to the data bus width of the processor which may improve performance. For example, a 32-bit processor may benefit from having buffers aligned on a 4-byte boundary.

L14-3(12) Transmit buffer offset. This setting configures an offset from the base transmit index to prepare loopback packets. The default offset of 0 *should* be configured. However, if loopback transmit packets are configured with an offset, the transmit buffer size *must* also be adjusted by the additional number of offset bytes.

L14-3(13) Memory Address. By default, this field is configured to 0x00000000. A value of 0 tells µC/TCP-IP to allocate buffers for the loopback interface from the µC/LIB Memory Manager default heap. If a faster, more specialized memory is available, the loopback interface buffers may be allocated into an alternate region if desired.

L14-3(14) Memory Size. By default, this field is configured to 0. A value of 0 tells µC/TCP-IP to allocate as much memory as required from the µC/LIB Memory Manager default heap. If an alternate memory region is specified in the 'Memory Address' field above, then the maximum size of the specified memory segment must be specified.

L14-3(15) Optional configuration flags. Configure (optional) loopback features by logically **OR**'ing bit-field flags :

`NET_DEV_CFG_FLAG_NONE`	No loopback configuration flags selected

14-6-2 ETHERNET DEVICE MAC CONFIGURATION

Listing 14-4 shows a sample configuration structure for a single MAC.

```
const  NET_DEV_CFG_ETHER  NetDev_Cfg_<DevName>[_Nbr] = {

    NET_IF_MEM_TYPE_MAIN,                                  (1)
    1518,                                                  (2)
      10,                                                  (3)
       4,                                                  (4)
       0,                                                  (5)

    NET_IF_MEM_TYPE_MAIN,                                  (6)
    1594,                                                  (7)
       5,                                                  (8)
     152,                                                  (9)
       5,                                                 (10)
       4,                                                 (11)
       0,                                                 (12)

    0x00000000,                                           (13)
             0,                                           (14)

    NET_DEV_CFG_FLAG_NONE,                                (15)

    10,                                                   (16)
     4,                                                   (17)

    0x40001000,                                           (18)
    0,                                                    (19)

   "00:50:C2:25:60:02"                                    (20)

};
```

Listing 14-4 **Example Ethernet device MAC configuration**

L14-4(1) Receive buffer pool type. This configuration setting controls the memory placement of the receive data buffers. Buffers may either be placed in main memory or in a dedicated memory region. Non-DMA based Ethernet controllers should be configured to use the main memory pool. DMA based Ethernet controllers may or may not require dedicated memory (see L14-4(13)). This depends on the type of controller being configured. This field should be set to one of two macros:

NET_IF_MEM_TYPE_MAIN
NET_IF_MEM_TYPE_DEDICATED

L14-4(2) Receive buffer size. For Ethernet this setting is generally configured to 1518 bytes which represents the MTU of an Ethernet network. For DMA based Ethernet controllers, the developer *must* configure the receive data buffer size greater or equal to the size of the largest receivable frame.

L14-4(3) Number of receive buffers. This setting controls the number of receive buffers that will be allocated to the device. For DMA devices, this number *must* be greater than 1. If the size of the total buffer allocation is greater than the amount of available memory in the chosen memory region, a run-time error will be generated when the device is initialized.

L14-4(4) Receive buffer alignment. This setting controls the alignment of the receive buffers in bytes. Some devices, such as the one used in this example require that the receive buffers be aligned to a specific byte boundary. Additionally, some processor architectures do not allow multi-byte reads and writes across word boundaries and therefore may require buffer alignment. In general, it is probably best practice to align buffers to the data bus width of the processor which may improve performance. For example, a 32-bit processor may benefit from having buffers aligned on a 4-byte boundary.

L14-4(5) Receive buffer offset. Most devices receive packets starting at base index 0 in the network buffer data areas. However, some devices may buffer additional bytes prior to the actual received Ethernet packet. This setting configures an offset to ignore these additional bytes. If a device does *not* buffer any additional bytes ahead of the received Ethernet packet, then the default offset of 0 *must* be configured. However, if a device does buffer additional bytes ahead of the received Ethernet packet, then configure this offset with the number of additional bytes. Also, the receive buffer size *must* also be adjusted by the number of additional bytes.

L14-4(6) Transmit buffer pool type. This configuration setting controls the memory placement of the transmit data buffers. Buffers may either be placed in main memory or in a dedicated memory region. Non-DMA based Ethernet controllers should be configured to use the main memory pool. DMA based Ethernet controllers may or may not require dedicated memory (see L14-4(13)).

In some cases, DMA based Ethernet controllers with dedicated memory may be able to transmit from main memory. If so, then the remaining dedicated memory may be allocated to additional receive buffers. This field should be set to one of two macros:

```
NET_IF_MEM_TYPE_MAIN
NET_IF_MEM_TYPE_DEDICATED
```

L14-4(7) Large transmit buffer size. This field controls the size of the large transmit buffers allocated to the device in bytes. This field has no effect if the number of large transmit buffers is configured to zero. Setting the size of the large transmit buffers below 1594 bytes may hinder the stack's ability to transmit full sized IP datagrams since IP transmit fragmentation is not yet supported. We recommend setting this field to 1594 to 1614 bytes in order to accommodate the maximum transmit packet sizes all µC/TCP-IP's protocols. See section 15-3 "Network Buffer Sizes" on page 337 for more details.

L14-4(8) Number of large transmit buffers. This field controls the number of large transmit buffers allocated to the device. The developer may set this field to 0 to make room for additional large transmit buffers, however, the size of the maximum transmittable UDP packet will then depend on the size of the small transmit buffers (see L14-4(9)).

L14-4(9) Small transmit buffer size. For devices with a minimal amount of RAM, it is possible to allocate small transmit buffers as well as large transmit buffers. In general, we recommend 152 byte small transmit buffers, however, the developer may adjust this value according to the application requirements. This field has no effect if the number of small transmit buffers is configured to 0.

L14-4(10) Number of small transmit buffers. This field controls the number of small transmit buffers allocated to the device. The developer may set this field to 0 to make room for additional large transmit buffers if required.

L14-4(11) Transmit buffer alignment. This setting controls the alignment of the transmit buffers in bytes. Some devices, such as the one used in this example require that the transmit buffers be aligned to a specific byte boundary. Additionally, some processor architectures do not allow multi-byte reads and writes across word boundaries and therefore may require buffer alignment. In general, it is probably best practice to align buffers to the data bus width of the processor which may improve performance. For example, a 32-bit processor may benefit from having buffers aligned on a 4-byte boundary.

L14-4(12) Transmit buffer offset. Most devices only need to transmit the actual Ethernet packets as prepared by the higher network layers. However, some devices may need to transmit additional bytes prior to the actual Ethernet packet. This setting configures an offset to prepare space for these additional bytes. If a device does *not* transmit any additional bytes ahead of the Ethernet packet, the default offset of 0 *should* be configured. However, if a device does transmit additional bytes ahead of the Ethernet packet then configure this offset with the number of additional bytes. Also, the transmit buffer size *must* be adjusted by the number of additional bytes.

L14-4(13) Memory Address. For devices with dedicated memory, this field represents the starting address of the dedicated memory region. Non dedicated memory based devices may initialize this field to 0.

L14-4(14) Memory Size. For devices with dedicated memory, this field represents the size of the dedicated memory region in bytes. Non dedicated memory based devices may initialize this field to 0.

L14-4(15) Optional configuration flags. Configure (optional) device features by logically **OR**'ing bit-field flags:

NET_DEV_CFG_FLAG_NONE	No device configuration flags selected.
NET_DEV_CFG_FLAG_SWAP_OCTETS	Swap data bytes (i.e., swap data words' high-order bytes with data words' low-order bytes, and vice-versa) if required by device-to-CPU data bus wiring and/or CPU endian word order.

L14-4(16) Number of receive descriptors. For DMA based devices, this value is utilized by the device driver during initialization in order to allocate a fixed size pool of receive descriptors to be used by the device. The number of descriptors *must* be less than the number of configured receive buffers. We recommend setting this value to between 60% to 70% of the number of receive buffers. Non-DMA based devices may configure this value to 0.

L14-4(17) Number of transmit descriptors. For DMA based devices, this value is utilized by the device driver during initialization to allocate a fixed size pool of transmit descriptors to be used by the device. For best performance, the number of transmit descriptors should be equal to the number of small, plus the number of large transmit buffers configured for the device. Non-DMA based devices may configure this value to 0.

L14-4(18) Device base address. This field represents the base register address of the device. This field is used by the device driver to determine the address of device registers given this base address and pre-defined register offset within the driver.

L14-4(19) Device data bus size configured in number of bits. For devices with configurable data bus sizes, it may be desirable to specify the width of the data bus in order for well written device drivers to correctly configure the device during initialization. For devices that abstract the data bus from the developer, such as MCU-integrated MAC's, this value should be specified as 0 and ignored by the driver; for all external devices, this value should be defined to 8, 16, 32, or 64.

L14-4(20) Hardware address. For Ethernet devices, the hardware address field provides a location to hard code the device's MAC address in string format. This must be configured in one of the following three ways:

(a) `"aa:bb:cc:dd:ee:ff"` where **aa**, **bb**, **cc**, **dd**, **ee**, and `ff` represent the desired static MAC address bytes which are to be configured to the device during initialization.

(b) `"00:00:00:00:00:00"` where a zero value MAC address string disables static configuration of the device MAC address. If this mechanism is used, the driver must check to see if the you have configured a MAC address during run-time, or if the MAC address is automatically loaded from a non-volatile memory source. We recommend this method of configuring the MAC address when the MAC address is to be determined during run-time via hard coding in software, or loading from an external memory device.

(c) `""` where an empty MAC address disables static configuration of the device MAC address. If this mechanism is used, then the driver must check to see if you have configured a MAC address during run-time, or if the MAC address is automatically loaded from a non-volatile memory source.

14-6-3 ETHERNET PHY CONFIGURATION

Listing 14-5 shows a typical Ethernet PHY configuration structure.


```
NET_PHY_CFG_ETHER NetPhy_Cfg_FEC_0= {
  1,                                        (1)
  NET_PHY_BUS_MODE_MII,                     (2)
  NET_PHY_TYPE_EXT                          (3)
  NET_PHY_SPD_AUTO,                         (4)
  NET_PHY_DUPLEX_AUTO,                      (5)
};
```

Listing 14-5 **Sample Ethernet PHY Configuration**

L14-5(1) PHY Address. This field represents the address of the PHY on the (R)MII bus. The value configured depends on the PHY and the state of the PHY pins during power-up. Developers may need to consult the schematics for their board to determine the configured PHY address. Alternatively, the PHY address may be detected automatically by specifying **NET_PHY_ADDR_AUTO**; however, this will increase the initialization latency of µC/TCP-IP and possibly the rest of the application depending on where the application places the call to `NetIF_Start()`.

L14-5(2) PHY bus mode. This value should be set to one of the following values depending on the hardware capabilities and schematics of the development board. The network device BSP should configure the Phy-level hardware based on this configuration value.

```
NET_PHY_BUS_MODE_MII
NET_PHY_BUS_MODE_RMII
NET_PHY_BUS_MODE_SMII
```

L14-5(3) PHY bus type. This field represents the type of electrical attachment of the PHY to the Ethernet controller. In some cases, the PHY may be internal to the network controller, while in other cases, it may be attached via an external MII or RMII bus. It is desirable to specify which attachment method is in use so that a device driver can initialize additional hardware resources if an external PHY is attached to a device that also has an internal PHY. Available settings for this field are:

```
NET_PHY_TYPE_INT
NET_PHY_TYPE_EXT
```

L14-5(4) Initial PHY link speed. This configuration setting will force the PHY to link to the specified link speed. Optionally, auto-negotiation may be enabled. This field must be set to one of the following values:

```
NET_PHY_SPD_AUTO
NET_PHY_SPD_10
NET_PHY_SPD_100
NET_PHY_SPD_1000
```

L14-5(5) Initial PHY link duplex. This configuration setting will force the PHY to link using the specified duplex. This setting must be set to one of the following values:

```
NET_PHY_DUPLEX_AUTO
NET_PHY_DUPLEX_HALF
NET_PHY_DUPLEX_FULL
```

14-7 NETWORK BSP

In order for device drivers to be platform independent, it is necessary to provide a layer of code that abstracts details such as configuring clocks, interrupt controllers, general-purpose input/ouput (GPIO) pins, direct-memory access (DMA) modules, and other such hardware modules. With this board support package (BSP) code layer, it is possible to implement certain high-level functionality in µC/TCP-IP that is independent of any specific hardware and to reuse device drivers on various architectures and bus configurations without having to uniquely modify µC/TCP-IP or device driver source code for each architecture or hardware platform.

14-7-1 NETWORK DEVICE BSP

For each Ethernet interface/device, an application must implement in **net_bsp.c** a unique, device-specific implementation of each of the following BSP functions:

```
void        NetDev_CfgClk    (NET_IF   *pif,
                              NET_ERR  *perr);
void        NetDev_CfgIntCtrl(NET_IF   *pif,
                              NET_ERR  *perr);
void        NetDev_CfgGPIO   (NET_IF   *pif,
                              NET_ERR  *perr);
CPU_INT32U  NetDev_ClkFreqGet(NET_IF   *pif,
                              NET_ERR  *perr);
```

Since each of these functions is called from a unique instantiation of its corresponding device driver, a pointer to the corresponding network interface (**pif**) is passed in order to access the specific interface's device configuration or data.

Network device driver BSP functions may be arbitrarily named but since development boards with multiple devices require unique BSP functions for each device, it is recommended that each device's BSP functions be named using the following convention:

`NetDev_[Device]<Function>[Number]()`

`[Device]` Network device name or type, e.g. MACB (optional if the development board does not support multiple devices)

`<Function>` Network device BSP function, e.g. **`CfgClk`**

`[Number]` Network device number for each specific instance of device (optional if the development board does not support multiple instances of the specific device)

For example, the **`NetDev_CfgClk()`** function for the #2 MACB Ethernet controller on an Atmel AT91SAM9263-EK should be named **`NetDev_MACB_CfgClk2()`**, or **`NetDev_MACB_CfgClk_2()`** with additional underscore optional.

Similarly, network devices' BSP-level interrupt service routine (ISR) handlers should be named using the following convention:

`NetDev_[Device]ISR_Handler[Type][Number]()`

`[Device]` Network device name or type, e.g. MACB (optional if the development board does not support multiple devices)

`[Type]` Network device interrupt type, e.g. receive interrupt (optional if interrupt type is generic or unknown)

`[Number]` Network device number for each specific instance of device (optional if the development board does not support multiple instances of the specific device)

For example, the receive ISR handler for the #2 MACB Ethernet controller on an Atmel AT91SAM9263-EK should be named **`NetDev_MACB_ISR_HandlerRx2()`**, or **`NetDev_MACB_ISR_HandlerRx_2()`** with additional underscore optional.

Next, each device's/interface's BSP functions must be organized into an interface structure used by the device driver to call specific devices' BSP functions via function pointer instead of by name. This allows applications to add, initialize, and configure any number of instances of various devices and drivers by creating similar but unique BSP functions and interface structures for each network device/interface. (See Appendix B, "NetIF_Add()" on page 514 for details on how applications add interfaces to μC/TCP-IP.)

Each device's/interface's BSP interface structure must be declared in the application's/ development board's network BSP source file, **net_bsp.c**, as well as externally declared in network BSP header file, **net_bsp.h**, with the exact same name and type as declared in **net_bsp.c**. These BSP interface structures and their corresponding functions must be uniquely named and should clearly identify the development board, device name, function name, and possibly the specific device number (assuming the development board supports multiple instances of any given device). BSP interface structures may be arbitrarily named but it is recommended that they be named using the following convention:

```
NetDev_BSP_<Board><Device>[Number]{}
```

<Board> Development board name, e.g. Atmel AT91SAM9263-EK

<Device> Network device name (or type), e.g. MACB

[Number] Network device number for each specific instance of the device (optional if the development board does not support multiple instances of the device)

For example, a BSP interface structure for the #2 MACB Ethernet controller on an Atmel AT91SAM9263-EK board should be named **NetDev_BSP_AT91SAM9263-EK_MACB_2{}** and declared in the AT91SAM9263-EK board's **net_bsp.c** :

```
                          /* AT91SAM9263-EK MACB #2's BSP fnct ptrs :  */
const  NET_DEV_BSP_ETHER  NetDev_BSP_AT91SAM9263-EK_MACB_2 = {
    NetDev_MACB_CfgClk_2,       /*   Cfg MACB #2's clk(s)              */
    NetDev_MACB_CfgIntCtrl_2,   /*   Cfg MACB #2's int ctrl(s)         */
    NetDev_MACB_CfgGPIO_2,      /*   Cfg MACB #2's GPIO                */
    NetDev_MACB_ClkFreqGet_2    /*   Get MACB #2's clk freq            */
};
```

And in order for the application to configure an interface with this BSP interface structure, the structure must be externally declared in the AT91SAM9263-EK board's **net_bsp.h** :

```
extern  const  NET_DEV_BSP_ETHER  NetDev_BSP_AT91SAM9263-EK_MACB_2;
```

Lastly, the AT91SAM9263-EK board's MACB #2 BSP functions must also be declared in **net_bsp.c** :

```
static  void        NetDev_MACB_CfgClk_2     (NET_IF   *pif,
                                               NET_ERR  *perr);
static  void        NetDev_MACB_CfgIntCtrl_2(NET_IF   *pif,
                                               NET_ERR  *perr);
static  void        NetDev_MACB_CfgGPIO_2    (NET_IF   *pif,
                                               NET_ERR  *perr);
static  CPU_INT32U  NetDev_MACB_ClkFreqGet_2(NET_IF   *pif,
                                               NET_ERR  *perr);
```

Note that since all network device BSP functions are accessed only by function pointer via their corresponding BSP interface structure, they don't need to be globally available and should therefore be declared as '**static**'.

Also note that although certain device drivers may not need to implement or call all of the above network device BSP function, we recommend that each device's BSP interface structure define all device BSP functions and not assign any of its function pointers to **NULL**. Instead, for any device's unused BSP functions, create empty functions that return **NET_DEV_ERR_NONE**. This way, if the device driver is ever modified to start using a previously-unused BSP function, there will at least be an empty function for the BSP function pointer to execute.

Details for these functions may be found in their respective sections in Appendix A, "Device Driver BSP Functions" on page 420 and templates for network device BSP functions and BSP interface structures are available in the **\Micrium\Software\uC-TCPIP-V2\BSP\Template** directories.

14-7-2 MISCELLANEOUS NETWORK BSP

µC/TCP-IP's BSP code layer also implements hardware abstraction code other than device driver BSP. The following functions *must* be declared and implemented in **net_bsp.c** :

```
NET_TS    NetUtil_TS_Get      (void);
NET_TS_MS NetUtil_TS_Get_ms   (void);
void      NetTCP_InitTxSeqNbr(void);
```


The first two functions provide internal timestamp µC/TCP-IP functionality (although **NetUtil_TS_Get()** is not absolutely required) while the latter function is only necessary if µC/TCP-IP is configured to include the TCP module. Details for these functions may be found in their respective sections in Appendix B, "µC/TCP-IP API Reference" on page 433 and templates for these BSP functions are available in the **\Micrium\Software\uC-TCPIP-V2\BSP\Template** directories.

14-8 MEMORY ALLOCATION

Memory is allocated to µC/TCP-IP device drivers through the µC/LIB memory module. The application developer must enable and configure the size of the µC/LIB memory heap available to the system. The following configuration constants should be defined from within **app_cfg.h** and set to match the application requirements.

```
#define LIB_MEM_CFG_ALLOC_EN        DEF_ENABLED
#define LIB_MEM_CFG_HEAP_SIZE             58000
```

The heap size is specified in bytes. If the heap size is not configured large enough, an error will be returned during the Network Protocol Stack initialization, or during interface addition.

Note: The memory module *must* be initialized by the application by calling **Mem_Init()** *prior* to calling **Net_Init()**. We recommend initializing the memory module before calling **OSStart()**, or near the top of the startup task.

For non-DMA based devices, additional memory allocation from within the device driver may not be necessary. However, DMA based devices should allocate memory from the µC/LIB memory module for descriptors. By using the µC/LIB memory module instead of declaring arrays, the driver developer can easily align descriptors to any required boundary and benefit from the run-time flexibility of the device configuration structure.

If you have access to the source code, see the µC/LIB documentation for additional information and usage notes.

14-9 DMA SUPPORT

A DMA controller is a unique peripheral devoted to moving data in a system. It is a controller that connects internal and external memories via a set of dedicated buses and a peripheral in the sense that the processor programs it to perform transfers.

In general, DMA controllers will include an address bus, a data bus, and control registers. An efficient DMA controller possesses the ability to request access to any resource it needs, without having the processor involved. It must have the capabilities to generate interrupts and to calculate addresses within the controller.

A processor might contain multiple DMA controllers. A DMA controller can have one or more DMA channels, as well as multiple buses that link directly to the memory banks and peripherals. One DMA channel can do one transfer of one or multiple, bytes or CPU words. Newer processors with an integrated Ethernet controller have a DMA controller for their Ethernet hardware.

Generally, the processor should only need to respond to DMA interrupts after the data transfers are completed. The DMA controller is programmed to move data in parallel while the processor is doing its basic processing task. The DMA controller generates an interrupt when the transfers are completed.

The DMA controller already has the capability to interface with memory, so it can get its own instruction from memory. Consider a DMA controller to be a simple processor with a simple instruction set. DMA channels have a finite number of registers that need to be filled with values, each of which gives a description of how to transfer the data.

There are two main classes of DMA transfer configuration: Register Mode and Descriptor Mode. In Register mode, the DMA controller is programmed by the CPU by writing the required parameters in the DMA registers. In Descriptor mode, the DMA can use its read memory circuitry to fetch the register values rather than burdening the CPU to write the values. The blocks of memory containing the required register parameters are called "descriptors." When the DMA runs in Register Mode, the DMA controller simply uses the values contained in the registers. The mode that provides the best results and the mode that is mostly found in microprocessor/microcontroller DMA controllers with integrated Ethernet controller is the Descriptor based mode. This is the mode described in details herein.

DMA transfers that are descriptor-based require a set of parameters stored within memory to initiate a DMA sequence. The descriptor contains all of the same parameters normally programmed into the DMA control registers set and descriptor information are described by the specific DMA controller. Descriptor-based model also allows the chaining together of multiple DMA sequences and can be programmed to automatically set up and start another DMA transfer after the current sequence completes. The descriptor-based model provides the most flexible configuration to manage a system's memory.

In general, DMA controller provides a main descriptor model method; normally called "Descriptor List". Depending of the DMA controller, the descriptor list may reside in consecutive memory location, but it is not mandatory. µC/TCP-IP reserves consecutive memory blocks for descriptors and both models can be used.

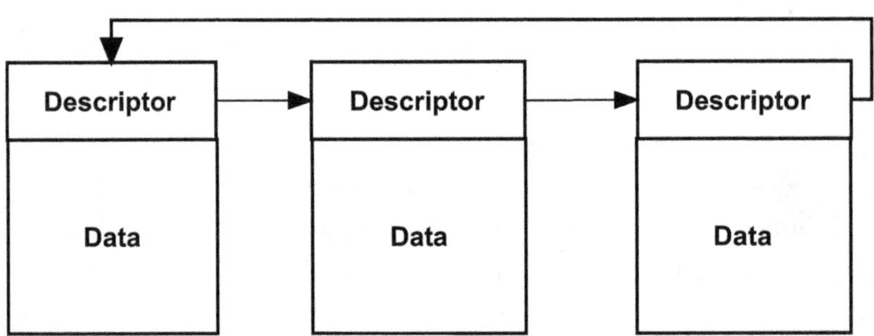

Figure 14-3 **Descriptor link list**

In the µC/TCP-IP device driver, a linked list of descriptors is created, as shown in Figure 14-3. The term linked implies that one descriptor points to the next descriptor, which is loaded automatically. To complete the chain, the last descriptor points back to the first descriptor, and the process repeats. This involves setting up multiple descriptors that are linked together. This mechanism is used for Ethernet frame reception.

14-9-1 RECEPTION WITH DMA

INITIALIZATION

When µC/TCP-IP is initialized, the Network Device Driver allocates a memory block for all receive descriptors; this is performed via calls to the µC/LIB.

Then, the Network Device Driver must allocate a list of descriptors and configure each address field to point to the start address of a receive buffers. At the same time, the Network Device Driver initializes three pointers. One to track the current descriptor which is expected to contain the next received frame, and two to remember the descriptor list boundaries. Finally, the DMA controller is initialized and hardware is informed of the descriptor list starting address.

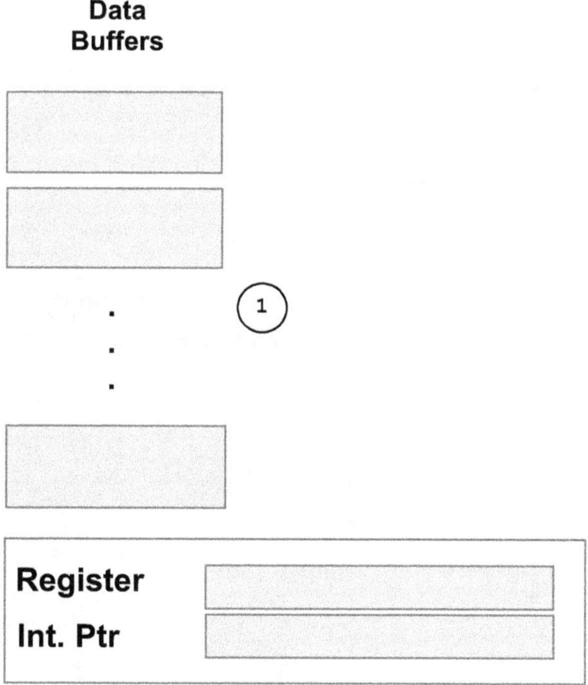

Figure 14-4 **Allocation of buffers**

F14-4(1) Figure 14-4(1) The result of `Mem_Init()` and the first step in the intialization of the Network Device Driver is the allocation of buffers.

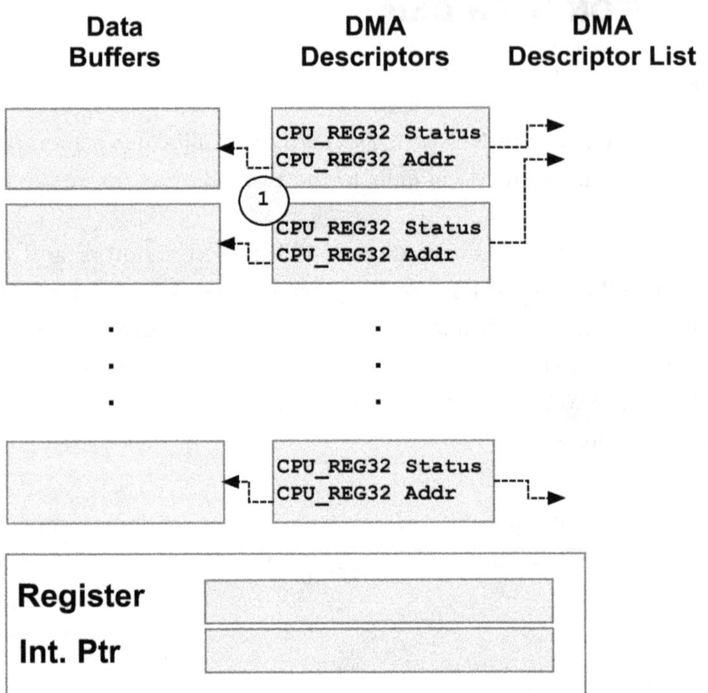

Figure 14-5 **Descriptor allocation**

Figure 14-5(1) µC/TCP-IP allocates a list of descriptors based on the Network Device Driver configuration and sets each address field to point to the start address of a receive buffer.

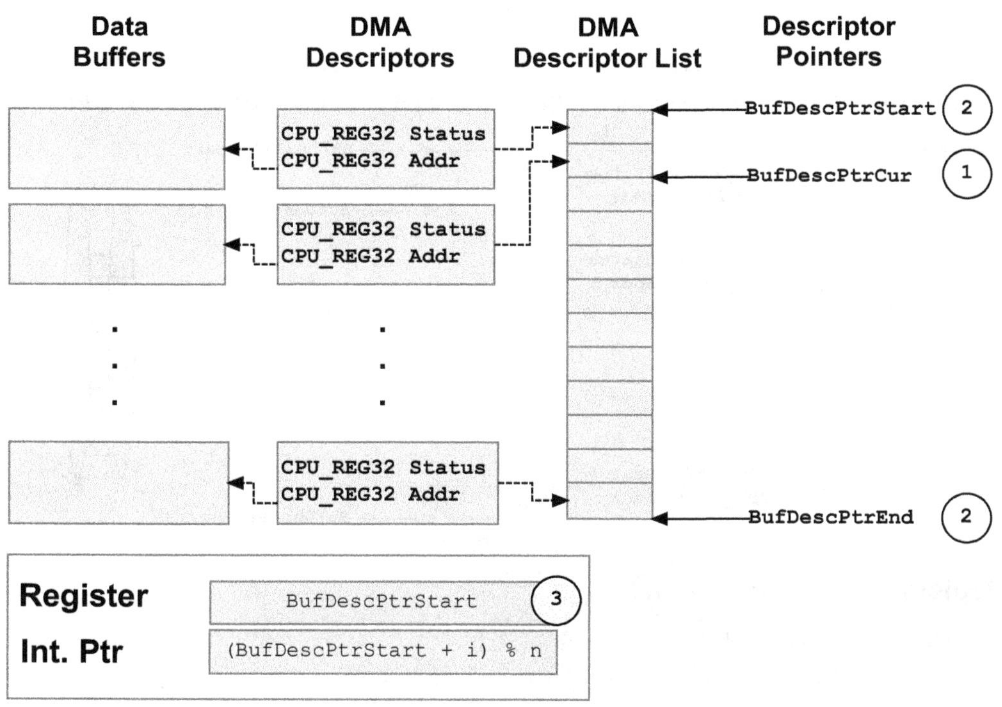

Figure 14-6 **Reception descriptor pointers initialization**

F14-6(1) The Network Device Driver initializes three pointers. One to track the current descriptor which is expected to contain the next received frame

F14-6(2) Two to remember the descriptor list boundaries.

F14-6(3) Finally, the DMA controller is initialized and hardware is informed of the descriptor list starting address.

RECEPTION

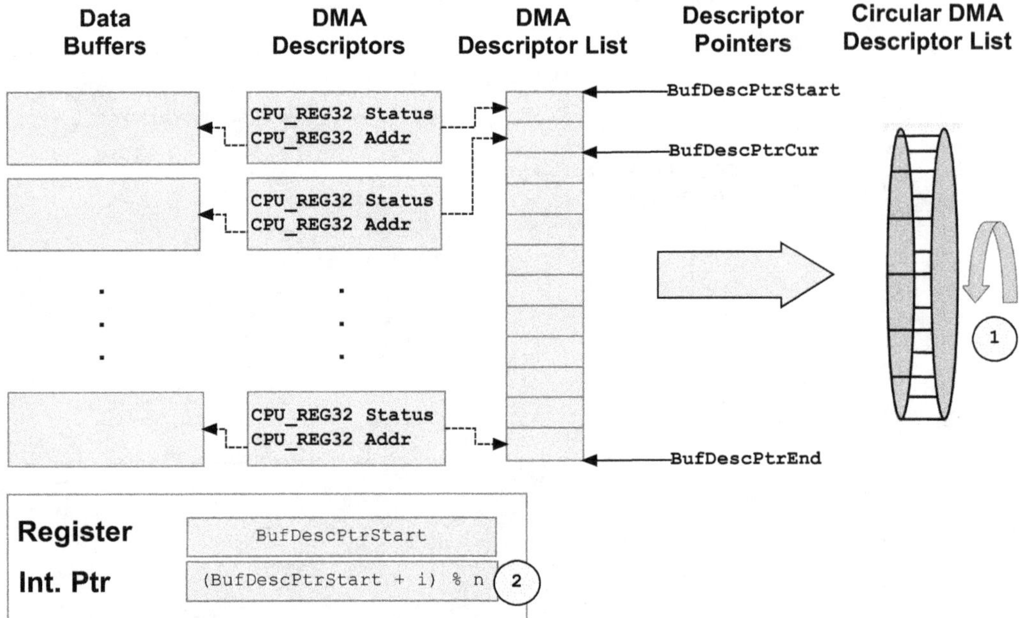

Figure 14-7 **Receiving an Ethernet frame with DMA**

F14-7(1) With each new received frame, the Network Device Driver increments BufDescPtrCur by 1 and wraps around the descriptor list as necessary

F14-7(2) The hardware applies the same logic to an internal descriptor pointer.

When a received frame is processed, the driver gets a pointer to a new data buffer and updates the current descriptor address field. The previous buffer address is passed to the protocol stack for processing. If a buffer pointer cannot be obtained, the existing pointer remains in place and the frame is dropped.

ISR HANDLER

When a frame is received, the DMA controller will generate an interrupt. The ISR handler must signal the network interface. The network interface will automatically call the receive function.

14-9-2 TRANSMISSION WITH DMA

When µC/TCP-IP has a packet to transmit, it updates an available descriptor in memory and then writes to a DMA register to start the stalled DMA channel. On transmissions, it is simpler to setup the descriptors. The number and length of the packets to transmit is well defined. This information determines the number of transmit descriptors required and the number of bytes to transmit on each descriptor. The transmit descriptor list is often used in a non-circular fashion. The initial descriptors in the descriptor list are setup for transmission, when the transmission is completed they are cleared, and the process starts over in the next transmission.

INITIALIZATION

Similarly to the receive descriptors, the Network Device Driver should allocate a memory block for all transmit buffers and descriptors shown in Figure 14-4.

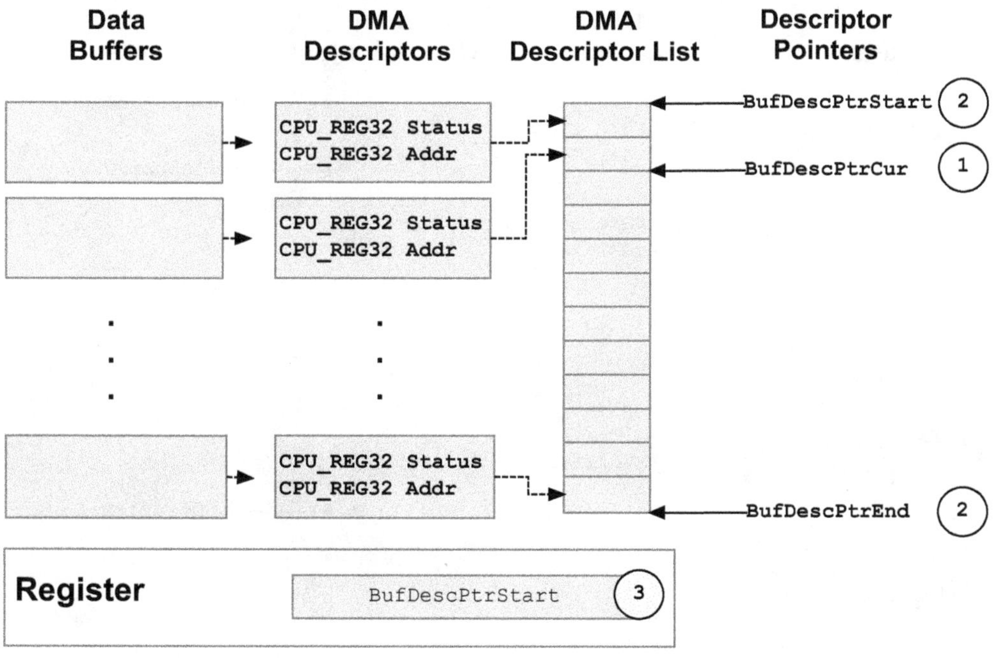

Figure 14-8 **Transmission descriptor pointers initialization**

F14-8(1) The Network Device Driver must allocate a list of descriptors and configure each address field to point to a null location.

F14-8(2) The Network Device Driver can initialize three pointers. One to track the current descriptor which is expected to contain the next buffer to transmit. A second points to the beginning of the descriptor list. The last pointer may point to the last descriptor in the list or depending on the implementation, it can also point to the last descriptor to transmit. Another method, depending on the DMA controller used, is to configure a parameter containing the number of descriptors to transmit in one of the DMA controller registers.

Finally, the DMA controller is initialized and hardware is informed of the descriptor list starting address.

TRANSMISSION

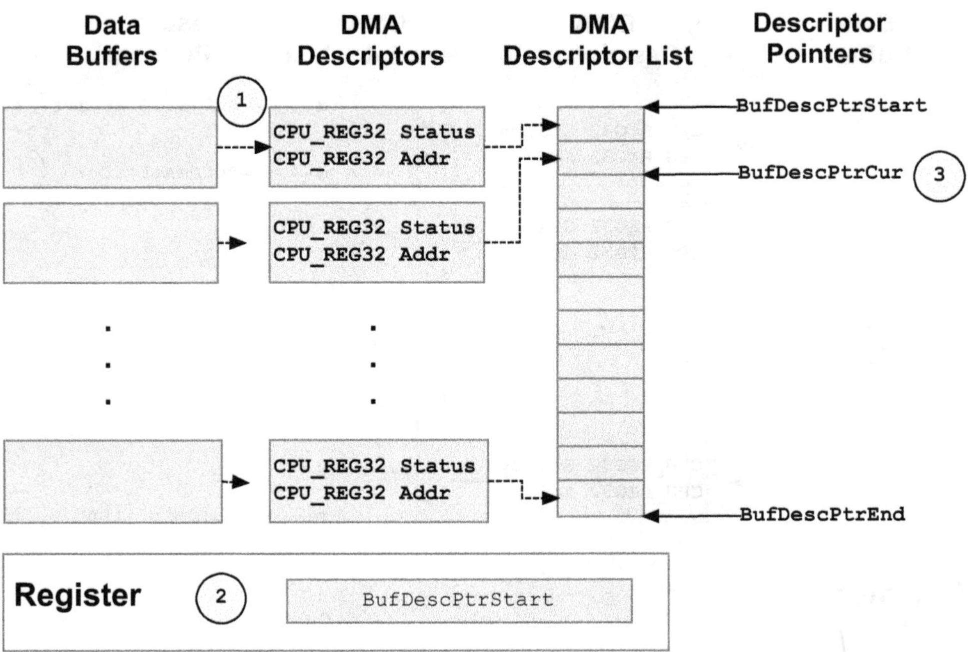

Figure 14-9 **Moving a buffer to the Ethernet controller with DMA**

F14-9(1) With each new transmit buffer, the current descriptor address is set to the buffer address.

F14-9(2) DMA transfer is enabled.

F14-9(3) The current descriptor pointer is set to the next descriptor for the next transmission.

If no descriptor is free an error should be returned to the Network Protocol stack.

ISR HANDLER

When the ISR handler receives a DMA interrupt after the transmission completion, a list of descriptors for the completed transmit buffers is determined. Each completed transmit buffer address is passed to the Network Transmit De-allocation Task, where the correspondent buffer gets released if it is not referenced by any other part of the Network stack. The Network interface is also signaled for each one of the completed transmit buffers to allow the Network stack to continue transmission of subsequent packets. To complete the operation, the transmit descriptors are cleared to make room for subsequent transmissions.

Chapter

15

Buffer Management

This chapter describe how µC/TCP-IP uses buffers to receive and transmit application data and network protocol control information.

15-1 NETWORK BUFFERS

µC/TCP-IP stores transmitted and received data in data structures known as Network Buffers. Each Network Buffer consists of two parts: the Network Buffer header and the Network Buffer Data Area pointer. Network Buffer headers contain information about the data pointed to via the data area pointer. Data to be received or transmitted is stored in the Network Buffer Data Area.

µC/TCP-IP is designed with the inherent constraints of an embedded system in mind, the most important being the restricted RAM space. µC/TCP-IP defines Network Buffers for the Maximum Transmission Unit (MTU) of the Data Link technology used, in this case typically Ethernet.

15-1-1 RECEIVE BUFFERS

Network Buffers used for reception for a Data Link technology are buffers that can hold one maximum frame size. Because it is impossible to predict how much data will be received, only large buffers can be configured. Even if the packet does not contain any payload, a large buffer must be used, as worst case must always be assumed.

15-1-2 TRANSMIT BUFFERS

On transmission, the number of bytes to transmit is always known so it is possible to use a Network Buffer size smaller than the maximum frame size. µC/TCP-IP allows the embedded developer to reduce the RAM usage of the system by defining small buffers. When the application does not require a full size frame to transmit, it is possible to use smaller

Network Buffers. Depending on the configuration, up to eight pools of Network Buffer related objects may be created per network interface. Only four pools are shown below and the remaining pools are used for maintaining Network Buffer usage statistics for each of the pools shown.

In transmission, the situation is different. The TCP/IP stack knows how much data is being transmitted. In addition to RAM being limited in embedded systems, another feature is the small amount of data that needs to be transmitted. For example, in the case of sensor data to be transmitted periodically, a few hundred bytes every second can be transferred. In this case, a small buffer can be used and save RAM instead of waste a large transmit buffer. Another example is the transmission of TCP acknowledgment packets, especially when they are not carrying any data back to the transmitter. These packets are also small and do not require a large transmit buffer. RAM is also saved.

15-2 NETWORK BUFFER ARCHITECTURE

µC/TCP-IP uses both small and large network buffers:

1 Network Buffers

2 Small Transmit Buffers

3 Large Transmit Buffers

4 Large Receive Buffers

A single Network Buffer is allocated for each small transmit, large transmit and large receive buffer. Network Buffers contain the control information for the network packet data in the Network Buffer Data Area. Currently, Network Buffers consume approximately 200 bytes each. The Network Buffers' Data Areas are used to buffer the actual transmit and receive packet data. The Network Buffer is connected to the data area via the Network Buffer Data Area pointer and both move through the Network Protocol Stack layers as a single entity. When the data area is no longer required, both the Network Buffer and the data area are freed. Figure 15-1 depicts the Network Buffer and Data Area objects.

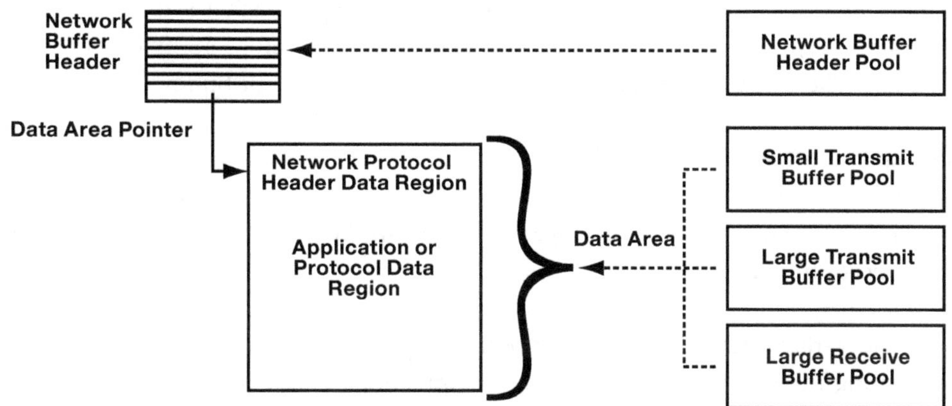

Figure 15-1 **Network Buffer Architecture**

All transmit data areas contain a small region of reserved space located at the top of the data area address space. The reserved space is used for network protocol header data and is currently fixed to 134 bytes in length. In general, not all of this space is required. However, the network protocol header region has been sized according to the maximum network protocol header usage for TCP/IP Ethernet packets.

µC/TCP-IP copies application-specified data from the application buffer into the application data region before writing network protocol header data to the protocol header region. Once the application data has been transferred into the Network Buffer Data Area by the highest required µC/TCP-IP layer, the Network Buffer descends through the remaining layers where additional protocol headers are added to the network protocol header data region.

15-3 NETWORK BUFFER SIZES

µC/TCP-IP requires that network buffer sizes configured in **`net_dev_cfg.c`** satisfy the minimum and maximum packet frame sizes of network interfaces/devices.

Assuming an Ethernet interface (with non-jumbo or VLAN-tagged frames), the minimum frame packet size is 64 bytes (including its 4-byte CRC). If an Ethernet frame is created such that the frame length is less than 60 bytes (before its 4-byte CRC is appended), frame padding must be appended by the Network Driver or the Ethernet Network Interface

Layer to the application data area to meet Ethernet's minimum packet size. For example, the ARP protocol typically creates packets of 42 bytes and therefore 18 bytes of padding must be added. The additional padding must fit within the network buffer's data area.

Ethernet's maximum transmit unit (MTU) size is 1500 bytes. When the TCP is used as the transport protocol, TCP and IP protocol header sizes are subtracted from Ethernet's 1500-byte MTU. A maximum of 1460 bytes of TCP application data may be sent in a full-sized Ethernet frame.

In addition, the variable size of network packet protocol headers must also be considered when configuring buffer sizes. The following computations demonstrate how to configure network buffer sizes to transmit and receive maximum sized network packets.

For transmit buffer size configuration, each layer's maximum header sizes must be assumed/included to achieve the maximum payload for each layer. The maximum header sizes for each layer are:

```
Max Ethernet header :  14 bytes  (this is a fixed size w/o CRC)
Max ARP header      :  28 bytes  (this is a fixed size for Ethernet/IPv4)
Max IP  header      :  60 bytes  (with maximum length IP  options)
Max TCP header      :  60 bytes  (with maximum length TCP options)
Max UDP header      :   8 bytes  (this is a fixed size)
```

Assuming both TCP and UDP are available as transport layer protocols, TCP's maximum header size is the value used as the maximum transport layer header size since it is greater than UDP's header size. Thus, the total maximum header size can then be computed as:

```
Max Hdr Size = Interface Max Header     (Ethernet hdr is 14 bytes)
             + Network   Max Header     (IP   max hdr is 60 bytes)
             + Transport Max Header     (TCP  max hdr is 60 bytes)
             = 14 + 60 + 60 = 134 bytes
```

µC/TCP-IP configures `NET_BUF_DATA_PROTOCOL_HDR_SIZE_MAX` with this value in `net_cfg_net.h` to use as the starting data area index for transmit buffers' application data.

The next step is to define transmit buffers' total data area size. The issue is that we used the maximum header size for the transport and network layers. However, most of the time, the network and transport layer headers typically do not have any options:

```
Typical IP  header :  20 bytes  (without IP  options)
Typical TCP header :  20 bytes  (without TCP options)
```

These header values are used to determine the maximum payload a Data Link frame can carry. Since a TCP header is larger than UDP headers, the following compures the TCP maximum payload, also known as TCP's Maximum Segment Size (MSS), over an Ethernet Data Link:

```
TCP payload (max) = Interface Max          (Ethernet 1514 bytes w/o CRC)
                  - Interface Header       (Ethernet   14 bytes w/o CRC)
                  - Min IP  Header         (IP  min hdr is 20 bytes)
                  - Min TCP Header         (TCP min hdr is 20 bytes)
                  = 1514 - 14 - 20 - 20 = 1460 bytes
```

When TCP is used in a system, it is recommended to configure the large buffer size to at least this size in order to transmit maximum size TCP MSS:

```
TCP Max Buf Size = Max TCP payload          (1460 bytes)
                 + Max Hdr sizes             (134 bytes)
                 = 1460 + 134 = 1594 bytes
```

If any IP or TCP options are used, it is possible that the payload must be reduced, but unfortunately, that cannot be known by the application when transmitting. It is possible that, when the packet is at the network layer and because the TCP or IP headers are larger than usual because an option is enabled, a packet is too large and needs to be fragmented to be transmitted. However, µC/TCP-IP does not yet support fragmentation; but since options are seldom used and the standard header sizes for TCP and IP are the ones supported, this is generally not a problem.

For UDP, the UDP header has no options and the size does not change – it is always 8 bytes. Thus, UDP's maximum payload is calculated as follows:

```
UDP payload (max) = Interface Max          (Ethernet 1514 bytes w/o CRC)
                  - Interface Header       (Ethernet   14 bytes w/o CRC)
                  - Min IP  Header         (IP  min hdr is 20 bytes)
                  - Min UDP Header         (UDP     hdr is  8 bytes)
                  = 1514 - 14 - 20 - 8 = 1472 bytes
```


So to transmit maximum-sized UDP packets, configure large buffer sizes to at least:

```
Max UDP Buf Size = Max UDP payload           (1472 bytes)
                 + Max Hdr sizes              (134 bytes)
                 = 1472 + 134 = 1606 bytes
```

ICMP packets which are encapsulated within IP datagrams also have variable-length header sizes from 8 to 20 bytes. However, for certain design reasons, ICMP headers are included in an IP datagram's data area and are not included in the maximum header size calculation. (IGMP packets have a fixed header size of 8 bytes but are also included in an IP datagram's data area.) Thus, ICMP's maximum payload is calculated as follows:

```
ICMP payload (max) = Interface Max          (Ethernet 1514 bytes w/o CRC)
                   - Interface Header       (Ethernet   14 bytes w/o CRC)
                   - Min IP Header          (IP min hdr is 20 bytes)
                   = 1514 - 14 - 20 = 1480 bytes
```

And to transmit maximum-sized ICMP packets, configure large buffer sizes to at least:

```
Max ICMP Buf Size = Max ICMP payload         (1480 bytes)
                  + Max Hdr  sizes            (134 bytes)
                  = 1480 + 134 = 1614 bytes
```

Small transmit buffer sizes must also be appropriately configured to at least the minimum packet frame size for the network interface/device. This means configuring a buffer size that supports sending a minimum sized packet for each layer's minimum header sizes. The minimum header sizes for each layer are:

```
Min Ethernet header :  14 bytes  (this is a fixed size w/o CRC)
Min ARP header      :  28 bytes  (this is a fixed size for Ethernet/IPv4)
Min IP  header      :  20 bytes  (with minimum length IP  options)
Min TCP header      :  20 bytes  (with minimum length TCP options)
Min UDP header      :   8 bytes  (this is a fixed size)
```

For Ethernet frames, the following computation shows that both ARP packets and UDP/IP packets share the smallest minimum header sizes of 42 bytes:

```
ARP packet (min) = Interface Min Header       (Ethernet 14 bytes w/o CRC)
                 + ARP Min Header             (ARP  min hdr is 28 bytes)
                 = 14 + 28 = 42 bytes

UDP packet (min) = Interface Min Header       (Ethernet 14 bytes w/o CRC)
                 + IP  Min Header             (IP   min hdr is 20 bytes)
                 + UDP Min Header             (UDP  min hdr is  8 bytes)
                 = 14 + 20 + 8 = 42 bytes
```

And since Ethernet packets must be at least 60 bytes in length (not including 4-byte CRC), small transmit buffers must be minimally configured to at least 152 bytes to receive the smallest payload for each layer:

```
Min Tx Pkt Size = Interface Min Size          (Ethernet 60 bytes w/o CRC)
                + Max Hdr Sizes               (134 bytes)
                - Min Pkt Size                 (42 bytes)
                = 60 + 134 - 42 = 152 bytes
```

Figure 15-2 shows transmit buffers with reserved space of 134 bytes/octets for the maximum protocol header sizes, application data sizes from 0 to 1472 bytes/octets, and the valid range of configured buffer data area sizes for Ethernet of 152 to 1614 bytes/octets

1

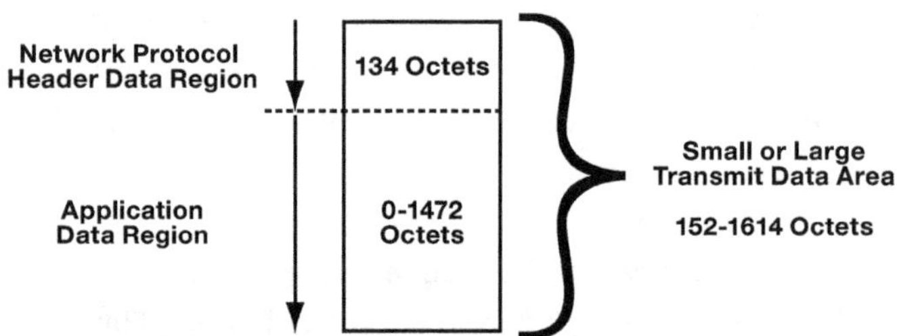

Figure 15-2 **Transmit Buffer Data Areas**

Note that the application data size range plus the maximum header sizes of 134 bytes do not exactly add up to the small or large transmit data area configuration total. This is due to certain protocols (e.g. ICMP) whose protocol headers are not included in the typical network protocol header region but start at index 134. Also note that if no small transmit buffer data areas are available, a data area from the large transmit data area pool is allocated if both small and large transmit data areas are configured.

µC/TCP-IP does *not* require receive buffer data areas to reserve space for maximum header sizes but *does* require that each receive buffer data area be configured to the maximum expected packet frame size for the network interface/device. For Ethernet interfaces, receive buffers must be configured to at least 1514 bytes, assuming the interface's Ethernet device is configured to discard and not buffer the packet's 4-byte CRC, or 1518 bytes, if the device does buffer the CRC. Although network buffers may require additional bytes to properly align each buffer, µC/TCP-IP creates the buffers with the appropriate alignment specified in **net_dev_cfg.c** so no additional bytes need be added to the receive buffer size.

Chapter

16

Network Interface Layer

The following sections describe how µC/TCP-IP manages the interaction between network devices, network device drivers, and network interfaces.

16-1 NETWORK INTERFACE CONFIGURATION

16-1-1 ADDING NETWORK INTERFACES

In µC/TCP-IP, the term Network Interfaces is used to represent an abstract view of the device hardware and data path that connects the hardware to the higher layers of the Network Protocol Stack. In order to communicate with hosts outside the local host, the application developer must add at least one Network Interface to the system. Note that the first interface added and started will be the default interface used for all default communication.

A typical call to **NetIF_Add()** is shown below. See section B-9-1 "NetIF_Add()" on page 514 for more details.

```
if_nbr = NetIF_Add((void    *)&NetIF_API_Ether,          (1)
                   (void    *)&NetDev_API_STR912,         (2)
                   (void    *)&NetDev_BSP_STR912_1,       (3)
                   (void    *)&NetDev_Cfg_STR912_1,       (4)
                   (void    *)&NetPHY_API_Generic,        (5)
                   (void    *)&NetPhy_Cfg_STR912_1,       (6)
                   (NET_ERR *)&err);                      (7)
```

Listing 16-1 **Calling NetIF_Add()**

L16-1(1) The first argument specifies the link layer API that will receive data from the hardware device. For an Ethernet interface, this value will always be defined as **NetIF_API_Ether**. This symbol is defined by µC/TCP-IP and it can be used to add as many Ethernet Network Interface's as necessary.

L16-1(2) The second argument represents the hardware device driver API which is defined as a fixed structure of function pointers of the type specified by Micrium for use with µC/TCP-IP. If Micrium supplies the device driver, the symbol name of the device API will be defined within the device driver documentation and at the top of the device driver source code file. Otherwise, the driver developer is responsible for creating the device driver and the API structure.

L16-1(3) The third argument specifies the specific device's board-specific (BSP) interface functions which is defined as a fixed structure of function pointers. The application developer must define both the BSP interface structure of function pointers and the actual BSP functions referenced by the BSP interface structure. Micrium may be able to supply example BSP interface structures and functions for certain evaluation boards. For more information about declaring BSP interface structures and BSP functions device, see section 14-7-1 "Network Device BSP" on page 320.

L16-1(4) The fourth argument specifies the device driver configuration structure that will be used to configure the device hardware for the interface being added. The device configuration structure format has been specified by Micrium and must be provided by the application developer since it is specific to the selection of device hardware and design of the evaluation board. Micrium may be able to supply example device configuration structures for certain evaluation boards. For more information about declaring a device configuration structure, see section 14-6-2 "Ethernet Device MAC Configuration" on page 313.

L16-1(5) The fifth argument represents the physical layer hardware device API. In most cases, when Ethernet is the link layer API specified in the first argument, the physical layer API may be defined as **NetPHY_API_Generic**. This symbol has been defined by the generic Ethernet physical layer device driver which can be supplied by Micrium. If a custom physical layer device driver is required, then the developer would be responsible for creating the API structure. Often Ethernet devices have built-in Physical layer devices which are *not* (R)MII compliant. In this circumstance, the Physical layer device driver API field may be left NULL and the Ethernet device driver may implement routines for the built-in PHY.

L16-1(6) The sixth argument represents the physical layer hardware device configuration structure. This structure is specified by the application developer and contains such information as the physical device connection type, address, and desired link state upon initialization. For devices with built in non (R)MII compliant Physical layer devices, this field may be left **NULL**. However, it may be convenient to declare a Physical layer device configuration structure and use some of the members for Physical layer device initialization from within the Ethernet device driver. For more information about declaring a physical layer hardware configuration structure, see section 14-6-3 "Ethernet PHY Configuration" on page 318.

L16-1(7) The last argument is a pointer to a **NET_ERR** variable that contains the return error code for **NetIF_Add()**. This variable *should* be checked by the application to ensure that no errors have occurred during network interface addition. Upon success, the return error code will be **NET_IF_ERR_NONE**.

Note: If an error occurs during the call to **NetIF_Add()**, the application *may* attempt to call **NetIF_Add()** a second time for the same interface but unless a temporary hardware fault occured, the application developer should observe the error code, determine and resolve the cause of the error, rebuild the application and try again. If a hardware failure occurred, the application may attempt to add an interface as many times as necessary, but a common problem to watch for is a µC/LIB Memory Manager heap out-of-memory condition. This may occur when adding network interfaces if there is insufficient memory to complete the operation. If this error occurs, the configured size of the µC/LIB heap within **app_cfg.h** must be increased.

Once an interface is added successfully, the next step is to configure the interface with one or more network layer protocol addresses.

16-1-2 CONFIGURING AN INTERNET PROTOCOL ADDRESS

Each Network Interface must be configured with at least one Internet Protocol address. This may be performed using µC/DHCPc or manually during run-time. If run-time configuration is chosen, the following functions may be utilized to set the IP, Net Mask, and Gateway address for a specific interface. More than one set of addresses may be configured for a specific network interface by calling the functions below. Note that on the default interface, the first IP address added will be the default address used for all default communication.

`NetASCII_Str_to_IP()`
`NetIP_CfgAddrAdd()`

The first function aids the developer by converting a string format IP address such as "192.168.1.2" to its hexadecimal equivalent. The second function is used to configure an interface with the specified IP, Net Mask and Gateway addresses. An example of each function call is shown below.

```
ip      = NetASCII_Str_to_IP((CPU_CHAR*)"192.168.1.2",   &err);        (1)
msk     = NetASCII_Str_to_IP((CPU_CHAR*)"255.255.255.0", &err);
gateway = NetASCII_Str_to_IP((CPU_CHAR*)"192.168.1.1",   &err);
```

Listing 16-2 **Calling NetASCII_Str_to_IP()**

L16-2(1) `NetASCII_Str_to_IP()` requires two arguments. The first function argument is a string representing a valid IP address, and the second argument is a pointer to a **NET_ERR** to contain the return error code. Upon successful conversion, the return error will contain the value **NET_ASCII_ERR_NONE** and the function will return a variable of type **NET_IP_ADDR** containing the hexadecimal equivalent of the specified address.

```
cfg_success = NetIP_CfgAddrAdd(if_nbr,          (1)
                               ip,              (2)
                               msk,             (3)
                               gateway,         (4)
                              &err);            (5)
```

Listing 16-3 **Calling NetIP_CfgAddrAdd()**

L16-3(1) The first argument is the number representing the Network Interface that is to be configured. This value is obtained as the result of a successful call to **NetIF_Add()**.

L16-3(2) The second argument is the **NET_IP_ADDR** value representing the IP address to be configured.

L16-3(3) The third argument is the **NET_IP_ADDR** value representing the Subnet Mask address that is to be configured.

L16-3(4) The fourth argument is the **NET_IP_ADDR** value representing the Default Gateway IP address that is to be configured.

L16-3(5) The fifth argument is a pointer to a **NET_ERR** variable containing the return error code for the function. If the interface address information is configured successfully, then the return error code will contain the value **NET_IP_ERR_NONE**. Additionally, function returns a Boolean value of **DEF_OK** or **DEF_FAIL** depending on the result. Either the return value or the **NET_ERR** variable may be checked for return status; however, the **NET_ERR** contains more detailed information and should therefore be the preferred check.

Note: The application may configure a Network Interface with more than one set of IP addresses. This may be desirable when a Network Interface and its paired device are connected to a switch or HUB with more than one network present. Additionally, an application may choose to *not* configure any interface addresses, and thus may *only* receive packets and should not attempt to transmit.

Additionally, addresses may be removed from an interface by calling **NetIP_CfgAddrRemove()** (see section B-11-5 “NetIP_CfgAddrRemove()” on page 556 and section B-11-6 “NetIP_CfgAddrRemoveAll()” on page 558).

Once a Network Interface has been successfully configured with Internet Protocol address information, the next step is to start the interface.

16-2 STARTING AND STOPPING NETWORK INTERFACES

16-2-1 STARTING NETWORK INTERFACES

When a Network Interface is 'Started', it becomes an active interface that is capable of transmitting and receiving data assuming an operational link to the network medium. A Network Interface may be started any time after the Network Interface has been successfully "added" to the system. A successful call to **NetIF_Start()** marks the end of the initialization sequence of µC/TCP-IP for a specific Network Interface. Recall that the first interface added and started will be the default interface.

The application developer may start a Network Interface by calling the **NetIF_Start()** API function with the necessary parameters. A call to **NetIF_Start()** is shown below.

```
NetIF_Start(if_nbr, &err);   (1)
```

Listing 16-4 **Calling NetIF_Start()**

L16-4(1) **NetIF_Start()** requires two arguments. The first function argument is the interface number that the application wants to start, and the second argument is a pointer to a **NET_ERR** to contain the return error code. The interface number is acquired upon successful addition of the interface and upon the successful start of the interface; the return error variable will contain the value **NET_IF_ERR_NONE**.

There are very few things that could cause a Network Interface to not start properly. The application developer should always inspect the return error code and take the appropriate action if an error occurs. Once the error is resolved, the application may again attempt to call **NetIF_Start()**.

16-2-2 STOPPING NETWORK INTERFACES

Under some circumstances, it may be desirable to stop a network interface. A Network Interface may be stopped any time after it has been successfully "added" to the system. Stopping an interface may be performed by calling **NetIF_Stop()** with the appropriate arguments shown below.

```
NetIF_Stop(if_nbr, &err);    (1)
```

Listing 16-5 **Calling NetIF_Stop()**

L16-5(1) **NetIF_Stop()** requires two arguments. The first function argument is the interface number that the application wants to stop, and the second argument is a pointer to a **NET_ERR** to contain the return error code. The interface number is acquired upon the successful addition of the interface and upon the successful stop of the interface; the return error variable will contain the value **NET_IF_ERR_NONE**.

There are very few things that may cause a Network Interface to not stop properly. The application developer should always inspect the return error code and take the appropriate action if an error occurs. Once the error is resolved, the application may attempt to call **NetIF_Stop()** again.

16-3 NETWORK INTERFACES' MTU

16-3-1 GETTING NETWORK INTERFACE MTU

On occasion, it may be desirable to have the application aware of an interface's Maximum Transmission Unit. The MTU for a particular interface may be acquired by calling **NetIF_MTU_Get()** with the appropriate arguments.

```
mtu = NetIF_MTU_Get(if_nbr, &err);    (1)
```

Listing 16-6 **Calling NetIF_MTU_Get()**

6

L16-6(1) **NetIF_MTU_Get()** requires two arguments. The first function argument is the interface number to get the current configured MTU, and the second argument is a pointer to a **NET_ERR** to contain the return error code. The interface number is acquired upon the successful addition of the interface, and upon the successful return of the function, the return error variable will contain the value **NET_IF_ERR_NONE**. The result is returned into a local variable of type **NET_MTU**.

16-3-2 SETTING NETWORK INTERFACE MTU

Some networks prefer to operate with a non-standard MTU. If this is the case, the application may specify the MTU for a particular interface by calling **NetIF_MTU_Set()** with the appropriate arguments.

```
NetIF_MTU_Set(if_nbr, mtu, &err);   (1)
```

Listing 16-7 **Calling NetIF_MTU_Set()**

L16-7(1) **NetIF_MTU_Set()** requires three arguments. The first function argument is the interface number of the interface to set the specified MTU. The second argument is the desired MTU to set, and the third argument is a pointer to a **NET_ERR** variable that will contain the return error code. The interface number is acquired upon the successful addition of the interface, and upon the successful return of the function, the return error variable will contain the value **NET_IF_ERR_NONE** and the specified MTU will be set.

Note: The configured MTU cannot be greater than the largest configured transmit buffer size associated with the specified interfaces' device minus overhead. Transmit buffer sizes are specified in the device configuration structure for the specified interface. For more information about configuring device buffer sizes, refer to Chapter 14, "Network Device Drivers" on page 299.

16-4 NETWORK INTERFACE HARDWARE ADDRESSES

16-4-1 GETTING NETWORK INTERFACE HARDWARE ADDRESSES

Many types of Network Interface hardware require the use of a link layer protocol address. In the case of Ethernet, this address is sometimes known as the Hardware Address or MAC Address. In some applications, it may be desirable to get the current configured hardware address for a specific interface. This may be performed by calling **NetIF_AddrHW_Get()** with the appropriate arguments.


```
NetIF_AddrHW_Get((NET_IF_NBR  ) if_nbr,                    (1)
                 (CPU_INT08U *)&addr_hw_sender[0],         (2)
                 (CPU_INT08U *)&addr_hw_len,               (3)
                 (NET_ERR    *) perr);                     (4)
```

Listing 16-8 **Calling NetIF_AddrHW_Get()**

L16-8(1) The first argument specifies the interface number from which to get the hardware address. The interface number is acquired upon the successful addition of the interface.

L16-8(2) The second argument is a pointer to a **CPU_INT08U** array used to provide storage for the returned hardware address. This array *must* be sized large enough to hold the returned number of bytes for the given interface's hardware address. The lowest index number in the hardware address array represents the most significant byte of the hardware address.

L16-8(3) The third function is a pointer to a **CPU_INT08U** variable that the function returns the length of the specified interface's hardware address.

L16-8(4) The fourth argument is a pointer to a **NET_ERR** variable containing the return error code for the function. If the hardware address is successfully obtained, then the return error code will contain the value **NET_IF_ERR_NONE**.

16-4-2 SETTING NETWORK INTERFACE HARDWARE ADDRESS

Some applications prefer to configure the hardware device's hardware address via software during run-time as opposed to a run-time auto-loading EEPROM as is common for many Ethernet devices. If the application is to set or change the hardware address during run-time, this may be performed by calling **NetIF_AddrHW_Set()** with the appropriate arguments. Alternatively, the hardware address may be statically configured via the device configuration structure and later changed during run-time.

```
NetIF_AddrHW_Set((NET_IF_NBR  ) if_nbr,              (1)
                 (CPU_INT08U *)&addr_hw[0],          (2)
                 (CPU_INT08U *)&addr_hw_len,         (3)
                 (NET_ERR    *) perr);               (4)
```

Listing 16-9 **Calling NetIF_AddrHW_Set()**

1

L16-9(1) The first argument specifies the interface number to set the hardware address. The interface number is acquired upon the successful addition of the interface.

L16-9(2) The second argument is a pointer to a **CPU_INT08U** array which contains the desired hardware address to set. The lowest index number in the hardware address array represents the most significant byte of the hardware address.

L16-9(3) The third function is a pointer to a **CPU_INT08U** variable that specifies the length of the hardware address being set. In most cases, this can be specified as **sizeof(addr_hw)** assuming **addr_hw** is declared as an array of **CPU_INT08U**.

L16-9(4) The fourth argument is a pointer to a **NET_ERR** variable containing the return error code for the function. If the hardware address is successfully obtained, then the return error code will contain the value **NET_IF_ERR_NONE**.

Note: In order to set the hardware address for a particular interface, it *must* first be stopped. The hardware address may then be set, and the interface re-started.

16-5 GETTING LINK STATE

Some applications may wish to get the physical link state for a specific interface. Link state information may be obtained by calling **NetIF_IO_Ctrl()** or **NetIF_LinkStateGet()** with the appropriate arguments.

Calling **NetIF_IO_Ctrl()** will poll the hardware for the current link state. Alternatively, **NetIF_LinkStateGet()** gets the approximate link state by reading the interface link state flag. Polling the Ethernet hardware for link state takes significantly longer due to the speed and latency of the MII bus. Consequently, it may not be desirable to poll the hardware in a tight loop. Reading the interface flag is fast, but the flag is only periodically updated by the Net IF every 250mS (default) when using the generic Ethernet PHY driver. PHY drivers that implement link state change interrupts may change the value of the interface flag immediately upon link state change detection. In this scenario, calling **NetIF_LinkStateGet()** is ideal for these interfaces.

16

```
NetIF_IO_Ctrl((NET_IF_NBR) if_nbr,                                    (1)
              (CPU_INT08U) NET_IF_IO_CTRL_LINK_STATE_GET_INFO,        (2)
              (void      *)&link_state,                               (3)
              (NET_ERR   *)&err);                                     (4)
```

Listing 16-10 **Calling NetIF_IO_Ctrl()**

L16-10(1) The first argument specifies the interface number from which to get the physical link state.

L16-10(2) The second argument specifies the desired function that **NetIF_IO_Ctrl()** will perform. In order to get the current interfaces' link state, the application should specify this argument as either:

NET_IF_IO_CTRL_LINK_STATE_GET
NET_IF_IO_CTRL_LINK_STATE_GET_INFO

L16-10(3) The third argument is a pointer to a link state variable that must be declared by the application and passed to **NetIF_IO_Ctrl()**.

Chapter

17

Socket Programming

The two network socket interfaces supported by µC/TCP-IP were previously introduced. Now, in this chapter, we will discuss socket programming, data structures, and API functions calls.

17-1 NETWORK SOCKET DATA STRUCTURES

Communication using sockets requires configuring or reading network addresses from network socket address structures. The BSD socket API defines a generic socket address structure as a blank template with no address-specific configuration…

```
struct  sockaddr {                          /* Generic BSD   socket address structure    */
    CPU_INT16U  sa_family;                  /*  Socket address family                    */
    CPU_CHAR    sa_data[14];                /*  Protocol-specific address informatio     */
};


typedef  struct  net_sock_addr {            /* Generic µC/TCP-IP socket address structure */
    NET_SOCK_ADDR_FAMILY   AddrFamily;
    CPU_INT08U             Addr[NET_SOCK_BSD_ADDR_LEN_MAX = 14];
} NET_SOCK_ADDR;
```

Listing 17-1 **Generic (non-address-specific) address structures**

…as well as specific socket address structures to configure each specific protocol address family's network address configuration (e.g., IPv4 socket addresses):

```
struct  in_addr {
    NET_IP_ADDR  s_addr;                            /* IPv4 address (32 bits)                    */
};


struct  sockaddr_in {                               /* BSD     IPv4 socket address structure     */
    CPU_INT16U          sin_family;                 /*  Internet address family (e.g. AF_INET) */
    CPU_INT16U          sin_port;                   /*  Socket  address port number (16 bits)  */
    struct in_addr      sin_addr;                   /*  IPv4     address         (32 bits)     */
    CPU_CHAR            sin_zero[8];                /*  Not used (all zeroes)                  */
};


typedef  struct  net_sock_addr_ip {                 /* µC/TCP-IP socket address structure      */
    NET_SOCK_ADDR_FAMILY     AddrFamily;
    NET_PORT_NBR             Port;
    NET_IP_ADDR              Addr;
    CPU_INT08U               Unused[NET_SOCK_ADDR_IP_NBR_OCTETS_UNUSED = 8];
} NET_SOCK_ADDR_IP;
```

17

Listing 17-2 **Internet (IPv4) address structures**

A socket address structure's **AddrFamily/sa_family/sin_family** value *must* be read/written in host CPU byte order, while all **Addr/sa_data** values *must* be read/written in network byte order (big endian).

Even though socket functions – both µC/TCP-IP and BSD – pass pointers to the generic socket address structure, applications *must* declare and pass an instance of the specific protocol's socket address structure (e.g., an IPv4 address structure). For microprocessors that require data access to be aligned to appropriate word boundaries, this forces compilers to declare an appropriately-aligned socket address structure so that all socket address members are correctly aligned to their appropriate word boundaries.

Caution: Applications should avoid, or be cautious when, declaring and configuring a generic byte array as a socket address structure, since the compiler may not correctly align the array to or the socket address structure's members to appropriate word boundaries.

Figure 17-1 shows an example IPv4 instance of the µC/TCP-IP **NET_SOCK_ADDR_IP (sockaddr_in)** structure overlaid on top of **NET_SOCK_ADDR (sockaddr) the** structure

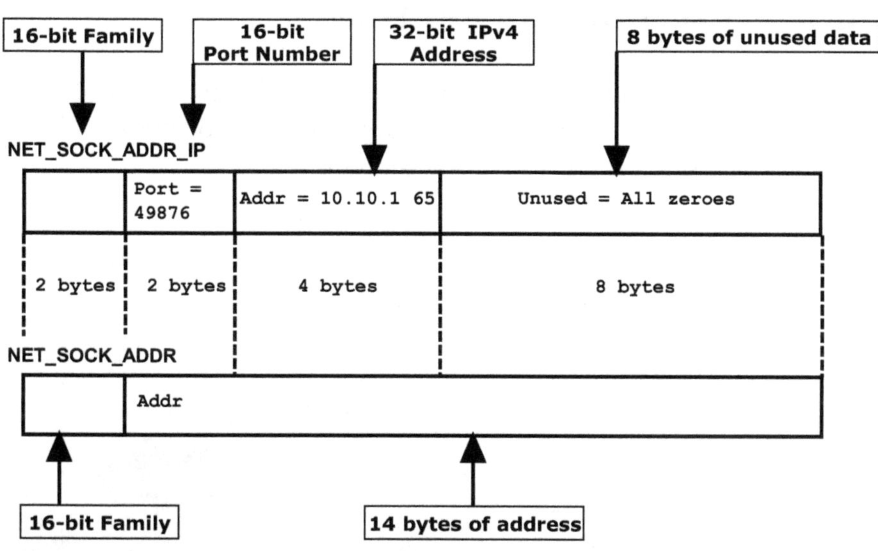

Figure 17-1 **NET_SOCK_ADDR_IP is the IPv4 specific instance of the generic NET_SOCK_ADDR data structure**

A socket could configure the example socket address structure in Figure 17-1 to bind on IP address 10.10.1.65 and port number 49876 with the following code:

```
NET_SOCK_ADDR_IP   addr_local;
NET_IP_ADDR        addr_ip;
NET_PORT_NBR       addr_port;
NET_SOCK_RTN_CODE  rtn_code;
NET_ERR            err;


addr_ip   = NetASCII_Str_to_IP("10.10.1.65", &err);
addr_port = 49876;
Mem_Clr((void    *)&addr_local,
        (CPU_SIZE_T) sizeof(addr_local));
addr_local.AddrFamily = NET_SOCK_ADDR_FAMILY_IP_V4;                 /* = AF_INET†† Figure 17-1
*/
addr_local.Addr       = NET_UTIL_HOST_TO_NET_32(addr_ip);
addr_local.Port       = NET_UTIL_HOST_TO_NET_16(addr_port);
rtn_code              = NetSock_Bind((NET_SOCK_ID       ) sock_id,
                             (NET_SOCK_ADDR    *)&addr_local,  /* Cast to generic addr† */
                             (NET_SOCK_ADDR_LEN) sizeof(addr_local),
                             (NET_ERR          *)&err);
```

Listing 17-3 **Bind on 10.10.1.65**

† The address of the specific IPv4 socket address structure is cast to a pointer to the generic socket address structure.

17-2 COMPLETE SEND() OPERATION

send() returns the number of bytes actually sent out. This might be less than the number that are available to send. The function will send as much of the data as it can. The developer must make sure that the rest of the packet is sent later.

```
{
    int  total     = 0;        /* how many bytes we've sent      */
    int  bytesleft = *len;     /* how many we have left to send  */
    int  n;

    while (total < *len) {
        n = send(s, buf + total, bytesleft, 0);                          (1)
        if (n == -1) {
            break;
        }
        total += n;                                                      (2)
        bytesleft -= n;                                                  (3)
    }
}
```

Listing 17-4 **Completing a send()**

L17-4(1) Send as many bytes as there are transmit network buffers available.

L17-4(2) Increase the number of bytes sent.

L17-4(3) Calculate how many bytes are left to send.

This is another example that, for a TCP/IP stack to operate smoothly, sufficient memory to define enough buffers for transmission and reception is a design decision that requires attention if optimum performance for the given hardware is desired.

17-3 SOCKET APPLICATIONS

Two socket types are identified: Datagram sockets and Stream sockets. The following sections provide sample code describing how these sockets work.

In addition to the BSD 4.x sockets application interface (API), the µC/TCP-IP stack gives the developer the opportunity to use Micrium's own socket functions with which to interact.

Although there is a great deal of similarity between the two APIs, the parameters of the two sets of functions differ slightly. The purpose of the following sections is o give developers a first look at Micrium's functions by providing concrete examples of how to use the API.

For those interested in BSD socket programming, there are plenty of books, online references, and articles dedicated to this subject.

The examples have been designed to be as simple as possible. Hence, only basic error checking is performed. When it comes to building real applications, those checks should be extended to deliver a product that is as robust as possible.

17

17-3-1 DATAGRAM SOCKET (UDP SOCKET)

Figure 17-2 reproduces a diagram that introduces sample code using the typical socket functions for a UDP client-server application. The example uses the Micrium proprietary socket API function calls. A similar example could be written using the BSD socket API.

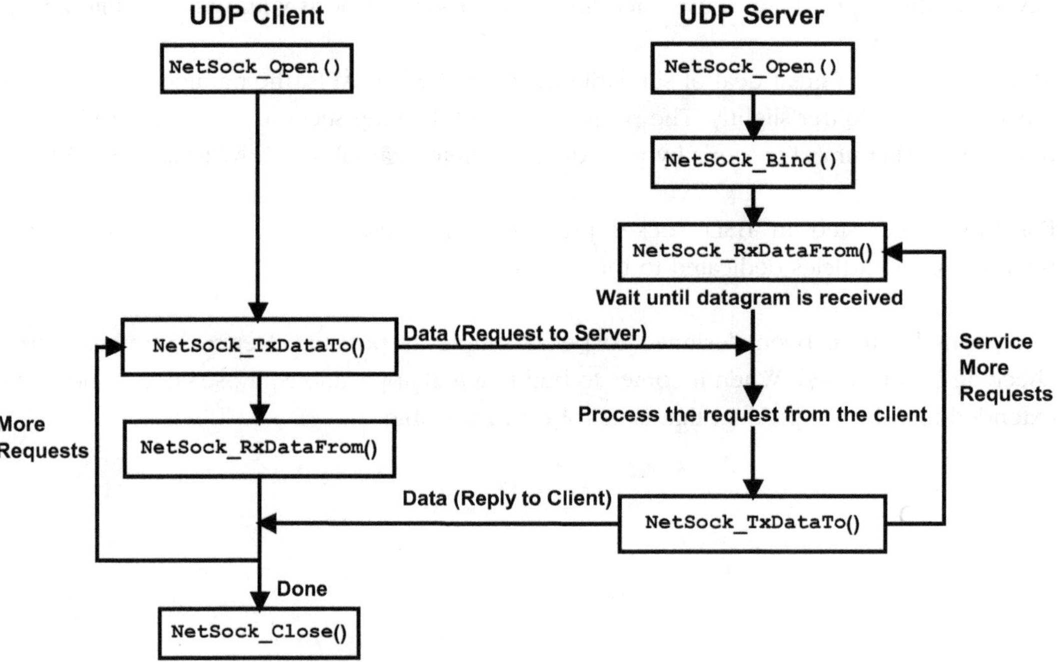

Figure 17-2 **μC/TCP-IP Socket calls used in a typical UDP client-server application**

The code in Listing 17-5 implements a UDP server. It opens a socket and binds an IP address, listens and waits for a packet to arrive at the specified port. See Appendix B, "μC/TCP-IP API Reference" on page 433 for a list of all μC/TCP-IP socket API functions.

DATAGRAM SERVER (UDP SERVER)

```
#define  UDP_SERVER_PORT  10001
#define  RX_BUF_SIZE         15
CPU_BOOLEAN  TestUDPServer (void)
{
    NET_SOCK_ID         sock;
    NET_SOCK_ADDR_IP    server_sock_addr_ip;
    NET_SOCK_ADDR_LEN   server_sock_addr_ip_size;
    NET_SOCK_ADDR_IP    client_sock_addr_ip;
    NET_SOCK_ADDR_LEN   client_sock_addr_ip_size;
    NET_SOCK_RTN_CODE   rx_size;
    CPU_CHAR            rx_buf[RX_BUF_SIZE];
    CPU_BOOLEAN         attempt_rx;
    NET_ERR             err;

    sock = NetSock_Open( NET_SOCK_ADDR_FAMILY_IP_V4,                          (1)
                         NET_SOCK_TYPE_DATAGRAM,
                         NET_SOCK_PROTOCOL_UDP,
                        &err);
    if (err != NET_SOCK_ERR_NONE) {
        return (DEF_FALSE);
    }

    server_sock_addr_ip_size = sizeof(server_sock_addr_ip);                   (2)
    Mem_Clr((void     *)&server_sock_addr_ip,
            (CPU_SIZE_T) server_sock_addr_ip_size);
    server_sock_addr_ip.AddrFamily = NET_SOCK_ADDR_FAMILY_IP_V4;
    server_sock_addr_ip.Addr       = NET_UTIL_HOST_TO_NET_32(NET_SOCK_ADDR_IP_WILD_CARD);
    server_sock_addr_ip.Port       = NET_UTIL_HOST_TO_NET_16(UDP_SERVER_PORT);

    NetSock_Bind((NET_SOCK_ID      ) sock,                                    (3)
                 (NET_SOCK_ADDR   *)&server_sock_addr_ip,
                 (NET_SOCK_ADDR_LEN) NET_SOCK_ADDR_SIZE,
                 (NET_ERR         *)&err);
    if (err != NET_SOCK_ERR_NONE) {
        NetSock_Close(sock, &err);
        return (DEF_FALSE);
    }
```

```
    do {
        client_sock_addr_ip_size = sizeof(client_sock_addr_ip);

        rx_size = NetSock_RxDataFrom((NET_SOCK_ID ) sock,                       (4)
                                     (void *) rx_buf,
                                     (CPU_INT16S ) RX_BUF_SIZE,
                                     (CPU_INT16S ) NET_SOCK_FLAG_NONE,
                                     (NET_SOCK_ADDR *)&client_sock_addr_ip,
                                     (NET_SOCK_ADDR_LEN *)&client_sock_addr_ip_size,
                                     (void *) 0,
                                     (CPU_INT08U ) 0,
                                     (CPU_INT08U *) 0,
                                     (NET_ERR *)&err);
        switch (err) {
            case NET_SOCK_ERR_NONE:
                attempt_rx = DEF_NO;
                break;
            case NET_SOCK_ERR_RX_Q_EMPTY:
            case NET_OS_ERR_LOCK:
                attempt_rx = DEF_YES;
                break;
            default:
                attempt_rx = DEF_NO;
                break;
        }
    } while (attempt_rx == DEF_YES);

    NetSock_Close(sock, &err);                                                  (5)

    if (err != NET_SOCK_ERR_NONE) {
        return (DEF_FALSE);
    }

    return (DEF_TRUE);
}
```

Listing 17-5 **Datagram Server**

L17-5(1) Open a datagram socket (UDP protocol).

L17-5(2) Populate the **NET_SOCK_ADDR_IP** structure for the server address and port, and convert it to network order.

L17-5(3) Bind the newly created socket to the address and port specified by **server_sock_addr_ip**.

L17-5(4) Receive data from any host on port **DATAGRAM_SERVER_PORT**.

L17-5(5) Close the socket.

DATAGRAM CLIENT (UDP CLIENT)

The code in Listing 17-6 implements a UDP client. It sends a **'Hello World!'** message to a server that listens on the **UDP_SERVER_PORT**.

```
#define  UDP_SERVER_IP_ADDR   "192.168.1.100"
#define  UDP_SERVER_PORT               10001
#define  UDP_SERVER_TX_STR     "Hello World!"


CPU_BOOLEAN  TestUDPClient (void)
{
    NET_SOCK_ID          sock;
    NET_IP_ADDR          server_ip_addr;
    NET_SOCK_ADDR_IP     server_sock_addr_ip;
    NET_SOCK_ADDR_LEN    server_sock_addr_ip_size;
    CPU_CHAR            *pbuf;
    CPU_INT16S           buf_len;
    NET_SOCK_RTN_CODE    tx_size;
    NET_ERR              err;
    pbuf     = UDP_SERVER_TX_STR;
    buf_len = Str_Len(UDP_SERVER_TX_STR);

    sock = NetSock_Open( NET_SOCK_ADDR_FAMILY_IP_V4,                        (1)
                         NET_SOCK_TYPE_DATAGRAM,
                         NET_SOCK_PROTOCOL_UDP,
                        &err);
    if (err != NET_SOCK_ERR_NONE) {
        return (DEF_FALSE);
    }

    server_ip_addr = NetASCII_Str_to_IP(UDP_SERVER_IP_ADDR, &err);          (2)
    if (err != NET_ASCII_ERR_NONE) {
        NetSock_Close(sock, &err);
        return (DEF_FALSE);
    }
```

```
    server_sock_addr_ip_size = sizeof(server_sock_addr_ip);                        (3)
    Mem_Clr((void      *)&server_sock_addr_ip,
            (CPU_SIZE_T) server_sock_addr_ip_size);
    server_sock_addr_ip.AddrFamily = NET_SOCK_ADDR_FAMILY_IP_V4;
    server_sock_addr_ip.Addr       = NET_UTIL_HOST_TO_NET_32(server_ip_addr);
    server_sock_addr_ip.Port       = NET_UTIL_HOST_TO_NET_16(UDP_SERVER_PORT);

    tx_size = NetSock_TxDataTo((NET_SOCK_ID ) sock,                               (4)
                               (void *) pbuf,
                               (CPU_INT16S ) buf_len,
                               (CPU_INT16S ) NET_SOCK_FLAG_NONE,
                               (NET_SOCK_ADDR *)&server_sock_addr_ip,
                               (NET_SOCK_ADDR_LEN) sizeof(server_sock_addr_ip),
                               (NET_ERR *)&err);

    NetSock_Close(sock, &err);                                                     (5)
    if (err != NET_SOCK_ERR_NONE) {
        return (DEF_FALSE);
    }
    return (DEF_TRUE);
}
```

Listing 17-6 **Datagram Client**

L17-6(1) Open a datagram socket (UDP protocol).

L17-6(2) Convert an IPv4 address from ASCII dotted-decimal notation to a network protocol IPv4 address in host-order.

L17-6(3) Populate the `NET_SOCK_ADDR_IP` structure for the server address and port, and convert it to network order.

L17-6(4) Transmit data to host `DATAGRAM_SERVER_IP_ADDR` on port `DATAGRAM_SERVER_PORT`.

L17-6(5) Close the socket.

17-3-2 STREAM SOCKET (TCP SOCKET)

Figure 17-3 reproduces Figure 8-8, which introduced sample code using typical socket functions for a TCP client-server application. The example uses the Micrium proprietary socket API function calls. A similar example could be written using the BSD socket API.

Typically, after a TCP server starts, TCP clients can connect and send requests to the server. A TCP server waits until client connections arrive and then creates a dedicated TCP socket connection to process the client's requests and reply back to the client (if necessary). This continues until either the client or the server closes the dedicated client-server connection. Also while handling multiple, simultaneous client-server connections, the TCP server can wait for new client-server connections

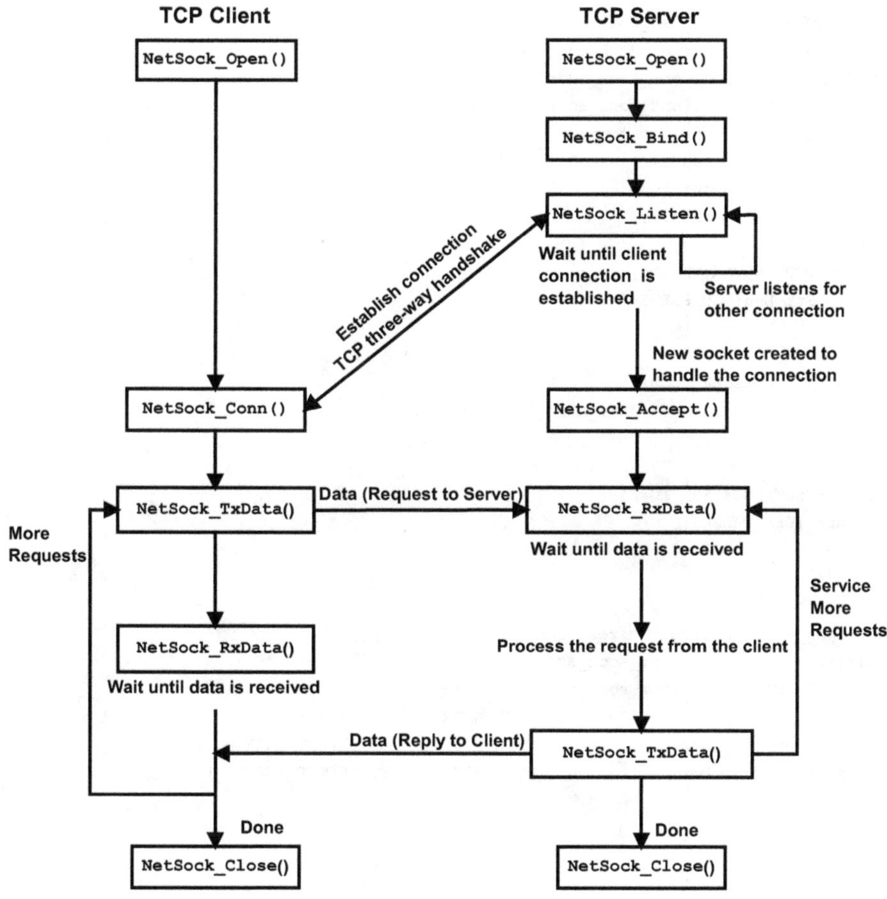

Figure 17-3 **μC/TCP-IP Socket calls used in a typical TCP client-server application**

STREAM SERVER (TCP SERVER)

This example presents a very basic client-server application over a TCP connection. The server presented is simply waits for a connection and send the string **'Hello World!'**. See section "µC/TCP-IP API Reference" on page 433 for a list of all µC/TCP-IP socket API functions.

```
#define  TCP_SERVER_PORT                     10000
#define  TCP_SERVER_CONN_Q_SIZE                  1
#define  TCP_SERVER_TX_STR             "Hello World!"

CPU_BOOLEAN  TestTCPServer (void)
{
    NET_SOCK_ID          sock_listen;
    NET_SOCK_ID          sock_req;
    NET_SOCK_ADDR_IP     server_sock_addr_ip;
    NET_SOCK_ADDR_LEN    server_sock_addr_ip_size;
    NET_SOCK_ADDR_IP     client_sock_addr_ip;
    NET_SOCK_ADDR_LEN    client_sock_addr_ip_size;
    CPU_BOOLEAN          attempt_conn;
    CPU_CHAR            *pbuf;
    CPU_INT16S           buf_len;
    NET_SOCK_RTN_CODE    tx_size;
    NET_ERR              err;
    pbuf    = TCP_SERVER_TX_STR;
    buf_len = Str_Len(TCP_SERVER_TX_STR);


    sock_listen = NetSock_Open( NET_SOCK_ADDR_FAMILY_IP_V4,                          (1)
                                NET_SOCK_TYPE_STREAM,
                                NET_SOCK_PROTOCOL_TCP,
                               &err);
    if (err != NET_SOCK_ERR_NONE) {
        return (DEF_FALSE);
    }


    server_sock_addr_ip_size = sizeof(server_sock_addr_ip);                          (2)
    Mem_Clr((void     *)&server_sock_addr_ip,
            (CPU_SIZE_T) server_sock_addr_ip_size);
    server_sock_addr_ip.AddrFamily = NET_SOCK_ADDR_FAMILY_IP_V4;
    server_sock_addr_ip.Addr       = NET_UTIL_HOST_TO_NET_32(NET_SOCK_ADDR_IP_WILD_CARD);
    server_sock_addr_ip.Port       = NET_UTIL_HOST_TO_NET_16(TCP_SERVER_PORT);
```

```
    NetSock_Bind((NET_SOCK_ID ) sock_listen,                              (3)
                 (NET_SOCK_ADDR *)&server_sock_addr_ip,
                 (NET_SOCK_ADDR_LEN) NET_SOCK_ADDR_SIZE,
                 (NET_ERR *)&err);
    if (err != NET_SOCK_ERR_NONE) {
        NetSock_Close(sock_listen, &err);
        return (DEF_FALSE);
}


    NetSock_Listen( sock_listen,                                          (4)
                    TCP_SERVER_CONN_Q_SIZE,
                   &err);
    if (err != NET_SOCK_ERR_NONE) {
        NetSock_Close(sock_listen, &err);
        return (DEF_FALSE);
    }

    do {
        client_sock_addr_ip_size = sizeof(client_sock_addr_ip);

        sock_req = NetSock_Accept((NET_SOCK_ID ) sock_listen,             (5)
                                  (NET_SOCK_ADDR *)&client_sock_addr_ip,
                                  (NET_SOCK_ADDR_LEN *)&client_sock_addr_ip_size,
                                  (NET_ERR *)&err);
        switch (err) {
            case NET_SOCK_ERR_NONE:
                attempt_conn = DEF_NO;
                break;
            case NET_ERR_INIT_INCOMPLETE:
            case NET_SOCK_ERR_NULL_PTR:
            case NET_SOCK_ERR_NONE_AVAIL:
            case NET_SOCK_ERR_CONN_ACCEPT_Q_NONE_AVAIL:
            case NET_SOCK_ERR_CONN_SIGNAL_TIMEOUT:
            case NET_OS_ERR_LOCK:
                attempt_conn = DEF_YES;
                break;

            default:
                attempt_conn = DEF_NO;
                break;
        }
    } while (attempt_conn == DEF_YES);

    if (err != NET_SOCK_ERR_NONE) {
        NetSock_Close(sock_req, &err);
        return (DEF_FALSE);
    }
```

```
    tx_size = NetSock_TxData( sock_req,                                    (6)
                              pbuf,
                              buf_len,
                              NET_SOCK_FLAG_NONE,
                             &err);

    NetSock_Close(sock_req, &err);                                         (7)
    NetSock_Close(sock_listen, &err);

    return (DEF_TRUE);
}
```

Listing 17-7 **Stream Server**

L17-7(1) Open a stream socket (TCP protocol).

L17-7(2) Populate the **NET_SOCK_ADDR_IP** structure for the server address and port, and convert it to network order.

L17-7(3) Bind the newly created socket to the address and port specified by **server_sock_addr_ip**.

L17-7(4) Set the socket to listen for a connection request coming on the specified port.

L17-7(5) Accept the incoming connection request, and return a new socket for this particular connection. Note that this function call is being called from inside a loop because it might timeout (no client attempts to connect to the server).

L17-7(6) One the connection has been established between the server and a client, transmit the message. Note that the return value of this function is not used here, but a real application should make sure all the message has been sent by comparing that value with the length of the message.

L17-7(7) Close both listen and request sockets. When the server need to stay active, the listen socket stays open so that I can accept additional connection requests. Usually, the server will wait for a connection, **accept()** it, and **OSTaskCreate()** a task to handle it.

STREAM CLIENT (TCP CLIENT)

The client of Listing 17-8 connects to the specified server and receives the string the server sends.

```
#define  TCP_SERVER_IP_ADDR  "192.168.1.101"
#define  TCP_SERVER_PORT               10000
#define  RX_BUF_SIZE                      15

CPU_BOOLEAN  TestTCPClient (void)
{
    NET_SOCK_ID         sock;
    NET_IP_ADDR         server_ip_addr;
    NET_SOCK_ADDR_IP    server_sock_addr_ip;
    NET_SOCK_ADDR_LEN   server_sock_addr_ip_size;
    NET_SOCK_RTN_CODE   conn_rtn_code;
    NET_SOCK_RTN_CODE   rx_size;
    CPU_CHAR            rx_buf[RX_BUF_SIZE];
    NET_ERR             err;


    sock = NetSock_Open( NET_SOCK_ADDR_FAMILY_IP_V4,                          (1)
                         NET_SOCK_TYPE_STREAM,
                         NET_SOCK_PROTOCOL_TCP,
                        &err);
    if (err != NET_SOCK_ERR_NONE) {
        return (DEF_FALSE);
    }

    server_ip_addr = NetASCII_Str_to_IP(TCP_SERVER_IP_ADDR, &err);            (2)
    if (err != NET_ASCII_ERR_NONE) {
        NetSock_Close(sock, &err);
        return (DEF_FALSE);
    }

    server_sock_addr_ip_size = sizeof(server_sock_addr_ip);                   (3)
    Mem_Clr((void     *)&server_sock_addr_ip,
            (CPU_SIZE_T) server_sock_addr_ip_size);
    server_sock_addr_ip.AddrFamily = NET_SOCK_ADDR_FAMILY_IP_V4;
    server_sock_addr_ip.Addr       = NET_UTIL_HOST_TO_NET_32(server_ip_addr);
    server_sock_addr_ip.Port       = NET_UTIL_HOST_TO_NET_16(TCP_SERVER_PORT);
```

```
    conn_rtn_code = NetSock_Conn((NET_SOCK_ID ) sock,                                          (4)
                                 (NET_SOCK_ADDR *)&server_sock_addr_ip,
                                 (NET_SOCK_ADDR_LEN) sizeof(server_sock_addr_ip),
                                 (NET_ERR *)&err);
    if (err != NET_SOCK_ERR_NONE) {
        NetSock_Close(sock, &err);
        return (DEF_FALSE);
    }

    rx_size = NetSock_RxData( sock,                                                            (5)
                              rx_buf,
                              RX_BUF_SIZE,
                              NET_SOCK_FLAG_NONE,
                             &err);
    if (err != NET_SOCK_ERR_NONE) {
        NetSock_Close(sock, &err);
        return (DEF_FALSE);
    }

    NetSock_Close(sock, &err);                                                                 (6)
    return (DEF_TRUE);
}
```

Listing 17-8 **Stream Client**

L17-8(1) Open a stream socket (TCP protocol).

L17-8(2) Convert an IPv4 address from ASCII dotted-decimal notation to a network protocol IPv4 address in host-order.

L17-8(3) Populate the **NET_SOCK_ADDR_IP** structure for the server address and port, and convert it to network order.

L17-8(4) Connect the socket to a remote host.

L17-8(5) Receive data from the connected socket. Note that the return value for this function is not used here.However, a real application should make sure everything has been received.

L17-8(6) Close the socket.

TCP CONNECTION CONFIGURATIONS

µC/TCP-IP provides a set of APIs to configure TCP connections on an individual basis. These APIs are listed below and detailed in section B-14 "TCP Functions" on page 667:

- NetTCP_ConnCfgIdleTimeout()
- NetTCP_ConnCfgMaxSegSizeLocal()
- NetTCP_ConnCfgReTxMaxTh()
- NetTCP_ConnCfgReTxMaxTimeout()
- NetTCP_ConnCfgRxWinSize()
- NetTCP_ConnCfgTxWinSize()
- NetTCP_ConnCfgTxAckImmedRxdPushEn()
- NetTCP_ConnCfgTxNagleEn()
- NetTCP_ConnCfgTxKeepAliveEn()
- NetTCP_ConnCfgTxKeepAliveTh()
- NetTCP_ConnCfgTxAckDlyTimeout()

17-4 SOCKET OPTIONS

µC/TCP-IP provides a set of APIs to configure sockets on an individual basis. These APIs are listed below and detailed in section B-13 "Network Socket Functions" on page 583:

- NetSock_CfgBlock() (TCP/UDP)
- NetSock_CfgSecure() (TCP)
- NetSock_CfgRxQ_Size() (TCP/UDP)

- NetSock_CfgTxQ_Size() (TCP/UDP)
- NetSock_CfgTxIP_TOS() (TCP/UDP)
- NetSock_CfgTxIP_TTL() (TCP/UDP)
- NetSock_CfgTxIP_TTL_Multicast() (TCP/UDP)
- NetSock_CfgTimeoutConnAcceptDflt() (TCP)
- NetSock_CfgTimeoutConnAcceptGet_ms() (TCP)
- NetSock_CfgTimeoutConnAcceptSet() (TCP)
- NetSock_CfgTimeoutConnCloseDflt() (TCP)
- NetSock_CfgTimeoutConnCloseGet_ms() (TCP)
- NetSock_CfgTimeoutConnCloseSet() (TCP)
- NetSock_CfgTimeoutConnReqDflt() (TCP)
- NetSock_CfgTimeoutConnReqGet_ms() (TCP)
- NetSock_CfgTimeoutConnReqSet() (TCP)
- NetSock_CfgTimeoutRxQ_Dflt() (TCP/UDP)
- NetSock_CfgTimeoutRxQ_Get_ms() (TCP/UDP)
- NetSock_CfgTimeoutRxQ_Set() (TCP/UDP)
- NetSock_CfgTimeoutTxQ_Dflt() (TCP)
- NetSock_CfgTimeoutTxQ_Get_ms() (TCP)
- NetSock_CfgTimeoutTxQ_Set() (TCP)

17-5 SECURE SOCKETS

If a network security module (i.e. µC/SSL) is available, µC/TCP-IP network security manager can be used to secure sockets. Basically, it provides APIs to install the required keying material and to set the secure flag on a specific socket. For details about the network security manager configuration, please refer to Appendix C, "Network Socket Configuration" on page 740. An example that shows how to use the network security manager can be found in section E-6 "Using Network Security Manager" on page 787.

17-6 2MSL

Maximum Segment Lifetime (MSL) is the time a TCP segment can exist in the network. It is arbitrarily defined to be two minutes. 2MSL is twice this lifetime. It is the maximum lifetime of a TCP segment on the network because it supposes segment transmission and acknowledgment.

Currently, Micrium does not support multiple sockets with exactly the same connection information. This prevents new sockets from binding to the same local addresses as other sockets. Thus, for TCP sockets, each **close()** incurs the TCP 2MSL timeout and prevents the next **bind()** from the same Client from occurring until after the timeout expires. This is why the 2MSL value is used. This can lead to a long delay before the socket resource is released and reused. µC/TCP-IP configures the TCP connection's default maximum segment lifetime (MSL) timeout value, specified in integer seconds. Micrium recommends starting with a value of 3 seconds.

If TCP connections are established and closed rapidly, it is possible that this timeout may further delay new TCP connections from becoming available. Thus, an even lower timeout value may be desirable to free TCP connections and make them available for new connections as rapidly as possible. However, a 0 second timeout prevents µC/TCP-IP from performing the complete TCP connection close sequence and will instead send TCP reset (RST) segments.

For UDP sockets, the sockets **close()** without delay. Thus, the next **bind()** is not blocked.

17-7 µC/TCP-IP SOCKET ERROR CODES

When socket functions return error codes, the error codes should be inspected to determine if the error is a temporary, non-fault condition (such as no data to receive) or fatal (such as the socket has been closed).

17-7-1 FATAL SOCKET ERROR CODES

Whenever any of the following fatal error codes are returned by any µC/TCP-IP socket function, that socket *must* be immediately **closed()**'d without further access by any other socket functions:


```
NET_SOCK_ERR_INVALID_FAMILY
NET_SOCK_ERR_INVALID_PROTOCOL
NET_SOCK_ERR_INVALID_TYPE
NET_SOCK_ERR_INVALID_STATE
NET_SOCK_ERR_FAULT
```

Whenever any of the following fatal error codes are returned by any µC/TCP-IP socket function, that socket *must not* be accessed by any other socket functions but must also *not* be **closed()**'d:

```
NET_SOCK_ERR_NOT_USED
```

17-7-2 SOCKET ERROR CODE LIST

See section D-7 "IP Error Codes" on page 756 for a brief explanation of all µC/TCP-IP socket error codes.

Chapter

18

Timer Management

μC/TCP-IP manages software timers used to keep track of various network-related timeouts. Timer management functions are found in **`net_tmr.*`**. Timers are required for:

- Network interface/device driver link-layer monitor 1 total
- Network interface performance statistics 1 total
- ARP cache management 1 per ARP cache entry
- IP fragment reassembly 1 per fragment chain
- Various TCP connection timeouts up to 7 per TCP connection
- Debug monitor task 1 total
- Performance monitor task 1 total

Of the three mandatory μC/TCP-IP tasks, one of them, the timer task, is used to manage and update timers. The timer task updates timers periodically. **`NET_TMR_CFG_TASK_FREQ`** determines how often (in Hz) network timers are to be updated. This value *must not* be configured as a floating-point number. This value is typically set to **10 Hz**.

See section C-5-1 on page 730 for more information on timer usage and configuration.

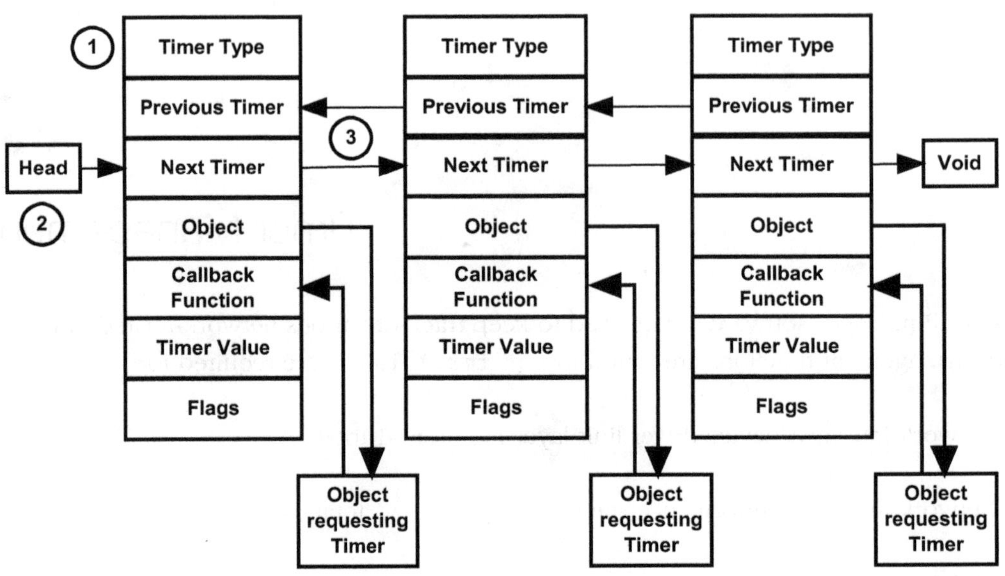

Figure 18-1 **Timer List**

L18-0(1) Timer types are either **NONE** or **TMR**, meaning unused or used. This field is defined as ASCII representations of network timer types. Memory displays of network timers will display the timer TYPEs with their chosen ASCII name.

L18-0(2) To manage the timers, the head of the timer list is identified by **NetTmr_TaskListHead**, a pointer to the head of the Timer List.

L18-0(3) **PrevPtr** and **NextPtr** doubly link each timer to form the Timer List.

The flags field is currently unused.

Network timers are managed by the Timer task in a doubly-linked Timer List. The function that executes these operation is the **NetTmr_TaskHandler()** function. This function is an operating system (OS) function and *should* be called only by appropriate network-operating system port function(s). **NetTmr_TaskHandler()** is blocked until network initialization completes.

NetTmr_TaskHandler() handles the network timers in the Timer List by acquiring the global network lock first. This function blocks all other network protocol tasks by pending on and acquiring the global network lock. Then it handles every network timer in Timer List by decrementing the network timer(s) and for any timer that expires, execute the timer's callback function and free the timer from Timer List. When a network timer expires, the timer is be freed *prior* to executing the timer callback function. This ensures that at least one timer is available if the timer callback function requires a timer. Finally, **NetTmr_TaskHandler()** releases the global network lock.

New timers are added at the head of the Timer List. As timers are added into the list, older timers migrate to the tail of the Timer List. Once a timer expires or is discarded, it is removed.

NetTmr_TaskHandler() handles of all the valid timers in the Timer List, up to the first corrupted timer. If a corrupted timer is detected, the timer is discarded/unlinked from the List. Consequently, any remaining valid timers are unlinked from Timer List and are not handled. Finally, the Timer Task is aborted.

Since **NetTmr_TaskHandler()** is asynchronous to ANY timer Get/Set, one additional tick is added to each timer's count-down so that the requested timeout is *always* satisfied. This additional tick is added by NOT checking for zero ticks after decrementing; any timer that expires is recognized at the next tick.

A timer value of 0 ticks/seconds is allowed. The next tick will expire the timer.

The **NetTmr_***()** functions are internal functions and should not be called by application functions. This is the reason they are not described here or in Appendix B, "µC/TCP-IP API Reference" on page 433. For more details on these functions, please refer to the **net_tmr.*** files.

Chapter

19

Debug Management

µC/TCP-IP contains debug constants and functions that may be used by applications to determine network RAM usage, check run-time network resource usage, and check network error or fault conditions. These constants and functions are found in **net_dbg.***. Most of these debug features must be enabled by appropriate configuration constants (see Appendix C, "µC/TCP-IP Configuration and Optimization" on page 723).

19-1 NETWORK DEBUG INFORMATION CONSTANTS

Network debug information constants provide the developer with run-time statistics on µC/TCP-IP configuration, data type and structure sizes, and data RAM usage. The list of debug information constants can be found in **net_dbg.c**, sections **GLOBAL NETWORK MODULE DEBUG INFORMATION CONSTANTS & GLOBAL NETWORK MODULE DATA SIZE CONSTANTS**. These debug constants are enabled by configuring **NET_DBG_CFG_DBG_INFO_EN** to **DEF_ENABLED**.

For example, these constants can be used as follows:

```
CPU_INT16U    net_version;
CPU_INT32U    net_data_size;
CPU_INT32U    net_data_nbr_if;


net_version      = Net_Version;
net_data_size    = Net_DataSize;
net_data_nbr_if = NetIF_CfgMaxNbrIF;
printf("µC/TCP-IP Version         : %05d\n", net_version);
printf("Total Network RAM Used    : %05d\n", net_data_size);
printf("Number Network Interfaces : %05d\n", net_data_nbr_if);
```

19-2 NETWORK DEBUG MONITOR TASK

The Network Debug Monitor Task periodically checks the current run-time status of certain µC/TCP-IP conditions and saves that status to global variables which may be queried by other network modules.

Currently, the Network Debug Monitor Task is only enabled when ICMP Transmit Source Quenches are enabled (see section C-10-1 on page 735) because this is the only network functionality that requires a periodic update of certain network status conditions. Applications do not need Debug Monitor Task functionality since applications have access to the same debug status functions that the Monitor Task calls and may call them asynchronously.

Chapter

20

Statistics and Error Counters

μC/TCP-IP maintains counters and statistics for a variety of expected or unexpected error conditions. Some of these statistics are optional since they require additional code and memory and are enabled only if **NET_CTR_CFG_STAT_EN** or **NET_CTR_CFG_ERR_EN** is enabled (see section C-4 "Network Counter Configuration" on page 729).

20-1 STATISTICS

μC/TCP-IP maintains run-time statistics on interfaces and most μC/TCP-IP object pools. If desired, an application can thus query μC/TCP-IP to find out how many frames have been processed on a particular interface, transmit and receive performance metrics, buffer utilization and more. An application can also reset the statistic pools back to their initialization values (see **net_stat.h**).

Applications may choose to monitor statistics for various reasons. For example, examining buffer statistics allows you to better manage the memory usage. Typically, more buffers can be allocated than necessary and, by examining buffer usage statistics, adjustments can be made to reduce their number.

Network protocol and interface statistics are kept in an instance of a data structure named **Net_StatCtrs**. This variable may be viewed within a debugger or referenced externally by the application for run-time analysis.

Unlike network protocol statistics, object pool statistics have functions to get a copy of the specified statistic pool and functions for resetting the pools to their default values. These statistics are kept in a data structure called **NET_STAT_POOL** which can be declared by the application and used as a return variable from the statistics API functions.

The data structure is shown below

```
typedef struct net_stat_pool {
    NET_TYPE            Type;
    NET_STAT_POOL_QTY   EntriesInit;
    NET_STAT_POOL_QTY   EntriesTotal;
    NET_STAT_POOL_QTY   EntriesAvail;
    NET_STAT_POOL_QTY   EntriesUsed;
    NET_STAT_POOL_QTY   EntriesUsedMax;
    NET_STAT_POOL_QTY   EntriesLostCur;
    NET_STAT_POOL_QTY   EntriesLostTotal;
    CPU_INT32U          EntriesAllocatedCtr;
    CPU_INT32U          EntriesDeallocatedCtr;
} NET_STAT_POOL;
```

NET_STAT_POOL_QTY is a data type currently set to **CPU_INT16U** and thus contains a maximum count of 65535.

Access to buffer statistics is obtained via interface functions that the application can call (described in the next sections). Most likely, only the following variables in **NET_STAT_POOL** need to be examined, because the **.Type** member is configured at initialization time as **NET_STAT_TYPE_POOL** :

.EntriesAvail
This variable indicates how many buffers are available in the pool.

.EntriesUsed
This variable indicates how many buffers are currently used by the TCP/IP stack.

.EntriesUsedMax
This variable indicates the maximum number of buffers used since it was last reset.

.EntriesAllocatedCtr
This variable indicates the total number of times buffers were allocated (i.e., used by the TCP/IP stack).

.EntriesDeallocatedCtr
This variable indicates the total number of times buffers were returned back to the buffer pool.

In order to enable run-time statistics, the macro **NET_CTR_CFG_STAT_EN** located within **net_cfg.h** must be defined to **DEF_ENABLED**.

20-2 ERROR COUNTERS

µC/TCP-IP maintains run-time counters for tracking error conditions within the Network Protocol Stack. If desired, the application may view the error counters in order to debug run-time problems such as low memory conditions, slow performance, packet loss, *etc*.

Network protocol error counters are kept in an instance of a data structure named **Net_ErrCtrs**. This variable may be viewed within a debugger or referenced externally by the application for run-time analysis (see **net_stat.h**).

In order to enable run-time error counters, the macro **NET_CTR_CFG_ERR_EN** located within **net_cfg.h** must be defined to **DEF_ENABLED**.

Appendix

µC/TCP-IP Device Driver APIs

This appendix provides a reference to the µC/TCP-IP Device Driver API. Each user-accessible service is presented in alphabetical order. The following information is provided for each of the services:

- A brief description
- The function prototype
- The filename of the source code
- A description of the arguments passed to the function
- A description of the returned value(s)
- Specific notes and warnings on the use of the service

A-1 DEVICE DRIVER FUNCTIONS FOR MAC

A-1-1 NetDev_Init()

The first function within the Ethernet API is the device driver initialization/`Init()` function. This function is called by `NetIF_Add()` exactly once for each specific network device added by the application. If multiple instances of the same network device are present on the development board, then this function is called for each instance of the device. However, applications should not try to add the same specific device more than once. If a network device fails to initialize, we recommend debugging to find and correct the cause of failure.

Note: This function relies heavily on the implementation of several network device board support package (BSP) functions. See Chapter 14, "Network Device BSP" on page 320 and Appendix A, "Device Driver BSP Functions" on page 420 for more information on network device BSP functions.

FILES

Every device driver's `net_dev.c`

PROTOTYPE

```
static void NetDev_Init (NET_IF  *pif,
                         NET_ERR *perr);
```

Note that since every device driver's `Init()` function is accessed only by function pointer via the device driver's API structure, it doesn't need to be globally available and should therefore be declared as '`static`'.

ARGUMENTS

`pif` Pointer to the interface to initialize a network device.

`perr` Pointer to variable that will receive the return error code from this function.

RETURNED VALUE

None.

REQUIRED CONFIGURATION

None.

NOTES / WARNINGS

The **Init()** function generally performs the following operations, however, depending on the device being initialized, functionality may need to be added or removed:

1 Configure clock gating to the MAC device, if applicable. This is generally performed via the network device's BSP function pointer, **CfgClk()**, implemented in **net_bsp.c** (see section A-3-1 on page 420).

2 Configure all necessary I/O pins for both an internal or external MAC and PHY, if present. This is generally performed via the network device's BSP function pointer, **CfgGPIO()**, implemented in **net_bsp.c** (see section A-3-2 on page 422).

- Configure the host interrupt controller for receive and transmit complete interrupts. Additional interrupt services may be initialized depending on the device and driver requirements. This is generally performed via the network device's BSP function pointer, **CfgIntCtrl()**, implemented in **net_bsp.c** (see section A-3-3 on page 424).

3 For DMA devices: Allocate memory for all necessary descriptors. This is performed via calls to µC/LIB's memory module.

4 For DMA devices: Initialize all descriptors to their ready states. This may be performed via calls to locally-declared, '**static**' functions.

5 Initialize the (R)MII bus interface, if applicable. This generally entails configuring the (R)MII bus frequency which is dependent on the system clock. Static values for clock frequencies should never be used when determining clock dividers. Instead, the driver should reference the associated clock function(s) for getting the system clock or peripheral bus frequencies, and use these values to compute the correct (R)MII bus clock divider(s). This is generally performed via the network device's BSP function pointer, **ClkFreqGet()**, implemented in **net_bsp.c** (see section A-3-4 on page 428).

6 Disable the transmitted and receiver (should already be disabled).

7 Disable and clear pending interrupts (should already be cleared).

8 Set **perr** to **NET_DEV_ERR_NONE** if initialization proceeded as expected. Otherwise, set **perr** to an appropriate network device error code.

A-1-2 NetDev_Start()

The second function is the device driver **Start()** function. This function is called once each time an interface is started.

FILES

Every device driver's net_dev.c

PROTOTYPE

```
static void NetDev_Start (NET_IF  *pif,
                          NET_ERR *perr);
```

Note that since every device driver's **Start()** function is accessed only by function pointer via the device driver's API structure, it doesn't need to be globally available and should therefore be declared as '**static**'.

ARGUMENTS

pif Pointer to the interface to start a network device.

perr Pointer to variable that will receive the return error code from this function.

RETURNED VALUE

None.

REQUIRED CONFIGURATION

None.

NOTES / WARNINGS

The **Start()** function performs the following items:

1 Configure the transmit ready semaphore count via a call to **NetOS_Dev_CfgTxRdySignal()**. This function call is optional and is generally performed when the hardware device supports the queuing of multiple transmit frames. By default, the count is initialized to one. However, DMA devices should set the semaphore count equal to the number of configured transmit descriptors for optimal

performance. Non-DMA devices that support the queuing of more than one transmit frame may also benefit from a non-default value.

2 Initialize the device MAC address if applicable. For Ethernet devices, this step is mandatory. The MAC address data may come from one of three sources and should be set using the following priority scheme:

a. Configure the MAC address using the string found within the device configuration structure. This is a form of static MAC address configuration and may be performed by calling **`NetASCII_Str_to_MAC()`** and **`NetIF_AddrHW_SetHandler()`**. If the device configuration string has been left empty, or is specified as all 0's, an error will be returned and the next method should be attempted.

b. Check if the application developer has called **`NetIF_AddrHW_Set()`** by making a call to **`NetIF_AddrHW_GetHandler()`** and **`NetIF_AddrHW_IsValidHandler()`** in order to check if the specified MAC address is valid. This method may be used as a static method for configuring the MAC address during run-time, or a dynamic method should a pre-programmed external memory device exist. If the acquired MAC address does not pass the check function, then:

c. Call **`NetIF_AddrHW_SetHandler()`** using the data found within the MAC individual address registers. If an auto-loading EEPROM is attached to the MAC, the registers will contain valid data. If not, then a configuration error has occurred. This method is often used with a production process where the MAC supports the automatic loading of individual address registers from a serial EEPROM. When using this method, the developer should specify an empty string for the MAC address within the device configuration and refrain from calling **`NetIF_AddrHW_Set()`** from within the application.

3 Initialize additional MAC registers required by the MAC for proper operation.

4 Clear all interrupt flags.

5 Locally enable interrupts on the hardware device. The host interrupt controller should have already been configured within the device driver **`Init()`** function.

6 Enable the receiver and transmitter.

7 Set **`perr`** equal to **`NET_DEV_ERR_NONE`** if no errors have occurred. Otherwise, set **`perr`** to an appropriate network device error code.

A-1-3 NetDev_Stop()

The next function within the device API structure is the device **Stop()** function. This function is called once each time an interface is stopped.

FILES

Every device driver's **net_dev.c**

PROTOTYPE

```
static void NetDev_Stop (NET_IF  *pif,
                         NET_ERR *perr);
```

Note that since every device driver's **Stop()** function is accessed only by function pointer via the device driver's API structure, it doesn't need to be globally available and should therefore be declared as '**static**'.

ARGUMENTS

pif Pointer to the interface to start a network device.

perr Pointer to variable that will receive the return error code from this function.

RETURNED VALUE

None.

REQUIRED CONFIGURATION

None.

NOTES / WARNINGS

The **Stop()** function must perform the following operations:

1. Disable the receiver and transmitter.
2. Disable all local MAC interrupt sources.
3. Clear all local MAC interrupt status flags.
4. For DMA devices, re-initialize all receive descriptors.
5. For DMA devices, free all transmit descriptors by calling **NetOS_IF_DeallocTaskPost()** with the address of the transmit descriptor data areas.
6. For DMA devices, re-initialize all transmit descriptors.
7. Set **perr** to **NET_DEV_ERR_NONE** if no error occurs. Otherwise, set **perr** to an appropriate network device error code.

A-1-4 NetDev_Rx()

The receive/`Rx()` function is called by µC/TCP-IP's Receive task after the Interrupt Service Routine handler has signaled to the Receive task that a receive event has occurred. The Receive function requires that the device driver return a pointer to the data area containing the received data and return the size of the received frame via pointer.

FILES

Every device driver's `net_dev.c`

PROTOTYPE

```
static void NetDev_Rx (NET_IF      *pif,
                       CPU_INT08U **p_data,
                       CPU_INT16U  *size,
                       NET_ERR     *perr);
```

Note that since every device driver's `Rx()` function is accessed only by function pointer via the device driver's API structure, it doesn't need to be globally available and should therefore be declared as '`static`'.

ARGUMENTS

`pif`Pointer to the interface to receive data from a network device.

`p_data`Pointer to return the address of the received data.

`size`Pointer to return the size of the received data.

`perr`Pointer to variable that will receive the return error code from this function.

RETURNED VALUE

None.

REQUIRED CONFIGURATION

None.

NOTES / WARNINGS

The receive function should perform the following actions:

1 Check for receive errors if applicable. If an error should occur during reception, the driver should set ***size** to 0 and ***p_data** to **(CPU_INT08U *)0** and return. Additional steps may be necessary depending on the device being serviced.

2 For Ethernet devices, get the size of the received frame and subtract 4 bytes for the CRC. It it always recommended that the frame size is checked to ensure that it is greater than 4 bytes before performing the subtraction to ensure that an underflow does not occur. Set ***size** equal to the adjusted frame size.

3 Get a new data buffer area by calling **NetBuf_GetDataPtr()**. If memory is not available, an error will be returned and the device driver should set ***size** to 0 and ***p_data** to (**CPU_INT08U *)0**. For DMA devices, the current receive descriptor should be marked as available or owned by hardware. The device driver should then return from the receive function.

4 If an error does not occur while getting a new data area, DMA devices should perform the following operations:

a. Set ***p_data** equal to the address of the data area within the descriptor being serviced.

b. Set the data area pointer within the receive descriptor to the address of the data area obtained by calling **NetBuf_GetDataPtr()**.

c. Update any descriptor ring pointers if applicable.

5 Non DMA devices should **Mem_Copy()** the data stored within the device to the address of the buffer obtained by calling **NetBuf_GetDataPtr()** and set ***p_data** equal to the address of the obtained data area.

6 Set **perr** to **NET_DEV_ERR_NONE** and return from the receive function. Otherwise, set **perr** to an appropriate network device error code.

A-1-5 NetDev_Tx()

The next function in the device API structure is the transmit/**Tx()** function.

FILES

Every device driver's **net_dev.c**

PROTOTYPE

```
static void NetDev_Tx (NET_IF      *pif,
                       CPU_INT08U *p_data,
                       CPU_INT16U  size,
                       NET_ERR    *perr);
```

Note that since every device driver's **Tx()** function is accessed only by function pointer via the device driver's API structure, it doesn't need to be globally available and should therefore be declared as '**static**'.

ARGUMENTS

pif Pointer to the interface to start a network device.

p_data Pointer to address of the data to transmit.

size Size of the data to transmit.

perr Pointer to variable that will receive the return error code from this function.

RETURNED VALUE

None.

REQUIRED CONFIGURATION

None.

NOTES / WARNINGS

The transmit function should perform the following actions:

1. For DMA-based hardware, the driver should select the next available transmit descriptor and set the pointer to the data area equal to the address pointer to by **p_data**.

2. Non-DMA hardware should **Mem_Copy()** the data stored within the buffer pointed to by **p_data** to the device's internal memory.

3. Once completed, the driver must configure the device with the number of bytes to transmit. This is passed directly by value within the size argument. DMA-based devices generally have a size field within the transmit descriptor. Non-DMA devices generally have a transmit size register that needs to be configured.

4. The driver should then take all necessary steps to initiate transmission of the data.

5. Set **perr** to **NET_DEV_ERR_NONE** and return from the transmit function.

A-1-6 NetDev_AddrMulticastAdd()

The next API function is the **AddrMulticastAdd()** function used to configure a device with an (IP-to-Ethernet) multicast hardware address.

FILES

Every device driver's net_dev.c

PROTOTYPE

```
static void NetDev_AddrMulticastAdd (NET_IF      *pif,
                                     CPU_INT08U *paddr_hw,
                                     CPU_INT08U  addr_hw_len,
                                     NET_ERR    *perr);
```

Note that since every device driver's **AddrMulticastAdd()** function is accessed only by function pointer via the device driver's API structure, it doesn't need to be globally available and should therefore be declared as '**static**'.

ARGUMENTS

pif Pointer to the interface to add/configure a multicast address.

paddr_hw Pointer to multicast hardware address to add.

addr_hw_len Length of multicast hardware address.

perr Pointer to variable that will receive the return error code from this function.

RETURNED VALUE

None.

REQUIRED CONFIGURATION

Necessary only if **NET_IP_CFG_MULTICAST_SEL** is configured for transmit and receive multicasting (see section C-9-2 on page 735).

NOTES / WARNINGS

Since many network controllers' documentation fail to properly indicate how to add/configure an Ethernet MAC device with a multicast address, the following methodology is recommended for determining and testing the correct multicast hash bit algorithm.

1 Configure a packet capture program or multicast application to broadcast a multicast packet with Ethernet destination address of 01:00:5E:00:00:01. This MAC address corresponds to the multicast group IP address of 224.0.0.1 which will be converted to a MAC address by higher layers and passed to this function.

2 Set a break point in the receive ISR handler and transmit one send packet to the target. The break point should *not* be reached as the result of the transmitted packet. Use caution to ensure that other network traffic is not the source of the interrupt when the button is pressed. Sometimes asynchronous network events happen very close in time and the end result can be deceiving. Ideally, these tests should be performed on an isolated network but disconnect as many other hosts from the network as possible.

3 Use the debugger to stop the application and program the MAC multicast hash register low bits to 0xFFFFFFFF. Go to step 2. Repeat for the hash bit high register if necessary. The goal is to bracket off which bit in either the high or low hash bit register causes the device to be interrupted when the broadcast frame is received by the target. Once the correct bit is known, the hash algorithm can be easily written and tested.

4 The following hash bit algorithm code below could be adjusted per the network controller's documentation in order to get the hash from the correct subset of CRC bits. Most of the code is similar between various devices and is thus reusable. The hash algorithm is the exlusive **OR** of every 6th bit of the destination address:

```
hash[5] = da[5] ^ da[11] ^ da[17] ^ da[23] ^ da[29] ^ da[35] ^ da[41] ^ da[47]
hash[4] = da[4] ^ da[10] ^ da[16] ^ da[22] ^ da[28] ^ da[34] ^ da[40] ^ da[46]
hash[3] = da[3] ^ da[09] ^ da[15] ^ da[21] ^ da[27] ^ da[33] ^ da[39] ^ da[45]
hash[2] = da[2] ^ da[08] ^ da[14] ^ da[20] ^ da[26] ^ da[32] ^ da[38] ^ da[44]
hash[1] = da[1] ^ da[07] ^ da[13] ^ da[19] ^ da[25] ^ da[31] ^ da[37] ^ da[43]
hash[0] = da[0] ^ da[06] ^ da[12] ^ da[18] ^ da[24] ^ da[30] ^ da[36] ^ da[42]
```

Where `da0` represents the least significant bit of the first byte of the destination address received and where `da47` represents the most significant bit of the last byte of the destination address received.

```
                                                  /* ---------- CALCULATE HASH CODE ---------- */
hash = 0;
for (i = 0; i < 6; i++) {                         /* For each row in the bit hash table:       */
    bit_val = 0;                                  /* Clear initial xor value for each row.     */
    for (j = 0; j < 8; j++) {                     /* For each bit in each octet:               */
        bit_nbr   = (j * 6) + i;                  /* Determine which bit in stream, 0-47.      */
        octet_nbr = bit_nbr / 8;                  /* Determine which octet bit belongs to.     */
        octet     = paddr_hw[octet_nbr];          /* Get octet value.                          */
        bit       = octet & (1 << (bit_nbr % 8)); /* Check if octet's bit is set.              */
        bit_val  ^= (bit > 0) ? 1 : 0;            /* Calculate table row's XOR hash value.     */
    }
     hash |= (bit_val << i);                      /* Add row's XOR hash value to final hash.   */
}
                                                  /* ---- ADD MULTICAST ADDRESS TO DEVICE ---- */
reg_sel = (hash >> 5) & 0x01;                     /* Determine hash register     to configure. */
reg_bit = (hash >> 0) & 0x1F;                     /* Determine hash register bit to configure. */
                                                  /* (Substitute '0x01'/'0x1F' with device's ..*/
                                                  /* .. actual hash register bit masks/shifts.)*/

  paddr_hash_ctrs = &pdev_data->MulticastAddrHashBitCtr[hash];
(*paddr_hash_ctrs)++;                             /* Increment hash bit reference counter.     */

if (reg_sel == 0) {                               /* Set multicast hash register bit.          */
    pdev->MCAST_REG_LO |= (1 << reg_bit);         /* (Substitute 'MCAST_REG_LO/HI' with ..     */
} else {                                          /* .. device's actual multicast registers.)  */
    pdev->MCAST_REG_HI |= (1 << reg_bit);
}
                                                  /* ---------- CALCULATE HASH CODE ---------- */
                                                  /* Calculate CRC.                            */
crc = NetUtil_32BitCRC_Calc((CPU_INT08U *)paddr_hw,
                            (CPU_INT32U  ) addr_hw_len,
                            (NET_ERR    *)perr);
```

Listing A-1 **Example device multicast address configuration using CRC hash code algorithm**

Alternatively, you may be able to compute the CRC hash with a call to **NetUtil_32BitCRC_CalcCpl()** followed by an optional call to **NetUtil_32BitReflect()**, with four possible combinations:

a. CRC without complement and without reflection
b. CRC without complement and with reflection
c. CRC with complement and without reflection
d. CRC with complement and with reflection

```
if (*perr != NET_UTIL_ERR_NONE) {
    return;
}
                                              /* ---- ADD MULTICAST ADDRESS TO DEVICE ---- */
crc     = NetUtil_32BitReflect(crc);          /* Optionally, complement CRC.              */
hash    = (crc >> 23u) & 0x3F;                /* Determine hash register     to configure. */
reg_bit = (hash % 32u);                       /* Determine hash register bit to configure. */
                                              /* (Substitute '23u'/'0x3F' with device's .. */
                                              /* .. actual hash register bit masks/shifts.)*/

 paddr_hash_ctrs = &pdev_data->MulticastAddrHashBitCtr[hash];
(*paddr_hash_ctrs)++;                         /* Increment hash bit reference counter.    */

if (hash <= 31u) {                            /* Set multicast hash register bit.          */
    pdev->MCAST_REG_LO |= (1 << reg_bit);     /* (Substitute 'MCAST_REG_LO/HI' with ..     */
} else {                                      /* .. device's actual multicast registers.)  */
    pdev->MCAST_REG_HI |= (1 << reg_bit);
}
```

Listing A-2 **Example device multicast address configuration using CRC and reflection functions**

Unfortunately, the product documentation will *not* likely tell you which combination of complement and reflection is necessary in order to properly compute the hash value. Most likely, the documentation will simply state 'Standard Ethernet CRC' which when compared to other documents, means any of the four combinations above; different than the actual frame CRC.

Fortunately, if the code is written to perform both the complement and reflection, then the debugger may be used to repeat the code block over and over skipping either the line that performs the complement or the function call to the reflection until the output hash bit is computed correctly.

5 Update the device driver's **AddrMulticastAdd()** function to calculate and configure the correct CRC.

6 Test the device driver's **AddrMulticastAdd()** function by ensuring that the group address 224.0.0.1, when joined from the application (see section B-10-1 on page 546), correctly configures the device to receive multicast packets destined to the 224.0.0.1 address. Then broadcast the 224.0.0.1 (see step 1) to test if the device receives the multicast packet.

A-1-7 NetDev_AddrMulticastRemove()

The next API function is the **AddrMulticastRemove()** function used to remove an (IP-to-Ethernet) multicast hardware address from a device.

FILES

Every device driver's **net_dev.c**

PROTOTYPE

```
static void NetDev_AddrMulticastRemove (NET_IF      *pif,
                                        CPU_INT08U *paddr_hw,
                                        CPU_INT08U  addr_hw_len,
                                        NET_ERR    *perr);
```

Note that since every device driver's **AddrMulticastRemove()** function is accessed only by function pointer via the device driver's API structure, it doesn't need to be globally available and should therefore be declared as '**static**'.

ARGUMENTS

pif Pointer to the interface to remove a multicast address.

paddr_hw Pointer to multicast hardware address to remove.

addr_hw_len Length of multicast hardware address.

perr Pointer to variable that will receive the return error code from this function.

RETURNED VALUE

None.

REQUIRED CONFIGURATION

Necessary only if **NET_IP_CFG_MULTICAST_SEL** is configured for transmit and receive multicasting (see section C-9-2 on page 735).

NOTES / WARNINGS

Use same exact code as in **`NetDev_AddrMulticastAdd()`** to calculate the device's CRC hash (see section A-1-6 on page 397), but remove a multicast address by decrementing the device's hash bit reference counters and clearing the appropriate bits in the device's multicast registers.

```
                                                   /* ---------- CALCULATE HASH CODE ---------- */
/* Use NetDev_AddrMulticastAdd()'s algorithm to calculate CRC hash.                            */
                                                   /* - REMOVE MULTICAST ADDRESS FROM DEVICE -- */
paddr_hash_ctrs = &pdev_data->MulticastAddrHashBitCtr[hash];
if (*paddr_hash_ctrs > 1u) {                       /* If multiple multicast addresses hashed, ..*/
   (*paddr_hash_ctrs)--;                           /* .. decrement hash bit reference counter ..*/
    *perr = NET_DEV_ERR_NONE;                      /* .. but do NOT unconfigure hash register.  */
     return;
}
*paddr_hash_ctrs = 0u;                             /* Clear hash bit reference counter.         */

if (hash <= 31u) {                                 /* Clear multicast hash register bit.        */
    pdev->MCAST_REG_LO &= ~(1u << reg_bit);        /* (Substitute 'MCAST_REG_LO/HI' with ..     */
} else {                                           /* .. device's actual multicast registers.)  */
    pdev->MCAST_REG_HI &= ~(1u << reg_bit);
}
```

Listing A-3 **Example device multicast address removal**

A-1-8 NetDev_ISR_Handler()

A device's `ISR_Handler()` function is used to handle each device's interrupts. See section 14-5-1 on page 304 for more details on how to handle each device's interrupts.

FILES

Every device driver's `net_dev.c`

PROTOTYPE

```
static void NetDev_ISR_Handler (NET_IF           *pif,
                                NET_DEV_ISR_TYPE  type);
```

Note that since every device driver's `ISR_Handler()` function is accessed only by function pointer via the device driver's API structure, it doesn't need to be globally available and should therefore be declared as '`static`'.

ARGUMENTS

`pif` Pointer to the interface to handle network device interrupts.

`type` Device's interrupt type:

```
NET_DEV_ISR_TYPE_UNKNOWN
NET_DEV_ISR_TYPE_RX
NET_DEV_ISR_TYPE_RX_RUNT
NET_DEV_ISR_TYPE_RX_OVERRUN
NET_DEV_ISR_TYPE_TX_RDY
NET_DEV_ISR_TYPE_TX_COMPLETE
NET_DEV_ISR_TYPE_TX_COLLISION_LATE
NET_DEV_ISR_TYPE_TX_COLLISION_EXCESS
NET_DEV_ISR_TYPE_JABBER
NET_DEV_ISR_TYPE_BABBLE
NET_DEV_ISR_TYPE_PHY
```

RETURNED VALUE

None.

REQUIRED CONFIGURATION

None.

NOTES / WARNINGS

Each device's **`NetDev_ISR_Handler()`** should never return early but check all applicable interrupt sources to see if they are active. This additional checking is necessary because multiple interrupt sources may be set within the interrupt response time and will reduce the number and overhead of handling interrupts.

A-1-9 NetDev_IO_Ctrl()

A device's input/output control/`IO_Ctrl()` function is used to implement miscellaneous functionality such as setting and getting the PHY link state, as well as updating the MAC link state registers when the PHY link state has changed. An optional void pointer to a data variable is passed into the function and may be used to get device parameters from the caller, or to return device parameters to the caller.

FILES

Every device driver's `net_dev.c`

PROTOTYPE

```
static void NetDev_IO_Ctrl (NET_IF      *pif,
                            CPU_INT08U  opt,
                            void        *p_data,
                            NET_ERR     *perr);
```

Note that since every device driver's `IO_Ctrl()` function is accessed only by function pointer via the device driver's API structure, it doesn't need to be globally available and should therefore be declared as '`static`'.

ARGUMENTS

`pif` Pointer to the interface to handle network device I/O operations.

`opt` I/O operation to perform.

`p_data` A pointer to a variable containing the data necessary to perform the operation or a pointer to a variable to store data associated with the result of the operation.

`perr` Pointer to variable that will receive the return error code from this function.

RETURNED VALUE

None.

REQUIRED CONFIGURATION

None.

NOTES / WARNINGS

µC/TCP-IP defines the following default options:

```
NET_DEV_LINK_STATE_GET_INFO
NET_DEV_LINK_STATE_UPDATE
```

The **NET_DEV_LINK_STATE_GET_INFO** option expects **p_data** to point to a variable of type **NET_DEV_LINK_ETHER** for the case of an Ethernet driver. This variable has two fields, **Spd** and **Duplex**, which are filled in by the PHY device driver via a call through the PHY API. µC/TCP-IP internally uses this option code in order to periodically poll the PHYs for link state.

The **NET_DEV_LINK_STATE_UPDATE** option is used by the PHY driver to communicate with the MAC when either µC/TCP-IP polls the PHY for link status, or when a PHY interrupt occurs. Not all MAC's require PHY link state synchronization. Should this be the case, then the device driver may not need to implement this option.

A-1-10 NetDev_MII_Rd()

The next function to implement is the (R)MII read/**Phy_RegRd()** function. This function is generally implemented within the Ethernet device driver file, since (R)MII bus reads are generally associated with the MAC device. In the case that the PHY communication mechanism is separate from the MAC, then a handler function may be provided within the **net_bsp.c** file and called from the device driver file instead.

Note: This function must be implemented with a timeout and should *not* block indefinitely should the PHY fail to respond.

FILES

Every device driver's **net_dev.c**

PROTOTYPE

```
static void NetDev_MII_Rd (NET_IF      *pif,
                           CPU_INT08U  phy_addr,
                           CPU_INT08U  reg_addr,
                           CPU_INT16U *p_data,
                           NET_ERR    *perr);
```

Note that since every device driver's **Phy_RegRd()/MII_Rd()** function is accessed only by function pointer via the device driver's API structure, it doesn't need to be globally available and should therefore be declared as '**static**'.

ARGUMENTS

pif Pointer to the interface to read a (R)MII PHY register.

phy_addr The bus address of the PHY.

reg_addr The MII register number to read.

p_data Pointer to a address to store the content of the PHY register being read.

perr Pointer to variable that will receive the return error code from this function.

RETURNED VALUE

None.

REQUIRED CONFIGURATION

None.

NOTES/WARNINGS

None.

A-1-11 NetDev_MII_Wr()

Next is the (R)MII write/**Phy_RegWr()** function. This function is generally implemented within the Ethernet device driver file since (R)MII bus writes are generally associated with the MAC device. In the case that the PHY communication mechanism is separate from the MAC, a handler function may be provided within the **net_bsp.c** file and called from the device driver file instead.

Note: This function must be implemented with a timeout and not block indefinitely should the PHY fail to respond.

FILES

Every device driver's **net_dev.c**

PROTOTYPE

```
static void NetDev_MII_Wr (NET_IF      *pif,
                           CPU_INT08U  phy_addr,
                           CPU_INT08U  reg_addr,
                           CPU_INT16U  data,
                           NET_ERR     *perr);
```

Note that since every device driver's **Phy_RegWr()/MII_Wr()** function is accessed only by function pointer via the device driver's API structure, it doesn't need to be globally available and should therefore be declared as '**static**'.

ARGUMENTS

pif Pointer to the interface to read a (R)MII PHY register.

phy_addr The bus address of the PHY.

reg_addr The MII register number to write to.

p_data Pointer to the data to write to the specified PHY register.

perr Pointer to variable that will receive the return error code from this function.

RETURNED VALUE

None.

REQUIRED CONFIGURATION

None.

NOTES/WARNINGS

None.

A-2 DEVICE DRIVER FUNCTIONS FOR PHY

A-2-1 NetPhy_Init()

The first function within the Ethernet PHY API is the PHY driver initialization/`Init()` function which is called by the Ethernet Network Interface Layer after the MAC device driver is initialized without error.

FILES

Every physical layer driver's `net_phy.c`

PROTOTYPE

```
static void NetPhy_Init (NET_IF  *pif,
                         NET_ERR *perr)
```

Note that since every PHY driver's `Init()` function is accessed only by function pointer via the PHY driver's API structure, it doesn't need to be globally available and should therefore be declared as '`static`'.

ARGUMENTS

`pif` Pointer to the interface to initialize a PHY.

`perr` Pointer to variable that will receive the return error code from this function.

RETURNED VALUE

None.

REQUIRED CONFIGURATION

None.

NOTES/WARNINGS

The PHY initialization function is responsible for the following actions:

1 Reset the PHY and wait with timeout for reset to complete. If a timeout occurs, return **perr** set to **NET_PHY_ERR_RESET_TIMEOUT**.

2 Start the auto-negotiation process. This should configure the PHY registers such that the desired link speed and duplex specified within the PHY configuration are respected. It is not necessary to wait until the auto-negotiation process has completed, as this can take upwards of many seconds. Generally, this action is performed by calling the PHY's **NetPhy_AutoNegStart()** function.

3 If no errors occur, return **perr** set to **NET_PHY_ERR_NONE**.

A-2-2 NetPhy_EnDis()

The next Ethernet PHY function is the enable-disable/**EnDis()** function. This function is called by the Ethernet Network Interface Layer when an interface is started or stopped.

FILES

Every physical layer driver's **net_phy.c**

PROTOTYPE

```
static void NetPhy_EnDis (NET_IF       *pif,
                          CPU_BOOLEAN  en,
                          NET_ERR      *perr);
```

Note that since every PHY driver's **EnDis()** function is accessed only by function pointer via the PHY driver's API structure, it doesn't need to be globally available and should therefore be declared as '**static**'.

ARGUMENTS

pif Pointer to the interface to enable/disable a PHY.

en A flag representing the next desired state of the PHY:

DEF_ENABLED
DEF_DISABLED

perr Pointer to variable that will receive the return error code from this function.

RETURNED VALUE

None.

REQUIRED CONFIGURATION

None.

NOTES/WARNINGS

Disabling the PHY will generally cause the PHY to power down which will cause link state to be disconnected.

A-2-3 NetPhy_LinkStateGet()

The Ethernet PHY's **LinkStateGet()** function determines the current Ethernet link state. Results are passed back to the caller in a **NET_DEV_LINK_ETHER** structure which contains fields for link speed and duplex. This function is called periodically by µC/TCP-IP.

FILES

Every physical layer driver's **net_phy.c**

PROTOTYPE

```
static void NetPhy_LinkStateGet (NET_IF              *pif,
                                 NET_DEV_LINK_ETHER *plink_state,
                                 NET_ERR             *perr);
```

Note that since every PHY driver's **LinkStateGet()** function is accessed only by function pointer via the PHY driver's API structure, it doesn't need to be globally available and should therefore be declared as '**static**'.

ARGUMENTS

pif Pointer to the interface to get a PHY's current link state.

plink_state Pointer to a link state structure to return link state information. The **NET_DEV_LINK_ETHER** structure contains two fields for link speed and duplex. Link speed is returned via **plink_state->Spd** :

NET_PHY_SPD_0
NET_PHY_SPD_10
NET_PHY_SPD_100

And link duplex is returned via **plink_state->Duplex** :

NET_PHY_DUPLEX_UNKNOWN
NET_PHY_DUPLEX_HALF
NET_PHY_DUPLEX_FULL

NET_PHY_SPD_0 and NET_PHY_DUPLEX_UNKNOWN represent an unlinked or unknown link state if an error occurs.

perr Pointer to variable that will receive the return error code from this function.

RETURNED VALUES

None.

REQUIRED CONFIGURATION

None.

NOTES/WARNINGS

The generic PHY driver does not return a link state. Instead, in order to avoid access to extended registers which are PHY specific, the driver attempts to determine link state by analyzing the PHY and PHY partner capabilities. The best combination of auto-negotiated link state is selected as the current link state.

A-2-4 NetPhy_LinkStateSet()

The Ethernet PHY's **LinkStateSet()** function determines the current Ethernet link state. Results are passed back to the caller within a **NET_DEV_LINK_ETHER** structure which contains fields for link speed and duplex. This function is called periodically by µC/TCP-IP.

FILES

Every physical layer driver's **net_phy.c**

PROTOTYPE

```
static void NetPhy_LinkStateSet (NET_IF              *pif,
                                 NET_DEV_LINK_ETHER *plink_state,
                                 NET_ERR            *perr);
```

Note that since every PHY driver's **LinkStateSet()** function is accessed only by function pointer via the PHY driver's API structure, it doesn't need to be globally available and should therefore be declared as '**static**'.

ARGUMENTS

pif Pointer to the interface to set a PHY's current link state.

plink_state Pointer to a link state structure with link state information to configure. The **NET_DEV_LINK_ETHER** structure contains two fields for link speed and duplex. Link speed is set via **plink_state->Spd** :

NET_PHY_SPD_10
NET_PHY_SPD_100

And link duplex is set via **plink_state->Duplex** :

NET_PHY_DUPLEX_HALF
NET_PHY_DUPLEX_FULL

perr Pointer to variable that will receive the return error code from this function.

RETURNED VALUE

None.

REQUIRED CONFIGURATION

None.

NOTES/WARNINGS

None.

A-2-5 NetPhy_ISR_Handler()

An Ethernet PHY's `ISR_Handler()` function is used to handle a PHY's interrupts. See section 14-5-2 on page 308 for more details on how to handle PHY interrupts. µC/TCP-IP does not require PHY drivers to enable or handle PHY interrupts. The generic PHY drivers does not even define a PHY interrupt handler function but instead handles all events by either periodic or event-triggered calls to other PHY API functions.

FILES

Every physical layer driver's `net_phy.c`

PROTOTYPE

```
static void NetPhy_ISR_Handler (NET_IF *pif);
```

Note that since every PHY driver's `ISR_Handler()` function is accessed only by function pointer via the PHY driver's API structure, it doesn't need to be globally available and should therefore be declared as '`static`'.

ARGUMENTS

`pif` Pointer to the interface to handle PHY interrupts.

RETURNED VALUE

None.

REQUIRED CONFIGURATION

None.

NOTES/WARNINGS

None.

A-3 DEVICE DRIVER BSP FUNCTIONS

A-3-1 NetDev_CfgClk()

This function is called by a device driver's **NetDev_Init()** to configure a specific network device's clocks on a specific interface.

FILES

net_bsp.c

PROTOTYPE

```
static void NetDev_CfgClk (NET_IF  *pif,
                           NET_ERR *perr);
```

Note: since **NetDev_CfgClk()** is accessed only by function pointer via a BSP interface structure, it doesn't need to be globally available and should therefore be declared as '**static**'.

ARGUMENTS

pif Pointer to specific interface to configure device's clocks.

perr Pointer to variable that will receive the return error code from this function:

NET_DEV_ERR_NONE
NET_DEV_ERR_FAULT

This is *not* an exclusive list of return errors and specific network device's or device BSP functions may return any other specific errors as required.

RETURNED VALUE

None.

REQUIRED CONFIGURATION

None.

NOTES / WARNINGS

Each network device's **NetDev_CfgClk()** should configure and enable all required clocks for the network device. For example, on some devices it may be necessary to enable clock gating for an embedded Ethernet MAC as well as various GPIO modules in order to configure Ethernet Phy pins for (R)MII mode and interrupts.

Since each network device requires a unique **NetDev_CfgClk()**, it is recommended that each device's **NetDev_CfgClk()** function be named using the following convention:

`NetDev_[Device]CfgClk[Number]()`

`[Device]` Network device name or type, e.g. MACB (optional if the development board does not support multiple devices)

`[Number]` Network device number for each specific instance of device (optional if the development board does not support multiple instances of the specific device)

For example, the **NetDev_CfgClk()** function for the #2 MACB Ethernet controller on an Atmel AT91SAM9263-EK should be named **NetDev_MACB_CfgClk2()**, or **NetDev_MACB_CfgClk_2()** with additional underscore optional.

See also section 14-7-1 "Network Device BSP" on page 320.

A-3-2 NetDev_CfgGPIO()

This function is called by a device driver's **NetDev_Init()** to configure a specific network device's general-purpose input/ouput (GPIO) on a specific interface.

FILES

net_bsp.c

PROTOTYPE

```
static void NetDev_CfgGPIO (NET_IF  *pif,
                            NET_ERR *perr);
```

Note that since **NetDev_CfgGPIO()** is accessed only by function pointer via a BSP interface structure, it doesn't need to be globally available and should therefore be declared as 'static'.

ARGUMENTS

pif Pointer to specific interface to configure device's GPIO.

perr Pointer to variable that will receive the return error code from this function:

NET_DEV_ERR_NONE
NET_DEV_ERR_FAULT

This is *not* an exclusive list of return errors and specific network device's or device BSP functions may return any other specific errors as required.

RETURNED VALUE

None.

REQUIRED CONFIGURATION

None.

NOTES / WARNINGS

Each network device's **NetDev_CfgGPIO()** should configure all required GPIO pins for the network device. For Ethernet devices, this function is usually necessary to configure the (R)MII bus pins, depending on whether you have configured an Ethernet interface to operate in the RMII or MII mode, and optionally the Ethernet Phy interrupt pin.

Since each network device requires a unique **NetDev_CfgGPIO()**, it is recommended that each device's **NetDev_CfgGPIO()** function be named using the following convention:

`NetDev_[Device]CfgGPIO[Number]()`

`[Device]`	Network device name or type, e.g. MACB (optional if the development board does not support multiple devices)
`[Number]`	Network device number for each specific instance of device (optional if the development board does not support multiple instances of the specific device)

For example, the **NetDev_CfgGPIO()** function for the #2 MACB Ethernet controller on an Atmel AT91SAM9263-EK should be named **NetDev_MACB_CfgGPIO2()**, or **NetDev_MACB_CfgGPIO_2()** with additional underscore optional.

See also section 14-7-1 "Network Device BSP" on page 320.

A-3-3 NetDev_CfgIntCtrl()

This function is called by a device driver's **NetDev_Init()** to configure a specific network device's interrupts and/or interrupt controller on a specific interface.

FILES

net_bsp.c

PROTOTYPE

```
static void NetDev_CfgIntCtrl (NET_IF  *pif,
                               NET_ERR *perr);
```

Note that since **NetDev_CfgIntCtrl()** is accessed only by function pointer via a BSP interface structure, it doesn't need to be globally available and should therefore be declared as '**static**'.

ARGUMENTS

pif Pointer to specific interface to configure device's interrupts.

perr Pointer to variable that will receive the return error code from this function:

NET_DEV_ERR_NONE
NET_DEV_ERR_FAULT

This is *not* an exclusive list of return errors and specific network device's or device BSP functions may return any other specific errors as required.

RETURNED VALUE

None.

REQUIRED CONFIGURATION

None.

NOTES / WARNINGS

Each network device's **NetDev_CfgIntCtrl()** should configure and enable all required interrupt sources for the network device. This usually means configuring the interrupt vector address of each corresponding network device BSP interrupt service routine (ISR) handler and enabling its corresponding interrupt source. Thus, for most **NetDev_CfgIntCtrl()**, the following actions *should* be performed:

1 Configure/store each device's network interface number to be available for all necessary **NetDev_ISR_Handler()** functions (see section A-3-5 "NetDev_ISR_Handler()" on page 430). Even though devices are added dynamically, the device's interface number must be saved in order for each device's ISR handlers to call **NetIF_ISR_Handler()** with the device's network interface number.

Since each network device maps to a unique network interface number, it is recommended that each instance of network devices' interface numbers be named using the following convention:

<Board><Device>[Number]_IF_Nbr

<Board>	Development board name
<Device>	Network device name (or type)
[Number]	Network device number for each specific instance of device (optional if the development board does not support multiple instances of the specific device)

For example, the network device interface number variable for the #2 MACB Ethernet controller on an Atmel AT91SAM9263-EK should be named **AT91SAM9263-EK_MACB_2_IF_Nbr**.

Network device interface number variables *should* be initialized to **NET_IF_NBR_NONE** at system initialization prior to being configured by their respective devices.

2 Configure each of the device's interrupts on either an external or CPU's integrated interrupt controller. However, vectored interrupt controllers may not require the explicit configuration and enabling of higher-level interrupt controller sources. In this case, the application developer may need to configure the system's interrupt vector table with the name of the ISR handler functions declared in **net_bsp.c**.

NetDev_CfgIntCtrl() should only enable each devices' interrupt sources but *not* the local device-level interrupts themselves, which are enabled by the device driver only after the device has been fully configured and started.

Since each network device requires a unique **NetDev_CfgIntCtrl()**, it is recommended that each device's **NetDev_CfgIntCtrl()** function be named using the following convention:

NetDev_[Device]CfgIntCtrl[Number]()

`[Device]` Network device name or type, e.g. MACB (optional if the development board does not support multiple devices)

`[Number]` Network device number for each specific instance of device (optional if the development board does not support multiple instances of the specific device)

For example, the **NetDev_CfgIntCtrl()** function for the #2 MACB Ethernet controller on an Atmel AT91SAM9263-EK should be named **NetDev_MACB_CfgIntCtrl2()**, or **NetDev_MACB_CfgIntCtrl_2()** with additional underscore optional.

See also section 14-7-1 "Network Device BSP" on page 320.

EXAMPLES

```
static  void  NetDev_MACB_CfgIntCtrl (NET_IF   *pif,
                                      NET_ERR  *perr)
{
                                /* Configure AT91SAM9263-EK MACB #2's specific IF number.      */
    AT91SAM9263-EK_MACB_2_IF_Nbr = pif->Nbr;
                                /* Configure AT91SAM9263-EK MACB #2's interrupts:              */
    BSP_IntVectSet(BSP_INT, &NetDev_MACB_ISR_Handler_2);/* Configure interrupt vector.         */
    BSP_IntEn(BSP_INT);                                 /* Enable    interrupts.               */

   *perr = NET_DEV_ERR_NONE;
}


static  void  NetDev_MACB_CfgIntCtrlRx_2 (NET_IF   *pif,
                                          NET_ERR  *perr)
{
                                /* Configure AT91SAM9263-EK MACB #2's specific IF number.      */
    AT91SAM9263-EK_MACB_2_IF_Nbr = pif->Nbr;
                                /* Configure AT91SAM9263-EK MACB #2's receive interrupt:       */
    BSP_IntVectSet(BSP_INT_RX, &NetDev_MACB_ISR_HandlerRx_2);   /* Configure interrupt vector. */
    BSP_IntEn(BSP_INT_RX);                                      /* Enable    interrupt.        */

   *perr = NET_DEV_ERR_NONE;
}
```

A-3-4 NetDev_ClkGetFreq()

This function is called by a device driver's **NetDev_Init()** to return a specific network device's clock frequency for a specific interface.

FILES

net_bsp.c

PROTOTYPE

```
static CPU_INT32U NetDev_ClkGetFreq (NET_IF  *pif,
                                     NET_ERR *perr);
```

Note that since **NetDev_ClkFreqGet()** is accessed only by function pointer via a BSP interface structure, it doesn't need to be globally available and should therefore be declared as '**static**'.

ARGUMENTS

pif Pointer to specific interface to return device's clock frequency.

perr Pointer to variable that will receive the return error code from this function:

NET_DEV_ERR_NONE
NET_DEV_ERR_FAULT

This is *not* an exclusive list of return errors and specific network device's or device BSP functions may return any other specific errors as required.

RETURNED VALUE

Network device's clock frequency (in Hz).

REQUIRED CONFIGURATION

None.

NOTES / WARNINGS

Each network device's **NetDev_ClkFreqGet()** should return the device's clock frequency (in Hz). For Ethernet devices, this is usually the clock frequency of the device's (R)MII bus. The device driver's **NetDev_Init()** uses the returned clock frequency to configure an appropriate bus divider to ensure that the (R)MII bus logic operates within an allowable range. In general, the device driver should not configure the divider such that the (R)MII bus operates faster than 2.5MHz.

Since each network device requires a unique **NetDev_ClkFreqGet()**, it is recommended that each device's **NetDev_ClkFreqGet()** function be named using the following convention:

NetDev_[Device]ClkGetFreq[Number]()

[Device]	Network device name or type, e.g. MACB (optional if the development board does not support multiple devices)
[Number]	Network device number for each specific instance of device (optional if the development board does not support multiple instances of the specific device)

For example, the **NetDev_ClkFreqGet()** function for the #2 MACB Ethernet controller on an Atmel AT91SAM9263-EK should be named **NetDev_MACB_ClkGetFreq2()**, or **NetDev_MACB_ClkGetFreq_2()** with additional underscore optional.

See also section 14-7-1 "Network Device BSP" on page 320.

A-3-5 NetDev_ISR_Handler()

Handle a network device's interrupts on a specific interface.

FILES

net_bsp.c

PROTOTYPE

```
static void NetDev_ISR_Handler (void);
```

Note that since **NetDev_ISR_Handler()** is accessed only by function pointer usually via an interrupt vector table, it doesn't need to be globally available and should therefore be declared as '**static**'.

ARGUMENTS

None.

RETURNED VALUE

None.

REQUIRED CONFIGURATION

None.

NOTES / WARNINGS

Each network device's interrupt, or set of device interrupts, must be handled by a unique BSP-level interrupt service routine (ISR) handler, **NetDev_ISR_Handler()**, which maps each specific device interrupt to its corresponding network interface ISR handler, **NetIF_ISR_Handler()**. For some CPUs this may be a first- or second-level interrupt handler. Generally, the application must configure the interrupt controller to call every network device's unique **NetDev_ISR_Handler()** when the device's interrupt occurs (see section A-3-3 on page 424). Every unique **NetDev_ISR_Handler()** *must* then perform the following actions:

1 Call **NetIF_ISR_Handler()** with the device's unique network interface number and appropriate interrupt type. The device's network interface number should be available after configuration in the device's **NetDev_CfgIntCtrl()** function (see section A-3-3 "NetDev_CfgIntCtrl()" on page 424). **NetIF_ISR_Handler()** in turn calls the appropriate device driver's interrupt handler.

   In most cases, each device requires only a single **NetDev_ISR_Handler()** which calls **NetIF_ISR_Handler()** with interrupt type code **NET_DEV_ISR_TYPE_UNKNOWN**. This is possible when the device's driver can determine the device's interrupt type to via internal device registers or the interrupt controller. However, some devices cannot generically determine the interrupt type when an interrupt occurs and may therefore require multiple, unique **NetDev_ISR_Handler()**'s each of which calls **NetIF_ISR_Handler()** with the appropriate interrupt type code.

   Ethernet Physical layer (Phy) interrupts should call **NetIF_ISR_Handler()** with interrupt type code **NET_DEV_ISR_TYPE_PHY**.

   See also section B-9-12 "NetIF_ISR_Handler()" on page 535.

2 Clear the device's interrupt source, possibly via an external or CPU-integrated interrupt controller source.

Since each network device requires a unique **NetDev_ISR_Handler()** for each device interrupt, it is recommended that each device's **NetDev_ISR_Handler()** function be named using the following convention:

NetDev_[Device]ISR_Handler[Type][Number]()

[Device]	Network device name or type, e.g., MACB (optional if the development board does not support multiple devices)
[Type]	Network device interrupt type, e.g., receive interrupt (optional if interrupt type is generic or unknown)
[Number]	Network device number for each specific instance of device (optional if the development board does not support multiple instances of the specific device)

For example, the receive ISR handler for the #2 MACB Ethernet controller on an Atmel AT91SAM9263-EK should be named **NetDev_MACB_ISR_HandlerRx2()**.

See also section 14-7-1 “Network Device BSP” on page 320.

EXAMPLES

```
static void NetDev_MACB_ISR_Handler_2 (void)
{
    NET_ERR  err;

    NetIF_ISR_Handler(AT91SAM9263-EK_MACB_2_IF_Nbr, NET_DEV_ISR_TYPE_UNKNOWN, &err);
    /* Clear external or CPU's integrated interrupt controller. */
}


static void NetDev_MACB_ISR_HandlerRx_2 (void)
{
    NET_ERR  err;

    NetIF_ISR_Handler(AT91SAM9263-EK_MACB_2_IF_Nbr, NET_DEV_ISR_TYPE_RX, &err);
    /* Clear external or CPU's integrated interrupt controller. */
}
```

Appendix

B

μC/TCP-IP API Reference

The application programming interfaces (APIs) to μC/TCP-IP using any of the functions or macros are described in this appendix. The functions/macros in this appendix are organized alphabetically with the exception of alphabetizing all BSD functions/macros in their own section, section B-18 on page 709.

B-1 GENERAL NETWORK FUNCTIONS

B-1-1 Net_Init()

Initializes µC/TCP-IP and *must* be called prior to calling any other µC/TCP-IP API functions.

FILES

net.h/net.c

PROTOTYPE

```
NET_ERR Net_Init(void);
```

ARGUMENTS

None.

RETURNED VALUE

NET_ERR_NONE,	if successful;
Specific initialization error code,	otherwise.

Return value *should* be inspected to determine whether or not µC/TCP-IP successfully initialized. If µC/TCP-IP did *not* successfully initialize, search for the returned error code in **net_err.h** and source files to locate where the µC/TCP-IP initialization failed.

REQUIRED CONFIGURATION

None.

NOTES / WARNINGS

µC/LIB memory management function **Mem_Init()** *must* be called prior to calling Net_Init().

B-1-2 Net_InitDflt()

Initialize default values for all µC/TCP-IP configurable parameters.

FILES

net.h/net.c

PROTOTYPE

```
void Net_InitDflt(void);
```

ARGUMENTS

None.

RETURNED VALUE

None.

REQUIRED CONFIGURATION

None.

NOTES / WARNINGS

Some default parameters are specified in **net_cfg.h** (see Appendix C, "µC/TCP-IP Configuration and Optimization" on page 723).

B-1-3 Net_VersionGet()

Get the µC/TCP-IP software version.

FILES

net.h/net.c

PROTOTYPE

```
CPU_INT16U Net_VersionGet(void);
```

ARGUMENTS

None.

RETURNED VALUE

µC/TCP-IP software version.

REQUIRED CONFIGURATION

None.

NOTES / WARNINGS

µC/TCP-IP's software version is denoted as follows:

Vx.yy.zz

where
V denotes Version label
x denotes major software version revision number
yy denotes minor software version revision number
zz denotes sub-minor software version revision number

The software version is returned as follows:

ver = x.yyzz * 100 * 100

where
ver denotes software version number scaled as an integer value

x.yyzz denotes software version number, where the unscaled integer portion denotes the major version number and the unscaled fractional portion denotes the (concatenated) minor version numbers

For example, (version) V2.11.01 would be returned as `21101`.

B-2 NETWORK APPLICATION INTERFACE FUNCTIONS

B-2-1 NetApp_SockAccept() (TCP)

Return a new application socket accepted from a listen application socket, with error handling. See section B-13-1 on page 583 for more information.

FILES

net_app.h/net_app.c

PROTOTYPE

```
NET_SOCK_ID  NetApp_SockAccept (NET_SOCK_ID          sock_id,
                                NET_SOCK_ADDR       *paddr_remote,
                                NET_SOCK_ADDR_LEN   *paddr_len,
                                CPU_INT16U           retry_max,
                                CPU_INT32U           timeout_ms,
                                CPU_INT32U           time_dly_ms,
                                NET_ERR             *perr);
```

ARGUMENTS

sock_id This is the socket ID returned by **NetApp_SockOpen()/NetSock_Open()/socket()** when the socket was created. This socket is assumed to be bound to an address and listening for new connections (see section B-13-34 on page 648).

paddr_remote Pointer to a socket address structure (see section 17-1 "Network Socket Data Structures" on page 355) to return the remote host address of the new accepted connection.

paddr_len Pointer to the size of the socket address structure which *must* be passed the size of the socket address structure [e.g., **sizeof(NET_SOCK_ADDR_IP)**]. Returns size of the accepted connection's socket address structure, if no errors; returns 0, otherwise.

retry_max Maximum number of consecutive socket accept retries.

`timeout_ms` Socket accept timeout value per attempt/retry.

`time_dly_ms` Socket accept delay value, in milliseconds.

`perr` Pointer to variable that will receive the error code from this function:

NET_APP_ERR_NONE
NET_APP_ERR_NONE_AVAIL
NET_APP_ERR_INVALID_ARG
NET_APP_ERR_INVALID_OP
NET_APP_ERR_FAULT
NET_APP_ERR_FAULT_TRANSITORY

RETURNED VALUE

Socket descriptor/handle identifier of new accepted socket, if no errors.

NET_SOCK_BSD_ERR_ACCEPT, otherwise.

REQUIRED CONFIGURATION

Available only if `NET_APP_CFG_API_EN` is enabled (see section C-18-1 on page 748) **AND** `NET_CFG_TRANSPORT_LAYER_SEL` is configured for TCP (see section C-12-1 on page 736).

NOTES / WARNINGS

Some socket arguments and/or operations are validated only if validation code is enabled (see section C-3-1 on page 729).

If a non-zero number of retries is requested (`retry_max`) **AND** socket blocking is configured for non-blocking operation (see section C-15-3 on page 741); then a non-zero timeout (`timeout_ms`) and/or a non-zero time delay (`time_dly_ms`) should also be requested. Otherwise, all retries will most likely fail immediately since no time will elapse to wait for and allow socket operations to successfully complete.

B-2-2 NetApp_SockBind() (TCP/UDP)

Bind an application socket to a local address, with error handling. See section B-13-2 on page 585 for more information.

FILES

net_app.h/net_app.c

PROTOTYPE

```
CPU_BOOLEAN  NetApp_SockBind (NET_SOCK_ID          sock_id,
                              NET_SOCK_ADDR        *paddr_local,
                              NET_SOCK_ADDR_LEN    addr_len,
                              CPU_INT16U           retry_max,
                              CPU_INT32U           time_dly_ms,
                              NET_ERR              *perr);
```

ARGUMENTS

sock_id This is the socket ID returned by **NetApp_SockOpen()/ NetSock_Open()/socket()** when the socket was created.

paddr_local Pointer to a socket address structure (see section 8-2 "Socket Interface" on page 208) which contains the local host address to bind the socket to.

addr_len Size of the socket address structure which *must* be passed the size of the socket address structure [for example, **sizeof(NET_SOCK_ADDR_IP)**].

retry_max Maximum number of consecutive socket bind retries.

time_dly_ms Socket bind delay value, in milliseconds.

`perr` Pointer to variable that will receive the error code from this function:

NET_APP_ERR_NONE
NET_APP_ERR_NONE_AVAIL
NET_APP_ERR_INVALID_ARG
NET_APP_ERR_INVALID_OP
NET_APP_ERR_FAULT

RETURNED VALUE

`DEF_OK`, Application socket successfully bound to a local address.

`DEF_FAIL`, otherwise.

REQUIRED CONFIGURATION

Available only if **NET_APP_CFG_API_EN** is enabled (see section C-18-1 on page 748) **AND** either **NET_CFG_TRANSPORT_LAYER_SEL** is configured for TCP (see section C-12-1 on page 736) and/or **NET_UDP_CFG_APP_API_SEL** is configured for sockets (see section C-13-1 on page 737).

NOTES / WARNINGS

Some socket arguments and/or operations are validated only if validation code is enabled (see section C-3-1 on page 729).

If a non-zero number of retries is requested (**retry_max**) then a non-zero time delay (**time_dly_ms**) should also be requested. Otherwise, all retries will most likely fail immediately since no time will elapse to wait for and allow socket operations to successfully complete.

B-2-3 NetApp_SockClose() (TCP/UDP)

Close an application socket, with error handling. See section B-13-25 on page 632 for more information.

FILES

net_app.h/net_app.c

PROTOTYPE

```
CPU_BOOLEAN  NetApp_SockClose (NET_SOCK_ID   sock_id,
                               CPU_INT32U    timeout_ms,
                               NET_ERR      *perr);
```

ARGUMENTS

sock_id — This is the socket ID returned by NetApp_SockOpen()/NetSock_Open()/socket() when the socket was created *or* by NetApp_SockAccept()/NetSock_Accept()/accept() when a connection was accepted.

timeout_ms — Socket close timeout value per attempt/retry.

perr — Pointer to variable that will receive the error code from this function:

NET_APP_ERR_NONE
NET_APP_ERR_INVALID_ARG
NET_APP_ERR_FAULT
NET_APP_ERR_FAULT_TRANSITORY

RETURNED VALUE

DEF_OK, — Application socket successfully closed.

DEF_FAIL, — otherwise.

REQUIRED CONFIGURATION

Available only if NET_APP_CFG_API_EN is enabled (see section C-18-1 on page 748) **AND** either NET_CFG_TRANSPORT_LAYER_SEL is configured for TCP (see section C-12-1 on page 736) and/or NET_UDP_CFG_APP_API_SEL is configured for sockets (see section C-13-1 on page 737).

NOTES / WARNINGS

Some socket arguments and/or operations are validated only if validation code is enabled (see section C-3-1 on page 729).

B-2-4 NetApp_SockConn() (TCP/UDP)

Connect an application socket to a remote address, with error handling. See section B-13-26 on page 634 for more information.

FILES

net_app.h/net_app.c

PROTOTYPE

```
CPU_BOOLEAN  NetApp_SockConn (NET_SOCK_ID          sock_id,
                              NET_SOCK_ADDR       *paddr_remote,
                              NET_SOCK_ADDR_LEN    addr_len,
                              CPU_INT16U           retry_max,
                              CPU_INT32U           timeout_ms,
                              CPU_INT32U           time_dly_ms,
                              NET_ERR             *perr);
```

ARGUMENTS

sock_id	This is the socket ID returned by **NetApp_SockOpen()/ NetSock_Open()/socket()** when the socket was created.
paddr_remote	Pointer to a socket address structure (see section 8-2 “Socket Interface” on page 208) which contains the remote socket address to connect the socket to.
addr_len	Size of the socket address structure which *must* be passed the size of the socket address structure [e.g., **sizeof(NET_SOCK_ADDR_IP)**].
retry_max	Maximum number of consecutive socket connect retries.
timeout_ms	Socket connect timeout value per attempt/retry.
time_dly_ms	Socket connect delay value, in milliseconds.

`perr`	Pointer to variable that will receive the error code from this function:

	`NET_APP_ERR_NONE`
	`NET_APP_ERR_NONE_AVAIL`
	`NET_APP_ERR_INVALID_ARG`
	`NET_APP_ERR_INVALID_OP`
	`NET_APP_ERR_FAULT`
	`NET_APP_ERR_FAULT_TRANSITORY`

RETURNED VALUE

`DEF_OK`, Application socket successfully connected to a remote address.

`DEF_FAIL`, otherwise.

REQUIRED CONFIGURATION

Available only if **`NET_APP_CFG_API_EN`** is enabled (see section C-18-1 on page 748) **AND** either **`NET_CFG_TRANSPORT_LAYER_SEL`** is configured for TCP (see section C-12-1 on page 736) and/or **`NET_UDP_CFG_APP_API_SEL`** is configured for sockets (see section C-13-1 on page 737).

NOTES / WARNINGS

Some socket arguments and/or operations are validated only if validation code is enabled (see section C-3-1 on page 729).

If a non-zero number of retries is requested (**`retry_max`**) **AND** socket blocking is configured for non-blocking operation (see section C-15-3 on page 741); then a non-zero timeout (**`timeout_ms`**) and/or a non-zero time delay (**`time_dly_ms`**) should also be requested. Otherwise, all retries will most likely fail immediately since no time will elapse to wait for and allow socket operations to successfully complete.

B-2-5 NetApp_SockListen() (TCP)

Set an application socket to listen for connection requests, with error handling. See section B-13-34 on page 648 for more information.

FILES

net_app.h/net_app.c

PROTOTYPE

```
CPU_BOOLEAN  NetApp_SockListen (NET_SOCK_ID        sock_id,
                                NET_SOCK_Q_SIZE    sock_q_size,
                                NET_ERR           *perr);
```

ARGUMENTS

sock_id This is the socket ID returned by **NetApp_SockOpen()/ NetSock_Open()/socket()** when the socket was created.

sock_q_size Maximum number of new connections allowed to be waiting. In other words, this argument specifies the maximum queue length of pending connections while the listening socket is busy servicing the current request.

perr Pointer to variable that will receive the error code from this function:

NET_APP_ERR_NONE
NET_APP_ERR_INVALID_ARG
NET_APP_ERR_INVALID_OP
NET_APP_ERR_FAULT
NET_APP_ERR_FAULT_TRANSITORY

RETURNED VALUE

DEF_OK, Application socket successfully set to listen.

DEF_FAIL, otherwise.

REQUIRED CONFIGURATION

Available only if `NET_APP_CFG_API_EN` is enabled (see section C-18-1 on page 748) **AND** `NET_CFG_TRANSPORT_LAYER_SEL` is configured for TCP (see section C-12-1 on page 736).

NOTES / WARNINGS

Some socket arguments and/or operations are validated only if validation code is enabled (see section C-3-1 on page 729).

B-2-6 NetApp_SockOpen() (TCP/UDP)

Open an application socket, with error handling. See section B-13-35 on page 650 for more information.

FILES

net_app.h/net_app.c

PROTOTYPE

```
NET_SOCK_ID  NetApp_SockOpen (NET_SOCK_PROTOCOL_FAMILY   protocol_family,
                              NET_SOCK_TYPE              sock_type,
                              NET_SOCK_PROTOCOL          protocol,
                              CPU_INT16U                 retry_max,
                              CPU_INT32U                 time_dly_ms,
                              NET_ERR                   *perr);
```

ARGUMENTS

protocol_family This field establishes the socket protocol family domain. Always use **NET_SOCK_FAMILY_IP_V4/PF_INET** for TCP/IP sockets.

sock_type Socket type:

NET_SOCK_TYPE_DATAGRAM/PF_DGRAM for datagram sockets (i.e., UDP)

NET_SOCK_TYPE_STREAM/PF_STREAM for stream sockets (i.e., TCP)

NET_SOCK_TYPE_DATAGRAM sockets preserve message boundaries. Applications that exchange single request and response messages are examples of datagram communication.

NET_SOCK_TYPE_STREAM sockets provides a reliable byte-stream connection, where bytes are received from the remote application in the same order as they were sent. File transfer and terminal emulation are examples of applications that require this type of protocol.

`protocol`	Socket protocol: `NET_SOCK_PROTOCOL_UDP/IPPROTO_UDP` for UDP `NET_SOCK_PROTOCOL_TCP/IPPROTO_TCP` for TCP `0` for default-protocol: UDP for `NET_SOCK_TYPE_DATAGRAM/PF_DGRAM` TCP for `NET_SOCK_TYPE_STREAM/PF_STREAM`
`retry_max`	Maximum number of consecutive socket open retries.
`time_dly_ms`	Socket open delay value, in milliseconds.

`perr`	Pointer to variable that will receive the error code from this function:
	
	`NET_APP_ERR_NONE`
	`NET_APP_ERR_NONE_AVAIL`
	`NET_APP_ERR_INVALID_ARG`
	`NET_APP_ERR_FAULT`

RETURNED VALUE

Socket descriptor/handle identifier of new socket, if no errors.

`NET_SOCK_BSD_ERR_OPEN`, otherwise.

REQUIRED CONFIGURATION

Available only if `NET_APP_CFG_API_EN` is enabled (see section C-18-1 on page 748) *and* either `NET_CFG_TRANSPORT_LAYER_SEL` is configured for TCP (see section C-12-1 on page 736) and/or `NET_UDP_CFG_APP_API_SEL` is configured for sockets (see section C-13-1 on page 737).

NOTES / WARNINGS

Some socket arguments and/or operations are validated only if validation code is enabled (see section C-3-1 on page 729).

If a non-zero number of retries is requested (`retry_max`) then a non-zero time delay (`time_dly_ms`) should also be requested. Otherwise, all retries will likely fail immediately since no time will elapse to wait for and allow socket operations to successfully complete.

B-2-7 NetApp_SockRx() (TCP/UDP)

Receive application data via socket, with error handling. See section B-13-38 on page 655 for more information.

FILES

net_app.h/net_app.c

PROTOTYPE

```
CPU_INT16U  NetApp_SockRx (NET_SOCK_ID         sock_id,
                           void               *pdata_buf,
                           CPU_INT16U          data_buf_len,
                           CPU_INT16U          data_rx_th,
                           CPU_INT16S          flags,
                           NET_SOCK_ADDR      *paddr_remote,
                           NET_SOCK_ADDR_LEN  *paddr_len,
                           CPU_INT16U          retry_max,
                           CPU_INT32U          timeout_ms,
                           CPU_INT32U          time_dly_ms,
                           NET_ERR            *perr);
```

ARGUMENTS

sock_id This is the socket ID returned by **NetApp_SockOpen()/NetSock_Open()/socket()** when the socket was created *or* by **NetApp_SockAccept()/NetSock_Accept()/accept()** when a connection was accepted.

pdata_buf Pointer to the application memory buffer to receive data.

data_buf_len Size of the destination application memory buffer (in bytes).

data_rx_th Application data receive threshold:

0, no minimum receive threshold; i.e. receive any amount of data. Recommended for datagram sockets;

Minimum amount of application data to receive (in bytes) within maximum number of retries, otherwise.

flags — Flag to select receive options; bit-field flags logically **OR**'d:

NET_SOCK_FLAG_NONE/0	No socket flags selected
NET_SOCK_FLAG_RX_DATA_PEEK/ MSG_PEEK	Receive socket data without consuming it
NET_SOCK_FLAG_RX_NO_BLOCK/ MSG_DONTWAIT	Receive socket data without blocking

In most cases, this flag would be set to NET_SOCK_FLAG_NONE/0.

paddr_remote — Pointer to a socket address structure (see section 8-2 "Socket Interface" on page 208) to return the remote host address that sent the received data.

paddr_len — Pointer to the size of the socket address structure which *must* be passed the size of the socket address structure [e.g., sizeof(NET_SOCK_ADDR_IP)]. Returns size of the accepted connection's socket address structure, if no errors; returns 0, otherwise.

retry_max — Maximum number of consecutive socket receive retries.

timeout_ms — Socket receive timeout value per attempt/retry.

time_dly_ms — Socket receive delay value, in milliseconds.

perr — Pointer to variable that will receive the error code from this function:

NET_APP_ERR_NONE
NET_APP_ERR_INVALID_ARG
NET_APP_ERR_INVALID_OP
NET_APP_ERR_FAULT
NET_APP_ERR_FAULT_TRANSITORY
NET_APP_ERR_CONN_CLOSED
NET_APP_ERR_DATA_BUF_OVF
NET_ERR_RX

RETURNED VALUE

Number of data bytes received, if no errors.

`0`, otherwise.

REQUIRED CONFIGURATION

Available only if `NET_APP_CFG_API_EN` is enabled (see section C-18-1 on page 748) *and* either `NET_CFG_TRANSPORT_LAYER_SEL` is configured for TCP (see section C-12-1 on page 736) and/or `NET_UDP_CFG_APP_API_SEL` is configured for sockets (see section C-13-1 on page 737).

NOTES / WARNINGS

Some socket arguments and/or operations are validated only if validation code is enabled (see section C-3-1 on page 729).

If a non-zero number of retries is requested (`retry_max`) *and* socket blocking is configured for non-blocking operation (see section C-15-3 on page 741); then a non-zero timeout (`timeout_ms`) and/or a non-zero time delay (`time_dly_ms`) should also be requested. Otherwise, all retries will most likely fail immediately since no time will elapse to wait for and allow socket operations to successfully complete.

B-2-8 NetApp_SockTx() (TCP/UDP)

Transmit application data via socket, with error handling. See section B-13-40 on page 662 for more information.

FILES

net_app.h/net_app.c

PROTOTYPE

```
CPU_INT16U  NetApp_SockTx (NET_SOCK_ID          sock_id,
                           void                *p_data,
                           CPU_INT16U           data_len,
                           CPU_INT16S           flags,
                           NET_SOCK_ADDR       *paddr_remote,
                           NET_SOCK_ADDR_LEN    addr_len,
                           CPU_INT16U           retry_max,
                           CPU_INT32U           timeout_ms,
                           CPU_INT32U           time_dly_ms,
                           NET_ERR             *perr);
```

ARGUMENTS

sock_id The socket ID returned by NetApp_SockOpen()/NetSock_Open()/socket() when the socket was created *or* by NetApp_SockAccept()/NetSock_Accept()/accept() when a connection was accepted.

p_data Pointer to the application data memory buffer to send.

data_len Size of the application data memory buffer (in bytes).

flags Flag to select transmit options; bit-field flags logically **OR**'d:

NET_SOCK_FLAG_NONE/0	
NET_SOCK_FLAG_TX_NO_BLOCK/	No socket flags selected
MSG_DONTWAIT	Send socket data without blocking

In most cases, this flag would be set to NET_SOCK_FLAG_NONE/0.

paddr_remote	Pointer to a socket address structure (see section 8-2 “Socket Interface” on page 208) which contains the remote socket address to send data to.
addr_len	Size of the socket address structure which *must* be passed the size of the socket address structure [e.g., **sizeof(NET_SOCK_ADDR_IP)**].
retry_max	Maximum number of consecutive socket transmit retries.
timeout_ms	Socket transmit timeout value per attempt/retry.
time_dly_ms	Socket transmit delay value, in milliseconds.
perr	Pointer to variable that will receive the error code from this function:

NET_APP_ERR_NONE
NET_APP_ERR_INVALID_ARG
NET_APP_ERR_INVALID_OP
NET_APP_ERR_FAULT
NET_APP_ERR_FAULT_TRANSITORY
NET_APP_ERR_CONN_CLOSED
NET_ERR_TX

RETURNED VALUE

Number of data bytes transmitted, if no errors.

0, otherwise.

REQUIRED CONFIGURATION

Available only if **NET_APP_CFG_API_EN** is enabled (see section C-18-1 on page 748) *and* either **NET_CFG_TRANSPORT_LAYER_SEL** is configured for TCP (see section C-12-1 on page 736) and/or **NET_UDP_CFG_APP_API_SEL** is configured for sockets (see section C-13-1 on page 737).

E

NOTES / WARNINGS

Some socket arguments and/or operations are validated only if validation code is enabled (see section C-3-1 on page 729).

If a non-zero number of retries is requested (`retry_max`) *and* socket blocking is configured for non-blocking operation (see section C-15-3 on page 741); then a non-zero timeout (`timeout_ms`) and/or a non-zero time delay (`time_dly_ms`) should also be requested. Otherwise, all retries will most likely fail immediately since no time will elapse to wait for and allow socket operations to successfully complete.

B-2-9 NetApp_TimeDly_ms()

Delay for specified time, in milliseconds.

FILES

net_app.h/net_app.c

PROTOTYPE

```
void  NetApp_TimeDly_ms (CPU_INT32U   time_dly_ms,
                         NET_ERR     *perr);
```

ARGUMENTS

time_dly_ms Time delay value, in milliseconds.

perr Pointer to variable that will receive the error code from this function:

NET_APP_ERR_NONE
NET_APP_ERR_INVALID_ARG
NET_APP_ERR_FAULT

RETURNED VALUE

None.

REQUIRED CONFIGURATION

Available only if NET_APP_CFG_API_EN is enabled (see section C-18-1 on page 748).

NOTES / WARNINGS

Time delay of 0 milliseconds allowed. Time delay limited to the maximum possible time delay supported by the system/OS.

B-3 ARP FUNCTIONS

B-3-1 NetARP_CacheCalcStat()

Calculate ARP cache found percentage statistics.

FILES

net_arp.h/net_arp.c

PROTOTYPE

```
CPU_INT08U NetARP_CacheCalcStat(void);
```

ARGUMENTS

None.

RETURNED VALUE

ARP cache found percentage, if no errors.

NULL cache found percentage, otherwise.

REQUIRED CONFIGURATION

Available only if an appropriate network interface layer is present (e.g., Ethernet; see section C-7-3 on page 732).

NOTES / WARNINGS

None.

B-3-2 NetARP_CacheGetAddrHW()

Get the hardware address corresponding to a specific ARP cache's protocol address.

FILES

net_arp.h/net_arp.c

PROTOTYPE

```
NET_ARP_ADDR_LEN NetARP_CacheGetAddrHW (CPU_INT08U        *paddr_hw
                                        NET_ARP_ADDR_LEN   addr_hw_len_buf,
                                        CPU_INT08U        *paddr_protocol,
                                        NET_ARP_ADDR_LEN   addr_protocol_len,
                                        NET_ERR           *perr);
```

ARGUMENTS

`paddr_hw` Pointer to a memory buffer that will receive the hardware address:

Hardware address that corresponds to the desired protocol address, if no errors; hardware address cleared to all zeros, otherwise.

`addr_hw_len_buf` Size of hardware address memory buffer (in bytes).

`paddr_protocol` Pointer to the specific protocol address.

`addr_protocol_len` Length of protocol address (in bytes).

`perr` Pointer to variable that will receive the error code from this function:

NET_ARP_ERR_NONE
NET_ARP_ERR_NULL_PTR
NET_ARP_ERR_INVALID_HW_ADDR_LEN
NET_ARP_ERR_INVALID_PROTOCOL_ADDR_LEN
NET_ARP_ERR_CACHE_NOT_FOUND
NET_ARP_ERR_CACHE_PEND

RETURNED VALUE

Length of returned hardware address, if available;

0, otherwise.

REQUIRED CONFIGURATION

Available only if an appropriate network interface layer is present (e.g., Ethernet; see section C-7-3 on page 732).

NOTES / WARNINGS

NetARP_CacheGetAddrHW() may be used in conjunction with **NetARP_ProbeAddrOnNet()** to determine if a specific protocol address is available on the local network.

B-3-3 NetARP_CachePoolStatGet()

Get ARP caches' statistics pool.

FILES

net_arp.h/net_arp.c

PROTOTYPE

```
NET_STAT_POOL NetARP_CachePoolStatGet(void);
```

ARGUMENTS

None.

RETURNED VALUE

ARP caches' statistics pool, if no errors.

NULL statistics pool, otherwise.

REQUIRED CONFIGURATION

Available only if an appropriate network interface layer is present (e.g., Ethernet; see section C-7-3 on page 732).

NOTES / WARNINGS

None.

B-3-4 NetARP_CachePoolStatResetMaxUsed()

Reset ARP caches' statistics pool's maximum number of entries used.

FILES

net_arp.h/net_arp.c

PROTOTYPE

```
void NetARP_CachePoolStatResetMaxUsed(void);
```

ARGUMENTS

None.

RETURNED VALUE

None.

REQUIRED CONFIGURATION

Available only if an appropriate network interface layer is present (e.g., Ethernet; see section C-7-3 on page 732).

NOTES / WARNINGS

None.

B-3-5 NetARP_CfgCacheAccessedTh()

Configure ARP cache access promotion threshold.

FILES

net_arp.h/net_arp.c

PROTOTYPE

```
CPU_BOOLEAN NetARP_CfgCacheAccessedTh(CPU_INT16U nbr_access);
```

ARGUMENTS

nbr_access — Desired number of ARP cache accesses before ARP cache entry is promoted.

RETURNED VALUE

DEF_OK, ARP cache access promotion threshold successfully configured;

DEF_FAIL, otherwise.

REQUIRED CONFIGURATION

Available only if an appropriate network interface layer is present (e.g., Ethernet; see section C-7-3 on page 732).

NOTES / WARNINGS

None.

B-3-6 NetARP_CfgCacheTimeout()

Configure ARP cache timeout for ARP Cache List. ARP cache entries will be retired if they are not used within the specified timeout.

FILES

`net_arp.h/net_arp.c`

PROTOTYPE

```
CPU_BOOLEAN NetARP_CfgCacheTimeout(CPU_INT16U timeout_sec);
```

ARGUMENTS

`timeout_sec` Desired value for ARP cache timeout (in seconds)

RETURNED VALUE

`DEF_OK`, ARP cache timeout successfully configured;

`DEF_FAIL`, otherwise.

REQUIRED CONFIGURATION

Available only if an appropriate network interface layer is present (e.g., Ethernet; see section C-7-3 on page 732).

NOTES / WARNINGS

None.

B-3-7 NetARP_CfgReqMaxRetries()

Configure maximum number of ARP request retries.

FILES

net_arp.h/net_arp.c

PROTOTYPE

```
CPU_BOOLEAN NetARP_CfgReqMaxRetries(CPU_INT08U max_nbr_retries);
```

ARGUMENTS

max_nbr_retries Desired maximum number of ARP request retries.

RETURNED VALUE

DEF_OK, maximum number of ARP request retries configured.

DEF_FAIL, otherwise.

REQUIRED CONFIGURATION

Available only if an appropriate network interface layer is present (e.g., Ethernet; see section C-7-3 on page 732).

NOTES / WARNINGS

None.

B-3-8 NetARP_CfgReqTimeout()

Configure timeout between ARP request timeouts.

FILES

net_arp.h/net_arp.c

PROTOTYPE

```
CPU_BOOLEAN NetARP_CfgReqTimeout(CPU_INT08U timeout_sec);
```

ARGUMENTS

timeout_sec   Desired value for ARP request pending ARP reply timeout (in seconds).

RETURNED VALUE

DEF_OK,   ARP request timeout successfully configured,

DEF_FAIL,   otherwise.

REQUIRED CONFIGURATION

Available only if an appropriate network interface layer is present (e.g., Ethernet; see section C-7-3 on page 732).

NOTES / WARNINGS

None.

B-3-9 NetARP_IsAddrProtocolConflict()

Check interface's protocol address conflict status between this interface's ARP host protocol address(es) and any other host(s) on the local network.

FILES

net_arp.h/net_arp.c

PROTOTYPE

```
CPU_BOOLEAN NetARP_IsAddrProtocolConflict (NET_IF_NBR  if_nbr,
                                           NET_ERR     *perr);
```

ARGUMENTS

if_nbr Interface number to get protocol address conflict status.

perr Pointer to variable that will receive the return error code from this function:

NET_ARP_ERR_NONE
NET_IF_ERR_INVALID_IF
NET_OS_ERR_LOCK

RETURNED VALUE

DEF_YES if address conflict detected;
DEF_NO otherwise.

REQUIRED CONFIGURATION

Available only if an appropriate network interface layer is present (e.g., Ethernet; see section C-7-3 on page 732).

NOTES / WARNINGS

None.

B-3-10 NetARP_ProbeAddrOnNet()

Transmit an ARP request to probe the local network for a specific protocol address.

FILES

net_arp.h/net_arp.c

PROTOTYPE

```
void NetARP_ProbeAddrOnNet(NET_PROTOCOL_TYPE  protocol_type,
                           CPU_INT08U        *paddr_protocol_sender,
                           CPU_INT08U        *paddr_protocol_target
                           NET_ARP_ADDR_LEN   addr_protocol_len,
                           NET_ERR           *perr);
```

ARGUMENTS

protocol_type Address protocol type.

paddr_protocol_sender Pointer to protocol address to send probe from.

paddr_protocol_target Pointer to protocol address to probe local network.

addr_protocol_len Length of protocol address (in bytes).

perr Pointer to variable that will receive the return error code from this function:

NET_ARP_ERR_NONE
NET_ARP_ERR_NULL_PTR
NET_ARP_ERR_INVALID_PROTOCOL_ADDR_LEN
NET_ARP_ERR_CACHE_INVALID_TYPE
NET_ARP_ERR_CACHE_NONE_AVAIL
NET_MGR_ERR_INVALID_PROTOCOL
NET_MGR_ERR_INVALID_PROTOCOL_ADDR
NET_MGR_ERR_INVALID_PROTOCOL_ADDR_LEN
NET_TMR_ERR_NULL_OBJ
NET_TMR_ERR_NULL_FNCT
NET_TMR_ERR_NONE_AVAIL
NET_TMR_ERR_INVALID_TYPE
NET_OS_ERR_LOCK

RETURNED VALUE

None.

REQUIRED CONFIGURATION

Available only if an appropriate network interface layer is present (e.g., Ethernet; see section C-7-3 on page 732).

NOTES / WARNINGS

`NetARP_ProbeAddrOnNet()` may be used in conjunction with **`NetARP_CacheGetAddrHW()`** to determine if a specific protocol address is available on the local network.

B-4 NETWORK ASCII FUNCTIONS

B-4-1 NetASCII_IP_to_Str()

Convert an IPv4 address in host-order into an IPv4 dotted-decimal notation ASCII string.

FILES

net_ascii.h/net_ascii.c

PROTOTYPE

```
void  NetASCII_IP_to_Str(NET_IP_ADDR    addr_ip,
                         CPU_CHAR      *paddr_ip_ascii,
                         CPU_BOOLEAN    lead_zeros,
                         NET_ERR       *perr);
```

ARGUMENTS

addr_ip IPv4 address (in host-order).

paddr_ip_ascii Pointer to a memory buffer of size greater than or equal to NET_ASCII_LEN_MAX_ADDR_IP bytes to receive the IPv4 address string. Note that the first ASCII character in the string is the most significant nibble of the IP address's most significant byte and that the last character in the string is the least significant nibble of the IP address's least significant byte. Example: "10.10.1.65" = 0x0A0A0141

lead_zeros Select formatting the IPv4 address string with leading zeros ('0') prior to the first non-zero digit in each IP address byte. The number of leading zeros added is such that each byte's total number of decimal digits is equal to the maximum number of digits for each byte (i.e., 3).

DEF_NO	Do *not* prepend leading zeros to each IP address byte
DEF_YES	Prepend leading zeros to each IP address byte

perr Pointer to variable that will receive the return error code from this function:

NET_ASCII_ERR_NONE
NET_ASCII_ERR_NULL_PTR
NET_ASCII_ERR_INVALID_CHAR_LEN

RETURNED VALUE

None.

REQUIRED CONFIGURATION

None.

NOTES / WARNINGS

RFC 1983 states that "dotted-decimal notation... refers [to] IP addresses of the form A.B.C.D; where each letter represents, in decimal, one byte of a four-byte IP address." In other words, the dotted-decimal notation separates four decimal byte values by the dot, or period, character ('.'). Each decimal value represents one byte of the IP address starting with the most significant byte in network order.

IPv4 Address Examples:

DOTTED DECIMAL NOTATION	HEXADECIMAL EQUIVALENT
127.0.0.1	0x7F000001
192.168.1.64	0xC0A80140
255.255.255.0	0xFFFFFF00
MSB .... LSB	MSB .... LSB

MSB Most Significant Byte in Dotted-Decimal IP Address

LSB Least Significant Byte in Dotted-Decimal IP Address

B-4-2 NetASCII_MAC_to_Str()

Convert a Media Access Control (MAC) address into a hexadecimal address string.

FILES

net_ascii.h/net_ascii.c

PROTOTYPE

```
void NetASCII_MAC_to_Str(CPU_INT08U   *paddr_mac,
                         CPU_CHAR     *paddr_mac_ascii,
                         CPU_BOOLEAN   hex_lower_case,
                         CPU_BOOLEAN   hex_colon_sep,
                         NET_ERR      *perr);
```

ARGUMENTS

paddr_mac

Pointer to a memory buffer of NET_ASCII_NBR_OCTET_ADDR_MAC bytes in size that contains the MAC address.

paddr_mac_ascii

Pointer to a memory buffer of size greater than or equal to NET_ASCII_LEN_MAX_ADDR_MAC bytes to receive the MAC address string. Note that the first ASCII character in the string is the most significant nibble of the MAC address's most significant byte and that the last character in the string is the least significant nibble of the MAC address's least significant address byte.

Example: "00:1A:07:AC:22:09" = 0x001A07AC2209

hex_lower_case

Select formatting the MAC address string with upper- or lower-case ASCII characters:

DEF_NO	Format MAC address string with upper-case characters
DEF_YES	Format MAC address string with lower-case characters

hex_colon_sep	Select formatting the MAC address string with colon (':') or dash ('-') characters to separate the MAC address hexadecimal bytes:	
	DEF_NO	Separate MAC address bytes with hyphen characters
	DEF_YES	Separate MAC address bytes with colon characters

perr Pointer to variable that will receive the return error code from this function:

NET_ASCII_ERR_NONE
NET_ASCII_ERR_NULL_PTR

RETURNED VALUE

None.

REQUIRED CONFIGURATION

None.

NOTES / WARNINGS

None.

B-4-3 NetASCII_Str_to_IP()

Convert a string of an IPv4 address in dotted-decimal notation to an IPv4 address in host-order.

FILES

net_ascii.h/net_ascii.c

PROTOTYPE

```
NET_IP_ADDR NetASCII_Str_to_IP(CPU_CHAR  *paddr_ip_ascii,
                               NET_ERR   *perr);
```

ARGUMENTS

paddr_ip_ascii

Pointer to an ASCII string that contains a dotted-decimal IPv4 address. Each decimal byte of the IPv4 address string must be separated by a dot, or period, character ('.'). Note that the first ASCII character in the string is the most significant nibble of the IP address's most significant byte and that the last character in the string is the least significant nibble of the IP address's least significant byte.

Example: "10.10.1.65" = 0x0A0A0141

perr

Pointer to variable that will receive the return error code from this function:

NET_ASCII_ERR_NONE
NET_ASCII_ERR_NULL_PTR
NET_ASCII_ERR_INVALID_STR_LEN
NET_ASCII_ERR_INVALID_CHAR
NET_ASCII_ERR_INVALID_CHAR_LEN
NET_ASCII_ERR_INVALID_CHAR_VAL
NET_ASCII_ERR_INVALID_CHAR_SEQ

RETURNED VALUE

Returns the IPv4 address, represented by the IPv3 address string, in host-order, if no errors.

`NET_IP_ADDR_NONE`, otherwise.

REQUIRED CONFIGURATION

None.

NOTES / WARNINGS

RFC 1983 states that "dotted decimal notation... refers [to] IP addresses of the form A.B.C.D; where each letter represents, in decimal, one byte of a four-byte IP address". In other words, the dotted-decimal notation separates four decimal byte values by the dot, or period, character ('.'). Each decimal value represents one byte of the IP address starting with the most significant byte in network order.

IPv4 Address Examples:

DOTTED DECIMAL NOTATION	HEXADECIMAL EQUIVALENT
127.0.0.1	0x7F000001
192.168.1.64	0xC0A80140
255.255.255.0	0xFFFFFF00
MSB .... LSB	MSB .... LSB

MSB Most Significant Byte in Dotted-Decimal IP Address

LSB Least Significant Byte in Dotted-Decimal IP Address

The IPv4 dotted-decimal ASCII string *must* include *only* decimal values and the dot, or period, character ('.'); all other characters are trapped as invalid, including any leading or trailing characters. The ASCII string *must* include exactly four decimal values separated by exactly three dot characters. Each decimal value *must not* exceed the maximum byte value (i.e., 255), or exceed the maximum number of digits for each byte (i.e., 3) including any leading zeros.

B-4-4 NetASCII_Str_to_MAC()

Convert a hexadecimal address string to a Media Access Control (MAC) address.

FILES

net_ascii.h/net_ascii.c

PROTOTYPE

```
void NetASCII_Str_to_MAC(CPU_CHAR    *paddr_mac_ascii,
                         CPU_INT08U  *paddr_mac,
                         NET_ERR     *perr);
```

ARGUMENTS

paddr_mac_ascii   Pointer to an ASCII string that contains hexadecimal bytes separated by colons or dashes that represents the MAC address. Each hexadecimal byte of the MAC address string must be separated by either the colon (':') or dash ('-') characters. Note that the first ASCII character in the string is the most significant nibble of the MAC address's most significant byte and that the last character in the string is the least significant nibble of the MAC address's least significant address byte.

Example: "00:1A:07:AC:22:09" = 0x001A07AC2209

paddr_mac   Pointer to a memory buffer of size greater than or equal to NET_ASCII_NBR_OCTET_ADDR_MAC bytes to receive the MAC address.

perr   Pointer to variable that will receive the return error code from this function:

NET_ASCII_ERR_NONE
NET_ASCII_ERR_NULL_PTR
NET_ASCII_ERR_INVALID_STR_LEN
NET_ASCII_ERR_INVALID_CHAR
NET_ASCII_ERR_INVALID_CHAR_LEN
NET_ASCII_ERR_INVALID_CHAR_SEQ

RETURNED VALUE

None.

REQUIRED CONFIGURATION

None.

NOTES / WARNINGS

None.

B-5 NETWORK BUFFER FUNCTIONS

B-5-1 NetBuf_PoolStatGet()

Get an interface's Network Buffers' statistics pool.

FILES

net_buf.h/net_buf.c

PROTOTYPE

```
NET_STAT_POOL NetBuf_PoolStatGet(NET_IF_NBR if_nbr);
```

ARGUMENTS

`if_nbr` Interface number to get Network Buffer statistics.

RETURNED VALUE

Network Buffers' statistics pool, if no errors.

NULL statistics pool, otherwise.

REQUIRED CONFIGURATION

None.

NOTES / WARNINGS

None.

B-5-2 NetBuf_PoolStatResetMaxUsed()

Reset an interface's Network Buffers' statistics pool's maximum number of entries used.

FILES

net_buf.h/net_buf.c

PROTOTYPE

```
void NetBuf_PoolStatResetMaxUsed(NET_IF_NBR if_nbr);
```

ARGUMENTS

if_nbr Interface number to reset Network Buffer statistics.

RETURNED VALUE

None.

REQUIRED CONFIGURATION

None.

NOTES / WARNINGS

None.

B-5-3 NetBuf_RxLargePoolStatGet()

Get an interface's large receive buffers' statistics pool.

FILES

net_buf.h/net_buf.c

PROTOTYPE

```
NET_STAT_POOL NetBuf_RxLargePoolStatGet(NET_IF_NBR if_nbr);
```

ARGUMENTS

if_nbr   Interface number to get Network Buffer statistics.

RETURNED VALUE

Large receive buffers' statistics pool, if no errors.

NULL statistics pool, otherwise.

REQUIRED CONFIGURATION

None.

NOTES / WARNINGS

None.

B-5-4 NetBuf_RxLargePoolStatResetMaxUsed()

Reset an interface's large receive buffers' statistics pool's maximum number of entries used.

FILES

net_buf.h/net_buf.c

PROTOTYPE

```
void NetBuf_RxLargePoolStatResetMaxUsed(NET_IF_NBR if_nbr);
```

ARGUMENTS

`if_nbr` Interface number to reset Network Buffer statistics.

RETURNED VALUE

None.

REQUIRED CONFIGURATION

None.

NOTES / WARNINGS

None.

B-5-5 NetBuf_TxLargePoolStatGet()

Get an interface's large transmit buffers' statistics pool.

FILES

net_buf.h/net_buf.c

PROTOTYPE

```
NET_STAT_POOL NetBuf_TxLargePoolStatGet(NET_IF_NBR if_nbr);
```

ARGUMENTS

if_nbr Interface number to get Network Buffer statistics.

RETURNED VALUE

Large transmit buffers' statistics pool, if no errors.

NULL statistics pool, otherwise.

REQUIRED CONFIGURATION

None.

NOTES / WARNINGS

None.

B-5-6 NetBuf_TxLargePoolStatResetMaxUsed()

Reset an interface's large transmit buffers' statistics pool's maximum number of entries used.

FILES

net_buf.h/net_buf.c

PROTOTYPE

```
void NetBuf_TxLargePoolStatResetMaxUsed(NET_IF_NBR if_nbr);
```

ARGUMENTS

if_nbr Interface number to reset Network Buffer statistics.

RETURNED VALUE

None.

REQUIRED CONFIGURATION

None.

NOTES / WARNINGS

None.

B-5-7 NetBuf_TxSmallPoolStatGet()

Get an interface's small transmit buffers' statistics pool.

FILES

net_buf.h/net_buf.c

PROTOTYPE

```
NET_STAT_POOL NetBuf_TxSmallPoolStatGet(NET_IF_NBR if_nbr);
```

ARGUMENTS

if_nbr   Interface number to get Network Buffer statistics.

RETURNED VALUE

Small transmit buffers' statistics pool, if no errors.

NULL statistics pool, otherwise.

REQUIRED CONFIGURATION

None.

NOTES / WARNINGS

None.

B-5-8 NetBuf_TxSmallPoolStatResetMaxUsed()

Reset an interface's small transmit buffers' statistics pool's maximum number of entries used.

FILES

net_buf.h/net_buf.c

PROTOTYPE

```
void NetBuf_TxSmallPoolStatResetMaxUsed(NET_IF_NBR if_nbr);
```

ARGUMENTS

`if_nbr` Interface number to reset Network Buffer statistics.

RETURNED VALUE

None.

REQUIRED CONFIGURATION

None.

NOTES / WARNINGS

None.

B-6 NETWORK CONNECTION FUNCTIONS

B-6-1 NetConn_CfgAccessedTh()

Configure network connection access promotion threshold.

FILES

net_conn.h/net_conn.c

PROTOTYPE

```
CPU_BOOLEAN NetConn_CfgAccessedTh(CPU_INT16U nbr_access);
```

ARGUMENTS

nbr_access   Desired number of accesses before network connection is promoted.

RETURNED VALUE

DEF_OK,   network connection access promotion threshold configured.

DEF_FAIL,   otherwise.

REQUIRED CONFIGURATION

Available only if either NET_CFG_TRANSPORT_LAYER_SEL is configured for TCP (see section C-12-1 on page 736) and/or NET_UDP_CFG_APP_API_SEL is configured for sockets (see section C-13-1 on page 737).

NOTES / WARNINGS

None.

B-6-2 NetConn_PoolStatGet()

Get Network Connections' statistics pool.

FILES

net_conn.h/net_conn.c

PROTOTYPE

```
NET_STAT_POOL NetConn_PoolStatGet(void);
```

ARGUMENTS

None.

RETURNED VALUE

Network Connections' statistics pool, if no errors.

NULL statistics pool, otherwise.

REQUIRED CONFIGURATION

Available only if either NET_CFG_TRANSPORT_LAYER_SEL is configured for TCP (see section C-12-1 on page 736) and/or NET_UDP_CFG_APP_API_SEL is configured for sockets (see section C-13-1 on page 737).

NOTES / WARNINGS

None.

B-6-3 NetConn_PoolStatResetMaxUsed()

Reset Network Connections' statistics pool's maximum number of entries used.

FILES

net_conn.h/net_conn.c

PROTOTYPE

```
void NetConn_PoolStatResetMaxUsed(void);
```

ARGUMENTS

None.

RETURNED VALUE

None.

REQUIRED CONFIGURATION

Available only if either NET_CFG_TRANSPORT_LAYER_SEL is configured for TCP (see section C-12-1 on page 736) and/or NET_UDP_CFG_APP_API_SEL is configured for sockets (see section C-13-1 on page 737).

NOTES / WARNINGS

None.

B-7 NETWORK DEBUG FUNCTIONS

B-7-1 NetDbg_CfgMonTaskTime()

Configure Network Debug Monitor time.

FILES

net_dbg.h/net_dbg.c

PROTOTYPE

```
CPU_BOOLEAN NetDbg_CfgMonTaskTime(CPU_INT16U time_sec);
```

ARGUMENTS

time_sec	Desired value for Network Debug Monitor Task time (in seconds).

RETURNED VALUE

DEF_OK,	Network Debug Monitor Task time successfully configured.
DEF_FAIL,	otherwise.

REQUIRED CONFIGURATION

Available only if the Network Debug Monitor Task is enabled (see section 19-2 "Network Debug Monitor Task" on page 380).

NOTES / WARNINGS

None.

B-7-2 NetDbg_CfgRsrcARP_CacheThLo()

Configure ARP caches' low resource threshold.

FILES

net_dbg.h/net_dbg.c

PROTOTYPE

```
CPU_BOOLEAN NetDbg_CfgRsrcARP_CacheThLo(CPU_INT08U th_pct,
                                        CPU_INT08U hyst_pct);
```

ARGUMENTS

th_pct Desired percentage of ARP caches available to trip low resources.

hyst_pct Desired percentage of ARP caches freed to clear low resources.

RETURNED VALUE

DEF_OK, ARP caches' low resource threshold successfully configured.

DEF_FAIL, otherwise.

REQUIRED CONFIGURATION

Available only if **NET_DBG_CFG_DBG_STATUS_EN** is enabled (see section C-2-2 on page 728) and/or if the Network Debug Monitor Task is enabled (Se section 19-2 on page 380) **AND** if an appropriate network interface layer is present (e.g., Ethernet; see section C-7-3 on page 732).

NOTES / WARNINGS

None.

B-7-3 NetDbg_CfgRsrcBufThLo()

Configure an interface's network buffers' low resource threshold.

FILES

net_dbg.h/net_dbg.c

PROTOTYPE

```
CPU_BOOLEAN NetDbg_CfgRsrcBufThLo(NET_IF_NBR if_nbr,
                                  CPU_INT08U th_pct,
                                  CPU_INT08U hyst_pct);
```

ARGUMENTS

if_nbr	Interface number to configure low threshold and hysteresis.
th_pct	Desired percentage of network buffers available to trip low resources.
hyst_pct	Desired percentage of network buffers freed to clear low resources.

RETURNED VALUE

DEF_OK,	Network buffers' low resource threshold successfully configured.
DEF_FAIL,	otherwise.

REQUIRED CONFIGURATION

Available only if **NET_DBG_CFG_DBG_STATUS_EN** is enabled (see section C-2-2 on page 728) and/or if the Network Debug Monitor Task is enabled (see section 19-2 on page 380).

NOTES / WARNINGS

None.

B-7-4 NetDbg_CfgRsrcBufRxLargeThLo()

Configure an interface's large receive buffers' low resource threshold.

FILES

net_dbg.h/net_dbg.c

PROTOTYPE

```
CPU_BOOLEAN NetDbg_CfgRsrcBufRxLargeThLo(NET_IF_NBR if_nbr,
                                         CPU_INT08U th_pct,
                                         CPU_INT08U hyst_pct);
```

ARGUMENTS

if_nbr	Interface number to configure low threshold & hysteresis.
th_pct	Desired percentage of large receive buffers available to trip low resources.
hyst_pct	Desired percentage of large receive buffers freed to clear low resources.

RETURNED VALUE

DEF_OK,	Large receive buffers' low resource threshold successfully configured.
DEF_FAIL,	otherwise.

REQUIRED CONFIGURATION

Available only if NET_DBG_CFG_DBG_STATUS_EN is enabled (see section C-2-2 on page 728) and/or if the Network Debug Monitor Task is enabled (see section 19-2 on page 380).

NOTES / WARNINGS

None.

B-7-5 NetDbg_CfgRsrcBufTxLargeThLo()

Configure an interface's large transmit buffers' low resource threshold.

FILES

net_dbg.h/net_dbg.c

PROTOTYPE

```
CPU_BOOLEAN NetDbg_CfgRsrcBufTxLargeThLo(NET_IF_NBR if_nbr,
                                         CPU_INT08U th_pct,
                                         CPU_INT08U hyst_pct);
```

ARGUMENTS

if_nbr	Interface number to configure low threshold and hysteresis.
th_pct	Desired percentage of large transmit buffers available to trip low resources.
hyst_pct	Desired percentage of large transmit buffers freed to clear low resources.

RETURNED VALUE

DEF_OK,	Large transmit buffers' low resource threshold successfully configured.
DEF_FAIL,	otherwise.

REQUIRED CONFIGURATION

Available only if NET_DBG_CFG_DBG_STATUS_EN is enabled (see section C-2-2 on page 728) and/or if the Network Debug Monitor Task is enabled (see section 19-2 on page 380).

NOTES / WARNINGS

None.

B-7-6 NetDbg_CfgRsrcBufTxSmallThLo()

Configure an interface's small transmit buffers' low resource threshold.

FILES

net_dbg.h/net_dbg.c

PROTOTYPE

```
CPU_BOOLEAN NetDbg_CfgRsrcBufTxSmallThLo(NET_IF_NBR if_nbr,
                                         CPU_INT08U th_pct,
                                         CPU_INT08U hyst_pct);
```

ARGUMENTS

if_nbr	Interface number to configure low threshold & hysteresis.
th_pct	Desired percentage of small transmit buffers available to trip low resources.
hyst_pct	Desired percentage of small transmit buffers freed to clear low resources.

RETURNED VALUE

DEF_OK,	Small transmit buffers' low resource threshold successfully configured.
DEF_FAIL,	otherwise.

REQUIRED CONFIGURATION

Available only if **NET_DBG_CFG_DBG_STATUS_EN** is enabled (see section C-2-2 on page 728) and/or if the Network Debug Monitor Task is enabled (see section 19-2 on page 380).

NOTES / WARNINGS

None.

B-7-7 NetDbg_CfgRsrcConnThLo()

Configure network connections' low resource threshold.

FILES

net_dbg.h/net_dbg.c

PROTOTYPE

```
CPU_BOOLEAN NetDbg_CfgRsrcConnThLo(CPU_INT08U th_pct,
                                   CPU_INT08U hyst_pct);
```

ARGUMENTS

th_pct Desired percentage of network connections available to trip low resources.

hyst_pct Desired percentage of network connections freed to clear low resources.

RETURNED VALUE

DEF_OK, Network connections' low resource threshold successfully configured.

DEF_FAIL, otherwise.

REQUIRED CONFIGURATION

Available only if NET_DBG_CFG_DBG_STATUS_EN is enabled (see section C-2-2 on page 728) and/or if the Network Debug Monitor Task is enabled (see section 19-2 on page 380) *and* if either NET_CFG_TRANSPORT_LAYER_SEL is configured for TCP (see section C-12-1 on page 736) and/or NET_UDP_CFG_APP_API_SEL is configured for sockets (see section C-13-1 on page 737).

NOTES / WARNINGS

None.

B-7-8 NetDbg_CfgRsrcSockThLo()

Configure network sockets' low resource threshold.

FILES

net_dbg.h/net_dbg.c

PROTOTYPE

```
CPU_BOOLEAN NetDbg_CfgRsrcSockThLo(CPU_INT08U th_pct,
                                   CPU_INT08U hyst_pct);
```

ARGUMENTS

th_pct   Desired percentage of network sockets available to trip low resources.

hyst_pct   Desired percentage of network sockets freed to clear low resources.

RETURNED VALUE

DEF_OK,   Network sockets' low resource threshold successfully configured.

DEF_FAIL,   otherwise.

REQUIRED CONFIGURATION

Available only if **NET_DBG_CFG_DBG_STATUS_EN** is enabled (see section C-2-2 on page 728) and/or if the Network Debug Monitor Task is enabled (see section 19-2 on page 380) **AND** if either **NET_CFG_TRANSPORT_LAYER_SEL** is configured for TCP (see section C-12-1 on page 736) and/or **NET_UDP_CFG_APP_API_SEL** is configured for sockets (see section C-13-1 on page 737).

NOTES / WARNINGS

None.

B-7-9 NetDbg_CfgRsrcTCP_ConnThLo()

Configure TCP connections' low resource threshold.

FILES

net_dbg.h/net_dbg.c

PROTOTYPE

```
CPU_BOOLEAN NetDbg_CfgRsrcTCP_ConnThLo(CPU_INT08U th_pct,
                                       CPU_INT08U hyst_pct);
```

ARGUMENTS

th_pct Desired percentage of TCP connections available to trip low resources.

hyst_pct Desired percentage of TCP connections freed to clear low resources.

RETURNED VALUE

DEF_OK, TCP connections' low resource threshold successfully configured.

DEF_FAIL, otherwise.

REQUIRED CONFIGURATION

Available only if NET_DBG_CFG_DBG_STATUS_EN is enabled (see section C-2-2 on page 728) and/or if the Network Debug Monitor Task is enabled (see section 19-2 on page 380) **AND** if NET_CFG_TRANSPORT_LAYER_SEL is configured for TCP (see section C-12-1 on page 736).

NOTES / WARNINGS

None.

B-7-10 NetDbg_CfgRsrcTmrThLo()

Configure network timers' low resource threshold.

FILES

net_dbg.h/net_dbg.c

PROTOTYPE

```
CPU_BOOLEAN NetDbg_CfgRsrcTmrThLo(CPU_INT08U th_pct,
                                  CPU_INT08U hyst_pct);
```

ARGUMENTS

th_pct Desired percentage of network timers available to trip low resources.

hyst_pct Desired percentage of network timers freed to clear low resources.

RETURNED VALUE

DEF_OK, Network timers' low resource threshold successfully configured.

DEF_FAIL, otherwise.

REQUIRED CONFIGURATION

Available only if NET_DBG_CFG_DBG_STATUS_EN is enabled (see section C-2-2 on page 728) and/or if the Network Debug Monitor Task is enabled (see section 19-2 on page 380).

NOTES / WARNINGS

None.

B-7-11 NetDbg_ChkStatus()

Return the current run-time status of certain µC/TCP-IP conditions.

FILES

net_dbg.h/net_dbg.c

PROTOTYPE

```
NET_DBG_STATUS NetDbg_ChkStatus(void);
```

ARGUMENTS

None.

RETURNED VALUE

NET_DBG_STATUS_OK, if all network conditions are OK (i.e., no warnings, faults, or errors currently exist);

Otherwise, returns the following status condition codes logically **OR**'d:

NET_DBG_STATUS_FAULT	Some network status fault(s)
NET_DBG_STATUS_RSRC_LOST	Some network resources lost.
NET_DBG_STATUS_RSRC_LO	Some network resources low.
NET_DBG_STATUS_FAULT_BUF	Some network buffer management fault(s).
NET_DBG_STATUS_FAULT_TMR	Some network timer management fault(s).
NET_DBG_STATUS_FAULT_CONN	Some network connection management fault(s).
NET_DBG_STATUS_FAULT_TCP	Some TCP layer fault(s).

REQUIRED CONFIGURATION

Available only if NET_DBG_CFG_DBG_STATUS_EN is enabled (see section C-2-2 on page 728).

NOTES / WARNINGS

None.

B-7-12 NetDbg_ChkStatusBufs()

Return the current run-time status of µC/TCP-IP network buffers.

FILES

net_dbg.h/net_dbg.c

PROTOTYPE

```
NET_DBG_STATUS NetDbg_ChkStatusBufs(void);
```

ARGUMENTS

None.

RETURNED VALUE

NET_DBG_STATUS_OK, if all network buffer conditions are OK (i.e., no warnings, faults, or errors currently exist);

Otherwise, returns the following status condition codes logically **OR**'d:

NET_DBG_SF_BUF	Some Network Buffer management fault(s).

REQUIRED CONFIGURATION

Available only if NET_DBG_CFG_DBG_STATUS_EN is enabled (see section C-2-2 on page 728).

NOTES / WARNINGS

Debug status information for network buffers has been deprecated in µC/TCP-IP.

B-7-13 NetDbg_ChkStatusConns()

Return the current run-time status of µC/TCP-IP network connections.

FILES

net_dbg.h/net_dbg.c

PROTOTYPE

```
NET_DBG_STATUS NetDbg_ChkStatusConns(void);
```

ARGUMENTS

None.

RETURNED VALUE

NET_DBG_STATUS_OK, if all network connection conditions are OK (i.e., no warnings, faults, or errors currently exist);

Otherwise, returns the following status condition codes logically **OR**'d:

NET_DBG_SF_CONN	Some network connection management fault(s).
NET_DBG_SF_CONN_TYPE	Network connection invalid type.
NET_DBG_SF_CONN_FAMILY	Network connection invalid family.
NET_DBG_SF_CONN_PROTOCOL_IX_NBR_MAX	Network connection invalid protocol list index number.
NET_DBG_SF_CONN_ID	Network connection invalid ID.
NET_DBG_SF_CONN_ID_NONE	Network connection with no connection IDs.

NET_DBG_SF_CONN_ID_UNUSED	Network connection linked to unused connection.
NET_DBG_SF_CONN_LINK_TYPE	Network connection invalid link type.
NET_DBG_SF_CONN_LINK_UNUSED	Network connection link unused.
NET_DBG_SF_CONN_LINK_BACK_TO_CONN	Network connection invalid link back to same connection.
NET_DBG_SF_CONN_LINK_NOT_TO_CONN	Network connection invalid link not back to same connection.
NET_DBG_SF_CONN_LINK_NOT_IN_LIST	Network connection not in appropriate connection list.
NET_DBG_SF_CONN_POOL_TYPE	Network connection invalid pool type.
NET_DBG_SF_CONN_POOL_ID	Network connection invalid pool id.
NET_DBG_SF_CONN_POOL_DUP	Network connection pool contains duplicate connection(s).
NET_DBG_SF_CONN_POOL_NBR_MAX	Network connection pool number of connections greater than maximum number of connections.
NET_DBG_SF_CONN_LIST_NBR_NOT_SOLITARY	Network connection lists number of connections not equal to solitary connection.
NET_DBG_SF_CONN_USED_IN_POOL	Network connection used but in pool.
NET_DBG_SF_CONN_USED_NOT_IN_LIST	Network connection used but not in list.
NET_DBG_SF_CONN_UNUSED_IN_LIST	Network connection unused but in list.

NET_DBG_SF_CONN_UNUSED_NOT_IN_POOL	Network connection unused but not in pool.
NET_DBG_SF_CONN_IN_LIST_IN_POOL	Network connection in list and in pool.
NET_DBG_SF_CONN_NOT_IN_LIST_NOT_IN_POOL	Network connection not in list nor in pool.

REQUIRED CONFIGURATION

Available only if **NET_DBG_CFG_DBG_STATUS_EN** is enabled (see section C-2-2 on page 728) *and* if either **NET_CFG_TRANSPORT_LAYER_SEL** is configured for TCP (see section C-12-1 on page 736) and/or **NET_UDP_CFG_APP_API_SEL** is configured for sockets (see section C-13-1 on page 737).

NOTES / WARNINGS

None.

B-7-14 NetDbg_ChkStatusRsrcLost() / NetDbg_MonTaskStatusGetRsrcLost()

Return whether any µC/TCP-IP resources are currently lost.

FILES

net_dbg.h/net_dbg.c

PROTOTYPES

```
NET_DBG_STATUS NetDbg_ChkStatusRsrcLost(void);
NET_DBG_STATUS NetDbg_MonTaskStatusGetRsrcLost(void);
```

ARGUMENTS

None.

RETURNED VALUE

NET_DBG_STATUS_OK, if no network resources are lost; otherwise, returns the following status condition codes logically **OR**'d:

NET_DBG_SF_RSRC_LOST	Some network resources lost.
NET_DBG_SF_RSRC_LOST_BUF_SMALL	Some network SMALL buffer resources lost.
NET_DBG_SF_RSRC_LOST_BUF_LARGE	Some network LARGE buffer resources lost.
NET_DBG_SF_RSRC_LOST_TMR	Some network timer resources lost.
NET_DBG_SF_RSRC_LOST_CONN	Some network connection resources lost.
NET_DBG_SF_RSRC_LOST_ARP_CACHE	Some network ARP cache resources lost.
NET_DBG_SF_RSRC_LOST_TCP_CONN	Some network TCP connection resources lost.
NET_DBG_SF_RSRC_LOST_SOCK	Some network socket resources lost.

REQUIRED CONFIGURATION

`NetDbg_ChkStatusRsrcLost()` available only if `NET_DBG_CFG_DBG_STATUS_EN` is enabled (see section C-2-2 on page 728). `NetDbg_MonTaskStatusGetRsrcLost()` available only if the Network Debug Monitor Task is enabled (see section 19-2 on page 380).

NOTES / WARNINGS

`NetDbg_ChkStatusRsrcLost()` checks network conditions lost status inline, whereas `NetDbg_MonTaskStatusGetRsrcLost()` checks the Network Debug Monitor Task's last known lost status.

B-7-15 NetDbg_ChkStatusRsrcLo() / NetDbg_MonTaskStatusGetRsrcLo()

Return whether any µC/TCP-IP resources are currently low.

FILES

net_dbg.h/net_dbg.c

PROTOTYPES

```
NET_DBG_STATUS NetDbg_ChkStatusRsrcLo(void);
NET_DBG_STATUS NetDbg_MonTaskStatusGetRsrcLo(void);
```

ARGUMENTS

None.

RETURNED VALUE

NET_DBG_STATUS_OK, if no network resources are low; otherwise, returns the following status condition codes logically **OR**'d:

NET_DBG_SF_RSRC_LO	Some network resources low.
NET_DBG_SF_RSRC_LO_BUF_SMALL	Network SMALL buffer resources low
NET_DBG_SF_RSRC_LO_BUF_LARGE	Network LARGE buffer resources low.
NET_DBG_SF_RSRC_LO_TMR	Network timer resources low.
NET_DBG_SF_RSRC_LO_CONN	Network connection resources low.
NET_DBG_SF_RSRC_LO_ARP_CACHE	Network ARP cache resources low.
NET_DBG_SF_RSRC_LO_TCP_CONN	Network TCP connection resources low.
NET_DBG_SF_RSRC_LO_SOCK	Network socket resources low.

REQUIRED CONFIGURATION

`NetDbg_ChkStatusRsrcLo()` available only if `NET_DBG_CFG_DBG_STATUS_EN` is enabled (see section C-2-2 on page 728). `NetDbg_MonTaskStatusGetRsrcLo()` available only if the Network Debug Monitor Task is enabled (see section 19-2 on page 380).

NOTES / WARNINGS

`NetDbg_ChkStatusRsrcLo()` checks network conditions low status inline, whereas `NetDbg_MonTaskStatusGetRsrcLo()` checks the Network Debug Monitor Task's last known low status.

B-7-16 NetDbg_ChkStatusTCP()

Return the current run-time status of µC/TCP-IP TCP connections.

FILES

net_dbg.h/net_dbg.c

PROTOTYPE

```
NET_DBG_STATUS NetDbg_ChkStatusTCP(void);
```

ARGUMENTS

None.

RETURNED VALUE

NET_DBG_STATUS_OK, if all TCP layer conditions are OK (i.e., no warnings, faults, or errors currently exist); otherwise, returns the following status condition codes logically **OR**'d:

NET_DBG_SF_TCP	Some TCP layer fault(s).
NET_DBG_SF_TCP_CONN_TYPE	TCP connection invalid type.
NET_DBG_SF_TCP_CONN_ID	TCP connection invalid id.
NET_DBG_SF_TCP_CONN_LINK_TYPE	TCP connection invalid link type.
NET_DBG_SF_TCP_CONN_LINK_UNUSED	TCP connection link unused.
NET_DBG_SF_TCP_CONN_POOL_TYPE	TCP connection invalid pool type.
NET_DBG_SF_TCP_CONN_POOL_ID	TCP connection invalid pool id.
NET_DBG_SF_TCP_CONN_POOL_DUP	TCP connection pool contains duplicate connection(s).

NET_DBG_SF_TCP_CONN_POOL_NBR_MAX	TCP connection pool number of connections greater than maximum number of connections.
NET_DBG_SF_TCP_CONN_USED_IN_POOL	TCP connection used in pool.
NET_DBG_SF_TCP_CONN_UNUSED_NOT_IN_POOL	TCP connection unused *not* in pool.
NET_DBG_SF_TCP_CONN_Q	Some TCP connection queue fault(s).
NET_DBG_SF_TCP_CONN_Q_BUF_TYPE	TCP connection queue buffer invalid type.
NET_DBG_SF_TCP_CONN_Q_BUF_UNUSED	TCP connection queue buffer unused.
NET_DBG_SF_TCP_CONN_Q_LINK_TYPE	TCP connection queue buffer invalid link type.
NET_DBG_SF_TCP_CONN_Q_LINK_UNUSED	TCP connection queue buffer link unused.
NET_DBG_SF_TCP_CONN_Q_BUF_DUP	TCP connection queue contains duplicate buffer(s).

REQUIRED CONFIGURATION

Available only if NET_DBG_CFG_DBG_STATUS_EN is enabled (see section C-2-2 on page 728) **AND** if NET_CFG_TRANSPORT_LAYER_SEL is configured for TCP (see section C-12-1 on page 736).

NOTES / WARNINGS

None.

B-7-17 NetDbg_ChkStatusTmrs()

Return the current run-time status of μC/TCP-IP network timers.

FILES

net_dbg.h/net_dbg.c

PROTOTYPE

```
NET_DBG_STATUS NetDbg_ChkStatusTmrs(void);
```

ARGUMENTS

None.

RETURNED VALUE

NET_DBG_STATUS_OK, if all network timer conditions are OK (i.e., no warnings, faults, or errors currently exist);

Otherwise, returns the following status condition codes logically **OR**'d:

NET_DBG_SF_TMR	Some network timer management fault(s).
NET_DBG_SF_TMR_TYPE	Network timer invalid type.
NET_DBG_SF_TMR_ID	Network timer invalid id.
NET_DBG_SF_TMR_LINK_TYPE	Network timer invalid link type.
NET_DBG_SF_TMR_LINK_UNUSED	Network timer link unused.
NET_DBG_SF_TMR_LINK_BACK_TO_TMR	Network timer invalid link back to same timer.
NET_DBG_SF_TMR_LINK_TO_TMR	Network timer invalid link back to timer.

NET_DBG_SF_TMR_POOL_TYPE	Network timer invalid pool type.
NET_DBG_SF_TMR_POOL_ID	Network timer invalid pool id.
NET_DBG_SF_TMR_POOL_DUP	Network timer pool contains duplicate timer(s).
NET_DBG_SF_TMR_POOL_NBR_MAX	Network timer pool number of timers greater than maximum number of timers.
NET_DBG_SF_TMR_LIST_TYPE	Network Timer Task list invalid type.
NET_DBG_SF_TMR_LIST_ID	Network Timer Task list invalid id.
NET_DBG_SF_TMR_LIST_DUP	Network Timer Task list contains duplicate timer(s).
NET_DBG_SF_TMR_LIST_NBR_MAX	Network Timer Task list number of timers greater than maximum number of timers.
NET_DBG_SF_TMR_LIST_NBR_USED	Network Timer Task list number of timers *not* equal to number of used timers.
NET_DBG_SF_TMR_USED_IN_POOL	Network timer used but in pool.
NET_DBG_SF_TMR_UNUSED_NOT_IN_POOL	Network timer unused but *not* in pool.
NET_DBG_SF_TMR_UNUSED_IN_LIST	Network timer unused but in Timer Task list.

REQUIRED CONFIGURATION

Available only if NET_DBG_CFG_DBG_STATUS_EN is enabled (see section C-2-2 on page 728).

NOTES / WARNINGS

None.

B-7-18 NetDbg_MonTaskStatusGetRsrcLost()

Return whether any µC/TCP-IP resources are currently lost.

See section B-7-14 on page 504 for more information.

FILES

net_dbg.h/net_dbg.c

PROTOTYPE

```
NET_DBG_STATUS NetDbg_MonTaskStatusGetRsrcLost(void);
```

B-7-19 NetDbg_MonTaskStatusGetRsrcLo()

Return whether any µC/TCP-IP resources are currently low.

See section B-7-15 on page 506 for more information.

FILES

net_dbg.h/net_dbg.c

PROTOTYPE

```
NET_DBG_STATUS NetDbg_MonTaskStatusGetRsrcLo(void);
```

B-8 ICMP FUNCTIONS

B-8-1 NetICMP_CfgTxSrcQuenchTh()

Configure ICMP transmit source quench entry's access transmit threshold.

FILES

net_icmp.h/net_icmp.c

PROTOTYPE

```
CPU_BOOLEAN NetICMP_CfgTxSrcQuenchTh(CPU_INT16U th);
```

ARGUMENTS

th   Desired number of received IP packets from a specific IP source host that trips the transmission of an additional ICMP Source Quench Error Message.

RETURNED VALUE

DEF_OK,   ICMP transmit source quench threshold configured.

DEF_FAIL,   otherwise.

REQUIRED CONFIGURATION

None.

NOTES / WARNINGS

None.

B-9 NETWORK INTERFACE FUNCTIONS

B-9-1 NetIF_Add()

Add a network device and hardware as a network interface.

FILES

net_if.h/net_if.c

PROTOTYPE

```
NET_IF_NBR NetIF_Add(void     *if_api,
                     void     *dev_api,
                     void     *dev_bsp,
                     void     *dev_cfg,
                     void     *phy_api,
                     void     *phy_cfg,
                     NET_ERR  *perr);
```

ARGUMENTS

if_api Pointer to the desired link-layer API for this network interface and device hardware. In most cases, the desired link-layer interface will point to the Ethernet API, **NetIF_API_Ether** (see also section L16-1(1) on page 344).

dev_api Pointer to the desired device driver API for this network interface (see also section 14-3 “Device Driver API for MAC” on page 300).

dev_bsp Pointer to the specific device's BSP interface for this network interface (see also section 14-7-1 “Network Device BSP” on page 320).

dev_cfg Pointer to a configuration structure used to configure the device hardware for the specific network interface (see also section 14-6-2 “Ethernet Device MAC Configuration” on page 313).

phy_api Pointer to an optional physical layer device driver API for this network interface. In most cases, the generic physical layer device API will be used, **NetPhy_API_Generic**, but for Ethernet devices that have non-MII or non-RMII compliant physical layer components, another device-specific physical layer device driver API may be necessary. See also section 14-4 "Device Driver API for PHY" on page 302.

`phy_cfg` Pointer to a configuration structure used to configure the physical layer hardware for the specific network interface (see also section 14-6-3 "Ethernet PHY Configuration" on page 318).

`perr` Pointer to variable that will receive the return error code from this function:

NET_IF_ERR_NONE
NET_IF_ERR_NULL_PTR
NET_IF_ERR_INVALID_IF
NET_IF_ERR_INVALID_CFG
NET_IF_ERR_NONE_AVAIL
NET_BUF_ERR_POOL_INIT
NET_BUF_ERR_INVALID_POOL_TYPE
NET_BUF_ERR_INVALID_POOL_ADDR
NET_BUF_ERR_INVALID_POOL_SIZE
NET_BUF_ERR_INVALID_POOL_QTY
NET_BUF_ERR_INVALID_SIZE
NET_OS_ERR_INIT_DEV_TX_RDY
NET_OS_ERR_INIT_DEV_TX_RDY_NAME
NET_OS_ERR_LOCK

RETURNED VALUE

Network interface number, if device and hardware successfully added;

NET_IF_NBR_NONE, otherwise.

REQUIRED CONFIGURATION

None.

NOTES / WARNINGS

The first network interface added and started is the default interface used for all default communication. See also section B-11-1 on page 549 and section B-11-2 on page 551.

Both physical layer API and configuration parameters *must* ,either be specified or passed `NULL` pointers.

Additional error codes may be returned by the specific interface or device driver.

See section 16-1-1 "Adding Network Interfaces" on page 343 for a detailed example of how to add an interface.

B-9-2 NetIF_AddrHW_Get()

Get network interface's hardware address.

FILES

net_if.h/net_if.c

PROTOTYPE

```
void NetIF_AddrHW_Get(NET_IF_NBR  if_nbr,
                      CPU_INT08U *paddr_hw,
                      CPU_INT08U *paddr_len,
                      NET_ERR    *perr);
```

ARGUMENTS

if_nbr Network interface number to get the hardware address.

paddr_hw Pointer to variable that will receive the hardware address.

paddr_len Pointer to a variable to pass the length of the address buffer pointed to by paddr_hw and return the size of the returned hardware address, if no errors.

perr Pointer to variable that will receive the return error code from this function:

NET_IF_ERR_NONE
NET_IF_ERR_NULL_PTR
NET_IF_ERR_NULL_FNCT
NET_IF_ERR_INVALID_IF
NET_IF_ERR_INVALID_CFG
NET_IF_ERR_INVALID_ADDR_LEN
NET_OS_ERR_LOCK

RETURNED VALUE

None.

REQUIRED CONFIGURATION

None.

NOTES / WARNINGS

The hardware address is returned in network-order; i.e., the pointer to the hardware address points to the highest-order byte. Additional error codes may be returned by the specific interface or device driver.

B-9-3 NetIF_AddrHW_IsValid()

Validate a network interface hardware address.

FILES

net_if.h/net_if.c

PROTOTYPE

```
CPU_BOOLEAN NetIF_AddrHW_IsValid(NET_IF_NBR  if_nbr,
                                 CPU_INT08U  *paddr_hw,
                                 NET_ERR     *perr);
```

ARGUMENTS

if_nbr Network interface number to validate the hardware address.

paddr_hw Pointer to a network interface hardware address.

perr Pointer to variable that will receive the return error code from this function:

NET_IF_ERR_NONE
NET_IF_ERR_NULL_PTR
NET_IF_ERR_NULL_FNCT
NET_IF_ERR_INVALID_IF
NET_IF_ERR_INVALID_CFG
NET_OS_ERR_LOCK

RETURNED VALUE

DEF_YES if hardware address valid;

DEF_NO otherwise.

REQUIRED CONFIGURATION

None.

NOTES / WARNINGS

None.

B-9-4 NetIF_AddrHW_Set()

Set network interface's hardware address.

FILES

net_if.h/net_if.c

PROTOTYPE

```
void NetIF_AddrHW_Set(NET_IF_NBR  if_nbr,
                      CPU_INT08U *paddr_hw,
                      CPU_INT08U  addr_len,
                      NET_ERR    *perr);
```

ARGUMENTS

if_nbr Network interface number to set hardware address.

paddr_hw Pointer to a hardware address.

addr_len Length of hardware address.

perr Pointer to variable that will receive the return error code from this function:

NET_IF_ERR_NONE
NET_IF_ERR_NULL_PTR
NET_IF_ERR_NULL_FNCT
NET_IF_ERR_INVALID_IF
NET_IF_ERR_INVALID_CFG
NET_IF_ERR_INVALID_STATE
NET_IF_ERR_INVALID_ADDR
NET_IF_ERR_INVALID_ADDR_LEN
NET_OS_ERR_LOCK

RETURNED VALUE

None.

REQUIRED CONFIGURATION

None.

NOTES / WARNINGS

The hardware address *must* be in network-order (i.e., the pointer to the hardware address *must* point to the highest-order byte).

The network interface *must* be stopped *before* setting a new hardware address, which does *not* take effect until the interface is re-started.

Additional error codes may be returned by the specific interface or device driver.

B-9-5 NetIF_CfgPerfMonPeriod()

Configure Network Interface Performance Monitor Handler timeout.

FILES

net_if.h/net_if.c

PROTOTYPE

```
CPU_BOOLEAN NetIF_CfgPerfMonPeriod(CPU_INT16U timeout_ms);
```

ARGUMENTS

timeout_ms Desired value for Network Interface Performance Monitor Handler timeout (in milliseconds).

RETURNED VALUE

DEF_OK, Network Interface Performance Monitor Handler timeout configured;

DEF_FAIL, otherwise.

REQUIRED CONFIGURATION

Available only if NET_CTR_CFG_STAT_EN is enabled (see section C-4-1 on page 730).

NOTES / WARNINGS

None.

B-9-6 NetIF_CfgPhyLinkPeriod()

Configure Network Interface Physical Link State Handler timeout.

FILES

net_if.h/net_if.c

PROTOTYPE

```
CPU_BOOLEAN NetIF_CfgPhyLinkPeriod(CPU_INT16U timeout_ms);
```

ARGUMENTS

timeout_ms Desired value for Network Interface Link State Handler timeout (in milliseconds).

RETURNED VALUE

DEF_OK, Network Interface Physical Link State Handler timeout configured;

DEF_FAIL, otherwise.

REQUIRED CONFIGURATION

None.

NOTES / WARNINGS

None.

B-9-7 NetIF_GetRxDataAlignPtr()

Get an aligned pointer into a receive application data buffer.

FILES

net_if.h/net_if.c

PROTOTYPE

```
void  *NetIF_GetRxDataAlignPtr(NET_IF_NBR   if_nbr,
                              void        *p_data,
                              NET_ERR     *perr);
```

ARGUMENTS

if_nbr   Network interface number to get a receive application buffer's aligned data pointer.

p_data   Pointer to receive application data buffer to get an aligned pointer into (see also Note #2).

perr   Pointer to variable that will receive the return error code from this function :

NET_IF_ERR_NONE
NET_IF_ERR_NULL_PTR
NET_IF_ERR_INVALID_IF
NET_IF_ERR_ALIGN_NOT_AVAIL
NET_ERR_INIT_INCOMPLETE
NET_ERR_INVALID_TRANSACTION
NET_OS_ERR_LOCK

RETURNED VALUE

Pointer to aligned receive application data buffer address, if no errors.

Pointer to NULL, otherwise.

NOTES/WARNINGS #1

1 Optimal alignment between application data buffers and the network interface's network buffer data areas is *not* guaranteed, and is possible if, and only if, all of the following conditions are true:

- Network interface's network buffer data areas *must* be aligned to a multiple of the CPU's data word size.

Otherwise, a single, fixed alignment between application data buffers and network interface's buffer data areas is *not* possible.

2 Even when application data buffers and network buffer data areas are aligned in the best case, optimal alignment is *not* guaranteed for every read/write of data to/from application data buffers and network buffer data areas.

For any single read/write of data to/from application data buffers and network buffer data areas, optimal alignment occurs if, and only if, all of the following conditions are true:

- Data read/written to/from application data buffers to network buffer data areas *must* start on addresses with the same relative offset from CPU word-aligned addresses.

  In other words, the modulus of the specific read/write address in the application data buffer with the CPU's data word size *must* be equal to the modulus of the specific read/write address in the network buffer data area with the CPU's data word size.

  This condition *might not* be satisfied whenever:

  - Data is read/written to/from fragmented packets
  - Data is *not* maximally read/written to/from stream-type packets (e.g., TCP data segments)
  - Packets include variable number of header options (e.g., IP options)

However, even though optimal alignment between application data buffers and network buffer data areas is *not* guaranteed for every read/write; optimal alignment SHOULD occur more frequently, leading to improved network data throughput.

NOTES/WARNINGS #2

Since the first aligned address in the application data buffer may be 0 to **(CPU_CFG_DATA_SIZE-1)** bytes after the application data buffer's starting address, the application data buffer *should* allocate and reserve an additional **(CPU_CFG_DATA_SIZE-1)** number of bytes.

However, the application data buffer's effective, useable size is still limited to its original declared size (before reserving additional bytes), and *should not* be increased by the additional, reserved bytes.

B-9-8 NetIF_GetTxDataAlignPtr()

Get an aligned pointer into a transmit application data buffer.

FILES

net_if.h/net_if.c

PROTOTYPE

```
void  *NetIF_GetTxDataAlignPtr(NET_IF_NBR   if_nbr,
                               void        *p_data,
                               NET_ERR     *perr);
```

ARGUMENTS

if_nbr Network interface number to get a transmit application buffer's aligned data pointer.

p_data Pointer to transmit application data buffer to get an aligned pointer into (see also Note #2b).

perr Pointer to variable that will receive the return error code from this function :

NET_IF_ERR_NONE
NET_IF_ERR_NULL_PTR
NET_IF_ERR_INVALID_IF
NET_IF_ERR_ALIGN_NOT_AVAIL
NET_ERR_INIT_INCOMPLETE
NET_ERR_INVALID_TRANSACTION
NET_OS_ERR_LOCK

RETURNED VALUE

Pointer to aligned transmit application data buffer address, if no errors.

Pointer to NULL, otherwise.

REQUIRED CONFIGURATION

None.

NOTES/WARNINGS #1

1 Optimal alignment between application data buffers and the network interface's network buffer data areas is *not* guaranteed, and is possible if, and only if, all of the following conditions are true:

- Network interface's network buffer data areas *must* be aligned to a multiple of the CPU's data word size.

Otherwise, a single, fixed alignment between application data buffers and network interface's buffer data areas is *not* possible.

2 Even when application data buffers and network buffer data areas are aligned in the best case, optimal alignment is *not* guaranteed for every read/write of data to/from application data buffers and network buffer data areas.

For any single read/write of data to/from application data buffers and network buffer data areas, optimal alignment occurs if, and only if, all of the following conditions are true:

- Data read/written to/from application data buffers to network buffer data areas *must* start on addresses with the same relative offset from CPU word-aligned addresses.

  In other words, the modulus of the specific read/write address in the application data buffer with the CPU's data word size *must* be equal to the modulus of the specific read/write address in the network buffer data area with the CPU's data word size.

  This condition *might not* be satisfied whenever:

  - Data is read/written to/from fragmented packets
  - Data is *not* maximally read/written to/from stream-type packets (e.g., TCP data segments)
  - Packets include variable number of header options (e.g., IP options)

However, even though optimal alignment between application data buffers and network buffer data areas is *not* guaranteed for every read/write; optimal alignment SHOULD NOT occur more frequently, leading to improved network data throughput.

NOTES/WARNINGS #2

Since the first aligned address in the application data buffer may be 0 to **(CPU_CFG_DATA_SIZE-1)** bytes after the application data buffer's starting address, the application data buffer *should* allocate and reserve an additional **(CPU_CFG_DATA_SIZE-1)** number of bytes.

However, the application data buffer's effective, useable size is still limited to its original declared size (before reserving additional bytes), and *should not* be increased by the additional, reserved bytes.

B-9-9 NetIF_IO_Ctrl()

Handle network interface &/or device specific (I/O) control(s).

FILES

net_if.h/net_if.c

PROTOTYPE

```
void NetIF_IO_Ctrl(NET_IF_NBR  if_nbr,
                   CPU_INT08U  opt,
                   void       *p_data,
                   NET_ERR    *perr);
```

ARGUMENTS

if_nbr — Network interface number to handle (I/O) controls.

opt — Desired I/O control option code to perform; additional control options may be defined by the device driver:

NET_IF_IO_CTRL_LINK_STATE_GET
NET_IF_IO_CTRL_LINK_STATE_UPDATE

p_data — Pointer to variable that will receive the I/O control information.

perr — Pointer to variable that will receive the return error code from this function:

NET_IF_ERR_NONE
NET_IF_ERR_NULL_PTR
NET_IF_ERR_NULL_FNCT
NET_IF_ERR_INVALID_IF
NET_IF_ERR_INVALID_CFG
NET_IF_ERR_INVALID_IO_CTRL_OPTNET_OS_ERR_LOCK

RETURNED VALUE

None.

REQUIRED CONFIGURATION

None.

NOTES / WARNINGS

Additional error codes may be returned by the specific interface or device driver.

B-9-10 NetIF_IsEn()

Validate network interface as enabled.

FILES

net_if.h/net_if.c

PROTOTYPE

```
CPU_BOOLEAN NetIF_IsEn(NET_IF_NBR  if_nbr,
                       NET_ERR    *perr);
```

ARGUMENTS

if_nbr Network interface number to validate.

perr Pointer to variable that will receive the return error code from this function:

NET_IF_ERR_NONE
NET_IF_ERR_INVALID_IF
NET_OS_ERR_LOCK

RETURNED VALUE

DEF_YES network interface valid and enabled;

DEF_NO network interface invalid or disabled.

REQUIRED CONFIGURATION

None.

NOTES / WARNINGS

None.

B-9-11 NetIF_IsEnCfgd()

Validate configured network interface as enabled.

FILES

net_if.h/net_if.c

PROTOTYPE

```
CPU_BOOLEAN NetIF_IsEnCfgd(NET_IF_NBR  if_nbr,
                           NET_ERR    *perr);
```

ARGUMENTS

if_nbr Network interface number to validate.

perr Pointer to variable that will receive the return error code from this function:

NET_IF_ERR_NONE
NET_IF_ERR_INVALID_IF
NET_OS_ERR_LOCK

RETURNED VALUE

DEF_YES network interface valid and enabled;

DEF_NO network interface invalid or disabled.

REQUIRED CONFIGURATION

None.

NOTES / WARNINGS

None.

B-9-12 NetIF_ISR_Handler()

Handle a network interface's device interrupts.

FILES

net_if.h/net_if.c

PROTOTYPE

```
void NetIF_ISR_Handler (NET_IF_NBR        if_nbr,
                        NET_DEV_ISR_TYPE  type,
                        NET_ERR          *perr);
```

ARGUMENTS

if_nbr Network interface number to handler device interrupts.

type Device interrupt type(s) to handle:

NET_DEV_ISR_TYPE_UNKNOWN	Handle unknown device interrupts.
NET_DEV_ISR_TYPE_RX	Handle device receive interrupts.
NET_DEV_ISR_TYPE_RX_OVERRUN	Handle device receive overrun interrupts.
NET_DEV_ISR_TYPE_TX_RDY	Handle device transmit ready interrupts.
NET_DEV_ISR_TYPE_TX_COMPLETE	Handle device transmit complete interrupts.

This is *not* an exclusive list of interrupt types and specific network device's may handle other types of interrupts.

perr Pointer to variable that will receive the return error code from this function:

NET_IF_ERR_NONE
NET_IF_ERR_INVALID_CFG
NET_IF_ERR_NULL_FNCT
NET_IF_ERR_INVALID_STATE
NET_ERR_INIT_INCOMPLETE
NET_IF_ERR_INVALID_IF

This is *not* an exclusive list of return errors and specific network interface's or device's may return any other specific errors as required.

RETURNED VALUE

None.

REQUIRED CONFIGURATION

None.

NOTES / WARNINGS

None.

B-9-13 NetIF_IsValid()

Validate network interface number.

FILES

net_if.h/net_if.c

PROTOTYPE

```
CPU_BOOLEAN NetIF_IsValid(NET_IF_NBR  if_nbr,
                          NET_ERR    *perr);
```

ARGUMENTS

if_nbr Network interface number to validate.

perr Pointer to variable that will receive the return error code from this function:

NET_IF_ERR_NONE
NET_IF_ERR_INVALID_IF
NET_OS_ERR_LOCK

RETURNED VALUE

DEF_YES network interface number valid;

DEF_NO network interface number invalid/*not* yet configured.

REQUIRED CONFIGURATION

None.

NOTES / WARNINGS

None.

B-9-14 NetIF_IsValidCfgd()

Validate configured network interface number.

FILES

net_if.h/net_if.c

PROTOTYPE

```
CPU_BOOLEAN NetIF_IsValidCfgd(NET_IF_NBR  if_nbr,
                              NET_ERR    *perr);
```

ARGUMENTS

if_nbr Network interface number to validate.

perr Pointer to variable that will receive the return error code from this function:

NET_IF_ERR_NONE
NET_IF_ERR_INVALID_IF
NET_OS_ERR_LOCK

RETURNED VALUE

DEF_YES network interface number valid;

DEF_NO network interface number invalid/*not* yet configured or reserved.

REQUIRED CONFIGURATION

None.

NOTES / WARNINGS

None.

B-9-15 NetIF_LinkStateGet()

Get network interface's last known physical link state.

FILES

net_if.h/net_if.c

PROTOTYPE

```
CPU_BOOLEAN NetIF_LinkStateGet(NET_IF_NBR  if_nbr,
                               NET_ERR    *perr);
```

ARGUMENTS

if_nbr Network interface number to get last known physical link state.

perr Pointer to variable that will receive the return error code from this function:

NET_IF_ERR_NONE
NET_IF_ERR_INVALID_IF
NET_OS_ERR_LOCK

RETURNED VALUE

NET_IF_LINK_UP if no errors and network interface's last known physical link state was 'UP';

NET_IF_LINK_DOWN otherwise.

REQUIRED CONFIGURATION

None.

NOTES / WARNINGS

Use NetIF_IO_Ctrl() with option NET_IF_IO_CTRL_LINK_STATE_GET to get a network interface's current physical link state.

B-9-16 NetIF_LinkStateWaitUntilUp()

Wait for a network interface's physical link state to be UP.

FILES

net_if.h/net_if.c

PROTOTYPE

```
CPU_BOOLEAN NetIF_LinkStateWaitUntilUp(NET_IF_NBR   if_nbr,
                                       CPU_INT16U   retry_max,
                                       CPU_INT32U   time_dly_ms,
                                       NET_ERR     *perr);
```

ARGUMENTS

if_nbr Network interface number to wait for link state to be UP.

retry_max Maximum number of consecutive socket open retries.

time_dly_ms Transitory socket open delay value, in milliseconds.

perr Pointer to variable that will receive the return error code from this function:

NET_IF_ERR_NONE
NET_IF_ERR_INVALID_IF
NET_IF_ERR_LINK_DOWN
NET_ERR_INIT_INCOMPLETE
NET_OS_ERR_LOCK

RETURNED VALUE

NET_IF_LINK_UP if no errors and network interface's physical link state is UP;

NET_IF_LINK_DOWN otherwise.

REQUIRED CONFIGURATION

None.

NOTES / WARNINGS

If a non-zero number of retries is requested (`retry_max`) then a non-zero time delay (`time_dly_ms`) should also be requested. Otherwise, all retries will most likely fail immediately since no time will elapse to wait for and allow the network interface's link state to successfully be `UP`.

B-9-17 NetIF_MTU_Get()

Get network interface's MTU.

FILES

net_if.h/net_if.c

PROTOTYPE

```
NET_MTU NetIF_MTU_Get(NET_IF_NBR  if_nbr,
                      NET_ERR    *perr);
```

ARGUMENTS

if_nbr   Network interface number to get MTU.

perr   Pointer to variable that will receive the return error code from this function:

NET_IF_ERR_NONE
NET_IF_ERR_INVALID_IF
NET_OS_ERR_LOCK

RETURNED VALUE

Network interface's MTU, if no errors.

0, otherwise.

REQUIRED CONFIGURATION

None.

NOTES / WARNINGS

None.

B-9-18 NetIF_MTU_Set()

Set network interface's MTU.

FILES

net_if.h/net_if.c

PROTOTYPE

```
void NetIF_MTU_Set(NET_IF_NBR  if_nbr,
                   NET_MTU     mtu,
                   NET_ERR    *perr);
```

ARGUMENTS

if_nbr   Network interface number to set MTU.

mtu   Desired maximum transmission unit size to configure.

perr   Pointer to variable that will receive the return error code from this function:

NET_IF_ERR_NONE
NET_IF_ERR_NULL_FNCT
NET_IF_ERR_INVALID_IF
NET_IF_ERR_INVALID_CFG
NET_IF_ERR_INVALID_MTU
NET_OS_ERR_LOCK

RETURNED VALUE

None.

REQUIRED CONFIGURATION

None.

NOTES / WARNINGS

Additional error codes may be returned by the specific interface or device driver.

B-9-19 NetIF_Start()

Start a network interface.

FILES

net_if.h/net_if.c

PROTOTYPE

```
void NetIF_Start(NET_IF_NBR  if_nbr,
                 NET_ERR    *perr);
```

ARGUMENTS

if_nbr Network interface number to start.

perr Pointer to variable that will receive the return error code from this function:

NET_IF_ERR_NONE
NET_IF_ERR_NULL_FNCT
NET_IF_ERR_INVALID_IF
NET_IF_ERR_INVALID_CFG
NET_IF_ERR_INVALID_STATE
NET_OS_ERR_LOCK

RETURNED VALUE

None.

REQUIRED CONFIGURATION

None.

NOTES / WARNINGS

Additional error codes may be returned by the specific interface or device driver.

B-9-20 NetIF_Stop()

Stop a network interface.

FILES

net_if.h/net_if.c

PROTOTYPE

```
void NetIF_Stop(NET_IF_NBR  if_nbr,
                NET_ERR    *perr);
```

ARGUMENTS

if_nbr   Network interface number to stop.

perr   Pointer to variable that will receive the return error code from this function:

NET_IF_ERR_NONE
NET_IF_ERR_NULL_FNCT
NET_IF_ERR_INVALID_IF
NET_IF_ERR_INVALID_CFG
NET_IF_ERR_INVALID_STATE
NET_OS_ERR_LOCK

RETURNED VALUE

None.

REQUIRED CONFIGURATION

None.

NOTES / WARNINGS

Additional error codes may be returned by the specific interface or device driver.

B-10 IGMP FUNCTIONS

B-10-1 NetIGMP_HostGrpJoin()

Join a host group.

FILES

net_igmp.h/net_igmp.c

PROTOTYPE

```
void NetIGMP_HostGrpJoin (NET_IF_NBR   if_nbr,
                          NET_IP_ADDR  addr_grp,
                          NET_ERR     *perr);
```

ARGUMENTS

if_nbr Interface number to join host group.

addr_grp IP address of host group to join.

perr Pointer to variable that will receive the return error code from this function:

NET_IGMP_ERR_NONE
NET_IGMP_ERR_INVALID_ADDR_GRP
NET_IGMP_ERR_HOST_GRP_NONE_AVAIL
NET_IGMP_ERR_HOST_GRP_INVALID_TYPE
NET_IF_ERR_INVALID_IF
NET_ERR_INIT_INCOMPLETE
NET_OS_ERR_LOCK

RETURNED VALUE

`DEF_OK`, if host group successfully joined.

`DEF_FAIL`, otherwise.

REQUIRED CONFIGURATION

Available only if `NET_IP_CFG_MULTICAST_SEL` is configured for transmit and receive multicasting (see section C-9-2 on page 735).

NOTES / WARNINGS

`addr_grp` *must* be in host-order.

B-10-2 NetIGMP_HostGrpLeave()

Leave a host group.

FILES

net_igmp.h/net_igmp.c

PROTOTYPE

```
void NetIGMP_HostGrpLeave (NET_IF_NBR   if_nbr,
                           NET_IP_ADDR  addr_grp,
                           NET_ERR     *perr);
```

ARGUMENTS

if_nbr   Interface number to leave host group.

addr_grp   IP address of host group to leave.

err   Pointer to variable that will receive the return error code from this function:

NET_IGMP_ERR_NONE
NET_IGMP_ERR_HOST_GRP_NOT_FOUND
NET_ERR_INIT_INCOMPLETE
NET_OS_ERR_LOCK

RETURNED VALUE

DEF_OK,   if host group successfully left.

DEF_FAIL,   otherwise.

REQUIRED CONFIGURATION

Available only if NET_IP_CFG_MULTICAST_SEL is configured for transmit and receive multicasting (see section C-9-2 on page 735).

NOTES / WARNINGS

addr_grp *must* be in host-order.

B-11 IP FUNCTIONS

B-11-1 NetIP_CfgAddrAdd()

Add a static IP host address, subnet mask, and default gateway to an interface.

FILES

net_ip.h/net_ip.c

PROTOTYPE

```
CPU_BOOLEAN NetIP_CfgAddrAdd(NET_IF_NBR   if_nbr,
                             NET_IP_ADDR  addr_host,
                             NET_IP_ADDR  addr_subnet_mask,
                             NET_IP_ADDR  addr_dflt_gateway,
                             NET_ERR     *perr);
```

ARGUMENTS

if_nbr Interface number to configure.

addr_host Desired IP address to add to this interface.

addr_subnet_mask Desired IP address subnet mask.

addr_dflt_gateway Desired IP default gateway address.

perr Pointer to variable that will receive the error code from this function:

NET_IP_ERR_NONE
NET_IP_ERR_INVALID_ADDR_HOST
NET_IP_ERR_INVALID_ADDR_GATEWAY
NET_IP_ERR_ADDR_CFG_STATE
NET_IP_ERR_ADDR_TBL_FULL
NET_IP_ERR_ADDR_CFG_IN_USE
NET_IF_ERR_INVALID_IF
NET_OS_ERR_LOCK

RETURNED VALUE

`DEF_OK`, if valid IP address, subnet mask, and default gateway statically-configured;

`DEF_FAIL`, otherwise.

REQUIRED CONFIGURATION

None.

NOTES / WARNINGS

IP addresses *must* be configured in host-order.

An interface may be configured with either:

- One or more statically- configured IP addresses (default configuration) **OR**
- Exactly one dynamically-configured IP address (see section B-11-2 on page 551).

If an interface's address(es) are dynamically-configured, no statically-configured address(es) may be added until all dynamically-configured address(es) are removed.

The maximum number of IP address(es) configured on any interface is limited to `NET_IP_CFG_IF_MAX_NBR_ADDR` (see section C-9-1 on page 734).

Note that on the default interface, the first IP address added will be the default address used for all default communication. See also section B-9-1 on page 514.

A host *may* be configured without a gateway address to allow communication only with other hosts on its local network. However, any configured gateway address *must* be on the same network as the configured host IP address (i.e., the network portion of the configured IP address and the configured gateway addresses *must* be identical).

B-11-2 NetIP_CfgAddrAddDynamic()

Add a dynamically-configured IP host address, subnet mask, and default gateway to an interface.

FILES

net_ip.h/net_ip.c

PROTOTYPE

```
CPU_BOOLEAN NetIP_CfgAddrAddDynamic(NET_IF_NBR   if_nbr,
                                    NET_IP_ADDR  addr_host,
                                    NET_IP_ADDR  addr_subnet_mask,
                                    NET_IP_ADDR  addr_dflt_gateway,
                                    NET_ERR     *perr);
```

ARGUMENTS

if_nbr Interface number to configure.

addr_host Desired IP address to add to this interface.

addr_subnet_mask Desired IP address subnet mask.

addr_dflt_gateway Desired IP default gateway address.

perr Pointer to variable that will receive the return error code from this function:

NET_IP_ERR_NONE
NET_IP_ERR_INVALID_ADDR_HOST
NET_IP_ERR_INVALID_ADDR_GATEWAY
NET_IP_ERR_ADDR_CFG_STATE
NET_IP_ERR_ADDR_CFG_IN_USE
NET_IF_ERR_INVALID_IF
NET_ERR_INIT_INCOMPLETE
NET_OS_ERR_LOCK

RETURNED VALUE

`DEF_OK`, if valid IP address, subnet mask, and default gateway dynamically configured;

`DEF_FAIL`, otherwise.

REQUIRED CONFIGURATION

None.

NOTES / WARNINGS

IP addresses *must* be configured in host-order.

An interface may be configured with either:

- One or more statically- configured IP addresses (see section B-11-1 on page 549) **OR**
- Exactly one dynamically-configured IP address.

This function should *only* be called by appropriate network application function(s) [e.g., DHCP initialization functions]. However, if the application attempts to dynamically configure IP address(es), it *must* call **`NetIP_CfgAddrAddDynamicStart()`** before calling **`NetIP_CfgAddrAddDynamic()`**. Note that on the default interface, the first IP address added will be the default address used for all default communication. See also section B-9-1 on page 514.

A host *may* be configured without a gateway address to allow communication only with other hosts on its local network. However, any configured gateway address *must* be on the same network as the configured host IP address (i.e., the network portion of the configured IP address and the configured gateway addresses *must* be identical).

B-11-3 NetIP_CfgAddrAddDynamicStart()

Start dynamic IP address configuration for an interface.

FILES

net_ip.h/net_ip.c

PROTOTYPE

```
CPU_BOOLEAN NetIP_CfgAddrAddDynamicStart(NET_IF_NBR  if_nbr,
                                         NET_ERR    *perr);
```

ARGUMENTS

if_nbr Interface number to start dynamic address configuration.

perr Pointer to variable that will receive the return error code from this function:

NET_IP_ERR_NONE
NET_IP_ERR_ADDR_CFG_STATE
NET_IP_ERR_ADDR_CFG_IN_PROGRESS
NET_IF_ERR_INVALID_IF
NET_OS_ERR_LOCK

RETURNED VALUE

DEF_OK, if dynamic IP address configuration successfully started;

DEF_FAIL, otherwise.

REQUIRED CONFIGURATION

None.

NOTES / WARNINGS

This function should *only* be called by appropriate network application function(s) [e.g., DHCP initialization functions]. However, if the application attempts to dynamically configure IP address(es), it *must* call **NetIP_CfgAddrAddDynamicStart()** before calling **NetIP_CfgAddrAddDynamic()**.

B-11-4 NetIP_CfgAddrAddDynamicStop()

Stop dynamic IP address configuration for an interface.

FILES

net_ip.h/net_ip.c

PROTOTYPE

```
CPU_BOOLEAN NetIP_CfgAddrAddDynamicStop(NET_IF_NBR  if_nbr,
                                        NET_ERR    *perr);
```

ARGUMENTS

if_nbr   Interface number to stop dynamic address configuration.

perr   Pointer to variable that will receive the return error code from this function:

NET_IP_ERR_NONE
NET_IP_ERR_ADDR_CFG_STATE
NET_IF_ERR_INVALID_IF
NET_OS_ERR_LOCK

RETURNED VALUE

DEF_OK,   if dynamic IP address configuration successfully stopped;

DEF_FAIL,   otherwise.

REQUIRED CONFIGURATION

None.

NOTES / WARNINGS

This function should *only* be called by appropriate network application function(s) [e.g., DHCP initialization functions]. However, if the application attempts to dynamically configure IP address(es), it must call **NetIP_CfgAddrAddDynamicStop()** *only* after calling **NetIP_CfgAddrAddDynamicStart()** and dynamic IP address configuration has failed.

B-11-5 NetIP_CfgAddrRemove()

Remove a configured IP host address from an interface.

FILES

net_ip.h/net_ip.c

PROTOTYPE

```
CPU_BOOLEAN NetIP_CfgAddrRemove(NET_IF_NBR   if_nbr,
                                NET_IP_ADDR  addr_host,
                                NET_ERR     *perr);
```

ARGUMENTS

if_nbr Interface number to remove configured IP host address.

addr_host IP address to remove.

perr Pointer to variable that will receive the return error code from this function:

NET_IP_ERR_NONE
NET_IP_ERR_INVALID_ADDR_HOST
NET_IP_ERR_ADDR_CFG_STATE
NET_IP_ERR_ADDR_TBL_EMPTY
NET_IP_ERR_ADDR_NOT_FOUND
NET_IF_ERR_INVALID_IF
NET_OS_ERR_LOCK

RETURNED VALUE

DEF_OK, if interface's configured IP host address successfully removed;

DEF_FAIL, otherwise.

REQUIRED CONFIGURATION

None.

NOTES / WARNINGS

None.

B-11-6 NetIP_CfgAddrRemoveAll()

Remove all configured IP host address(es) from an interface.

FILES

net_ip.h/net_ip.c

PROTOTYPE

```
CPU_BOOLEAN NetIP_CfgAddrRemoveAll(NET_IF_NBR  if_nbr,
                                   NET_ERR    *perr);
```

ARGUMENTS

if_nbr Interface number to remove all configured IP host address(es).

perr Pointer to variable that will receive the return error code from this function:

NET_IP_ERR_NONE
NET_IP_ERR_ADDR_CFG_STATE
NET_IF_ERR_INVALID_IF
NET_OS_ERR_LOCK

RETURNED VALUE

DEF_OK, if all interface's configured IP host address(es) successfully removed;

DEF_FAIL, otherwise.

REQUIRED CONFIGURATION

None.

NOTES / WARNINGS

None.

B-11-7 NetIP_CfgFragReasmTimeout()

Configure IP fragment reassembly timeout.

FILES

net_ip.h/net_ip.c

PROTOTYPE

```
CPU_BOOLEAN NetIP_CfgFragReasmTimeout(CPU_INT08U timeout_sec);
```

ARGUMENTS

timeout_sec Desired value for IP fragment reassembly timeout (in seconds).

RETURNED VALUE

DEF_OK, IP fragment reassembly timeout successfully configured.

DEF_FAIL, otherwise.

REQUIRED CONFIGURATION

None.

NOTES / WARNINGS

Fragment reassembly timeout is the maximum time allowed between received fragments of the same IP datagram.

B-11-8 NetIP_GetAddrDfltGateway()

Get the default gateway IP address for a host's configured IP address.

FILES

net_ip.h/net_ip.c

PROTOTYPE

```
NET_IP_ADDR NetIP_GetAddrDfltGateway(NET_IP_ADDR  addr,
                                     NET_ERR     *perr);
```

ARGUMENTS

addr Configured IP host address.

perr Pointer to variable that will receive the return error code from this function:

NET_IP_ERR_NONE
NET_IP_ERR_INVALID_ADDR_HOST
NET_OS_ERR_LOCK

RETURNED VALUE

Configured IP host address's default gateway (in host-order), if no errors.

NET_IP_ADDR_NONE, otherwise.

REQUIRED CONFIGURATION

None.

NOTES / WARNINGS

All IP addresses in host-order.

B-11-9 NetIP_GetAddrHost()

Get an interface's configured IP host address(es).

FILES

net_ip.h/net_ip.c

PROTOTYPE

```
CPU_BOOLEAN NetIP_GetAddrHost(NET_IF_NBR         if_nbr,
                              NET_IP_ADDR       *paddr_tbl,
                              NET_IP_ADDRS_QTY *paddr_tbl_qty,
                              NET_ERR           *perr);
```

ARGUMENTS

if_nbr Interface number to get configured IP host address(es).

paddr_tbl Pointer to IP address table that will receive the IP host address(es) in host-order for this interface.

paddr_tbl_qty Pointer to a variable to:

Pass the size of the address table, in number of IP addresses, pointed to by **paddr_tbl**.

Returns the actual number of IP addresses, if no errors.
Returns 0, otherwise.

perr Pointer to variable that will receive the error code from this function:

NET_IP_ERR_NONE
NET_IP_ERR_NULL_PTR
NET_IP_ERR_ADDR_NONE_AVAIL
NET_IP_ERR_ADDR_CFG_IN_PROGRESS
NET_IP_ERR_ADDR_TBL_SIZE
NET_IF_ERR_INVALID_IF
NET_OS_ERR_LOCK

RETURNED VALUE

DEF_OK,	if interface's configured IP host address(es) successfully returned;
DEF_FAIL,	otherwise.

REQUIRED CONFIGURATION

None.

NOTES / WARNINGS

IP addresses returned in host-order.

B-11-10 NetIP_GetAddrHostCfgd()

Get corresponding configured IP host address for a remote IP address.

FILES

net_ip.h/net_ip.c

PROTOTYPE

```
NET_IP_ADDR NetIP_GetAddrHostCfgd(NET_IP_ADDR addr_remote);
```

ARGUMENTS

addr_remote	Remote address to get configured IP host address

RETURNED VALUE

Configured IP host address,	if available;
NET_IP_ADDR_NONE,	otherwise.

REQUIRED CONFIGURATION

None.

NOTES / WARNINGS

IP addresses returned in host-order.

B-11-11 NetIP_GetAddrSubnetMask()

Get the IP address subnet mask for a host's configured IP address.

FILES

net_ip.h/net_ip.c

PROTOTYPE

```
NET_IP_ADDR NetIP_GetAddrSubnetMask(NET_IP_ADDR  addr,
                                    NET_ERR     *perr);
```

ARGUMENTS

addr Configured IP host address.

perr Pointer to variable that will receive the return error code from this function:

NET_IP_ERR_NONE
NET_IP_ERR_INVALID_ADDR_HOST
NET_OS_ERR_LOCK

RETURNED VALUE

Configured IP host address's subnet mask (in host-order), if no errors.

NET_IP_ADDR_NONE, otherwise.

REQUIRED CONFIGURATION

None.

NOTES / WARNINGS

IP addresses in host-order.

B-11-12 NetIP_IsAddrBroadcast()

Validate an IP address as the limited broadcast IP address.

FILES

net_ip.h/net_ip.c

PROTOTYPE

```
CPU_BOOLEAN NetIP_IsAddrBroadcast(NET_IP_ADDR addr);
```

ARGUMENTS

addr IP address to validate.

RETURNED VALUE

DEF_YES if IP address is a limited broadcast IP address;

DEF_NO otherwise.

REQUIRED CONFIGURATION

None.

NOTES / WARNINGS

IP address *must* be in host-order.

The broadcast IP address is 255.255.255.255.

B-11-13 NetIP_IsAddrClassA()

Validate an IP address as a Class-A IP address.

FILES

net_ip.h/net_ip.c

PROTOTYPE

```
CPU_BOOLEAN NetIP_IsAddrClassA(NET_IP_ADDR addr);
```

ARGUMENTS

addr IP address to validate.

RETURNED VALUE

DEF_YES if IP address is a Class-A IP address;

DEF_NO otherwise.

REQUIRED CONFIGURATION

None.

NOTES / WARNINGS

IP address *must* be in host-order.

Class-A IP addresses have their most significant bit be '0'.

B-11-14 NetIP_IsAddrClassB()

Validate an IP address as a Class-B IP address.

FILES

net_ip.h/net_ip.c

PROTOTYPE

```
CPU_BOOLEAN NetIP_IsAddrClassB(NET_IP_ADDR addr);
```

ARGUMENTS

addr	IP address to validate.

RETURNED VALUE

DEF_YES	if IP address is a Class-B IP address;
DEF_NO	otherwise.

REQUIRED CONFIGURATION

None.

NOTES / WARNINGS

IP address *must* be in host-order.

Class-B IP addresses have their most significant bits be '10'.

B-11-15 NetIP_IsAddrClassC()

Validate an IP address as a Class-C IP address.

FILES

net_ip.h/net_ip.c

PROTOTYPE

```
CPU_BOOLEAN NetIP_IsAddrClassC(NET_IP_ADDR addr);
```

ARGUMENTS

addr IP address to validate.

RETURNED VALUE

DEF_YES if IP address is a Class-C IP address;

DEF_NO otherwise.

REQUIRED CONFIGURATION

None.

NOTES / WARNINGS

IP address *must* be in host-order.

Class-C IP addresses have their most significant bits be ‘110’.

B-11-16 NetIP_IsAddrHost()

Validate an IP address as one the host's IP address(es).

FILES

net_ip.h/net_ip.c

PROTOTYPE

```
CPU_BOOLEAN NetIP_IsAddrHost(NET_IP_ADDR addr);
```

ARGUMENTS

addr IP address to validate.

RETURNED VALUE

DEF_YES if IP address is any one of the host's IP address(es);

DEF_NO otherwise.

REQUIRED CONFIGURATION

None.

NOTES / WARNINGS

IP address *must* be in host-order.

B-11-17 NetIP_IsAddrHostCfgd()

Validate an IP address as one the host's configured IP address(es).

FILES

net_ip.h/net_ip.c

PROTOTYPE

```
CPU_BOOLEAN NetIP_IsAddrHostCfgd(NET_IP_ADDR addr);
```

ARGUMENTS

addr IP address to validate.

RETURNED VALUE

DEF_YES if IP address is any one of the host's configured IP address(es);

DEF_NO otherwise.

REQUIRED CONFIGURATION

None.

NOTES / WARNINGS

IP address *must* be in host-order.

B-11-18 NetIP_IsAddrLocalHost()

Validate an IP address as a Localhost IP address.

FILES

net_ip.h/net_ip.c

PROTOTYPE

```
CPU_BOOLEAN NetIP_IsAddrLocalHost(NET_IP_ADDR addr);
```

ARGUMENTS

addr IP address to validate.

RETURNED VALUE

DEF_YES if IP address is a Localhost IP address;

DEF_NO otherwise.

REQUIRED CONFIGURATION

None.

NOTES / WARNINGS

IP address *must* be in host-order.

Localhost IP addresses are any host address in the '127.<host>' subnet.

B-11-19 NetIP_IsAddrLocalLink()

Validate an IP address as a link-local IP address.

FILES

net_ip.h/net_ip.c

PROTOTYPE

```
CPU_BOOLEAN NetIP_IsAddrLocalLink(NET_IP_ADDR addr);
```

ARGUMENTS

addr	IP address to validate.

RETURNED VALUE

DEF_YES	if IP address is a link-local IP address;
DEF_NO	otherwise.

REQUIRED CONFIGURATION

None.

NOTES / WARNINGS

IP address *must* be in host-order.

Link-local IP addresses are any host address in the '169.254.<host>' subnet.

B-11-20 NetIP_IsAddrsCfgdOnIF()

Check if any IP address(es) are configured on an interface.

FILES

net_ip.h/net_ip.c

PROTOTYPE

```
CPU_BOOLEAN NetIP_IsAddrsHostCfgdOnIF(NET_IF_NBR  if_nbr,
NET_ERR   *perr);
```

ARGUMENTS

if_nbr Interface number to check for configured IP host address(es).

perr Pointer to variable that will receive the return error code from this function:

NET_IP_ERR_NONE
NET_IF_ERR_INVALID_IF
NET_OS_ERR_LOCK

RETURNED VALUE

DEF_YES if ANY IP host address(es) are configured on the interface;

DEF_NO otherwise.

REQUIRED CONFIGURATION

None.

NOTES / WARNINGS

None.

B-11-21 NetIP_IsAddrThisHost()

Validate an IP address as the 'This Host' initialization IP address.

FILES

net_ip.h/net_ip.c

PROTOTYPE

```
CPU_BOOLEAN NetIP_IsAddrThisHost(NET_IP_ADDR addr);
```

ARGUMENTS

addr	IP address to validate.

RETURNED VALUE

DEF_YES	if IP address is a 'This Host' initialization IP address;
DEF_NO	otherwise.

REQUIRED CONFIGURATION

None.

NOTES / WARNINGS

IP address *must* be in host-order.

The 'This Host' initialization IP address is 0.0.0.0.

B-11-22 NetIP_IsValidAddrHost()

Validate an IP address as a valid IP host address.

FILES

net_ip.h/net_ip.c

PROTOTYPE

```
CPU_BOOLEAN NetIP_IsValidAddrHost(NET_IP_ADDR addr_host);
```

ARGUMENTS

addr_host IP host address to validate.

RETURNED VALUE

DEF_YES if valid IP host address;

DEF_NO otherwise.

REQUIRED CONFIGURATION

None.

NOTES / WARNINGS

IP address *must* be in host-order. A valid IP host address must *not* be one of the following:

- This Host (see section B-11-21 on page 574)
- Specified Host
- Localhost (see section B-11-18 on page 571)
- Limited Broadcast (see section B-11-12 on page 565)
- Directed Broadcast

B-11-23 NetIP_IsValidAddrHostCfgd()

Validate an IP address as a valid, configurable IP host address.

FILES

net_ip.h/net_ip.c

PROTOTYPE

```
CPU_BOOLEAN NetIP_IsValidAddrHostCfgd(NET_IP_ADDR addr_host,
                                      NET_IP_ADDR addr_subnet_mask);
```

ARGUMENTS

addr_host	IP host address to validate.
addr_subnet_mask	IP host address subnet mask.

RETURNED VALUE

DEF_YES	if configurable IP host address;
DEF_NO	otherwise.

REQUIRED CONFIGURATION

None.

NOTES / WARNINGS

IP addresses *must* be in host-order.

A configurable IP host address must *not* be one of the following:

- This Host (see section B-11-21 on page 574)
- Specified Host
- Localhost (see section B-11-18 on page 571)

- Limited Broadcast (see section B-11-12 on page 565)
- Directed Broadcast
- Subnet Broadcast

B-11-24 NetIP_IsValidAddrSubnetMask()

Validate an IP address subnet mask.

FILES

net_ip.h/net_ip.c

PROTOTYPE

```
CPU_BOOLEAN NetIP_IsValidAddrSubnetMask(NET_IP_ADDR addr_subnet_mask);
```

ARGUMENTS

addr_subnet_mask	IP host address subnet mask.

RETURNED VALUE

DEF_YES	if valid IP address subnet mask;
DEF_NO	otherwise.

REQUIRED CONFIGURATION

None.

NOTES / WARNINGS

IP address *must* be in host-order.

B-12 NETWORK SECURITY FUNCTIONS

B-12-1 NetSecureMgr_InstallBuf()

Install a certificate authority (CA), a certificate (CERT), or a private key (KEY) from a buffer.

FILE

net_secure_mgr.h/net_secure_mgr.c

CALLED FROM

Application

PROTOTYPE

```
CPU_BOOLEAN NetSecureMgr_InstallBuf(void        *p_buf,
                                    CPU_INT08U  type,
                                    CPU_INT08U  fmt,
                                    CPU_SIZE_T  size,
                                    NET_ERR     *p_err);
```

ARGUMENTS

p_buf   Pointer to the CA, CERT or KEY buffer to install.

type   Type of the CA, CERT or KEY to install:

NET_SECURE_MGR_INSTALL_TYPE_CA	Certificate authority (CA)
NET_SECURE_INSTALL_TYPE_CERT	Public key certificate
NET_SECURE_INSTALL_TYPE_KEY	Private key

fmt   Format of the CA, CERT or KEY to install:

NET_SECURE_MGR_INSTALL_FMT_PEM
NET_SECURE_MGR_INSTALL_FMT_DER

size Size of the CA, CERT or KEY buffer to install.

p_err Pointer to variable that will receive the return error code from this function:

NET_SECURE_MGR_ERR_NONE
NET_SECURE_MGR_ERR_NULL_PTR
NET_SECURE_MGR_ERR_TYPE
NET_SECURE_MGR_ERR_FMT
NET_SECURE_ERR_INSTALL_NOT_TRUSTED
NET_SECURE_ERR_INSTALL_DATE_EXPIRATION
NET_SECURE_ERR_INSTALL_DATE_CREATION
NET_SECURE_ERR_INSTALL_CA_SLOT
NET_SECURE_ERR_INSTALL

RETURNED VALUE

DEF_OK, CA, CERT or KEY successfully installed;

DEF_FAIL, otherwise.

REQUIRED CONFIGURATION

Available only if **NET_SECURE_CFG_EN** is enabled (see section C-16-1 on page 744) *and* **NET_CFG_TRANSPORT_LAYER_SEL** is configured for TCP (see section C-12-1 on page 736).

NOTES / WARNINGS

None.

E

B-12-2 NetSecureMgr_InstallFile()

Install a certificate authority (CA), a certificate (CERT), or a private key (KEY) from a file.

FILE

net_secure_mgr.h/net_secure_mgr.c

CALLED FROM

Application

PROTOTYPE

```
CPU_BOOLEAN NetSecureMgr_InstallFile(CPU_CHAR    *p_filename,
                                     CPU_INT08U  type,
                                     CPU_INT08U  fmt,
                                     NET_ERR     *p_err);
```

ARGUMENTS

p_filename Pointer to the CA, CERT or KEY filename to install.

type Type of the CA, CERT or KEY to install:

NET_SECURE_MGR_INSTALL_TYPE_CA	Certificate authority (CA)
NET_SECURE_INSTALL_TYPE_CERT	Public key certificate
NET_SECURE_INSTALL_TYPE_KEY	Private key

fmt Format of the CA, CERT or KEY to install:

NET_SECURE_MGR_INSTALL_FMT_PEM
NET_SECURE_MGR_INSTALL_FMT_DER

p_err — Pointer to variable that will receive the return error code from this function:

NET_SECURE_MGR_ERR_NONE
NET_SECURE_MGR_ERR_NULL_PTR
NET_SECURE_MGR_ERR_TYPE
NET_SECURE_MGR_ERR_FMT
NET_SECURE_ERR_INSTALL_NOT_TRUSTED
NET_SECURE_ERR_INSTALL_DATE_EXPIRATION
NET_SECURE_ERR_INSTALL_DATE_CREATION
NET_SECURE_INSTALL_CA_SLOT
NET_SECURE_ERR_INSTALL

RETURNED VALUE

DEF_OK, — CA, CERT or KEY successfully installed;

DEF_FAIL, — otherwise.

REQUIRED CONFIGURATION

Available only if NET_SECURE_CFG_EN is enabled (see section C-16-1 on page 744) *and* NET_CFG_TRANSPORT_LAYER_SEL is configured for TCP (see section C-12-1 on page 736).

NOTES / WARNINGS

p_filename must point to the full path filename of the CA, CERT or KEY file to install. The following are some example files:

```
\server-cert.der
\<Your Target Path>\server-key.pem
```

...and corresponding filename strings:

```
"\\server-cert.der"
"\\<Your Target Path>\\server-key.pem"
```

where:

<Your Target Path> — directory path on your target file system (FS)

B-13 NETWORK SOCKET FUNCTIONS

B-13-1 NetSock_Accept() / accept() (TCP)

Wait for new socket connections on a listening server socket (see section B-13-34 on page 648). When a new connection arrives and the TCP handshake has successfully completed, a new socket ID is returned for the new connection with the remote host's address and port number returned in the socket address structure.

FILES

net_sock.h/net_sock.c
net_bsd.h/net_bsd.c

PROTOTYPES

```
NET_SOCK_ID NetSock_Accept(NET_SOCK_ID          sock_id,
                           NET_SOCK_ADDR        *paddr_remote,
                           NET_SOCK_ADDR_LEN    *paddr_len,
                           NET_ERR              *perr);


int accept(int                    sock_id,
           struct sockaddr  *paddr_remote,
           socklen_t        *paddr_len);
```

ARGUMENTS

sock_id This is the socket ID returned by **NetSock_Open()/socket()** when the socket was created. This socket is assumed to be bound to an address and listening for new connections (see section B-13-34 on page 648).

paddr_remote Pointer to a socket address structure (see section 17-1 "Network Socket Data Structures" on page 355) to return the remote host address of the new accepted connection.

paddr_len Pointer to the size of the socket address structure which *must* be passed the size of the socket address structure [e.g., **sizeof(NET_SOCK_ADDR_IP)**]. Returns size of the accepted connection's socket address structure, if no errors; returns 0, otherwise.

perr Pointer to variable that will receive the return error code from this function:

NET_SOCK_ERR_NONE
NET_SOCK_ERR_NULL_PTR
NET_SOCK_ERR_NONE_AVAIL
NET_SOCK_ERR_NOT_USED
NET_SOCK_ERR_CLOSED
NET_SOCK_ERR_INVALID_SOCK
NET_SOCK_ERR_INVALID_FAMILY
NET_SOCK_ERR_INVALID_TYPE
NET_SOCK_ERR_INVALID_STATE
NET_SOCK_ERR_INVALID_OP
NET_SOCK_ERR_CONN_ACCEPT_Q_NONE_AVAIL
NET_SOCK_ERR_CONN_SIGNAL_TIMEOUT
NET_SOCK_ERR_CONN_FAIL
NET_SOCK_ERR_FAULT
NET_ERR_INIT_INCOMPLETE
NET_OS_ERR_LOCK

RETURNED VALUE

Returns a non-negative socket descriptor ID for the new accepted connection, if successful;

NET_SOCK_BSD_ERR_ACCEPT/-1, otherwise.

If the socket is configured for non-blocking, a return value of NET_SOCK_BSD_ERR_ACCEPT/-1 may indicate that the no requests for connection were queued when NetSock_Accept()/accept() was called. In this case, the server can "poll" for a new connection at a later time.

REQUIRED CONFIGURATION

NetSock_Accept() is available only if NET_CFG_TRANSPORT_LAYER_SEL is configured for TCP (see section C-12-1 on page 736).

In addition, accept() is available only if NET_BSD_CFG_API_EN is enabled (see section C-17-1 on page 747).

NOTES / WARNINGS

See section 8-2 "Socket Interface" on page 208 for socket address structure formats.

E

B-13-2 NetSock_Bind() / bind() (TCP/UDP)

Assign network addresses to sockets. Typically, server sockets bind to addresses but client sockets do not. Servers may bind to one of the local host's addresses but usually bind to the wildcard address (**NET_SOCK_ADDR_IP_WILDCARD/INADDR_ANY**) on a specific, well-known port number. Whereas client sockets usually bind to one of the local host's addresses but with a random port number (by configuring the socket address structure's port number field with a value of **0**).

FILES

net_sock.h/net_sock.c
net_bsd.h/net_bsd.c

PROTOTYPES

```
NET_SOCK_RTN_CODE NetSock_Bind(NET_SOCK_ID          sock_id,
                               NET_SOCK_ADDR       *paddr_local,
                               NET_SOCK_ADDR_LEN    addr_len,
                               NET_ERR             *perr);

int bind(int                    sock_id,
         struct sockaddr       *paddr_local,
         socklen_t              addr_len);
```

ARGUMENTS

sock_id This is the socket ID returned by **NetSock_Open()/socket()** when the socket was created.

paddr_local Pointer to a socket address structure (see section 8-2 "Socket Interface" on page 208) which contains the local host address to bind the socket to.

addr_len Size of the socket address structure which *must* be passed the size of the socket address structure [for example, **sizeof(NET_SOCK_ADDR_IP)**].

perr Pointer to variable that will receive the return error code from this function:

NET_SOCK_ERR_NONE
NET_SOCK_ERR_NOT_USED
NET_SOCK_ERR_CLOSED
NET_SOCK_ERR_INVALID_SOCK
NET_SOCK_ERR_INVALID_FAMILY
NET_SOCK_ERR_INVALID_PROTOCOL
NET_SOCK_ERR_INVALID_TYPE
NET_SOCK_ERR_INVALID_STATE
NET_SOCK_ERR_INVALID_OP
NET_SOCK_ERR_INVALID_ADDR
NET_SOCK_ERR_ADDR_IN_USE
NET_SOCK_ERR_PORT_NBR_NONE_AVAIL
NET_SOCK_ERR_CONN_FAIL
NET_IF_ERR_INVALID_IF
NET_IP_ERR_ADDR_NONE_AVAIL
NET_IP_ERR_ADDR_CFG_IN_PROGRESS
NET_CONN_ERR_NULL_PTR
NET_CONN_ERR_NOT_USED
NET_CONN_ERR_NONE_AVAIL
NET_CONN_ERR_INVALID_CONN
NET_CONN_ERR_INVALID_FAMILY
NET_CONN_ERR_INVALID_TYPE
NET_CONN_ERR_INVALID_PROTOCOL_IX
NET_CONN_ERR_INVALID_ADDR_LEN
NET_CONN_ERR_ADDR_NOT_USED
NET_CONN_ERR_ADDR_IN_USE
NET_ERR_INIT_INCOMPLETE
NET_OS_ERR_LOCK

RETURNED VALUE

NET_SOCK_BSD_ERR_NONE/0, if successful;

NET_SOCK_BSD_ERR_BIND/-1, otherwise.

REQUIRED CONFIGURATION

`NetSock_Bind()` is available only if either `NET_CFG_TRANSPORT_LAYER_SEL` is configured for TCP (see section C-12-1 on page 736) and/or `NET_UDP_CFG_APP_API_SEL` is configured for sockets (see section C-13-1 on page 737).

In addition, `bind()` is available only if `NET_BSD_CFG_API_EN` is enabled (see section C-17-1 on page 747).

NOTES / WARNINGS

See section 8-2 "Socket Interface" on page 208 for socket address structure formats.

Sockets may bind to any of the host's configured addresses, any localhost address (127.x.y.z network; e.g., 127.0.0.1), any link-local address (169.254.y.z network; e.g., 169.254.65.111), as well as the wildcard address (`NET_SOCK_ADDR_IP_WILDCARD/INADDR_ANY`, i.e., 0.0.0.0).

Sockets may bind to specific port numbers or request a random, ephemeral port number by configuring the socket address structure's port number field with a value of 0. Sockets may *not* bind to a port number that is within the configured range of random port numbers (see section C-15-2 on page 740 and section C-15-7 on page 742):

```
 NET_SOCK_CFG_PORT_NBR_RANDOM_BASE <= RandomPortNbrs <=
(NET_SOCK_CFG_PORT_NBR_RANDOM_BASE + NET_SOCK_CFG_NBR_SOCK + 10)
```

B-13-3 NetSock_CfgBlock() (TCP/UDP)

Configure a socket's blocking mode.

FILES

net_sock.h/net_sock.c

PROTOTYPE

```
CPU_BOOLEAN NetSock_CfgBlock(NET_SOCK_ID  sock_id,
                             CPU_INT08U   block,
                             NET_ERR     *perr);
```

ARGUMENTS

sock_id This is the socket ID returned by **NetSock_Open()/socket()** when the socket was created *or* by **NetSock_Accept()/accept()** when a connection was accepted.

block Desired value for socket blocking mode:

NET_SOCK_BLOCK_SEL_DFLT	Socket operations will block
NET_SOCK_BLOCK_SEL_BLOCK	Socket operations will block
NET_SOCK_BLOCK_SEL_NO_BLOCK	Socket operations will not block

perr Pointer to variable that will receive the return error code from this function:

NET_SOCK_ERR_NONE
NET_SOCK_ERR_NOT_USED
NET_SOCK_ERR_INVALID_SOCK
NET_SOCK_ERR_INVALID_ARG
NET_ERR_INIT_INCOMPLETE
NET_OS_ERR_LOCK

RETURNED VALUE

DEF_OK, Socket blocking mode successfully configured;

DEF_FAIL, otherwise.

E

REQUIRED CONFIGURATION

Available only if `NET_CFG_TRANSPORT_LAYER_SEL` is configured for TCP (see section C-12-1 on page 736) and/or `NET_UDP_CFG_APP_API_SEL` is configured for sockets (see section C-13-1 on page 737).

NOTES / WARNINGS

None.

B-13-4 NetSock_CfgSecure() (TCP)

Configure a socket's secure mode.

FILES

net_sock.h/net_sock.c

PROTOTYPE

```
CPU_BOOLEAN NetSock_CfgBlock(NET_SOCK_ID  sock_id,
                             CPU_INT08U   secure,
                             NET_ERR     *perr);
```

ARGUMENTS

sock_id This is the socket ID returned by **NetSock_Open()/socket()** when the socket was created.

block Desired value for socket secure mode:

DEF_ENABLED	Socket operations will be secured.
DEF_DISABLED	Socket operations will not be secured.

perr Pointer to variable that will receive the return error code from this function:

NET_SOCK_ERR_NONE
NET_SOCK_ERR_NOT_USED
NET_SOCK_ERR_INVALID_ARG
NET_SOCK_ERR_INVALID_TYPE
NET_SOCK_ERR_INVALID_STATE
NET_SOCK_ERR_INVALID_SOCK
NET_ERR_INIT_INCOMPLETE
NET_SECURE_ERR_NOT_AVAIL
NET_OS_ERR_LOCK

RETURNED VALUE

DEF_OK, Socket secure mode successfully configured;

DEF_FAIL, otherwise.

REQUIRED CONFIGURATION

Available only if **NET_CFG_TRANSPORT_LAYER_SEL** is configured for TCP (see section C-12-1 on page 736) *and* if **NET_SECURE_CFG_EN** is enabled (see section C-15 on page 740).

NOTES / WARNINGS

Available only for stream-type sockets (e.g., TCP sockets).

B-13-5 NetSock_CfgRxQ_Size() (TCP/UDP)

Configure socket's receive queue size.

FILES

net_sock.h/net_sock.c

PROTOTYPE

```
CPU_BOOLEAN NetSock_CfgRxQ_Size(NET_SOCK_ID          sock_id,
                                NET_SOCK_DATA_SIZE   size
                                NET_ERR             *perr);
```

ARGUMENTS

sock_id This is the socket ID of socket to configure receive queue size.

size Desired receive queue size.

perr Pointer to variable that will receive the return error code from this function:

NET_SOCK_ERR_NONE
NET_SOCK_ERR_INVALID_TYPE
NET_SOCK_ERR_INVALID_PROTOCOL
NET_SOCK_ERR_INVALID_DATA_SIZE
NET_ERR_INIT_INCOMPLETE
NET_SOCK_ERR_INVALID_SOCK
NET_SOCK_ERR_NOT_USED
NET_TCP_ERR_INVALID_CONN
NET_TCP_ERR_INVALID_ARG
NET_TCP_ERR_CONN_NOT_USED
NET_CONN_ERR_INVALID_CONN
NET_CONN_ERR_NOT_USED
NET_OS_ERR_LOCK

RETURNED VALUE

`DEF_OK`, Socket receive queue size successfully configured;

`DEF_FAIL`, otherwise.

REQUIRED CONFIGURATION

None.

NOTES / WARNINGS

For datagram sockets, configured size does NOT:

- Limit or remove any received data currently queued but becomes effective for later received data.
- Partially truncate any received data but instead allows data from exactly one received packet buffer to overflow the configured size since each datagram MUST be received atomically (see section B-13-38 "NetSock_RxData() / recv() (TCP) NetSock_RxDataFrom() / recvfrom() (UDP)" on page 655).

For steam sockets, size MAY be required to be configured prior to connecting (see section B-14-5 "NetTCP_ConnCfgRxWinSize()" on page 675).

B-13-6 NetSock_CfgTxQ_Size() (TCP/UDP)

Configure socket's transmit queue size.

FILES

net_sock.h/net_sock.c

PROTOTYPE

```
CPU_BOOLEAN NetSock_CfgTxQ_Size(NET_SOCK_ID        sock_id,
                                NET_SOCK_DATA_SIZE size
                                NET_ERR           *perr);
```

ARGUMENTS

sock_id This is the socket ID of socket to configure transmit queue size.

size Desired transmit queue size.

perr Pointer to variable that will receive the return error code from this function:

NET_SOCK_ERR_NONE
NET_SOCK_ERR_INVALID_TYPE
NET_SOCK_ERR_INVALID_PROTOCOL
NET_SOCK_ERR_INVALID_DATA_SIZE
NET_ERR_INIT_INCOMPLETE
NET_SOCK_ERR_INVALID_SOCK
NET_SOCK_ERR_NOT_USED
NET_TCP_ERR_INVALID_CONN
NET_TCP_ERR_INVALID_ARG
NET_TCP_ERR_CONN_NOT_USED
NET_CONN_ERR_INVALID_CONN
NET_CONN_ERR_NOT_USED
NET_OS_ERR_LOCK

RETURNED VALUE

`DEF_OK`, Socket transmit queue size successfully configured;

`DEF_FAIL`, otherwise.

REQUIRED CONFIGURATION

None.

NOTES / WARNINGS

For datagram sockets, configured size does NOT:

- Partially truncate any transmitted data but instead allows data from exactly one transmitted packet buffer to overflow the configured size since each datagram MUST be transmitted atomically (see section B-13-40 "NetSock_TxData() / send() (TCP) NetSock_TxDataTo() / sendto() (UDP)" on page 662).

For steam sockets, size MAY be required to be configured prior to connecting (see section B-14-6 "NetTCP_ConnCfgTxWinSize()" on page 677).

B-13-7 NetSock_CfgTxIP_TOS() (TCP/UDP)

Configure socket's transmit IP TOS.

FILES

net_sock.h/net_sock.c

PROTOTYPE

```
CPU_BOOLEAN NetSock_CfgTxIP_TOS(NET_SOCK_ID  sock_id,
                                NET_IP_TOS   ip_tos
                                NET_ERR     *perr);
```

ARGUMENTS

sock_id This is the socket ID of socket to configure transmit IP TOS.

size Desired transmit IP TOS.

perr Pointer to variable that will receive the return error code from this function:

NET_SOCK_ERR_NONE
NET_SOCK_ERR_NOT_USED
NET_SOCK_ERR_INVALID_STATE
NET_SOCK_ERR_INVALID_OP
NET_ERR_INIT_INCOMPLETE
NET_SOCK_ERR_INVALID_SOCK
NET_CONN_ERR_INVALID_ARG
NET_CONN_ERR_INVALID_CONN
NET_CONN_ERR_NOT_USED
NET_OS_ERR_LOCK

RETURNED VALUE

DEF_OK, Socket transmit IP TOS successfully configured;

DEF_FAIL, otherwise.

REQUIRED CONFIGURATION

None.

NOTES / WARNINGS

None.

B-13-8 NetSock_CfgTxIP_TTL() (TCP/UDP)

Configure socket's transmit IP TTL.

FILES

net_sock.h/net_sock.c

PROTOTYPE

```
CPU_BOOLEAN NetSock_CfgTxIP_TTL(NET_SOCK_ID  sock_id,
                                NET_IP_TTL   ip_ttl
                                NET_ERR     *perr);
```

ARGUMENTS

sock_id This is the socket ID of socket to configure transmit IP TTL.

size Desired transmit IP TTL:

NET_IP_TTL_MIN	Minimum TTL transmit value (1)
NET_IP_TTL_MAX	Maximum TTL transmit value (255)
NET_IP_TTL_DFLT	Default TTL transmit value (128)
NET_IP_TTL_NONE	Replace with default TTL

perr Pointer to variable that will receive the return error code from this function:

NET_SOCK_ERR_NONE
NET_SOCK_ERR_NOT_USED
NET_SOCK_ERR_INVALID_STATE
NET_SOCK_ERR_INVALID_OP
NET_ERR_INIT_INCOMPLETE
NET_SOCK_ERR_INVALID_SOCK
NET_CONN_ERR_INVALID_ARG
NET_CONN_ERR_INVALID_CONN
NET_CONN_ERR_NOT_USED
NET_OS_ERR_LOCK

RETURNED VALUE

DEF_OK, Socket transmit IP TTL successfully configured;

DEF_FAIL, otherwise.

REQUIRED CONFIGURATION

None.

NOTES / WARNINGS

None.

B-13-9 NetSock_CfgTxIP_TTL_Multicast() (TCP/UDP)

Configure socket's transmit IP multicast TTL.

FILES

net_sock.h/net_sock.c

PROTOTYPE

```
CPU_BOOLEAN NetSock_CfgTxIP_TTL_Multicast(NET_SOCK_ID  sock_id,
                                          NET_IP_TTL   ip_ttl
                                          NET_ERR     *perr);
```

ARGUMENTS

sock_id This is the socket ID of socket to configure transmit IP TTL.

size Desired transmit IP multicast TTL:

NET_IP_TTL_MIN	Minimum TTL transmit value (1)
NET_IP_TTL_MAX	Maximum TTL transmit value (255)
NET_IP_TTL_DFLT	Default TTL transmit value (1)
NET_IP_TTL_NONE	Replace with default TTL

perr Pointer to variable that will receive the return error code from this function:

NET_SOCK_ERR_NONE
NET_SOCK_ERR_NOT_USED
NET_SOCK_ERR_INVALID_STATE
NET_SOCK_ERR_INVALID_OP
NET_SOCK_ERR_API_DIS
NET_ERR_INIT_INCOMPLETE
NET_SOCK_ERR_INVALID_SOCK
NET_CONN_ERR_INVALID_ARG
NET_CONN_ERR_INVALID_CONN
NET_CONN_ERR_NOT_USED
NET_OS_ERR_LOCK

RETURNED VALUE

`DEF_OK`, Socket transmit IP multicast TTL successfully configured;

`DEF_FAIL`, otherwise.

REQUIRED CONFIGURATION

Available only if NET_SOCK_CFG_FAMILY is configured for IPv4 sockets (see section C-15-1 "NET_SOCK_CFG_FAMILY" on page 740).

NOTES / WARNINGS

None.

B-13-10 NetSock_CfgTimeoutConnAcceptDflt() (TCP)

Set socket's connection accept timeout to configured-default value.

FILES

net_sock.h/net_sock.c

PROTOTYPE

```
CPU_BOOLEAN NetSock_CfgTimeoutConnAcceptDflt(NET_SOCK_ID  sock_id,
                                              NET_ERR     *perr);
```

ARGUMENTS

sock_id This is the socket ID returned by **NetSock_Open()/socket()** when the socket was created *or* by **NetSock_Accept()/accept()** when a connection was accepted.

perr Pointer to variable that will receive the return error code from this function:

NET_SOCK_ERR_NONE
NET_SOCK_ERR_NOT_USED
NET_SOCK_ERR_INVALID_SOCK
NET_ERR_INIT_INCOMPLETE
NET_OS_ERR_INVALID_TIME
NET_OS_ERR_LOCK

RETURNED VALUE

DEF_OK, Socket connection accept configured-default timeout successfully set;

DEF_FAIL, otherwise.

REQUIRED CONFIGURATION

Available only if NET_CFG_TRANSPORT_LAYER_SEL is configured for TCP (see section C-12-1 on page 736).

NOTES / WARNINGS

None.

B-13-11 NetSock_CfgTimeoutConnAcceptGet_ms() (TCP)

Get socket's connection accept timeout value.

FILES

net_sock.h/net_sock.c

PROTOTYPE

```
CPU_INT32U NetSock_CfgTimeoutConnAcceptGet_ms(NET_SOCK_ID  sock_id,
                                              NET_ERR     *perr);
```

ARGUMENTS

sock_id This is the socket ID returned by **NetSock_Open()/socket()** when the socket was created *or* by **NetSock_Accept()/accept()** when a connection was accepted.

perr Pointer to variable that will receive the return error code from this function:

NET_SOCK_ERR_NONE
NET_SOCK_ERR_NOT_USED
NET_SOCK_ERR_INVALID_SOCK
NET_ERR_INIT_INCOMPLETE
NET_OS_ERR_LOCK

RETURNED VALUE

0, on any errors;

NET_TMR_TIME_INFINITE, if infinite (i.e., no timeout) value configured.

Timeout in number of milliseconds, otherwise.

E

REQUIRED CONFIGURATION

Available only if NET_CFG_TRANSPORT_LAYER_SEL is configured for TCP (see section C-12-1 on page 736).

NOTES / WARNINGS

None.

B-13-12 NetSock_CfgTimeoutConnAcceptSet() (TCP)

Set socket's connection accept timeout value.

FILES

net_sock.h/net_sock.c

PROTOTYPE

```
CPU_BOOLEAN NetSock_CfgTimeoutConnAcceptSet(NET_SOCK_ID  sock_id,
                                            CPU_INT32U   timeout_ms,
                                            NET_ERR     *perr);
```

ARGUMENTS

sock_id — This is the socket ID returned by NetSock_Open()/socket() when the socket was created *or* by NetSock_Accept()/accept() when a connection was accepted.

timeout_ms — Desired timeout value:

NET_TMR_TIME_INFINITE, if infinite (i.e., no timeout) value desired.

In number of milliseconds, otherwise.

perr — Pointer to variable that will receive the return error code from this function:

NET_SOCK_ERR_NONE
NET_SOCK_ERR_NOT_USED
NET_SOCK_ERR_INVALID_SOCK
NET_ERR_INIT_INCOMPLETE
NET_OS_ERR_INVALID_TIME
NET_OS_ERR_LOCK

RETURNED VALUE

`DEF_OK`, Socket connection accept timeout successfully set;

`DEF_FAIL`, otherwise.

REQUIRED CONFIGURATION

Available only if `NET_CFG_TRANSPORT_LAYER_SEL` is configured for TCP (see section C-12-1 on page 736).

NOTES / WARNINGS

None.

B-13-13 NetSock_CfgTimeoutConnCloseDflt() (TCP)

Set socket's connection close timeout to configured-default value.

FILES

net_sock.h/net_sock.c

PROTOTYPE

```
CPU_BOOLEAN NetSock_CfgTimeoutConnCloseDflt(NET_SOCK_ID  sock_id,
                                             NET_ERR     *perr);
```

ARGUMENTS

sock_id This is the socket ID returned by **NetSock_Open()/socket()** when the socket was created *or* by **NetSock_Accept()/accept()** when a connection was accepted.

perr Pointer to variable that will receive the return error code from this function:

NET_SOCK_ERR_NONE
NET_SOCK_ERR_NOT_USED
NET_SOCK_ERR_INVALID_SOCK
NET_ERR_INIT_INCOMPLETE
NET_OS_ERR_INVALID_TIME
NET_OS_ERR_LOCK

RETURNED VALUE

DEF_OK, Socket connection close configured-default timeout successfully set;

DEF_FAIL, otherwise.

REQUIRED CONFIGURATION

Available only if `NET_CFG_TRANSPORT_LAYER_SEL` is configured for TCP (see section C-12-1 on page 736).

NOTES / WARNINGS

None.

B-13-14 NetSock_CfgTimeoutConnCloseGet_ms() (TCP)

Get socket's connection close timeout value.

FILES

net_sock.h/net_sock.c

PROTOTYPE

```
CPU_INT32U NetSock_CfgTimeoutConnCloseGet_ms(NET_SOCK_ID  sock_id,
                                             NET_ERR     *perr);
```

ARGUMENTS

sock_id This is the socket ID returned by NetSock_Open()/socket() when the socket was created *or* by NetSock_Accept()/accept() when a connection was accepted.

perr Pointer to variable that will receive the return error code from this function:

NET_SOCK_ERR_NONE
NET_SOCK_ERR_NOT_USED
NET_SOCK_ERR_INVALID_SOCK
NET_ERR_INIT_INCOMPLETE
NET_OS_ERR_LOCK

RETURNED VALUE

0, on any errors;

NET_TMR_TIME_INFINITE, if infinite (i.e., no timeout) value configured;

Timeout in number of milliseconds, otherwise.

REQUIRED CONFIGURATION

Available only if NET_CFG_TRANSPORT_LAYER_SEL is configured for TCP (see section C-12-1 on page 736).

NOTES / WARNINGS

None.

B-13-15 NetSock_CfgTimeoutConnCloseSet() (TCP)

Set socket's connection close timeout value.

FILES

net_sock.h/net_sock.c

PROTOTYPE

```
CPU_BOOLEAN NetSock_CfgTimeoutConnCloseSet(NET_SOCK_ID  sock_id,
                                           CPU_INT32U   timeout_ms,
                                           NET_ERR     *perr);
```

ARGUMENTS

sock_id This is the socket ID returned by **NetSock_Open()/socket()** when the socket was created *or* by **NetSock_Accept()/accept()** when a connection was accepted.

timeout_ms Desired timeout value:

NET_TMR_TIME_INFINITE, if infinite (i.e., no timeout) value desired.
In number of milliseconds, otherwise.

perr Pointer to variable that will receive the return error code from this function:

NET_SOCK_ERR_NONE
NET_SOCK_ERR_NOT_USED
NET_SOCK_ERR_INVALID_SOCK
NET_ERR_INIT_INCOMPLETE
NET_OS_ERR_INVALID_TIME
NET_OS_ERR_LOCK

RETURNED VALUE

DEF_OK, Socket connection close timeout successfully set;

DEF_FAIL, otherwise.

REQUIRED CONFIGURATION

Available only if NET_CFG_TRANSPORT_LAYER_SEL is configured for TCP (see section C-12-1 on page 736).

NOTES / WARNINGS

None.

B-13-16 NetSock_CfgTimeoutConnReqDflt() (TCP)

Set socket's connection request timeout to configured-default value.

FILES

net_sock.h/net_sock.c

PROTOTYPE

```
CPU_BOOLEAN NetSock_CfgTimeoutConnReqDflt(NET_SOCK_ID  sock_id,
                                          NET_ERR     *perr);
```

ARGUMENTS

sock_id This is the socket ID returned by **NetSock_Open()/socket()** when the socket was created *or* by **NetSock_Accept()/accept()** when a connection was accepted.

perr Pointer to variable that will receive the return error code from this function:

NET_SOCK_ERR_NONE
NET_SOCK_ERR_NOT_USED
NET_SOCK_ERR_INVALID_SOCK
NET_ERR_INIT_INCOMPLETE
NET_OS_ERR_INVALID_TIME
NET_OS_ERR_LOCK

RETURNED VALUE

DEF_OK, Socket connection request configured-default timeout successfully set;

DEF_FAIL, otherwise.

REQUIRED CONFIGURATION

Available only if **NET_CFG_TRANSPORT_LAYER_SEL** is configured for TCP (see section C-12-1 on page 736).

NOTES / WARNINGS

None.

B-13-17 NetSock_CfgTimeoutConnReqGet_ms() (TCP)

Get socket's connection request timeout value.

FILES

net_sock.h/net_sock.c

PROTOTYPE

```
CPU_INT32U NetSock_CfgTimeoutConnReqGet_ms(NET_SOCK_ID  sock_id,
                                           NET_ERR     *perr);
```

ARGUMENTS

sock_id This is the socket ID returned by **NetSock_Open()/socket()** when the socket was created *or* by **NetSock_Accept()/accept()** when a connection was accepted.

perr Pointer to variable that will receive the return error code from this function:

NET_SOCK_ERR_NONE
NET_SOCK_ERR_NOT_USED
NET_SOCK_ERR_INVALID_SOCK
NET_ERR_INIT_INCOMPLETE
NET_OS_ERR_LOCK

RETURNED VALUE

0, on any errors;

NET_TMR_TIME_INFINITE, if infinite (i.e., no timeout) value configured;

Timeout in number of milliseconds, otherwise.

REQUIRED CONFIGURATION

Available only if **NET_CFG_TRANSPORT_LAYER_SEL** is configured for TCP (see section C-12-1 on page 736).

NOTES / WARNINGS

None.

B-13-18 NetSock_CfgTimeoutConnReqSet() (TCP)

Set socket's connection request timeout value.

FILES

net_sock.h/net_sock.c

PROTOTYPE

```
CPU_BOOLEAN NetSock_CfgTimeoutConnReqSet(NET_SOCK_ID  sock_id,
                                         CPU_INT32U   timeout_ms,
                                         NET_ERR     *perr);
```

ARGUMENTS

sock_id This is the socket ID returned by **NetSock_Open()/socket()** when the socket was created *or* by **NetSock_Accept()/accept()** when a connection was accepted.

timeout_ms Desired timeout value:

NET_TMR_TIME_INFINITE, if infinite (i.e., no timeout) value desired.
In number of milliseconds, otherwise.

perr Pointer to variable that will receive the return error code from this function:

NET_SOCK_ERR_NONE
NET_SOCK_ERR_NOT_USED
NET_SOCK_ERR_INVALID_SOCK
NET_ERR_INIT_INCOMPLETE
NET_OS_ERR_INVALID_TIME
NET_OS_ERR_LOCK

RETURNED VALUE

`DEF_OK`, Socket connection request timeout successfully set;

`DEF_FAIL`, otherwise.

REQUIRED CONFIGURATION

Available only if `NET_CFG_TRANSPORT_LAYER_SEL` is configured for TCP (see section C-12-1 on page 736).

NOTES / WARNINGS

None.

B-13-19 NetSock_CfgTimeoutRxQ_Dflt() (TCP/UDP)

Set socket's connection receive queue timeout to configured-default value.

FILES

net_sock.h/net_sock.c

PROTOTYPE

```
CPU_BOOLEAN NetSock_CfgTimeoutRxQ_Dflt(NET_SOCK_ID  sock_id,
                                       NET_ERR     *perr);
```

ARGUMENTS

sock_id This is the socket ID returned by **NetSock_Open()/socket()** when the socket was created *or* by **NetSock_Accept()/accept()** when a connection was accepted.

perr Pointer to variable that will receive the return error code from this function:

NET_SOCK_ERR_NONE
NET_SOCK_ERR_NOT_USED
NET_SOCK_ERR_INVALID_SOCK
NET_SOCK_ERR_INVALID_TYPE
NET_SOCK_ERR_INVALID_PROTOCOL
NET_TCP_ERR_CONN_NOT_USED
NET_TCP_ERR_INVALID_CONN
NET_CONN_ERR_NOT_USED
NET_CONN_ERR_INVALID_CONN
NET_ERR_INIT_INCOMPLETE
NET_OS_ERR_INVALID_TIME
NET_OS_ERR_LOCK

RETURNED VALUE

`DEF_OK`, Socket receive queue configured-default timeout successfully set;

`DEF_FAIL`, otherwise.

REQUIRED CONFIGURATION

Available only if either **NET_CFG_TRANSPORT_LAYER_SEL** is configured for TCP (see section C-12-1 on page 736) and/or **NET_UDP_CFG_APP_API_SEL** is configured for sockets (see section C-13-1 on page 737).

NOTES / WARNINGS

None.

B-13-20 NetSock_CfgTimeoutRxQ_Get_ms() (TCP/UDP)

Get socket's receive queue timeout value.

FILES

net_sock.h/net_sock.c

PROTOTYPE

```
CPU_INT32U NetSock_CfgTimeoutRxQ_Get_ms(NET_SOCK_ID  sock_id,
                                        NET_ERR     *perr);
```

ARGUMENTS

sock_id This is the socket ID returned by **NetSock_Open()/socket()** when the socket was created *or* by **NetSock_Accept()/accept()** when a connection was accepted.

perr Pointer to variable that will receive the return error code from this function:

NET_SOCK_ERR_NONE
NET_SOCK_ERR_NOT_USED
NET_SOCK_ERR_INVALID_SOCK
NET_SOCK_ERR_INVALID_TYPE
NET_SOCK_ERR_INVALID_PROTOCOL
NET_TCP_ERR_CONN_NOT_USED
NET_TCP_ERR_INVALID_CONN
NET_CONN_ERR_NOT_USED
NET_CONN_ERR_INVALID_CONN
NET_ERR_INIT_INCOMPLETE
NET_OS_ERR_LOCK

RETURNED VALUE

0, on any errors;

NET_TMR_TIME_INFINITE, if infinite (i.e., no timeout) value configured;

Timeout in number of milliseconds, otherwise.

REQUIRED CONFIGURATION

Available only if either NET_CFG_TRANSPORT_LAYER_SEL is configured for TCP (see section C-12-1 on page 736) and/or NET_UDP_CFG_APP_API_SEL is configured for sockets (see section C-13-1 on page 737).

NOTES / WARNINGS

None.

B-13-21 NetSock_CfgTimeoutRxQ_Set() (TCP/UDP)

Set socket's connection receive queue timeout value.

FILES

net_sock.h/net_sock.c

PROTOTYPE

```
CPU_BOOLEAN NetSock_CfgTimeoutRxQ_Set(NET_SOCK_ID  sock_id,
                                      CPU_INT32U   timeout_ms,
                                      NET_ERR     *perr);
```

ARGUMENTS

sock_id This is the socket ID returned by **NetSock_Open()/socket()** when the socket was created *or* by **NetSock_Accept()/accept()** when a connection was accepted.

timeout_ms Desired timeout value:

NET_TMR_TIME_INFINITE, if infinite (i.e., no timeout) value desired.

In number of milliseconds, otherwise.

perr Pointer to variable that will receive the return error code from this function:

NET_SOCK_ERR_NONE
NET_SOCK_ERR_NOT_USED
NET_SOCK_ERR_INVALID_SOCK
NET_SOCK_ERR_INVALID_TYPE
NET_SOCK_ERR_INVALID_PROTOCOL
NET_TCP_ERR_CONN_NOT_USED
NET_TCP_ERR_INVALID_CONN
NET_CONN_ERR_NOT_USED
NET_CONN_ERR_INVALID_CONN
NET_ERR_INIT_INCOMPLETE
NET_OS_ERR_INVALID_TIME
NET_OS_ERR_LOCK

E

RETURNED VALUE

DEF_OK, Socket receive queue timeout successfully set;

DEF_FAIL, otherwise.

REQUIRED CONFIGURATION

Available only if either **NET_CFG_TRANSPORT_LAYER_SEL** is configured for TCP (see section C-12-1 on page 736) and/or **NET_UDP_CFG_APP_API_SEL** is configured for sockets (see section C-13-1 on page 737).

NOTES / WARNINGS

None.

B-13-22 NetSock_CfgTimeoutTxQ_Dflt() (TCP)

Set socket's connection transmit queue timeout to configured-default value.

FILES

net_sock.h/net_sock.c

PROTOTYPE

```
CPU_BOOLEAN NetSock_CfgTimeoutTxQ_Dflt(NET_SOCK_ID  sock_id,
                                       NET_ERR     *perr);
```

ARGUMENTS

sock_id This is the socket ID returned by **NetSock_Open()/socket()** when the socket was created *or* by **NetSock_Accept()/accept()** when a connection was accepted.

perr Pointer to variable that will receive the return error code from this function:

NET_SOCK_ERR_NONE
NET_SOCK_ERR_NOT_USED
NET_SOCK_ERR_INVALID_SOCK
NET_SOCK_ERR_INVALID_TYPE
NET_SOCK_ERR_INVALID_PROTOCOL
NET_TCP_ERR_CONN_NOT_USED
NET_TCP_ERR_INVALID_CONN
NET_CONN_ERR_NOT_USED
NET_CONN_ERR_INVALID_CONN
NET_ERR_INIT_INCOMPLETE
NET_OS_ERR_INVALID_TIME
NET_OS_ERR_LOCK

RETURNED VALUE

DEF_OK, Socket transmit queue configured-default timeout successfully set;

DEF_FAIL, otherwise.

REQUIRED CONFIGURATION

Available only if NET_CFG_TRANSPORT_LAYER_SEL is configured for TCP (see section C-12-1 on page 736).

NOTES / WARNINGS

None.

B-13-23 NetSock_CfgTimeoutTxQ_Get_ms() (TCP)

Get socket's transmit queue timeout value.

FILES

net_sock.h/net_sock.c

PROTOTYPE

```
CPU_INT32U NetSock_CfgTimeoutTxQ_Get_ms(NET_SOCK_ID  sock_id,
                                        NET_ERR     *perr);
```

ARGUMENTS

sock_id This is the socket ID returned by **NetSock_Open()/socket()** when the socket was created *or* by **NetSock_Accept()/accept()** when a connection was accepted.

perr Pointer to variable that will receive the return error code from this function:

NET_SOCK_ERR_NONE
NET_SOCK_ERR_NOT_USED
NET_SOCK_ERR_INVALID_SOCK
NET_SOCK_ERR_INVALID_TYPE
NET_SOCK_ERR_INVALID_PROTOCOL
NET_TCP_ERR_CONN_NOT_USED
NET_TCP_ERR_INVALID_CONN
NET_CONN_ERR_NOT_USED
NET_CONN_ERR_INVALID_CONN
NET_ERR_INIT_INCOMPLETE
NET_OS_ERR_LOCK

RETURNED VALUE

0, on any errors;

NET_TMR_TIME_INFINITE, if infinite (i.e., no timeout) value configured;

Timeout in number of milliseconds, otherwise.

REQUIRED CONFIGURATION

Available only if NET_CFG_TRANSPORT_LAYER_SEL is configured for TCP (see section C-12-1 on page 736).

NOTES / WARNINGS

None.

B-13-24 NetSock_CfgTimeoutTxQ_Set() (TCP)

Set socket's connection transmit queue timeout value.

FILES

net_sock.h/net_sock.c

PROTOTYPE

```
CPU_BOOLEAN NetSock_CfgTimeoutTxQ_Set(NET_SOCK_ID  sock_id,
                                      CPU_INT32U   timeout_ms,
                                      NET_ERR     *perr);
```

ARGUMENTS

sock_id This is the socket ID returned by **NetSock_Open()/socket()** when the socket was created *or* by **NetSock_Accept()/accept()** when a connection was accepted.

timeout_ms Desired timeout value:

NET_TMR_TIME_INFINITE, if infinite (i.e., no timeout) value desired.
In number of milliseconds, otherwise.

perr Pointer to variable that will receive the return error code from this function:

NET_SOCK_ERR_NONE
NET_SOCK_ERR_NOT_USED
NET_SOCK_ERR_INVALID_SOCK
NET_SOCK_ERR_INVALID_TYPE
NET_SOCK_ERR_INVALID_PROTOCOL
NET_TCP_ERR_CONN_NOT_USED
NET_TCP_ERR_INVALID_CONN
NET_CONN_ERR_NOT_USED
NET_CONN_ERR_INVALID_CONN
NET_ERR_INIT_INCOMPLETE
NET_OS_ERR_INVALID_TIME
NET_OS_ERR_LOCK

RETURNED VALUE

`DEF_OK`, Socket transmit queue timeout successfully set;

`DEF_FAIL`, otherwise.

REQUIRED CONFIGURATION

Available only if `NET_CFG_TRANSPORT_LAYER_SEL` is configured for TCP (see section C-12-1 on page 736).

NOTES / WARNINGS

None.

B-13-25 NetSock_Close() / close() (TCP/UDP)

Terminate communication and free a socket.

FILES

net_sock.h/net_sock.c
net_bsd.h/net_bsd.c

PROTOTYPES

```
NET_SOCK_RTN_CODE NetSock_Close(NET_SOCK_ID  sock_id,
                                NET_ERR     *perr);

int close(int sock_id);
```

ARGUMENTS

sock_id	This is the socket ID returned by NetSock_Open()/socket() when the socket was created *or* by NetSock_Accept()/accept() when a connection was accepted.

perr	Pointer to variable that will receive the return error code from this function:

NET_SOCK_ERR_NONE
NET_SOCK_ERR_NOT_USED
NET_SOCK_ERR_CLOSED
NET_SOCK_ERR_INVALID_SOCK
NET_SOCK_ERR_INVALID_FAMILY
NET_SOCK_ERR_INVALID_STATE
NET_SOCK_ERR_CLOSE_IN_PROGRESS
NET_SOCK_ERR_CONN_SIGNAL_TIMEOUT
NET_SOCK_ERR_CONN_FAIL
NET_SOCK_ERR_FAULT
NET_CONN_ERR_NULL_PTR
NET_CONN_ERR_NOT_USED
NET_CONN_ERR_INVALID_CONN
NET_CONN_ERR_INVALID_ADDR_LEN

NET_CONN_ERR_ADDR_IN_USE
NET_ERR_INIT_INCOMPLETE
NET_OS_ERR_LOCK

RETURNED VALUE

NET_SOCK_BSD_ERR_NONE/0, if successful;

NET_SOCK_BSD_ERR_CLOSE/-1, otherwise.

REQUIRED CONFIGURATION

NetSock_Close() is available only if either **NET_CFG_TRANSPORT_LAYER_SEL** is configured for TCP (see section C-12-1 on page 736) and/or **NET_UDP_CFG_APP_API_SEL** is configured for sockets (see section C-13-1 on page 737).

In addition, **close()** is available only if **NET_BSD_CFG_API_EN** is enabled (see section C-17-1 on page 747).

NOTES / WARNINGS

After closing a socket, no further operations should be performed with the socket.

B-13-26 NetSock_Conn() / connect() (TCP/UDP)

Connect a local socket to a remote socket address. If the local socket was not previously bound to a local address and port, the socket is bound to the default interface's default address and a random port number. When successful, a connected socket has access to both local and remote socket addresses.

Although both UDP and TCP sockets may both connect to remote servers or hosts, UDP and TCP connections are inherently different:

For TCP sockets, `NetSock_Conn()/connect()` returns successfully only after completing the three-way TCP handshake with the remote TCP host. Success implies the existence of a dedicated connection to the remote socket similar to a telephone connection. This dedicated connection is maintained for the life of the connection until one or both sides close the connection.

For UDP sockets, `NetSock_Conn()/connect()` merely saves the remote socket's address for the local socket for convenience. All UDP datagrams from the socket will be transmitted to the remote socket. This pseudo-connection is not permanent and may be re-configured at any time.

FILES

`net_sock.h/net_sock.c`
`net_bsd.h/net_bsd.c`

PROTOTYPES

```
NET_SOCK_RTN_CODE NetSock_Conn(NET_SOCK_ID          sock_id,
                               NET_SOCK_ADDR       *paddr_remote,
                               NET_SOCK_ADDR_LEN    addr_len,
                               NET_ERR             *perr);


int connect(int                sock_id,
            struct sockaddr   *paddr_remote,
            socklen_t          addr_len);
```

ARGUMENTS

sock_id This is the socket ID returned by **NetSock_Open()/socket()** when the socket was created.

paddr_remote Pointer to a socket address structure (see section 8-2 "Socket Interface" on page 208) which contains the remote socket address to connect the socket to.

addr_len Size of the socket address structure which *must* be passed the size of the socket address structure [e.g., **sizeof(NET_SOCK_ADDR_IP)**].

perr Pointer to variable that will receive the return error code from this function:

NET_SOCK_ERR_NONE
NET_SOCK_ERR_NOT_USED
NET_SOCK_ERR_CLOSED
NET_SOCK_ERR_INVALID_SOCK
NET_SOCK_ERR_INVALID_FAMILY
NET_SOCK_ERR_INVALID_PROTOCOL
NET_SOCK_ERR_INVALID_TYPE
NET_SOCK_ERR_INVALID_STATE
NET_SOCK_ERR_INVALID_OP
NET_SOCK_ERR_INVALID_ADDR
NET_SOCK_ERR_INVALID_ADDR_LEN
NET_SOCK_ERR_ADDR_IN_USE
NET_SOCK_ERR_PORT_NBR_NONE_AVAIL
NET_SOCK_ERR_CONN_SIGNAL_TIMEOUT
NET_SOCK_ERR_CONN_IN_USE
NET_SOCK_ERR_CONN_FAIL
NET_SOCK_ERR_FAULT
NET_IF_ERR_INVALID_IF
NET_IP_ERR_ADDR_NONE_AVAIL
NET_IP_ERR_ADDR_CFG_IN_PROGRESS
NET_CONN_ERR_NULL_PTR
NET_CONN_ERR_NOT_USED
NET_CONN_ERR_NONE_AVAIL
NET_CONN_ERR_INVALID_CONN
NET_CONN_ERR_INVALID_FAMILY
NET_CONN_ERR_INVALID_TYPE

NET_CONN_ERR_INVALID_PROTOCOL_IX
NET_CONN_ERR_INVALID_ADDR_LEN
NET_CONN_ERR_ADDR_NOT_USED
NET_CONN_ERR_ADDR_IN_USE
NET_ERR_INIT_INCOMPLETE
NET_OS_ERR_LOCK

RETURNED VALUE

NET_SOCK_BSD_ERR_NONE/0, if successful;

NET_SOCK_BSD_ERR_CONN/-1, otherwise.

REQUIRED CONFIGURATION

NetSock_Conn() is available only if either NET_CFG_TRANSPORT_LAYER_SEL is configured for TCP (see section C-12-1 on page 736) and/or NET_UDP_CFG_APP_API_SEL is configured for sockets (see section C-13-1 on page 737).

In addition, connect() is available only if NET_BSD_CFG_API_EN is enabled (see section C-17-1 on page 747).

NOTES / WARNINGS

See section 8-2 “Socket Interface” on page 208 for socket address structure formats.

B-13-27 NET_SOCK_DESC_CLR() / FD_CLR() (TCP/UDP)

Remove a socket file descriptor ID as a member of a file descriptor set. See also section B-13-39 "NetSock_Sel() / select() (TCP/UDP)" on page 659.

FILES

net_sock.h

PROTOTYPE

```
NET_SOCK_DESC_CLR(desc_nbr, pdesc_set);
```

ARGUMENTS

desc_nbr This is the socket file descriptor ID returned by **NetSock_Open()/socket()** when the socket was created *or* by **NetSock_Accept()/accept()** when a connection was accepted.

pdesc_set Pointer to a socket file descriptor set.

RETURNED VALUE

None.

REQUIRED CONFIGURATION

Available only if either **NET_CFG_TRANSPORT_LAYER_SEL** is configured for TCP (see section C-12-1 on page 736) and/or **NET_UDP_CFG_APP_API_SEL** is configured for sockets (see section C-13-1 on page 737) *and* if **NET_SOCK_CFG_SEL_EN** is enabled (see section C-15-4 on page 741).

In addition, **FD_CLR()** is available only if **NET_BSD_CFG_API_EN** is enabled (see section C-17-1 on page 747).

NOTES / WARNINGS

`NetSock_Sel()/select()` checks or waits for available operations or error conditions on any of the socket file descriptor members of a socket file descriptor set.

No errors are returned even if the socket file descriptor ID or the file descriptor set is invalid, or the socket file descriptor ID is *not* set in the file descriptor set.

B-13-28 NET_SOCK_DESC_COPY() (TCP/UDP)

Copy a file descriptor set to another file descriptor set. See also section B-13-39 "NetSock_Sel() / select() (TCP/UDP)" on page 659.

FILES

net_sock.h

PROTOTYPE

```
NET_SOCK_DESC_COPY(pdesc_set_dest, pdesc_set_src);
```

ARGUMENTS

pdesc_set_dest — Pointer to the destination socket file descriptor set.

pdesc_set_src — Pointer to the source socket file descriptor set to copy.

RETURNED VALUE

None.

REQUIRED CONFIGURATION

Available only if either **NET_CFG_TRANSPORT_LAYER_SEL** is configured for TCP (see section C-12-1 on page 736) and/or **NET_UDP_CFG_APP_API_SEL** is configured for sockets (see section C-13-1 on page 737) ***and* if NET_SOCK_CFG_SEL_EN** is enabled (see section C-15-4 on page 741).

NOTES / WARNINGS

NetSock_Sel()/select() checks or waits for available operations or error conditions on any of the socket file descriptor members of a socket file descriptor set.

No errors are returned even if either file descriptor set is invalid.

B-13-29 NET_SOCK_DESC_INIT() / FD_ZERO() (TCP/UDP)

Initialize/zero-clear a file descriptor set. See also section B-13-39 "NetSock_Sel() / select() (TCP/UDP)" on page 659.

FILES

net_sock.h

PROTOTYPE

```
NET_SOCK_DESC_INIT(pdesc_set);
```

ARGUMENTS

pdesc_set   Pointer to a socket file descriptor set.

RETURNED VALUE

None.

REQUIRED CONFIGURATION

Available only if either NET_CFG_TRANSPORT_LAYER_SEL is configured for TCP (see section C-12-1 on page 736) and/or NET_UDP_CFG_APP_API_SEL is configured for sockets (see section C-13-1 on page 737) *and* if NET_SOCK_CFG_SEL_EN is enabled (see section C-15-4 on page 741).

In addition, FD_ZERO() is available only if NET_BSD_CFG_API_EN is enabled (see section C-17-1 on page 747).

NOTES / WARNINGS

NetSock_Sel()/select() checks or waits for available operations or error conditions on any of the socket file descriptor members of a socket file descriptor set.

No errors are returned even if the file descriptor set is invalid.

B-13-30 NET_SOCK_DESC_IS_SET() / FD_IS_SET() (TCP/UDP)

Check if a socket file descriptor ID is a member of a file descriptor set. See also section B-13-39 "NetSock_Sel() / select() (TCP/UDP)" on page 659.

FILES

net_sock.h

PROTOTYPE

```
NET_SOCK_DESC_IS_SET(desc_nbr, pdesc_set);
```

ARGUMENTS

desc_nbr This is the socket file descriptor ID returned by NetSock_Open()/socket() when the socket was created *or* by NetSock_Accept()/accept() when a connection was accepted.

pdesc_set Pointer to a socket file descriptor set.

RETURNED VALUE

1, if the socket file descriptor ID is a member of the file descriptor set;

0, otherwise.

REQUIRED CONFIGURATION

Available only if either NET_CFG_TRANSPORT_LAYER_SEL is configured for TCP (see section C-12-1 on page 736) and/or NET_UDP_CFG_APP_API_SEL is configured for sockets (see section C-13-1 on page 737) *and* if NET_SOCK_CFG_SEL_EN is enabled (see section C-15-4 on page 741).

In addition, FD_IS_SET() is available only if NET_BSD_CFG_API_EN is enabled (see section C-17-1 on page 747).

NOTES / WARNINGS

NetSock_Sel()/select() checks or waits for available operations or error conditions on any of the socket file descriptor members of a socket file descriptor set.

0 is returned if the socket file descriptor ID or the file descriptor set is invalid.

B-13-31 NET_SOCK_DESC_SET() / FD_SET() (TCP/UDP)

Add a socket file descriptor ID as a member of a file descriptor set. See also section B-13-39 "NetSock_Sel() / select() (TCP/UDP)" on page 659.

FILES

`net_sock.h`

PROTOTYPE

```
NET_SOCK_DESC_SET(desc_nbr, pdesc_set);
```

ARGUMENTS

desc_nbr This is the socket file descriptor ID returned by `NetSock_Open()/socket()` when the socket was created *or* by `NetSock_Accept()/accept()` when a connection was accepted.

pdesc_set Pointer to a socket file descriptor set.

RETURNED VALUE

None.

REQUIRED CONFIGURATION

Available only if either `NET_CFG_TRANSPORT_LAYER_SEL` is configured for TCP (see section C-12-1 on page 736) and/or `NET_UDP_CFG_APP_API_SEL` is configured for sockets (see section C-13-1 on page 737) *and* if `NET_SOCK_CFG_SEL_EN` is enabled (see section C-15-4 on page 741). In addition, `FD_SET()` is available only if `NET_BSD_CFG_API_EN` is enabled (see section C-17-1 on page 747).

NOTES / WARNINGS

`NetSock_Sel()/select()` checks or waits for available operations or error conditions on any of the socket file descriptor members of a socket file descriptor set.

No errors are returned even if the socket file descriptor ID or the file descriptor set is invalid, or the socket file descriptor ID is *not* cleared in the file descriptor set.

B-13-32 NetSock_GetConnTransportID()

Gets a socket's transport layer connection handle ID (e.g., TCP connection ID) if available.

FILES

net_sock.h/net_sock.c

PROTOTYPE

```
NET_CONN_ID NetSock_GetConnTransportID(NET_SOCK_ID  sock_id,
                                       NET_ERR     *perr);
```

ARGUMENTS

sock_id — This is the socket ID returned by NetSock_Open()/socket() when the socket was created *or* by NetSock_Accept()/accept() when a connection was accepted.

perr — Pointer to variable that will receive the return error code from this function:

NET_SOCK_ERR_NONE
NET_SOCK_ERR_NOT_USED
NET_SOCK_ERR_INVALID_SOCK
NET_SOCK_ERR_INVALID_TYPE
NET_CONN_ERR_NOT_USED
NET_CONN_ERR_INVALID_CONN
NET_ERR_INIT_INCOMPLETE
NET_OS_ERR_LOCK

RETURNED VALUE

Socket's transport connection handle ID (e.g., TCP connection ID), if no errors.

NET_CONN_ID_NONE, otherwise.

REQUIRED CONFIGURATION

Available only if either NET_CFG_TRANSPORT_LAYER_SEL is configured for TCP (see section C-12-1 on page 736) and/or NET_UDP_CFG_APP_API_SEL is configured for sockets (see section C-13-1 on page 737).

NOTES / WARNINGS

None.

B-13-33 NetSock_IsConn() (TCP/UDP)

Check if a socket is connected to a remote socket.

FILES

net_sock.h/net_sock.c

PROTOTYPE

```
CPU_BOOLEAN NetSock_IsConn(NET_SOCK_ID  sock_id,
                           NET_ERR     *perr);
```

ARGUMENTS

sock_id This is the socket ID returned by **NetSock_Open()/socket()** when the socket was created *or* by **NetSock_Accept()/accept()** when a connection was accepted.

perr Pointer to variable that will receive the return error code from this function:

NET_SOCK_ERR_NONE
NET_SOCK_ERR_NOT_USED
NET_SOCK_ERR_INVALID_SOCK
NET_ERR_INIT_INCOMPLETE
NET_OS_ERR_LOCK

RETURNED VALUE

DEF_YES if the socket is valid and connected;

DEF_NO otherwise.

REQUIRED CONFIGURATION

Available only if either NET_CFG_TRANSPORT_LAYER_SEL is configured for TCP (see section C-12-1 on page 736) and/or NET_UDP_CFG_APP_API_SEL is configured for sockets (see section C-13-1 on page 737).

NOTES / WARNINGS

None.

B-13-34 NetSock_Listen() / listen() (TCP)

Set a socket to accept incoming connections. The socket must already be bound to a local address. If successful, incoming TCP connection requests addressed to the socket's local address will be queued until accepted by the socket (see section B-13-1 "NetSock_Accept() / accept() (TCP)" on page 583).

FILES

net_sock.h/net_sock.c
net_bsd.h/net_bsd.c

PROTOTYPES

```
NET_SOCK_RTN_CODE NetSock_Listen(NET_SOCK_ID      sock_id,
                                 NET_SOCK_Q_SIZE  sock_q_size,
                                 NET_ERR         *perr);


int listen(int sock_id,
           int sock_q_size);
```

ARGUMENTS

sock_id This is the socket ID returned by **NetSock_Open()/socket()** when the socket was created.

sock_q_size Maximum number of new connections allowed to be waiting. In other words, this argument specifies the maximum queue length of pending connections while the listening socket is busy servicing the current request.

perr Pointer to variable that will receive the return error code from this function:

NET_SOCK_ERR_NONE
NET_SOCK_ERR_NOT_USED
NET_SOCK_ERR_CLOSED
NET_SOCK_ERR_INVALID_SOCK
NET_SOCK_ERR_INVALID_FAMILY
NET_SOCK_ERR_INVALID_PROTOCOL
NET_SOCK_ERR_INVALID_TYPE
NET_SOCK_ERR_INVALID_STATE

NET_SOCK_ERR_INVALID_OP
NET_SOCK_ERR_CONN_FAIL
NET_CONN_ERR_NOT_USED
NET_CONN_ERR_INVALID_CONN
NET_ERR_INIT_INCOMPLETE
NET_OS_ERR_LOCK

RETURNED VALUE

NET_SOCK_BSD_ERR_NONE/0, if successful;

NET_SOCK_BSD_ERR_LISTEN/-1, otherwise.

REQUIRED CONFIGURATION

NetSock_Listen() is available only if either **NET_CFG_TRANSPORT_LAYER_SEL** is configured for TCP (see section C-12-1 on page 736) and/or **NET_UDP_CFG_APP_API_SEL** is configured for sockets (see section C-13-1 on page 737).

In addition, **listen()** is available only if **NET_BSD_CFG_API_EN** is enabled (see section C-17-1 on page 747).

NOTES / WARNINGS

None.

B-13-35 NetSock_Open() / socket() (TCP/UDP)

Create a datagram (i.e., UDP) or stream (i.e., TCP) type socket.

FILES

net_sock.h/net_sock.c
net_bsd.h/net_bsd.c

PROTOTYPES

```
NET_SOCK_ID NetSock_Open(NET_SOCK_PROTOCOL_FAMILY  protocol_family,
                         NET_SOCK_TYPE             sock_type,
                         NET_SOCK_PROTOCOL         protocol,
                         NET_ERR                  *perr);

int socket(int protocol_family,
           int sock_type,
           int protocol);
```

ARGUMENTS

`protocol_family` This field establishes the socket protocol family domain. Always use `NET_SOCK_FAMILY_IP_V4/PF_INET` for TCP/IP sockets.

`sock_type` Socket type:

`NET_SOCK_TYPE_DATAGRAM/PF_DGRAM` for datagram sockets (i.e., UDP)

`NET_SOCK_TYPE_STREAM/PF_STREAM` for stream sockets (i.e., TCP)

`NET_SOCK_TYPE_DATAGRAM` sockets preserve message boundaries. Applications that exchange single request and response messages are examples of datagram communication.

`NET_SOCK_TYPE_STREAM` sockets provides a reliable byte-stream connection, where bytes are received from the remote application in the same order as they were sent. File transfer and terminal emulation are examples of applications that require this type of protocol.

protocol Socket protocol:

NET_SOCK_PROTOCOL_UDP/IPPROTO_UDP for UDP

NET_SOCK_PROTOCOL_TCP/IPPROTO_TCP for TCP

0 for default-protocol:

UDP for NET_SOCK_TYPE_DATAGRAM/PF_DGRAM

TCP for NET_SOCK_TYPE_STREAM/PF_STREAM

perr Pointer to variable that will receive the return error code from this function:

NET_SOCK_ERR_NONE
NET_SOCK_ERR_NONE_AVAIL
NET_SOCK_ERR_INVALID_FAMILY
NET_SOCK_ERR_INVALID_PROTOCOL
NET_SOCK_ERR_INVALID_TYPE
NET_ERR_INIT_INCOMPLETE
NET_OS_ERR_LOCK

The table below shows you the different ways you can specify the three arguments.

TCP/IP Protocol	Arguments		
	protocol_family	**sock_type**	**protocol**
UDP	NET_SOCK_FAMILY_IP_V4	NET_SOCK_TYPE_DATAGRAM	NET_SOCK_PROTOCOL_UDP
UDP	NET_SOCK_FAMILY_IP_V4	NET_SOCK_TYPE_DATAGRAM	0
TCP	NET_SOCK_FAMILY_IP_V4	NET_SOCK_TYPE_STREAM	ET_SOCK_PROTOCOL_TCP
TCP	NET_SOCK_FAMILY_IP_V4	NET_SOCK_TYPE_STREAM	0

RETURNED VALUE

Returns a non-negative socket descriptor ID for the new socket connection, if successful;

NET_SOCK_BSD_ERR_OPEN/-1 otherwise.

REQUIRED CONFIGURATION

NetSock_Open() is available only if either **NET_CFG_TRANSPORT_LAYER_SEL** is configured for TCP (see section C-12-1 on page 736) and/or **NET_UDP_CFG_APP_API_SEL** is configured for sockets (see section C-13-1 on page 737).

In addition, **socket()** is available only if **NET_BSD_CFG_API_EN** is enabled (see section C-17-1 on page 747).

NOTES / WARNINGS

The family, type, and protocol of a socket is fixed once a socket is created. In other words, you cannot change a TCP stream socket to a UDP datagram socket (or vice versa) at run-time.

To connect two sockets, both sockets must share the same socket family, type, and protocol.

B-13-36 NetSock_PoolStatGet()

Get Network Sockets' statistics pool.

FILES

net_sock.h/net_sock.c

PROTOTYPE

```
NET_STAT_POOL NetSock_PoolStatGet(void);
```

ARGUMENTS

None.

RETURNED VALUE

Network Sockets' statistics pool, if no errors.

NULL statistics pool, otherwise.

REQUIRED CONFIGURATION

Available only if either NET_CFG_TRANSPORT_LAYER_SEL is configured for TCP (see section C-12-1 on page 736) and/or NET_UDP_CFG_APP_API_SEL is configured for sockets (see section C-13-1 on page 737).

NOTES / WARNINGS

None.

B-13-37 NetSock_PoolStatResetMaxUsed()

Reset Network Sockets' statistics pool's maximum number of entries used.

FILES

net_sock.h/net_sock.c

PROTOTYPE

```
void NetSock_PoolStatResetMaxUsed(void);
```

ARGUMENTS

None.

RETURNED VALUE

None.

REQUIRED CONFIGURATION

Available only if either NET_CFG_TRANSPORT_LAYER_SEL is configured for TCP (see section C-12-1 on page 736) and/or NET_UDP_CFG_APP_API_SEL is configured for sockets (see section C-13-1 on page 737).

NOTES / WARNINGS

None.

B-13-38 NetSock_RxData() / recv() (TCP) NetSock_RxDataFrom() / recvfrom() (UDP)

Copy up to a specified number of bytes received from a remote socket into an application memory buffer.

FILES

net_sock.h/net_sock.c
net_bsd.h/net_bsd.c

PROTOTYPES

```
NET_SOCK_RTN_CODE NetSock_RxData(NET_SOCK_ID      sock_id,
                                 void            *pdata_buf,
                                 CPU_INT16U       data_buf_len,
                                 CPU_INT16S       flags,
                                 NET_ERR         *perr);

NET_SOCK_RTN_CODE NetSock_RxDataFrom(NET_SOCK_ID      sock_id,
                                     void            *pdata_buf,
                                     CPU_INT16U       data_buf_len,
                                     CPU_INT16S       flags,
                                     NET_SOCK_ADDR   *paddr_remote,
                                     NET_SOCK_ADDR_  *paddr_len,
                                     void            *pip_opts_buf,
                                     CPU_INT08U       ip_opts_buf_len,
                                     CPU_INT08U      *pip_opts_len,
                                     NET_ERR         *perr);

ssize_t recv(int      sock_id,
             void    *pdata_buf,
             _size_t  data_buf_len,
             int      flags);

ssize_t recvfrom(int                sock_id,
                 void              *pdata_buf,
                 _size_t            data_buf_len,
                 int                flags,
                 struct sockaddr   *paddr_remote,
                 socklen_t         *paddr_len);
```

ARGUMENTS

sock_id This is the socket ID returned by **NetSock_Open()/socket()** when the socket was created *or* by **NetSock_Accept()/accept()** when a connection was accepted.

pdata_buf Pointer to the application memory buffer to receive data.

data_buf_len Size of the destination application memory buffer (in bytes).

flags Flag to select receive options; bit-field flags logically **OR**'d:

NET_SOCK_FLAG_NONE/0	No socket flags selected
NET_SOCK_FLAG_RX_DATA_PEEK/ MSG_PEEK	Receive socket data without consuming it
NET_SOCK_FLAG_RX_NO_BLOCK/ MSG_DONTWAIT	Receive socket data without blocking

In most cases, this flag would be set to **NET_SOCK_FLAG_NONE/0**.

paddr_remote Pointer to a socket address structure (see section 8-2 "Socket Interface" on page 208) to return the remote host address that sent the received data.

paddr_len Pointer to the size of the socket address structure which *must* be passed the size of the socket address structure [e.g., **sizeof(NET_SOCK_ADDR_IP)**]. Returns size of the accepted connection's socket address structure, if no errors; returns 0, otherwise.

pip_opts_buf Pointer to buffer to receive possible IP options.

pip_opts_len Pointer to variable that will receive the return size of any received IP options.

perr Pointer to variable that will receive the return error code from this function:

NET_SOCK_ERR_NONE
NET_SOCK_ERR_NULL_PTR
NET_SOCK_ERR_NULL_SIZE
NET_SOCK_ERR_NOT_USED
NET_SOCK_ERR_CLOSED

NET_SOCK_ERR_INVALID_SOCK
NET_SOCK_ERR_INVALID_FAMILY
NET_SOCK_ERR_INVALID_PROTOCOL
NET_SOCK_ERR_INVALID_TYPE
NET_SOCK_ERR_INVALID_STATE
NET_SOCK_ERR_INVALID_OP
NET_SOCK_ERR_INVALID_FLAG
NET_SOCK_ERR_INVALID_ADDR_LEN
NET_SOCK_ERR_INVALID_DATA_SIZE
NET_SOCK_ERR_CONN_FAIL
NET_SOCK_ERR_FAULT
NET_SOCK_ERR_RX_Q_EMPTY
NET_SOCK_ERR_RX_Q_CLOSED
NET_ERR_RX
NET_CONN_ERR_NULL_PTR
NET_CONN_ERR_NOT_USED
NET_CONN_ERR_INVALID_CONN
NET_CONN_ERR_INVALID_ADDR_LEN
NET_CONN_ERR_ADDR_NOT_USED
NET_ERR_INIT_INCOMPLETE
NET_OS_ERR_LOCK

RETURNED VALUE

Positive number of bytes received, if successful;

NET_SOCK_BSD_RTN_CODE_CONN_CLOSED/0, if the socket is closed;

NET_SOCK_BSD_ERR_RX/-1, otherwise.

BLOCKING VS NON-BLOCKING

The default setting for µC/TCP-IP is blocking. However, this setting can be changed at compile time by setting the NET_SOCK_CFG_BLOCK_SEL (see section C-15-3 on page 741) to one of the following values:

NET_SOCK_BLOCK_SEL_DFLT sets blocking mode to the default, or blocking, unless modified by run-time options.

NET_SOCK_BLOCK_SEL_BLOCK sets the blocking mode to blocking. This means that a socket receive function will wait forever, until at least one byte of data is available to return or the socket connection is closed, unless a timeout is specified by NetSock_CfgTimeoutRxQ_Set() [See section B-13-21 on page 624].

NET_SOCK_BLOCK_SEL_NO_BLOCK sets the blocking mode to non-blocking. This means that a socket receive function will *not* wait but immediately return either any available data, socket connection closed, or an error indicating no available data or other possible socket faults. Your application will have to "poll" the socket on a regular basis to receive data.

The current version of µC/TCP-IP selects blocking or non-blocking at compile time for all sockets. A future version may allow the selection of blocking or non-blocking at the individual socket level. However, each socket receive call can pass the NET_SOCK_FLAG_RX_NO_BLOCK/MSG_DONTWAIT flag to disable blocking on that call.

REQUIRED CONFIGURATION

NetSock_RxData()/NetSock_RxDataFrom() is available only if NET_CFG_TRANSPORT_LAYER_SEL is configured for TCP (see section C-12-1 on page 736) and/or NET_UDP_CFG_APP_API_SEL is configured for sockets (see section C-13-1 on page 737).

In addition, recv()/recvfrom() is available only if NET_BSD_CFG_API_EN is enabled (see section C-17-1 on page 747).

NOTES / WARNINGS

TCP sockets typically use NetSock_RxData()/recv(), whereas UDP sockets typically use NetSock_RxDataFrom()/recvfrom().

For stream sockets (i.e., TCP), bytes are guaranteed to be received in the same order as they were transmitted, without omissions.

For datagram sockets (i.e., UDP), each receive returns the data from exactly one send but datagram order and delivery is not guaranteed. Also, if the application memory buffer is not big enough to receive an entire datagram, the datagram's data is truncated to the size of the memory buffer and the remaining data is discarded.

Only some receive flag options are implemented. If other flag options are requested, an error is returned so that flag options are *not* silently ignored.

E

B-13-39 NetSock_Sel() / select() (TCP/UDP)

Check if any sockets are ready for available read or write operations or error conditions.

FILES

net_sock.h/net_sock.c
net_bsd.h/net_bsd.c

PROTOTYPES

```
NET_SOCK_RTN_CODE NetSock_Sel(NET_SOCK_QTY      sock_nbr_max,
                              NET_SOCK_DESC    *psock_desc_rd,
                              NET_SOCK_DESC    *psock_desc_wr,
                              NET_SOCK_DESC    *psock_desc_err,
                              NET_SOCK_TIMEOUT *ptimeout,
                              NET_ERR          *perr);

int select(int             desc_nbr_max,
           struct fd_set   *pdesc_rd,
           struct fd_set   *pdesc_wr,
           struct fd_set   *pdesc_err,
           struct timeval  *ptimeout);
```

ARGUMENTS

sock_nbr_max Specifies the maximum number of socket file descriptors in the file descriptor sets.

psock_desc_rd Pointer to a set of socket file descriptors to:

- Check for available read operations.
- Returns the actual socket file descriptors ready for available read operations, if no errors;
    - Returns the initial, non-modified set of socket file descriptors, on any errors;
    - Returns a null-valued (i.e., zero-cleared) descriptor set, if any timeout expires.

psock_desc_wr Pointer to a set of socket file descriptors to:

- Check for available write operations.
- Returns the actual socket file descriptors ready for available write operations, if no errors;
  - Returns the initial, non-modified set of socket file descriptors, on any errors;
  - Returns a null-valued (i.e., zero-cleared) descriptor set, if any timeout expires.

psock_desc_err Pointer to a set of socket file descriptors to:

- Check for any available socket errors.
- Returns the actual socket file descriptors ready with any pending errors;
  - Returns the initial, non-modified set of socket file descriptors, on any errors;
  - Returns a null-valued (i.e., zero-cleared) descriptor set, if any timeout expires.

ptimeout Pointer to a timeout argument.

perr Pointer to variable that will receive the error code from this function:

```
NET_SOCK_ERR_NONE
NET_SOCK_ERR_TIMEOUT
NET_ERR_INIT_INCOMPLETE
NET_SOCK_ERR_INVALID_DESC
NET_SOCK_ERR_INVALID_TIMEOUT
NET_SOCK_ERR_INVALID_SOCK
NET_SOCK_ERR_INVALID_TYPE
NET_SOCK_ERR_NOT_USED
NET_SOCK_ERR_EVENTS_NBR_MAX
NET_OS_ERR_LOCK
```

RETURNED VALUE

Returns the number of sockets ready with available operations, if successful;

NET_SOCK_BSD_RTN_CODE_TIMEOUT/0, upon timeout;

NET_SOCK_BSD_ERR_SEL/-1, otherwise.

REQUIRED CONFIGURATION

NetSock_Sel() is available only if either NET_CFG_TRANSPORT_LAYER_SEL is configured for TCP (see section C-12-1 on page 736) and/or NET_UDP_CFG_APP_API_SEL is configured for sockets (see section C-13-1 on page 737) *and* if NET_SOCK_CFG_SEL_EN is enabled (see section C-15-4 on page 741).

In addition, select() is available only if NET_BSD_CFG_API_EN is enabled (see section C-17-1 on page 747).

NOTES / WARNINGS

Supports socket file descriptors *only* (i.e., socket ID numbers).

The descriptor macro's is used to prepare and decode socket file descriptor sets (see section B-13-27 on page 637 through section B-13-31 on page 643).

See "net_sock.c NetSock_Sel() Note #3" for more details.

B-13-40 NetSock_TxData() / send() (TCP) NetSock_TxDataTo() / sendto() (UDP)

Copy bytes from an application memory buffer into a socket to send to a remote socket.

FILES

net_sock.h/net_sock.c
net_bsd.h/net_bsd.c

PROTOTYPES

```
NET_SOCK_RTN_CODE NetSock_TxData(NET_SOCK_ID  sock_id,
                                 void        *p_data,
                                 CPU_INT16U   data_len,
                                 CPU_INT16S   flags,
                                 NET_ERR     *perr);

NET_SOCK_RTN_CODE NetSock_TxDataTo(NET_SOCK_ID        sock_id,
                                   void              *p_data,
                                   CPU_INT16U         data_len,
                                   CPU_INT16S         flags,
                                   NET_SOCK_ADDR     *paddr_remote,
                                   NET_SOCK_ADDR_LEN  addr_len,
                                   NET_ERR           *perr);

ssize_t send (int    sock_id,
              void  *p_data,
             _size_t  data_len,
             int    flags);

ssize_t sendto(int               sock_id,
               void             *p_data,
               _size_t           data_len,
               int               flags,
               struct sockaddr  *paddr_remote,
               socklen_t         addr_len);
```

ARGUMENTS

sock_id This is the socket ID returned by **NetSock_Open()/socket()** when the socket was created *or* by **NetSock_Accept()/accept()** when a connection was accepted.

p_data Pointer to the application data memory buffer to send.

data_len Size of the application data memory buffer (in bytes).

flags Flag to select transmit options; bit-field flags logically **OR**'d:

NET_SOCK_FLAG_NONE/0	
NET_SOCK_FLAG_TX_NO_BLOCK/	No socket flags selected
MSG_DONTWAIT	Send socket data without blocking

In most cases, this flag would be set to NET_SOCK_FLAG_NONE/0.

paddr_remote Pointer to a socket address structure (see section 8-2 "Socket Interface" on page 208) which contains the remote socket address to send data to.

addr_len Size of the socket address structure which *must* be passed the size of the socket address structure [e.g., sizeof(NET_SOCK_ADDR_IP)].

perr Pointer to variable that will receive the return error code from this function:

NET_SOCK_ERR_NONE
NET_SOCK_ERR_NULL_PTR
NET_SOCK_ERR_NOT_USED
NET_SOCK_ERR_CLOSED
NET_SOCK_ERR_INVALID_SOCK
NET_SOCK_ERR_INVALID_FAMILY
NET_SOCK_ERR_INVALID_PROTOCOL
NET_SOCK_ERR_INVALID_TYPE
NET_SOCK_ERR_INVALID_STATE
NET_SOCK_ERR_INVALID_OP
NET_SOCK_ERR_INVALID_FLAG
NET_SOCK_ERR_INVALID_DATA_SIZE
NET_SOCK_ERR_INVALID_CONN
NET_SOCK_ERR_INVALID_ADDR
NET_SOCK_ERR_INVALID_ADDR_LEN
NET_SOCK_ERR_INVALID_PORT_NBR
NET_SOCK_ERR_ADDR_IN_USE
NET_SOCK_ERR_PORT_NBR_NONE_AVAIL
NET_SOCK_ERR_CONN_FAIL
NET_SOCK_ERR_FAULT

NET_ERR_TX
NET_IF_ERR_INVALID_IF
NET_IP_ERR_ADDR_NONE_AVAIL
NET_IP_ERR_ADDR_CFG_IN_PROGRESS
NET_CONN_ERR_NULL_PTR
NET_CONN_ERR_NOT_USED
NET_CONN_ERR_INVALID_CONN
NET_CONN_ERR_INVALID_FAMILY
NET_CONN_ERR_INVALID_TYPE
NET_CONN_ERR_INVALID_PROTOCOL_IX
NET_CONN_ERR_INVALID_ADDR_LEN
NET_CONN_ERR_ADDR_IN_USE
NET_ERR_INIT_INCOMPLETE
NET_OS_ERR_LOCK

RETURNED VALUE

Positive number of bytes (queued to be) sent, if successful;

NET_SOCK_BSD_RTN_CODE_CONN_CLOSED/0, if the socket is closed;

NET_SOCK_BSD_ERR_TX/-1, otherwise.

Note that a positive return value does not mean that the message was successfully delivered to the remote socket, just that it was sent or queued for sending.

BLOCKING VS NON-BLOCKING

The default setting for µC/TCP-IP is blocking. However, this setting can be changed at compile time by setting the NET_SOCK_CFG_BLOCK_SEL (see section C-15-3 on page 741) to one of the following values:

NET_SOCK_BLOCK_SEL_DFLT sets blocking mode to the default, or blocking, unless modified by run-time options.

NET_SOCK_BLOCK_SEL_BLOCK sets the blocking mode to blocking. This means that a socket transmit function will wait forever, until it can send (or queue to send) at least one byte of data or the socket connection is closed, unless a timeout is specified by NetSock_CfgTimeoutTxQ_Set() [See section B-13-24 on page 630].

NET_SOCK_BLOCK_SEL_NO_BLOCK sets the blocking mode to non-blocking. This means that a socket transmit function will *not* wait but immediately return as much data sent (or queued to be sent), socket connection closed, or an error indicating no available memory to send (or queue) data or other possible socket faults. The application will have to "poll" the socket on a regular basis to transmit data.

The current version of µC/TCP-IP selects blocking or non-blocking at compile time for all sockets. A future version may allow the selection of blocking or non-blocking at the individual socket level. However, each socket transmit call can pass the **NET_SOCK_FLAG_TX_NO_BLOCK/MSG_DONTWAIT** flag to disable blocking on that call.

Despite these socket-level blocking options, the current version of µC/TCP-IP possibly blocks at the device driver when waiting for the availability of a device's transmitter.

REQUIRED CONFIGURATION

NetSock_TxData()/NetSock_TxDataTo() is available only if:

- **NET_CFG_TRANSPORT_LAYER_SEL** is configured for TCP (see section C-12-1 on page 736), and/or

- **NET_UDP_CFG_APP_API_SEL** is configured for sockets (see section C-13-1 on page 737).

In addition, **send()/sendto()** is available only if **NET_BSD_CFG_API_EN** is enabled (see section C-17-1 on page 747).

NOTES / WARNINGS

TCP sockets typically use **NetSock_TxData()/send()**, whereas UDP sockets typically use **NetSock_TxDataTo()/sendto()**.

For datagram sockets (i.e., UDP), each receive returns the data from exactly one send but datagram order and delivery is not guaranteed. Also, if the receive memory buffer is not large enough to receive an entire datagram, the datagram's data is truncated to the size of the memory buffer and the remaining data is discarded.

For datagram sockets (i.e., UDP), all data is sent atomically – i.e., each call to send data *must* be sent in a single, complete datagram. Since µC/TCP-IP does *not* currently support IP transmit fragmentation, if a datagram socket attempts to send data greater than a single datagram, then the socket send is aborted and no socket data is sent.

Only some transmit flag options are implemented. If other flag options are requested, an error is returned so that flag options are *not* silently ignored.

B-14 TCP FUNCTIONS

B-14-1 NetTCP_ConnCfgIdleTimeout()

Configure TCP connection's idle timeout.

FILES

net_tcp.h/net_tcp.c

PROTOTYPE

```
CPU_BOOLEAN NetTCP_ConnCfgIdleTimeout(NET_TCP_CONN_ID      conn_id_tcp,
                                      NET_TCP_TIMEOUT_SEC  timeout_sec,
                                      NET_ERR             *perr);
```

ARGUMENTS

conn_id_tcp TCP connection handle ID to configure connection handle timeout.

timeout_sec Desired value for TCP connection idle timeout (in seconds).

perr Pointer to variable that will receive the return error code from this function:

NET_TCP_ERR_NONE
NET_TCP_ERR_INVALID_ARG
NET_TCP_ERR_INVALID_CONN
NET_TCP_ERR_CONN_NOT_USED
NET_ERR_INIT_INCOMPLETE
NET_OS_ERR_LOCK

RETURNED VALUE

DEF_OK, TCP connection's idle timeout successfully configured.

DEF_FAIL, otherwise.

REQUIRED CONFIGURATION

Available only if **NET_CFG_TRANSPORT_LAYER_SEL** is configured for TCP (see section C-12-1 on page 736).

NOTES / WARNINGS

Configured timeout does not reschedule any current idle timeout in progress but becomes effective the next time a TCP connection sets its idle timeout.

The **conn_id_tcp** argument represents the TCP connection handle – *not* the socket handle. The following code may be used to get the TCP connection handle and configure TCP connection parameters (see also section B-13-32 "NetSock_GetConnTransportID()" on page 644):

```
NET_SOCK_ID     sock_id;
NET_TCP_CONN_ID conn_id_tcp;
NET_ERR         err;

sock_id     = Application's TCP socket ID; /* Get application's TCP socket     ID. */
                                           /* Get socket's      TCP connection ID. */
conn_id_tcp = (NET_TCP_CONN_ID)NetSock_GetConnTransportID(sock_id, &err);

if (err == NET_SOCK_ERR_NONE) {/* If NO errors, ...                                */
                               /* ... configure TCP connection maximum re-transmit threshold. */
    NetTCP_ConnCfgReTxMaxTh(conn_id_tcp, 4u);
}
```

NetTCP_ConnCfgIdleTimeout() is called by application function(s) and *must not* be called with the global network lock already acquired. It *must* block *all* other network protocol tasks by pending on and acquiring the global network lock (see "**net.h** Note #3"). This is required since an application's network protocol suite API function access is asynchronous to other network protocol tasks.

B-14-2 NetTCP_ConnCfgMaxSegSizeLocal()

Configure TCP connection's local maximum segment size.

FILES

net_tcp.h/net_tcp.c

PROTOTYPE

```
CPU_BOOLEAN NetTCP_ConnCfgMaxSegSizeLocal(NET_TCP_CONN_ID   conn_id_tcp,
                                          NET_TCP_SEG_SIZE  max_seg_size,
                                          NET_ERR          *perr);
```

ARGUMENTS

conn_id_tcp TCP connection handle ID to configure local maximum segment size.

max_seg_size Desired maximum segment size.

perr Pointer to variable that will receive the return error code from this function:

NET_TCP_ERR_NONE
NET_TCP_ERR_CONN_NOT_USED
NET_TCP_ERR_INVALID_CONN_STATE
NET_TCP_ERR_INVALID_CONN_OP
NET_TCP_ERR_INVALID_CONN_ARG
NET_TCP_ERR_INVALID_CONN
NET_TCP_ERR_CONN_NOT_USED
NET_ERR_INIT_INCOMPLETE
NET_OS_ERR_LOCK

RETURNED VALUE

DEF_OK, TCP connection's local maximum segment size successfully configured, if no errors.

DEF_FAIL, otherwise.

REQUIRED CONFIGURATION

Available only if **NET_CFG_TRANSPORT_LAYER_SEL** is configured for TCP (see section C-12-1 on page 736).

NOTES / WARNINGS

The **conn_id_tcp** argument represents the TCP connection handle — *not* the socket handle. The following code may be used to get the TCP connection handle and configure TCP connection parameters (see also section B-13-32 "NetSock_GetConnTransportID()" on page 644):

```
NET_SOCK_ID      sock_id;
NET_TCP_CONN_ID conn_id_tcp;
NET_ERR          err;

sock_id     = Application's TCP socket ID; /* Get application's TCP socket     ID. */
                                            /* Get socket's      TCP connection ID. */
conn_id_tcp = (NET_TCP_CONN_ID)NetSock_GetConnTransportID(sock_id, &err);

if (err == NET_SOCK_ERR_NONE) { /* If NO errors, ...                               */
                                /* ... configure TCP connection local maximum segment size. */
    NetTCP_ConnCfgMaxSegSizeLocal(conn_id_tcp, 1360u);
}
```

NetTCP_ConnCfgMaxSegSizeLocal() is called by application function(s) and *must not* be called with the global network lock already acquired. It *must* block *all* other network protocol tasks by pending on and acquiring the global network lock (see "**net.h** Note #3"). This is required since an application's network protocol suite API function access is asynchronous to other network protocol tasks.

B-14-3 NetTCP_ConnCfgReTxMaxTh()

Configure TCP connection's maximum number of same segment retransmissions.

FILES

net_tcp.h/net_tcp.c

PROTOTYPE

```
CPU_BOOLEAN NetTCP_ConnCfgReTxMaxTh(NET_TCP_CONN_ID  conn_id_tcp,
                                    NET_PKT_CTR      nbr_max_re_tx,
                                    NET_ERR         *perr);
```

ARGUMENTS

conn_id_tcp TCP connection handle ID to configure maximum number of same segment retransmissions.

nbr_max_re_tx Desired maximum number of same segment retransmissions.

perr Pointer to variable that will receive the return error code from this function:

NET_TCP_ERR_NONE
NET_TCP_ERR_INVALID_ARG
NET_TCP_ERR_INVALID_CONN
NET_TCP_ERR_CONN_NOT_USED
NET_ERR_INIT_INCOMPLETE
NET_OS_ERR_LOCK

RETURNED VALUE

DEF_OK, TCP connection's maximum number of retransmissions successfully configured, if no errors.

DEF_FAIL, otherwise.

REQUIRED CONFIGURATION

Available only if **NET_CFG_TRANSPORT_LAYER_SEL** is configured for TCP (see section C-12-1 on page 736).

NOTES / WARNINGS

The **conn_id_tcp** argument represents the TCP connection handle – *not* the socket handle. The following code may be used to get the TCP connection handle and configure TCP connection parameters (see also section B-13-32 "NetSock_GetConnTransportID()" on page 644):

```
NET_SOCK_ID     sock_id;
NET_TCP_CONN_ID conn_id_tcp;
NET_ERR         err;

sock_id     = Application's TCP socket ID; /* Get application's TCP socket     ID. */
                                           /* Get socket's      TCP connection ID. */
conn_id_tcp = (NET_TCP_CONN_ID)NetSock_GetConnTransportID(sock_id, &err);

if (err == NET_SOCK_ERR_NONE) {/* If NO errors, ...                                    */
                              /* ... configure TCP connection maximum re-transmit threshold. */
    NetTCP_ConnCfgReTxMaxTh(conn_id_tcp, 4u);
}
```

NetTCP_ConnCfgReTxMaxTh() is called by application function(s) and *must not* be called with the global network lock already acquired. It *must* block *all* other network protocol tasks by pending on and acquiring the global network lock (see "**net.h** Note #3"). This is required since an application's network protocol suite API function access is asynchronous to other network protocol tasks.

B-14-4 NetTCP_ConnCfgReTxMaxTimeout()

Configure TCP connection's maximum retransmission timeout.

FILES

net_tcp.h/net_tcp.c

PROTOTYPE

```
CPU_BOOLEAN NetTCP_ConnCfgReTxMaxTimeout(NET_TCP_CONN_ID      conn_id_tcp,
                                         NET_TCP_TIMEOUT_SEC  timeout_sec,
                                         NET_ERR             *perr);
```

ARGUMENTS

conn_id_tcp TCP connection handle ID to configure maximum retransmission timeout value.

timeout_sec Desired value for TCP connection maximum retransmission timeout (in seconds).

perr Pointer to variable that will receive the return error code from this function:

NET_TCP_ERR_NONE
NET_TCP_ERR_INVALID_ARG
NET_TCP_ERR_INVALID_CONN
NET_TCP_ERR_CONN_NOT_USED
NET_ERR_INIT_INCOMPLETE
NET_OS_ERR_LOCK

RETURNED VALUE

DEF_OK, TCP connection's maximum retransmission timeout successfully configured, if no errors.

DEF_FAIL, otherwise.

REQUIRED CONFIGURATION

Available only if **NET_CFG_TRANSPORT_LAYER_SEL** is configured for TCP (see section C-12-1 on page 736).

NOTES / WARNINGS

The conn_id_tcp argument represents the TCP connection handle — *not* the socket handle. The following code may be used to get the TCP connection handle and configure TCP connection parameters (see also section B-13-32 "NetSock_GetConnTransportID()" on page 644):

```
NET_SOCK_ID     sock_id;
NET_TCP_CONN_ID conn_id_tcp;
NET_ERR         err;

sock_id     = Application's TCP socket ID; /* Get application's TCP socket     ID. */
                                           /* Get socket's      TCP connection ID. */
conn_id_tcp = (NET_TCP_CONN_ID)NetSock_GetConnTransportID(sock_id, &err);

if (err == NET_SOCK_ERR_NONE) { /* If NO errors, ...                                */
                                /* ... configure TCP connection maximum re-transmit timeout. */
    NetTCP_ConnCfgReTxMaxTimeout(conn_id_tcp, 30u);
}
```

NetTCP_ConnCfgReTxMaxTimeout() is called by application function(s) and *must not* be called with the global network lock already acquired. It *must* block *all* other network protocol tasks by pending on and acquiring the global network lock (see "**net.h** Note #3"). This is required since an application's network protocol suite API function access is asynchronous to other network protocol tasks.

E

B-14-5 NetTCP_ConnCfgRxWinSize()

Configure TCP connection's receive window size.

FILES

net_tcp.h/net_tcp.c

PROTOTYPE

```
CPU_BOOLEAN NetTCP_ConnCfgRxWinSize(NET_TCP_CONN_ID   conn_id_tcp,
                                    NET_TCP_WIN_SIZE  win_size,
                                    NET_ERR          *perr);
```

ARGUMENTS

conn_id_tcp TCP connection handle ID to configure receive window size.

win_size Desired receive window size.

perr Pointer to variable that will receive the return error code from this function:

NET_TCP_ERR_NONE
NET_TCP_ERR_CONN_NOT_USED
NET_TCP_ERR_INVALID_CONN_STATE
NET_TCP_ERR_INVALID_CONN_OP
NET_TCP_ERR_INVALID_ARG
NET_TCP_ERR_INVALID_CONN
NET_TCP_ERR_CONN_NOT_USED
NET_ERR_INIT_INCOMPLETE
NET_OS_ERR_LOCK

RETURNED VALUE

DEF_OK, TCP connection's receive window size successfully configured, if no errors.

DEF_FAIL, otherwise.

REQUIRED CONFIGURATION

Available only if **NET_CFG_TRANSPORT_LAYER_SEL** is configured for TCP (see section C-12-1 on page 736).

NOTES / WARNINGS

The conn_id_tcp argument represents the TCP connection handle – *not* the socket handle. The following code may be used to get the TCP connection handle and configure TCP connection parameters (see also section B-13-32 “NetSock_GetConnTransportID()” on page 644):

```
NET_SOCK_ID     sock_id;
NET_TCP_CONN_ID conn_id_tcp;
NET_ERR         err;

sock_id     = Application's TCP socket ID; /* Get application's TCP socket     ID. */
                                           /* Get socket's      TCP connection ID. */
conn_id_tcp = (NET_TCP_CONN_ID)NetSock_GetConnTransportID(sock_id, &err);

if (err == NET_SOCK_ERR_NONE) { /* If NO errors, ...                              */
                                /* ... configure TCP connection receive window size. */
    NetTCP_ConnCfgRxWinSize(conn_id_tcp, (4u * 1460u));
}
```

NetTCP_ConnCfgRxWindowsSize() is called by application function(s) and *must not* be called with the global network lock already acquired. It *must* block *all* other network protocol tasks by pending on and acquiring the global network lock (see “**net.h** Note #3”). This is required since an application's network protocol suite API function access is asynchronous to other network protocol tasks.

B-14-6 NetTCP_ConnCfgTxWinSize()

Configure TCP connection's transmit window size.

FILES

net_tcp.h/net_tcp.c

PROTOTYPE

```
CPU_BOOLEAN NetTCP_ConnCfgTxWinSize(NET_TCP_CONN_ID   conn_id_tcp,
                                    NET_TCP_WIN_SIZE  win_size,
                                    NET_ERR          *perr);
```

ARGUMENTS

conn_id_tcp TCP connection handle ID to configure transmit window size.

win_size Desired transmit window size.

perr Pointer to variable that will receive the return error code from this function:

NET_TCP_ERR_NONE
NET_TCP_ERR_CONN_NOT_USED
NET_TCP_ERR_INVALID_CONN_STATE
NET_TCP_ERR_INVALID_CONN_OP
NET_TCP_ERR_INVALID_ARG
NET_TCP_ERR_INVALID_CONN
NET_TCP_ERR_CONN_NOT_USED
NET_ERR_INIT_INCOMPLETE
NET_OS_ERR_LOCK

RETURNED VALUE

DEF_OK, TCP connection's transmit window size successfully configured, if no errors.

DEF_FAIL, otherwise.

REQUIRED CONFIGURATION

Available only if **NET_CFG_TRANSPORT_LAYER_SEL** is configured for TCP (see section C-12-1 on page 736).

NOTES / WARNINGS

The conn_id_tcp argument represents the TCP connection handle – *not* the socket handle. The following code may be used to get the TCP connection handle and configure TCP connection parameters (see also section B-13-32 "NetSock_GetConnTransportID()" on page 644):

```
NET_SOCK_ID     sock_id;
NET_TCP_CONN_ID conn_id_tcp;
NET_ERR         err;

sock_id     = Application's TCP socket ID; /* Get application's TCP socket     ID. */
                                           /* Get socket's      TCP connection ID. */
conn_id_tcp = (NET_TCP_CONN_ID)NetSock_GetConnTransportID(sock_id, &err);

if (err == NET_SOCK_ERR_NONE) { /* If NO errors, ...                               */
                                /* ... configure TCP connection receive window size. */
    NetTCP_ConnCfgRxWinSize(conn_id_tcp, (4u * 1460u));
}
```

NetTCP_ConnCfgTxWindowsSize() is called by application function(s) and *must not* be called with the global network lock already acquired. It *must* block *all* other network protocol tasks by pending on and acquiring the global network lock (see "**net.h** Note #3"). This is required since an application's network protocol suite API function access is asynchronous to other network protocol tasks.

B-14-7 NetTCP_ConnCfgTxAckImmedRxdPushEn()

Configure TCP connection's transmit immediate acknowledgement for received and pushed TCP segments.

FILES

net_tcp.h/net_tcp.c

PROTOTYPE

```
CPU_BOOLEAN NetTCP_ConnCfgTxAckImmedRxdPushEn(NET_TCP_CONN_ID  conn_id_tcp,
                                              CPU_BOOLEAN      tx_immed_ack_en,
                                              NET_ERR         *perr);
```

ARGUMENTS

conn_id_tcp — TCP connection handle ID to configure transmit immediate acknowledgement for received and pushed TCP segments.

tx_immed_ack_en — Desired value for TCP connection transmit immediate acknowledgement for received and pushed TCP segments:

DEF_ENABLED	TCP connection acknowledgements immediately transmitted for any pushed TCP segments received.
DEF_DISABLED	TCP connection acknowledgements *not* immediately transmitted for any pushed TCP segments received.

perr — Pointer to variable that will receive the return error code from this function:

NET_TCP_ERR_NONE
NET_TCP_ERR_INVALID_ARG
NET_TCP_ERR_INVALID_CONN
NET_TCP_ERR_CONN_NOT_USED
NET_ERR_INIT_INCOMPLETE
NET_OS_ERR_LOCK

RETURNED VALUE

DEF_OK, TCP connection's transmit immediate acknowledgement for received and pushed TCP segments successfully configured, if no errors.

DEF_FAIL, otherwise.

REQUIRED CONFIGURATION

Available only if **NET_CFG_TRANSPORT_LAYER_SEL** is configured for TCP (see section C-12-1 on page 736).

NOTES / WARNINGS

The **conn_id_tcp** argument represents the TCP connection handle – *not* the socket handle. The following code may be used to get the TCP connection handle and configure TCP connection parameters (see also section B-13-32 on page 644):

```
NET_SOCK_ID     sock_id;
NET_TCP_CONN_ID conn_id_tcp;
NET_ERR         err;

sock_id     = Application's TCP socket ID; /* Get application's TCP socket     ID. */
                                           /* Get socket's      TCP connection ID. */
conn_id_tcp = (NET_TCP_CONN_ID)NetSock_GetConnTransportID(sock_id, &err);

if (err == NET_SOCK_ERR_NONE) {
                   /* If NO errors, ...                                             */
                   /* ... configure TCP connection transmit immediate ACK for received PUSH. */
    NetTCP_ConnCfgTxAckImmedRxdPushEn(conn_id_tcp, DEF_NO);
}
```

NetTCP_ConnCfgTxAckImmedRxdPushEn() is called by application function(s) and *must not* be called with the global network lock already acquired. It *must* block *all* other network protocol tasks by pending on and acquiring the global network lock (see "**net.h** Note #3"). This is required since an application's network protocol suite API function access is asynchronous to other network protocol tasks.

B-14-8 NetTCP_ConnCfgTxNagleEn()

Configure TCP connection's transmit Nagle algorithm enable.

FILES

net_tcp.h/net_tcp.c

PROTOTYPE

```
CPU_BOOLEAN NetTCP_ConnCfgTxNagleEn(NET_TCP_CONN_ID  conn_id_tcp,
                                    CPU_BOOLEAN      nagle_en,
                                    NET_ERR         *perr);
```

ARGUMENTS

conn_id_tcp Handle identifier of TCP connection to configure transmit Nagle enable.

nagle_en Desired value for TCP connection transmit Nagle enable :

DEF_ENABLED	TCP connections delay transmitting next data segment(s) until all unacknowledged data is acknowledged **OR** an MSS-sized segment can be transmitted.
DEF_DISABLED	TCP connections transmit all data segment(s) when permitted by local & remote hosts' congestion controls.

perr Pointer to variable that will receive the return error code from this function:

NET_TCP_ERR_NONE
NET_TCP_ERR_INVALID_ARG
NET_TCP_ERR_INVALID_CONN
NET_TCP_ERR_CONN_NOT_USED
NET_ERR_INIT_INCOMPLETE
NET_OS_ERR_LOCK

RETURNED VALUE

DEF_OK, TCP connection's transmit Nagle enable successfully configured;

DEF_FAIL, otherwise.

REQUIRED CONFIGURATION

Available only if **NET_CFG_TRANSPORT_LAYER_SEL** is configured for TCP (see section C-12-1 on page 736).

NOTES / WARNINGS

The **conn_id_tcp** argument represents the TCP connection handle – *not* the socket handle. The following code may be used to get the TCP connection handle and configure TCP connection parameters (see also section B-13-32 "NetSock_GetConnTransportID()" on page 644):

```
NET_SOCK_ID      sock_id;
NET_TCP_CONN_ID conn_id_tcp;
NET_ERR          err;

sock_id     = Application's TCP socket ID; /* Get application's TCP socket      ID. */
                                            /* Get socket's      TCP connection ID. */
conn_id_tcp = (NET_TCP_CONN_ID)NetSock_GetConnTransportID(sock_id, &err);

if (err == NET_SOCK_ERR_NONE) { /* If NO errors, ...                              */
                                /* ... configure TCP connection Nagle algorithm. */
    NetTCP_ConnCfgTxNagleEn(conn_id_tcp, DEF_NO);
}
```

NetTCP_ConnCfgTxNagleEn() is called by application function(s) and *must not* be called with the global network lock already acquired. It *must* block *all* other network protocol tasks by pending on and acquiring the global network lock (see "**net.h** Note #3"). This is required since an application's network protocol suite API function access is asynchronous to other network protocol tasks.

B-14-9 NetTCP_ConnCfgTxKeepAliveEn()

Configure TCP connection's transmit keep-alive enable.

FILES

net_tcp.h/net_tcp.c

PROTOTYPE

```
CPU_BOOLEAN NetTCP_ConnCfgTxKeepAliveEn(NET_TCP_CONN_ID  conn_id_tcp,
                                        CPU_BOOLEAN      keep_alive_en,
                                        NET_ERR         *perr);
```

ARGUMENTS

conn_id_tcp — Handle identifier of TCP connection to configure transmit keep-alive.

keep_alive_en — Desired value for TCP connection transmit keep-alive enable:

DEF_ENABLED — TCP connections transmit periodic keep-alive segments if no data segments have been received within the keep-alive timeout.

DEF_DISABLED — TCP connections transmit a reset segment and close if no data segments have been received within the keep-alive timeout.

perr — Pointer to variable that will receive the return error code from this function:

NET_TCP_ERR_NONE
NET_TCP_ERR_INVALID_ARG
NET_TCP_ERR_INVALID_CONN
NET_TCP_ERR_CONN_NOT_USED
NET_ERR_INIT_INCOMPLETE
NET_OS_ERR_LOCK

RETURNED VALUE

DEF_OK, TCP connection's transmit keep-alive enable successfully configured;

DEF_FAIL, otherwise.

REQUIRED CONFIGURATION

Available only if **NET_CFG_TRANSPORT_LAYER_SEL** is configured for TCP (see section C-12-1 on page 736).

NOTES / WARNINGS

The **conn_id_tcp** argument represents the TCP connection handle – *not* the socket handle. The following code may be used to get the TCP connection handle and configure TCP connection parameters (see also section B-13-32 "NetSock_GetConnTransportID()" on page 644):

```
NET_SOCK_ID     sock_id;
NET_TCP_CONN_ID conn_id_tcp;
NET_ERR         err;

sock_id     = Application's TCP socket ID; /* Get application's TCP socket     ID. */
                                           /* Get socket's      TCP connection ID. */
conn_id_tcp = (NET_TCP_CONN_ID)NetSock_GetConnTransportID(sock_id, &err);

if (err == NET_SOCK_ERR_NONE) {  /* If NO errors, ...                              */
                                 /* ... configure TCP connection Nagle algorithm. */
    NetTCP_ConnCfgTxNagleEn(conn_id_tcp, DEF_NO);
}
```

NetTCP_ConnCfgTxKeepAliveEn() is called by application function(s) and *must not* be called with the global network lock already acquired. It *must* block *all* other network protocol tasks by pending on and acquiring the global network lock (see "**net.h** Note #3"). This is required since an application's network protocol suite API function access is asynchronous to other network protocol tasks.

B-14-10 NetTCP_ConnCfgTxKeepAliveTh()

Configure TCP connection's maximum number of consecutive keep-alives to transmit.

FILES

net_tcp.h/net_tcp.c

PROTOTYPE

```
CPU_BOOLEAN NetTCP_ConnCfgTxKeepAliveTh(NET_TCP_CONN_ID  conn_id_tcp,
                                        NET_PKT_CTR      nbr_max_keep_alive,
                                        NET_ERR         *perr);
```

ARGUMENTS

conn_id_tcp — Handle identifier of TCP connection to configure transmit keep-alive threshold.

keep_alive_en — Desired maximum number of consecutive keep-alives to transmit.

perr — Pointer to variable that will receive the return error code from this function:

NET_TCP_ERR_NONE
NET_TCP_ERR_INVALID_ARG
NET_TCP_ERR_INVALID_CONN
NET_TCP_ERR_CONN_NOT_USED
NET_ERR_INIT_INCOMPLETE
NET_OS_ERR_LOCK

RETURNED VALUE

DEF_OK, — TCP connection's transmit keep-alive enable successfully configured;

DEF_FAIL, — otherwise.

REQUIRED CONFIGURATION

Available only if **NET_CFG_TRANSPORT_LAYER_SEL** is configured for TCP (see section C-12-1 on page 736).

NOTES / WARNINGS

The **conn_id_tcp** argument represents the TCP connection handle – *not* the socket handle. The following code may be used to get the TCP connection handle and configure TCP connection parameters (see also section B-13-32 "NetSock_GetConnTransportID()" on page 644):

```
NET_SOCK_ID     sock_id;
NET_TCP_CONN_ID conn_id_tcp;
NET_ERR         err;

sock_id     = Application's TCP socket ID; /* Get application's TCP socket     ID. */
                                           /* Get socket's      TCP connection ID. */
conn_id_tcp = (NET_TCP_CONN_ID)NetSock_GetConnTransportID(sock_id, &err);

if (err == NET_SOCK_ERR_NONE) { /* If NO errors, ...                              */
                                /* ... configure TCP connection Nagle algorithm. */
    NetTCP_ConnCfgTxNagleEn(conn_id_tcp, DEF_NO);
}
```

NetTCP_ConnCfgTxKeepAliveTh() is called by application function(s) and *must not* be called with the global network lock already acquired. It *must* block *all* other network protocol tasks by pending on and acquiring the global network lock (see "**net.h** Note #3"). This is required since an application's network protocol suite API function access is asynchronous to other network protocol tasks.

B-14-11 NetTCP_ConnCfgTxKeepAliveRetryTimeout()

Configure TCP connection's transmit keep-alive retry timeout.

FILES

net_tcp.h/net_tcp.c

PROTOTYPE

```
CPU_BOOLEAN NetTCP_ConnCfgTxKeepAliveRetryTimeout(NET_TCP_CONN_ID      conn_id_tcp,
                                                   NET_TCP_TIMEOUT_SEC  timeout_sec,
                                                   NET_ERR             *perr);
```

ARGUMENTS

conn_id_tcp — Handle identifier of TCP connection to configure transmit keep-alive retry timeout.

timeout_sec — Desired value for TCP connection transmit keep-alive retry timeout (in seconds).

perr — Pointer to variable that will receive the return error code from this function:

NET_TCP_ERR_NONE
NET_TCP_ERR_INVALID_ARG
NET_TCP_ERR_INVALID_CONN
NET_TCP_ERR_CONN_NOT_USED
NET_ERR_INIT_INCOMPLETE
NET_OS_ERR_LOCK

RETURNED VALUE

DEF_OK, TCP connection's transmit keep-alive retry timeout successfully configured;

DEF_FAIL, otherwise.

REQUIRED CONFIGURATION

Available only if **NET_CFG_TRANSPORT_LAYER_SEL** is configured for TCP (see section C-12-1 on page 736).

NOTES / WARNINGS

The **conn_id_tcp** argument represents the TCP connection handle – *not* the socket handle. The following code may be used to get the TCP connection handle and configure TCP connection parameters (see also section B-13-32 "NetSock_GetConnTransportID()" on page 644):

```
NET_SOCK_ID     sock_id;
NET_TCP_CONN_ID conn_id_tcp;
NET_ERR         err;

sock_id     = Application's TCP socket ID; /* Get application's TCP socket     ID. */
                                           /* Get socket's      TCP connection ID. */
conn_id_tcp = (NET_TCP_CONN_ID)NetSock_GetConnTransportID(sock_id, &err);

if (err == NET_SOCK_ERR_NONE) { /* If NO errors, ...                              */
                                /* ... configure TCP connection Nagle algorithm. */
    NetTCP_ConnCfgTxNagleEn(conn_id_tcp, DEF_NO);
}
```

NetTCP_ConnCfgTxKeepAliveRetryTimeout() is called by application function(s) and *must not* be called with the global network lock already acquired. It *must* block *all* other network protocol tasks by pending on and acquiring the global network lock (see "**net.h** Note #3"). This is required since an application's network protocol suite API function access is asynchronous to other network protocol tasks.

B-14-12 NetTCP_ConnCfgTxAckDlyTimeout()

Configure TCP connection's transmit acknowledgement delay timeout.

FILES

net_tcp.h/net_tcp.c

PROTOTYPE

```
CPU_BOOLEAN NetTCP_ConnCfgTxAckDlyTimeout(NET_TCP_CONN_ID     conn_id_tcp,
                                          NET_TCP_TIMEOUT_MS  timeout_ms,
                                          NET_ERR            *perr);
```

ARGUMENTS

conn_id_tcp — Handle identifier of TCP connection to configure transmit acknowledgement delay timeout.

timeout_sec — Desired value for TCP connection transmit acknowledgement delay timeout (in milliseconds).

perr — Pointer to variable that will receive the return error code from this function:

NET_TCP_ERR_NONE
NET_TCP_ERR_INVALID_ARG
NET_TCP_ERR_INVALID_CONN
NET_TCP_ERR_CONN_NOT_USED
NET_ERR_INIT_INCOMPLETE
NET_OS_ERR_LOCK

RETURNED VALUE

DEF_OK, — TCP connection's transmit acknowledgement delay timeout successfully configured;

DEF_FAIL, — otherwise.

REQUIRED CONFIGURATION

Available only if **NET_CFG_TRANSPORT_LAYER_SEL** is configured for TCP (see section C-12-1 on page 736).

NOTES / WARNINGS

The **conn_id_tcp** argument represents the TCP connection handle – *not* the socket handle. The following code may be used to get the TCP connection handle and configure TCP connection parameters (see also section B-13-32 "NetSock_GetConnTransportID()" on page 644):

```
NET_SOCK_ID     sock_id;
NET_TCP_CONN_ID conn_id_tcp;
NET_ERR         err;

sock_id     = Application's TCP socket ID; /* Get application's TCP socket     ID. */
                                           /* Get socket's      TCP connection ID. */
conn_id_tcp = (NET_TCP_CONN_ID)NetSock_GetConnTransportID(sock_id, &err);

if (err == NET_SOCK_ERR_NONE) { /* If NO errors, ...                              */
                                /* ... configure TCP connection Nagle algorithm. */
    NetTCP_ConnCfgTxNagleEn(conn_id_tcp, DEF_NO);
}
```

NetTCP_ConnCfgTxAckDlyTimeout() is called by application function(s) and *must not* be called with the global network lock already acquired. It *must* block *all* other network protocol tasks by pending on and acquiring the global network lock (see "**net.h** Note #3"). This is required since an application's network protocol suite API function access is asynchronous to other network protocol tasks.

B-14-13 NetTCP_ConnPoolStatGet()

Get TCP connections' statistics pool.

FILES

net_tcp.h/net_tcp.c

PROTOTYPE

```
NET_STAT_POOL NetTCP_ConnPoolStatGet(void);
```

ARGUMENTS

None.

RETURNED VALUE

TCP connections' statistics pool, if no errors.

NULL statistics pool, otherwise.

REQUIRED CONFIGURATION

Available only if NET_CFG_TRANSPORT_LAYER_SEL is configured for TCP (see section C-12-1 on page 736).

NOTES / WARNINGS

None.

B-14-14 NetTCP_ConnPoolStatResetMaxUsed()

Reset TCP connections' statistics pool's maximum number of entries used.

FILES

net_tcp.h/net_tcp.c

PROTOTYPE

```
void NetTCP_ConnPoolStatResetMaxUsed(void);
```

ARGUMENTS

None.

RETURNED VALUE

None.

REQUIRED CONFIGURATION

Available only if NET_CFG_TRANSPORT_LAYER_SEL is configured for TCP (see section C-12-1 on page 736).

NOTES / WARNINGS

None.

B-14-15 NetTCP_InitTxSeqNbr()

Application-defined function to initialize TCP's Initial Transmit Sequence Number Counter.

FILES

net_tcp.h/net_bsp.c

PROTOTYPE

```
void NetTCP_InitTxSeqNbr(void);
```

ARGUMENTS

None.

RETURNED VALUE

None.

REQUIRED CONFIGURATION

Available only if NET_CFG_TRANSPORT_LAYER_SEL is configured for TCP (see section C-12-1 on page 736).

NOTES / WARNINGS

If TCP module is included, the application is required to initialize TCP's Initial Transmit Sequence Number Counter. Possible initialization methods include:

- Time-based initialization is one preferred method since it more appropriately provides a pseudo-random initial sequence number.
- Hardware-generated random number initialization is *not* a preferred method since it tends to produce a discrete set of pseudo-random initial sequence numbers – often the same initial sequence number.
- Hard-coded initial sequence number is *not* a preferred method since it is *not* random.

B-15 NETWORK TIMER FUNCTIONS

B-15-1 NetTmr_PoolStatGet()

Get Network Timers' statistics pool.

FILES

net_tmr.h/net_tmr.c

PROTOTYPE

```
NET_STAT_POOL NetTmr_PoolStatGet(void);
```

ARGUMENTS

None.

RETURNED VALUE

Network Timers' statistics pool, if no errors.

NULL statistics pool, otherwise.

REQUIRED CONFIGURATION

None.

NOTES / WARNINGS

None.

B-15-2 NetTmr_PoolStatResetMaxUsed()

Reset Network Timers' statistics pool's maximum number of entries used.

FILES

net_tmr.h/net_tmr.c

PROTOTYPE

```
void NetTmr_PoolStatResetMaxUsed(void);
```

ARGUMENTS

None.

RETURNED VALUE

None.

REQUIRED CONFIGURATION

None.

NOTES / WARNINGS

None.

B-16 UDP FUNCTIONS

B-16-1 NetUDP_RxAppData()

Copy up to a specified number of bytes from received UDP packet buffer(s) into an application memory buffer.

FILES

net_udp.h/net_udp.c

PROTOTYPE

```
CPU_INT16U    NetUDP_RxAppData(NET_BUF     *pbuf,
                               void        *pdata_buf,
                               CPU_INT16U   data_buf_len,
                               CPU_INT16U   flags,
                               void        *pip_opts_buf,
                               CPU_INT08U   ip_opts_buf_len,
                               CPU_INT08U  *pip_opts_len,
                               NET_ERR     *perr);
```

ARGUMENTS

pbuf Pointer to network buffer that received UDP datagram.

pdata_buf Pointer to application buffer to receive application data.

data_buf_len Size of application receive buffer (in bytes).

flags Flag to select receive options; bit-field flags logically **OR**'d:

NET_UDP_FLAG_NONE	No UDP receive flags selected.
NET_UDP_FLAG_RX_DATA_PEEK	Receive UDP application data without consuming the data; i.e., do *not* free any UDP receive packet buffer(s).

pip_opts_buf Pointer to buffer to receive possible IP options, if no errors.

`ip_opts_buf_len` Size of IP options receive buffer (in bytes).

`pip_opts_len` Pointer to variable that will receive the return size of any received IP options, if no errors.

`perr` Pointer to variable that will receive the return error code from this function:

```
NET_UDP_ERR_NONE
NET_UDP_ERR_NULL_PTR
NET_UDP_ERR_INVALID_DATA_SIZE
NET_UDP_ERR_INVALID_FLAG
NET_ERR_INIT_INCOMPLETE
NET_ERR_RX
```

RETURNED VALUE

Positive number of bytes received, if successful;

0, otherwise.

REQUIRED CONFIGURATION

None.

NOTES / WARNINGS

NetUDP_RxAppData() *must* be called with the global network lock already acquired. Expected to be called from application's custom **NetUDP_RxAppDataHandler()** (see section B-16-2 on page 698).

Each UDP receive returns the data from exactly one send but datagram order and delivery is not guaranteed. Also, if the application memory buffer is not large enough to receive an entire datagram, the datagram's data is truncated to the size of the memory buffer and the remaining data is discarded. Therefore, the application memory buffer should be large enough to receive either the maximum UDP datagram size (i.e., 65,507 bytes) *or* the application's expected maximum UDP datagram size.

Only some UDP receive flag options are implemented. If other flag options are requested, an error is returned so that flag options are *not* silently ignored.

B-16-2 NetUDP_RxAppDataHandler()

Application-defined handler to demultiplex and receive UDP packet(s) to application without sockets.

FILES

net_udp.h/net_bsp.c

PROTOTYPE

```
void NetUDP_RxAppDataHandler(NET_BUF           *pbuf,
                             NET_IP_ADDR        src_addr,
                             NET_UDP_PORT_NBR   src_port,
                             NET_IP_ADDR        dest_addr,
                             NET_UDP_PORT_NBR   dest_port,
                             NET_ERR           *perr);
```

ARGUMENTS

pbuf Pointer to network buffer that received UDP datagram.

src_addr Receive UDP packet's source IP address.

src_port Receive UDP packet's source UDP port.

dest_addr Receive UDP packet's destination IP address.

dest_port Receive UDP packet's destination UDP port.

perr Pointer to variable that will receive the return error code from this function:

NET_APP_ERR_NONE
NET_ERR_RX_DEST
NET_ERR_RX

RETURNED VALUE

None.

E

REQUIRED CONFIGURATION

Available only if NET_UDP_CFG_APP_API_SEL is configured for application demultiplexing (see section C-13-1 on page 737).

NOTES / WARNINGS

NetUDP_RxAppDataHandler() *already* called with the global network lock acquired and expects to call NetUDP_RxAppData() to copy data from received UDP packets (see section B-16-1 on page 696).

If NetUDP_RxAppDataHandler() services the application data immediately within the handler function, it should do so as quickly as possible since the network's global lock remains acquired for the full duration. Thus, no other network receives or transmits can occur while NetUDP_RxAppDataHandler() executes.

NetUDP_RxAppDataHandler() may delay servicing the application data but *must* then:

- Acquire the network's global lock *prior* to calling NetUDP_RxAppData()

- Release the network's global lock *after* calling NetUDP_RxAppData()

If NetUDP_RxAppDataHandler() successfully demultiplexes the UDP packets, it should eventually call NetUDP_RxAppData() to deframe the UDP packet application data. If NetUDP_RxAppData() successfully deframes the UDP packet application data, NetUDP_RxAppDataHandler() *must not* call NetUDP_RxPktFree() to free the UDP packet's network buffer(s), since NetUDP_RxAppData() already frees the network buffer(s). And if the UDP packets were successfully demultiplexed and deframed, NetUDP_RxAppDataHandler() must return NET_APP_ERR_NONE.

However, if NetUDP_RxAppDataHandler() does *not* successfully demultiplex the UDP packets and therefore does *not* call NetUDP_RxAppData(), then NetUDP_RxAppDataHandler() should return NET_ERR_RX_DEST but must *not* free or discard the UDP packet network buffer(s).

But if NetUDP_RxAppDataHandler() or NetUDP_RxAppData() fails for any other reason, NetUDP_RxAppDataHandler() should call NetUDP_RxPktDiscard() to discard the UDP packet's network buffer(s) and should return NET_ERR_RX.

B-16-3 NetUDP_TxAppData()

Copy bytes from an application memory buffer to send via UDP packet(s).

FILES

net_udp.h/net_udp.c

PROTOTYPE

```
CPU_INT16U
NetUDP_TxAppData(void             *p_data,
                 CPU_INT16U        data_len,
                 NET_IP_ADDR       src_addr,
                 NET_UDP_PORT_NBR  src_port,
                 NET_IP_ADDR       dest_addr,
                 NET_UDP_PORT_NBR  dest_port,
                 NET_IP_TOS        TOS,
                 NET_IP_TTL        TTL,
                 CPU_INT16U        flags_udp,
                 CPU_INT16U        flags_ip,
                 void             *popts_ip,
                 NET_ERR          *perr);
```

ARGUMENTS

p_data Pointer to application data.

data_len Length of application data (in bytes).

src_addr Source IP address.

src_port Source UDP port.

dest_addr Destination IP address.

dest_port Destination UDP port.

TOS Specific TOS to transmit UDP/IP packet.

TTL Specific TTL to transmit UDP/IP packet:

NET_IP_TTL_MIN	1	minimum	TTL transmit value
NET_IP_TTL_MAX	255	maximum	TTL transmit value
NET_IP_TTL_DFLT		default	TTL transmit value
NET_IP_TTL_NONE	0	replace with default TTL	

flags_udp Flags to select UDP transmit options; bit-field flags logically **OR**'d:

NET_UDP_FLAG_NONE	No UDP transmit flags selected.
NET_UDP_FLAG_TX_CHK_SUM_DIS	Disable UDP transmit check-sums.
NET_UDP_FLAG_TX_BLOCK	Transmit UDP application data with blocking, if flag set; without blocking, if flag clear.

flags_ip Flags to select IP transmit options; bit-field flags logically **OR**'d:

NET_IP_FLAG_NONE	No IP transmit flags selected.
NET_IP_FLAG_TX_DONT_FRAG	Set IP 'Don't Frag' flag.

popts_ip Pointer to one or more IP options configuration data structures:

NULL	No IP transmit options configuration.
NET_IP_OPT_CFG_ROUTE_TS	Route and/or Internet Timestamp options configuration.
NET_IP_OPT_CFG_SECURITY	Security options configuration.

perr Pointer to variable that will receive the return error code from this function:

NET_UDP_ERR_NONE
NET_UDP_ERR_NULL_PTR
NET_UDP_ERR_INVALID_DATA_SIZE
NET_UDP_ERR_INVALID_LEN_DATA
NET_UDP_ERR_INVALID_PORT_NBR
NET_UDP_ERR_INVALID_FLAG
NET_BUF_ERR_NULL_PTR
NET_BUF_ERR_NONE_AVAIL

```
NET_BUF_ERR_INVALID_TYPE
NET_BUF_ERR_INVALID_SIZE
NET_BUF_ERR_INVALID_IX
NET_BUF_ERR_INVALID_LEN
NET_UTIL_ERR_NULL_PTR
NET_UTIL_ERR_NULL_SIZE
NET_UTIL_ERR_INVALID_PROTOCOL
NET_ERR_TX
NET_ERR_INIT_INCOMPLETE
NET_ERR_INVALID_PROTOCOL
NET_OS_ERR_LOCK
```

RETURNED VALUE

Positive number of bytes sent, if successful;

0, otherwise.

REQUIRED CONFIGURATION

None.

NOTES / WARNINGS

Each UDP datagram is sent atomically – i.e., each call to send data *must* be sent in a single, complete datagram. Since µC/TCP-IP does *not* currently support IP transmit fragmentation, if the application attempts to send data greater than a single UDP datagram, then the send is aborted and no data is sent.

Only some UDP transmit flag options are implemented. If other flag options are requested, an error is returned so that flag options are *not* silently ignored.

B-17 GENERAL NETWORK UTILITY FUNCTIONS

B-17-1 NET_UTIL_HOST_TO_NET_16()

Convert 16-bit integer values from CPU host-order to network-order.

FILES

net_util.h

PROTOTYPE

```
NET_UTIL_HOST_TO_NET_16(val);
```

ARGUMENTS

val 16-bit integer data value to convert.

RETURNED VALUE

16-bit integer value in network-order.

REQUIRED CONFIGURATION

None.

NOTES / WARNINGS

For microprocessors that require data access to be aligned to appropriate word boundaries, val and any variable to receive the returned 16-bit integer *must* start on appropriately-aligned CPU addresses. This means that all 16-bit words *must* start on addresses that are multiples of 2 bytes.

B-17-2 NET_UTIL_HOST_TO_NET_32()

Convert 32-bit integer values from CPU host-order to network-order.

FILES

net_util.h

PROTOTYPE

```
NET_UTIL_HOST_TO_NET_32(val);
```

ARGUMENTS

val 32-bit integer data value to convert.

RETURNED VALUE

32-bit integer value in network-order.

REQUIRED CONFIGURATION

None.

NOTES / WARNINGS

For microprocessors that require data access to be aligned to appropriate word boundaries, val and any variable to receive the returned 32-bit integer *must* start on appropriately-aligned CPU addresses. This means that all 32-bit words *must* start on addresses that are multiples of 4 bytes.

B-17-3 NET_UTIL_NET_TO_HOST_16()

Convert 16-bit integer values from network-order to CPU host- order.

FILES

`net_util.h`

PROTOTYPE

```
NET_UTIL_NET_TO_HOST_16(val);
```

ARGUMENTS

`val` 16-bit integer data value to convert.

RETURNED VALUE

16-bit integer value in CPU host-order.

REQUIRED CONFIGURATION

None.

NOTES / WARNINGS

For microprocessors that require data access to be aligned to appropriate word boundaries, val and any variable to receive the returned 16-bit integer *must* start on appropriately-aligned CPU addresses. This means that all 16-bit words *must* start on addresses that are multiples of 2 bytes.

B-17-4 NET_UTIL_NET_TO_HOST_32()

Convert 32-bit integer values from network-order to CPU host- order.

FILES

net_util.h

PROTOTYPE

```
NET_UTIL_NET_TO_HOST_32(val);
```

ARGUMENTS

`val` 32-bit integer data value to convert.

RETURNED VALUE

32-bit integer value in CPU host-order.

REQUIRED CONFIGURATION

None.

NOTES / WARNINGS

For microprocessors that require data access to be aligned to appropriate word boundaries, val and any variable to receive the returned 32-bit integer *must* start on appropriately-aligned CPU addresses. This means that all 32-bit words *must* start on addresses that are multiples of 4 bytes.

B-17-5 NetUtil_TS_Get()

Application-defined function to get the current Internet Timestamp.

FILES

net_util.h/net_bsp.c

PROTOTYPE

```
NET_TS NetUtil_TS_Get (void);
```

ARGUMENTS

None.

RETURNED VALUE

Current Internet Timestamp, if available;

NET_TS_NONE, otherwise.

REQUIRED CONFIGURATION

None.

NOTES / WARNINGS

RFC #791, Section 3.1 'Options: Internet Timestamp' states that "the [Internet] Timestamp is a right-justified, 32-bit timestamp in milliseconds since midnight UT [Universal Time]".

The application is responsible for providing a real-time clock with correct time-zone configuration to implement the Internet Timestamp, if possible. In order to implement this feature, the target hardware must usually include a real-time clock with the correct time zone configuration. However, NetUtil_TS_Get() is not absolutely required and may return NET_TS_NONE if real-time clock hardware is not available.

B-17-6 NetUtil_TS_Get_ms()

Application-defined function to get the current millisecond timestamp.

FILES

net_util.h/net_bsp.c

PROTOTYPE

```
NET_TS_MS NetUtil_TS_Get_ms (void);
```

ARGUMENTS

None.

RETURNED VALUE

Current millisecond timestamp.

REQUIRED CONFIGURATION

None.

NOTES / WARNINGS

The application is responsible for providing a millisecond timestamp clock with adequate resolution and range to satisfy the minimum/maximum TCP RTO values (see 'net_bsp.c `NetUtil_TS_Get_ms()` Note #1a').

µC/TCP-IP includes µC/OS-II and µC/OS-III implementations which use their OS tick counters as the source for the millisecond timestamp. These implementations can be found in the following directories:

```
\Micrium\Software\uC-TCPIP-V2\BSP\Template\OS\uCOS-II
\Micrium\Software\uC-TCPIP-V2\BSP\Template\OS\uCOS-III
```

B-18 BSD FUNCTIONS

B-18-1 accept() (TCP)

Wait for new socket connections on a listening server socket. See section B-13-1 on page 583 for more information.

FILES

net_bsd.h/net_bsd.c

PROTOTYPE

```
int accept(int              sock_id,
           struct sockaddr *paddr_remote,
           socklen_t       *paddr_len);
```

B-18-2 bind() (TCP/UDP)

Assign network addresses to sockets. See section B-13-2 on page 585 for more information.

FILES

net_bsd.h/net_bsd.c

PROTOTYPE

```
int bind(int              sock_id,
         struct sockaddr *paddr_local,
         socklen_t        addr_len);
```

B-18-3 close() (TCP/UDP)

Terminate communication and free a socket. See section B-13-25 on page 632 for more information.

FILES

net_bsd.h/net_bsd.c

PROTOTYPE

```
int close(int sock_id);
```

B-18-4 connect() (TCP/UDP)

Connect a local socket to a remote socket address. See section B-13-26 on page 634 for more information.

FILES

net_bsd.h/net_bsd.c

PROTOTYPE

```
int connect(int              sock_id,
            struct sockaddr *paddr_remote,
            socklen_t        addr_len);
```

B-18-5 FD_CLR() (TCP/UDP)

Remove a socket file descriptor ID as a member of a file descriptor set. See section B-13-27 on page 637 for more information.

FILES

net_bsd.h

PROTOTYPE

```
FD_CLR(fd, fdsetp);
```

REQUIRED CONFIGURATION

Available only if NET_BSD_CFG_API_EN is enabled (see section C-17-1 on page 747).

B-18-6 FD_ISSET() (TCP/UDP)

Check if a socket file descriptor ID is a member of a file descriptor set. See section B-13-30 on page 641 for more information.

FILES

net_bsd.h

PROTOTYPE

```
FD_ISSET(fd, fdsetp);
```

REQUIRED CONFIGURATION

Available only if NET_BSD_CFG_API_EN is enabled (see section C-17-1 on page 747).

B-18-7 FD_SET() (TCP/UDP)

Add a socket file descriptor ID as a member of a file descriptor set. See section B-13-31 on page 643 for more information.

FILES

net_bsd.h

PROTOTYPE

```
FD_SET(fd, fdsetp);
```

REQUIRED CONFIGURATION

Available only if NET_BSD_CFG_API_EN is enabled (see section C-17-1 on page 747).

B-18-8 FD_ZERO() (TCP/UDP)

Initialize/zero-clear a file descriptor set. See section B-13-29 on page 640 for more information.

FILES

net_bsd.h

PROTOTYPE

```
FD_ZERO(fdsetp);
```

REQUIRED CONFIGURATION

Available only if NET_BSD_CFG_API_EN is enabled (see section C-17-1 on page 747).

B-18-9 htonl()

Convert 32-bit integer values from CPU host-order to network-order. See section B-17-2 on page 704 for more information.

FILES

net_bsd.h

PROTOTYPE

```
htonl(val);
```

REQUIRED CONFIGURATION

Available only if NET_BSD_CFG_API_EN is enabled (see section C-17-1 on page 747).

B-18-10 htons()

Convert 16-bit integer values from CPU host-order to network-order. See section B-17-1 on page 703 for more information.

FILES

net_bsd.h

PROTOTYPE

```
htons(val);
```

B-18-11 inet_addr() (IPv4)

Convert a string of an IPv4 address in dotted-decimal notation to an IPv4 address in host-order. See section B-4-3 on page 473 for more information.

FILES

net_bsd.h/net_bsd.c

PROTOTYPE

```
in_addr_t inet_addr(char *paddr);
```

ARGUMENTS

paddr Pointer to an ASCII string that contains a dotted-decimal IPv4 address.

RETURNED VALUE

Returns the IPv4 address represented by ASCII string in host-order, if no errors.

-1 (i.e., 0xFFFFFFFF), otherwise.

REQUIRED CONFIGURATION

Available only if either NET_CFG_TRANSPORT_LAYER_SEL is configured for TCP (see section C-12-1 on page 736) and/or NET_UDP_CFG_APP_API_SEL is configured for sockets (see section C-13-1 on page 737) *and* if NET_BSD_CFG_API_EN is enabled (see section C-17-1 on page 747).

NOTES / WARNINGS

RFC 1983 states that "dotted decimal notation... refers [to] IP addresses of the form A.B.C.D; where each letter represents, in decimal, one byte of a four byte IP address". In other words, the dotted-decimal notation separates four decimal byte values by the dot, or period, character ('.'). Each decimal value represents one byte of the IP address starting with the most significant byte in network order.

E

IPv4 Address Examples

DOTTED DECIMAL NOTATION	HEXADECIMAL EQUIVALENT
127.0.0.1	0x7F000001
192.168.1.64	0xC0A80140
255.255.255.0	0xFFFFFF00
MSB .... LSB	MSB .... LSB

MSB Most Significant Byte in Dotted-Decimal IP Address

LSB Least Significant Byte in Dotted-Decimal IP Address

The IPv4 dotted-decimal ASCII string *must* include *only* decimal values and the dot, or period, character ('.'); all other characters are trapped as invalid, including any leading or trailing characters. The ASCII string *must* include exactly four decimal values separated by exactly three dot characters. Each decimal value *must not* exceed the maximum byte value (i.e., 255), or exceed the maximum number of digits for each byte (i.e., 3) including any leading zeros.

B-18-12 inet_ntoa() (IPv4)

Convert an IPv4 address in host-order into an IPv4 dotted-decimal notation ASCII string. See section B-4-1 on page 469 for more information.

FILES

net_bsd.h/net_bsd.c

PROTOTYPE

```
char *inet_ntoa(struct in_addr addr);
```

ARGUMENTS

in_addr   IPv4 address (in host-order).

RETURNED VALUE

Pointer to ASCII string of converted IPv4 address (see Notes / Warnings), if no errors.

Pointer to NULL, otherwise.

REQUIRED CONFIGURATION

Available only if either NET_CFG_TRANSPORT_LAYER_SEL is configured for TCP (see section C-12-1 on page 736) and/or NET_UDP_CFG_APP_API_SEL is configured for sockets (see section C-13-1 on page 737) *and* if NET_BSD_CFG_API_EN is enabled (see section C-17-1 on page 747).

NOTES / WARNINGS

RFC 1983 states that "dotted decimal notation... refers [to] IP addresses of the form A.B.C.D; where each letter represents, in decimal, one byte of a four-byte IP address". In other words, the dotted-decimal notation separates four decimal byte values by the dot, or period, character ('.'). Each decimal value represents one byte of the IP address starting with the most significant byte in network order.

IPv4 Address Examples

DOTTED DECIMAL NOTATION	HEXADECIMAL EQUIVALENT
`127.0.0.1`	`0x7F000001`
`192.168.1.64`	`0xC0A80140`
`255.255.255.0`	`0xFFFFFF00`
MSB .... LSB	MSB .... LSB

MSB Most Significant Byte in Dotted-Decimal IP Address

LSB Least Significant Byte in Dotted-Decimal IP Address

Since the returned ASCII string is stored in a single, global ASCII string array, this function is *not* reentrant or thread-safe. Therefore, the returned string should be copied as soon as possible before other calls to inet_ntoa() are needed.

B-18-13 listen() (TCP)

Set a socket to accept incoming connections. See section B-13-34 on page 648 for more information.

FILES

net_bsd.h/net_bsd.c

PROTOTYPE

```
int listen(int sock_id,
           int sock_q_size);
```

B-18-14 ntohl()

Convert 32-bit integer values from network-order to CPU host-order. See section B-17-4 on page 706 for more information.

FILES

net_bsd.h

PROTOTYPE

```
ntohl(val);
```

REQUIRED CONFIGURATION

Available only if **NET_BSD_CFG_API_EN** is enabled (see section C-17-1 on page 747).

B-18-15 ntohs()

Convert 16-bit integer values from network-order to CPU host-order. See section B-17-3 on page 705 for more information.

FILES

net_bsd.h

PROTOTYPE

```
ntohs(val);
```

REQUIRED CONFIGURATION

Available only if NET_BSD_CFG_API_EN is enabled (see section C-17-1 on page 747).

B-18-16 recv() / recvfrom() (TCP/UDP)

Copy up to a specified number of bytes received from a remote socket into an application memory buffer. See section B-13-38 on page 655 for more information.

FILES

net_bsd.h/net_bsd.c

PROTOTYPES

```
ssize_t recv(int      sock_id,
             void    *pdata_buf,
            _size_t  data_buf_len,
             int      flags);

ssize_t recvfrom(int               sock_id,
                 void             *pdata_buf,
                _size_t            data_buf_len,
                 int               flags,
                 struct sockaddr  *paddr_remote,
                 socklen_t        *paddr_len);
```

B-18-17 select() (TCP/UDP)

Check if any sockets are ready for available read or write operations or error conditions. See section B-13-39 "NetSock_Sel() / select() (TCP/UDP)" on page 659 for more information.

FILES

net_bsd.h/net_bsd.c

PROTOTYPE

```
int select(int             desc_nbr_max,
           struct fd_set   *pdesc_rd,
           struct fd_set   *pdesc_wr,
           struct fd_set   *pdesc_err,
           struct timeval  *ptimeout);
```

B-18-18 send() / sendto() (TCP/UDP)

Copy bytes from an application memory buffer into a socket to send to a remote socket. See section B-13-40 on page 662 for more information.

FILES

net_bsd.h/net_bsd.c

PROTOTYPES

```
ssize_t send (int      sock_id,
              void    *p_data,
             _size_t   data_len,
              int      flags);

ssize_t sendto(int              sock_id,
               void            *p_data,
              _size_t           data_len,
               int              flags,
               struct sockaddr *paddr_remote,
               socklen_t        addr_len);
```

B-18-19 socket() (TCP/UDP)

Create a datagram (i.e., UDP) or stream (i.e., TCP) type socket. See section B-13-35 on page 650 for more information.

FILES

net_bsd.h/net_bsd.c

PROTOTYPE

```
int socket(int protocol_family,
           int sock_type,
           int protocol);
```

Appendix

C

μC/TCP-IP Configuration and Optimization

μC/TCP-IP is configurable at compile time via approximately 70 **#defines** in an application's **net_cfg.h** and **app_cfg.h** files. μC/TCP-IP uses **#defines** because they allow code and data sizes to be scaled at compile time based on enabled features and the configured number of network objects. This allows the ROM and RAM footprints of μC/TCP-IP to be adjusted based on application requirements.

Most of the **#defines** should be configured with the default configuration values. A handful of values may likely never change because there is currently only one configuration choice available. This leaves approximately a dozen values that should be configured with values that may deviate from the default configuration.

It is recommended that the configuration process begins with the recommended or default configuration values which are shown in **bold**.

Unlike Appendix B on page 433, the sections in this appendix are organized following the order in μC/TCP-IP's template configuration file, **net_cfg.h**.

C-1 NETWORK CONFIGURATION

C-1-1 NET_CFG_INIT_CFG_VALS

NET_CFG_INIT_CFG_VALS is used to determine whether internal TCP/IP parameters are set to default values or are set by the user:

NET_INIT_CFG_VALS_DFLT µC/TCP-IP initializes all parameters with default values

NET_INIT_CFG_VALS_APP_INIT Application initializes all µC/TCP-IP parameters with application-specific values

NET_INIT_CFG_VALS_DFLT
Configure µC/TCP-IP's network parameters with default values. The application only needs to call **Net_Init()** to initialize both µC/TCP-IP and its configurable parameters. This configuration is highly recommended since configuring network parameters requires in-depth knowledge of the protocol stack. In fact, most references recommend many of the default values we have selected.

Parameter	Units	Min	Max	Default	Configuration Function
Interface's Network Buffer Low Threshold	% of the Total Number of an Interface's Network Buffers	5%	50%	5%	NetDbg_CfgRsrcBufThLo()
Interface's Network Buffer Low Threshold Hysteresis	% of the Total Number of an Interface's Network Buffers	0%	15%	3%	NetDbg_CfgRsrcBufThLo()
Interface's Large Receive Buffer Low Threshold	% of the Total Number of an Interface's Large Receive Buffers	5%	50%	5%	NetDbg_CfgRsrcBufRxLargeThLo()
Interface's Large Receive Buffer Low Threshold Hysteresis	% of the Total Number of an Interface's Large Receive Buffers	0%	15%	3%	NetDbg_CfgRsrcBufRxLargeThLo()
Interface's Small Transmit Buffer Low Threshold	% of the Total Number of an Interface's Small Transmit Buffers	5%	50%	5%	NetDbg_CfgRsrcBufTxSmallThLo()

Parameter	Units	Min	Max	Default	Configuration Function
Interface's Small Transmit Buffer Low Threshold Hysteresis	% of the Total Number of an Interface's Small Transmit Buffers	0%	15%	3%	`NetDbg_CfgRsrcBufTxSmallThLo()`
Interface's Large Transmit Buffer Low Threshold	% of the Total Number of an Interface's Large Transmit Buffers	5%	50%	5%	`NetDbg_CfgRsrcBufTxLargeThLo()`
Interface's Large Transmit Buffer Low Threshold Hysteresis	% of the Total Number of an Interface's Large Transmit Buffers	0%	15%	3%	`NetDbg_CfgRsrcBufTxLargeThLo()`
Network Timer Low Threshold	% of the Total Number of Network Timers	5%	50%	5%	`NetDbg_CfgRsrcTmrLoTh()`
Network Timer Low Threshold Hysteresis	% of the Total Number of Network Timers	0%	15%	3%	`NetDbg_CfgRsrcTmrLoTh()`
Network Connection Low Threshold	% of the Total Number of Network Connections	5%	50%	5%	`NetDbg_CfgRsrcConnLoTh()`
Network Connection Low Threshold Hysteresis	% of the Total Number of Network Connections	0%	15%	3%	`NetDbg_CfgRsrcConnLoTh()`
ARP Cache Low Threshold	% of the Total Number of ARP Caches	5%	50%	5%	`NetDbg_CfgRsrcARP_CacheLoTh()`
ARP Cache Low Threshold Hysteresis	% of the Total Number of ARP Caches	0%	15%	3%	`NetDbg_CfgRsrcARP_CacheLoTh()`
TCP Connection Low Threshold	% of the Total Number of TCP Connections	5%	50%	5%	`NetDbg_CfgRsrcTCP_ConnLoTh()`
TCP Connection Low Threshold Hysteresis	% of the Total Number of TCP Connections	0%	15%	3%	`NetDbg_CfgRsrcTCP_ConnLoTh()`
Socket Low Threshold	% of the Total Number of Sockets	5%	50%	5%	`NetDbg_CfgRsrcSockLoTh()`
Socket Low Threshold Hysteresis	% of the Total Number of Sockets	0%	15%	3%	`NetDbg_CfgRsrcSockLoTh()`
Resource Monitor Task Time	Seconds	1	600	60	`NetDbg_CfgMonTaskTime()`
Network Connection Accessed Threshold	Number of Network Connections	10	6500 0	100	`NetConn_CfgAccessTh()`

Parameter	Units	Min	Max	Default	Configuration Function
Network Interface Physical Link Monitor Period	Milliseconds	50	60000	250	`NetIF_CfgPhyLinkPeriod()`
Network Interface Performance Monitor Period	Milliseconds	50	60000	250	`NetIF_CfgPerfMonPeriod()`
ARP Cache Timeout	Seconds	60	600	600	`NetARP_CfgCacheTimeout()`
ARP Cache Accessed Threshold	Number of ARP Caches	100	65000	100	`NetARP_CfgCacheAccessedTh()`
ARP Request Timeout	Seconds	1	10	5	`NetARP_CfgReqTimeout()`
ARP Request Maximum Number of Retries	Maximum Number of Transmitted ARP Request Retries	0	5	3	`NetARP_CfgReqMaxRetries()`
IP Receive Fragments Reassembly Timeout	Seconds	1	15	5	`NetIP_CfgFragReasmTimeout()`
ICMP Transmit Source Quench Threshold	Number of Transmitted ICMP Source Quenches	1	100	5	`NetICMP_CfgTxSrcQuenchTh()`

Table C-1 **µC/TCP-IP Internal Configuration Parameters**

`NET_INIT_CFG_VALS_APP_INIT`

It is possible to change the parameters listed in by calling the above configuration functions. These values could be stored in non-volatile memory and recalled at power up (*e.g.*, using EEPROM or battery-backed RAM) by the application. Similarly the values could be hard-coded directly in the application. Regardless of how the application configures the values, if this option is selected, the application must initialize **all** of the above configuration parameters using the configuration functions listed above.

Alternatively, the application could call `Net_InitDflt()` to initialize all of the internal configuration parameters to their default values and then call the configuration functions for only the values to be modified.

C-1-2 NET_CFG_OPTIMIZE

Select portions of µC/TCP-IP code may be optimized for better performance or for smallest code size by configuring NET_CFG_OPTIMIZE:

NET_OPTIMIZE_SPD	Optimizes µC/TCP-IP for best speed performance
NET_OPTIMIZE_SIZE	Optimizes µC/TCP-IP for best binary image size

C-1-3 NET_CFG_OPTIMIZE_ASM_EN

Select portions of µC/TCP-IP code may even call optimized assembly functions by configuring NET_CFG_OPTIMIZE_ASM_EN:

DEF_DISABLED — No optimized assembly files/functions are included in the µC/TCP-IP build

or

DEF_ENABLED — Optimized assembly files/functions are included in the µC/TCP-IP build

C-1-4 NET_CFG_BUILD_LIB_EN

µC/TCP-IP can be compiled on some toolchains into a linkable library by configuring NET_CFG_BUILD_LIB_EN:

DEF_DISABLED — µC/TCP-IP **not** compiled as a linkable library

or

DEF_ENABLED — Build µC/TCP-IP as a linkable library

C-2 DEBUG CONFIGURATION

A fair amount of code in μC/TCP-IP has been included to simplify debugging. There are several configuration constants used to aid debugging.

C-2-1 NET_DBG_CFG_INFO_EN

NET_DBG_CFG_INFO_EN is used to enable/disable μC/TCP-IP debug information:

- Internal constants assigned to global variables
- Internal variable data sizes calculated and assigned to global variables

NET_DBG_CFG_INFO_EN can be set to either **DEF_DISABLED** or DEF_ENABLED.

C-2-2 NET_DBG_CFG_STATUS_EN

NET_DBG_CFG_STATUS_EN is used to enable/disable μC/TCP-IP run-time status information:

- Internal resource usage – low or lost resources
- Internal faults or errors

NET_DBG_CFG_STATUS_EN can be set to either **DEF_DISABLED** or DEF_ENABLED.

C-2-3 NET_DBG_CFG_MEM_CLR_EN

NET_DBG_CFG_MEM_CLR_EN is used to clear internal network data structures when allocated or de-allocated. By clearing, all bytes in internal data structures are set to '0' or to default initialization values. NET_DBG_CFG_MEM_CLR_EN can be set to either **DEF_DISABLED** or DEF_ENABLED. This configuration is typically set it to DEF_DISABLED unless the contents of the internal network data structures need to be examined for debugging purposes. Having the internal network data structures cleared generally helps to differentiate between "proper" data and "pollution".

C-2-4 NET_DBG_CFG_TEST_EN

NET_DBG_CFG_TEST_EN is used internally for testing/debugging purposes and can be set to either **DEF_DISABLED** or DEF_ENABLED.

C-3 ARGUMENT CHECKING CONFIGURATION

Most functions in µC/TCP-IP include code to validate arguments that are passed to it. Specifically, µC/TCP-IP checks to see if passed pointers are NULL, if arguments are within valid ranges, etc. The following constants configure additional argument checking.

C-3-1 NET_ERR_CFG_ARG_CHK_EXT_EN

NET_ERR_CFG_ARG_CHK_EXT_EN allows code to be generated to check arguments for functions that can be called by the user and, for functions which are internal but receive arguments from an API that the user can call. Also, enabling this check verifies that µC/TCP-IP is initialized before API tasks and functions perform the desired function.

NET_ERR_CFG_ARG_CHK_EXT_EN can be set to either DEF_DISABLED or **DEF_ENABLED**.

C-3-2 NET_ERR_CFG_ARG_CHK_DBG_EN

NET_ERR_CFG_ARG_CHK_DBG_EN allows code to be generated which checks to make sure that pointers passed to functions are not NULL, and that arguments are within range, etc. NET_ERR_CFG_ARG_CHK_DBG_EN can be set to either **DEF_DISABLED** or DEF_ENABLED.

C-4 NETWORK COUNTER CONFIGURATION

µC/TCP-IP contains code that increments counters to keep track of statistics such as the number of packets received, the number of packets transmitted, etc. Also, µC/TCP-IP contains counters that are incremented when error conditions are detected. The following constants enable or disable network counters.

C-4-1 NET_CTR_CFG_STAT_EN

NET_CTR_CFG_STAT_EN determines whether the code and data space used to keep track of statistics will be included. NET_CTR_CFG_STAT_EN can be set to either DEF_DISABLED or **DEF_ENABLED**.

C-4-2 NET_CTR_CFG_ERR_EN

NET_CTR_CFG_ERR_EN determines whether the code and data space used to keep track of errors will be included. NET_CTR_CFG_ERR_EN can be set to either **DEF_DISABLED** or DEF_ENABLED.

C-5 NETWORK TIMER CONFIGURATION

µC/TCP-IP manages software timers used to keep track of timeouts and execute callback functions when needed.

C-5-1 NET_TMR_CFG_NBR_TMR

NET_TMR_CFG_NBR_TMR determines the number of timers that µC/TCP-IP will be managing. Of course, the number of timers affect the amount of RAM required by µC/TCP-IP. Each timer requires 12 bytes plus 4 pointers. Timers are required for:

- The Network Debug Monitor Task 1 total
- The Network Performance Monitor 1 total
- The Network Link State Handler 1 total
- Each ARP cache entry 1 per ARP cache
- Each IP fragment reassembly 1 per IP fragment chain
- Each TCP connection 7 per TCP connection

It is recommended to set NET_TMR_CFG_NBR_TMR with at least **12 timers**, but a better starting point may be to allocate the maximum number of timers for all resources.

For instance, if the Network Debug Monitor Task is enabled (see section 19-2 "Network Debug Monitor Task" on page 380), 20 ARP caches are configured (NET_ARP_CFG_NBR_CACHE = 20), & 10 TCP connections are configured (NET_TCP_CFG_NBR_CONN = 10); the maximum number of timers for these resources is 1 for the Network Debug Monitor Task, 1 for the Network Performance Monitor, 1 for the Link State Handler, (20 * 1) for the ARP caches and, (10 * 7) for TCP connections:

 # Timers = 1 + 1 + 1 + (20 * 1) + (10 * 7) = 93

C-5-2 NET_TMR_CFG_TASK_FREQ

NET_TMR_CFG_TASK_FREQ determines how often (in Hz) network timers are to be updated. This value *must not* be configured as a floating-point number. NET_TMR_CFG_TASK_FREQ is typically set to **10 Hz**.

C-6 NETWORK BUFFER CONFIGURATION

µC/TCP-IP manages Network Buffers to read data to and from network applications and network devices. Network Buffers are specially configured with network devices as described in Chapter 14, "Network Device Drivers" on page 299.

C-7 NETWORK INTERFACE LAYER CONFIGURATION

C-7-1 NET_IF_CFG_MAX_NBR_IF

NET_IF_CFG_MAX_NBR_IF determines the maximum number of network interfaces that µC/TCP-IP may create at run-time. The default value of **1** is for a single network interface.

C-7-2 NET_IF_CFG_LOOPBACK_EN

NET_IF_CFG_LOOPBACK_EN determines whether the code and data space used to support the loopback interface for internal-only communication only will be included. NET_IF_CFG_LOOPBACK_EN can be set to either **DEF_DISABLED** or DEF_ENABLED.

C-7-3 NET_IF_CFG_ETHER_EN

NET_IF_CFG_ETHER_EN determines whether the code and data space used to support Ethernet interfaces and devices will be included. NET_IF_CFG_ETHER_EN can be set to either DEF_DISABLED or **DEF_ENABLED**, but must be enabled if the target expects to communicate over Ethernet networks.

C-7-4 NET_IF_CFG_WIFI_EN

NET_IF_CFG_WIFI_EN determines whether the code and data space used to support wireless interfaces and devices will be included. NET_IF_CFG_WIFI_EN can be set to either DEF_DISABLED or **DEF_ENABLED**, but must be enabled if the target expects to communicate over wireless networks.

C-7-5 NET_IF_CFG_ADDR_FLTR_EN

NET_IF_CFG_ADDR_FLTR_EN determines whether address filtering is enabled or not:

DEF_DISABLED Addresses are *not* filtered

or

DEF_ENABLED Addresses are filtered

C-7-6 NET_IF_CFG_TX_SUSPEND_TIMEOUT_MS

NET_IF_CFG_TX_SUSPEND_TIMEOUT_MS configures the network interface transmit suspend timeout value. The value is specified in integer milliseconds. It is recommended to initially set NET_IF_CFG_TX_SUSPEND_TIMEOUT_MS with a value of **1 millisecond**.

C-8 ARP (ADDRESS RESOLUTION PROTOCOL) CONFIGURATION

ARP is only required for some network interfaces such as Ethernet.

C-8-1 NET_ARP_CFG_HW_TYPE

The current version of μC/TCP-IP only supports Ethernet-type networks, and thus NET_ARP_CFG_HW_TYPE should *always* be set to **NET_ARP_HW_TYPE_ETHER**.

C-8-2 NET_ARP_CFG_PROTOCOL_TYPE

The current version of μC/TCP-IP only supports IPv4, and thus NET_ARP_CFG_PROTOCOL_TYPE should *always* be set to **NET_ARP_PROTOCOL_TYPE_IP_V4**.

C-8-3 NET_ARP_CFG_NBR_CACHE

ARP caches the mapping of IP addresses to physical (i.e., MAC) addresses. NET_ARP_CFG_NBR_CACHE configures the number of ARP cache entries. Each cache entry requires approximately 18 bytes of RAM, plus five pointers, plus a hardware address and protocol address (10 bytes assuming Ethernet interfaces and IPv4 addresses).

The number of ARP caches required by the application depends on how many different hosts are expected to communicate. If the application *only* communicates with hosts on remote networks via the local network's default gateway (i.e., router), then only a single ARP cache needs to be configured.

To test µC/TCP-IP with a smaller network, a default number of 3 ARP caches should be sufficient.

C-8-4 NET_ARP_CFG_ADDR_FLTR_EN

NET_ARP_CFG_ADDR_FLTR_EN determines whether to enable address filtering:

DEF_DISABLED Addresses are *not* filtered

or

DEF_ENABLED Addresses are filtered

C-9 IP (INTERNET PROTOCOL) CONFIGURATION

C-9-1 NET_IP_CFG_IF_MAX_NBR_ADDR

NET_IP_CFG_IF_MAX_NBR_ADDR determines the maximum number of IP addresses that may be configured per network interface at run-time. It is recommended to set NET_IP_CFG_IF_MAX_NBR_ADDR to the initial, default value of **1 IP address** per network interface and increased if the µC/TCP-IP target requires more addresses on each interface.

C-9-2 NET_IP_CFG_MULTICAST_SEL

NET_IP_CFG_MULTICAST_SEL is used to determine the IP multicast support level. The allowable values for this parameter are:

NET_IP_MULTICAST_SEL_NONE	No multicasting
NET_IP_MULTICAST_SEL_TX	Transmit multicasting only
NET_IP_MULTICAST_SEL_TX_RX	Transmit and receive multicasting

C-10 ICMP (INTERNET CONTROL MESSAGE PROTOCOL) CONFIGURATION

C-10-1 NET_ICMP_CFG_TX_SRC_QUENCH_EN

ICMP transmits ICMP source quench messages to other hosts when the Network Resources are low (see section 19-2 "Network Debug Monitor Task" on page 380). NET_ICMP_CFG_TX_SRC_QUENCH_EN can be set to either:

DEF_DISABLED ICMP does not transmit any Source Quenches

or

DEF_ENABLED ICMP transmits Source Quenches when necessary

C-10-2 NET_ICMP_CFG_TX_SRC_QUENCH_NBR

NET_ICMP_CFG_TX_SRC_QUENCH_NBR configures the number of ICMP transmit source quench entries. Each source quench entry requires approximately 12 bytes of RAM plus two pointers.

The number of entries depends on the number of different hosts to communicate with. It is recommended to set NET_ICMP_CFG_TX_SRC_QUENCH_NBR with an initial value of **5** and adjusted if the µC/TCP-IP target communicates with more or less hosts.

C-11 IGMP (INTERNET GROUP MANAGEMENT PROTOCOL) CONFIGURATION

C-11-1 NET_IGMP_CFG_MAX_NBR_HOST_GRP

NET_IGMP_CFG_MAX_NBR_HOST_GRP configures the maximum number of IGMP host groups that may be joined at any one time. Each group entry requires approximately 12 bytes of RAM, plus three pointers, plus a protocol address (4 bytes assuming IPv4 address).

The number of IGMP host groups required by the application depends on how many host groups are expected to be joined at a given time. Since each configured multicast address requires its own IGMP host group, it is recommended to configure at least one host group per multicast address used by the application, plus one additional host group. Thus for a single multicast address, it is recommended to set NET_IGMP_CFG_MAX_NBR_HOST_GRP with an initial value of **2**.

C-12 TRANSPORT LAYER CONFIGURATION

C-12-1 NET_CFG_TRANSPORT_LAYER_SEL

µC/TCP-IP allows you to include code for either UDP alone or for both UDP and TCP. Most application software requires TCP as well as UDP. However, enabling UDP only reduces both the code and data size required by µC/TCP-IP. NET_CFG_TRANSPORT_LAYER_SEL can be set to either:

NET_TRANSPORT_LAYER_SEL_UDP_TCP UDP and TCP transport layers included

or

NET_TRANSPORT_LAYER_SEL_UDP Only UDP transport layer included

C-13 UDP (USER DATAGRAM PROTOCOL) CONFIGURATION

C-13-1 NET_UDP_CFG_APP_API_SEL

NET_UDP_CFG_APP_API_SEL is used to determine where to send the de-multiplexed UDP datagram. Specifically, the datagram may be sent to the socket layer, to a function at the application level, or both. NET_UDP_CFG_APP_API_SEL can be set to one of the following values:

NET_UDP_APP_API_SEL_SOCK	De-multiplex receive datagrams to socket layer only
NET_UDP_APP_API_SEL_APP	De-multiplex receive datagrams to the application only
NET_UDP_APP_API_SEL_SOCK_APP	De-multiplex receive datagrams to socket layer first, then to the application

If either NET_UDP_APP_API_SEL_APP or NET_UDP_APP_API_SEL_SOCK_APP is configured, the application must define **NetUDP_RxAppDataHandler()** to de-multiplex receive datagrams by the application (see section B-16-2 on page 698).

C-13-2 NET_UDP_CFG_RX_CHK_SUM_DISCARD_EN

NET_UDP_CFG_RX_CHK_SUM_DISCARD_EN is used to determine whether received UDP packets without a valid checksum are discarded or are handled and processed. Before a UDP Datagram Check-Sum is validated, it is necessary to check whether the UDP datagram was transmitted with or without a computed Check-Sum (see RFC #768, Section 'Fields: Checksum').

NET_UDP_CFG_RX_CHK_SUM_DISCARD_EN can be set to either:

DEF_DISABLED	UDP Layer processes but flags all UDP datagrams received without a checksum so that "an application may optionally discard datagrams without checksums" (see RFC #1122, Section 4.1.3.4).

or

DEF_ENABLED	All UDP datagrams received without a checksum are discarded.

C-13-3 NET_UDP_CFG_TX_CHK_SUM_EN

NET_UDP_CFG_TX_CHK_SUM_EN is used to determine whether UDP checksums are computed for transmission to other hosts. An application MAY optionally be able to control whether a UDP checksum will be generated (see RFC #1122, Section 4.1.3.4).

NET_UDP_CFG_TX_CHK_SUM_EN can be set to either:

DEF_DISABLED — All UDP datagrams are transmitted without a computed checksum

or

DEF_ENABLED — All UDP datagrams are transmitted with a computed checksum

C-14 TCP (TRANSPORT CONTROL PROTOCOL) CONFIGURATION

C-14-1 NET_TCP_CFG_NBR_CONN

NET_TCP_CFG_NBR_CONN configures the maximum number of TCP connections that µC/TCP-IP can handle concurrently. This number depends entirely on how many simultaneous TCP connections the application requires. Each TCP connection requires approximately 220 bytes of RAM plus 16 pointers. It is recommended to set NET_TCP_CFG_NBR_CONN with an initial value of **10** and adjust this value if more or less TCP connections are required.

C-14-2 NET_TCP_CFG_RX_WIN_SIZE_OCTET

NET_TCP_CFG_RX_WIN_SIZE_OCTET configures each TCP connection's receive window size. It is recommended to set TCP window sizes to integer multiples of each TCP connection's maximum segment size (MSS). For example, systems with an Ethernet MSS of 1460, a value 5840 (4 * 1460) is probably a better configuration than the default window size of **4096** (4K).

C-14-3 NET_TCP_CFG_TX_WIN_SIZE_OCTET

NET_TCP_CFG_TX_WIN_SIZE_OCTET configures each TCP connection's transmit window size. It is recommended to set TCP window sizes to integer multiples of each TCP connection's maximum segment size (MSS). For example, systems with an Ethernet MSS of 1460, a value 5840 (4 * 1460) is probably a better configuration than the default window size of **4096** (4K).

C-14-4 NET_TCP_CFG_TIMEOUT_CONN_MAX_SEG_SEC

NET_TCP_CFG_TIMEOUT_CONN_MAX_SEG_SEC configures TCP connections' default maximum segment lifetime timeout (MSL) value, specified in integer seconds. It is recommended to start with a value of **3 seconds**.

If TCP connections are established and closed rapidly, it is possible that this timeout may further delay new TCP connections from becoming available. Thus, an even lower timeout value may be desirable to free TCP connections and make them available as quickly as possible. However, a 0 second timeout prevents µC/TCP-IP from performing the complete TCP connection close sequence and will instead send TCP reset (RST) segments.

C-14-5 NET_TCP_CFG_TIMEOUT_CONN_FIN_WAIT_2_SEC

NET_TCP_CFG_TIMEOUT_CONN_FIN_WAIT_2_SEC configures the TCP connection default FIN-WAIT-2 timeout (in seconds *or* no timeout if configured with NET_TMR_TIME_INFINITE). On a typical connection close (FIN/ACK/FIN/ACK), this timeout defines the maximum delay between the ACK/FIN packets sent by the remote host. It is recommended to set NET_TCP_CFG_TIMEOUT_CONN_FIN_WAIT_2_SEC with a value of 15 seconds.

C-14-6 NET_TCP_CFG_TIMEOUT_CONN_ACK_DLY_MS

NET_TCP_CFG_TIMEOUT_CONN_ACK_DLY_MS configures the TCP acknowledgement delay in integer milliseconds. It is recommended to configure the default value of **500 milliseconds** since RFC #2581, Section 4.2 states that "an ACK *must* be generated within 500 ms of the arrival of the first unacknowledged packet".

C-14-7 NET_TCP_CFG_TIMEOUT_CONN_RX_Q_MS

NET_TCP_CFG_TIMEOUT_CONN_RX_Q_MS configures each TCP connection's receive timeout (in milliseconds *or* no timeout if configured with NET_TMR_TIME_INFINITE). It is recommended to start with a value of 3000 milliseconds *or* the no-timeout value of **NET_TMR_TIME_INFINITE**.

C-14-8 NET_TCP_CFG_TIMEOUT_CONN_TX_Q_MS

NET_TCP_CFG_TIMEOUT_CONN_TX_Q_MS configures each TCP connection's transmit timeout (in milliseconds *or* no timeout if configured with NET_TMR_TIME_INFINITE). It is recommended to start with a value of 3000 milliseconds *or* the no-timeout value of **NET_TMR_TIME_INFINITE**.

C-15 NETWORK SOCKET CONFIGURATION

µC/TCP-IP supports BSD 4.x sockets and basic socket API for the TCP/UDP/IP protocols.

C-15-1 NET_SOCK_CFG_FAMILY

The current version of µC/TCP-IP only supports IPv4 BSD sockets, and thus NET_SOCK_CFG_FAMILY should *always* be set to **NET_SOCK_FAMILY_IP_V4**.

C-15-2 NET_SOCK_CFG_NBR_SOCK

NET_SOCK_CFG_NBR_SOCK configures the maximum number of sockets that µC/TCP-IP can handle concurrently. This number depends entirely on how many simultaneous socket connections the application requires. Each socket requires approximately 28 bytes of RAM plus three pointers. It is recommended to set NET_SOCK_CFG_NBR_SOCK with an initial value of **10** and adjust this value if more or less sockets are required.

C-15-3 NET_SOCK_CFG_BLOCK_SEL

NET_SOCK_CFG_BLOCK_SEL determines the default blocking (or non-blocking) behavior for sockets:

NET_SOCK_BLOCK_SEL_DFLT	Sockets will be blocking by default, but may be individually configured in a future release
NET_SOCK_BLOCK_SEL_BLOCK	Sockets will be blocking by default
NET_SOCK_BLOCK_SEL_NO_BLOCK	Sockets will be non-blocking by default

If blocking mode is enabled, a timeout can be specified. The amount of time for the timeout is determined by various timeout functions implemented in **net_sock.c**:

NetSock_CfgTimeoutRxQ_Set()	Configure datagram socket receive timeout
NetSock_CfgTimeoutConnReqSet()	Configure socket connection timeout
NetSock_CfgTimeoutConnAcceptSet()	Configure socket accept timeout
NetSock_CfgTimeoutConnClOSset()	Configure socket close timeout

C-15-4 NET_SOCK_CFG_SEL_EN

NET_SOCK_CFG_SEL_EN determines whether or not the code and data space used to support socket **select()** functionality is enabled:

DEF_DISABLED BSD **select()** API disabled

or

DEF_ENABLED BSD **select()** API enabled

C-15-5 NET_SOCK_CFG_SEL_NBR_EVENTS_MAX

NET_SOCK_CFG_SEL_NBR_EVENTS_MAX is used to configure the maximum number of socket events/operations that the socket **select()** functionality can wait on. It is recommended to set NET_SOCK_CFG_SEL_NBR_EVENTS_MAX with an initial value of at least **10** and adjust this value if more or less socket **select()** events are required.

C-15-6 NET_SOCK_CFG_CONN_ACCEPT_Q_SIZE_MAX

NET_SOCK_CFG_CONN_ACCEPT_Q_SIZE_MAX is used to configure the absolute maximum queue size of **accept()** connections for stream-type sockets. It is recommended to set NET_SOCK_CFG_CONN_ACCEPT_Q_SIZE_MAX with an initial value of at least **5** and adjust this value if more or less socket connections need to be queued.

C-15-7 NET_SOCK_CFG_PORT_NBR_RANDOM_BASE

NET_SOCK_CFG_PORT_NBR_RANDOM_BASE is used to configure the starting base socket number for "ephemeral" or "random" port numbers. Since two times the number of random ports are required for each socket, the base value for the random port number must be:

```
Random Port Number Base <= 65535 – (2 * NET_SOCK_CFG_NBR_SOCK)
```

The arbitrary default value of **65000** is recommended as a good starting point.

C-15-8 NET_SOCK_CFG_RX_Q_SIZE_OCTET

NET_SOCK_CFG_RX_Q_SIZE_OCTET configures datagram sockets default receive queue buffer size in integer number of octets. According to 4.3BSD, it is recommended to set NET_SOCK_CFG_RX_Q_SIZE_OCTET with a value of 4096 octets. However, systems such as 4.4BSD use larger default buffer sizes, such as 8192 or 16384 bytes. This configuration does not impact TCP default receive windows size.

C-15-9 NET_SOCK_CFG_TX_Q_SIZE_OCTET

NET_SOCK_CFG_TX_Q_SIZE_OCTET configures datagram sockets default transmit queue buffer size in integer number of octets. According to 4.3BSD, it is recommended to set NET_SOCK_CFG_TX_Q_SIZE_OCTET with a value of 4096 octets. However, systems such as 4.4BSD use larger default buffer sizes, such as 8192 or 16384 bytes. This configuration does not impact TCP default transmit windows size.

C-15-10 NET_SOCK_CFG_TIMEOUT_RX_Q_MS

NET_SOCK_CFG_TIMEOUT_RX_Q_MS configures socket timeout value (in milliseconds *or* no timeout if configured with NET_TMR_TIME_INFINITE) for UDP datagram socket recv() operations. It is recommended to set NET_SOCK_CFG_TIMEOUT_RX_Q_MS with a value of 3000 milliseconds *or* the no-timeout value of **NET_TMR_TIME_INFINITE**.

C-15-11 NET_SOCK_CFG_TIMEOUT_CONN_REQ_MS

NET_SOCK_CFG_TIMEOUT_CONN_REQ_MS configures socket timeout value (in milliseconds *or* no timeout if configured with NET_TMR_TIME_INFINITE) for stream socket connect() operations. It is recommended to set NET_SOCK_CFG_TIMEOUT_CONN_REQ_MS with a value of 3000 milliseconds *or* the no-timeout value of **NET_TMR_TIME_INFINITE**.

C-15-12 NET_SOCK_CFG_TIMEOUT_CONN_ACCEPT_MS

NET_SOCK_CFG_TIMEOUT_CONN_ACCEPT_MS configures socket timeout value (in milliseconds *or* no timeout if configured with NET_TMR_TIME_INFINITE) for socket accept() operations. It is recommended to set NET_SOCK_CFG_TIMEOUT_CONN_ACCEPT_MS with a value of 3000 milliseconds *or* the no-timeout value of **NET_TMR_TIME_INFINITE**.

C-15-13 NET_SOCK_CFG_TIMEOUT_CONN_CLOSE_MS

NET_SOCK_CFG_TIMEOUT_CONN_CLOSE_MS configures socket timeout value (in milliseconds *or* no timeout if configured with NET_TMR_TIME_INFINITE) for socket close() operations. It is recommended to set NET_SOCK_CFG_TIMEOUT_CONN_CLOSE_MS with a value of **10000 milliseconds** *or* the no-timeout value of NET_TMR_TIME_INFINITE.

C-16 NETWORK SECURITY MANAGER CONFIGURATION

C-16-1 NET_SECURE_CFG_EN

NET_SECURE_CFG_EN determines whether or not the network security manager is enabled. When the network security manager is enabled, a network security module (e.g., µC/SSL) must be present in the build. NET_SECURE_CFG_EN can be set to either:

DEF_DISABLED	Network security manager and security port layer disabled

or

DEF_ENABLED	Network security manager and security port layer enabled

C-16-2 NET_SECURE_CFG_FS_EN

NET_SECURE_CFG_FS_EN determines whether or not file system operations can be used to install keying material. When NET_SECURE_CFG_FS_EN is enabled, a file system (e.g., µC/FS) must be present in the build. NET_SECURE_CFG_FS_EN can be set to either:

DEF_DISABLED	Keying material cannot be installed from file system

or

DEF_ENABLED	Keying material can be installed from file system

C-16-3 NET_SECURE_CFG_VER

NET_SECURE_CFG_VER determines the default protocol version of the network security layer and can be set to one of the following values:

NET_SECURE_SSL_V2_0	SSL V2.0
NET_SECURE_SSL_V3_0	SSL V3.0
NET_SECURE_TLS_V1_0	TLS V1.0

NET_SECURE_TLS_V1_1	TLS V1.1
NET_SECURE_TLS_V1_2	TLS V1.2

Please refer to the specific network security module (e.g., µC/SSL) to determine which protocol versions are supported.

C-16-4 NET_SECURE_CFG_WORD_SIZE

NET_SECURE_CFG_WORD_SIZE configures an optimized word size for the network security port, if applicable:

CPU_WORD_SIZE_08	8-bit word size
CPU_WORD_SIZE_16	16-bit word size
CPU_WORD_SIZE_32	32-bit word size
CPU_WORD_SIZE_64	64-bit word size

NET_SECURE_CFG_WORD_SIZE should be configured to CPU_WORD_SIZE_64 **only if** 64-bit data types and optimization is available by the specific network security module (e.g., µC/SSL).

C-16-5 NET_SECURE_CFG_CLIENT_DOWNGRADE_EN

NET_SECURE_CFG_CLIENT_DOWNGRADE_EN determines whether or not the client downgrade option is enabled. If client downgrading is enabled, client applications will be allowed to connect on a server that is using a protocol version older than NET_SECURE_CFG_VER. NET_SECURE_CFG_CLIENT_DOWNGRADE_EN can be set to either **DEF_DISABLED** or DEF_ENABLED but it is recommended to disable client downgrading.

C-16-6 NET_SECURE_CFG_SERVER_DOWNGRADE_EN

NET_SECURE_CFG_SERVER_DOWNGRADE_EN determines whether or not the server downgrade option is enabled. If server downgrading is enabled, server will be allowed to accept connection request coming from clients that are using a protocol version older than NET_SECURE_CFG_VER. NET_SECURE_CFG_SERVER_DOWNGRADE_EN can be set to either DEF_DISABLED or **DEF_ENABLED** but it is recommended to enable server downgrading.

C-16-7 NET_SECURE_CFG_MAX_NBR_SOCK

NET_SECURE_CFG_MAX_NBR_SOCK configures the maximum number of sockets that can be secured. If your application is a simple TCP server, you need to have two secure sockets (one listening socket and one accepted socket). If your application is a simple TCP client, you will only need to have one secure socket to connect. It is recommended to set NET_SECURE_CFG_MAX_NBR_SOCK to the initial value of **5 sockets** and adjust this value if more or less sockets are required. However, the maximum number of secure sockets must be less than or equal to NET_SOCK_CFG_NBR_SOCK (see section C-15-2 on page 740).

C-16-8 NET_SECURE_CFG_MAX_NBR_CA

NET_SECURE_CFG_MAX_NBR_CA configures the maximum number of certificate authorities (CAs) that can be installed. If many CAs are installed, they are saved into a linked-list. When the client receives the server public key certificate, it scans the linked-list to see if it is trusted by one of the installed CAs.

C-16-9 NET_SECURE_CFG_MAX_KEY_LEN

NET_SECURE_CFG_MAX_KEY_LEN configures the maximum length (in bytes) of a certificate authority, a public key certificate or a private key. It is recommended to set NET_SECURE_CFG_MAX_KEY_LEN to the default value of **1500** for standard keying material and adjust this value if required. You can find the size of any certificate authority, public key or private key by right clicking on the DER or PEM file on a Windows environment and by choosing 'Properties'. Usually DER encoded keying material is smaller than PEM encoded keying material.

C-16-10 NET_SECURE_CFG_MAX_ISSUER_CN_LEN

NET_SECURE_CFG_MAX_ISSUER_CN_LEN configures the maximum length (in bytes) of common names. The common name is chosen during the creation of the certificate. Most of the time, it is the name of the company that is using the certificate (i.e, Micrium, Google, Paypal, etc.). It is recommended to set NET_SECURE_CFG_MAX_ISSUER_CN_LEN with an initial value of **20** and adjust this value if longer or shorter common names are required.

C-16-11 NET_SECURE_CFG_MAX_PUBLIC_KEY_LEN

NET_SECURE_CFG_MAX_PUBLIC_KEY_LEN configures the maximum length (in bytes) of public key. The public key is part of the public key certificate and is chosen during the creation of the certificate. It is recommended to set NET_SECURE_CFG_MAX_PUBLIC_KEY_LEN with an initial value of **256** and adjust this value if longer or shorter public keys are required.

C-17 BSD SOCKETS CONFIGURATION

C-17-1 NET_BSD_CFG_API_EN

NET_BSD_CFG_API_EN determines whether or not the standard BSD 4.x socket API is included in the build:

DEF_DISABLED BSD 4.x layer API disabled

or

DEF_ENABLED BSD 4.x layer API enabled

C-18 NETWORK APPLICATION INTERFACE CONFIGURATION

C-18-1 NET_APP_CFG_API_EN

NET_APP_CFG_API_EN determines whether or not a simplified network application programming interface (API) is included in the build:

DEF_DISABLED Network API layer disabled

or

DEF_ENABLED Network API layer enabled

C-19 NETWORK CONNECTION MANAGER CONFIGURATION

C-19-1 NET_CONN_CFG_FAMILY

The current version of µC/TCP-IP only supports IPv4 connections, and thus NET_CONN_CFG_FAMILY should *always* be set to **NET_CONN_FAMILY_IP_V4_SOCK**.

C-19-2 NET_CONN_CFG_NBR_CONN

NET_CONN_CFG_NBR_CONN configures the maximum number of connections that µC/TCP-IP can handle concurrently. This number depends entirely on how many simultaneous connections the application requires and *must* be at least greater than the configured number of application (socket) connections and transport layer (TCP) connections. Each connection requires approximately **28** bytes of RAM, plus five pointers, plus two protocol addresses (8 bytes assuming IPv4 addresses). It is recommended to set NET_CONN_CFG_NBR_CONN with an initial value of **20** and adjust this value if more or less connections are required.

C-20 APPLICATION-SPECIFIC CONFIGURATION

This section defines the configuration constants related to µC/TCP-IP but that are application-specific. Most of these configuration constants relate to the various ports for µC/TCP-IP such as the CPU, OS, device, or network interface ports. Other configuration constants relate to the compiler and standard library ports.

These configuration constants should be defined in an application's `app_cfg.h` file.

C-20-1 OPERATING SYSTEM CONFIGURATION

The following configuration constants relate to the µC/TCP-IP OS port. For many OSs, the µC/TCP-IP task priorities, stack sizes, and other options will need to be explicitly configured for the particular OS (consult the specific OS's documentation for more information).

The priority of µC/TCP-IP tasks is dependent on the network communication requirements of the application. For most applications, the priority for µC/TCP-IP tasks is typically lower than the priority for other application tasks.

For µC/OS-II and µC/OS-III, the following macros must be configured within `app_cfg.h`:

```
NET_OS_CFG_IF_TX_DEALLOC_PRIO              10    (highest priority)
NET_OS_CFG_TMR_TASK_PRIO                   51
NET_OS_CFG_IF_RX_TASK_PRIO                 52    (lowest  priority)
```

The arbitrary task priorities of **10**, **51**, and **52** are a good starting point for most applications, where the Network Interface Transmit De-allocation Task is assigned a higher priority than all application tasks that use µC/TCP-IP network services but the Network Timer Task and Network Interface Receive Task are assigned lower priorities than almost all other application tasks.

```
NET_OS_CFG_IF_TX_DEALLOC_TASK_STK_SIZE  1000
NET_OS_CFG_IF_RX_TASK_STK_SIZE          1000
NET_OS_CFG_TMR_TASK_STK_SIZE            1000
```

The arbitrary stack size of **1000** is a good starting point for most applications.

The only guaranteed method of determining the required task stack sizes is to calculate the maximum stack usage for each task. Obviously, the maximum stack usage for a task is the total stack usage along the task's most-stack-greedy function path plus the (maximum) stack usage for interrupts. Note that the most-stack-greedy function path is not necessarily the longest or deepest function path.

The easiest and best method for calculating the maximum stack usage for any task/function should be performed statically by the compiler or by a static analysis tool since these can calculate function/task maximum stack usage based on the compiler's actual code generation and optimization settings. So for optimal task stack configuration, we recommend to invest in a task stack calculator tool compatible with your build toolchain.

C-20-2 µC/TCP-IP CONFIGURATION

The following configuration constants relate to the µC/TCP-IP OS port. For many OSs, the µC/TCP-IP maximum queue sizes may need to be explicitly configured for the particular OS (consult the specific OS's documentation for more information).

For µC/OS-II and µC/OS-III, the following macros must be configured within `app_cfg.h`:

`NET_OS_CFG_IF_RX_Q_SIZE`

`NET_OS_CFG_IF_TX_DEALLOC_Q_SIZE`

The values configured for these macros depend on additional application dependent information such as the number of transmit or receive buffers configured for the total number of interfaces.

The following configuration for the above macros are recommended:

`NET_OS_CFG_IF_RX_Q_SIZE` should be configured such that it reflects the total number of DMA receive descriptors on all physical interfaces. If DMA is not available, or a combination of DMA and I/O based interfaces are configured then this number reflects the maximum number of packets than can be acknowledged and signaled for during a single receive interrupt event for all interfaces.

For example, if one interface has 10 receive descriptors and another interface is I/O based but is capable of receiving 4 frames within its internal memory and issuing a single interrupt request, then the `NET_OS_CFG_IF_RX_Q_SIZE` macro should be configured to `14`. Defining a number in excess of the maximum number of receivable frames per interrupt across all interfaces would not be harmful, but the additional queue space will not be utilized.

`NET_OS_CFG_IF_TX_DEALLOC_Q_SIZE` should be defined to be the total number of small and large transmit buffers declared for all interfaces.

C-21 µC/TCP-IP OPTIMIZATION

C-21-1 OPTIMIZING µC/TCP-IP FOR ADDITIONAL PERFORMANCE

There are several configuration combinations that can improve overall µC/TCP-IP performance. The following items can be used as a starting point:

1 Enable the assembly port optimizations, if available in the architecture.

2 Configure the µC/TCP-IP for speed optimization.

3 Configure optimum TCP window sizes for TCP communication. Disable argument checking, statistics and error counters.

ASSEMBLY OPTIMIZATION

First, if using the ARM architecture, or other supported optimized architecture, the files `net_util_a.asm` and `lib_mem_a.asm` may be included into the project and the following macros should be defined and enabled:

```
app_cfg.h: #define LIB_MEM_CFG_OPTIMIZE_ASM_EN
net_cfg.h: Set NET_CFG_OPTIMIZE_ASM_EN to DEF_ENABLED
```

These files are generally located in the following directories:

```
\Micrium\Software\uC-LIB\Ports\ARM\IAR\lib_mem_a.asm
\Micrium\Software\uC-TCPIP-V2\Ports\ARM\IAR\net_util_a.asm
```

ENABLE SPEED OPTIMIZATION

Second, you may compile the Network Protocol Stack with speed optimizations enabled.

This can be accomplished by configuring the `net_cfg.h` macro `NET_CFG_OPTIMIZE` to `NET_OPTIMIZE_SPD`.

TCP OPTIMIZATION

Third, the two `net_cfg.h` macros `NET_TCP_CFG_RX_WIN_SIZE_OCTET` and `NET_TCP_CFG_TX_WIN_SIZE_OCTET` **should** configure each TCP connection's receive and transmit window sizes. It is recommended to set TCP window sizes to integer multiples of each TCP connection's maximum segment size (MSS). For example, systems with an Ethernet MSS of 1460, a value `5840` (4 * 1460) is probably a better configuration than the default window size of `4096` (4K).

DISABLE ARGUMENT CHECKING

Finally, once the application has been validated, argument checking, statistics and error counters may optionally be disabled by configuring the following macros to `DEF_DISABLED`:

```
NET_ERR_CFG_ARG_CHK_EXT_EN
NET_ERR_CFG_ARG_CHK_DBG_EN
NET_CTR_CFG_STAT_EN
NET_CTR_CFG_ERR_EN
```

Appendix

D

µC/TCP-IP Error Codes

This appendix provides a brief explanation of µC/TCP-IP error codes defined in `net_err.h`. Any error codes not listed here may be searched in `net_err.h` for both their numerical value and usage.

Each error has a numerical value. The error codes are grouped. The definition of the groups are:

Error code group	Numbering serie
NETWORK-OS LAYER	1000
NETWORK UTILITY LIBRARY	2000
ASCII LIBRARY	3000
NETWORK STATISTIC MANAGEMENT	4000
NETWORK TIMER MANAGEMENT	5000
NETWORK BUFFER MANAGEMENT	6000
NETWORK CONNECTION MANAGEMENT	6000
NETWORK BOARD SUPPORT PACKAGE (BSP)	10000
NETWORK DEVICE	11000
NETWORK PHYSICAL LAYER	12000
NETWORK INTERFACE LAYER	13000
ARP LAYER	15000
NETWORK LAYER MANAGEMENT	20000
IP LAYER	21000
ICMP LAYER	22000

Error code group	Numbering serie
IGMP LAYER	23000
UDP LAYER	30000
TCP LAYER	31000
APPLICATION LAYER	40000
NETWORK SOCKET LAYER	41000
NETWORK SECURITY MANAGER LAYER	50000
NETWORK SECURITY LAYER	51000

D-1 NETWORK ERROR CODES

10	NET_ERR_INIT_INCOMPLETE	Network initialization *not* complete.
20	NET_ERR_INVALID_PROTOCOL	Invalid/unknown network protocol type.
30	NET_ERR_INVALID_TRANSACTION	Invalid/unknown network buffer pool type.
400	NET_ERR_RX	General receive error. Receive data discarded.
450	NET_ERR_RX_DEST	Destination address and/or port -number not available on this host.
500	NET_ERR_TX	General transmit error. No data transmitted. A momentarily delay should be performed to allow additional buffers to be de-allocated before calling send(), NetSock_TxData() or NetSock_TxDataTo().

D-2 ARP ERROR CODES

15000	NET_ARP_ERR_NONE	ARP operation completed successfully.
15020	NET_ARP_ERR_NULL_PTR	Argument(s) passed NULL pointer.
15102	NET_ARP_ERR_INVALID_HW_ADDR_LEN	Invalid ARP hardware address length.
15105	NET_ARP_ERR_INVALID_PROTOCOL_LEN	Invalid ARP protocol address length.
15150	NET_ARP_ERR_CACHE_NONE_AVAIL	No ARP cache entry structures available.
15151	NET_ARP_ERR_CACHE_INVALID_TYPE	ARP cache type invalid or unknown.

15155	NET_ARP_ERR_CACHE_NOT_FOUND	ARP cache entry not found.
15156	NET_ARP_ERR_CACHE_PEND	ARP cache resolution pending.

D-3 NETWORK ASCII ERROR CODES

3000	NET_ASCII_ERR_NONE	ASCII operation completed successfully.
3020	NET_ASCII_ERR_NULL_PTR	Argument(s) passed NULL pointer.
3100	NET_ASCII_ERR_INVALID_STR_LEN	Invalid ASCII string length.
3101	NET_ASCII_ERR_INVALID_CHAR_LEN	Invalid ASCII character length.
3102	NET_ASCII_ERR_INVALID_CHAR_VAL	Invalid ASCII character value.
3103	NET_ASCII_ERR_INVALID_CHAR_SEQ	Invalid ASCII character sequence.
3200	NET_ASCII_ERR_INVALID_CHAR	Invalid ASCII character.

D-4 NETWORK BUFFER ERROR CODES

6010	NET_BUF_ERR_NONE_AVAIL	No network buffers of required size available.
6031	NET_BUF_ERR_INVALID_SIZE	Invalid network buffer pool size.
6032	NET_BUF_ERR_INVALID_IX	Invalid buffer index outside data area.
6033	NET_BUF_ERR_INVALID_LEN	Invalid buffer length specified outside of data area.
6040	NET_BUF_ERR_POOL_INIT	Network buffer pool initialization failed.
6050	NET_BUF_ERR_INVALID_POOL_TYPE	Invalid network buffer pool type.
6051	NET_BUF_ERR_INVALID_POOL_ADDR	Invalid network buffer pool address.
6053	NET_BUF_ERR_INVALID_POOL_QTY	Invalid number of pool buffers configured.

D-5 ICMP ERROR CODES

D-6 NETWORK INTERFACE ERROR CODES

13000	NET_IF_ERR_NONE	Network interface operation completed successfully.
13010	NET_IF_ERR_NONE_AVAIL	No network interfaces available. The value of NET_IF_CFG_MAX_NBR_IF should be increased in net_cfg.h.
13020	NET_IF_ERR_NULL_PTR	Argument(s) passed NULL pointer.
13021	NET_IF_ERR_NULL_FNCT	NULL interface API function pointer encountered.
13100	NET_IF_ERR_INVALID_IF	Invalid network interface number specified.
13101	NET_IF_ERR_INVALID_CFG	Invalid network interface configuration specified.
13110	NET_IF_ERR_INVALID_STATE	Invalid network interface state for specified operation.
13120	NET_IF_ERR_INVALID_IO_CTRL_OPT	Invalid I/O control option parameter specified.
13200	NET_IF_ERR_INVALID_MTU	Invalid hardware MTU specified.
13210	NET_IF_ERR_INVALID_ADDR	Invalid hardware address specified.
13211	NET_IF_ERR_INVALID_ADDR_LEN	Invalid hardware address length specified.

D-7 IP ERROR CODES

21000	NET_IP_ERR_NONE	IP operation completed successfully.
21020	NET_IP_ERR_NULL_PTR	Argument(s) passed NULL pointer.
21115	NET_IP_ERR_INVALID_ADDR_HOST	Invalid host IP address.
21117	NET_IP_ERR_INVALID_ADDR_GATEWAY	Invalid gateway IP address.
21201	NET_IP_ERR_ADDR_CFG_STATE	Invalid IP address state for attempted operation.
21202	NET_IP_ERR_ADDR_CFG_IN_PROGRESS	Interface address configuration in progress.
21203	NET_IP_ERR_ADDR_CFG_IN_USE	Specified IP address currently in use.
21210	NET_IP_ERR_ADDR_NONE_AVAIL	No IP addresses configured.
21211	NET_IP_ERR_ADDR_NOT_FOUND	IP address not found.
21220	NET_IP_ERR_ADDR_TBL_SIZE	Invalid IP address table size argument passed.

21221	NET_IP_ERR_ADDR_TBL_EMPTY	IP address table empty.
21222	NET_IP_ERR_ADDR_TBL_FULL	IP address table full.

D-8 IGMP ERROR CODES

23000	NET_IGMP_ERR_NONE	IGMP operation completed successfully.
23100	NET_IGMP_ERR_INVALID_VER	Invalid IGMP version.
23101	NET_IGMP_ERR_INVALID_TYPE	Invalid IGMP message type.
23102	NET_IGMP_ERR_INVALID_LEN	Invalid IGMP message lenth.
23103	NET_IGMP_ERR_INVALID_CHK_SUM	Invalid IGMP checksum.
23104	NET_IGMP_ERR_INVALID_ADDR_SRC	Invalid IGMP IP source address.
23105	NET_IGMP_ERR_INVALID_ADDR_DEST	Invalid IGMP IP destination address.
23106	NET_IGMP_ERR_INVALID_ADDR_GRP	Invalid IGMP IP host group address
23200	NET_IGMP_ERR_HOST_GRP_NONE_AVAIL	No host group available.
23201	NET_IGMP_ERR_HOST_GRP_INVALID_TYPE	Invalid or unknown IGMP host group type.
23202	NET_IGMP_ERR_HOST_GRP_NOT_FOUND	No IGMP host group found.

D-9 OS ERROR CODES

1010	NET_OS_ERR_LOCK	Network global lock access *not* acquired. OS-implemented lock may be corrupted.

D-10 UDP ERROR CODES

30040	NET_UDP_ERR_INVALID_DATA_SIZE	UDP receive or transmit data does not fit into the receive or transmit buffer.In the case of receive, excess data bytes are dropped; for transmit, no data is sent.
30105	NET_UDP_ERR_INVALID_FLAG	Invalid UDP flags specified.
30101	NET_UDP_ERR_INVALID_LEN_DATA	Invalid protocol/data length.
30103	NET_UDP_ERR_INVALID_PORT_NBR	Invalid UDP port number.
30000	NET_UDP_ERR_NONE	UDP operation completed successfully.
30020	NET_UDP_ERR_NULL_PTR	Argument(s) passed NULL pointer.
	NET_UDP_ERR_NULL_SIZE	Argument(s) passed NULL size.

D-11 NETWORK SOCKET ERROR CODES

41072	NET_SOCK_ERR_ADDR_IN_USE	Socket address (IP / port number) already in use.
41020	NET_SOCK_ERR_CLOSED	Socket already/previously closed.
41106	NET_SOCK_ERR_CLOSE_IN_PROGRESS	Socket already closing.
41130	NET_SOCK_ERR_CONN_ACCEPT_Q_NONE _AVAIL	Accept connection handle identifier not available.
41110	NET_SOCK_ERR_CONN_FAIL	Socket operation failed.
41100	NET_SOCK_ERR_CONN_IN_USE	Socket address (IP / port number) already connected.
41122	NET_SOCK_ERR_CONN_SIGNAL_TIMEOUT	Socket operation not signaled before specified timeout.
41091	NET_SOCK_ERR_EVENTS_NBR_MAX	Number of configured socket events is greater than the maximum number of socket events.
41021	NET_SOCK_ERR_FAULT	Fatal socket fault; close socket immediately.
41070	NET_SOCK_ERR_INVALID_ADDR	Invalid socket address specified.
41071	NET_SOCK_ERR_INVALID_ADDR_LEN	Invalid socket address length specified.
41055	NET_SOCK_ERR_INVALID_CONN	Invalid socket connection.
41040	NET_SOCK_ERR_INVALID_DATA_SIZE	Socket receive or transmit data does not fit into the receive or transmit buffer.In the case of receive, excess data bytes are dropped; for transmit, no data is sent.
41054	NET_SOCK_ERR_INVALID_DESC	Invalid socket descriptor number.
41050	NET_SOCK_ERR_INVALID_FAMILY	Invalid socket family; close socket immediately.

41058	NET_SOCK_ERR_INVALID_FLAG	Invalid socket flags specified.
41057	NET_SOCK_ERR_INVALID_OP	Invalid socket operation; e.g., socket not in the correct state for specified socket call.
41080	NET_SOCK_ERR_INVALID_PORT_NBR	Invalid port number specified.
41051	NET_SOCK_ERR_INVALID_PROTOCOL	Invalid socket protocol; close socket immediately.
41053	NET_SOCK_ERR_INVALID_SOCK	Invalid socket number specified.
41056	NET_SOCK_ERR_INVALID_STATE	Invalid socket state; close socket immediately.
41059	NET_SOCK_ERR_INVALID_TIMEOUT	Invalid or no timeout specified.
41052	NET_SOCK_ERR_INVALID_TYPE	Invalid socket type; close socket immediately.
41000	NET_SOCK_ERR_NONE	Socket operation completed successfully.
41010	NET_SOCK_ERR_NONE_AVAIL	No available socket resources to allocate; NET_SOCK_CFG_NBR_SOCK should be increased in net_cfg.h.
41011	NET_SOCK_ERR_NOT_USED	Socket not used; do not close or use the socket for further operations.
41030	NET_SOCK_ERR_NULL_PTR	Argument(s) passed NULL pointer.
41031	NET_SOCK_ERR_NULL_SIZE	Argument(s) passed NULL size.
41085	NET_SOCK_ERR_PORT_NBR_NONE_AVAIL	Random local port number not available.
41400	NET_SOCK_ERR_RX_Q_CLOSED	Socket receive queue closed (received FIN from peer).
41401	NET_SOCK_ERR_RX_Q_EMPTY	Socket receive queue empty.
41022	NET_SOCK_ERR_TIMEOUT	No socket events occurred before timeout expired.

D-12 NETWORK SECURITY MANAGER ERROR CODES

50005	NET_SECURE_MGR_ERR_FORMAT	Invalid keying material format.
50002	NET_SECURE_MGR_ERR_INIT	Failed to initialize network security manager.
50000	NET_SECURE_MGR_ERR_NONE	Network security manager operation successful.
50001	NET_SECURE_MGR_ERR_NOT_AVAIL	Network security manager not available.
50003	NET_SECURE_MGR_ERR_NULL_PTR	Argument(s) passed NULL pointer.
50004	NET_SECURE_MGR_ERR_TYPE	Invalid keying material type.

D-13 NETWORK SECURITY ERROR CODES

51011	NET_SECURE_ERR_BLK_FREE	Failed to free block from memory pool.
51010	NET_SECURE_ERR_BLK_GET	Failed to get block from memory pool.
51013	NET_SECURE_ERR_HANDSHAKE	Failed to perform secure handshake.
51002	NET_SECURE_ERR_INIT_POOL	Failed to initialize memory pool.
51020	NET_SECURE_ERR_INSTALL	Failed to install keying material.
51024	NET_SECURE_ERR_INSTALL_CA_SLOT	No more CA slot available.
51023	NET_SECURE_ERR_INSTALL_DATE_CREATION	Keying material creation date is invalid.
51022	NET_SECURE_ERR_INSTALL_DATE_EXPIRATION	Keying material is expired.
51021	NET_SECURE_ERR_INSTALL_NOT_TRUSTED	Keying material is not trusted.
50000	NET_SECURE_ERR_NONE	Network security operation successful.
51001	NET_SECURE_ERR_NOT_AVAIL	Failed to get secure session from memory pool.
51012	NET_SECURE_ERR_NULL_PTR	Argument(s) passed NULL pointer.

Appendix

E

µC/TCP-IP Typical Usage

This appendix provides a brief explanation to a variety of common questions regarding how to use µC/TCP-IP.

E-1 µC/TCP-IP CONFIGURATION AND INITIALIZATION

E-1-1 µC/TCP-IP STACK CONFIGURATION

Refer to Appendix C, "µC/TCP-IP Configuration and Optimization" on page 723 for information on this topic.

E-1-2 µC/LIB MEMORY HEAP INITIALIZATION

The µC/LIB memory heap is used for allocation of the following objects:

1 Transmit small buffers

2 Transmit large buffers

3 Receive large buffers

4 Network Buffers (Network Buffer header and pointer to data area)

5 DMA receive descriptors

6 DMA transmit descriptors

7 Interface data area

8 Device driver data area

E

In the following example, the use of a Network Device Driver with DMA support is assumed. DMA descriptors are included in the analysis. The size of Network Buffer Data Areas (1, 2, 3) vary based on configuration. Refer to Chapter 15, "Buffer Management" on page 335. However, for this example, the following object sizes in bytes are assumed:

- Small transmit buffers: 152
- Large transmit buffers: 1594 for maximum sized TCP packets
- Large receive buffers: 1518
- Size of DMA receive descriptor: 8
- Size of DMA transmit descriptor: 8
- Ethernet interface data area: 7
- Average Ethernet device driver data area: 108

With a 4-byte alignment on all memory pool objects, it results in a worst case disposal of three leading bytes for each object. In practice this is not usually true since the size of most objects tend to be even multiples of four. Therefore, the alignment is preserved after having aligned the start of the pool data area. However, this makes the case for allocating objects with size to the next greatest multiple of four in order to prevent lost space due to misalignment.

The approximate memory heap size may be determined according to the following expressions:

```
nbr buf per interface      = nbr small Tx buf +
                             nbr large Tx buf +
                             nbr large Rx buf

nbr net buf per interface = nbr buf per interface
```

```
nbr objects    = nbr buf per interface     +
                 nbr net buf per interface +
                 nbr Rx descriptors        +
                 nbr Tx descriptors        +
                 1 Ethernet       data area +
                 1 Device driver data area

interface mem = (nbr small Tx buf        *  152) +
                (nbr large Tx buf        * 1594) +
                (nbr large Rx buf        * 1518) +
                (nbr Rx descriptors      *    8) +
                (nbr Tx descriptors      *    8) +
                (Ethernet IF  data area  *    7) +
                (Ethernet Drv data area  *  108) +
                (nbr objects             *    3)

total mem required = nbr interfaces * interface mem
```

EXAMPLE

With the following configuration, the memory heap required is:

- 10 small transmit buffers
- 10 large transmit buffers
- 10 large receive buffers
- 6 receive descriptors
- 20 transmit descriptors
- Ethernet interface (interface + device driver data area required)

```
nbr     buf per interface = 10 + 10 + 10                 = 30
nbr net buf per interface = nbr buf per interface        = 30
nbr objects               = (30 + 30 + 6 + 20 + 1 + 1) = 88
interface mem             = (10 *  152) +
                            (10 * 1594) +
                            (10 * 1518) +
                            ( 6 *    8) +
                            (20 *    8) +
                            ( 1 *    7) +
                            ( 1 *  108) +
                            (88 *    3) = 33,227 bytes

total mem required = 33,227 ( + localhost memory, if enabled)
```

The localhost interface, when enabled, requires a similar amount of memory except that it does not require Rx and Tx descriptors, an IF data area, or a device driver data area.

The value determined by these expressions is only an estimate. In some cases, it may be possible to reduce the size of the µC/LIB memory heap by inspecting the variable **Mem_PoolHeap.SegSizeRem** after all interfaces have been successfully initialized and any additional application allocations (if applicable) have been completed.

Excess heap space, if present, may be subtracted from the lib heap size configuration macro, **LIB_MEM_CFG_HEAP_SIZE**, present in **app_cfg.h**.

E-1-3 µC/TCP-IP TASK STACKS

In general, the size of µC/TCP-IP task stacks is dependent on the CPU architecture and compiler used.

On ARM processors, experience has shown that configuring the task stacks to 1024 **OS_STK** entries (4,096 bytes) is sufficient for most applications. Certainly, the stack sizes may be examined and reduced accordingly once the run-time behavior of the device has been analyzed and additional stack space deemed to be unnecessary.

The only guaranteed method of determining the required task stack sizes is to calculate the maximum stack usage for each task. Obviously, the maximum stack usage for a task is the total stack usage along the task's most-stack-greedy function path plus the (maximum) stack usage for interrupts. Note that the most-stack-greedy function path is not necessarily the longest or deepest function path.

The easiest and best method for calculating the maximum stack usage for any task/function should be performed statically by the compiler or by a static analysis tool since these can calculate function/task maximum stack usage based on the compiler's actual code generation and optimization settings. So for optimal task stack configuration, we recommend to invest in a task stack calculator tool compatible with your build toolchain.

See also section C-20-1 "Operating System Configuration" on page 749.

E-1-4 µC/TCP-IP TASK PRIORITIES

We recommend to configure the Network Protocol Stack task priorities as follows:

```
NET_OS_CFG_IF_TX_DEALLOC_TASK_PRIO   (highest priority)
NET_OS_CFG_TMR_TASK_PRIO
NET_OS_CFG_IF_RX_TASK_PRIO           (lowest  priority)
```

We recommend that the µC/TCP-IP Timer Task and Network Interface Receive Task be lower priority than almost all other application tasks; but we recommend that the Network Interface Transmit De-allocation Task be higher priority than all application tasks that use µC/TCP-IP network services.

See also section C-20-1 "Operating System Configuration" on page 749.

E-1-5 µC/TCP-IP QUEUE SIZES

Refer to section C-20-2 "µC/TCP-IP Configuration" on page 750.

E

E-1-6 µC/TCP-IP INITIALIZATION

The following example code demonstrates the initialization of two identical Network Interface Devices via a local, application developer provided function named **AppInit_TCPIP()**. Another example of this method can also be found in section 13-3 “Application Code” on page 291

The first interface is bound to two different sets of network addresses on two separate networks. The second interface is configured to operate on one of the same networks as the first interface, but could easily be plugged into a separate network that happens to use the same address ranges.

```
static void AppInit_TCPIP (void)
{
  NET_IF_NBR   if_nbr;
  NET_IP_ADDR  ip;
  NET_IP_ADDR  msk;
  NET_IP_ADDR  gateway;
  CPU_BOOLEAN  cfg_success;
  NET_ERR      err;

  Mem_Init();                                                                    (1)
  err = Net_Init();                                                              (2)
  if (err != NET_ERR_NONE) {
      return;
  }

  if_nbr = NetIF_Add((void     *)&NetIF_API_Ether,                               (3)
                     (void     *)&NetDev_API_FEC,
                     (void     *)&NetDev_BSP_FEC_0,
                     (void     *)&NetDev_Cfg_FEC_0,
                     (void     *)&NetPHY_API_Generic,
                     (void     *)&NetPhy_Cfg_FEC_0,
                     (NET_ERR *)&err);

  if (err == NET_IF_ERR_NONE) {
      ip          = NetASCII_Str_to_IP((CPU_CHAR *)"192.168.1.2",     &err);    (4)
      msk         = NetASCII_Str_to_IP((CPU_CHAR *)"255.255.255.0", &err);
      gateway     = NetASCII_Str_to_IP((CPU_CHAR *)"192.168.1.1",     &err);
      cfg_success = NetIP_CfgAddrAdd(if_nbr, ip, msk, gateway, &err);          (5)

      ip          = NetASCII_Str_to_IP((CPU_CHAR *)"10.10.1.2",       &err);    (6)
      msk         = NetASCII_Str_to_IP((CPU_CHAR *)"255.255.255.0", &err);
      gateway     = NetASCII_Str_to_IP((CPU_CHAR *)"10.10.1.1",       &err);
      cfg_success = NetIP_CfgAddrAdd(if_nbr, ip, msk, gateway, &err);          (7)

      NetIF_Start(if_nbr, &err);                                                (8)
  }
```

```
    if_nbr = NetIF_Add((void     *)&NetIF_API_Ether,                              (9)
                       (void     *)&NetDev_API_FEC,
                       (void     *)&NetDev_BSP_FEC_1,
                       (void     *)&NetDev_Cfg_FEC_1,
                       (void     *)&NetPHY_API_Generic,
                       (void     *)&NetPhy_Cfg_FEC_1,
                       (NET_ERR *)&err);

    if (err == NET_IF_ERR_NONE) {
        ip          = NetASCII_Str_to_IP((CPU_CHAR *)"192.168.1.3",   &err);     (10)
        msk         = NetASCII_Str_to_IP((CPU_CHAR *)"255.255.255.0", &err);
        gateway     = NetASCII_Str_to_IP((CPU_CHAR *)"192.168.1.1",   &err);
        cfg_success = NetIP_CfgAddrAdd(if_nbr, ip, msk, gateway, &err);          (11)

        NetIF_Start(if_nbr, &err);                                               (12)
    }
}
```

Listing E-1 **Complete Initialization Example**

LE-1(1) Initialize µC/LIB memory management. Most applications call this function PRIOR to **AppInit_TCPIP()** so that other parts of the application may benefit from memory management functionality prior to initializing µC/TCP-IP.

LE-1(2) Initialize µC/TCP-IP. This function must only be called once following the call to µC/LIB **Mem_Init()**. The return error code should be checked for **NET_ERR_NONE** before proceeding

LE-1(3) Add the first network interface to the system. In this case, an Ethernet interface bound to a Freescale FEC hardware device and generic (MII or RMII) compliant physical layer device is being configured. The interface uses a different device configuration structure than the second interface being added in Step 8. Each interface requires a unique device BSP interface and configuration structure. Physical layer device configuration structures however could be re-used if the Physical layer configurations are exactly the same. The return error should be checked before starting the interface.

LE-1(4) Obtain the hexadecimal equivalents for the first set of Internet addresses to configure on the first added interface.

LE-1(5) Configure the first added interface with the first set of specified addresses.

LE-1(6) Obtain the hexadecimal equivalents for the second set of Internet addresses to configure on the first added interface. The same local variables have been used as when the first set of address information was configured. Once the address set is configured to the interface, as in Step 4, the local copies of the configured addresses are no longer necessary and can be overwritten with the next set of addresses to configure.

LE-1(7) Configure the first added interface with the second set of specified addresses.

LE-1(8) Start the first interface. The return error code should be checked, but this depends on whether the application will attempt to restart the interface should an error occur. This example assumes that no error occurs when starting the interface. Initialization for the first interface is now complete, and if no further initialization takes place, the first interface will respond to ICMP Echo (ping) requests on either of its configured addresses.

LE-1(9) Add the second network interface to the system. In this case, an Ethernet interface bound to a Freescale FEC hardware device and generic (MII or RMII) compliant physical layer device is being configured. The interface uses a different device configuration structure than the first interface added in Step 2. Each interface requires a unique device BSP interface and configuration structure. Physical layer device configuration structures, however, could be re-used if the Physical layer configurations are exactly the same. The return error should be checked before starting the interface.

LE-1(10) Obtain the hexadecimal equivalents for the first and only set of Internet addresses to configure on the second added interface.

LE-1(11) Configure the second interface with the first and only set of specified addresses.

LE-1(12) Start the second interface. The return error code should be checked, but this depends on whether the application will attempt to restart the interface should an error occur. This example assumes that no error occurs when starting the interface. Initialization for the second interface is now complete and it will respond to ICMP Echo (ping) requests on its configured address.

E

E-2 NETWORK INTERFACES, DEVICES, AND BUFFERS

E-2-1 NETWORK INTERFACE CONFIGURATION

ADDING AN INTERFACE

Interfaces may be added to the stack by calling **NetIF_Add()**. Each new interface requires additional BSP. The order of addition is critical to ensure that the interface number assigned to the new interface matches the code defined within **net_bsp.c**. See section 16-1 "Network Interface Configuration" on page 343 for more information on configuring and adding interfaces.

STARTING AN INTERFACE

Interfaces may be started by calling **NetIF_Start()**. See section 16-2-1 "Starting Network Interfaces" on page 348 for more information on starting interfaces.

STOPPING AN INTERFACE

Interfaces may be started by calling **NetIF_Stop()**. See section 16-2-2 "Stopping Network Interfaces" on page 349 for more information on stopping interfaces.

CHECKING FOR ENABLED INTERFACE

The application may check if an interface is enabled by calling **NetIF_IsEn()** or **NetIF_IsEnCfgd()**. See section B-9-10 "NetIF_IsEn()" on page 533 and section B-9-11 "NetIF_IsEnCfgd()" on page 534 for more information.

E

E-2-2 NETWORK AND DEVICE BUFFER CONFIGURATION

LARGE TRANSMIT BUFFERS ARE 1594 BYTES

Refer to the section 15-3 "Network Buffer Sizes" on page 337 for more information.

NUMBER OF RX PR TX BUFFERS TO CONFIGURE

The number of large receive, small transmit and large transmit buffers configured for a specific interface depend on several factors.

1 Desired level of performance.

2 Amount of data to be either transmitted or received.

3 Ability of the target application to either produce or consume transmitted or received data.

4 Average CPU utilization.

5 Average network utilization.

The discussion on the bandwidth-delay product is always valid. In general, the more buffers the better. However, the number of buffers can be tailored based on the application. For example, if an application receives a lot of data but transmits very little, then it may be sufficient to define a number of small transmit buffers for operations such as TCP acknowledgements and allocate the remaining memory to large receive buffers. Similarly, if an application transmits and receives little, then the buffer allocation emphasis should be on defining more transmit buffers. However, there is a caveat:

If the application is written such that the task that consumes receive data runs infrequently or the CPU utilization is high and the receiving application task(s) becomes starved for CPU time, then more receive buffers will be required.

To ensure the highest level of performance possible, it makes sense to define as many buffers as possible and use the interface and pool statistics data in order to refine the number after having run the application for a while. A busy network will require more receive buffers in order to handle the additional broadcast messages that will be received.

In general, at least two large and two small transmit buffers should be configured. This assumes that neither the network or CPU are very busy.

Many applications will receive properly with four or more large receive buffers. However, for TCP applications that move a lot of data between the target and the peer, this number may need to be higher.

Specifying too few transmit or receive buffers may lead to stalls in communication and possibly even dead-lock. Care should be taken when configuring the number of buffers. µC/TCP-IP is often tested with configurations of 10 or more small transmit, large transmit, and large receive buffers.

All device configuration structures and declarations are in the provided files named **net_dev_cfg.c** and **net_dev_cfg.h**. Each configuration structure must be completely initialized in the specified order. The following listing shows where to define the number of buffers per interface as calculated

```
const  NET_DEV_CFG_ETHER  NetDev_Cfg_Processor_0 = {
    NET_IF_MEM_TYPE_MAIN,
    1518,                                           (1)
      10,                                           (2)
      16,
       0,

    NET_IF_MEM_TYPE_MAIN,
    1594,                                           (3)
       5,                                           (4)
     256,                                           (5)
       5,                                           (6)
      16,
       0,

    0x00000000,
             0,

    10,                                             (7)
     5,                                             (8)

    0x40001000,
             0,

   "00:50:C2:25:60:02"
};
```

Listing E-2 **Network Device Driver buffer configuration**

LE-2(1) Receive buffer size. This field sets the size of the largest receivable packet and may be set to match the application's requirements.

LE-2(2) Number of receive buffers. This setting controls the number of receive buffers that will be allocated to the interface. This value *must* be set greater than or equal to one buffer if the interface is receiving *only* UDP. If TCP data is expected to be transferred across the interface, then there *must* be the minimum of receive buffers as calculated by the BDP.

LE-2(3) Large transmit buffer size. This field controls the size of the large transmit buffers allocated to the device in bytes. This field has no effect if the number of large transmit buffers is configured to zero. Setting the size of the large transmit buffers below 1594, bytes may hinder the stack's ability to transmit full-sized IP datagrams since IP transmit fragmentation is not yet supported. Micrium recommends setting this field to 1594 bytes in order to accommodate µC/TCP-IPs internal packet building mechanisms.

LE-2(4) Number of large transmit buffers. This field controls the number of large transmit buffers allocated to the device. The developer may set this field to zero to make room for additional small transmit buffers, however, the size of the maximum transmittable UDP packet will depend on the size of the small transmit buffers, (see #5).

LE-2(5) Small transmit buffer size. For devices with a minimal amount of RAM, it is possible to allocate small transmit buffers as well as large transmit buffers. In general, Micrium recommends 256 byte small transmit buffers, however, the developer may adjust this value according to the application requirements. This field has no effect if the number of small transmit buffers is configured to zero.

LE-2(6) Number of small transmit buffers. This field controls the number of small transmit buffers allocated to the device. The developer may set this field to zero to make room for additional large transmit buffers if required.

E

NUMBER OF DMA DESCRIPTORS TO CONFIGURE

If the hardware device is an Ethernet MAC that supports DMA, then the number of configured receive descriptors will play an important role in determining overall performance for the configured interface.

For applications with 10 or less large receive buffers, it is desirable to configure the number of receive descriptors to that of 60% to 70% of the number of configured receive buffers.

In this example, 60% of 10 receive buffers allows for four receive buffers to be available to the stack waiting to be processed by application tasks. While the application is processing data, the hardware may continue to receive additional frames up to the number of configured receive descriptors.

There is, however, a point in which configuring additional receive descriptors no longer greatly impacts performance. For applications with 20 or more buffers, the number of descriptors can be configured to 50% of the number of configured receive buffers. After this point, only the number of buffers remains a significant factor; especially for slower or busy CPUs and networks with higher utilization.

In general, if the CPU is not busy and the µC/TCP-IP Receive Task has the opportunity to run often, the ratio of receive descriptors to receive buffers may be reduced further for very high numbers of available receive buffers (e.g., 50 or more).

The number of transmit descriptors should be configured such that it is equal to the number of small plus the number of large transmit buffers.

These numbers only serve as a starting point. The application and the environment that the device will be attached to will ultimately dictate the number of required transmit and receive descriptors necessary for achieving maximum performance.

Specifying too few descriptors can cause communication delays. See Listing E-2 for descriptors configuration.

LE-2(7) Number of receive descriptors. For DMA-based devices, this value is utilized by the device driver during initialization in order to allocate a fixed-size pool of receive descriptors to be used by the device. The number of descriptors *must* be less than the number of configured receive buffers. Micrium recommends setting this value to approximately 60% to 70%f of the number of receive buffers. Non DMA based devices may configure this value to zero.

LE-2(8) Number of transmit descriptors. For DMA-based devices, this value is utilized by the device driver during initialization in order to allocate a fixed-size pool of transmit descriptors to be used by the device. For best performance, the number of transmit descriptors should be equal to the number of small, plus the number of large transmit buffers configured for the device. Non DMA based devices may configure this value to zero.

CONFIGURING TCP WINDOW SIZES

Once number and size of the transmit and receive buffers are configured, as explained in the previous section, the last thing that need to be done is to configure the TCP Transmit and Receive Window sizes. These parameters are found in the **net_cfg.h** file in the **TRANSMISSION CONTROL PROTOCOL LAYER CONFIGURATION** section.

```
#define  NET_TCP_CFG_RX_WIN_SIZE_OCTET   4096  /* Configure TCP connection receive  window size.
*/  (1)
#define  NET_TCP_CFG_TX_WIN_SIZE_OCTET   4096  /* Configure TCP connection transmit window size.
*/  (2)
```

Listing E-3 **TCP Transmit and Receive Window Size configuration**

LE-3(1) This **#define** configures the TCP Receive Window size. It is recommended to set this parameter to the number of receive descriptors in the case of DMA or to the number of receive buffers in the case of non-DMA, multiplied by the MSS. For example, if 4 descriptors or 4 receive buffers are required, the TCP Receive WIndow size is 4 * 1460 = 5840 bytes.

LE-3(2) This **#define** configures the TCP Transmit Window size. It is recommended to set this parameter to the number of transmit descriptors in the case of DMA or to the number of transmit buffers in the case of non-DMA, multiplied by the MSS. For example, if 2 descriptors or 2 receive buffers are required, the TCP Receive WIndow size is 2 * 1460 = 2920 bytes.

E

WRITING OR OBTAINING ADDITIONAL DEVICE DRIVERS

Contact Micrium for information regarding obtaining additional device drivers. If a specific driver is not available, Micrium may develop the driver by providing engineering consulting services.

Alternately, a new device driver may be developed by filling in a template driver provided with the µC/TCP-IP source code.

See Chapter 14, "Network Device Drivers" on page 299 for more information.

E-2-3 ETHERNET MAC ADDRESS

GETTING AN INTERFACE MAC ADDRESS

The application may call **NetIF_AddrHW_Get()** to obtain the MAC address for a specific interface.

CHANGING AN INTERFACE MAC ADDRESS

The application may call **NetIF_AddrHW_Set()** in order to set the MAC address for a specific interface.

GETTING A HOST MAC ADDRESS ON MY NETWORK

In order to determine the MAC address of a host on the network, the Network Protocol Stack must have an ARP cache entry for the specified host protocol address. An application may check to see if an ARP cache entry is present by calling **NetARP_CacheGetAddrHW()**.

If an ARP cache entry is not found, the application may call **NetARP_ProbeAddrOnNet()** to send an ARP request to all hosts on the network. If the target host is present, an ARP reply will be received shortly and the application should wait and then call **NetARP_CacheGetAddrHW()** to determine if the ARP reply has been entered into the ARP cache.

The following example shows how to obtain the Ethernet MAC address of a host on the local area network:

```
void AppGetRemoteHW_Addr (void)
{
  NET_IP_ADDR   addr_ip_local;
  NET_IP_ADDR   addr_ip_remote;
  CPU_CHAR     *paddr_ip_remote;
  CPU_CHAR      addr_hw_str[NET_IF_ETHER_ADDR_SIZE_STR];
  CPU_INT08U    addr_hw[NET_IF_ETHER_ADDR_SIZE];
  NET_ERR       err;

                                   /* ------------- PREPARE IP ADDRs ------------- */
  paddr_ip_local = "10.10.1.10";   /* MUST be one of host's configured IP addrs.   */
   addr_ip_local = NetASCII_Str_to_IP((CPU_CHAR *) paddr_ip_local,
                                      (NET_ERR  *)&err);
  if (err != NET_ASCII_ERR_NONE) {
    printf(" Error #%d converting IP address %s", err, paddr_ip_local);
    return;
  }

  paddr_ip_remote = "10.10.1.50";   /* Remote host's IP addr to get hardware addr. */
   addr_ip_remote = NetASCII_Str_to_IP((CPU_CHAR *) paddr_ip_remote,
                                       (NET_ERR  *)&err);
  if (err != NET_ASCII_ERR_NONE) {
    printf(" Error #%d converting IP address %s", err, paddr_ip_remote);
    return;
  }

  addr_ip_local  = NET_UTIL_HOST_TO_NET_32(addr_ip_local);
  addr_ip_remote = NET_UTIL_HOST_TO_NET_32(addr_ip_remote);

                                    /* ------------ PROBE ADDR ON NET ------------- */
  NetARP_ProbeAddrOnNet((NET_PROTOCOL_TYPE) NET_PROTOCOL_TYPE_IP_V4,
                        (CPU_INT08U      *)&addr_ip_local,
                        (CPU_INT08U      *)&addr_ip_remote,
                        (NET_ARP_ADDR_LEN ) sizeof(addr_ip_remote),
                        (NET_ERR         *)&err);
  if (err != NET_ARP_ERR_NONE) {
    printf(" Error #%d probing address %s on network", err, addr_ip_remote);
    return;
  }

  OSTimeDly(2);                     /* Delay short time for ARP to probe network.   */
```

```
                                     /* ---- QUERY ARP CACHE FOR REMOTE HW ADDR ---- */
(void)NetARP_CacheGetAddrHW((CPU_INT08U      *)&addr_hw[0],
                            (NET_ARP_ADDR_LEN) sizeof(addr_hw_str),
                            (CPU_INT08U      *)&addr_ip_remote,
                            (NET_ARP_ADDR_LEN) sizeof(addr_ip_remote),
                            (NET_ERR         *)&err);
  switch (err) {
    case NET_ARP_ERR_NONE:
       NetASCII_MAC_to_Str((CPU_INT08U *)&addr_hw[0],
                           (CPU_CHAR    *)&addr_hw_str[0],
                           (CPU_BOOLEAN ) DEF_NO,
                           (CPU_BOOLEAN ) DEF_YES,
                           (NET_ERR    *)&err);
       if (err != NET_ASCII_ERR_NONE) {
         printf(" Error #%d converting hardware address", err);
         return;
       }

       printf(" Remote IP Addr %s @ HW Addr %s\n\r", paddr_ip_remote, &addr_hw_str[0]);
       break;

    case NET_ARP_ERR_CACHE_NOT_FOUND:
       printf("  Remote IP Addr %s NOT found on network\n\r", paddr_ip_remote);
       break;

    case NET_ARP_ERR_CACHE_PEND:
       printf("  Remote IP Addr %s NOT YET found on network\n\r", paddr_ip_remote);
       break;

    case NET_ARP_ERR_NULL_PTR:
    case NET_ARP_ERR_INVALID_HW_ADDR_LEN:
    case NET_ARP_ERR_INVALID_PROTOCOL_ADDR_LEN:
    default:
       printf(" Error #%d querying ARP cache", err);
       break;
  }
}
```

Listing E-4 **Obtaining the Ethernet MAC address of a host**

E-2-4 ETHERNET PHY LINK STATE

INCREASING THE RATE OF LINK STATE POLLING

The application may increase the µC/TCP-IP link state polling rate by calling -**NetIF_CfgPhyLinkPeriod()** (see section B-9-6 on page 524). The default value is 250ms.

GETTING THE CURRENT LINK STATE FOR AN INTERFACE

µC/TCP-IP provides two mechanisms for obtaining interface link state.

1 A function which reads a global variable that is periodically updated.

2 A function which reads the current link state from the hardware.

Method 1 provides the fastest mechanism to obtain link state since it does not require communication with the physical layer device. For most applications, this mechanism is suitable and if necessary, the polling rate can be increased by calling **NetIF_CfgPhyLinkPeriod()**. In order to utilize Method 1, the application may call **NetIF_LinkStateGet()** which returns **NET_IF_LINK_UP** or **NET_IF_LINK_DOWN**.

The accuracy of Method 1 can be improved by using a physical layer device and driver combination that supports link state change interrupts. In this circumstance, the value of the global variable containing the link state is updated immediately following a link state change. Therefore, the polling rate can be reduced further if desired and a call to **NetIF_LinkStateGet()** will return the actual link state.

Method 2 requires the application to call **NetIF_IO_Ctrl()** with the option parameter set to either **NET_IF_IO_CTRL_LINK_STATE_GET** or **NET_IF_IO_CTRL_LINK_STATE_GET_INFO**.

- If the application specifies **NET_IF_IO_CTRL_LINK_STATE_GET**, then **NET_IF_LINK_UP** or **NET_IF_LINK_DOWN** will be returned.

- Alternatively, if the application specifies **NET_IF_IO_CTRL_LINK_STATE_GET_INFO**, the link state details such as speed and duplex will be returned.

The advantage to Method 2 is that the link state returned is the actual link state as reported by the hardware at the time of the function call. However, the overhead of communicating with the physical layer device may be high and therefore some cycles may be wasted waiting for the result since the connection bus between the CPU and the physical layer device is often only a couple of MHz.

FORCING AN ETHERNET PHY TO A SPECIFIC LINK STATE

The generic PHY driver that comes with µC/TCP-IP does not provide a mechanism for disabling auto-negotiation and specifying a desired link state. This restriction is required in order to remain MII register block compliant with all (R)MII compliant physical layer devices.

However, µC/TCP-IP does provide a mechanism for coaching the physical layer device into advertising only the desired auto-negotiation states. This may be achieved by adjusting the physical layer device configuration as specified in **net_dev_cfg.c** with alternative link speed and duplex values.

The following is an example physical layer device configuration structure.

```
NET_PHY_CFG_ETHER NetPhy_Cfg_Generic_0 = {
    0,
    NET_PHY_BUS_MODE_MII,
    NET_PHY_TYPE_EXT,
    NET_PHY_SPD_AUTO,
    NET_PHY_DUPLEX_AUTO
};
```

The parameters **NET_PHY_SPD_AUTO** and **NET_PHY_DUPLEX_AUTO** may be changed to match any of the following settings:

NET_PHY_SPD_10
NET_PHY_SPD_100
NET_PHY_SPD_1000
NET_PHY_SPD_AUTO
NET_PHY_DUPLEX_HALF
NET_PHY_DUPLEX_FULL
NET_PHY_DUPLEX_AUTO

This mechanism is only effective when both the physical layer device attached to the target and the remote link state partner support auto-negotiation.

E-3 IP ADDRESS CONFIGURATION

E-3-1 CONVERTING IP ADDRESSES TO AND FROM THEIR DOTTED DECIMAL REPRESENTATION

µC/TCP-IP contains functions to perform various string operations on IP addresses.

The following example shows how to use the NetASCII module in order to convert IP addresses to and from their dotted-decimal representations:

```
NET_IP_ADDR ip;
CPU_INT08U  ip_str[16];
NET_ERR     err;
ip = NetASCII_Str_to_IP((CPU_CHAR *)"192.168.1.65", &err);
NetASCII_IP_to_Str(ip, &ip_str[0], DEF_NO, &err);
```

E-3-2 ASSIGNING STATIC IP ADDRESSES TO AN INTERFACE

The constant `NET_IP_CFG_IF_MAX_NBR_ADDR` specified in `net_cfg.h` determines the maximum number of IP addresses that may be assigned to an interface. Many IP addresses may be added up to the specified maximum by calling `NetIP_CfgAddrAdd()`.

Configuring an IP gateway address is not necessary when communicating only within your local network.

```
CPU_BOOLEAN cfg_success;


ip          = NetASCII_Str_to_IP((CPU_CHAR *)"192.168.1.65", perr);
msk         = NetASCII_Str_to_IP((CPU_CHAR *)"255.255.255.0", perr);
gateway     = NetASCII_Str_to_IP((CPU_CHAR *)"192.168.1.1",  perr);
cfg_success = NetIP_CfgAddrAdd(if_nbr, ip, msk, gateway, perr);
```

E-3-3 REMOVING STATICALLY ASSIGNED IP ADDRESSES FROM AN INTERFACE

Statically assigned IP addresses for a specific interface may be removed by calling `NetIP_CfgAddrRemove()`.

Alternatively, the application may call `NetIP_CfgAddrRemoveAll()` to remove all configured static addresses for a specific interface.

E-3-4 GETTING A DYNAMIC IP ADDRESS

µC/DHCPc must be obtained and integrated into the application to dynamically assign an IP address to an interface.

E-3-5 GETTING ALL THE IP ADDRESSES CONFIGURED ON A SPECIFIC INTERFACE

The application may obtain the protocol address information for a specific interface by calling `NetIP_GetAddrHost()`. This function may return one or more configured addresses.

Similarly, the application may call `NetIP_GetAddrSubnetMask()` and `NetIP_GetAddrDfltGateway()` in order to determine the subnet mask and gateway information for a specific interface.

E-4 SOCKET PROGRAMMING

E-4-1 USING µC/TCP-IP SOCKETS

Refer to Chapter 17, "Socket Programming" on page 355 for code examples on this topic.

E-4-2 JOINING AND LEAVING AN IGMP HOST GROUP

µC/TCP-IP supports IP multicasting with IGMP. In order to receive packets addressed to a given IP multicast group address, the stack must have been configured to support multicasting in **net_cfg.h**, and that host group has to be joined.

The following examples show how to join and leave an IP multicast group with µC/TCP-IP:

```
NET_IF_NBR  if_nbr;
NET_IP_ADDR group_ip_addr;
NET_ERR     err;


if_nbr        = NET_IF_NBR_BASE_CFGD;
group_ip_addr = NetASCII_Str_to_IP("233.0.0.1", &err);
if (err != NET_ASCII_ERR_NONE) {
  /* Handle error. */
}
NetIGMP_HostGrpJoin(if_nbr, group_ip_addr, &err);
if (err != NET_IGMP_ERR_NONE) {
  /* Handle error. */
}
[...]
NetIGMP_HostGrpLeave(if_nbr, group_ip_addr, &err);
if (err != NET_IGMP_ERR_NONE) {
  /* Handle error. */
}
```

E-4-3 TRANSMITTING TO A MULTICAST IP GROUP ADDRESS

Transmitting to an IP multicast group is identical to transmitting to a unicast or broadcast address. However, the stack must be configured to enable multicast transmit.

E-4-4 RECEIVING FROM A MULTICAST IP GROUP

An IP multicast group must be joined before packets can be received from it from it (see section E-4-2 "Joining and Leaving an IGMP Host Group" on page 782 for more information). Once this is done, receiving from a multicast group only requires a socket bound to the **NET_SOCK_ADDR_IP_WILDCARD** address, as shown in the following example:

```
NET_SOCK_ID        sock;
NET_SOCK_ADDR_IP   sock_addr_ip;
NET_SOCK_ADDR      addr_remote;
NET_SOCK_ADDR_LEN addr_remote_len;
CPU_CHAR           rx_buf[100];
CPU_INT16U         rx_len;
NET_ERR            err;


sock = NetSock_Open((NET_SOCK_PROTOCOL_FAMILY) NET_SOCK_ADDR_FAMILY_IP_V4,
                    (NET_SOCK_TYPE            ) NET_SOCK_TYPE_DATAGRAM,
                    (NET_SOCK_PROTOCOL        ) NET_SOCK_PROTOCOL_UDP,
                    (NET_ERR                 *)&err);
if (err != NET_SOCK_ERR_NONE) {
  /* Handle error. */
}
Mem_Set(&sock_addr_ip, (CPU_CHAR)0, sizeof(sock_addr_ip));
sock_addr_ip.AddrFamily = NET_SOCK_ADDR_FAMILY_IP_V4;
sock_addr_ip.Addr       = NET_UTIL_HOST_TO_NET_32(NET_SOCK_ADDR_IP_WILDCARD);
sock_addr_ip.Port       = NET_UTIL_HOST_TO_NET_16(10000);
NetSock_Bind((NET_SOCK_ID       ) sock,
             (NET_SOCK_ADDR    *)&sock_addr_ip,
             (NET_SOCK_ADDR_LEN) NET_SOCK_ADDR_SIZE,
             (NET_ERR          *)&err);
if (err != NET_SOCK_ERR_NONE) {
  /* Handle error. */
}

rx_len = NetSock_RxDataFrom((NET_SOCK_ID        ) sock,
                            (void              *)&rx_buf [0],
                            (CPU_INT16U         ) BUF_SIZE,
                            (CPU_INT16S         ) NET_SOCK_FLAG_NONE,
                            (NET_SOCK_ADDR     *)&addr_remote,
                            (NET_SOCK_ADDR_LEN *)&addr_remote_len,
                            (void              *) 0,
                            (CPU_INT08U         ) 0,
                            (CPU_INT08U        *) 0,
                            (NET_ERR           *)&err);
```

E

E-4-5 THE APPLICATION RECEIVE SOCKET ERRORS IMMEDIATELY AFTER REBOOT

Immediately after a network interface is added, the physical layer device is reset and network interface and device initialization begins. However, it may take up to three seconds for the average Ethernet physical layer device to complete auto-negotiation. During this time, the socket layer will return NET_SOCK_ERR_LINK_DOWN for sockets that are bound to the interface in question.

The application should attempt to retry the socket operation with a short delay between attempts until network link has been established.

E-4-6 REDUCING THE NUMBER OF TRANSITORY ERRORS (NET_ERR_TX)

The number of transmit buffer should be increased. Additionally, it may be helpful to add a short delay between successive calls to socket transmit functions.

E-4-7 CONTROLLING SOCKET BLOCKING OPTIONS

Socket blocking options may be configured during compile time by adjusting the net_cfg.h macro NET_SOCK_CFG_BLOCK_SEL to the following values:

```
NET_SOCK_BLOCK_SEL_DFLT
NET_SOCK_BLOCK_SEL_BLOCK
NET_SOCK_BLOCK_SEL_NO_BLOCK
```

NET_SOCK_BLOCK_SEL_DFLT selects blocking as the default option, however, allows run-time code to override blocking settings by specifying additional socket.

NET_SOCK_BLOCK_SEL_BLOCK configures all sockets to always block.

NET_SOCK_BLOCK_SEL_NO_BLOCK configures all sockets to non blocking.

See the section B-13-38 on page 655 and section B-13-40 on page 662 for more information about sockets and blocking options.

E-4-8 DETECTING IF A SOCKET IS STILL CONNECTED TO A PEER

Applications may call `NetSock_IsConn()` to determine if a socket is (still) connected to a remote socket (see section B-13-33 on page 646).

Alternatively, applications may make a non-blocking call to `recv()`, `NetSock_RxData()`, or `NetSock_RxDataFrom()` and inspect the return value. If data or a non-fatal, transitory error is returned, then the socket is still connected; otherwise, if '0' or a fatal error is returned, then the socket is disconnected or closed.

E-4-9 RECEIVING -1 INSTEAD OF 0 WHEN CALLING RECV() FOR A CLOSED SOCKET

When a remote peer closes a socket, and the target application calls one of the receive socket functions, µC/TCP-IP will first report that the receive queue is empty and return a -1 for both BSD and µC/TCP-IP socket API functions. The next call to receive will indicate that the socket has been closed by the remote peer.

This is a known issue and will be corrected in subsequent versions of µC/TCP-IP.

E-4-10 DETERMINE THE INTERFACE FOR RECEIVED UDP DATAGRAM

If a UDP socket server is bound to the "any" address, then it is not currently possible to know which interface received the UDP datagram. This is a limitation in the BSD socket API and therefore no solution has been implemented in the µC/TCP-IP socket API.

In order to guarantee which interface a UDP packet was received on, the socket server must bind a specific interface address.

In fact, if a UDP datagram is received on a listening socket bound to the "any" address and the application transmits a response back to the peer using the same socket, then the newly transmitted UDP datagram will be transmitted from the default interface. The default interface may or may not be the interface in which the UDP datagram originated.

E-5 µC/TCP-IP STATISTICS AND DEBUG

E-5-1 PERFORMANCE STATISTICS DURING RUN-TIME

µC/TCP-IP periodically measures and estimates run-time performance on a per interface basis. The performance data is stored in the global µC/TCP-IP statistics data structure, **Net_StatCtrs** which is of type **NET_CTR_STATS**.

Each interface has a performance metric structure which is allocated within a single array of **NET_CTR_IF_STATS**. Each index in the array represents a different interface.

In order to access the performance metrics for a specific interface number, the application may externally access the array by viewing the variable **Net_StatCtrs.NetIF_StatCtrs[if_nbr].field_name**, where **if_nbr** represents the interface number in question, 0 for the loopback interface, and where **field_name** corresponds to one of the fields below.

Possible field names:

```
NetIF_StatRxNbrOctets
NetIF_StatRxNbrOctetsPerSec
NetIF_StatRxNbrOctetsPerSecMax
NetIF_StatRxNbrPktCtr
NetIF_StatRxNbrPktCtrPerSec
NetIF_StatRxNbrPktCtrPerSecMax
NetIF_StatRxNbrPktCtrProcessed
NetIF_StatTxNbrOctets
NetIF_StatTxNbrOctetsPerSec
NetIF_StatTxNbrOctetsPerSecMax
NetIF_StatTxNbrPktCtr
NetIF_StatTxNbrPktCtrPerSec
NetIF_StatTxNbrPktCtrPerSecMax
NetIF_StatTxNbrPktCtrProcessed
```

See Chapter 20, "Statistics and Error Counters" on page 381 for more information.

E-5-2 VIEWING ERROR AND STATISTICS COUNTERS

In order to access the statistics and error counters, the application may externally access the global µC/TCP-IP statistics array by referencing the members of the structure variable `Net_StatCtrs`.

See Chapter 20, "Statistics and Error Counters" on page 381 for more information.

E-5-3 USING NETWORK DEBUG FUNCTIONS TO CHECK NETWORK STATUS CONDITIONS

Example(s) demonstrating how to use the network debug status functions include:

```
NET_DBG_STATUS net_status;
CPU_BOOLEAN    net_fault;
CPU_BOOLEAN    net_fault_conn;
CPU_BOOLEAN    net_rsrc_lost;
CPU_BOOLEAN    net_rsrc_low;

net_status     = NetDbg_ChkStatus();
net_fault      = DEF_BIT_IS_SET(net_status, NET_DBG_STATUS_FAULT);
net_fault_conn = DEF_BIT_IS_SET(net_status, NET_DBG_STATUS_FAULT_CONN);
net_rsrc_lost  = DEF_BIT_IS_SET(net_status, NET_DBG_STATUS_RSRC_LOST);
net_rsrc_lo    = DEF_BIT_IS_SET(net_status, NET_DBG_STATUS_RSRC_LO);
net_status     = NetDbg_ChkStatusTmrs();
```

E-6 USING NETWORK SECURITY MANAGER

The network security manager requires the presence of a network security layer such as µC/SSL. The port layer developed for the network security layer is reponsible of securing the sockets and applying the security strategy over typical socket programming functions. From an application point of view, the usage of µC/TCP-IP network security manager is very simple. It requires two basic step. The application code shipped with µC/TCP-IP includes a project that shows how to use the network security manager.

E-6-1 KEYING MATERIAL INSTALLATION

In order to acheive secure handshake connections, some keying material must be installed before performing any secure socket operation. With µC/SSL, the client side needs to install certificates authorities to validate the identity of the public key certificate sent by the server side. On the opposite, a server needs to install a public key certificare / private key pair to send the the clients that wants to connect. This keying material can be installed using the network security manager APIs decribed in section B-12-1 on page 579 and section B-12-2 on page 581 of µC/TCP-IP user manual. The following example demonstrates how to install a PEM certificate authority from a constant buffer.

```
CPU_SIZE_T  Micrium_Ca_Cert_Pem_Len = 994;
CPU_CHAR    Micrium_Ca_Cert_Pem[] =
"-----BEGIN CERTIFICATE-----\r\n"
"MIICpTCCAg4CCQDNdHgFKaYRWDANBgkqhkiG9w0BAQUFADCBljELMAkGA1UEBhMC\r\n"
"Q0ExDzANBgNVBAgMBlF1ZWJlYzERMA8GA1UEBwwITW9udHJlYWwxFTATBgNVBAoM\r\n"
"DE1pY3JpdW0gSW5jLjEZMBcGA1UECwwQRW1iZWRkZWQgU3lzdGVtczEQMA4GA1UE\r\n"
"AwwHTW1jcml1bTEfMB0GCSqGSIb3DQEJARYQaW5mb0BtaWNyaXVtLmNvbTAeFw0x\r\n"
"aXVtMR8wHQYJKoZIhvcNAQkBFhBpbmZvQG1pY3JpdW0uY29tMIGfMA0GCSqGSIb3\r\n"
[...]
"CZFtP3vbY0SA6gFrCvCcKjTWRapzQKwSYknMu1QorP4mdwZDeCYsikkn8bI5//zn\r\n"
"CInLCmrWdbrCEtj23t0wefw8fyNQxkKi9JdbzLVwxjIQt8wMq1CnTOQRa7aGX5Uw\r\n"
"QQIDAQABMA0GCSqGSIb3DQEBBQUAA4GBACqyJeSDQ3j5KohXIvV+iBOrl5qbIlPS\r\n"
"WAHf4PSyiTX0Spa58VSdhM4sestd/FELBWo/MHKIfBdoLMhg2frDZE5e7m8Ftq1R\r\n"
"1YBKNbTzIJNjwTajkUPz38BjXb5sqLyPK8wRbjadm2pOlw1f7bIFunpbHpV+1XAl\r\n"
"tk3W32BqKfzy\r\n"
"-----END CERTIFICATE-----\r\n";

void  Task (void)
{
    NET_ERR  err;


    NetSecureMgr_InstallBuf((CPU_INT08U *)Micrium_Ca_Cert_Pem,
                                          NET_SECURE_INSTALL_TYPE_CA,
                                          NET_SECURE_INSTALL_FORMAT_PEM,
                                          Micrium_Ca_Cert_Pem_Len,
                                         &err);
    if (err != NET_SECURE_MGR_ERR_NONE) {
        APP_TRACE_INFO(("    uC/TCP-IP:NetSecureMgr_InstallBuf() error %d \n", err));
        return;
    }
}
```

The following example demonstrates how to install a DER certificate authority, PEM public key certificate and a DER private key from the file system.

```
#define  Micrium_Ca_Cert_File_Der               "\\ca-cert.der"
#define  Micrium_Srv_Cert_File_Pem              "\\server-cert.pem"
#define  Micrium_Srv_Key_File_Der               "\\server-key.der"
void  Task (void  *p_arg)
{
    NET_ERR  err;


    NetSecureMgr_InstallFile(Micrium_Ca_Cert_File_Der,
                             NET_SECURE_INSTALL_TYPE_CA,
                             NET_SECURE_INSTALL_FORMAT_DER,
                            &err);
    if (err != NET_SECURE_MGR_ERR_NONE) {
        APP_TRACE_INFO(("    uC/TCP-IP:NetSecureMgr_InstallFile() error %d \n", err));
        return;
    }

    NetSecureMgr_InstallFile(Micrium_Srv_Cert_File_Pem,
                             NET_SECURE_INSTALL_TYPE_CERT,
                             NET_SECURE_INSTALL_FORMAT_PEM,
                            &err);
    if (err != NET_SECURE_MGR_ERR_NONE) {
        APP_TRACE_INFO(("    uC/TCP-IP:NetSecureMgr_InstallFile() error %d \n", err));
        return;
    }

    NetSecureMgr_InstallFile(Micrium_Srv_Key_File_Der,
                             NET_SECURE_INSTALL_TYPE_KEY,
                             NET_SECURE_INSTALL_FORMAT_DER,
                            &err);
    if (err != NET_SECURE_MGR_ERR_NONE) {
        APP_TRACE_INFO(("    uC/TCP-IP:NetSecureMgr_InstallFile() error %d \n", err));
        return;
    }
}
```

E-6-2 SECURING A SOCKET

Once the appropriate keying material is installed, a TCP socket can be secured if it has been successfully open. A simple function call is used to setup the secure flag on the socket. This function is documented in section B-13-4 on page 590 of µC/TCP-IP user manual. With this simple API, you can secure your custom TCP client or server application. Pleae note that all Micrium applications running over TCP has already been modified to support secure sockets (µC/HTTPs, µC/TELNETs, µC/FTPs, µC/FTPc, µC/SMTPc, µC/POP3c). The following example demonstrates how to open and secure a TCP socket

```
void  Task (void  *p_arg)
{
    NET_ERR  net_err;
    sock_id = NetSock_Open(NET_SOCK_ADDR_FAMILY_IP_V4,
                           NET_SOCK_TYPE_STREAM,
                           NET_SOCK_PROTOCOL_TCP,
                          &net_err);
    if (net_err == NET_SOCK_ERR_NONE) {

#ifdef  NET_SECURE_MODULE_PRESENT
        (void)NetSock_CfgSecure((NET_SOCK_ID    ) sock_id,
                                (CPU_BOOLEAN    ) DEF_YES,
                                (NET_ERR       *)&net_err);
        if (net_err != NET_SOCK_ERR_NONE) {
            APP_TRACE_INFO(("Open socket failed. No secure socket available.\n"));
            return (DEF_FAIL);
        }
#endif
    }
}
```

E-7 MISCELLANEOUS

E-7-1 SENDING AND RECEIVING ICMP ECHO REQUESTS FROM THE TARGET

From the user application, µC/TCP-IP does not support sending and receiving ICMP Echo Request and Reply messages However, the target is capable of receiving externally generated ICMP Echo Request messages and replying them accordingly. At this time, there are no means to generate an ICMP Echo Request from the target.

E-7-2 TCP KEEP-ALIVES

µC/TCP-IP does not currently support TCP Keep-Alives. If both ends of the connection are running different Network Protocol Stacks, you may attempt to enable TCP Keep-Alives on the remote side. Alternatively, the application will have to send something through the socket to the remote peer in order to ensure that the TCP connection remains open.

E-7-3 USING µC/TCP-IP FOR INTER-PROCESS COMMUNICATION

It is possible for tasks to communicate with sockets via the localhost interface which must be enabled.

Appendix

F

Bibliography

Labrosse, Jean J. 2009, *μC/OS-III, The Real-Time Kernel*, Micrium Press, 2009, ISBN 978-0-98223375-3-0.

Douglas E. Comer. 2006, *Internetworking With TCP/IP Volume 1: Principles Protocols, and Architecture, 5th edition,* 2006. (Hardcover - Jul 10, 2005) ISBN 0-13-187671-6.

W. Richard Stevens. 1993, *TCP/IP Illustrated, Volume 1: The Protocols*, Addison-Wesley Professional Computing Series, Published Dec 31, 1993 by Addison-Wesley Professional, Hardcover , ISBN-10: 0-201-63346-9

W. Richard Stevens, Bill Fenner, Andrew M. Rudoff. *Unix Network Programming, Volume 1: The Sockets Networking API (3rd Edition)* (Addison-Wesley Professional Computing Series) (Hardcover), ISBN-10: 0-13-141155-1

IEEE Standard 802.3-1985, *Technical Committee on Computer Communications of the IEEE Computer Society.* (1985), IEEE Standard 802.3-1985, IEEE, pp. 121, ISBN 0-471-82749-5

Request for Comments (RFCs), Internet Engineering Task Force (IETF). The complete list of RFCs can be found at http://www.faqs.org/rfcs/.

Brian "Beej Jorgensen" Hall, 2009, *Beej's Guide to Network Programming, Version 3.0.13,* March 23, 2009, http://beej.us/guide/bgnet/

The Motor Industry Software Reliability Association, *MISRA-C:2004*, Guidelines for the Use of the C Language in Critical Systems, October 2004. www.misra-c.com.

Appendix

G

µC/TCP-IP Licensing Policy

G-1 µC/TCP-IP LICENSING

G-1-1 µC/OS-III AND µC/TCP-IP LICENSING

This book includes µC/OS-III in source form for free short-term evaluation, for educational use or for peaceful research. We provide ALL the source code for your convenience and to help you experience µC/OS-III. The fact that the source is provided does *not* mean that you can use it commercially without paying a licensing fee. Knowledge of the source code may NOT be used to develop a similar product either.

This book also contains µC/TCP-IP, precompiled in linkable object form. It is not necessary to purchase anything else, as long as the initial purchase is used for educational purposes. Once the code is used to create a commercial project/product for profit, however, it is necessary to purchase a license.

You are required to purchase this license when the decision to use µC/OS-III and/or µC/TCP-IP in a design is made, not when the design is ready to go to production.

If you are unsure about whether you need to obtain a license for your application, please contact Micrium and discuss the intended use with a sales representative.

G-1-2 μC/TCP-IP MAINTENANCE RENEWAL

Licensing μC/TCP-IP provides one year of limited technical support and maintenance and source code updates. Renew the maintenance agreement for continued support and source code updates.Contact sales@Micrium.com for additional information.

G-1-3 μC/TCP-IP SOURCE CODE UPDATES

If you are under maintenance, you will be automatically emailed when source code updates become available. You can then download your available updates from the Micrium FTP server. If you are no longer under maintenance, or forget your Micrium FTP user name or password, please contact sales@Micrium.com.

G-1-4 μC/TCP-IP SUPPORT

Support is available for licensed customers. Please visit the customer support section in www.Micrium.com. If you are not a current user, please register to create your account. A web form will be offered to you to submit your support question,

Licensed customers can also use the following contact:

CONTACT MICRIUM

Micrium
1290 Weston Road, Suite 306
Weston, FL 33326

+1 954 217 2036
+1 954 217 2037 (FAX)

and the

Renesas RX62N

Christian Légaré

Weston, FL 33326

Micrium Press
1290 Weston Road, Suite 306
Weston, FL 33326
USA
www.Micrium.com

For bulk orders, please contact Micrium Press at: +1 954 217 2036

ISBN: 978-1-935772-06-4
100-uC-TCPIP-Renesas-RX62N-001

Foreword to Part II

The sophistication, capabilities, performance, and system design opportunities offered by Renesas RX™ microcontrollers are quite astounding and continue to grow. A good TCP/IP stack — especially a well-proven TCP/IP stack — can shorten the time to market and help achieve the enormous solution potential of these connected devices.

What is needed for many applications is a TCP/IP stack with features honed to deliver the kind of fast, reliable system that takes full advantage of the microcontroller and turns them into actions and operations that make successful end products, equipment and electronic systems. Micriµm, one of our Platinum Partners, delivers this key software in the form of their popular µC/TCP-IP embedded protocol stack. And to better support this product, Christian Légaré, vice president of Micriµm Inc., has written this incredibly informative book.

Academic theory for creating a TCP/IP stack is quite straightforward. But a world of difference exists between theory and practice. There are a myriad of practical issues related to designing, testing and implementing a TCP/IP stack that delivers all the capabilities essential for today's embedded systems, especially for those that are mission-critical or bear huge safety burdens. Moreover, of necessity, there are complexities associated with ensuring the optimum use of the features that the protocol stack delivers. Mr. Légaré's book is a tremendous body of work; an amazing investment of effort produced to make it easier for system engineers to create powerful and reliable new products for diverse global markets, while also saving valuable time in the development cycle.

Micriµm's µC/TCP-IP stack and all its modules are compact, portable designs used in thousands of products, including safety-critical systems. Scalable and ROM-able, and they support most MISRA-C rules. Among the wide range of middleware products offered by Micriµm, µC/OS-III, µC/USB Host and Device, µC/FS, and µC/CAN conform to applicable standards, are highly reliable, and specifically put the processing power of microcontrollers like the Renesas RX62N chip to work with high efficiency.

This package, containing Mr. Légaré's book, the companion Renesas Demo Kit YRDKRX62N, μC/TCP-IP embedded protocol stack and the latest Eclipse-based IDE from Renesas called e^2 Studio (**e**clipse **e**mbedded **Studio**), combines Renesas' strengths and Micriμm's strengths in a very synergistic way. Based on true out-of-the-box thinking, it is much more than just a convenient entry point for meeting the requirements of even the most challenging new design projects. It's also a valuable tutorial for getting the most out of the system implementation, as well as a valuable reference for analysis and troubleshooting.

Renesas and Micriμm had two primary goals in creating this package. We wanted to simplify and facilitate the application of RX600 series microcontrollers, and wanted to help you build the highest possible level of quality into your system designs. If we've been successful in meeting these objectives, you will enjoy using the system development resources delivered herein and be able to put them to good use easily, again and again.

Thank you for your interest in Renesas microcontrollers and advanced embedded system solutions.

Ali Sebt
Executive Vice President
Renesas Electronics America, Inc.

Chapter

1

Introduction

This book explains the embedded TCP/IP stack and its inner workings using Micrium's μC/TCP-IP.

As previously discussed in the first part of the book Chapter 10, "Introduction to μC/TCP-IP" on page 243, μC/TCP-IP requires the use of an RTOS capable of supporting multiple tasks, semaphores and message queues like μC/OS-II or μC/OS-III. For the examples in this book, μC/OS-III is used and it is provided in source form for free short-term evaluation. Refer to Appendix B on page 1029 for more details about licensing μC/OS-III in a commercial product.

For developers that immediately want to get their hands on the code and run it on real hardware, the next chapters are for you. For readers interested in the theory of IP networking and issues related to embedding the technology, the first chapters in Part I should be consulted.

1-1 PART II - READY-TO-RUN EXAMPLES

Application examples contained in Part II use the Renesas Demonstration Kit YRDKRX62N which can be purchased separately. The board contains a Renesas RX62N microcontroller with Ethernet, CAN and USB connectivity.

This μC/TCP-IP book and board are complemented by a full set of tools provided free of charge and downloadable through the Internet from the following links:

- www.micrium.com/page/downloads/uc-tcp-ip_files
- www.renesas.com
- www.kpitgnutools.com

To build the example code provided in Part II of this book, you download the IDE from the Renesas website, the GNU-RX-ELF compiler from the KPIT GNU tools website and the examples source code from the Micrium website.

µC/TCP-IP is provided as a library for the evaluation board. The tools and the use of µC/TCP-IP are free as long as they are used with the evaluation board, and there is no commercial intent to use them on a project. For educational purposes, this book is ideal for an IP networking class.

The book also comes with a trial version of a tool from Micrium called µC/Probe. The trial version allows the user to monitor and change up to five variables in a target system, in addition to the µC/OS-III and µC/TCP-IP variables.

1-2 µC/PROBE

µC/Probe is a Microsoft Windows™ based application that enables the user to visualize, display, or change the value of any variable in a system while the target is running. These variables can be displayed using such graphical elements as gauges, meters, bar graphs, virtual LEDs, numeric indicators, and many more. Sliders, switches, and buttons can be used to change variables--all without the user writing a single line of code.

µC/Probe interfaces to any target (8-, 16-, 32-, 64-bit, or even DSPs) through one of the many interfaces supported (J-Tag, RS-232C, USB, Ethernet, etc.). µC/Probe displays or changes any variable (as long as they are global) in the application, including µC/OS-III's and µC/TCP-IP's internal variables.

µC/Probe works with any compiler/assembler/linker able to generate an ELF/DWARF or IEEE695 file. This is the exact same file that the user will download to the evaluation board or a final target. From this file, µC/Probe is able to extract symbolic information about variables, and determine where variables are stored in RAM or ROM.

µC/Probe enables users to log the data displayed into a file for data analysis at a later time. µC/Probe also provides µC/OS-III kernel awareness as a built-in feature. Data screens monitoring the main µC/TCP-IP variables are also provided.

µC/Probe is a tool that serious embedded software engineers should have in their toolbox. The full version of µC/Probe is included when licensing µC/OS-III. See www.Micrium.com for more details.

1-3 PART II CHAPTER CONTENTS

Figure 1-1 illustrates the layout and flow of Part II of the book. This diagram should be useful in understanding the relationship between chapters and appendices.

The first column on the left indicates chapters that should be read in order to understand the example projects and provides excellent templates on how to configure and use µC/TCP-IP with UDP or TCP. The second column consists of miscellaneous appendices.

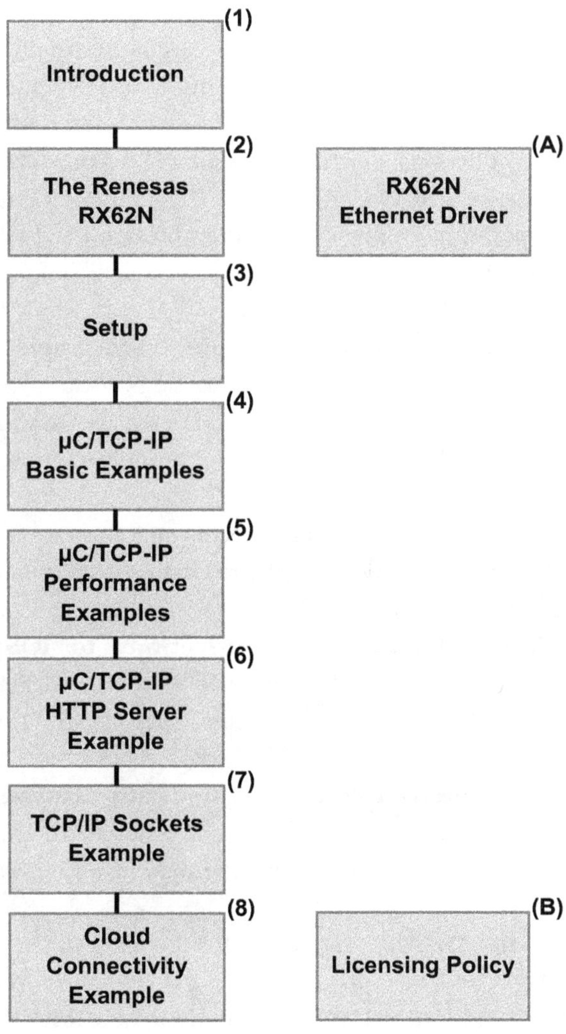

Figure 1-1 **Part II Chapter Layout**

Chapter 1, "Introduction". This chapter.

Chapter 2, "The Renesas RX600 MCU". The chapter describes the Renesas' RX600 32-bit MCU/DSP hybrid also known as Digital Signal Controller (DSC).

Chapter 3, "Setup". The chapter explains how to set up the evaluation environment to run µC/TCP-IP examples. The chapter describes how to download the tools, how to obtain the example code that accompanies the book, and how to connect the Renesas Demonstration Kit YRDKRX62N and a PC to the network.

Chapter 4, "µC/TCP-IP Basic Examples". This chapter explains how to get µC/TCP-IP up and running. Both projects blink LEDs on the board when running. At this point, the external host (the PC) can PING the target board to validate that the Ethernet interface and the TCP/IP stack are functional. Example project #1 uses a static IP configuration while example project #2 uses a DHCP configuration. The example demonstrates how easy it is to use µC/Probe to display run-time data in a target through the J-Link interface. The example #3 in this chapter introduces a faster µC/Probe interface through UDP.

Chapter 5, "µC/TCP-IP Performance Examples". The chapter uses µC/IPerf to run UDP and TCP tests. Wireshark captures are used to demonstrate the exchange between the YRDKRX62N and the PC. µC/Probe can also be used to view the TCP/IP stack resource utilization. Again, µC/Probe is used to show run-time information.

Chapter 6, "Example #5 HTTP Server". In this chapter, an HTTP server is built showing how data from and to the embedded target can be transferred using a web browser.

Chapter 7, "TCP/IP Sockets: Push Notifications to iOS devices". The chapter demonstrates the use of TCP sockets in order to send Growl/Prowl notifications from the YRDKRX62N target board to an iOS based system such as an iPhone or iPad.

Chapter 8, "Cloud Connectivity: Interfacing with Exosite's One Platform". The chapter demonstrates the use of TCP sockets in order to interface with an XMPP based portal that delivers notifications and presents the data in a web-based dashboard.

Appendix A, "Ethernet Driver". The driver for the YRDKRX62N Ethernet controller.

Appendix B, "µC/OS-III and µC/TCP-IP Licensing Policy". Information about licensing µC/OS-III and µC/TCP-IP in commercial products.

Chapter

2

The Renesas RX600 MCU

Renesas' RX600 32-bit CPU enables a new class of microcontrollers which meets many demands of today's embedded real time control applications including: high performance yet very low power consumption; the smallest possible code and data size; the lowest cost; and the need for digital signal processing.

The RX600 is an MCU/DSP hybrid, or Digital Signal Controller (DSC), producing 1.65 Dhrystone MIPS/MHz as an MCU, but it is also a very powerful signal processor because of the integrated Floating Point Unit (FPU) and Multiply-Accumulate (MAC) unit. This unified processor has 73 basic instructions, plus eight floating point and nine DSP instructions. Code for both traditional real time embedded control tasks as well as DSP algorithms are developed for the RX600 in C/C++ using a single, easy-to-use Integrated Development Environment (IDE).

DSC capability spans many applications, including energy efficient motor control in home appliances, medical patient monitoring, smart metering, factory/building/home automation, personal audio, barcode and image scanning, point-of-sale terminals, human-machine interfacing, and many more.

2-1 ORIGINS OF RX600

The design team at Renesas has combined the advantages of high-speed RISC CPU designs refined in the SuperH family with those of the flexible, code-efficient CISC designs nurtured in the H8S/H8SX and the M16C/R32C families. Specifically, to create a next-generation CPU architecture, the RX design team combined a RISC-like 32-bit general purpose register-based Modified Harvard architecture machine having a five-stage pipeline, with a set of CISC-like variable-length instructions ranging from 8-bits to 64-bits and a rich set of addressing modes. The result, a minimum execution time of one clock-per-instruction was achieved while maintaining ultra-compact code and data size. And as a natural extension, the FPU and MAC were included from SuperH and M16C heritage to complete the DSC capability of RX600. This CPU is capable of up to 200 MHz maximum frequency producing 1.65 Dhrystone MIPS/MHz, and the core uses just 30 µA/MHz (on 90 nm flash memory technology). This clever design approach was made possible by building on decades of MCU design experience and applying a large library of accumulated IP.

2-2 RX600 SERIES DEVICES

As of June 2010, Renesas has introduced 3 major groups within the RX600 Series, the RX610, RX620, RX62N, and RX62T. All of these MCUs currently have a maximum frequency of 100 MHz, and are based on the proven 90 nm MONOS (Metal Oxide Nitride Oxide Silicon) embedded flash memory technology capable of read access up to 100 MHz with no wait-states. This means the RX600 CPU core will have full performance with no stalls due to reading code from on-chip flash memory, and no need for memory acceleration techniques.

Key attributes for each of these RX600 groups:

- RX610 group has very large memory with flash memory up to 2 MB and SRAM of 128 kB, and fast ADCs up to 4M samples/second.
- RX620 group enables connectivity with USB Host/Device and CAN.
- RX62N group enables connectivity with Ethernet, USB-FS Host/Device/OTG, and CAN, plus the ability to drive a color TFT-LCD.
- RX62T has special timers and analog functions optimizing motor control, including embedded op-amps with programmable gain. This MCU can drive two motors at once.

Figure 2-1 shows the current RX600 Series line-up. Many more RX600 devices are coming in 2012, expanding choices for connectivity, memory size, package selection, and additional low-power modes. Please check the web for the latest offerings at www.renesas.com/rx.

		Advanced Peripherals							Basic Peripheral Set																			
		Connectivity				Advanced Motor			Memory			Analog				Timers								Communication				
	Group	Ethernet 10/100 MAC	USB 2.0 Host/Device/OTG	CAN 2.0B	Graphics ExDMA	Advanced ADC 12-bit	MTU3	GPT	Flash (max)	SRAM (max)	Data Flash	ADC 10-bit	DAC 10-bit	ADC 12-bit	Temp Sensor	MTU2	TPU	PPG	TMR	CMT	WDT	I-WDT	RTC	I2C	SCI	ExBus	SPI	LIN
Connectivity	RX621	–	1	1	1	–	–	–	512KB	96KB	32KB	–	2	8	–	12	–	8	4	4	1	1	1	2	6	8/16/32	2	–
	RX631	–	2	3	1	–	–	–	2MB	128KB	32KB	8	2	21	1	6	12	8	4	4	1	1	1	4	13	8/16/32	3	–
	RX62N	1	2	1	1	–	–	–	512KB	96KB	32KB	–	2	8	–	12	–	8	4	4	1	1	1	2	6	8/16/32	2	–
	RX63N	1	2	3	1	–	–	–	2MB	128KB	32KB	8	2	21	1	6	12	8	4	4	1	1	1	4	13	8/16/32	3	–
General Purpose	RX610	–	–	–	–	–	–	–	2MB	128KB	32KB	16	2	–	–	–	12	8	4	4	1	–	–	2	7	8/16	–	–
	RX630	–	1*	3	–	–	–	–	2MB	128KB	32KB	8	2	21	1	6	12	8	4	4	1	1	1	4	13	8/16	3	–
Motor Control	RX62T	–	–	1	–	8	8	4	256KB	16KB	8KB	12	–	–	–	–	–	–	–	4	1	1	–	1	3	–	1	1

Figure 2-1 **RX600 Groups and Peripheral Set**

The new RX200 Series, which was released in 2011, maintains the common RX CPU core and carries many of the same peripherals of the RX600 Series, but the RX200 is based on an ultra-low leakage 130 nm flash memory process for very low-power portable applications with enhanced analog capabilities. The RX600 and RX200 Series complement each other in applications needing the most performance and the least power consumption, as shown in Figure 2-2.

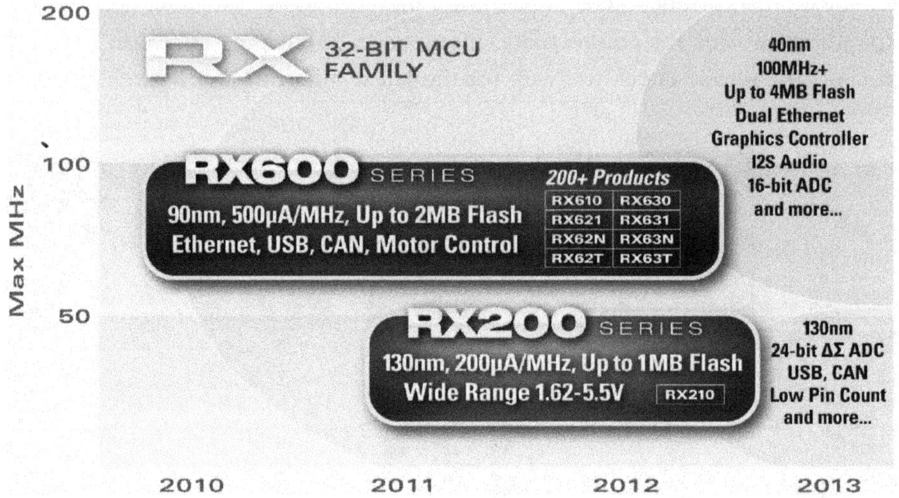

Figure 2-2 **RX Family Roadmap**

2-3 RX600 FEATURES

CPU

- 32-bit Modified Harvard architecture CPU core
- 5-stage instruction pipeline
- Minimum execution time One CPU clock per instruction
- 1.65 DMIPS/MHz (Dhrystone v2.1)
- 200 MHz Maximum operating frequency
- 4-Gbyte linear address space
- CPU Register Set
  - Sixteen general 32-bit registers
  - Nine 32-bit control registers
  - One 64-bit accumulator
- Memory-protection unit (MPU)

- Single precision (32-bit) floating point unit (FPU)
    - Data types and floating-point exceptions in conformance IEEE754
- 16 x 16 + 48 → 48 bits Multiply Accumulate (MAC), single-cycle
- 32 x 32 + 80 → 80 bits Repeated Multiply Accumulate (RMPA)
- On-chip 32-bit multiplier: 32 x 32 → 64 bits
- On-chip divider: 32 / 32 → 32 bits
- Barrel shifter: 32 bits
- 73 Basic instructions including:
    - arithmetic/logic
    - data-transfer
    - relative branches to optimize for branch distances
    - bit-manipulation
    - string-manipulation
    - system control
- 8 Floating-point instructions including:
    - Addition
    - Subtraction
    - Multiplication
    - Division
    - Compare
    - Integer conversion
    - Floating Point conversion
    - Rounding
- 9 DSP instructions including:
    - Multiply Accumulate
    - Repeated Multiply Accumulate

- Saturating math
- Barrel Shift
- Accumulator data rounding

- 10 Addressing modes including:
  - Immediate
  - Register direct
  - Register indirect
  - Register relative
  - Post-increment register indirect
  - Pre-decrement register indirect
  - Indexed register indirect
  - Control register direct
  - PSW direct
  - Program counter relative
- Data arrangement
  - Instructions: Little endian
  - Data: Selectable as little endian or big endian

2-4 ZERO WAIT-STATE FLASH UP TO 100MHz

At the time of printing, all RX600 MCUs from Renesas are designed with high speed 90 nm flash memory that operates up to 100 MHz (10 ns) read speed. Most other MCU manufacturers use flash memory technology that has a limited read speed of around 20 to 50 MHz. A slower flash memory requires more wait states than a faster flash memory as MCU operating frequency is increased beyond the flash read speed. For every wait state addition, the CPU has to wait longer and longer to fetch instructions from the flash memory and ultimately, the MCU performance at higher frequency suffers. Figure 2-3 shows the impact of wait states on the MCU performance. To minimize the performance penalty due to slower flash, most MCU manufacturers use 64-bit or wider prefetch buffer with cache memory. This technique, however, does not completely overcome the performance penalty when the CPU executes non-sequential code, like happens so often in embedded control applications. The RX600 MCUs use a combination of a fast 100 MHz 64-bit wide flash memory and a simple 64-bit wide by 4-deep prefetch queue containing up to 32 instructions to provide a constant stream of instruction flow to the CPU at all speeds. For non-linear execution of code (a branch for example), the maximum delay in flash memory access for RX600 is only one CPU clock (10 ns) if the instruction of the branch is not already in the prefetch queue. This one CPU clock is all that it takes to reload the prefetch queue with the new instruction stream started by the branch operation. If the instruction from the branch is already in the prefetch queue, there is no extra CPU clock needed and execution progresses without delay. Therefore, the RX requires no wait states, and needs no caching methods to reduce the latency on non-linear code execution.

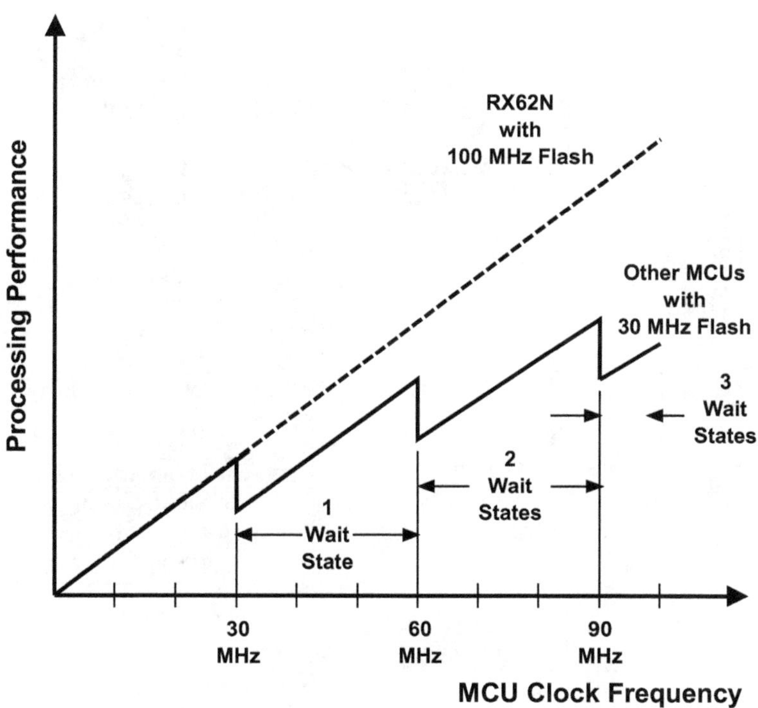

Figure 2-3 **RX62N with 100MHz on-chip flash**

2-5 THE RENESAS RX62N

The specific RX600 MCU group member used in this book for demonstration is the RX62N. This 100 MHz MCU has the RX CPU core just described, plus up to 512 kB of Zero Wait-State flash memory, up to 96 kB of SRAM, 32 kB of data flash memory, and connectivity with 10/100 Ethernet, USB-FS Host/Device/OTG, CAN, and others.

The block diagram is shown in Figure 2-4.

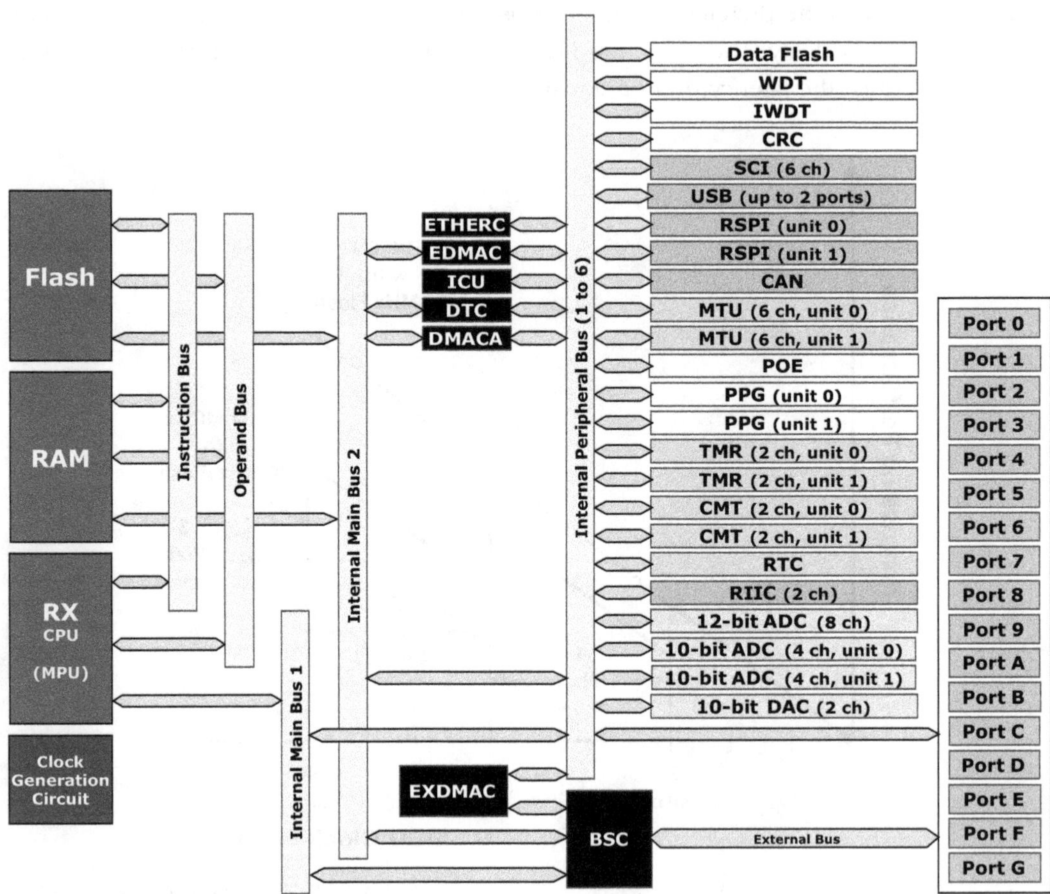

Figure 2-4 **RX62N Block Diagram**

The following is a brief description of just a few of many peripherals found on the RX62N, which significantly off-load work from the CPU and enhance connectivity.

DMAC (DIRECT MEMORY ACCESS CONTROLLER)

There are four programmable DMAC channels on the RX62N to manage movement of data between peripherals and memory, memory to memory, and peripheral to peripheral, with very minimal overhead of CPU involvement. These transfers occur in the background on separate physical busses inside the RX62N, removing any restrictions on the RX CPU's immediate local busses for code and data access. The DMAC channels operate in many flexible modes, including Normal Transfer, Repeat Transfer, and Block Transfer with burst and cycle-stealing options. There is also a very useful option to automatically update the data transfer address after each transfer by incrementing, decrementing, or offset addition. The DMAC can be set to activate automatically by on-chip peripherals, including timers, serial channels, A/D Converters, as well as external interrupt pins and by software.

EXDMAC (EXTERNAL DIRECT MEMORY ACCESS CONTROLLER)

There are two EXDMAC channels on the RX62N, which are very similar to the DMACs, but instead of operating on data internal to the RX62N chip, the EXDMAC channels control movement of data outside the RX62N chip. This means the RX62N can orchestrate data movement from one external memory or device to another memory or external device, and the data never enters the RX chip. A good example of this is when the RX62N drives a TFT-LCD panel with EXDMAC. The graphic image data is stored in an external SDRAM (frame buffer), and the EXDMAC automatically moves the graphic data from the SDRAM (one external device) to the TFT-LCD panel (the other external device), refreshing the panel at a 60 Hz rate. All this happens with very little CPU overhead because the graphic data never enters the RX62N chip.

DTC (DATA TRANSFER CONTROLLER)

The DTC performs a task similar to that of a DMAC. That is, when triggered, the DTC transfers data from one memory location to another without CPU intervention. This eases the load on the CPU, freeing up processing power for applications and control tasks. It differs from the DMAC in that the configuration data for a data transfer is loaded on the fly from RAM based tables. This has the advantage of offering more transfer channels than a DMAC as the number of channels is limited only by available RAM. Data transfer activated by an on-chip peripheral module interrupt can be done independently of the CPU. The transfer mode is selectable for each interrupt source. The DTC supports multiple transfer modes: Normal mode, repeat mode, or block transfer mode. The data transfer can be specified as byte (8-bit), word (16-bit), or longword (32-bit). The interrupt that activated the DTC can also be issued to the CPU. A CPU interrupt can be requested after one data transfer is complete. Finally, a CPU interrupt can be requested after all specified data transfers are complete.

MTU2 (MULTI-FUNCTION TIMER UNIT)

The RX62N has two MTU timer units which can be used for sophisticated motor control, or for general timer/counter/PWM functions. Each one provides a maximum of 16 lines of pulse input/output and three lines of pulse input based on six channels of 16-bit timers. The MTU can be configured to provide 21 output compare and input capture registers. The pulse output modes can be set to: Toggle, PWM, and complementary PWM. The MTU allows the synchronization of multiple counters. The complementary PWM output mode allows for non-overlapping waveforms output for 3-phase inverter control, automatic dead time setting, 0% to 100% PWM duty cycle value specifiable, A/D conversion delaying function, and interrupt skipping at crest or trough. The reset-synchronized PWM mode allows three-phase PWM waveforms in positive and negative phases and can be output with a required duty value. The phase counting mode allows for two-phase encoder pulse counting. Each MTU2 unit is supported by the DMAC and DTC units.

TMR (8-BIT TIMER)

There are two TMR channels on the RX62N, each timer unit is 8-bits and supports counting, comparing, pulse and PWM outputs. These timer units are frequently used for baud rate generation for the SCI serial interfaces. TMR channels are supported by the DTC.

CMT (COMPARE MATCH TIMER)

The RX62N provides two 16-bit compare match timers. Each CMT channel is supported by the DMAC and DTC units. These are actually used by µC/OS-III: CMT0 is used to generate the tick rate interrupt, and CMT1 is used for time measurements.

RSPI (RENESAS SERIAL PERIPHERAL INTERFACE)

There are two RSPI channels on the RX62N. Each one supports Master, Slave, and Multi-master modes up to 18 MHz clock rate. All standard SPI clock synchronous transfer modes are supported and configured at run-time, including all combinations of clock phase, clock polarity, and MSB/LSB bit ordering. Variable data length transfers are supported from 8 to 32 bits. Up to four slaves can be controlled in single master mode. Up to three slaves can be controlled in multi-master mode. Data is double-buffered for higher throughput. There is a simple interface to the RX CPU with a number of registers and four interrupts per RSPI channel. RSPI channels are supported by the DMAC and DTC units.

RIIC (RENESAS I²C BUS)

There are two RIIC channels on the RX62N. Each one supports Master, Slave, and Multi-master modes up to 1 Mbps transfer rates. There is a simple interface to the RX CPU with a number of registers and four interrupts per RIIC channel. The hardware takes care of all low-level I^2C data transfers including bus arbitration, time-outs, re-starts, handshaking, clock stretching and clock holding to adjust dissimilar speeds of master and slave devices, as well as use of the acknowledge bit. RIIC channels are supported by the DMAC and DTC units.

SERIAL COMMUNICATIONS INTERFACE (SCI)

RX62N has six SCI channels, each one capable of asynchronous and clock synchronous transfers. The SCI channels can also handle smartcard ISO/IEC 7816-3 protocol for ID cards. Various UART modes are supported, including Multi-Processor Communications (9-bit UART), and speeds over 3 Mbps. There is a simple interface to the RX CPU with a number of registers and four interrupts per SCI channel. The hardware takes care of all low-level SCI data transfers, and data is double-buffered in the transmit and receive paths for higher throughput. SCI channels are supported by the DMAC and DTC units.

USB (UNIVERSAL SERIAL BUS – HOST/DEVICE/OTG)

There are up to two USB interfaces on the RX62N, each one supports USB 2.0 full-speed mode (12 Mbps) Host, Device, or OTG operation selectable by firmware. Each interface provides 10 endpoints (EP0 to EP9) and contains on-chip transceivers for Host and Device modes (OTG needs external circuit). Standard commands are automatically processed by hardware. The USB peripheral supports four USB transfer types: control transfer, bulk transfer, isochronous transfer, and interrupt transfer. DMAC and DTC transfers are supported and the data can be automatically streamed to or from the common SRAM in the RX62N chip. There is also a 2 kB FIFO dedicated to the data transmitted and received by the USB peripheral to maximize throughput. The RX62N USB controller is supported by Micrium's µC/USB-Host/Device/OTG.

ETHERNET CONTROLLER (MEDIA ACCESS CONTROLLER OR MAC)

The RX62N has a single Media Access Control (MAC) unit which assembles and disassembles data frames based on the IEEE-802.3 format at either 10 or 100 Mbps. The MAC contains a 2 kbytes FIFO for transmission and a separate 2 kbytes FIFO for reception. The MAC allows for full duplex and half-duplex communication. The Ethernet controller supports the MII standard (Media Independent Interface) and the RMII standard (Reduced

Media Independent Interface) connection to an external PHY device. Data to and from the Ethernet controller is managed by a dedicated DMA controller, the EDMAC, to maximize data throughput. The RX62N Ethernet controller is supported by Micrium's µC/TCP-IP and complementary protocol stacks (DHCP, DNS, FTP, HTTP, POP3, SMTP, SNTP, Telnet, etc.).

CAN (CONTROLLER AREA NETWORK)

The RX62N has a single CAN interface supporting the ISO118998-1 CAN protocol standard operating at 1 Mbps. This interface supports 32 message mailboxes, each one can be configured for transmit or receive, and up to eight of them can have FIFO support to increase throughput. There are eight acceptance filters to apply to these mailboxes to reduce overhead of the CPU in filtering which messages are destined for the RX62N on the CAN bus. An automatic time-stamp for messages is also supported. The RX62N CAN controller is supported by Micrium's µC/CAN.

EXTERNAL BUS

The RX62N supports an external, non-multiplexed, data bus in the larger packages (144-pin and 176-pin) with up to 32 data lines and 24 address lines. Eight memory regions are available, each one with a separate chip-select signal and programmable timing. SDRAM memory is also supported.

2-6 SUMMARY

The RX CPU is a unique architecture taking an ideal blend of CISC and RISC ideas to achieve the lowest clock-per-instruction rate at the same time making the smallest memory footprint size possible. Since this RX core, at 1.65 DMIPS/MHz, is built on a platform of 100 MHz no wait-states flash memory, it provides a tremendous amount of deterministic CPU processing power to add rich capabilities to embedded systems. In addition to this, the presence of RX's hardware floating point (FPU) and multiply-accumulate (MAC) units push RX's capabilities beyond standard real-time embedded control, and into the Digital Signal Controller category.

The RX62N MCU on the Renesas Demonstration Kit featured in this book is one of many varieties of RX600 devices available now, with many more new varieties coming in the future. A wide range of RX600 devices is available, covering many memory and packages sizes, as well as many different communication and analog capabilities. To learn more about the entire RX MCU series, visit `www.renesas.com/rx`.

Chapter

3

Setup

The following sections explain where to obtain the hardware and how to setup the tools.

3-1 HARDWARE

This book assumes the use of the Renesas Demonstration Kit YRDKRX62N available for purchase from the Renesas website.

Figure 3-1 **YRDKRX62N demonstration kit**

Besides the board, the hardware components required are:

1 A Windows-based PC running Windows-XP, Vista or Windows 7

2 The Renesas YRDKRX62N demonstration kit

3 The USB cable that accompanies the YRDKRX62N

4 An Ethernet cross-over cable or an Ethernet switch with two Ethernet cables

3-1-1 CONNECTING THE YRDKRX62N TO A PC

There are three ways to connect the YRDKRX62N to the PC:

1 Using an RS-232C connection for µC/Probe

2 Using an Ethernet cable connected directly to the PC

3 Using an Ethernet cable connected through a router

The following sections illustrate each setup for future reference.

CONNECTING THE YRDKRX62N (RS-232C)

Figure 3-2 shows a simple block diagram of how to connect the YRDKRX62N to a PC using an RS-232C cable in order to use µC/Probe through a serial interface.

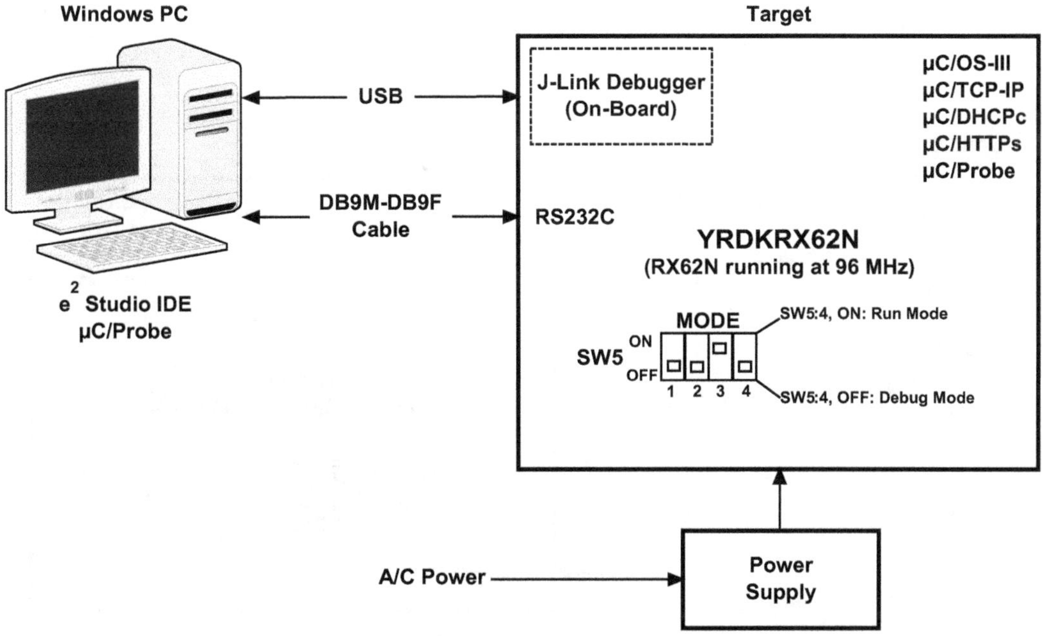

Figure 3-2 **YRDKRX62N setup with RS-232C for µC/Probe**

CONNECTING THE YRDKRX62N (ETHERNET - AUTO IP)

Figure 3-3 shows a simple block diagram of how to connect the YRDKRX62N to a PC using an Ethernet crossover cable in order to create a UDP interface with µC/Probe without requiring a switch/router.

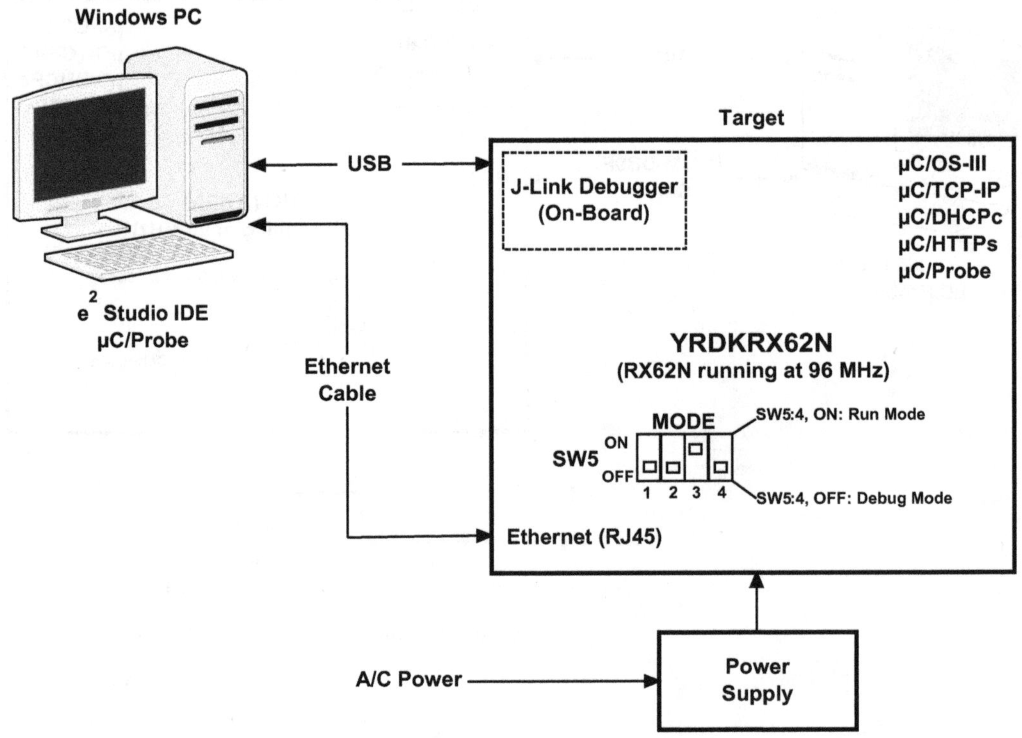

Figure 3-3 **YRDKRX62N setup with Ethernet for µC/Probe (no router)**

CONNECTING THE YRDKRX62N (ETHERNET & ROUTER)

Figure 3-4 shows a simple block diagram of how to connect the YRDKRX62N to a PC using a regular Ethernet cable in order to create a UDP interface with µC/Probe, using a router with a built-in DHCP server to obtain an IP address.

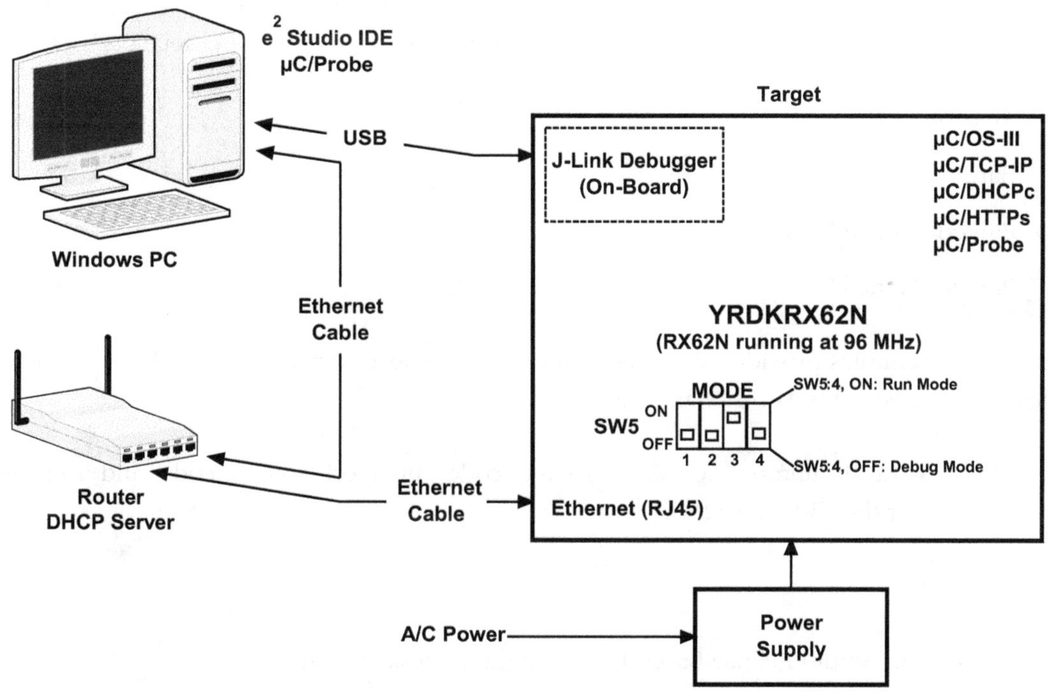

Figure 3-4 **YRDKRX62N setup with Ethernet for µC/Probe (using a router to obtain an IP address)**

3-2 SOFTWARE

µC/TCP-IP requires the use of an RTOS and for the examples in this book, µC/OS-III is used. While the µC/OS-III book is not mandatory as µC/OS-III is delivered as source available ready to run TCP/IP examples, should the reader want to know how the µC/OS-III real-time kernel works, having the book handy is a good idea.

You can purchase the book *µC/OS-III: The Real-Time Kernel for the Renesas RX62N by Jean J. Labrosse* identified by ISBN 978-0-9823375-7-8 from one of the following retailers:

- Amazon
- Barnes & Noble
- EmbeddedDeveloper.com
- Premier Farnell

To run the examples provided with this book, it will be necessary to download a number of files from the Micrium web site and other sites:

- The µC/TCP-IP library, µC/OS-III source code, µC/IPerf source code and sample projects for the YRDKRX62N
- µC/Probe
- The new e^2 Studio Eclipse-based IDE from the Renesas website
- Tera Term Pro terminal emulator. A different terminal emulator can also be used
- The IPerf network performance test tool for Windows
- WireShark, Network Protocol Analyzer from the Wireshark website
- RX62N documentation from the Renesas website

The code for the examples in this book is provided to help readers gain first-hand experience with TCP/IP concepts. Additional tools are provided to help visualize these same concepts. In this chapter, code and tools are used to create an environment that facilitates the analysis of µC/TCP-IP based projects.

3-3 DOWNLOADING μC/TCP-IP PROJECTS FOR THIS BOOK

The μC/TCP-IP book and Renesas YRDKRX62N Demonstration Kit rely on project files that are downloadable from the Micrium website. This allows samples to be kept up to date.

To obtain the μC/TCP-IP software and examples for the projects provided, simply go to:

`www.micrium.com/page/downloads/uc-tcp-ip_files`

You will be required to register. The required information will be used for market research purposes and will allow us to contact you should updates of μC/TCP-IP for this book be available. Your information will not be shared or sold.

Download and execute the following file:

`Micrium-Book-YRDKRX62N-uC-TCPIP.exe`

Figure 3-5 shows the directory structure created by this executable.

The files included in this executable are meant to be built with Renesas e^2 Studio and the workspace uses path variables that are necessary to configure according to the location in your file system where the files were extracted. More information about this configuration step is available in section 3-6-1 "Configuring the Micriμm folder path variable" on page 835.

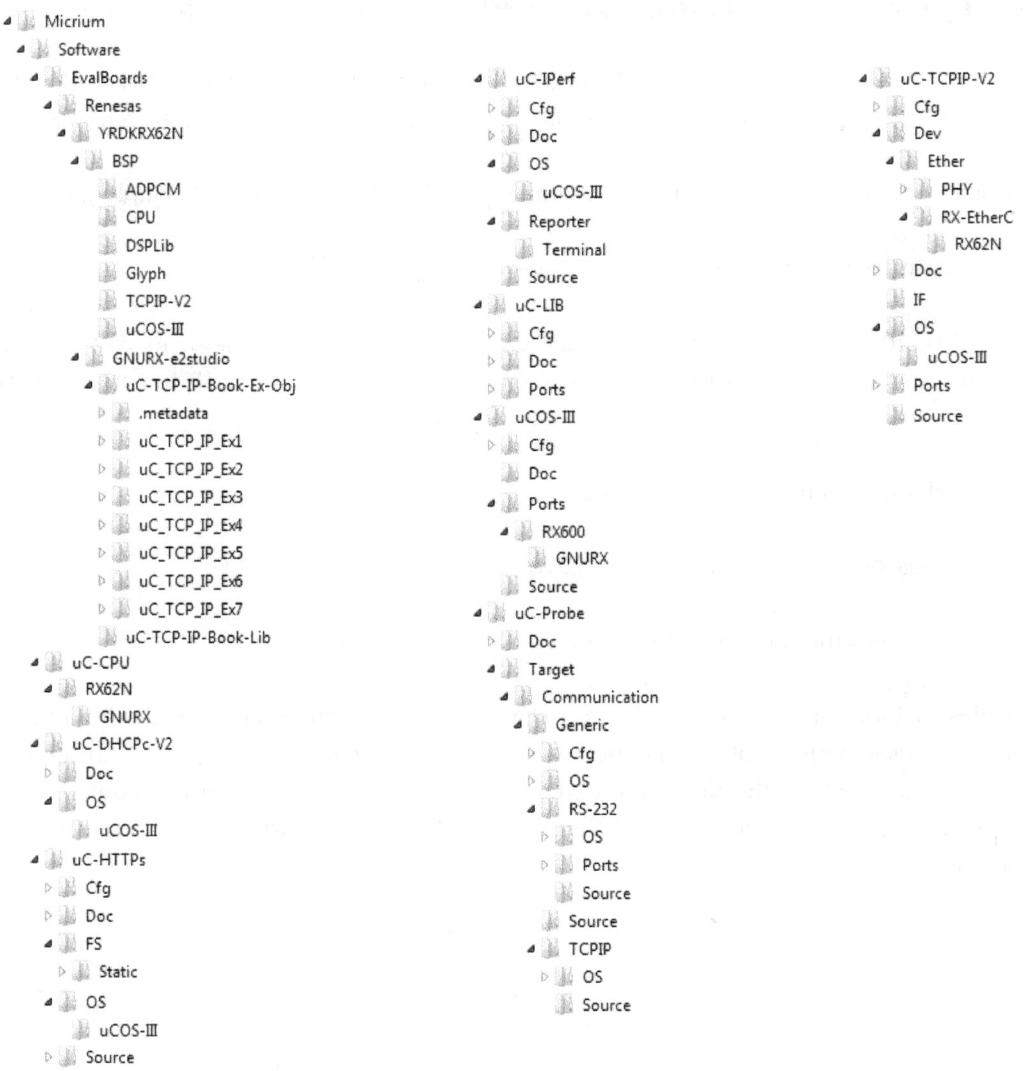

Figure 3-5 **µC/TCP-IP Project Directories**

All files are placed under the `\Micrium\Software` directory. There are five main sub-directories: `\EvalBoards`, `\uC-CPU`, `\uC-LIB`, `\uCOS-III` and `\uC-TCPIP-V2`. They are described below. Other directories are also present but are not used for all projects. The directories are `\uC-DHCPc-V2` used in Example #2, `\uC-HTTPs` used in Example #5, `\uC-IPerf` used in Example #4 and `\uC-Probe` in Examples #3 and #4.

3-3-1 \EvalBoards

This is the standard Micrium sub-directory where all evaluation board examples are placed. The sub-directory contains additional sub-directories organizing evaluation boards by manufacturers. In this case, **\Renesas** is the manufacturer of the YRDKRX62N board, and projects for this board are placed under: **\YRDKRX62N**.

The `\EvalBoards\Renesas\YRDKRX62N` sub-directory contains further directories. It contains:

\EvalBoards\Renesas\YRDKRX62N\Datasheets contains a series of datasheets and reference manuals:

```
RX62N-ReferenceManual.pdf
YRDKRX62N-Schematics.pdf
YRDKRX62N-Datasheet.pdf
```

\EvalBoards\Renesas\YRDKRX62N\GNURX-e2studio contains all the code for the YRDKRX62N written using the Renesas Eclipse-based IDE. This sub-directory contains two additional sub-directories:

```
\BSP
\uC-TPCPIP-V2-Book
```

\EvalBoards\Renesas\YRDKRX62N\GNURX-e2studio\BSP contains Board Support Package (BSP) files used to support the peripherals found on the YRDKRX62N. Specifically, functions are available to turn on or off the onboard LEDs, display characters or strings on the LCD and more. The contents of these files will be described as needed within the sample projects. This sub-directory contains the following files:

```
bsp.c
bsp.h
bsp_adt7420.c
bsp_adt7420.h
bsp_adxl345.c
bsp_adxl345.h
bsp_glcd.c
bsp_glcd.h
bsp_ser_a.s
```

```
bsp_ser_c.c
bsp_ser_c.h
bsp_tick_a.s
bsp_tick_c.c
\DSPLib
    rtadsplib.h
    SPLib_rx600_sl.a
\Glyph
\TCPIP-V2
    net_bsp.c
    net_bsp.h
    net_bsp_a.s
    net_phy_dp83640.c
    net_phy_dp83640.h
\uCOS-III
    bsp_os.c
    bsp_os.h
```

\EvalBoards\Renesas\YRDKRX62N\GNURX-e2studio\uC-TCP-IP-Book-Ex-Obj contains the main Eclipse IDE workspace, which includes the projects provided with this book. Specifically, the folder .metadata contains all the files that make up the workspace that contains the seven example projects.

Projects will be described in the next three chapters. This sub-directory contains five additional sub-directories:

```
\.metadata
\uC-TCP-IP-Ex1
\uC-TCP-IP-Ex2
\uC-TCP-IP-Ex3
\uC-TCP-IP-Ex4
\uC-TCP-IP-Ex5
\uC-TCP-IP-Ex6
\uC-TCP-IP-Ex7
```

\EvalBoards\Renesas\YRDKRX62N\GNURX-e2studio\uC-TCP-IP-Book-Lib is the directory from which all the libraries were built. The following files are found in this directory and these files are referenced in the projects presented in the examples:

```
app_cfg.h
cpu_cfg.h
dhcp-c_cfg.h
http-s_cfg.h
includes.h
net_cfg.h
net_dev_cfg.c
net_dev_cfg.h
os_app_hooks.c
os_app_hooks.h
os_cfg.h
os_cfg_app.h
probe_com_cfg.h
uC-DHCPc-V2.a
uC-HTTPs.a
uC-Probe-TCPIP.a
uC-TCPIP-V2.a
```

The header files contain all the definitions that we used to compile the libraries below:

uC-DHCPc-V2.a is a linkable object file containing code for the μC/DHCPc module which is used by the TCP/IP stack to obtain the IP address from a router or, a Windows based PC using AutoIP or Link-Local address assignment.

uC-HTTPs.a is a linkable object file containing code for the μC/HTTPs module which is used by the Web Server example.

uC-TCPIP-V2.a is a linkable object file containing code for the μC/TCP-IP stack which is used to run μC/Probe.

\EvalBoards\Renesas\YRDKRX62N\GNURX-e2studio\uC-TCP-IP-Book-Ex-Obj\uC-TCP-IP-Ex1 presents a simple project that demonstrates how to properly initialize and start a μC/TCP-IP-based application. This project is described in Chapter 4, "μC/TCP-IP Example #1" on page 841.

\EvalBoards\Renesas\YRDKRX62N\GNURX-e2studio\uC-TCP-IP-Book-Ex-Obj\uC-TCP-IP-Ex2 presents a project similar to example #1 with the exception that IP address configuration is accomplished via DHCP. This project is described in Chapter 4, "µC/TCP-IP Example #2" on page 876.

\EvalBoards\Renesas\YRDKRX62N\GNURX-e2studio\uC-TCP-IP-Book-Ex-Obj\uC-TCP-IP-Ex3 presents a project featuring µC/Probe over the TCP/IP connection instead of the J-Link connection. This project is described in Chapter 4, "µC/TCP-IP Example #3" on page 886.

\EvalBoards\Renesas\YRDKRX62N\GNURX-e2studio\uC-TCP-IP-Book-Ex-Obj\uC-TCP-IP-Ex4 presents a project that uses µC/IPerf to measure the performance of the application using UDP or TCP. This project is described in Chapter 5, "µC/TCP-IP Performance Examples" on page 895.

\EvalBoards\Renesas\YRDKRX62N\GNURX-e2studio\uC-TCP-IP-Book-Ex-Obj\uC-TCP-IP-Ex5 presents a project that uses µC/HTTPs implementing a web server. This project will be described in Chapter 6, "Example #5 HTTP Server" on page 935.

\EvalBoards\Renesas\YRDKRX62N\GNURX-e2studio\uC-TCP-IP-Book-Ex-Obj\uC-TCP-IP-Ex6 presents a project that uses µC/TCP-IP sockets to send push notifications to an iOS mobile device such as the iPhone or iPad. This project will be described in Chapter 7, "TCP/IP Sockets: Push Notifications to iOS devices" on page 949.

\EvalBoards\Renesas\YRDKRX62N\GNURX-e2studio\uC-TCP-IP-Book-Ex-Obj\uC-TCP-IP-Ex7 presents a project that uses µC/TCP-IP sockets to interface with a cloud-based system to send real-time data and develop very impressive web dashboards for monitoring purposes. This project will be described in Chapter 8, "Cloud Connectivity: Interfacing with Exosite's One Platform" on page 969.

3-3-2 \uC-CPU

This sub-directory contains generic and RX62N-specific files for the µC/CPU module. These are described in Appendix B of the µC/OS-III book. This sub-directory contains the following files:

```
cpu_core.c
cpu_core.h
cpu_def.h
\Cfg\Template\cpu_cfg.h
\RX62N\GNURX\cpu.h
\RX62N\GNURX\cpu_a.asm
\RX62N\GNURX\cpu_c.c
```

3-3-3 \uC-LIB

This sub-directory contains compiler-independent library functions to manipulate ASCII strings, initialize memory pools, perform memory copies, and more. We refer to these files as being part of the µC/LIB module. **lib_def.h** contains a number of useful #defines such as **DEF_FALSE**, **DEF_TRUE**, **DEF_ON**, **DEF_OFF**, **DEF_ENABLED**, **DEF_DISABLED**, and dozens more. µC/LIB also declares such macros as **DEF_MIN()**, **DEF_MAX()**, **DEF_ABS()**, and more.

This sub-directory contains the following files:

```
lib_ascii.c
lib_ascii.h
lib_def.h
lib_math.c
lib_math.h
lib_mem.c
lib_mem.h
lib_str.c
lib_str.h
\Doc\uC-Lib_Manual.pdf
\Doc\uC-Lib-ReleaseNotes.pdf
\Ports\RX62N\GNURX\lib_mem_a.asm
```

3-3-4 \uCOS-III

µC/OS-III is provided in source form for free short-term evaluation, for educational use or for peaceful research. If you plan or intend to use µC/OS-III in a commercial application or product then, you need to contact Micrium to properly license µC/OS-III for its use in your application/product. We provide all the source code for your convenience and to help you experience µC/OS-III. This sub-directory contains the following files:

```
\Source\os.h
\Source\os_cfg_app.c
\Source\os_core.c
\Source\os_dbg.c
\Source\os_flag.c
\Source\os_int.c
\Source\os_mem.c
\Source\os_msg.c
\Source\os_mutex.c
\Source\os_pend_multi.c
\Source\os_prio.c
\Source\os_q.c
\Source\os_sem.c
\Source\os_stat.c
\Source\os_task.c
\Source\os_tick.c
\Source\os_time.c
\Source\os_tmr.c
\Source\os_type.h
\Source\os_var.c
```

The fact that the source is provided does not mean that you can use it commercially without paying a licensing fee.

Knowledge of the source code may not be used to develop a similar product.

Please refer to Appendix B, "µC/OS-III and µC/TCP-IP Licensing Policy" on page 1029 for more details.

3-3-5 \uC-iperf

This sub-directory contains files used to perform UDP and TCP performance testing. See chapter 5 for a short description of μC/IPerf. The μC/IPerf user manual is also available.

This module is delivered in source code. It performs UDP and TCP testing but it is also the best code sample to demonstrate how to code a client or server application.

This sub-directory contains the following files:

```
\Doc\IPerf-Manual.pdf
\Doc\IPerf-ReleaseNotes.pdf
\OS\uCOS-III\iperf_os.c
\Reporter\Terminal\iperf_rep.c
\Reporter\Terminal\iperf_rep.h
\Source\iperf.c
\Source\iperf.h
\Source\iperf-c.c
\Source\iperf-s.c
```

3-3-6 \uC-DHCPc-v2

This sub-directory contains the files for the DHCP client. The client is provided in the form of a linkable object and contains the following files:

```
\Doc\DHCPc-V2-Manual.pdf
\Doc\DHCPc-V2-ReleaseNotes.pdf
\Source\dhcp-c.h
```

3-3-7 \uC-HTTPs

This sub-directory contains the files for the HTTP server. The server is provided in the form of a linkable object and contains the following files:

```
\Doc\HTTPs-Manual.pdf
\Doc\HTTPs-ReleaseNotes.pdf
\OS\uCOS-III\https_os.c
\Source\http-s.h
```

3-3-8 \uC-TCPIP-v2

This sub-directory contains the files for the TCP-IP stack. The stack is provided in the form of a linkable object and contains the following files:

```
\IF\net_if.h
\IF\net_if_ether.h
\IF\net_if_loopback.h
\OS\Template\net_os.c
\OS\Template\net_os.h
\Ports\Renesas\RX600\GNURX\os_cpu.h
\Source\os.h
\Source\net_cfg_net.h
\Source\net_def.h
\Source\net_type.h
```

The only source files from the \Source sub-directory that are provided with this book are **net.h and net_type.h**. The remaining source files are available to μC/TCP-IP licensees only. Contact Micrium for licensing details and pricing.

The TCP-IP stack library is called **uC-TCPIP.a**. The library supports two sockets with 4 receive buffers. 2 transmit buffers, 2 DMA receive descriptors and 2 DMA transmit descriptors. The library was compiled using the KPIT GNURX v11.02 Windows Toolchain (ELF) and options were set to 'no-optimization,' as this offers greater debug flexibility.

3-4 DOWNLOADING μC/PROBE

μC/Probe is a Windows-based application that allows users to display or change the value (at run time) of virtually any variable or memory location on a connected embedded target.

μC/Probe is used to gain run-time visibility in all of the examples described in Chapters 3, 4 and 5. There are two versions of μC/Probe:

The *Full Version* of μC/Probe is included with all μC/TCP-IP licenses. The full version supports J-Link, RS-232C, TCP/IP, USB, and other interfaces. The *Full Version* allows users to display or change an unlimited number of variables.

The *Trial Version* is not time limited, but allows users to display or change up to 5 application variables. However, the trial version allows users to monitor any µC/TCP-IP and µC/OS-III variables because µC/Probe is µC/TCP-IP and µC/OS-III aware.

Both versions are available from Micrium's website. Simply visit:

`www.micrium.com/page/downloads/windows_probe_trial`

Follow the links to download the desired version. If not already registered on the Micrium website, you will be asked to do so. Once downloaded, execute the appropriate µC/Probe setup file:

```
Micrium-uC-Probe-Setup-Full.exe
Micrium-uC-Probe-Setup-Trial.exe
```

A link to these two µC/Probe versions is also available on the Companion Software link for this book:

`www.micrium.com/page/downloads/uc-tcp-ip_files`

3-5 DOWNLOADING THE KPIT GNURX TOOLCHAIN

Examples provided with this book were tested using the KPIT GNURX v11.02 Windows Toolchain (ELF). The GNURX is a collection of GNU tools required for the development of embedded system applications running on Renesas RX that includes a cross-compiler, assembler, linker, libraries and associated tools. The GNURX v11.02 toolchain has support for command line, HEW and Eclipse-based IDEs integration. Documentation is also supplied by the installer, backed up by free worldwide support.

Some of the benefits and features of this toolchain are:

- Completely free of charge GNU Tools. Please check Terms of Use.
- Completely free worldwide technical support for KPIT GNU Tools.
- Free toolchain based on Free Software Foundation sources.

- Ready-to-use Installers on Windows & Linux platforms.
- Windows users can use the tools with Renesas Eclipse-based IDE, their high-performance Embedded Workshop (HEW) IDE and other Renesas tools (such as the HDI Debugging Interface).
- HDI as supplied with many Hitachi and Renesas EDKs.
- Useful utilities, documentation, FAQs and sample tutorials to accelerate your development.
- Full source code available.
- Free GDB debugger and simulators supplied with the toolchains.
- Full ANSI/ISO C and C++ Support.
- Supports H8/300, H8/300H, H8/300H Tiny Series, H8/300L, H8/S 2XXX, H8/S 26XX, H8/SX (ELF), SH-1, SH-2, SH-2A, SH-2E, SH2-DSP, SH-3, SH-3E, SH3-DSP, SH-4, SH-4A, R8C (ELF), M16C (ELF), M32CM (ELF) and M32C (ELF) targets.
- Extensively tested and optimized for Renesas processors.
- RFlash, a tool for flash programming Renesas' FZTAT devices for the GNU/Linux operating system.

The toolchain is available for download from the KPIT Cummins website at:

`www.kpitgnutools.com`

If you are installing the toolchain on a Windows Vista or Windows 7 operating system, we strongly suggest to install it in a folder different than the typical “C:\Program Files” because of security-related issues. Since both, the toolchain and e^2 Studio Eclipse-based IDE need to be inside the same folder we recommend to call this installation folder something like “C:\GNU-RX-Eclipse”.

3-6 DOWNLOADING THE ECLIPSE EMBEDDED STUDIO (E^2 STUDIO) IDE

The GNURX v11.02 toolchain has support for integration with the new Eclipse-based IDE from Renesas e^2 Studio. Go to the link below to download the IDE:

```
http://www.renesas.com/e2studio
```

3-6-1 Configuring the Micriµm folder path variable

Path variables specify locations on the file system. The location of linked resources may be specified relative to these path variables. They allow you to avoid references to a fixed location on your file system.

By using a path variable, you can share projects containing linked resources with team members without requiring the exact same directory structure as on your file system.

Path variables can be either defined at the project level or at the workspace level. Creating path variables at the project level ensures that projects that contain linked resources using those path variables remain portable across workspace and computers.

You can load a project that uses path variables even if you do not currently have all the path variables defined in the project or workspace. A linked resource that uses a missing path variable is flagged using a special decorator icon. In addition, the File > Properties > Resource property page and the Properties view (Window > Show View > Other... > General > Properties) for a linked resource indicate the variable and whether it is defined or not. A path variable can also specify a location that does not currently exist on the file system. Linked resources that use such a path variable are indicated using the same decorator icon mentioned above.

You can create new path variables and edit and remove existing path variables in the File > Properties > Resource > Linked Resources property page for a project resource and at the workspace level on the General > Workspace > Linked Resources preference page as shown in Figure 3-6.

Edit the path variable called *MicriumFolder* with the location in your file system where you extracted the project files as shown in Figure 3-7.

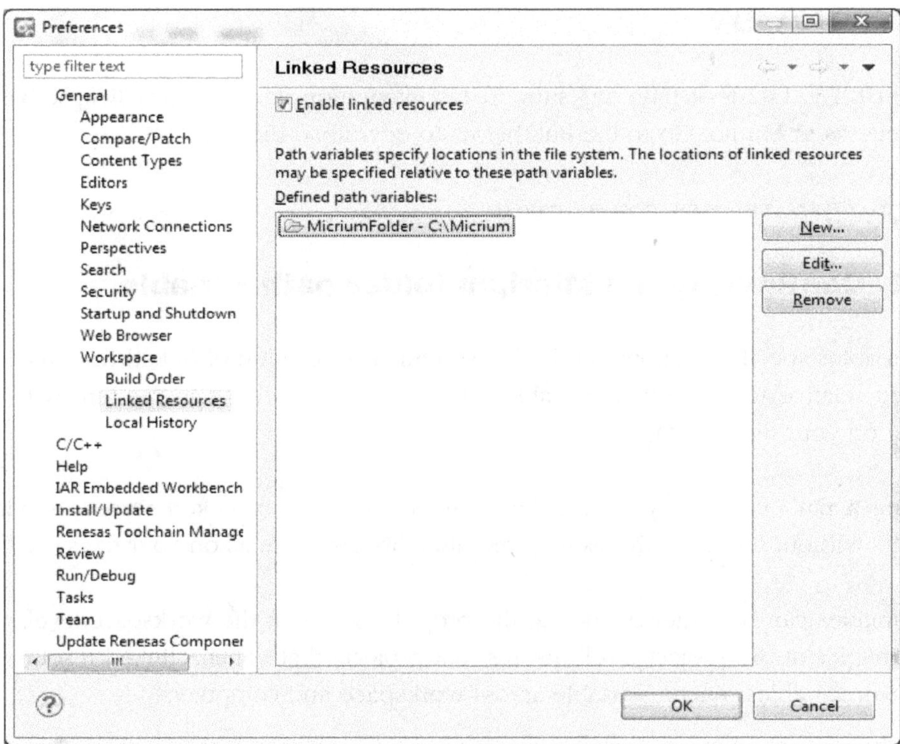

Figure 3-6 **Linked Resources: Path Variables**

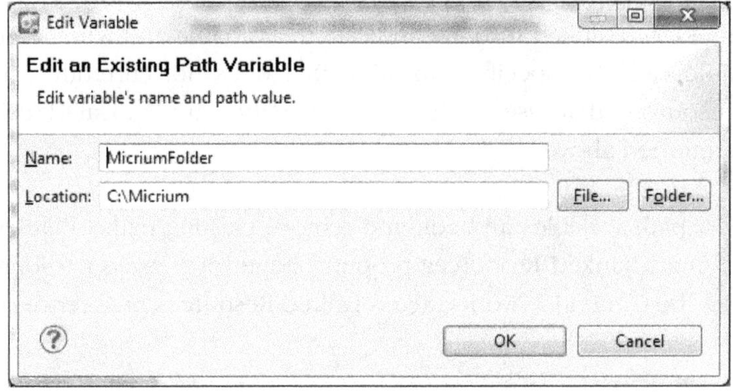

Figure 3-7 **Configuring your Micriμm Folder**

3-7 DOWNLOADING TERA TERM PRO

On the PC, any terminal window application can be used. The user selects a terminal emulator of choice. For the purpose of the examples in this book, TeraTerm Pro was used. TeraTerm is an open-source, free software implemented, terminal emulator (communications) program. It emulates different types of terminals, from DEC VT100 to DEC VT382. Tera Term Pro is available from Micrium's website. Simply visit:

```
www.micrium.com/page/downloads/uc-tcp-ip_files
```

Follow the link to download TeraTerm Pro. If not already registered on the Micrium website, you will be asked to do so. Once downloaded, execute the Tera Term Pro setup file:

```
ttermp23.zip
```

If you choose to use this terminal emulation software, select the TeraTerm Pro install file (`ttermp23.zip`). Unzip the file and install the software on your PC.

3-8 DOWNLOADING IPERF FOR WINDOWS

IPerf is an unbiased benchmarking tool used for the comparison of wired and wireless networking performance. With IPerf, a user can create TCP and UDP data streams and measure the throughput of a network for these streams. IPerf test engine has client and server functionality and can measure the throughput between two hosts, either uni-directionally or bi-directionally.

The IPerf PC implementation used in this book project uses a graphical user interface (GUI) front end called Jperf (the install file is named Kperf, a Java variant).

The Kperf install file is available from Micrium's website. Simply visit:

```
www.micrium.com/page/downloads/uc-tcp-ip_files
```

Follow the link to download KPerf. If not already registered on the Micrium website, you will be asked to do so. Once downloaded, execute the Kperf setup file (Kperf is a Java variant of Jperf but will install as Jperf on your PC):

```
kperf_setup.exe
```

Install it on your PC. When Jperf is installed it creates an entry in the Windows Start menu and a desktop shortcut. Launch Jperf either way. Figure 3-8 shows the desktop shortcut.

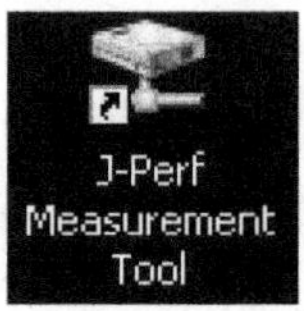

Figure 3-8 **Jperf desktop shortcut**

3-9 DOWNLOADING WIRESHARK

There are multiple commercial network protocol analyzers. We at Micrium typically use Wireshark, a free network protocol analyzer. Wireshark uses **p**acket **cap**ture (**pcap**) and consists of an API for capturing network traffic. Unix-like systems implement pcap in the libpcap library, while Windows uses a port of libpcap known as WinPcap to configure the NIC in promiscuous mode to capture packets. Wireshark runs on Microsoft Windows and on various Unix-like operating systems including Linux, Mac OS X, BSD, and Solaris. Wireshark is released under the terms of the GNU General Public License.

To download and install Wireshark on a Windows host, the WinPcap utility is installed by the installer tool. Download Wireshark from:

```
http://www.wireshark.org/download.html
```

3-10 DOWNLOADING THE RENESAS YRDKRX62N DOCUMENTATION

You can download the latest RX62N datasheets and programming manuals from:

```
http://am.renesas.com/products/tools/
introductory_evaluation_tools/renesas_demo_kits/
yrdkrx62n/yrdkrx62n.jsp
```

For additional documentation and example projects for the Renesas Demonstration Kit for the RX62N, please visit the associated online community located at

`http://www.RenesasRulz.com/RDKRX62N`

Chapter

4

µC/TCP-IP Basic Examples

In this chapter, we demonstrate how easy it is to put together a µC/TCP-IP based application. The Renesas YRDKRX62N Demonstration Kit as introduced in Chapter 3, "Setup" on page 817, provides the basis for the examples.

The instructions to access the tools and code to run the examples described in this chapter are also provided in Chapter 3, "Software" on page 822. Follow these instructions carefully.

The first project introduces the use of Renesas e^2 Studio Eclipse-based IDE, Wireshark and µC/Probe. These tools are used by all projects. The tools introduction provided in Example #1 will not be reproduced in every example.

4-1 µC/TCP-IP EXAMPLE #1

This project initializes and configures µC/TCP-IP on the YRDKRX62N board. The IP configuration is a static configuration (see Listing 3-3). Once this code is running, LEDs on the board will blink. It is now possible for the PC connected to the same network as the board (see Chapter 3, "Connecting the YRDKRX62N to a PC" on page 818) to PING the board. This project does not do anything exciting however, it allows the reader to put all of the pieces together.

Installing Renesas e^2 Studio on the PC creates an entry in the Windows Start menu and/or placed an icon on the desktop. Start the e^2 Studio IDE and open the following workspace:

```
$\Micrium\Software\EvalBoards\Renesas\YRDKRX62N\GNURX-e2studio\uC-TCP-IP-Book-Ex-Obj
```

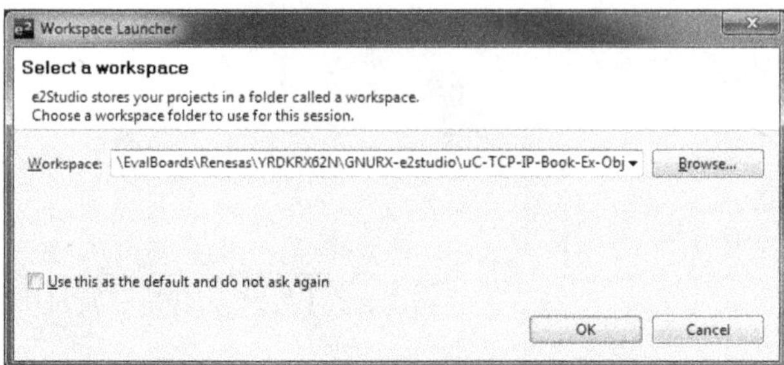

Figure 4-1 **Open Workspace**

Make sure you have followed the instructions to configure the path to linked resources in section 3-6-1 "Configuring the Micriμm folder path variable" on page 835 and click the uC-TCP-IP-Ex1 item at the top of the workspace explorer to select the first project as shown in Figure 4-2.

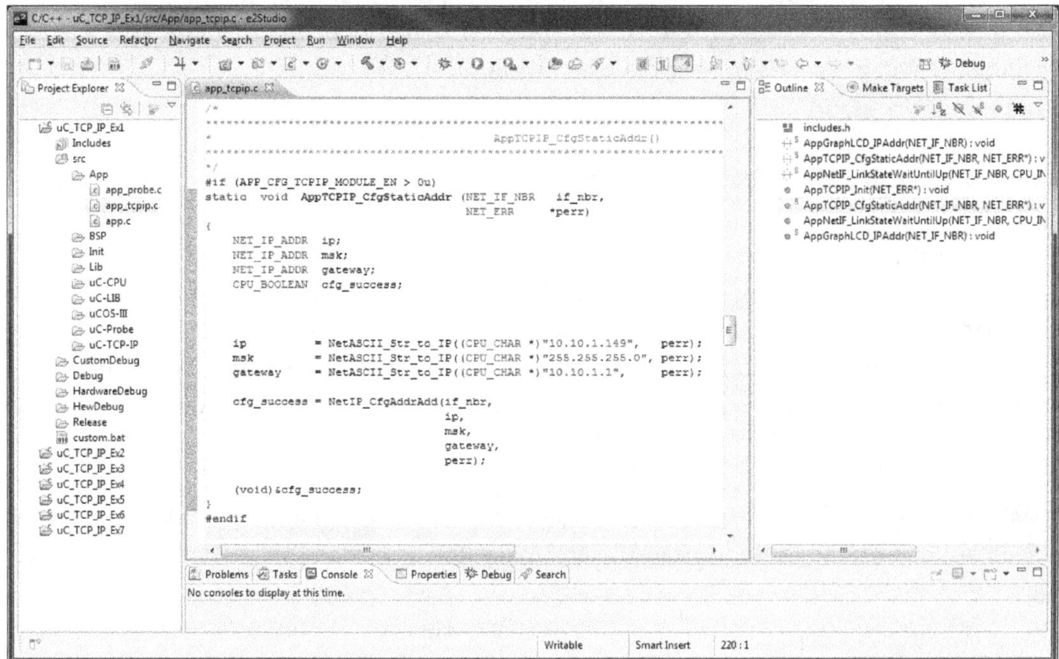

Figure 4-2 **Open project uC-TCPIP-Ex1**

Figure 4-3 shows the workspace explorer with groups expanded. Groups allow us to neatly organize projects.

The App group is where the actual code for the example is located.

The BSP group contains the 'Board Support Package' code to use for several of the Input/Output (I/O) devices on the YRDKRX62N board. Under the BSP group, you will find the subfolders CPU, Glyph, TCP-IP and uCOS-III.

The Init group contains the hardware initialization files provided by Renesas.

The uC-CPU group contains header files, as well as the µC/CPU source code.

The uC-LIB group contains the header files, as well as the µC/LIB source code.

The uCOS-III group contains header files and the µC/OS-III source code.

The uC-TCP-IP group contains the header files and the µC/TCP-IP object code library. The header files are needed as some of the application code requires definitions and declarations found in these files.

The Lib group contains the files that were used to configure the µC/TCP-IP object code libraries. You must not change these files.

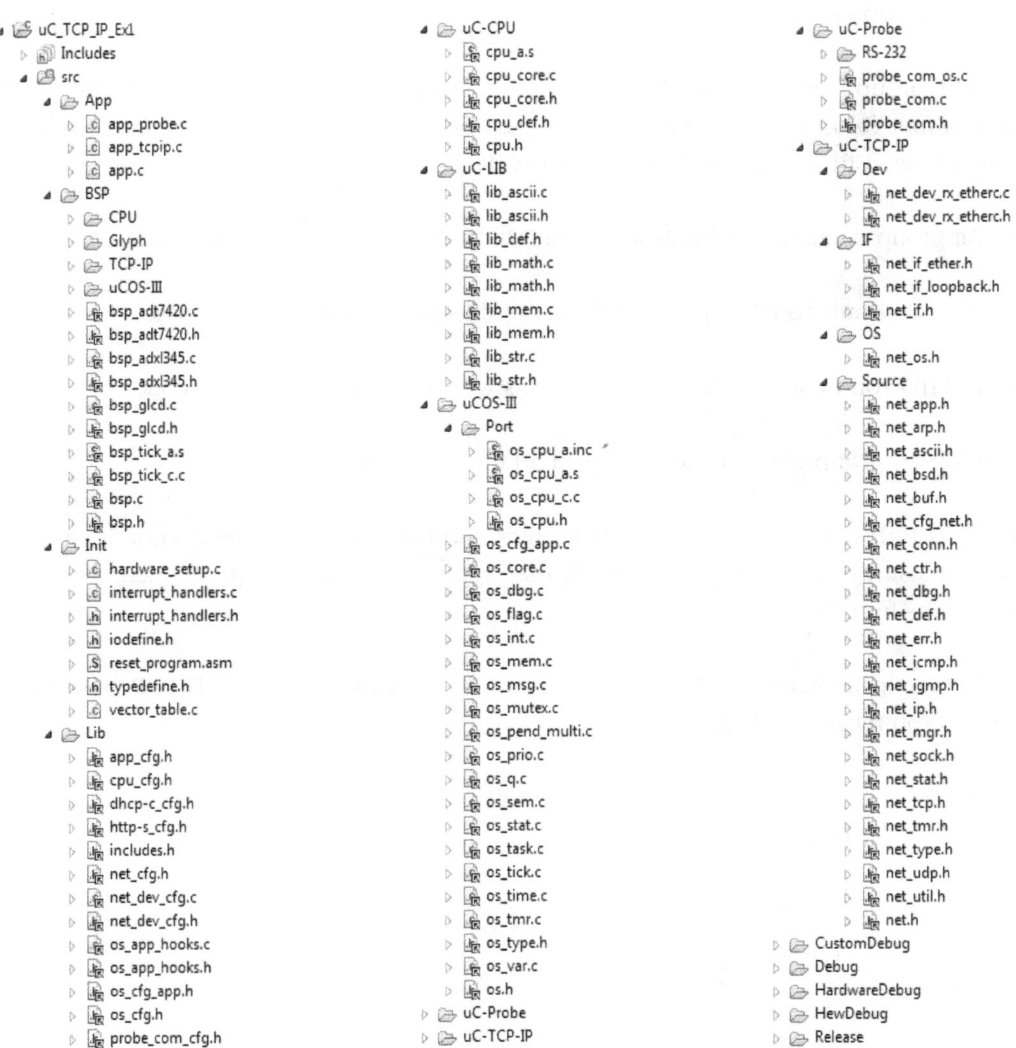

Figure 4-3 **Expanded Workspace for uC-TCP-IP-Ex1 Project**

4-1-1 HOW THE EXAMPLE PROJECT WORKS

As with most C programs, code execution starts at **main()** which is shown in Listing 4-1. The application code starts multitasking. This code is typical to µC/OS-II and µC/OS-III multitasking. Detailed information is found in the µC/OS-II and µC/OS-III books.

```
int  main (void)
{
    OS_ERR  err;


    CPU_IntDis();                                     /* Disable all interrupts.           */  (1)

    OSInit(&err);                                     /* Initialize uC/OS-III.             */  (2)

    App_OS_SetAllHooks();

    OSTaskCreate((OS_TCB      *)&AppTaskStartTCB,     /* Create the start task             */  (3)
                 (CPU_CHAR    *)"App Task Start",                                              (4)
                 (OS_TASK_PTR ) AppTaskStart,                                                  (5)
                 (void        *) 0,                                                            (6)
                 (OS_PRIO     ) APP_TASK_START_PRIO,                                           (7)
                 (CPU_STK     *)&AppTaskStartStk[0],                                           (8)
                 (CPU_STK_SIZE) APP_TASK_START_STK_SIZE / 10u,                                 (9)
                 (CPU_STK_SIZE) APP_TASK_START_STK_SIZE,                                      (10)
                 (OS_MSG_QTY  ) 0u,
                 (OS_TICK     ) 0u,
                 (void        *) 0,
                 (OS_OPT      )(OS_OPT_TASK_STK_CHK | OS_OPT_TASK_STK_CLR),                   (11)
                 (OS_ERR      *)&err);                                                        (12)

    OSStart(&err);                                    /* Start multitasking                */ (13)
                                                      /* (i.e. give control to uC/OS-III).*/

    while (DEF_ON) {
        ;
    }

    return (0);
}
```

Listing 4-1 **Code execution starts at main()**

L4-1(1) Start **main()** by calling a function that disables all interrupts. On most processors, interrupts are disabled at startup until explicitly enabled by application code. However, it is safer to turn off all peripheral interrupts during startup.

L4-1(2) Call **OSInit()**, which is responsible for initializing µC/OS-III. **OSInit()** initializes internal variables and data structures, and also creates two (2) to five (5) internal tasks. At a minimum, µC/OS-III creates the idle task (**OS_IdleTask()**), which executes when no other task is ready to run. µC/OS-III also creates the tick task, which is responsible for keeping track of time.

Depending on the value of **#define** constants, µC/OS-III will create the statistic task (**OS_StatTask()**), the timer task (**OS_TmrTask()**), and the interrupt handler queue management task (**OS_IntQTask()**). These are discussed in Chapter 4, "Task Management" of the µC/OS-III book.

Most of µC/OS-III's functions return an error code via a pointer to an **OS_ERR** variable, err in this case. If **OSInit()** is successful, err will be set to **OS_ERR_NONE**. If **OSInit()** encounters a problem during initialization, it will return immediately upon detecting the problem and set err accordingly. If this occurs, look up the error code value in **os.h**. Specifically, all error codes start with **OS_ERR_**.

It is important to note that **OSInit()** must be called before any other µC/OS-III function.

L4-1(3) Create a task by calling **OSTaskCreate()**. **OSTaskCreate()** requires 13 arguments. The first argument is the address of the **OS_TCB** that is declared for this task. Chapter 4, "Task Management" of the µC/OS-III book, provides additional information about tasks.

L4-1(4) **OSTaskCreate()** allows a name to be assigned to each of the tasks. µC/OS-III stores a pointer to the task name inside the **OS_TCB** of the task. There is no limit on the number of ASCII characters used for the name.

L4-1(5) The third argument is the address of the task code. A typical µC/OS-III task is implemented as an infinite loop as shown below:

```
void  MyTask (void *p_arg)
{
    while (1) {
        /* Task body */
    }
}
```

The task receives an argument when it first starts. As far as the task is concerned, it looks like any other C function that can be called by the code. However, the code *must not* call **MyTask()**. The call is actually performed through µC/OS-III.

L4-1(6) The fourth argument of **OSTaskCreate()** is the actual argument that the task receives when it first begins. In other words, the **p_arg** of **MyTask()**. In the example a NULL pointer is passed, and thus **p_arg** for **AppTaskStart()** will be a NULL pointer.

The argument passed to the task can actually be any pointer. For example, the user may pass a pointer to a data structure containing parameters for the task.

L4-1(7) The next argument to **OSTaskCreate()** is the priority of the task. The priority establishes the relative importance of this task with respect to the other tasks in the application. A low-priority number indicates a high priority (or more important) task. Set the priority of the task to any value between 1 and **OS_CFG_PRIO_MAX-2**, inclusively. Avoid using priority #0, and priority **OS_CFG_PRIO_MAX-1**, because these are reserved for µC/OS-III. **OS_CFG_PRIO_MAX** is a compile time configuration constant, which is declared in **os_cfg.h**.

L4-1(8) The sixth argument to **OSTaskCreate()** is the base address of the stack assigned to this task. The base address is always the lowest memory location of the stack.

L4-1(9) The next argument specifies the location of a "watermark" in the task's stack that can be used to determine the allowable stack growth of the task. See Chapter 4, "Task Management" of the µC/OS-III book for more details on using this feature. In the code listed in Listing 4-1, the value represents the amount of stack space (in **CPU_STK** elements) before the stack is empty. In other words, in the example, the limit is reached when there is 10% of the stack left.

L4-1(10) The eighth argument to **OSTaskCreate()** specifies the size of the task's stack in number of **CPU_STK** elements (not bytes). For example, if allocating 1 Kbytes of stack space for a task and the **CPU_STK** is a 32-bit word, then pass 256.

L4-1(11) The next three arguments are skipped as they are not relevant for the current discussion. The next argument to **OSTaskCreate()** specifies options. In this example, it is specified that the stack will be checked at run time (assuming the statistic task was enabled in **os_cfg.h**), and that the contents of the stack will be cleared when the task is created.

L4-1(12) The last argument of **OSTaskCreate()** is a pointer to a variable that will receive an error code. If **OSTaskCreate()** is successful, the error code will be **OS_ERR_NONE** otherwise, the value of the error code can be looked up in **os.h** (see **OS_ERR_xxxx**) to determine the problem with the call.

L4-1(13) The final step in **main()** is to call **OSStart()**, which starts the multitasking process.

You may create as many tasks as you like before calling **OSStart()**. However, it is recommended to only create one task as shown in the example. Notice that interrupts are not enabled. µC/OS-III and µC/OS-II always start a task with interrupts enabled. As soon as the first task executes, the interrupts are enabled. The first task is **AppTaskStart()** and its contents are examined in Listing 4-2.

```
static  void  AppTaskStart (void *p_arg)                            (1)
{
    OS_ERR      err;
    NET_ERR     net_err;

   (void)&p_arg;
    BSP_Init();                                                     (2)
    CPU_Init();                                                     (3)
    OS_CPU_TickInit(cnts);                                          (4)

#if (OS_CFG_STAT_TASK_EN > 0u)
    OSStatTaskCPUUsageInit(&err_os);                                (5)
#endif

#ifdef CPU_CFG_INT_DIS_MEAS_EN
    CPU_IntDisMeasMaxCurReset();                                    (6)
#endif

    Mem_Init();                                                     (7)

#if (APP_CFG_PROBE_COM_MODULE_EN == DEF_ENABLED)
    AppProbe_Init();                                                (8)
#endif

    BSP_GraphLCD_Init();                                            (9)
    AppGraphLCD_Hdr();                                             (10)

    AppTCPIP_Init(&net_err);                                       (11)

    OSTaskDel(&AppTaskStartTCB, &err);                             (12)

    while (DEF_ON) {                                               (13)
        ;
    }
}
```

Listing 4-2 **AppTaskStart**

L4-2(1) As previously mentioned, a task looks like any other C function. The argument **p_arg** is passed to **AppTaskStart()** by **OSTaskCreate()**, as discussed in the previous listing description.

L4-2(2) **BSP_Init()** is a Board Support Package (BSP) function that is responsible for initializing the hardware on an evaluation or target board. The evaluation board might have General Purpose Input Output (GPIO) lines to be configured, relays, sensors and more. This function is found in a file called **bsp.c**.

L4-2(3) **CPU_Init()** initializes the µC/CPU services. µC/CPU provides services to measure interrupt latency, receive time stamps, and provides emulation of the count leading zeros instruction if the processor used does not have that instruction.

L4-2(4) **OS_CPU_SysTickInit()** sets up the periodic µC/OS-III tick interrupt.

L4-2(5) **OSStatTaskCPUUsageInit()** computes the CPU capacity with no task running to establish a reference for the statistics.

L4-2(6) **CPU_IntDisMeasMaxCurReset()** enables Interrupt disable time measurement. The information gathered by this function can be displayed with µC/Probe kernel awareness for µC/OS-III.

L4-2(7) **Mem_Init()** initializes the memory management module. µC/TCP-IP object creation uses this module. This function is part of µC/LIB. The memory module *must* be initialized by calling **Mem_Init()** PRIOR to calling **net_init()**. It is recommended to initialize the memory module before calling **OSStart()**, or near the top of the startup task. The application developer must enable and configure the size of the µC/LIB memory heap available to the system. **LIB_MEM_CFG_HEAP_SIZE** should be defined from within **app_cfg.h** and set to match application requirements.

L4-2(8) **AppProbe_Init()** initializes the modules required by µC/Probe over RS-232.

L4-2(9) **BSP_GraphLCD_Init()** is declared in **bsp_glcd.c** and it initializes the graphic LCD.

L4-2(10) **AppGraphLCD_Hdr()** is an application function declared in **app.c** that displays the header on the LCD. For example, Micrµm, µC/TCP-IP, Example # 1.

L4-2(11) **AppTCPIP_Init()** initializes the TCP/IP stack and the initial parameters to configure it. See Listing 4-3 for more details.

L4-2(12) When a task is no longer needed, it can be deleted by calling **OS_TaskDel()**. Deleting a task does not mean that the code is removed, but that the task code is no longer managed by µC/OS-III.

L4-2(13) Most µC/OS-III tasks will need to be written as an infinite loop.

AppTaskStart() calls the **AppTCPIP_Init()**, a function declared in **app_tcpip.c** responsible of initializing and starting the TCP/IP stack. This function is shown in Listing 4-3:

```
void  AppTCPIP_Init (NET_ERR  *perr)
{
    NET_IF_NBR   if_nbr;
    CPU_INT32U   timeout;
    CPU_INT32U   retry_dly_ms;
    CPU_INT16U   retry_max;
    CPU_INT16U   retry_sec;
    CPU_BOOLEAN  link_state;
    CPU_CHAR     err_msg[]   = "  ret err = xxxxx  ";
    CPU_CHAR     retry_msg[] = "Retrying for xx sec";

                                    /* ------------- INIT NET PROTOCOL STACK -------------- */
   *perr = Net_Init();                                                                     (1)
    if (*perr != NET_ERR_NONE) {
         Str_FmtNbr_Int32U(*perr,
                           5u,
                           DEF_NBR_BASE_DEC,
                           ASCII_CHAR_NULL,
                           DEF_NO,
                           DEF_YES,
                          &err_msg[12]);
         BSP_GraphLCD_ClrLine(4);                                                          (2)
         BSP_GraphLCD_ClrLine(5);
         BSP_GraphLCD_String(4, "Net Init failed!");                                       (3)
         BSP_GraphLCD_String(5, err_msg);
         return;
    }
                                    /* ------------------- ADD IF NBR 1 ------------------- */
    if_nbr  = NetIF_Add((void    *)&NetIF_API_Ether,         /* Ethernet API                */   (4)
                        (void    *)&NetDev_API_RX_EtherC,    /* Device API structure        */   (5)
                        (void    *)&NetDev_BSP_RSK2_RX62N,   /* Device BSP structure        */   (6)
                        (void    *)&NetDev_Cfg_RX_Ether_0,   /* Device Config structure     */   (7)
                        (void    *)&NetPhy_API_DP83640,      /* PHY API structure           */   (8)
                        (void    *)&NetPhy_Cfg_Generic_0,    /* PHY Configuration structure */   (9)
                        (NET_ERR *) perr);                   /* Return error variable       */  (10)
    if (*perr != NET_IF_ERR_NONE) {
         Str_FmtNbr_Int32U(*perr,
                           5u,
                           DEF_NBR_BASE_DEC,
                           ASCII_CHAR_NULL,
                           DEF_NO,
                           DEF_YES,
                          &err_msg[12]);
         BSP_GraphLCD_ClrLine(4);
         BSP_GraphLCD_ClrLine(5);
         BSP_GraphLCD_String(4, "NetIF Add failed!");
         BSP_GraphLCD_String(5, err_msg);
         return;
    }
```

```
AppTCPIP_CfgStaticAddr(if_nbr, perr);                                                  (11)
if (*perr != NET_IP_ERR_NONE) {
    Str_FmtNbr_Int32U(*perr,
                       5u,
                       DEF_NBR_BASE_DEC,
                       ASCII_CHAR_NULL,
                       DEF_NO,
                       DEF_YES,
                      &err_msg[12]);
    BSP_GraphLCD_ClrLine(4);
    BSP_GraphLCD_ClrLine(5);
    BSP_GraphLCD_String(4, "Static Addr failed!");
    BSP_GraphLCD_String(5, err_msg);
    return;
}
                                /* ---------------- START IF NBR 1 ---------------- */
NetIF_Start(if_nbr, perr);                                                             (12)
if (*perr != NET_IF_ERR_NONE) {
    Str_FmtNbr_Int32U(*perr,
                       5u,
                       DEF_NBR_BASE_DEC,
                       ASCII_CHAR_NULL,
                       DEF_NO,
                       DEF_YES,
                      &err_msg[12]);
    BSP_GraphLCD_ClrLine(4);
    BSP_GraphLCD_ClrLine(5);
    BSP_GraphLCD_String(4, "NetIF Start failed!");
    BSP_GraphLCD_String(5, err_msg);
    return;
}

                                /* --------------- WAIT FOR LINK UP --------------- */
                                                 /* Chk link state.                 */
link_state = NetIF_LinkStateGet(if_nbr,
                                perr);                                                 (13)
if (link_state == NET_IF_LINK_DOWN) {
   BSP_GraphLCD_ClrLine(4);
   BSP_GraphLCD_String(4, "Ethernet Link Down!");

   timeout      =  30u;
   retry_dly_ms =  50u;
   retry_sec    =   1u;
   retry_max    = (retry_sec * DEF_TIME_NBR_mS_PER_SEC) / retry_dly_ms;
```

```
        while ((timeout    >  0u) &&
               (link_state == NET_IF_LINK_DOWN)) {

            Str_FmtNbr_Int32U(timeout,
                              2u,
                              DEF_NBR_BASE_DEC,
                              ASCII_CHAR_SPACE,
                              DEF_NO,
                              DEF_NO,
                             &retry_msg[13]);
            BSP_GraphLCD_ClrLine(5);
            BSP_GraphLCD_String(5, retry_msg);

            timeout--;
            link_state = AppNetIF_LinkStateWaitUntilUp(if_nbr,
                                                       retry_max,
                                                       retry_dly_ms,
                                                      perr);                    (14)
        }

        if (link_state == NET_IF_LINK_UP) {
            BSP_GraphLCD_ClrLine(4);
            BSP_GraphLCD_String(4, "Ethernet Link Up!");
        }
        BSP_GraphLCD_ClrLine(5);
        BSP_GraphLCD_String(5, "");
    }
    if (*perr == NET_IF_ERR_NONE) {             /* Translate successful return error   */
        *perr  = NET_ERR_NONE;                  /* to NET_ERR_NONE.                    */
    }
                                /* ---------------- MANUALLY CFG'D ADDR --------------- */
    BSP_GraphLCD_ClrLine(4);
    BSP_GraphLCD_String(4, "Manually Configured");
    AppGraphLCD_IPAddr(if_nbr);                                                        (15)
}
```

Listing 4-3 **AppTCPIP_Init()**

L4-3(1) `Net_Init()` is the Network Protocol stack initialization function.

L4-3(2) `BSP_GraphLCD_ClrLine()` is a function declared in `bsp_glcd.c` responsible of clearing a line on the LCD display. This function will be used extensively right before writing a message on the display.

L4-3(3) `BSP_GraphLCD_String()` is also declared in `bsp_glcd.c` and is responsible of printing a string of characters on the LCD display.

L4-3(4) **NetIF_Add()** is a Network Interface function responsible for initializing a Network Device driver. The architecture of the Network Device driver is defined in Chapter 14, "Network Device Drivers" on page 299. The first parameter is the **address of** the Ethernet API function. **if_nbr** is the interface index number. The first interface is index number 1. If the loopback interface is configured it has interface index number 0.

The architecture of the Network Device driver defined in Chapter 14, "Network Device Drivers" on page 299, also applies to the next seven parameters.

L4-3(5) The second parameter is the address of the device API function.

L4-3(6) The third parameter is the address of the device BSP data structure.

L4-3(7) The third parameter is the address of the device configuration data structure.

L4-3(8) The fourth parameter is the address of the PHY API function.

L4-3(9) The fifth and last parameter is the address of the PHY configuration data structure.

L4-3(10) The error code is used to validate the result of the function execution.

L4-3(11) **AppTCPIP_CfgStaticAddr()** is an application function that calls the stack's API function **NetIP_CfgAddrAdd()** to add a static IP host address, subnet mask, and default gateway to an interface. The function is declared in **app_tcpip.c** and is shown in Listing 4-4.

L4-3(12) **NetIF_Start()** makes the network interface ready to receive and transmit.

L4-3(13) **NetIF_LinkStateGet()** is a function that gets the interface's last known physical link state. It returns either Up or Down state.

L4-3(14) **AppNetIF_LinkStateWaitUntilUp()** is an application function that waits for the network interface's link state to be up. This function is declared in **app_tcpip.c.**

L4-3(15) **AppGraphLCD_IPAddr()** is an application function responsible of displaying the interface's configuration on the LCD display.

```
static  void  AppTCPIP_CfgStaticAddr (NET_IF_NBR   if_nbr,
                                      NET_ERR      *perr)
{
    NET_IP_ADDR  ip;
    NET_IP_ADDR  msk;
    NET_IP_ADDR  gateway;
    CPU_BOOLEAN  cfg_success;


    ip          = NetASCII_Str_to_IP((CPU_CHAR *)"10.10.1.149",   perr);                 (1)
    msk         = NetASCII_Str_to_IP((CPU_CHAR *)"255.255.255.0", perr);
    gateway     = NetASCII_Str_to_IP((CPU_CHAR *)"10.10.1.1",     perr);

    cfg_success = NetIP_CfgAddrAdd(if_nbr,                                               (2)
                                   ip,
                                   msk,
                                   gateway,
                                   perr);

    (void)&cfg_success;
}
```

Listing 4-4 **AppTCPIP_CfgStaticAddr() function**

L4-4(1) The **NetASCII_Str_to_IP()** converts the human readable address into the format required by the protocol stack. In this example the **10.10.1.149** address out of the 10.10.1.1 network with a subnet mask of **255.255.255.0** is used. To match a different network, this address, the subnet mask and the default gateway IP address must be customized.

L4-4(2) **NetIP_CfgAddrAdd()** configures the network parameters (IP address, subnet mask and default gateway IP address) required for the interface. More than one set of network parameters can be configured per interface. Once the source code is built and loaded into the target, the target will respond to ICMP Echo (ping) requests to 10.10.1.149.

4-1-2 BUILDING AND LOADING THE APPLICATION

Everything should be in place to run the example project. Connect the USB cable that accompanies the RX62N board to J14 (JLINK USB) on the board, right beside the network connector, and the other end to a free USB port on a PC.

Right click on the project name at the top of the workspace explorer tree and select *Build Project* as shown in Figure 4-4.

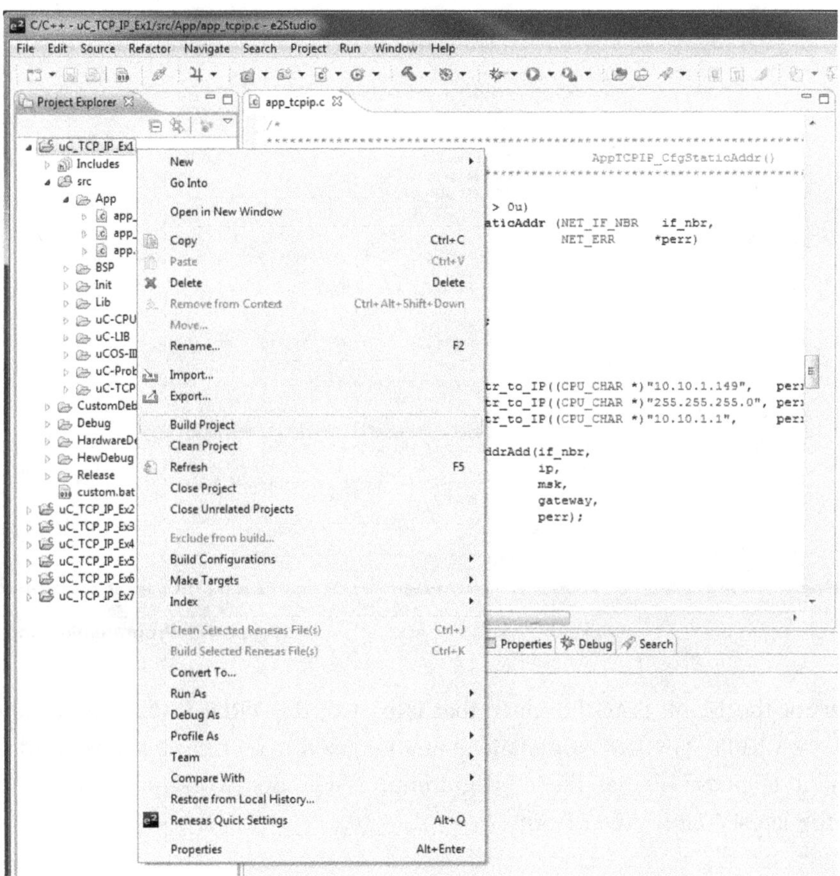

Figure 4-4 **Building the Project**

The KPIT GNURX toolchain will compile and link the example code and a new item will appear on the workspace explorer tree under the new group *Binaries*. Select the new item under the Binaries group called uC-TCP-IP-Ex1.x and click on the button with the Bug icon in order to download the code into the RX62N flash and start a debug session.

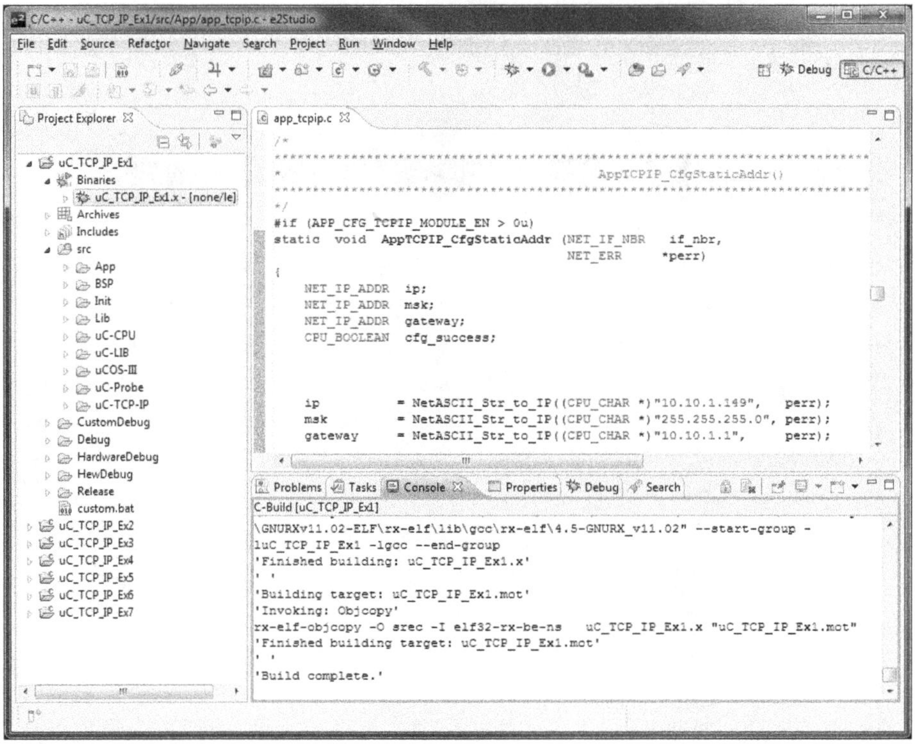

Figure 4-5 **Programming and Debugging**

If the driver for the J-Link JTAG interface that is part of the YRDKRX62N board is not up to date with the KPIT GNURX toolchain version used to compile, link and load the application, it is possible that flash programming will not work properly. In this case, download the latest J-Link driver from:

```
http://www.segger.com/jlink-software.html
```

The code will start executing and stop at `main()` in `app.c`. Click on the debugger's Go button to continue execution and verify that the LEDs are blinking and the static IP address is shown in the LCD display as illustrated in Figure 4-6:

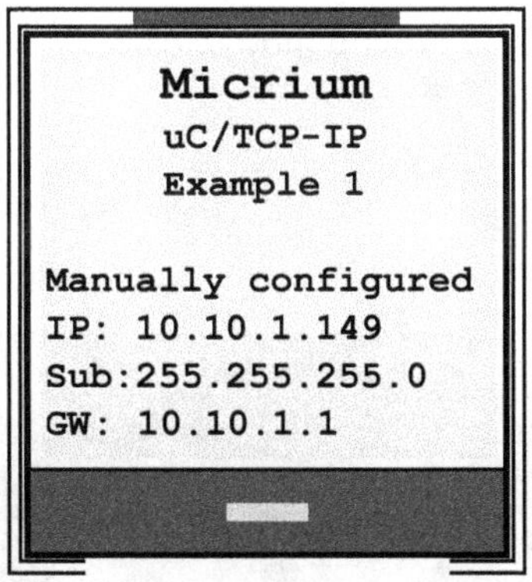

Figure 4-6 **Example #1 LCD screen: Static IP configuration**

4-1-3 RUNNING THE APPLICATION

Now that the project is running, the next step is to use the application. This project only implements the TCP/IP stack. As described in Listing 4-4, the static IP address 10.10.1.149 is assigned to the target board. The PC and the target board must be able to reach each other, and the easiest way, is to connect them to the same network as illustrated in Figure 3-2, in section 3-1-1 "Connecting the YRDKRX62N to a PC" on page 818. The PC is used to PING the board. It is also possible to place the PC and the target board on two different networks. As long as you know the IP addresses for each network, everything is fine. Let's first concentrate on placing the PC and the target in the same LAN. There are two possibilities:

- Change the target board IP parameters so that the target board is on the same network as the PC, or:
- Change the PC IP parameters so that it is on the same network as the target board.

Here, it is assumed that the host facing the target board in this PING test is a PC running Windows. If your host is not running Windows, the equivalent method to configure the IP parameters will have to be determined.

CHANGING THE TARGET BOARD IP PARAMETERS

In this case, the goal is to configure the target board IP parameters to match the network used by the PC. To achieve this, first we need to find the PC IP parameters. With Windows, the easiest way to determine a host IP parameters is to use the **`ipconfig`** command from a Command Prompt window. To open this window, click Start -> All Programs -> Accessories -> Command Prompt

The following window is displayed:

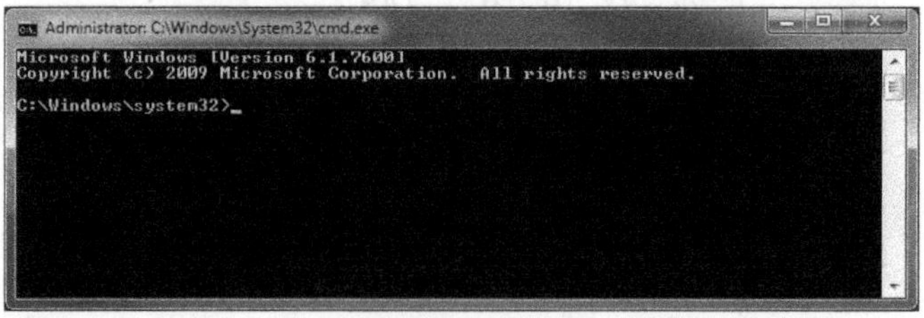

```
Administrator: C:\Windows\System32\cmd.exe
Microsoft Windows [Version 6.1.7600]
Copyright (c) 2009 Microsoft Corporation.  All rights reserved.

C:\Windows\system32>_
```

Figure 4-7 **Command Prompt**

Type **`ipconfig`** after the prompt and press Enter. The IP configuration for all the PC interfaces is displayed. Select the interface used to connect the PC to the network used for this PING test.

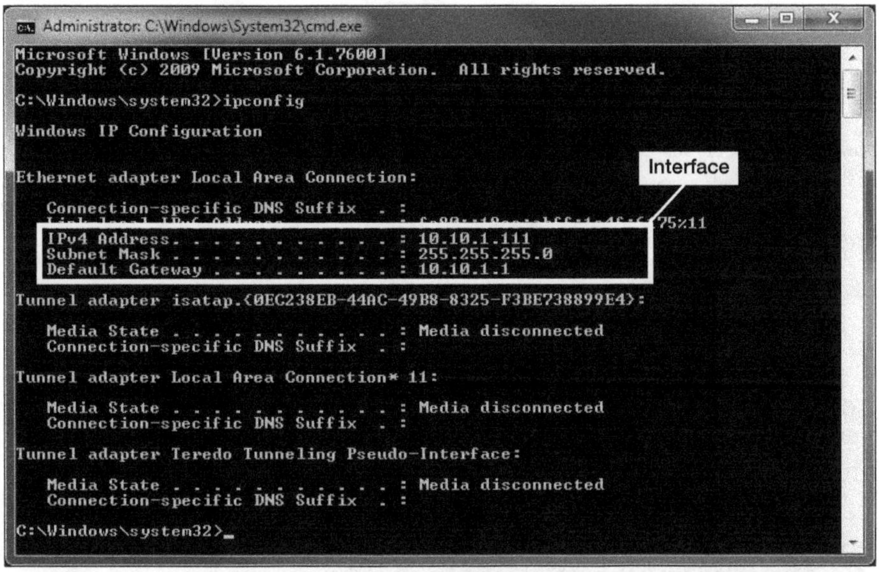

```
Administrator: C:\Windows\System32\cmd.exe
Microsoft Windows [Version 6.1.7600]
Copyright (c) 2009 Microsoft Corporation.  All rights reserved.

C:\Windows\system32>ipconfig

Windows IP Configuration

Ethernet adapter Local Area Connection:

   Connection-specific DNS Suffix  . :
   IPv4 Address. . . . . . . . . . . : 10.10.1.111
   Subnet Mask . . . . . . . . . . . : 255.255.255.0
   Default Gateway . . . . . . . . . : 10.10.1.1

Tunnel adapter isatap.{0EC238EB-44AC-49B8-8325-F3BE738899E4}:

   Media State . . . . . . . . . . . : Media disconnected
   Connection-specific DNS Suffix  . :

Tunnel adapter Local Area Connection* 11:

   Media State . . . . . . . . . . . : Media disconnected
   Connection-specific DNS Suffix  . :

Tunnel adapter Teredo Tunneling Pseudo-Interface:

   Media State . . . . . . . . . . . : Media disconnected
   Connection-specific DNS Suffix  . :

C:\Windows\system32>_
```

Interface

Figure 4-8 **ipconfig results**

In Figure 4-8, the white box identifies the IP parameters associated with the network interface of the PC connected to the test network. Make sure to properly identify the interface used in your system. The IP parameters are:

IP Address	10.10.1.111
Subnet Mask	255.255.255.0
Default Gateway	10.10.1.1

Table 4-1 **PC IP parameters**

From this information, the network address used for the network to which the PC is connected is 10.10.1.111 with a subnet mask of 255.255.255.0. We can now assign an IP address to the target board, an IP address that will work in this network. As the IP address to assign to the target board is selected manually, make sure the selected address is not already in use by another host. Let's say IP address 10.10.1.149 is chosen. Modify **AppInit_TCPIP()** in to statically configure this IP address. Here is the code snippet for this:

```
ip      = NetASCII_Str_to_IP((CPU_CHAR *)"10.10.1.149",
                             (NET_ERR *)&err_net);
msk     = NetASCII_Str_to_IP((CPU_CHAR *)"255.255.255.0",
                             (NET_ERR *)&err_net);
gateway = NetASCII_Str_to_IP((CPU_CHAR *)"10.10.1.1",
                             (NET_ERR *)&err_net);

NetIP_CfgAddrAdd(if_nbr, ip, msk, gateway, &err_net);
```

Listing 4-5 **Changing the target board IP parameters**

Compile, load and run the code on the target board. The next step is for the PC to issue the PING command. In a Command Prompt window on the PC, issue the following command: "ping 10.10.1.149".

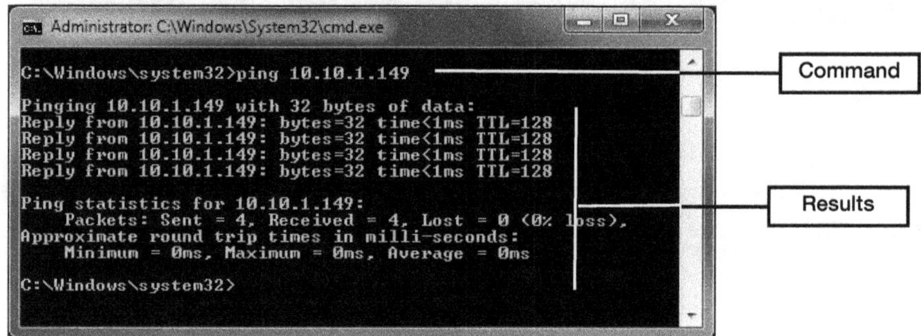

Figure 4-9 **Example #1, PING results**

If the output of the PING command is similar to the result shown in Figure 4-9, then the Example #1 was successfully installed, compiled, loaded and executed.

CHANGING THE PC IP PARAMETERS

The second method to install the PC and the target board on the same network is to keep the target board's configured address as shown in Listing 4-4 and to change the PC IP parameters. In Figure 4-8, the target board IP parameters are:

IP Address	10.10.1.111
Subnet Mask	255.255.255.0
Default Gateway	10.10.1.1

Table 4-2 **Target IP parameters**

With this information, the network address defined for the target board network is 10.10.1.0 with a subnet mask of 255.255.255.0. The IP address can now be assigned to the PC, selecting an IP address that will work in this network. As the IP address to assign to the PC is selected manually, make sure the address is not already in use by another host. Let's say IP address 10.10.1.100 is chosen. To change the IP parameters for an interface in a Windows PC, launch the Control Panel and click on "View network status and tasks" under the Network and Internet group.

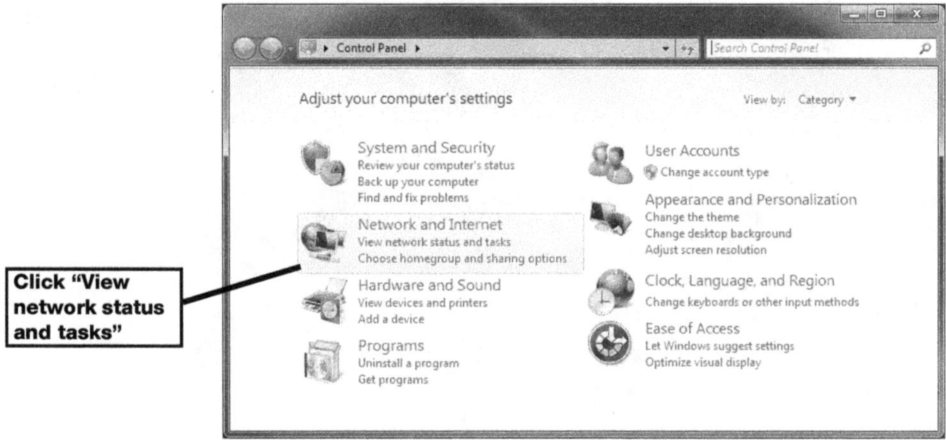

Figure 4-10 **Windows Control Panel**

In the Network Connections window, select the network interface card that is used to connect to the network to which the target board is connected.

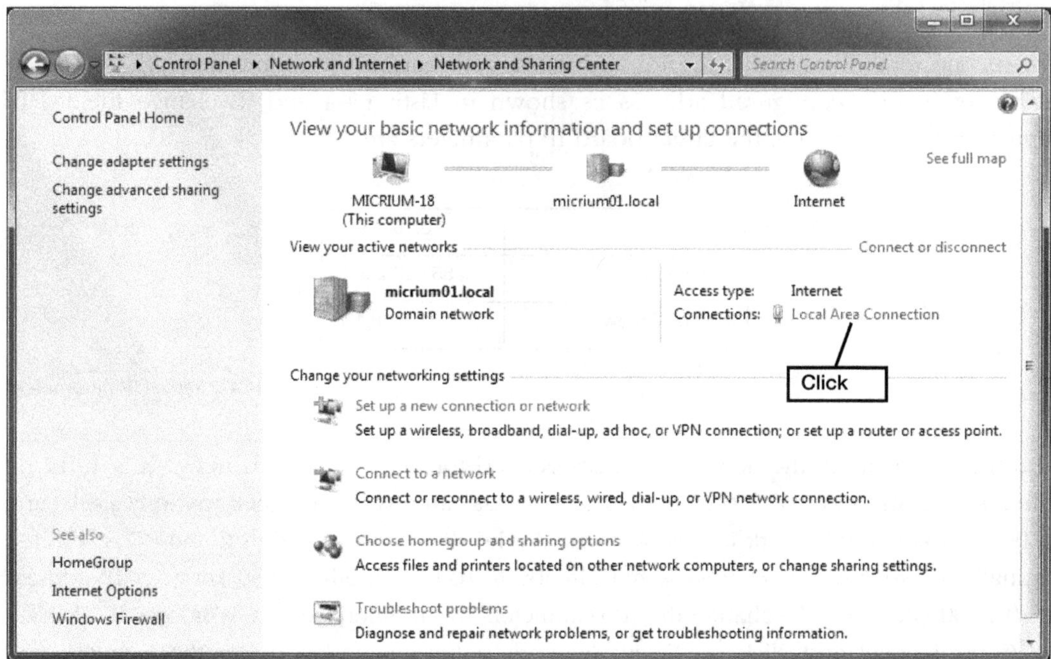

Figure 4-11 **Network Connections**

The “Local Area Connection Status” window opens up as shown in Figure 4-12. Then click on Properties. This opens the Local Area Connection Properties for the network interface as shown in Figure 4-13. Select the item labeled as Internet Protocol Version 4 (TCP/IPv4) and click on the Properties button.

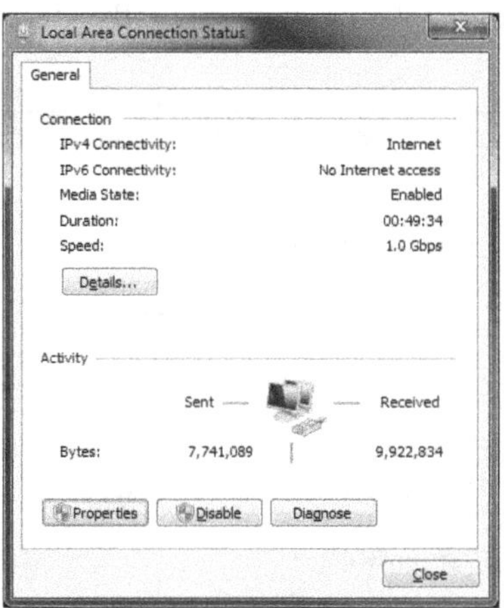

Figure 4-12 **Local Area Connection Status**

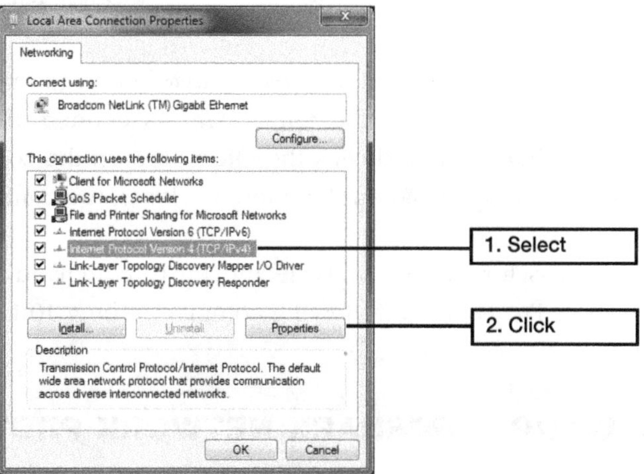

Figure 4-13 **Local Area Connection Properties**

Once you click on the properties button, the screen shown in Figure 4-14 will open.

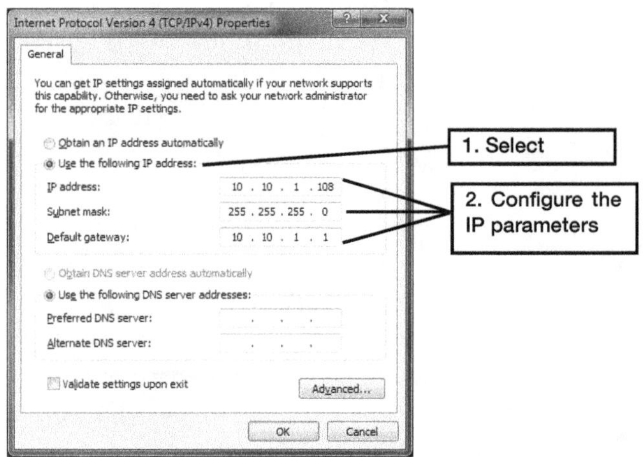

Figure 4-14 **Internet Protocol (TCP/IP) Properties**

Select the "Use the following IP address:" radio button to manually assign IP parameters to the network interface. Enter the parameters as defined above. Click the OK button to confirm the configuration and click the OK button on the Local Area Connection Properties window that is still open. When the window closes, the configuration is effective.

The next step is for the PC to issue the PING command. In a DOS Command Prompt window on the PC, issue the following command: "ping 10.10.1.149". The result is shown in Figure 4-9.

4-1-4 USING WIRESHARK NETWORK PROTOCOL ANALYZER

It is recommended to follow the guidelines for Wireshark installation and configuration provided in section 6-2-2 "Wireshark" on page 152. Wireshark is installed on the PC that is part of this example setup (see Chapter 3, "Connecting the YRDKRX62N to a PC" on page 818). The main Wireshark configuration steps are:

- Install and launch Wireshark.
- Configure Name resolution to see the MAC address and Transport port numbers instead of their associated names.

- Configure the Capture or Display filter to view only relevant traffic. In this example, ARP and ICMP packets are of interest.

- Configure to view the Packet List and Packet Details frame. Packet Bytes frame is not required.

- Select the Network Interface that is participating in the example.

- Start the capture.

While Wireshark is capturing the traffic between the PC and the target board, use a Command prompt window on the PC and issue a PING command similar to the one in Figure 4-9, but with the IP address determined for your network configuration. When the PING execution is complete, the capture can be stopped. The capture result should look like this:

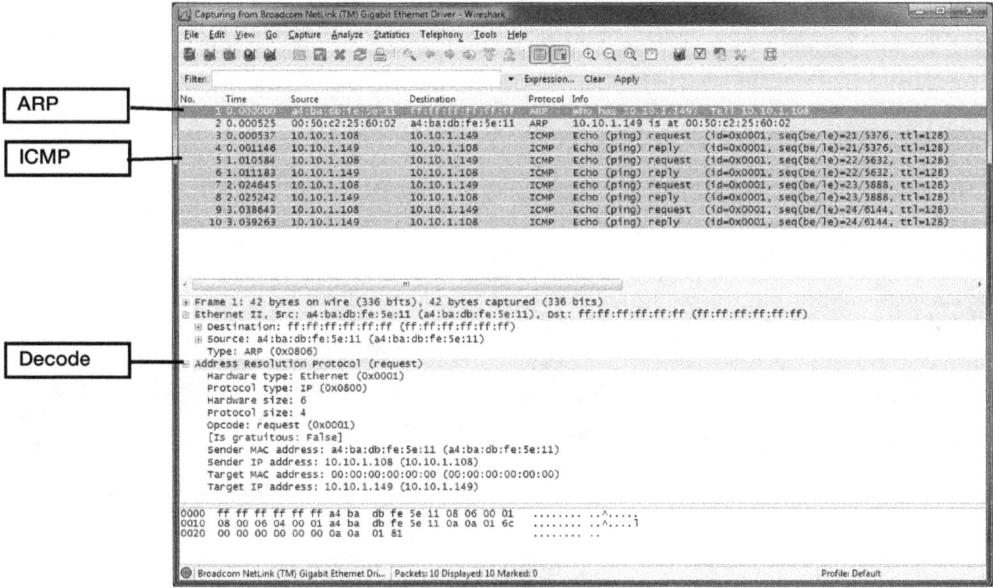

Figure 4-15 **Wireshark capture**

The first two packets in the test are the ARP request from the PC and the ARP reply from the target board. The first packet is highlighted and it is expanded in the Packet Detail pane in the bottom half of the screen. To decode another packet, select it in the Packet List pane and its content will be displayed in the Packet Detail pane. Every level of the packet is first represented and the complete packet encapsulation is collapsed. To expand a level, click the plus sign beside it. Figure 4-15 shows the ARP request completely decoded. The ARP concepts introduced in section 4-8 "ARP Packet" on page 107 of the first part of this book are well exposed in this figure. The second packet in the list in light blue is the ARP reply. To decode it, select it and see its content in the Packet Detail pane. The same can be done for an ICMP Echo request

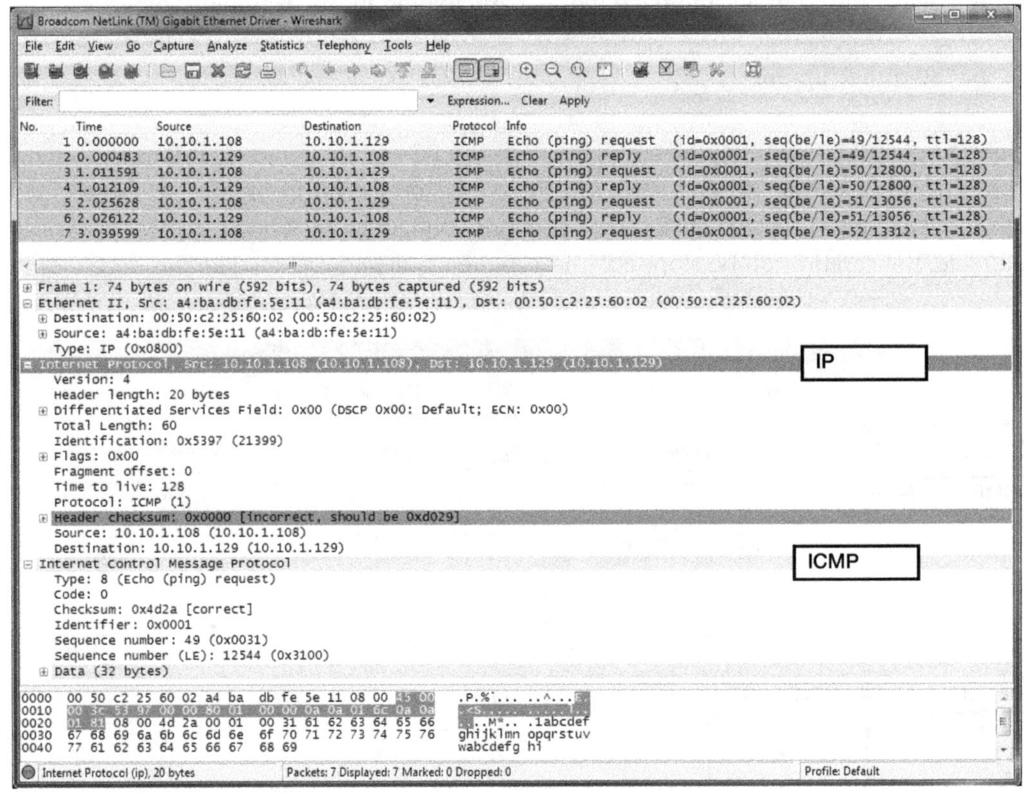

Figure 4-16 **Wireshark ICMP Echo Request capture**

Decoding the ICMP Echo request in Figure 4-16 demonstrates the concept of the IP header introduced in section Figure 5-2 "IP version 4 Header and Packet" on page 115 and the concept of the ICMP message introduced in section 6-1-1 "Internet Control Message Protocol (ICMP)" on page 136.

4-1-5 MONITORING VARIABLES USING μC/PROBE

Click the Go button in the IAR C-Spy debugger to resume execution of the code if it was stopped. To use μC/Probe, the target code must be running. A short introduction to μC/Probe is provided in the next pages. Complete μC/Probe user manuals are in the following directory after installation:

```
$\Micrium\uC-Probe\uC-Probe-Protocol.pdf
$\Micrium\uC-Probe\uC-Probe-Target-Manual.pdf
$\Micrium\uC-Probe\uC-Probe-User-Manual.pdf
```

Now start μC/Probe by locating the μC/Probe icon on your PC illustrated in Figure 4-17.

Figure 4-17 **μC/Probe icon**

Figure 4-18 shows the initial screen when μC/Probe is first started.

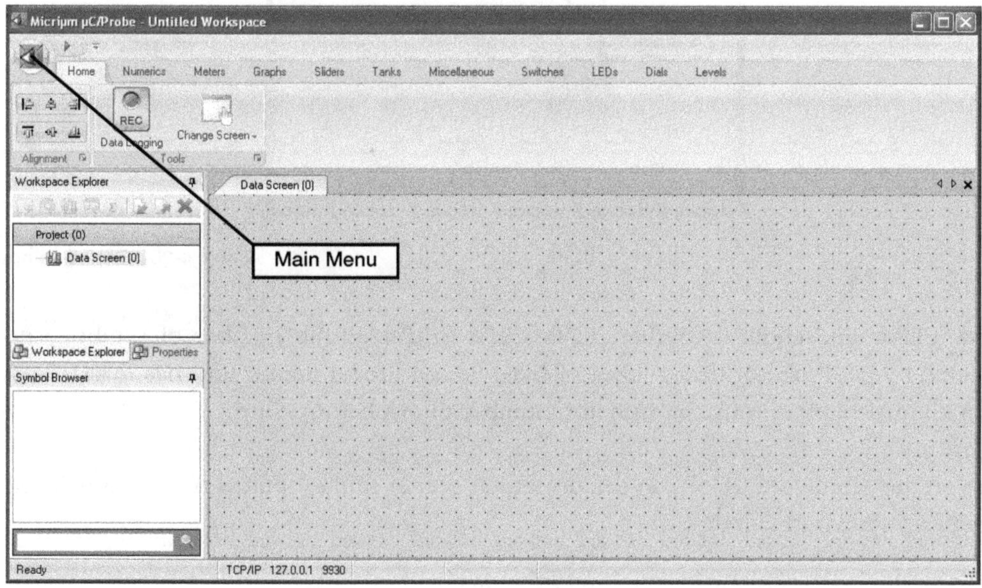

Figure 4-18 **μC/Probe startup screen**

Click on the 'Main Menu' button to open up the main menu as shown in Figure 4-19.

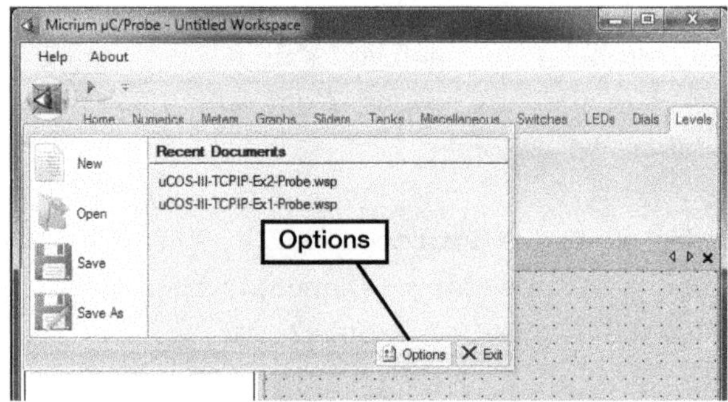

Figure 4-19 **µC/Probe's main menu**

Click on the Options button to setup options as shown in Figure 4-20.

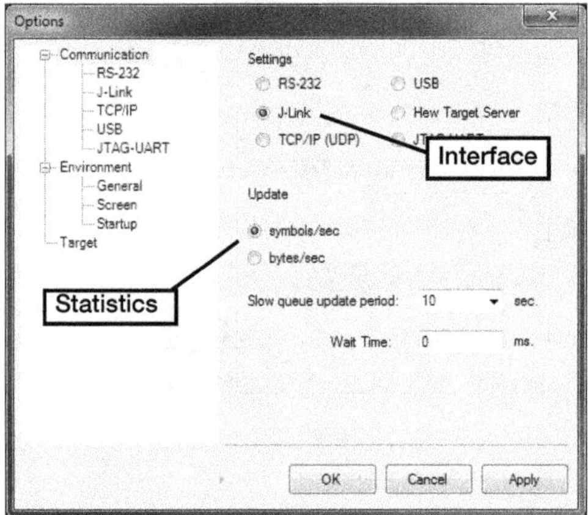

Figure 4-20 **µC/Probe's options**

Select 'J-Link' and choose whether µC/Probe is to display the number of symbols/second collected by µC/Probe or the number of bytes/second for run-time statistics in µC/Probe. It generally makes more sense to view the number of symbols/second.

Click on the 'Configure J-Link' on the upper-left corner in the options tree. You will see the dialog box shown in Figure 4-21.

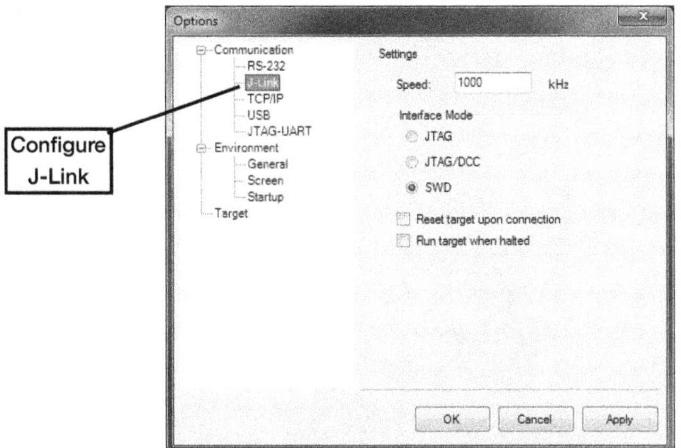

Figure 4-21 **µC/Probe's J-Link options**

The speed of the J-Link interface is set by default at 500 KHz. We have tested it up to 12000 KHz with success. The faster the speed, the better the µC/Probe display rate. Make sure you select the 'SWD interface mode. Finally click on the OK button at the bottom.

Now go back to the 'Main Menu' and open the **uC-TCP-IP-Ex1-Probe.wsp** workspace found in the following directory:

$\Micrium\Software\EvalBoards\Renesas\YRDKRX62N\GNURX-e2studio\uC-TCP-IP-Book-Ex-Obj\uC-TCP-IP-Ex1

When opening a workspace, the location of compiler output is required. This file contains all the variable information used by µC/Probe for this project. This project workspace was created and saved with the name and location of this file. The user will not be prompted for this file, in this case. The µC/Probe screen should appear as the one shown in Figure 4-22.

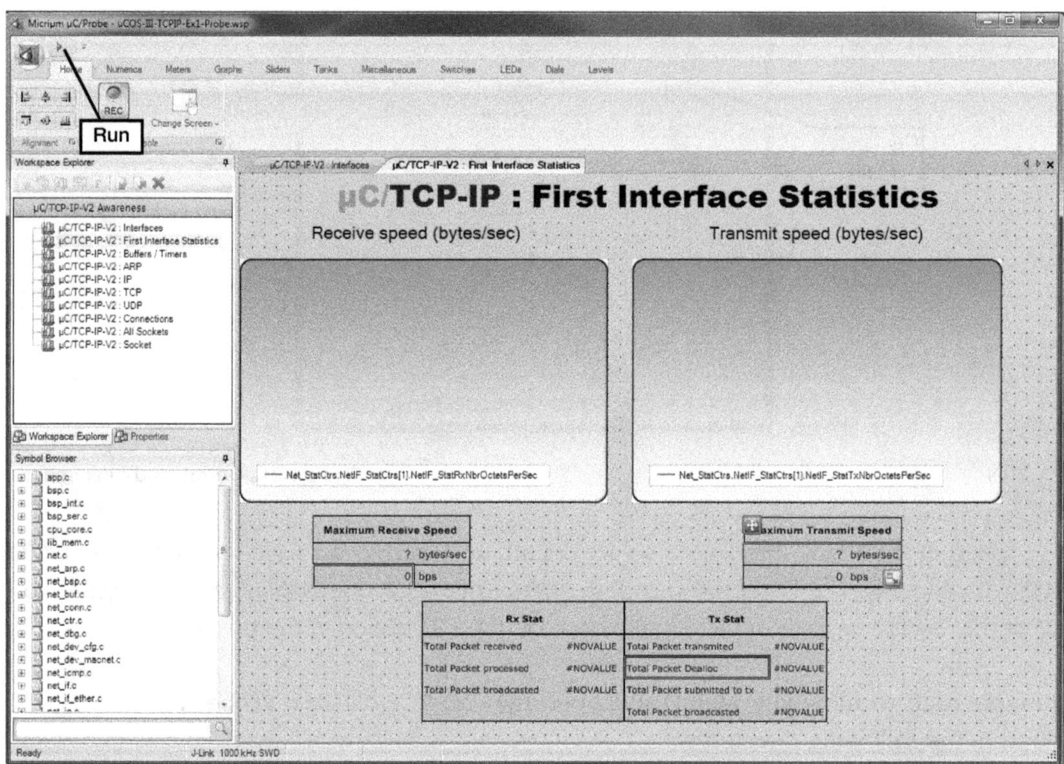

Figure 4-22 **µC/Probe Example #1 Edit Mode Screen**

µC/TCP-IP collects statistics on various modules. The following screens are used to display these statistics. Example #1 does not put any stress on the target board. The description of all of the screens is kept for the examples in Part II, Chapter 5, "µC/TCP-IP Performance Examples" on page 895, where more traffic is generated in the examples. Performance examples will provide more data and will make the screens more meaningful.

For this example, selecting the Interface screen is a good example of how µC/Probe works and what a screen does. Click on the Run button and see µC/Probe collect run-time data from the YRDKRX62N board as shown in Figure 4-23.

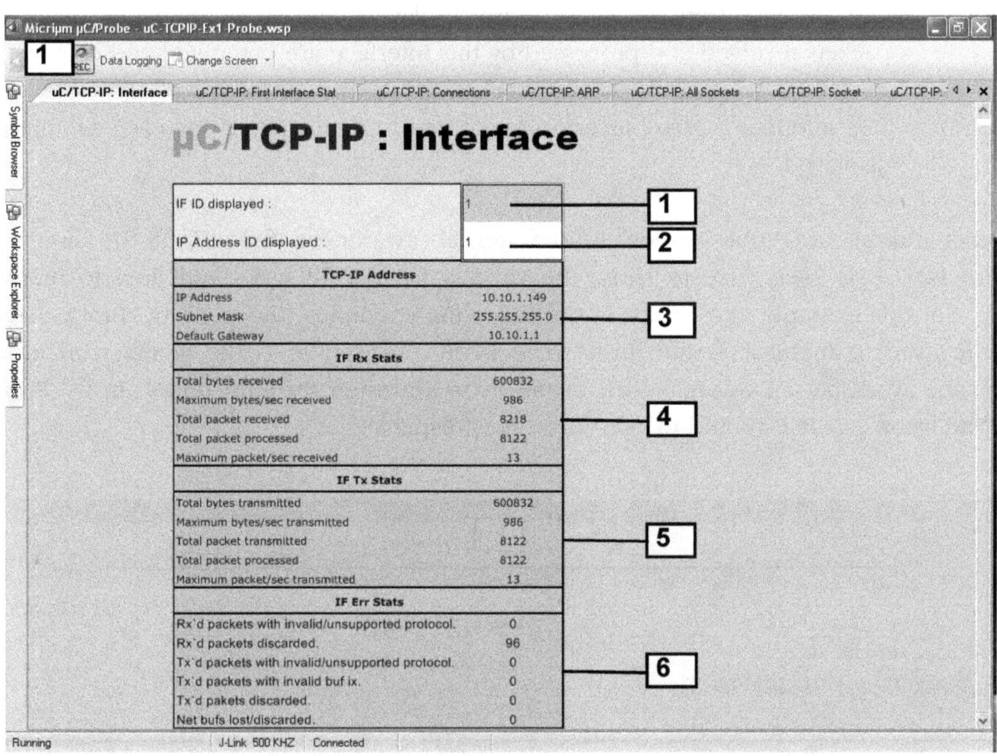

Figure 4-23 **µC/Probe Example #1 Run Mode Screen #1 - Interface statistics**

F4-23(1) This field is used to identify the interface index number. The information about this interface is displayed in the fields below. The YRDKRX62N has a single network interface.

F4-23(2) A network interface can have more than one IP address assigned. This field identifies which IP address the display of information pertains to. In this example, there is a single IP address used. It is the IP address that was determined in section 4-1-3 "Running the Application" on page 859. IF #0 is reserved for the loopback interface.

F4-23(3) This section displays the IP parameters associated with the interface.

F4-23(4) The interface receive statistics are displayed here. The number of bytes and packets received and processed by this interface are computed and displayed.

F4-23(5) The interface transmit statistics are displayed here. The number of bytes and packets received and processed by this interface are computed and displayed.

F4-23(6) The interface's possible errors are listed and the count for each of them is displayed.

Another useful µC/Probe screen is the kernel awareness for µC/OS-III shown in Figure 4-24. It is used here to show the various µC/TCP-IP tasks and how to monitor them. For this example and for all of the following examples, the same µC/Probe screen can be used to monitor system tasks. The kernel awareness is the Sigma icon in the µC/Probe Workspace Explorer. Click on the icon and then the Run button in µC/Probe, and the list of µC/TCP-IP and µC/OS-III tasks is displayed

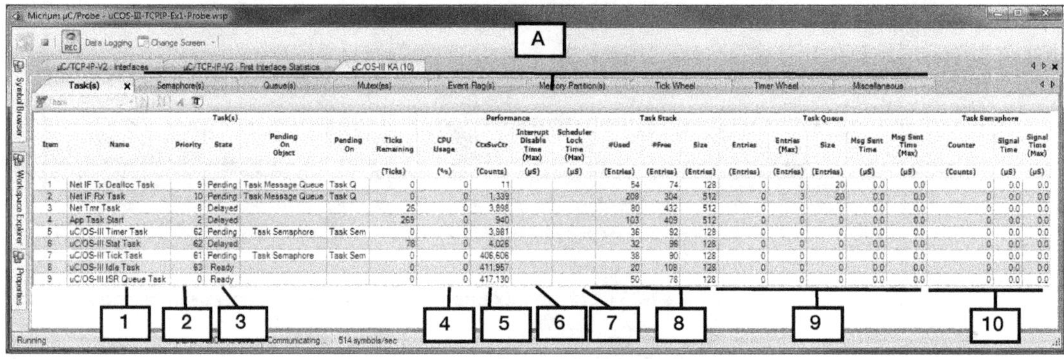

Figure 4-24 **µC/Probe Example #1 Run Mode - Kernel Awareness Screens**

F4-24(1) The first column after the line item number displays the name of the task.

F4-24(2) The priority of each task is displayed in the second column. The idle task is always assigned the lowest priority (i.e., 31). The statistic and timer tasks are executing at the same priority.

F4-24(3) The next column indicates the state of each task. A task can be in one of eight states as described in Chapter 4, *Task Management* in Part I of the µC/OS-III book.

The idle task will always show that the task is ready. The tick and timer tasks will either be ready or pending because both tasks wait (i.e., pend) on their internal task semaphore. The statistics task will show delayed because it calls **OSTimeDly()** every 1/10th of a second.

F4-24(4) The CPU Usage column indicates the CPU usage of each task relative to other tasks. The example consumes approximately 1% of the CPU. The idle task consumes 95% of that 1% or, 0.94% of the CPU. The tick task 0.05% and the other tasks consume nearly nothing.

F4-24(5) The `CtxSwCtr` column indicates the number of times the task executed.

F4-24(6) This column indicates the maximum amount of time interrupts were disabled when running the corresponding task.

F4-24(7) This column indicates the maximum amount of time the scheduler was locked when running the corresponding task.

F4-24(8) The next three columns indicate the stack usage of each task. This information is collected by the statistics task 10 times per second.

F4-24(9) The next five columns provide statistics about each task's internal message queue. Because none of the internal μC/OS-III tasks make use of the internal message queue, the corresponding values are not displayed. In fact, they would all be 0 anyway.

F4-24(10) The last three columns provide run-time statistics regarding each task's internal semaphore.

F3-24(A) The μC/Probe Kernel Awareness has more than the task screen. As indicated by the A reference in the figure, Semaphore(s), Queue(s), Mutex(es), EvenFlag(s), Memory Partition(s), Tick Wheel, Timer Wheel and Miscellaneous μC/OS-III elements can also be monitored.

4-2 µC/TCP-IP EXAMPLE #2

The µC/DHCPc module is part of the µC/TCP-IP family and implements the DHCP protocol to enable embedded systems to get their IP configuration from a centralized database rather than configuring it by hand as shown in the previous example. This second project is similar to Example #1 with the exception that the IP configuration uses DHCP to dynamically configure the IP address, the subnet mask and the default gateway IP address (see Listing 3-3). This assumes that there is a DHCP server on the network.

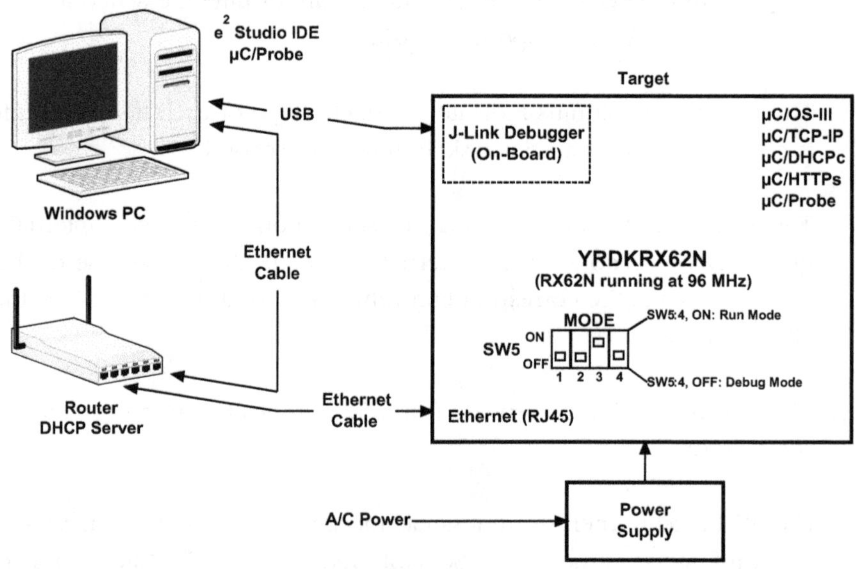

Figure 4-25 **Connecting a PC and the YRDKRX62N, using a DHCP server**

The difference in this project is how to determine the target board IP address. Because DHCP is used, the IP address will only be known once the project is running and DHCP has completed its process. The project uses Micrium µC/DHCPc DHCP Client. The section 4-2-1 "How the Example Project Works" on page 878 gives the major points concerning the µC/DHCPc usage. The complete µC/DHCPc user manual is included in the package downloaded to obtain the tools and software for these examples (see section 3-3 "Downloading µC/TCP-IP Projects for this Book" on page 823).

The same Renesas e^2 Studio workspace as is in Example #1 workspace is used. Open it as described in the previous section (Chapter 4, on page 841). Click on the uC-TCP-IP-Ex2 item of the project explorer to select the second project. The workspace is very similar to the Example #1 workspace with one exception. Figure 4-26 shows the additional folder for uC/DHCPc present in the Example #2 workspace.

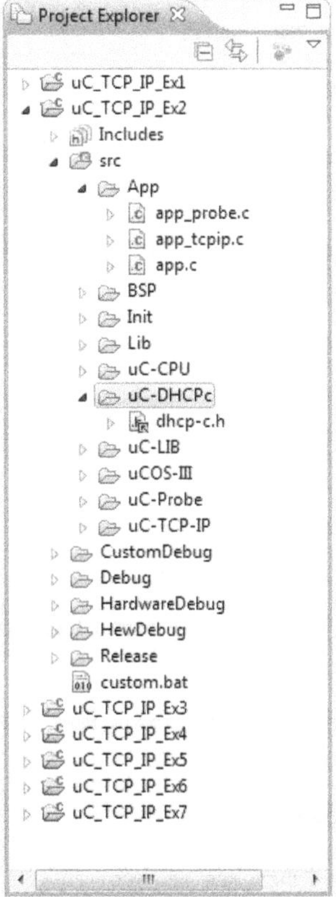

Figure 4-26 **Expanded Workspace for uC-TCPIP-V2-Ex2**

The groups are identical to Example #1 with the addition of the uC/DHCPc group. It contains the header file. The µC/DHCPc object code library used in this example is located in:

```
$\Micrium\Software\EvalBoards\Renesas\YRDKRX62N\
GNURX-e2studio\uC-TCP-IP-Book-Lib\uC-DHCPc-V2.a
```

```
                case DHCP_STATUS_CFGD_NO_TMR:     /* IF configured (no timer set)      */
                     if_dhcp_init_tbl[if_done_ix] = DEF_YES;
                     nbr_if_init++;
                     AppTCPIP_CfgStaticAddr(nbr_if_init,
                                            &err_addr_cfg);
                    (void)&err_addr_cfg;

                     BSP_GraphLCD_ClrLine(4);
                     BSP_GraphLCD_String(4, "Assigned by DHCP*");
                     AppGraphLCD_IPAddr(if_nbr_cur);
                     break;

                case DHCP_STATUS_CFGD_LOCAL_LINK:  /* IF configured (link-local addr)  */
                     if_dhcp_init_tbl[if_done_ix] = DEF_YES;
                     nbr_if_init++;

                     BSP_GraphLCD_ClrLine(4);
                     BSP_GraphLCD_String(4, "Link-Local Address");
                     AppGraphLCD_IPAddr(if_nbr_cur);
                     break;

                case DHCP_STATUS_FAIL:             /* IF configuration failed          */
                     if_dhcp_init_tbl[if_done_ix] = DEF_YES;
                     nbr_if_init++;
                     AppTCPIP_CfgStaticAddr(nbr_if_init,
                                            &err_addr_cfg);
                    (void)&err_addr_cfg;

                     BSP_GraphLCD_ClrLine(4);
                     BSP_GraphLCD_String(4, "Manually Configured");
                     AppGraphLCD_IPAddr(if_nbr_cur);
                     break;

                default:
                     break;
            }
        }

        if_done_ix++;
        if_nbr_cur++;
    }
  }
}
```

Listing 4-6 **AppInit_DHCPc()**

L4-6(1) `DHCPc_Init()` initializes the DHCP client module.

L4-6(2) Set the DHCP options.

L4-6(3) Start the DHCP Client for the selected interface.

L4-6(4) Delay until the configuration is completed.

L4-6(5) Check the interface DHCP configuration status.

L4-6(6) Display the IP address as configured by the DHCP server on the LCD.

4-3 RUNNING THE APPLICATION

Once this code is running and DHCP has completed its process, LEDs on the board will blink. It is now possible for the PC connected to the same network as the board (see Figure 4-25) to PING the board. The IP address, subnet mask and default gateway IP address are assigned to the target board once the code is running and DHCP has completed its process. To PING the target board, the board IP address is required.

4-3-1 DISPLAYING IP PARAMETERS

Two methods can be used to display the IP parameters:

- Using µC/Probe
- Looking at the LCD display

USING µC/PROBE TO DISPLAY THE IP PARAMETERS

Launch µC/Probe as demonstrated in Example #1. Now go back to the µC/Probe 'Main Menu' and open the **uC-TCP-IP-Ex2-Probe.wsp** workspace found in the following directory:

```
$\Micrium\Software\EvalBoards\Renesas\YRDKRX62N\GNURX-e2studio\
uC-TCP-IP-Book-Ex-Obj\uC-TCP-IP-Ex2
```

Select the Interface screen and click on the Run button. The µC/Probe screen will be similar to the one in Figure 4-27. The values for the IP address, subnet mask and default gateway depend on your network configuration. The network that was used to produce this example, the network is 10.10.1.1.

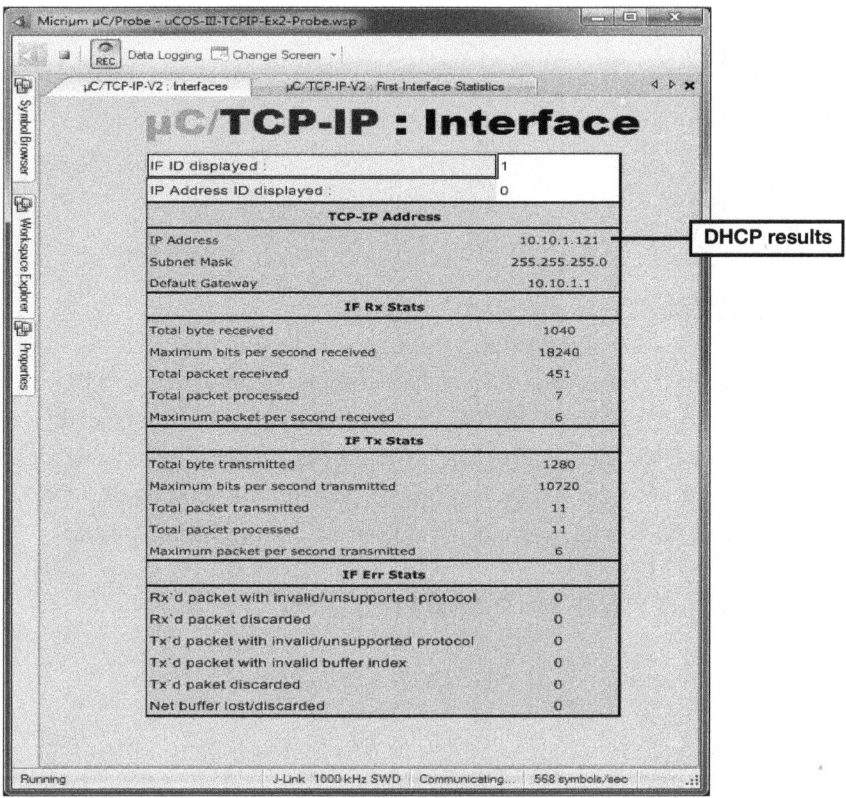

Figure 4-27 **Example #2 DHCP results**

LOOKING AT THE LCD DISPLAY TO FIND OUT THE IP PARAMETERS

This project includes a BSP module for the Graphic LCD onboard the YRDKRX62N. In this and most examples using DHCP, the LCD display is used to show the parameters provided by DHCP.

Figure 4-28 illustrates the process of IP configuration through DHCP as seen from the LCD display:

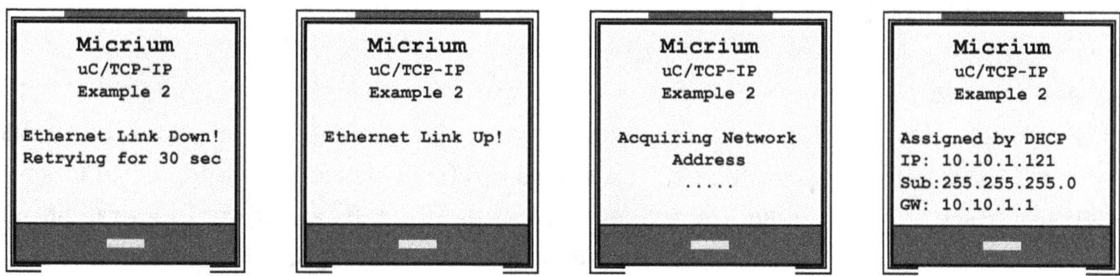

Figure 4-28 **Example #2 LCD screens: DHCP process**

The last screen is displayed once the DHCP process has completed. It may take thirty to forty-five seconds, depending on your network.

4-3-2 PINGING THE TARGET BOARD

Now that the target board IP parameters are known, the PC or any other devices having access to the network can now PING the target board. Open a Command Prompt window and issue the PING command using the IP address of the target board in a similar manner to Example #1 (Figure 4-9).

4-4 USING WIRESHARK TO VISUALIZE THE DHCP PROCESS

It is not possible to capture the DHCP process with the existing setup (Figure 4-25). The DHCP process happens between the target board and the PC. To capture this traffic, Wireshark needs to be between the two hosts. This can be achieved with a hub or an Ethernet switch where the traffic to either the target board or the PC can be mirrored to a monitoring port where the host running Wireshark is connected. In this example, a hub is used.

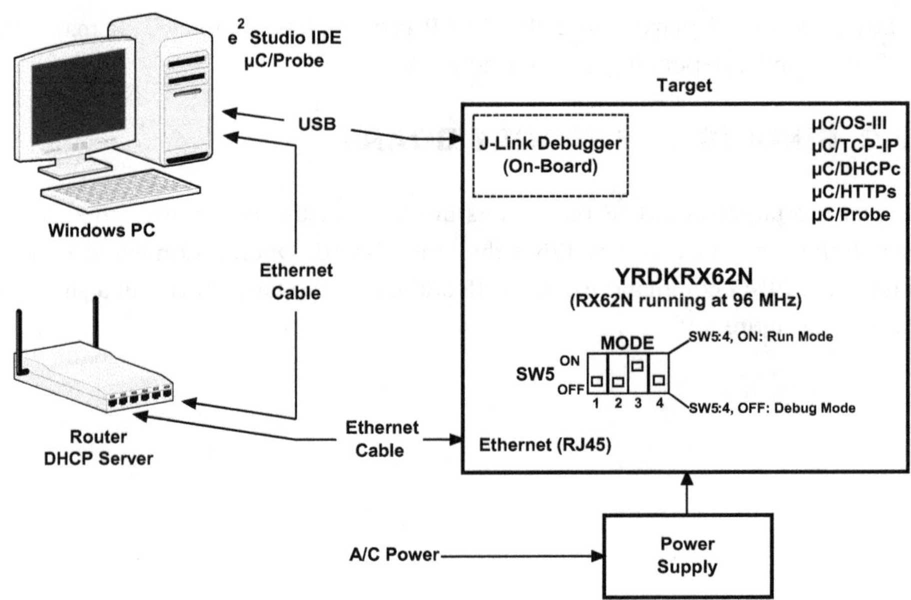

Figure 4-29 **DHCP process capture using a hub**

With this network setup, Wireshark captures all the traffic on this Ethernet LAN. The issue here is that there may be a lot of undesirable traffic generated by all of the hosts on this network. To view only the DHCP traffic between the target board and the DHCP server, a capture filter or a display filter is required. In the following figure, a display filter is used.

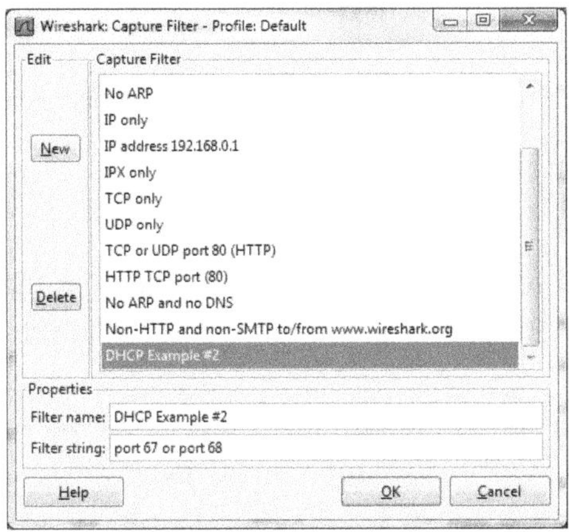

Figure 4-30 **Wireshark display filter for DHCP only**

UDP port 67 and 68 are the port numbers used by the client and server in a DHCP exchange. The DHCP process has four messages. First, the target board sends a DHCP Discover message using Ethernet broadcast. To complete the DHCP process, the Offer, Request and ACK messages follow.

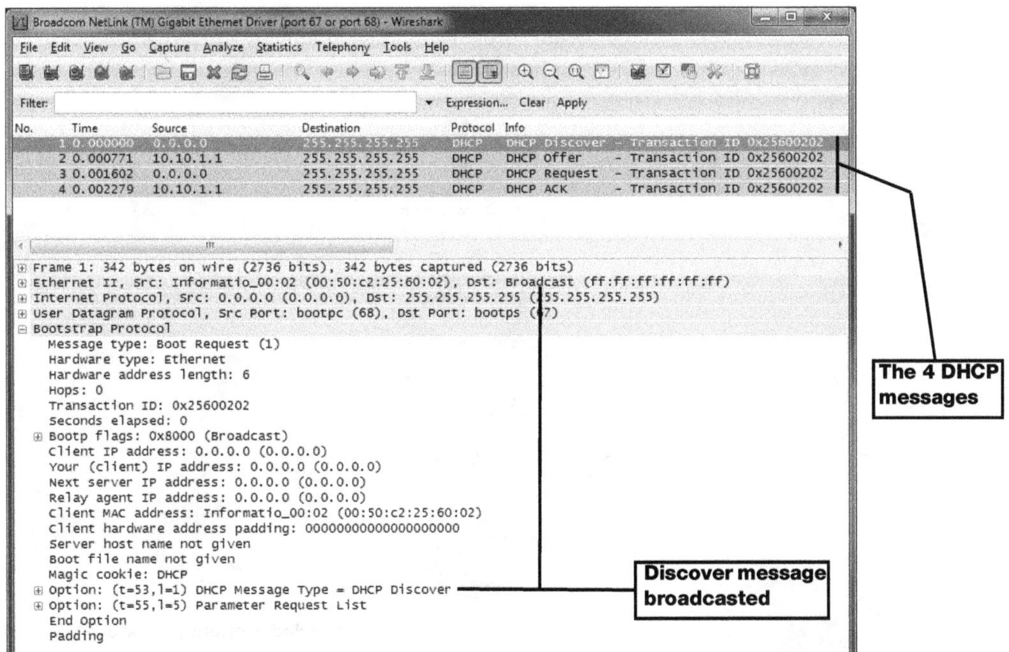

Figure 4-31 **DHCP process and Discover message decoded**

4-5 µC/TCP-IP EXAMPLE #3

µC/Probe is a windows application that allows developers to prototype GUIs by using drag-and-drop virtual controls and indicators to display run-time values of application variables, memory locations and I/O ports.

This third project is similar to Example #2 with the exception that the interface to µC/Probe uses the Ethernet interface instead of the J-Link or RS-232 interfaces.

All the examples are contained within the same workspace. Open the workspace as described in the previous section (Chapter 4, on page 844). Click on the uC-TCP-IP-Ex3 item in the Project Explorer tree to select the third project.

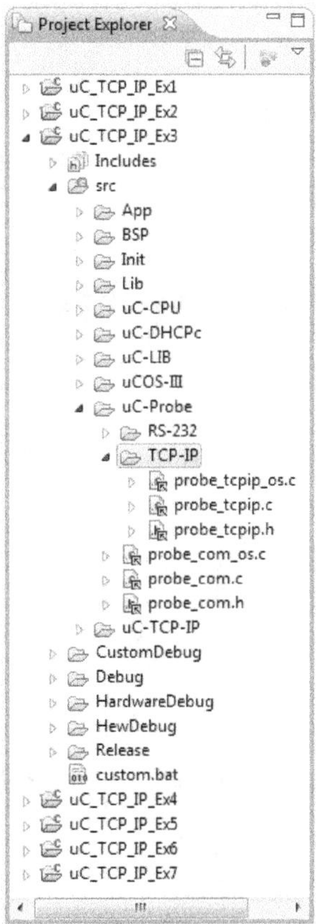

Figure 4-32 **Expanded Workspace for uC-TCP-IP-Ex3**

The workspace is very similar to the Example #2 workspace with one exception. Figure 4-32 shows the additional folder for uC/Probe present in the Example #3 workspace. The μC/Probe group contains header files, as well as the μC/Probe object code library used in this example. The μC/Probe library is a UDP server that implements the communication protocol between the target board and μC/Probe on the PC. The header files are needed since some of the application code requires definitions and declarations found in these files.

4-5-1 HOW THE EXAMPLE PROJECT WORKS

The code from **main()** and **AppTaskStart()** in this example are identical to Example #2. However, the use of μC/Probe over TCP/IP in this example modifies **AppProbe_Init()** where the communication protocol used by μC/Probe is initialized as shown in Listing 4-7.

```
void  AppProbe_Init (void)
{
#if (APP_CFG_PROBE_COM_MODULE_EN > 0)
    ProbeCom_Init();                    /* Initialize the uC/Probe communications module    */

#if (PROBE_COM_CFG_RS232_EN > 0)
    ProbeRS232_Init(PROBE_BAUD_RATE);
    ProbeRS232_RxIntEn();
#endif

#if (PROBE_COM_CFG_TCPIP_EN > 0)
    ProbeTCPIP_Init();
#endif
#endif
}


void  ProbeTCPIP_Init (void)
{
    ProbeTCPIP_OS_Init();
}
```

Listing 4-7 **AppProbeInit() and ProbeTCP_Init()**

Ultimately the function **ProbeTCPIP_OS_Init()** basically initializes a UDP server task that will serve any requests from μC/Probe to read or write run-time values of application variables and target's memory locations.

4-6 RUNNING THE APPLICATION

Execute the code in the same way you did for Example #1. Once this code is running, LEDs on the board will be blinking. It is now possible for the PC connected to the same network as the board to connect µC/Probe through UDP.

By default, it is assumed a DHCP server in the network just like the previous example setup and the IP address that you need to configure µC/Probe is displayed on the LCD screen as illustrated in Figure 4-33:

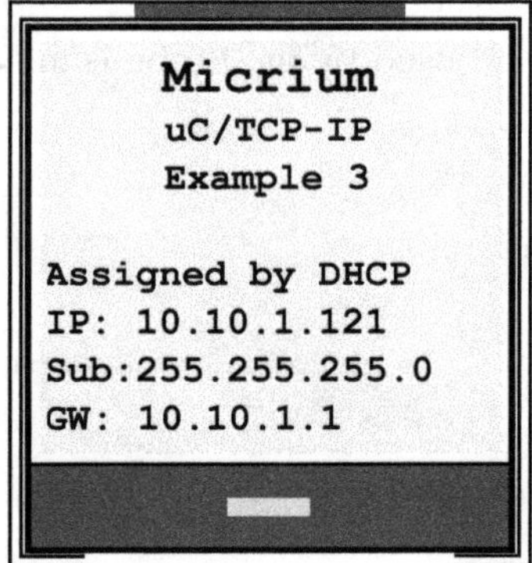

Figure 4-33 **Example #3 LCD screen**

In case you want to configure the target IP address manually, all you need to do is disable the DHCP process through a definition declared in **app_cfg.h** shown in Listing 4-8 and update the IP parameters in **AppTCPIP_CfgStaticAddr()** as described in the first example.

```
#define  APP_CFG_DHCPc_MODULE_EN            DEF_ENABLED
```

Listing 4-8 **Enabling and Disabling DHCP**

4-6-1 MONITORING VARIABLES USING µC/PROBE

To use µC/Probe, the target code must be running. Launch µC/Probe as demonstrated in Example #1.

In Example #1, the interface to µC/Probe is configured to use J-Link. In this example, it is configured to use TCP/IP. Click on the 'Main Menu' button to open up the main menu as shown in Figure 4-34.

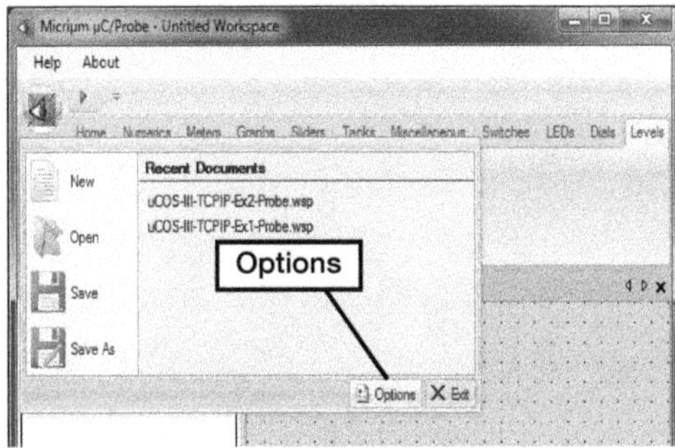

Figure 4-34 **µC/Probe's main menu**

Click on the Options button to setup options as shown in Figure 4-35.

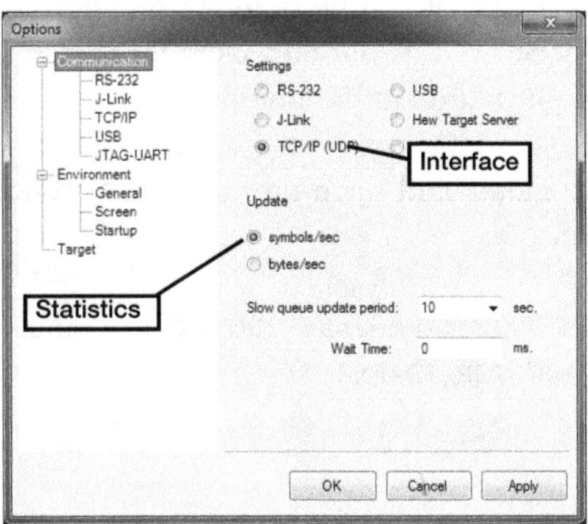

Figure 4-35 **µC/Probe's options**

Select 'TCP/IP' and select whether μC/Probe is to display the number of symbols/second collected by μC/Probe or the number of bytes/second for run-time statistics in μC/Probe. It generally makes more sense to view the number of symbols/second.

Click on the 'Configure TCP/IP' on the upper-left corner in the options tree. You will see the dialog box shown in Figure 4-36.

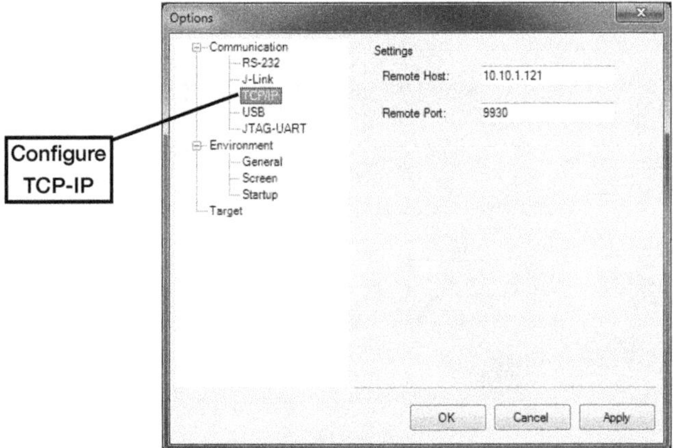

Figure 4-36 **μC/Probe's TCP/IP options**

The Remote Host field is the IP address of the target board. According to Figure 4-33 the target's IP address is 10.10.1.121. (it will be different on your network). Make sure not to modify the Remote Port (9930) as it is the port used for the μC/Probe UDP server on the target board. Click on the OK button at the bottom.

Now go back to the 'Main Menu' and open the **uC-TCPIP-V2-Ex3-Probe.wsp** workspace found in the following directory:

```
$\Micrium\Software\EvalBoards\Renesas\YRDKRX62N\GNURX-e2studio\
uC-TCP-IP-Book-Ex-Obj\uC-TCP-IP-Ex3
```

The µC/Probe screen should appear as the one shown in Figure 4-37.

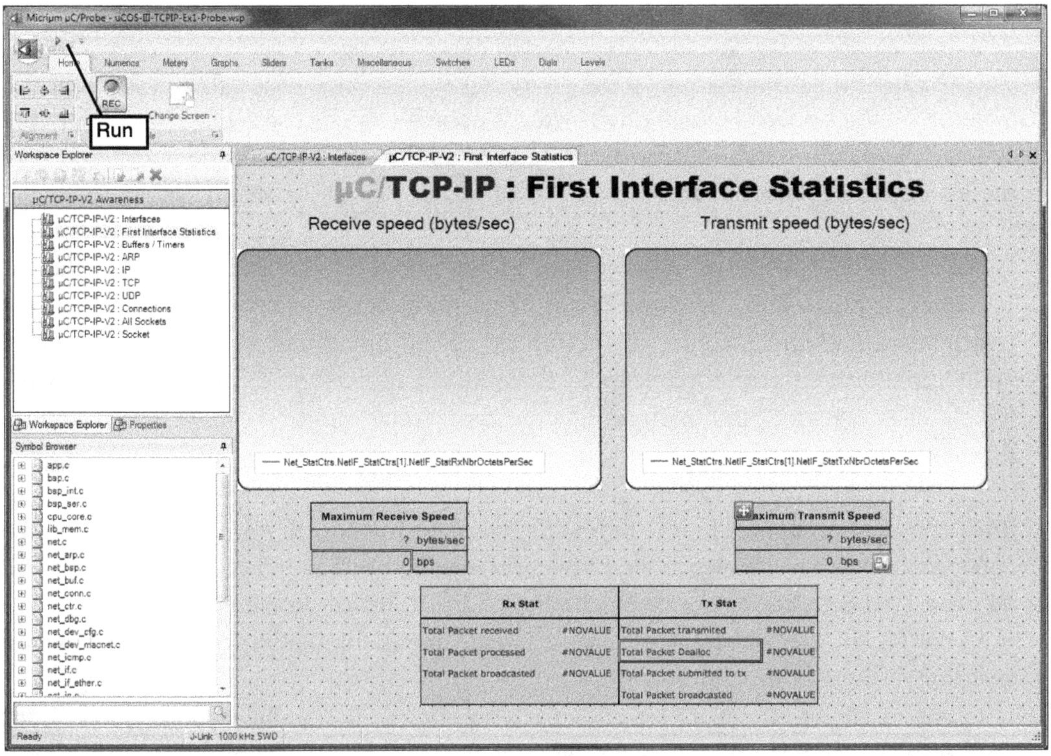

Figure 4-37 **µC/Probe Example #1 Edit Mode Screen**

The same screens in Example #1 are used for this example. The only difference is that with a TCP/IP connection, the refresh rate is higher which can be useful depending on the type of monitoring used.

When measuring the throughput of an Ethernet interface, note that when using TCP/IP as the interface for µC/Probe, that µC/Probe communication is included in the measurement. It may distort the result, but it can also create traffic on the interface, helping to visualize what is happening on the target board.

4-7 SUMMARY

There are several interesting things to notice.

1 The µC/TCP-IP IP parameters configuration can be done statically or dynamically. When the target board is configured with IP parameters corresponding to the network to which it is connected, it can participate in this network. This was demonstrated with the use of the PING command.

2 Wireshark can be used to monitor and decode the network traffic between the PC running Wireshark and the target board. If the traffic to be monitored is between the target board and another host, this traffic cannot be monitored with Wireshark unless an Ethernet hub is used. Another solution is to use a more sophisticated Ethernet switch which allows network traffic on an Ethernet port to be mirrored on another port used for monitoring.

3 With the on-board J-Link and the SWD interface, you can run Renesas e^2 Studio concurrently with µC/Probe, even if you are stepping through the code. In other words, you can stop the debugger at a breakpoint and µC/Probe will continue reading values from the target. This allows you to see changes in variables as they are updated when stepping through code.

4 The display screens in µC/Probe only show µC/OS-III variables and µC/TCP-IP variables. A µC/TCP-IP project implements three tasks. It is possible to view these task attributes using µC/Probe. However, µC/Probe allows you to “see” any variable in the target as long as the variable is declared global or static. In fact, it is fairly easy to add the application task to the task list.

5 Variables are updated on the µC/Probe data screen as quickly as the interface permits. The J-Link interface should update variables at about 300 or so symbols per second. If µC/Probe uses the serial port (RS-232C) instead, updates should be approximately twice as fast. With TCP/IP, we’ve seen updates easily exceeding 10,000 symbols/second. With RS-232C and TCP/IP, however, you will need to add target resident code and µC/Probe would only be able to update the display when the target is running.

The on-board J-Link and the debugger make it easy to download the application to the target and Flash the RX62N.

This chapter only covered the IP configuration and basic setup for a target board. What is very important in embedding a TCP/IP stack is the performance achieved. This step involves the configuration of the TCP/IP stack network buffers. In the case of DMA support by the network device driver, it also involves the configuration of the descriptors. Finally, the configuration of the TCP transmit and receive window size must be analyzed. This is the topic of the next chapter.

Chapter

5

μC/TCP-IP Performance Examples

In this chapter, we learn how to obtain performance measurements for your system using μC/IPerf, a simple command line network testing tool to measure network performance. UDP and TCP tests are described and performance results are compared for different system configurations.

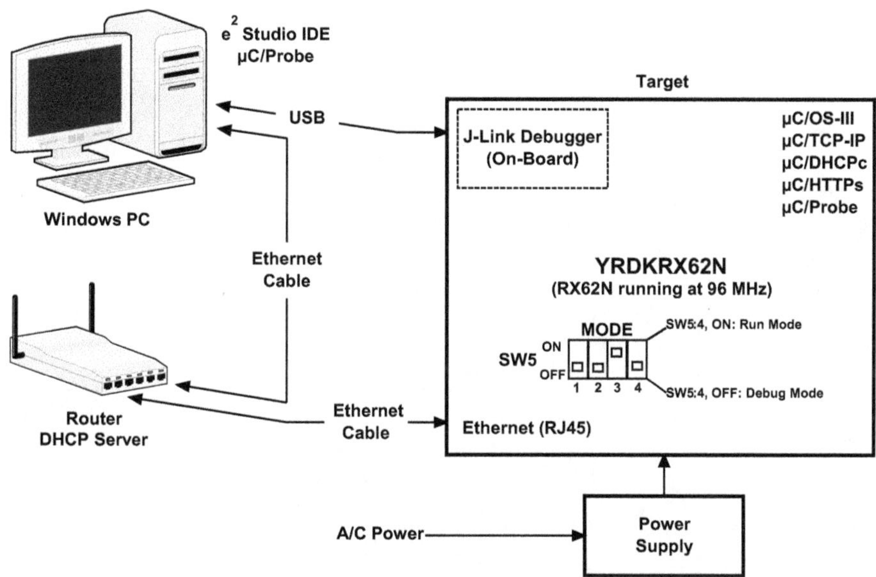

Figure 5-1 **Equipment configuration for Example #4**

This project uses IPerf for TCP and UDP performance benchmarking. The μC/IPerf test environment is illustrated in Figure 5-1. You can replace the Ethernet router with a cross-over cable — an Ethernet cable with the TX and RX wires crossed so that two devices have a face-to-face connection without the use of a hub or switch. This type of cable is useful for troubleshooting, but it must be used carefully as it may not work with certain Ethernet switches. More recent computers and Ethernet switches automatically sense the TX and RX wires. With this type of equipment, you can use any Ethernet cable to connect two devices.

5-1 µC/TCP-IP EXAMPLE #4

The same Renesas e² Studio workspace as the one used for section 4-1 "µC/TCP-IP Example #1" on page 841, is used:

```
$\Micrium\Software\EvalBoards\Renesas\YRDKRX62N\
GNURX-e2studio\uC-TCP-IP-Book-Ex-Obj
```

Click on the uC-TCP-IP-Ex4 item in the project explorer tree to select the example #4. Figure 5-2 shows the project explorer. The groups are the same as for Example #1 with the addition of the uC-IPerf group.

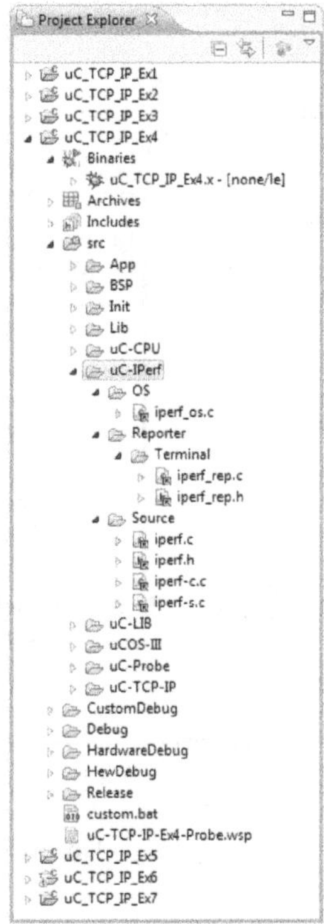

Figure 5-2 **Additional group for uC-TCP-IP-Ex4 Expanded Project**

The uC-IPerf group contains the header files and µC/IPerf source code. These files are needed as some of the application code requires definitions and declarations found in the files.

5-1-1 HOW THE EXAMPLE PROJECT WORKS

As with most C programs, code execution starts at **main()**. The code from **main()** in this example is identical to the examples in previous chapters. The use of µC/IPerf in this example modifies **AppTaskStart()** which is shown in Listing 5-1.

```
static  void  AppTaskStart (void *p_arg)                                                (1)
{
    OS_ERR     err;
#if (APP_CFG_TCPIP_MODULE_EN > 0u)
    NET_ERR    net_err;
#endif
    IPERF_ERR err_iperf;


   (void)&p_arg;

    BSP_Init();                         /* Initialize BSP functions                        */   (2)
    CPU_Init();                         /* Initialize the uC/CPU services                  */   (3)
    OS_CPU_TickInit();                  /* Init uC/OS periodic time src (SysTick).         */   (4)

#if (OS_CFG_STAT_TASK_EN > 0u)
    OSStatTaskCPUUsageInit(&err);       /* Compute CPU capacity with no task running       */   (5)
#endif
                                        /* Initialize serial port.                         */   (6)
    BSP_Ser_Init(APP_CFG_SERIAL_BAUDRATE);
    Mem_Init();                         /* Initialize mem mgmt module, required for TCP-IP. */   (8)

    BSP_GraphLCD_Init();                /* Initialize the graphic LCD.                     */   (9)
    AppGraphLCD_Hdr();

#if (APP_CFG_TCPIP_MODULE_EN > 0u)
    AppTCPIP_Init(&net_err);            /* Initialize uC/TCP-IP & associated applications.  */  (10)
#endif

    IPerf_Init(&err_iperf);             /* Initialize uC/IPerf modules.                    */  (11)
```

```
/* Create the Terminal I/O task.                                   */    (12)
    OSTaskCreate((OS_TCB       *)&AppTaskTerminalTCB,
                 (CPU_CHAR     *) "Terminal",
                 (OS_TASK_PTR  ) AppTaskTerminal,
                 (void         *) 0,
                 (OS_PRIO       ) APP_CFG_TASK_TERMINAL_PRIO,
                 (CPU_STK      *)&AppTaskTerminalStk[0],
                 (CPU_STK_SIZE)(APP_TASK_TERMINAL_STK_SIZE / 10u),
                 (CPU_STK_SIZE) APP_TASK_TERMINAL_STK_SIZE,
                 (OS_MSG_QTY   ) 0u,
                 (OS_TICK       ) 0u,
                 (void         *) 0,
                 (OS_OPT        )(OS_OPT_TASK_STK_CHK | OS_OPT_TASK_STK_CLR),
                 (OS_ERR       *)&err);

#ifdef CPU_CFG_INT_DIS_MEAS_EN
    CPU_IntDisMeasMaxCurReset();                                                (13)
#endif

    AppTCPIP_Cfg = DEF_TRUE;

    OSTaskDel(&AppTaskStartTCB,    /* Delete task because its work is complete    */    (14)
              &err);

    while (DEF_ON) {
        ;                          /* Should not get here!                         */
    }
}
```

Listing 5-1 **AppTaskStart()**

Interrupts are disabled in **main()**. µC/OS-III and µC/OS-II always start a task with interrupts enabled. When the first task executes, interrupts are enabled from that point on.

Steps 1 to 9 are identical to the code found in Example #1 for **AppTaskStart()**.

L5-1(10) **IPerf_Init()** initializes µC/IPerf modules.

The remaining steps are identical to the code found in Example #1 for **AppTaskStart()**.

AppTaskStart() calls the **AppTCPIP_Init()** to initialize and start the TCP/IP stack. This function is identical to the same function in example #1 and #3. See Chapter 4, “” on page 852.

```
static  void  AppTaskTerminal (void  *p_arg)
{
    CPU_CHAR        cmd_str[TASK_TERMINAL_CMD_STR_MAX_LEN];
    CPU_INT16S      cmp_str;
    CPU_SIZE_T      cmd_len;
    IPERF_TEST_ID   test_id_iperf;
    IPERF_ERR       err_iperf;

    APP_TRACE_INFO(("\n\rTerminal I/O\n\r\n\r"));                                    (1)

    while (DEF_ON) {
        APP_TRACE(("\n\r>  "));

        BSP_Ser_RdStr((CPU_CHAR *)&cmd_str[0],                                         (2)
                      (CPU_INT16U) TASK_TERMINAL_CMD_STR_MAX_LEN);

        cmp_str = Str_Cmp_N((CPU_CHAR *)&cmd_str[0],                                   (3)
                            (CPU_CHAR *) IPERF_STR_CMD,
                            (CPU_SIZE_T) IPERF_STR_CMD_LEN);

        cmd_len = Str_Len(&cmd_str[0]);
        if (cmp_str == 0) {                                                            (4)
            APP_TRACE_INFO(("\n\r\n\r"));

            test_id_iperf = IPerf_Start((CPU_CHAR        *)&cmd_str[0],                (5)
                                        (IPERF_OUT_FNCT   )&AppOutputFnct,
                                        (IPERF_OUT_PARAM *) 0,
                                        (IPERF_ERR       *)&err_iperf);

            if (err_iperf == IPERF_ERR_NONE) {                                         (6)
                IPerf_Reporter((IPERF_TEST_ID    ) test_id_iperf,
                               (IPERF_OUT_FNCT   )&AppOutputFnct,
                               (IPERF_OUT_PARAM *) 0);
                APP_TRACE_INFO(("\n\r"));
            }
        } else if (cmd_len > 1u) {
            APP_TRACE_INFO(("Command is not recognized."));
        }
    }
}
```

Listing 5-2 **AppTaskTerminal()**

L5-2(1) When this application runs, the terminal emulation session lets the user know it is ready to accept IPerf commands by displaying its prompt preceded by the words “Terminal I/O”.

L5-2(2) Using the serial port functions available in the BSP, the application checks if a command was received. The application will loop until a command is received.

L5-2(3) A command was entered. This line parses the command to verify that IPerf was invoked by checking the first word of the command.

L5-2(4) If the command entered is an IPerf command it will be executed otherwise an error message is displayed.

L5-2(5) **IPerf_Start()** checks the command-line parameters. The **AppOutputFnct** is used to report any error in the parameters. When the parameters are valid, **IPERF_ERR takes the IPERF_ERR_NONE** value. When all parameters are correct, the test is executed by the IPerf task created and initialized in **AppTaskStart()**.

L5-2(6) **IPerf_Reporter()** loops until the test is completed. This function outputs the test interim results every second and the test summary results once the test has completed, using the same **AppOutputFnct** function. It then exits. The **IPerf_Reporter()** function in this example uses the target board and uses the serial port. It could be replaced by a function that would use a web server or a Telnet server if that would be more appropriate to the user.

5-1-2 RUNNING THE APPLICATION

For the first IPerf example, the PC is configured as a client and the target board under test as a server.

Start a terminal emulation session with Tera Term PRO or the terminal program of your choice and configure an RS-232 connection at 38400 8-N-1.

Select and right click the item in the Project Explorer tree labeled as uC-TCP-IP-Ex4 in order to build the project. Just like previous examples, selecting the new file named uC-TCP-IP-Ex4.x under the Binaries folder and clicking on the Debug button downloads the code into the RX62N flash memory and starts a debug session.

Click F8 or the Resume button in the debug tool bar to start the application.

The example is configured to setup the IP address in static mode, in order to minimize the data footprint and in turn maximize performance. The LCD display onboard the YRDKRX62N should look like the one illustrated in Figure 5-3 while the firmware application configures the IP address:

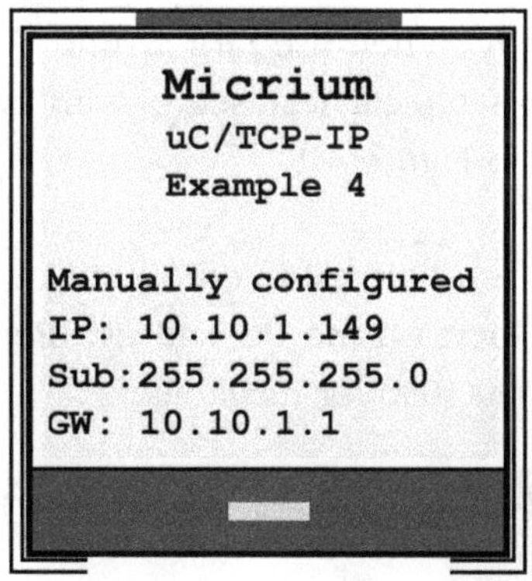

Figure 5-3 **Example #4 LCD screen: Static IP address**

Now that the project is running, the next step is to use the application.

The Terminal I/O window shown in Figure 5-4 will be used to control µC/IPerf running on the target board.

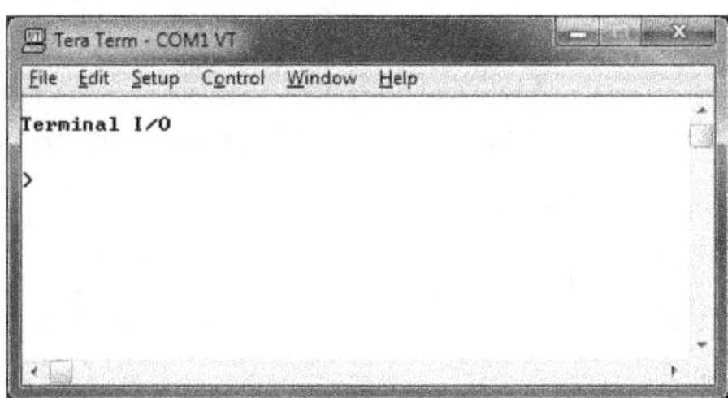

Figure 5-4 **µC/IPerf Command Prompt**

5-1-3 IPERF

This project implements IPerf. IPerf is an unbiased benchmarking tool for comparison of wired and wireless networking performances. With IPerf, a user can create TCP and UDP data streams and measure the throughput of a network for these streams. IPerf has client and server functionality.

The IPerf test engine can measure the throughput between two hosts, either uni-directionally or bi-directionally. When used for testing TCP capacity, IPerf measures the throughput of the payload. In a typical test setup with two hosts, one of them is the embedded system under test as in Figure 5-1.

Typically, an IPerf report contains a time stamped output of the amount of data transferred and the throughput measured. Jperf on the PC and µC/IPerf on the embedded target use 1024*1024 for megabytes and 1000*1000 for megabits.

The µC/IPerf source code, is also an excellent example of how to write a client and/or a server application for µC/TCP-IP.

In any IPerf test, it is always recommended to start the server first. This way, the server "waits" for the connection request from the client. Otherwise, the client will be looking for a server and if none is present, it will abort. To avoid having the IPerf client to abort, start the server first.

5-1-4 IPERF ON THE PC

The IPerf PC implementation in this example project uses a graphical user interface (GUI) front end called Jperf. This tool is part of the download package described in section 3-2 "Software" on page 822.

Start the Jperf utility on the PC. When Jperf was installed, it created an entry in the Windows Start menu and a desktop shortcut. Launch Jperf either way. Look for a shortcut similar to the one in the figure below.

Figure 5-5 **Jperf desktop shortcut**

Launching Jperf opens a window named "Jperf Measurement Tool".

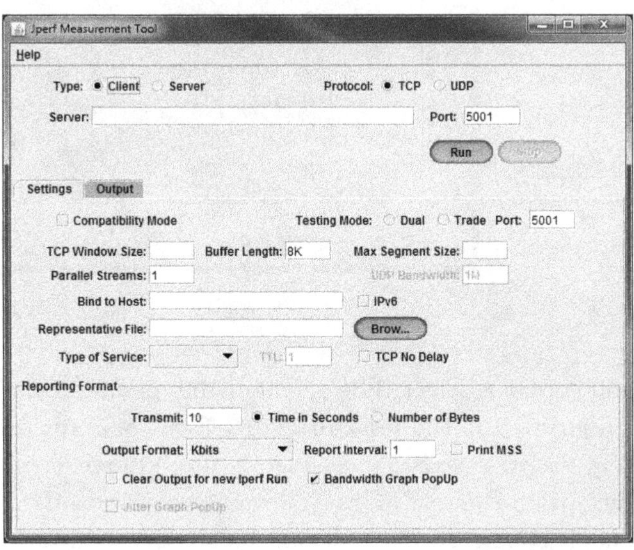

Figure 5-6 **Jperf on PC in Client mode (default)**

Jperf opens in client mode with the radio button already selected. The default transport protocol is TCP. Port number 5001 is the default port for the connection.

5

The best documentation for IPerf is the user manual included in the IPerf install script located at: **`C:\Program Files\iperf-2.0.2\doc\iperf-2.0.2\index.html`**

When performing a simple test with the default parameter settings, one item is missing: the IP address for the IPerf server. The IP address of the target board is 10.10.1.149 as shown in the LCD display (unless it was modified to match your environment). Enter this address in the Server input box and click on the "Run" button. As this test is a Client test from the PC, the server must be running on the target board before IPerf on the PC can be started in Client mode.

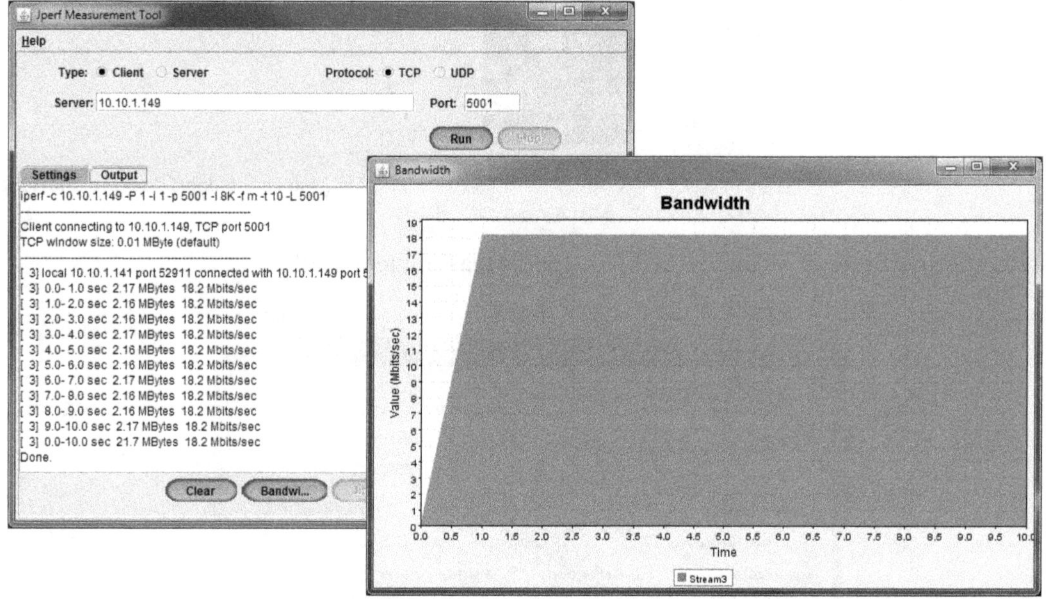

Figure 5-7 **Jperf sample test results**

The Bandwidth Graph PopUp is selected by default in the Jperf Measurement Tool window. This is the graphic in Figure 5-7. The test in Figure 5-7 was performed with all the default settings. One of them that is possible to change is the "Output format". The value that makes sense for this parameter is "Mbits" (Megabits per second). As Ethernet is the ubiquitous LAN technology and as Ethernet link bandwidth is always reported in Mbits, configuring the output with the same scale gives a measurement of the tested interface performance versus line speed.

In the following sections, multiple tests will be presented using this tool. All possible network configurations can be tested: TCP or UDP tests in client-to-server or server-to-client mode, using different parameter settings. For your reference, all the screen captures were taken with IP addresses configured as follows:

- PC Computer: 10.10.1.141
- Embedded Target: 10.10.1.149

5-1-5 µC/IPERF ON THE TARGET BOARD

The project code presented in section 5-1-1 "How the Example Project Works" on page 897 implements IPerf. It is packaged as a µC/TCP-IP add-on called µC/IPerf. The µC/IPerf I/O uses the serial interface. It is the same interface that was used in Example #2 (section 4-2 "µC/TCP-IP Example #2" on page 876). Configure a terminal emulation session as specified in Example #2 and connect it to the YRDKRX62N board RS-232 interface. As soon as the code runs on the target, the terminal window will look like Figure 5-4.

µC/IPerf documentation is part of the µC/IPerf package that was downloaded with the software and tools package for this book. Look for **IPerf_manual.pdf** in the **\Micrium\Software\uC-IPerf\Doc** directory.

The input to µC/IPerf is done in a command line using the Terminal I/O. To view all the µC/IPerf options, enter the following command: **iperf -h**.

```
Tera Term - COM1 VT
File  Edit  Setup  Control  Window  Help

Terminal I/O

>  iperf -h

Server specific:
  -s                  Run in server mode
  -D                  Run the server as persistent
  -w                  Rx TCP window size (IGNORED with UDP option)

Client specific:
  -c                  Run in client mode
  -t                  Time in seconds to transmit for (default 10 secs)
  -n                  Number of bytes to transmit (instead of -t)
<host>                IP address of <host> to connect to

Options:
  -f     [kmKM]       Format to report: kbits, mbits, Kbytes, MBytes
  -l                  Length of buffer to read or write (default 8 KB)
  -p                  Server port to listen on/connect to
  -u                  Use UDP rather than TCP
  -i                  MILISECONDS between periodic bandwidth report

Miscellaneous:
  -h                  Print this message
  -v                  Print version information

>
```

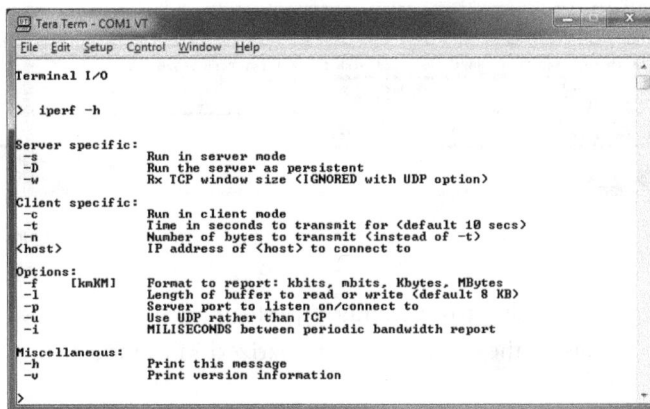

Figure 5-8 **µC/IPerf options**

From the list of command options, let's launch µC/IPerf in server mode using default settings. The command is **iperf -s**. The TCP Receive Window size is 8760 bytes (or 6 MSS – 6 times 1460) and the buffer size is 8192 bytes. The server is now waiting for a connection request from a client (Figure 5-9).

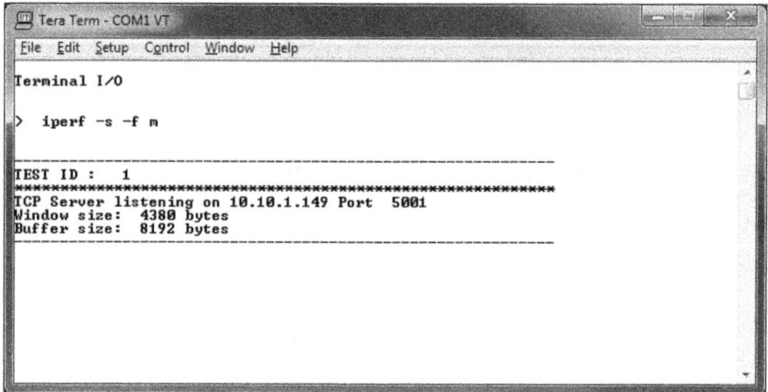

Figure 5-9 **µC/IPerf in server mode**

Starting the equivalent client on the PC executes the test. The default test duration is ten seconds with an automatic interim report every second. The test produces the results shown in Figure 5-10.

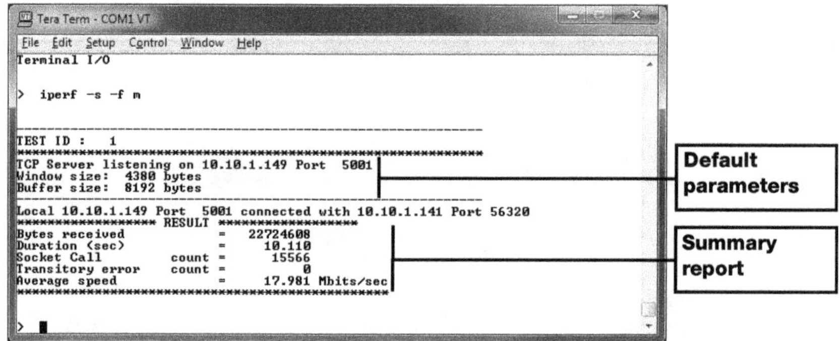

Figure 5-10 **µC/IPerf results**

µC/IPerf is used extensively to generate performance data with three different configurations. The results of these tests are summarized in the following sections.

5-2 MONITORING VARIABLES WITH μC/PROBE

There are ten μC/Probe screens provided by Micrium to monitor μC/TCP-IP variables. In this example, μC/Probe uses the J-Link interface to the YRDKRX62N board. The μC/Probe screens provided are:

Screen title	Description
Interface	This screen provides the basic information for each interface configured. It has two input fields. The first input field is used to select the interface index within μC/TCP-IP. Remember that interface index 0 is the loopback interface. It can only be displayed if it was configured. The second input field is used to select the IP address index. A network interface can be assigned more than one IP address.
First interface statistics	To retrieve the statistics for one interface, the interface index must be predefined in μC/Probe. This is why Micrium has provided this screen. It is very useful as most systems have a single interface. And, at the same time, it could be used as a template to build screens for additional interfaces. This screen provides the transmit and receive bytes per second as computed by the network interface driver. This screen is updated as frequently as μC/Probe can. Remember that μC/Probe is limited by the interface speed connecting μC/Probe to the target board.
ARP	This screen provides basic information about ARP and the ARP table.
Buffers/Timers	This screen summarizes the use of buffers and timers. The number of buffers and timers configured is displayed as the number of buffers and timers currently used and the maximum number used during program execution.
IP	This screen provides the summary statistics for the number of IP packets transmitted and received plus the number of events per IP error type.
UDP	This screen provides the summary statistics for the number of UDP datagrams transmitted and received.
TCP	This screen provides the summary statistics for the number of TCP segments transmitted and received.
Connections	Connection is an internal μC/TCP-IP data structure used to retain the information about a host's participation in a connection. This screen provides the summary usage statistics for this μC/TCP-IP internal resource.
All sockets	This screen summarizes the sockets defined and the information for the active sockets is displayed. For more detailed information on a specific socket, the Socket screen is used.
Socket	This screen provides the information relative to a specific socket ID. The input field on this screen allows to select the socket ID.

Launch µC/Probe as explained in Chapter 4, "Monitoring Variables Using µC/Probe" on page 869. Go to the µC/Probe 'Main Menu' and open the **`uC-TCP-IP-Ex4-Probe.wsp`** workspace found in the following directory:

```
$\Micrium\Software\EvalBoards\Renesas\YRDKRX62N\GNURX-e2studio\
uC-TCP-IP-Book-Ex-Obj
```

Click on the µC/Probe "Run" button and select the screen you want to view. The following figures are examples of each of the µC/TCP-IP screen provided.

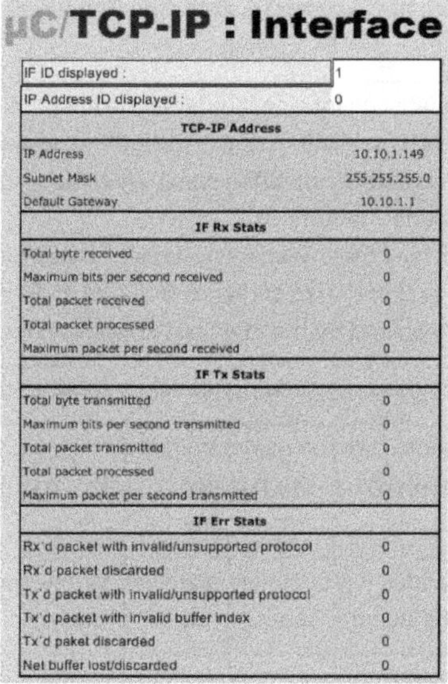

Figure 5-11 **µC/Probe Interface screen**

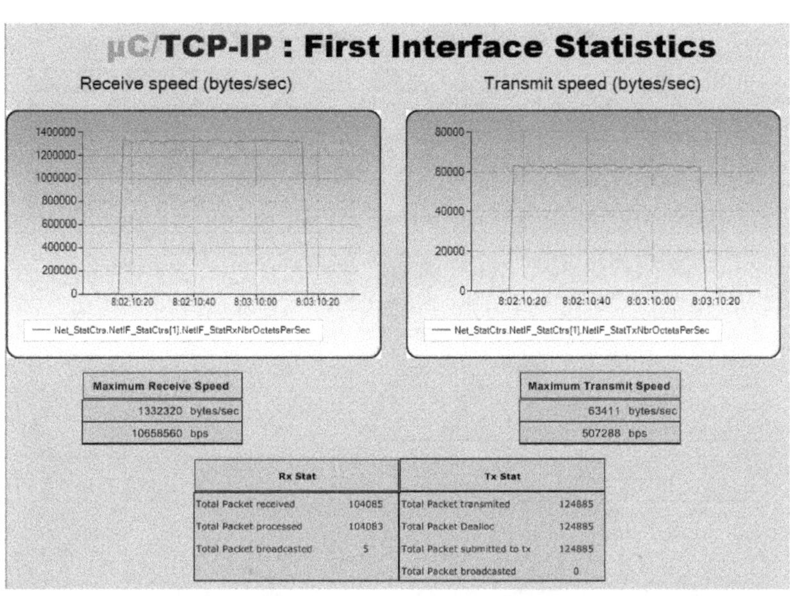

Figure 5-12 **µC/Probe First Interface Statistics screen**

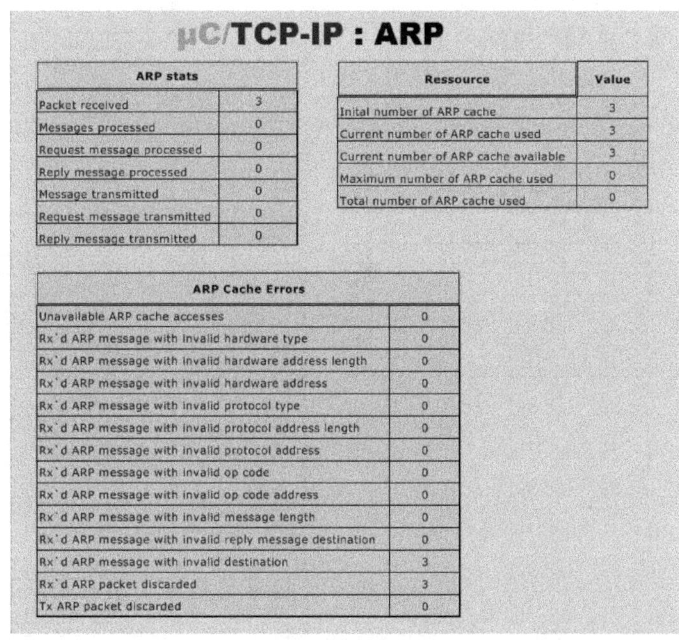

µC/TCP-IP : ARP
ARP stats
Packet received 3
Messages processed 0
Request message processed 0
Reply message processed 0
Message transmitted 0
Request message transmitted 0
Reply message transmitted 0
Ressource | Value
Inital number of ARP cache 3
Current number of ARP cache used 3
Current number of ARP cache available 3
Maximum number of ARP cache used 0
Total number of ARP cache used 0
ARP Cache Errors
Unavailable ARP cache accesses 0
Rx'd ARP message with invalid hardware type 0
Rx'd ARP message with invalid hardware address length 0
Rx'd ARP message with invalid hardware address 0
Rx'd ARP message with invalid protocol type 0
Rx'd ARP message with invalid protocol address length 0
Rx'd ARP message with invalid protocol address 0
Rx'd ARP message with invalid op code 0
Rx'd ARP message with invalid op code address 0
Rx'd ARP message with invalid message length 0
Rx'd ARP message with invalid reply message destination 0
Rx'd ARP message with invalid destination 3
Rx'd ARP packet discarded 3
Tx ARP packet discarded 0

Figure 5-13 **µC/Probe ARP screen**

µC/TCP-IP-V2 : Buffers / Timers

Ressource Item	Value
Initial number of receive buffer	12
Current number of receive buffer used	6
Current number of receive buffer available	6
Maximum number of receive buffer used	7
Total number of receive buffer used	48
Initial number of transmit small buffer	4
Current number of transmit small buffer used	0
Current number of transmit small buffer available	4
Maximum number of transmit small buffer used	0
Total number of transmit small buffer used	0
Initial number of transmit large buffer	4
Current number of transmit large buffer used	0
Current number of transmit large buffer available	4
Maximum number of transmit large buffer used	0
Total number of transmit large buffer used	0

Timer ressources	Value
Initial number of timer	30
Current number of timer used	3
Current number of timer available	30
Maximum number of timer used	3
Total number of timer used	2252

Timer Errors	
Unavailable net timer accesse	0

Buffers errors	
Unavailable net buffer accesse	0
Invalid net buffer type accesse	0
Net buffer with invalid size	0
Net buffer with invalid length	0

Figure 5-14 **µC/Probe Buffers/Timers screen**

µC/TCP-IP : IP

Rx IP	
Number of received IP datagram	52
Number of received IP datagram delivered to supported protocol	0
Number of received IP datagram from localhost	0
Number of received IP datagram via broadcast	52
Number of received IP fragment	0
Number of received IP fragment reassembled	0

Tx IP	
Number of transmitted IP datagram	0
Number of transmitted IP datagram to this host	0
Number of transmitted IP datagram to local host	0
Number of transmitted IP datagram to local link address	0
Number of transmitted IP datagram to local net	0
Number of transmitted IP datagram to remote net	0
Number of transmitted IP datagram broadcast to destination	0

IP errors	
Null IP pointer access	0
Invalid IP host address attempt	0
Invalid IP default gateway address attempt	0
In use IP host address attempt	0
Invalid IP address state access	0
Invalid IP address not found access	0
Invalid IP address size access	0
Invalid IP address table empty access	0
Invalid IP address table full access	0
Rx'd IP datagram with invalid IP version	0
Rx'd IP datagram with invalid header length	0
Rx'd IP datagram with invalid/inconsistent total length	0
Rx'd IP datagram with invalid flag	0
Rx'd IP datagram with invalid fragmentation	0
Rx'd IP datagram with invalid/unsupported protocol	0
Rx'd IP datagram with invalid check sum	0
Rx'd IP datagram with invalid source address	0
Rx'd IP datagram with unknown/invalid option	0
Rx'd IP datagram with no options buffers available	0
Rx'd IP datagram with write options buffer error	0
Rx'd IP datagram not for this IP destination	0
Rx'd IP datagram illegally broadcast to this destination	0
Rx'd IP fragment with invalid size	0
Rx'd IP fragments discarded	0
Rx'd IP fragmented datagrams discarded	0
Rx'd IP fragmented datagrams timed out	0
Rx'd IP packet with invalid/unsupported protocol	0
Rx'd IP packet discarded	52
Tx packet with invalid/unsupported protocol	0
Tx packet with invalid option type	0
Tx datagram with invalid destination address	0
Tx packet discarded	0

Figure 5-15 **µC/Probe IP screen**

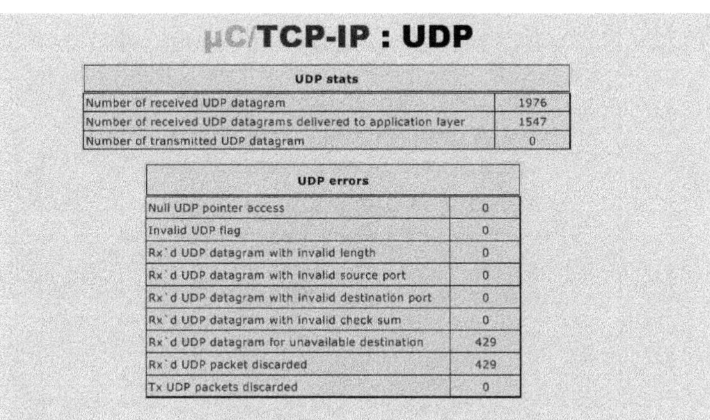

µC/TCP-IP : UDP

UDP stats	
Number of received UDP datagram	1976
Number of received UDP datagrams delivered to application layer	1547
Number of transmitted UDP datagram	0

UDP errors	
Null UDP pointer access	0
Invalid UDP flag	0
Rx`d UDP datagram with invalid length	0
Rx`d UDP datagram with invalid source port	0
Rx`d UDP datagram with invalid destination port	0
Rx`d UDP datagram with invalid check sum	0
Rx`d UDP datagram for unavailable destination	429
Rx`d UDP packet discarded	429
Tx UDP packets discarded	0

Figure 5-16 **µC/Probe UDP screen**

µC/TCP-IP : TCP

TCP Ressources	Value
Initial number of TCP connection	5
Current number of TCP connections used	2
Current number of TCP connections available	3
Maximum number of TCP connections used	2
Total number of TCP connection used	2

Connections Errors	
Unavailable net connection access	0
Unused net connection access	0
Net connections close	0
Invalid net connection ID access	0
Net connection with invalid address length	0
Net connection with address already in use	0
Net connection with invalid connection family	0
Net connection with invalid protocol index	0

TCP Rx Stats	
Number of received TCP segment	25865
Number of received TCP segments delivered to application layer	25867
TCP Tx Stats	
Number of transmitted TCP segment	31040
Number of transmitted TCP connection sync. segment	1
Number of transmitted TCP connection close segment	0
Number of transmitted TCP connection ack. segment	31045
Number of transmitted TCP connection reset segment	0
Number of transmitted TCP connection probe segment	0
Number of transmitted TCP connection transmit queue segment	0
Number of transmitted TCP connection re-transmit queue segment	0

Figure 5-17 **µC/Probe TCP screen**

µC/TCP-IP : Connections

Connections Ressources	Value
Initial number of connection	10
Current number of connection used	2
Current number of connection available	8
Maximum number of connection used	2
Total number of connection used	4

Connections errors	
Unavaillable net connection access	0
Unused net connection access	0
Net connection close	0
Invalid net connection ID access	0
Net connection with invalid address length	0
Net connection with address already in use	0
Net connection with invalid connection family	0
Net connection with invalid protocol index	0

Figure 5-18 **µC/Probe Connections screen**

µC/TCP-IP : Sockets

ID	Socket Type	Socket State	Conn ID	TCP ID	Local Addr	Local Port	Remote Addr	Remote Port	TCP State
0	NONE	FREE	----	----	----	----	----	----	----
1	NONE	FREE	----	----	----	----	----	----	----
2	NONE	FREE	----	----	----	----	----	----	----
3	STREAM	CONN	8	3	10.10.1.149	5001	10.10.1.141	2775	NONE
4	STREAM	LISTEN	9	4	0.0.0.0	5001	0.0.0.0	0	NONE
----	----	----	----	----	----	----	----	----	----
----	----	----	----	----	----	----	----	----	----
----	----	----	----	----	----	----	----	----	----
----	----	----	----	----	----	----	----	----	----
----	----	----	----	----	----	----	----	----	----

Ressource	Value
Inital number of socket	5
Current number of socket used	2
Current number of socket available	3
Maximum number of socket used	2
Total number of socket used	0

Sockets Errors	
Null socket pointer access	0
Null socket size access	0
Unavailable socket access	0
Unused socket access	0
Fault sock close	0
Socket with invalid socket family	0
Socket with invalid socket protocol	0
Socket with invalid socket type	0
Socket with invalid socket ID access	0
Socket with invalid flag	0
Socket with invalid op	0
Socket with invalid state	0
Socket with invalid address	0
Socket with invalid address length	0
Socket with invalid address already in use	0
Socket with invalid port number	0
Socket with invalid connection already in use	0
Unavailable socket random port number access	0
Rx'd socket packets for unavailable destination	0
Rx'd socket packets discarded	16

Figure 5-19 **µC/Probe All Sockets screen**

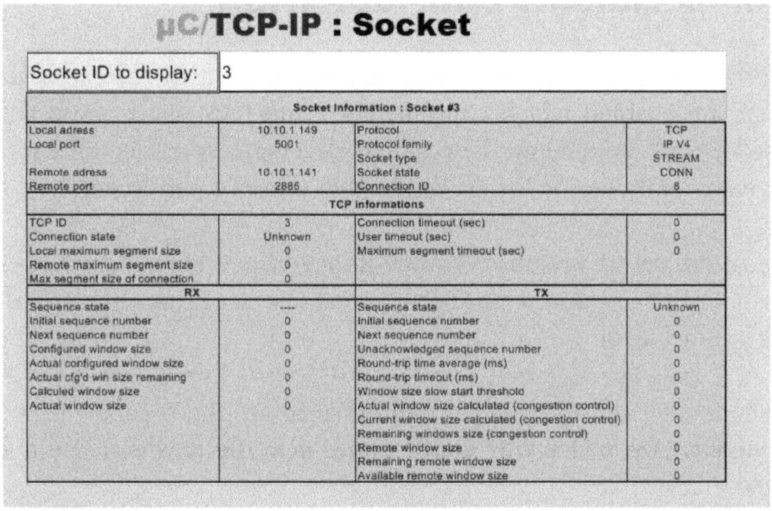

μC/TCP-IP : Socket

Socket ID to display:	3		
Socket Information : Socket #3			
Local adress	10.10.1.149	Protocol	TCP
Local port	5001	Protocol family	IP V4
		Socket type	STREAM
Remote adress	10.10.1.141	Socket state	CONN
Remote port	2885	Connection ID	8
TCP informations			
TCP ID	3	Connection timeout (sec)	0
Connection state	Unknown	User timeout (sec)	0
Local maximum segment size	0	Maximum segment timeout (sec)	0
Remote maximum segment size	0		
Max segment size of connection	0		
RX		**TX**	
Sequence state	----	Sequence state	Unknown
Initial sequence number	0	Initial sequence number	0
Next sequence number	0	Next sequence number	0
Configured window size	0	Unacknowledged sequence number	0
Actual configured window size	0	Round-trip time average (ms)	0
Actual cfg'd win size remaining	0	Round-trip timeout (ms)	0
Calculed window size	0	Window size slow start threshold	0
Actual window size	0	Actual window size calculated (congestion control)	0
		Current window size calculated (congestion control)	0
		Remaining windows size (congestion control)	0
		Remote window size	0
		Remaining remote window size	0
		Available remote window size	0

Figure 5-20 **μC/Probe Socket screen**

The μC/Probe socket data screen is based on a spreadsheet that uses many μC/TCP-IP variables to compute the information displayed in this screen. It is possible that this screen display operation is slow when other data screens are open. It is strongly recommended to close the other screens and keep only the socket screen open.

It is also possible that this μC/Probe data screen does not display correctly when the user clicks on the “Run” button. It is suggested to end this session by clicking on the μC/Probe “Stop” button and then select the “Run” button again. This operation may have to be done a few times before the complete table is populated and updated.

5-3 µC/TCP-IP LIBRARY CONFIGURATION

The µC/TCP-IP library provided with this book is provided for use with the examples. Multiple options are enabled which consume code and RAM space, especially the debug options. These options are mainly used in the development cycle. In a typical product configuration, many of these options are disabled to improve performance.

Because many of the debug options consume RAM space, it limits the number of network buffers that can be configured in the RX62N internal 69K RAM, once the application and all other modules are included.

The main configuration settings affecting performance are the number of buffers and the TCP receive window size which can not be larger than the maximum number of receive buffers available.

Three µC/TCP-IP configurations will be used to provide the reader with performance numbers for different TCP/IP stack configuration parameters. The description of the three configurations used in the following sections for the performance tests are:

Configuration	**Description**
#1	Optimized for Size: minimal configuration, very few resources used by the TCP/IP stack.
#2	Configuration for the examples in this book. Resources are allocated so that all the examples work well.
#3	Optimized for Speed: configuration considering all the resources available on the YRDKRX62N board are meant for the TCP/IP stack.

The μC/TCP-IP library produced for this book has the following parameter settings:

File	Parameter	Value
app_cfg.h	IPERF_CFG_ALIGN_BUF_EN	DEF_DISABLED
cpu_cfg.h	CPU_CFG_INT_DIS_MEAS_EN	DEF_ENABLED
	CPU_CFG_LEAD_ZEROS_ASM_PRESENT	DEF_ENABLED
os_cfg.h	OS_CFG_APP_HOOKS_EN	DEF_ENABLED
	OS_CFG_ARG_CHK_EN	DEF_ENABLED
	OS_CFG_CALLED_FROM_ISR_CHK_EN	DEF_ENABLED
	OS_CFG_DBG_EN	DEF_ENABLED
	OS_CFG_OBJ_TYPE_CHK_EN	DEF_ENABLED
	OS_CFG_SCHED_LOCK_TIME_MEAS_EN	DEF_ENABLED
net_cfg.h	NET_CFG_OPTIMIZE	NET_OPTIMIZE_SPD
	NET_CFG_OPTIMIZE_ASM_EN	DEF_ENABLED
	NET_DBG_CFG_INFO_EN	DEF_ENABLED
	NET_DBG_CFG_STATUS_EN	DEF_ENABLED
	NET_DBG_CFG_MEM_CLR_EN	DEF_ENABLED
	NET_DBG_CFG_TEST_EN	DEF_ENABLED
	NET_ERR_CFG_ARG_CHK_EXT_EN	DEF_ENABLED
	NET_ERR_CFG_ARG_CHK_DBG_EN	DEF_ENABLED
	NET_CTR_CFG_STAT_EN	DEF_ENABLED
	NET_CTR_CFG_ERR_EN	DEF_ENABLED
	NET_TCP_CFG_RX_WIN_SIZE_OCTET	3 * 1460
	NET_TCP_CFG_TX_WIN_SIZE_OCTET	3 * 1460

Table 5-1 **Configuration #2: Default**

In addition to the configuration parameters, the network device driver interface configuration also contributes to the system performance. The network device driver configuration is done in **net_dev_cfg.c** (see section 14-6-2 "Ethernet Device MAC Configuration" on page 313). The main parameters contributing to the performance and their values are given in the table below. The minimum number of DMA descriptors that can be defined is two.

Number of device's large receive buffers	12
Number of device's large transmit buffers	6
Number of device's small transmit buffers	4
Number of receive DMA descriptors	6
Number of transmit DMA descriptors	6

Table 5-2 **Configuration #2: Default**

The examples provided with this book use the library configuration described above. This default library is identified as Configuration #2. To provide the reader with an idea of what can be achieved with µC/TCP-IP in various hardware configurations, two additional µC/TCP-IP configurations were defined and used, however not provided with this book. UDP and TCP performance measurement results are provided in the respective following sections, using these three configurations.

The following are the definitions of the two additional configurations:

CONFIGURATION #1: OPTIMIZED FOR SIZE

File	Parameter	Value
app_cfg.h	IPERF_CFG_ALIGN_BUF_EN	DEF_DISABLED
cpu_cfg.h	CPU_CFG_INT_DIS_MEAS_EN	DEF_ENABLED
	CPU_CFG_LEAD_ZEROS_ASM_PRESENT	DEF_ENABLED
os_cfg.h	OS_CFG_APP_HOOKS_EN	DEF_ENABLED
	OS_CFG_ARG_CHK_EN	DEF_ENABLED
	OS_CFG_CALLED_FROM_ISR_CHK_EN	DEF_ENABLED
	OS_CFG_DBG_EN	DEF_ENABLED
	OS_CFG_OBJ_TYPE_CHK_EN	DEF_ENABLED
	OS_CFG_SCHED_LOCK_TIME_MEAS_EN	DEF_ENABLED
net_cfg.h	NET_CFG_OPTIMIZE	NET_OPTIMIZE_SIZE
	NET_CFG_OPTIMIZE_ASM_EN	DEF_ENABLED
	NET_DBG_CFG_INFO_EN	DEF_ENABLED
	NET_DBG_CFG_STATUS_EN	DEF_ENABLED
	NET_DBG_CFG_MEM_CLR_EN	DEF_ENABLED
	NET_DBG_CFG_TEST_EN	DEF_ENABLED
	NET_ERR_CFG_ARG_CHK_EXT_EN	DEF_ENABLED
	NET_ERR_CFG_ARG_CHK_DBG_EN	DEF_ENABLED
	NET_CTR_CFG_STAT_EN	DEF_ENABLED
	NET_CTR_CFG_ERR_EN	DEF_ENABLED
	NET_TCP_CFG_RX_WIN_SIZE_OCTET	1 * 1460
	NET_TCP_CFG_TX_WIN_SIZE_OCTET	1 * 1460

Number of device's large receive buffers	3
Number of device's large transmit buffers	1
Number of device's small transmit buffers	1
Number of receive DMA descriptors	2
Number of transmit DMA descriptors	1

Table 5-3 **Configuration #1: Optimized for Size**

CONFIGURATION #3: OPTIMIZED FOR SPEED

File	Parameter	Value
app_cfg.h	IPERF_CFG_ALIGN_BUF_EN	DEF_ENABLED
cpu_cfg.h	CPU_CFG_INT_DIS_MEAS_EN	DEF_DISABLED
	CPU_CFG_LEAD_ZEROS_ASM_PRESENT	DEF_ENABLED
os_cfg.h	OS_CFG_APP_HOOKS_EN	DEF_DISABLED
	OS_CFG_ARG_CHK_EN	DEF_DISABLED
	OS_CFG_CALLED_FROM_ISR_CHK_EN	DEF_DISABLED
	OS_CFG_DBG_EN	DEF_DISABLED
	OS_CFG_OBJ_TYPE_CHK_EN	DEF_DISABLED
	OS_CFG_SCHED_LOCK_TIME_MEAS_EN	DEF_DISABLED
net_cfg.h	NET_CFG_OPTIMIZE	NET_OPTIMIZE_SPD
	NET_CFG_OPTIMIZE_ASM_EN	DEF_ENABLED
	NET_DBG_CFG_INFO_EN	DEF_DISABLED
	NET_DBG_CFG_STATUS_EN	DEF_DISABLED
	NET_DBG_CFG_MEM_CLR_EN	DEF_DISABLED
	NET_DBG_CFG_TEST_EN	DEF_DISABLED
	NET_ERR_CFG_ARG_CHK_EXT_EN	DEF_DISABLED
	NET_ERR_CFG_ARG_CHK_DBG_EN	DEF_DISABLED
	NET_CTR_CFG_STAT_EN	DEF_DISABLED
	NET_CTR_CFG_ERR_EN	DEF_DISABLED
	NET_TCP_CFG_RX_WIN_SIZE_OCTET	5 * 1460
	NET_TCP_CFG_TX_WIN_SIZE_OCTET	8 * 1460

Number of device's large receive buffers	12
Number of device's large transmit buffers	8
Number of device's small transmit buffers	4
Number of receive DMA descriptors	6
Number of transmit DMA descriptors	8

Table 5-4 **Configuration #3: Optimized for Speed**

5-4 UDP PERFORMANCE

When used for testing UDP capacity, IPerf allows users to specify datagram size, and it provides results for datagram throughput and packet loss.

5-4-1 TARGET BOARD AS THE SERVER

With the target board as the server, the PC is the client. The client is set for a 3-second test. As for all tests, the output is set to the **-m** value (Mbits). Other parameters have default values. Here are the results with the µC/TCP-IP library available for the Example #4.

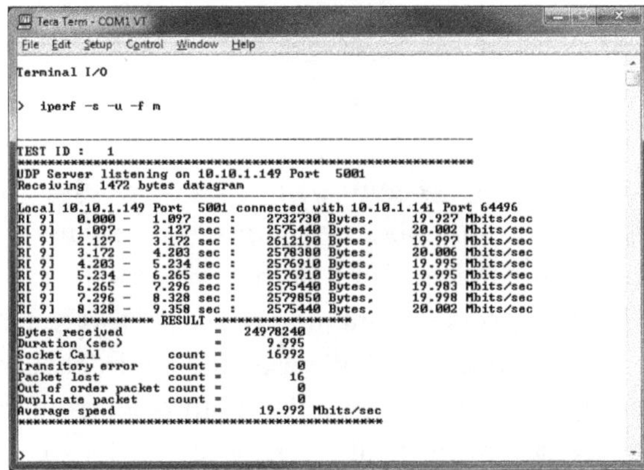

Figure 5-21 **Target board as the server**

The Client is configured to send 20 Megabits per second. This is set in the UDP Bandwidth input box. This number is chosen to make sure that the embedded target will not be able to receive all the UDP datagrams. The Client is also configured to not display the bandwidth graph and to clear the output for a new IPerf run. This is done by checking or unchecking the boxes at the bottom of the Settings window.

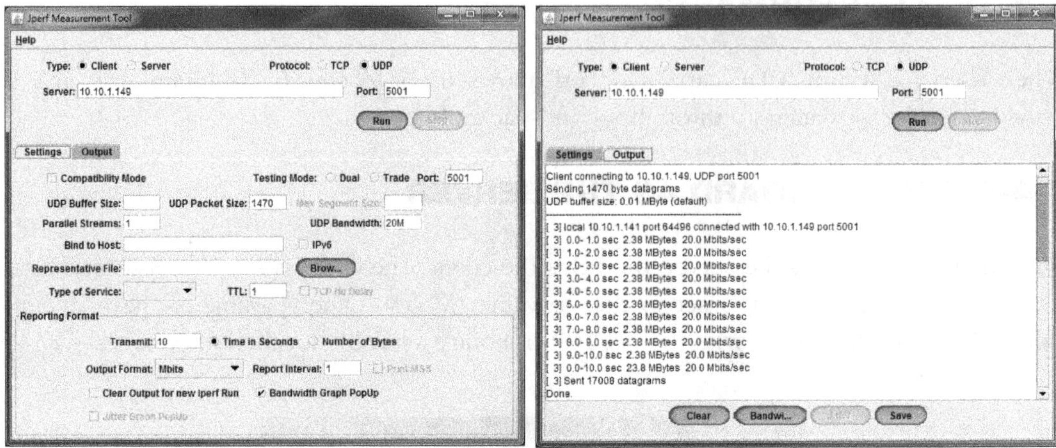

Figure 5-22 **PC as the client**

Comparing Figure 5-22 results to Figure 5-21 numbers, the Client is sending at approximately 20.0 Mbps while the embedded target is receiving at 19.992 Mpbs. Where have these UDP datagrams gone? Remember that the embedded target is a slower consumer compared to the faster PC producer. The missing datagrams were just not received by the embedded target. Because UDP does not have a guaranteed delivery, these datagrams are lost. The developer wanting to build an application with guaranteed delivery with UDP has to implement a control mechanism in its application code. This is the case, for example, with the Trivial File Transfer Protocol (TFTP).

5-4-2 TARGET BOARD AS THE CLIENT

Start the server first, which in this case is the PC at 10.10.1.111.

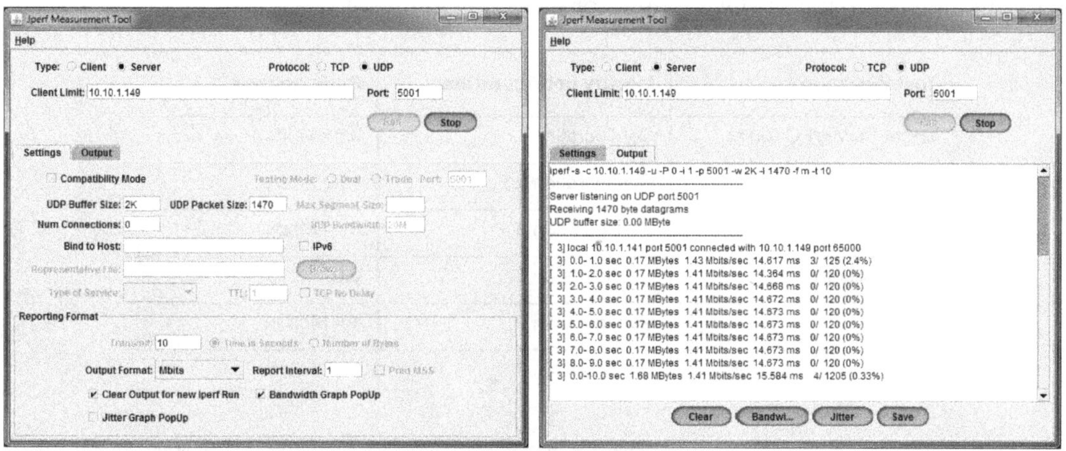

Figure 5-23 **PC as the server**

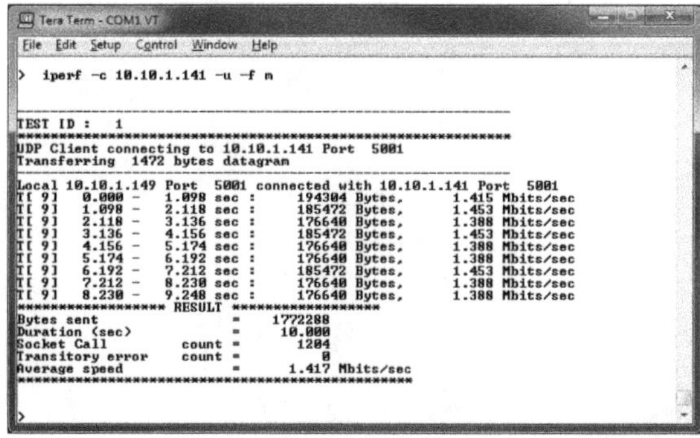

Figure 5-24 **Target board as the client**

Comparing Figure 5-23 results to Figure 5-24 numbers, the embedded target can transmit approximately 1.4 Mbps and it is clear that the PC can sustain the rate imposed by the embedded target.

5

5-4-3 UDP TESTS SUMMARY

The same Client/Server and Server/Client tests were performed using different µC/TCP-IP configurations. Three µC/TCP-IP configurations (see section 5-3 "µC/TCP-IP Library Configuration" on page 914) were used for the following results.

Test direction	Library configuration	Performance
Target Server/PC Client	Configuration 1	0.01 Mpbs
	Configuration 2	19.9 Mbps
	Configuration 3	31.4 Mbps
Target Client/PC Server	Configuration 1	0.01 Mbps
	Configuration 2	1.4 Mbps
	Configuration 3	11.2 Mbps

Table 5-5 **UDP performance with various TCP/IP stack configuration**

5-5 TCP PERFORMANCE

TCP performance measurements require the configuration of more parameters to achieve optimal performance. In the following tests, the configuration of the binary library delivered with this book is used. It is described as Configuration #2 in a previous section.

5-5-1 TARGET BOARD AS THE SERVER

Start the server before the client so that it can wait for a connection request from the client.

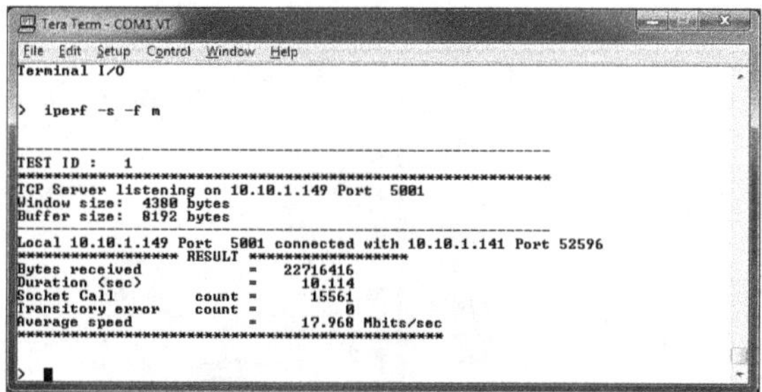

Figure 5-25 **Target board as the server**

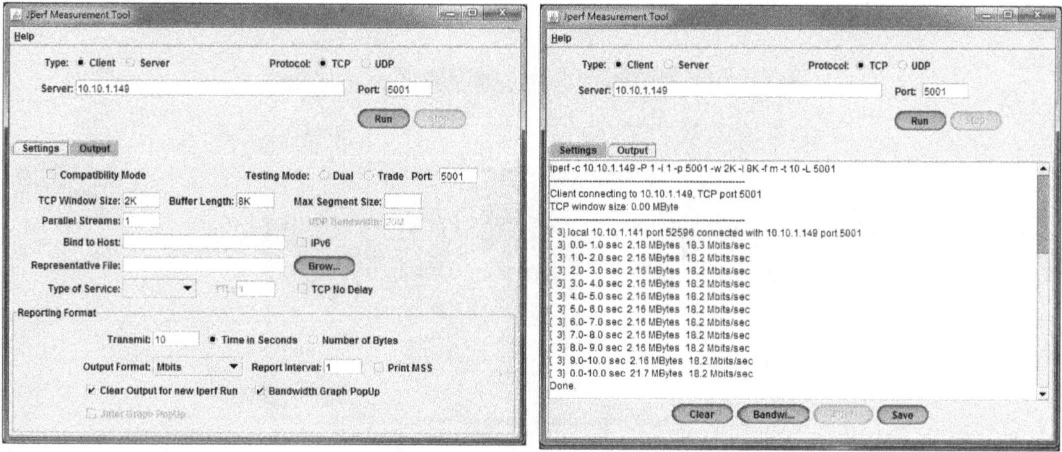

Figure 5-26 **PC as the client**

TCP performance numbers are similar in Figure 5-25 and Figure 5-26. This is no surprise as TCP implements guaranteed delivery and no data is lost in the process.

5

5-5-2 TARGET BOARD AS THE CLIENT

Start the server first, which in this case is the PC.

Note that IPerf on the PC can sometimes not react as expected. In this case, you may have to close the application or kill the process running even if the application is closed or even worst, reboot the computer.

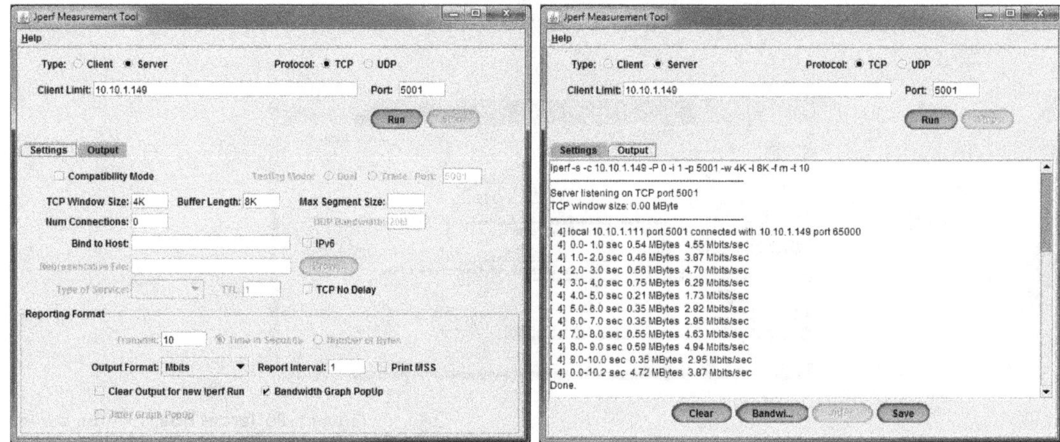

Figure 5-27 **PC as the server**

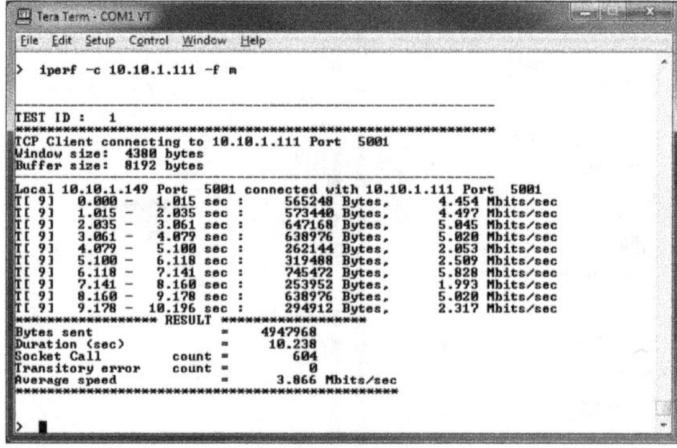

Figure 5-28 **Target board as the client**

This test shows that the embedded target is able to receive TCP segments faster that it can transmit them.

5-6 TCP TESTS SUMMARY

The same Client/Server and Server/Client tests were performed using different µC/TCP-IP configurations. Three µC/TCP-IP configurations (see section 5-3 "µC/TCP-IP Library Configuration" on page 914) were used for the following results.

Test direction	Library configuration	Performance
Target Server/PC Client	Configuration 1	6.13 Mpbs
	Configuration 2	17.96 Mbps
	Configuration 3	20.3 Mbps
Target Client/PC Server	Configuration 1	0.01 Mbps
	Configuration 2	3.86 Mbps
	Configuration 3	7.32 Mpbs

Figure 5-29 **TCP performance with various TCP/IP stack configuration**

5-7 USING WIRESHARK NETWORK PROTOCOL ANALYZER

The installation and introduction to using Wireshark for this book example applications is covered in Part II, Chapter 4, "Using Wireshark Network Protocol Analyzer" on page 866. In this chapter, IPerf is used to run UDP and TCP performance tests. IPerf in conjunction with Wireshark allows us to demonstrate transport protocol concepts presented in this book. Wireshark captures are demonstrated, once for each UDP and TCP test configuration.

5-7-1 TCP 3-WAY HANDSHAKE

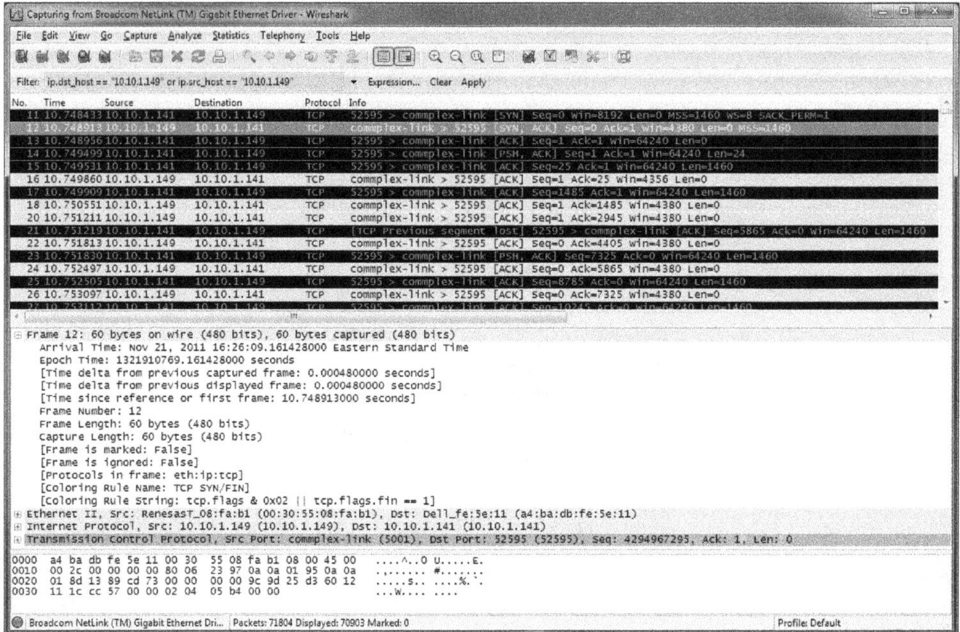

Figure 5-30 **Wireshark capture of an IPerf test**

Figure 5-30 represents a typical TCP connection exchange. Take a look at packets number 3 to 5 as it is the capture of the TCP three-way handshake.

5-7-2 TCP FLOW CONTROL

The next figure shows a number of TCP messages because the TCP receive window size is of a dimension that is easily filled by the Ethernet controller and driver. Note the ZEROWINDOW and the WINDOW UPDATE messages. The configuration to generate this result is different than the configuration used for the library delivered for the examples in this book The configuration is as follows:.

File	Parameter	Value
cpu_cfg.h	CPU_CFG_INT_DIS_MEAS_EN	DEF_ENABLED
	CPU_CFG_LEAD_ZEROS_ASM_PRESENT	DEF_ENABLED
os_cfg.h	OS_CFG_APP_HOOKS_EN	DEF_ENABLED
	OS_CFG_ARG_CHK_EN	DEF_ENABLED
	OS_CFG_CALLED_FROM_ISR_CHK_EN	DEF_ENABLED
	OS_CFG_DBG_EN	DEF_ENABLED
	OS_CFG_OBJ_TYPE_CHK_EN	DEF_ENABLED
	OS_CFG_SCHED_LOCK_TIME_MEAS_EN	DEF_ENABLED
net_cfg.h	NET_CFG_OPTIMIZE	NET_OPTIMIZE_SIZE
	NET_CFG_OPTIMIZE_ASM_EN	DEF_DISABLED
	NET_DBG_CFG_INFO_EN	DEF_ENABLED
	NET_DBG_CFG_STATUS_EN	DEF_ENABLED
	NET_DBG_CFG_MEM_CLR_EN	DEF_ENABLED
	NET_DBG_CFG_TEST_EN	DEF_ENABLED
	NET_ERR_CFG_ARG_CHK_EXT_EN	DEF_ENABLED
	NET_ERR_CFG_ARG_CHK_DBG_EN	DEF_ENABLED
	NET_CTR_CFG_STAT_EN	DEF_ENABLED
	NET_CTR_CFG_ERR_EN	DEF_ENABLED
	NET_TCP_CFG_RX_WIN_SIZE_OCTET	1 * 1460
	NET_TCP_CFG_TX_WIN_SIZE_OCTET	1 * 1460

The embedded target receive window size is set to one TCP segment (1460 and the PC client is configured to send buffers of 7300 bytes.

Number of device's large receive buffers	3
Number of device's large transmit buffers	1
Number of device's small transmit buffers	1
Number of receive DMA descriptors	2
Number of transmit DMA descriptors	1

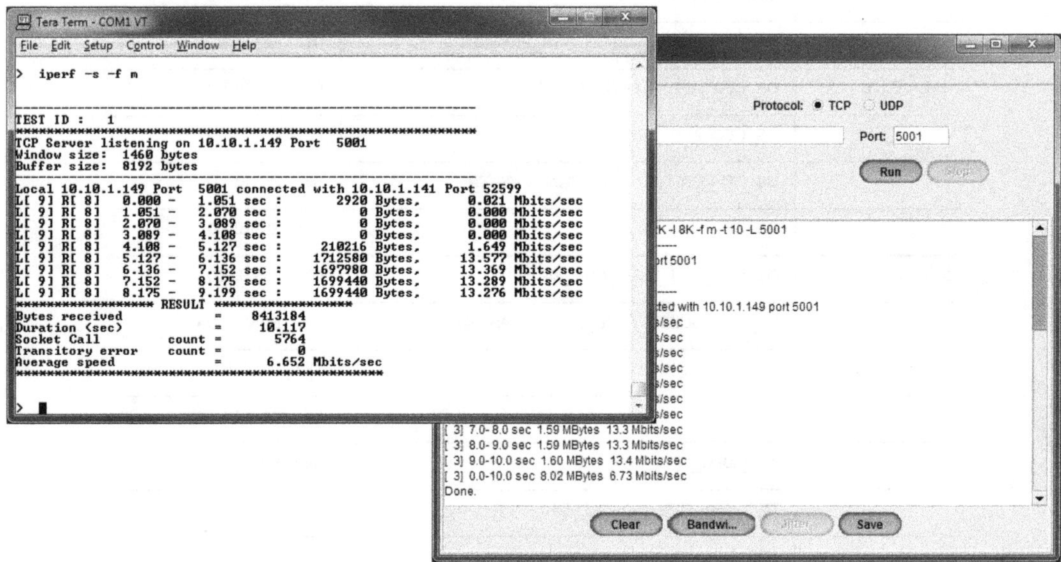

Figure 5-31 **Small Receive Window Size demonstration TCP flow control**

The Wireshark capture demonstrating this behavior looks like:

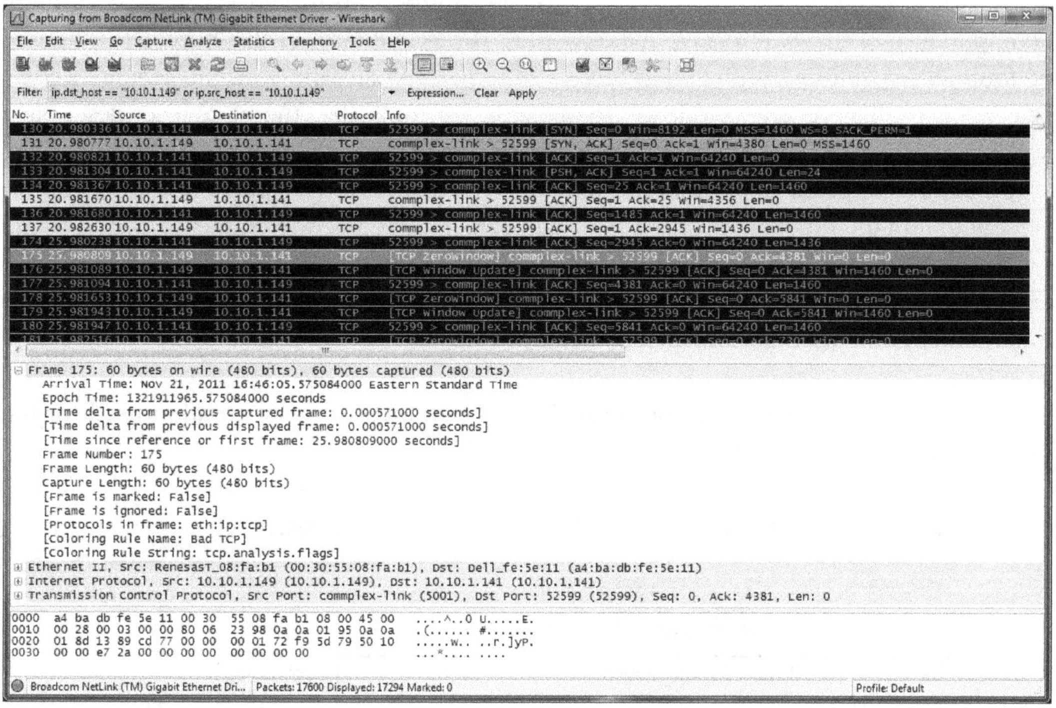

Figure 5-32 **Wireshark capture of TCP flow control**

The additional flow control messages are the cause of the performance degradation versus a similar test with the receive window size matching the number of receive descriptors.

5-7-3 WRONG TCP RECEIVE WINDOW SIZE TEST

The next test is the demonstration of the concepts introduced in Part I of this book about the importance of the TCP receive window size. The µC/Library for this book is configured for four receive buffers and two receive DMA descriptors. The tests in section 5-5 on page 923 use a TCP receive window size of 2920, which matches the number of descriptors available. Let's do a test with the TCP receive window size larger and see how the performance is affected by such a configuration. In other words, we are using the receive window to fool the PC client sending TCP segments to the embedded target to believe it can send more segments than the embedded target can receive. In this case, some segments will be lost (i.e., not received). TCP's mechanisms enters into play and recuperates from this situation but at the cost of performance degradation.

The configuration to generate these results is different than the configuration used for the library delivered for the examples in this book.

File	Parameter	Value
cpu_cfg.h	CPU_CFG_INT_DIS_MEAS_EN	DEF_ENABLED
	CPU_CFG_LEAD_ZEROS_ASM_PRESENT	DEF_ENABLED
os_cfg.h	OS_CFG_APP_HOOKS_EN	DEF_ENABLED
	OS_CFG_ARG_CHK_EN	DEF_ENABLED
	OS_CFG_CALLED_FROM_ISR_CHK_EN	DEF_ENABLED
	OS_CFG_DBG_EN	DEF_ENABLED
	OS_CFG_OBJ_TYPE_CHK_EN	DEF_ENABLED
	OS_CFG_SCHED_LOCK_TIME_MEAS_EN	DEF_ENABLED
net_cfg.h	NET_CFG_OPTIMIZE	NET_OPTIMIZE_SIZE
	NET_CFG_OPTIMIZE_ASM_EN	DEF_DISABLED
	NET_DBG_CFG_INFO_EN	DEF_ENABLED
	NET_DBG_CFG_STATUS_EN	DEF_ENABLED
	NET_DBG_CFG_MEM_CLR_EN	DEF_ENABLED
	NET_DBG_CFG_TEST_EN	DEF_ENABLED
	NET_ERR_CFG_ARG_CHK_EXT_EN	DEF_ENABLED
	NET_ERR_CFG_ARG_CHK_DBG_EN	DEF_ENABLED
	NET_CTR_CFG_STAT_EN	DEF_ENABLED

File	Parameter	Value
	NET_CTR_CFG_ERR_EN	DEF_ENABLED
	NET_TCP_CFG_RX_WIN_SIZE_OCTET	4 * 1460
	NET_TCP_CFG_TX_WIN_SIZE_OCTET	2 * 1460

Number of device's large receive buffers	4
Number of device's large transmit buffers	2
Number of device's small transmit buffers	2
Number of receive DMA descriptors	2
Number of transmit DMA descriptors	2

The next figure shows a number of TCP segments not being acknowledged by the target which generates a lot of retransmitions from the PC.

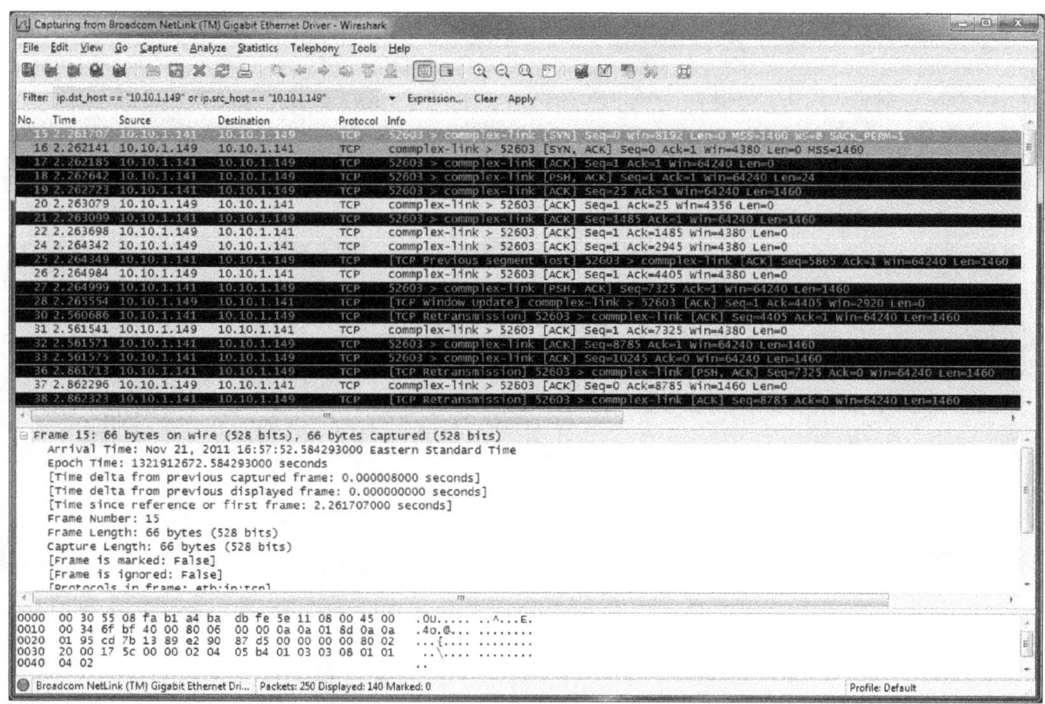

Figure 5-33 **Simulating network congestion with the TCP receive window size larger than the number of receive descriptors**

Note the packets highlighted in black. These are typical messages seen when TCP flow control is resolving a network problem.

Packet #28 is a TCP Window update. TCP used the receive window and is now able to increase it after having processed one or more packets.

Packet #30 is the re-transmission from the client. A re-transmission can happen because the acknowledgement was not received before the TCP re-transmission time-out (RTO) or because it is re-asked by the other host with a duplicate ACK.

Packet #36 is another example of a retransmission.

With all these extra flow control messages, the throughput can not be sustained compared to the previous performance we were able to achieve with our TCP/IP stack configuration. Remember that with our typical configuration we are able to achieve about 18 Mbps. Note the lower than 1 Mbps result in Figure 5-34 indicates that there are configuration or networking problems:

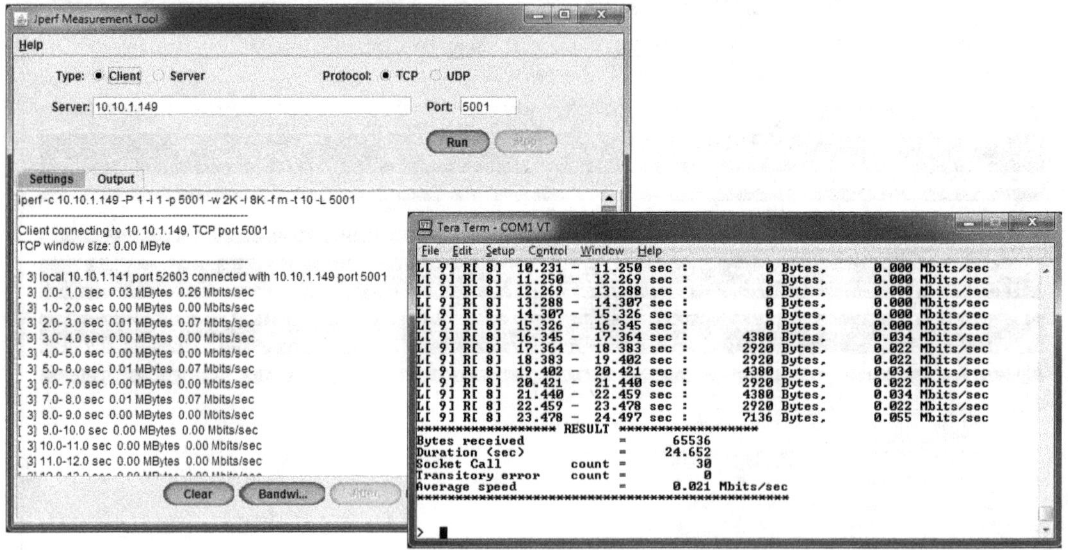

Figure 5-34 **Performance degradation in presence of networking problems**

5-8 SUMMARY

There are several interesting things to notice.

- IPerf is an excellent tool to exercise the stack for system validation. It can be used as a traffic generator and to stress the system in order to identify any design issues and limitations.

- IPerf is also an excellent tool to obtain performance statistics. Its usefulness also comes from the fact that it is a standard tool. Tests done with this tool can be compared to similar tests with the same tool.

- TCP and UDP performance is dependant on multiple TCP/IP stack configuration parameters. IPerf allows us to test all the possible permutations and values for these configurable parameters.

- The µC/Probe workspace provided with this example project delivers valuable data screens to help understand what is going on in the embedded system. It also provides enough information to view most of the internal µC/TCP-IP operations

- While IPerf is used to exercise the embedded TCP/IP stack, Wireshark can be used to monitor and decode the network traffic and protocol operations.

This chapter covered UDP and TCP operations on a target board. UDP and TCP are the transport layers used as the foundation for any application. µC/IPerf is a fun application, but it does not provide a useful service for a commercial product. µC/IPerf is an application residing above the socket interface. Most of the useful services for any embedded system are of a similar type. The best example is the famous web server, also called HTTP server. The next chapter is an example of the implementation of a web server using Micrium's µC/HTTPs.

Chapter

6

Example #5 HTTP Server

The following project builds on previous examples by providing a popular service in embedded systems -- a web server. Using a web browser to configure an embedded system, or to read parameters from the same system, is a common practice in the industry. Graphical representation of information from or to an embedded system is definitely a useful tool.

6-1 µC/TCP-IP EXAMPLE #5 HTTP SERVER

Start e^2 Studio and open the following workspace:

```
$\Micrium\Software\EvalBoards\Renesas\YRDKRX62N\
GNURX-e2studio\uC-TCP-IP-Book-Ex-Obj
```

Click on the uC-TCP-IP-Ex5 item in the project explorer tree to select the example #5. The project structure is similar to the examples provided in the previous chapter. However, for the purpose of this example, one additional module from the µC/TCP-IP family is included: µC/HTTPs.

The µC/HTTPs user manual is part of the documentation package downloaded for these examples (see Chapter 3, “Software” on page 822).

The project explorer with the additional expanded group for µC/HTTPs and the webpage compared to Example #2 workspace is shown in Figure 6-1. The uC/HTTPs group contains header files, and the µC/HTTPs object code library for this example is located in:

```
$\Micrium\Software\EvalBoards\Renesas\YRDKRX62N\
GNURX-e2studio\uC-TCP-IP-Book-Lib
```

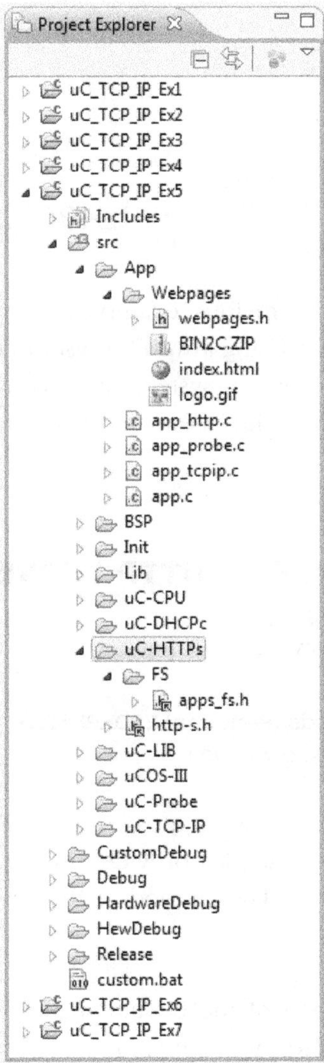

Figure 6-1 **Example #5 Project Explorer**

Under the **App** group you will find a new folder called **Webpages**. This is where you store the actual html and media files. This example features a simple server that includes the **index.html** and a **logo.gif**. Both files have been converted to binary using the tool **Bin2C** that has been included for your convenience within the **BIN2C.zip** file. The tool converts a the html and gif file into 2 C arrays declared in the header file **webpages.h**. Ultimately, this is the file that gets compiled with the rest of the application.

6-1-1 HOW THE EXAMPLE PROJECT WORKS

Since this example uses DHCP to configure the IP address, the code from **main()** in this example is identical to Example #2. However, **AppTaskStart()** differs because the HTTP server must be initialized. In order to initialize µC/HTTPs it is necessary to call the function **AppHTTPs_Init()** shown in Listing 6-1 right after the IP address is configured.

```
void  AppHTTPs_Init (void)
{
    CPU_BOOLEAN  cfg_success;


    cfg_success = HTTPs_Init(DEF_NO);                                         (1)
    APP_TEST_FAULT(cfg_success, DEF_OK);                                      (2)

    cfg_success = Apps_FS_Init();                                             (3)
    APP_TEST_FAULT(cfg_success, DEF_OK);

    cfg_success = Apps_FS_AddFile((CPU_CHAR *)&STATIC_INDEX_HTML_NAME,
                                  (CPU_CHAR *)&Index_html,
                                  (CPU_INT32U) STATIC_INDEX_HTML_LEN);        (4)
    APP_TEST_FAULT(cfg_success, DEF_OK);

    cfg_success = Apps_FS_AddFile((CPU_CHAR *)&STATIC_LOGO_GIF_NAME,
                                  (CPU_CHAR *)&Logo_Gif,
                                  (CPU_INT32U) STATIC_LOGO_GIF_LEN);          (5)
    APP_TEST_FAULT(cfg_success, DEF_OK);

    BSP_Temp_Init();                                                          (6)
    App_TempSensorUpdate();                                                   (7)

    BSP_GraphLCD_ClrLine(3);                                                  (8)
    BSP_GraphLCD_ClrLine(4);
    BSP_GraphLCD_ClrLine(5);
    BSP_GraphLCD_String(3, "Open a browser and");                             (9)
    BSP_GraphLCD_String(4, "go to the address");
    BSP_GraphLCD_String(5, "below:");
}
```

Listing 6-1 **AppHTTPs_Init()**

L6-1(1) **HTTPs_Init()** starts the HTTP server.

L6-1(2) **APP_TEST_FAULT()** is a macro definition that you can use to define your own error handlers. For the sake of simplicity, this example just stops the task by getting it in an infinite loop.

L6-1(3) **Apps_FS_Init()** initializes the file system. The HTTP server requires a file system to serve the web pages. In this example, the file system is configured to use static pages loaded into the RX62N Flash memory.

L6-1(4) The **index.html** file is compiled with the example and is loaded in Flash. **Apps_FS_AddFile()** loads this file for use by the HTTP server. This is done to save RAM space. On this processor, as with many microcontrollers, Flash is always in a larger quantity than RAM.

L6-1(5) The **index.html** web page for this example uses an image called **logo.gif** which is also compiled with the application and loaded in Flash. **Apps_FS_AddFile()** loads this file for use by the HTTP server.

L6-1(6) The function **BSP_Temp_Init()** is declared in **bsp_adt7420.c** and it is responsible of initializing the temperature sensor onboard the YRDKRX62N board. This example will display the current temperature reading on the web page.

L6-1(7) **App_TempSensorUpdate()** is an application function declared in **app_http.c** responsible of updating the HTTP server variables with the current reading from the temperature sensor.

L6-1(8) The function **BSP_GraphLCD_ClrLine()** has been used in previous examples and it is used to clear a line on the LCD display.

L6-1(9) In order to instruct the user to open a browser and go to the web page served by the target, we call **BSP_Graph_LCD_String()** to print strings of characters on the LCD display.

The web page built for this example displays µC/OS-III and µC/TCP-IP version numbers. These two fields are static. To display a dynamic value, the web page uses the temperature sensor on the YRDKRX62N board to display the temperature in Fahrenheit and Celsius.

For the web page to send and receive data from the embedded target, two additional functions need to be defined in the application. There are both located in **`app_http.c`**. The first one is **`HTTPs_ValReq()`**. **`HTTPs_ValReq()`** is a callback function that *must* be implemented in the application and *should* return the value corresponding to the token. A token is added to the HTML page under the form ${TOKEN}. It is used to take variable data from the embedded target and to send it to the web page. The following listing describes this callback function.

```
CPU_BOOLEAN  HTTPs_ValReq (CPU_CHAR   *p_tok,
                           CPU_CHAR  **p_val)
{
    static  CPU_CHAR    val_buf[HTTPs_VAL_REQ_BUF_LEN];                                  (1)
#if   (LIB_VERSION >= 126u)
            CPU_INT32U  ver;
#elif (LIB_STR_CFG_FP_EN == DEF_ENABLED)
            CPU_FP32    ver;
#endif
            OS_TICK     os_time_tick;
#if (LIB_STR_CFG_FP_EN == DEF_ENABLED)
            CPU_FP32    os_time_sec;
#else
            CPU_INT32U  os_time_sec;
            CPU_INT32U  os_time_ms;
            CPU_SIZE_T  os_time_len;
#endif
            OS_ERR      os_err;


   (void)Str_Copy(&val_buf[0], "%%%%%%%%");
   *p_val = &val_buf[0];                                                                 (2)

                                           /* --------------- OS VALUES -------------- */ (3)
    if (Str_Cmp(p_tok, "OS_VERSION")                 == 0) {                              (4)
#if (LIB_VERSION >=   126u)
#if (OS_VERSION  >= 30200u)
        ver =  OS_VERSION / 10000;
       (void)Str_FmtNbr_Int32U(ver, 2, DEF_NBR_BASE_DEC, ' ', DEF_NO, DEF_NO, &val_buf[0]);
        val_buf[2] = '.';

        ver = (OS_VERSION /   100) % 100;
       (void)Str_FmtNbr_Int32U(ver, 2, DEF_NBR_BASE_DEC, '0', DEF_NO, DEF_NO, &val_buf[3]);
        val_buf[5] = '.';

        ver = (OS_VERSION /     1) %  10;
       (void)Str_FmtNbr_Int32U(ver, 2, DEF_NBR_BASE_DEC, '0', DEF_NO, DEF_YES, &val_buf[6]);
        val_buf[8] = '\0';
```

```
#elif (OS_VERSION >   300u)
        ver =  OS_VERSION / 1000;
       (void)Str_FmtNbr_Int32U(ver,   2, DEF_NBR_BASE_DEC, ' ', DEF_NO, DEF_NO,  &val_buf[0]);
        val_buf[2] = '.';

        ver = (OS_VERSION /   10) % 100;
       (void)Str_FmtNbr_Int32U(ver,   2, DEF_NBR_BASE_DEC, '0', DEF_NO, DEF_NO,  &val_buf[3]);
        val_buf[5] = '.';

        ver = (OS_VERSION /    1) %  10;
       (void)Str_FmtNbr_Int32U(ver,   1, DEF_NBR_BASE_DEC, '0', DEF_NO, DEF_YES, &val_buf[6]);
        val_buf[8] = '\0';

#else
        ver =  OS_VERSION /  100;
       (void)Str_FmtNbr_Int32U(ver,   2, DEF_NBR_BASE_DEC, ' ', DEF_NO, DEF_NO,  &val_buf[0]);
        val_buf[2] = '.';

        ver = (OS_VERSION /    1) % 100;
       (void)Str_FmtNbr_Int32U(ver,   2, DEF_NBR_BASE_DEC, '0', DEF_NO, DEF_YES, &val_buf[3]);
        val_buf[5] = '\0';
#endif

#elif (LIB_STR_CFG_FP_EN == DEF_ENABLED)
#if   (OS_VERSION > 30200u)
        ver = (CPU_FP32)OS_VERSION / 10000;
       (void)Str_FmtNbr_32(ver,  2,  2, ' ',  DEF_NO,  &val_buf[0]);

        ver = (CPU_FP32)OS_VERSION /   100;
       (void)Str_FmtNbr_32(ver,  0,  2, '\0', DEF_YES, &val_buf[6]);

#elif (OS_VERSION >   300u)
        ver = (CPU_FP32)OS_VERSION / 1000;
       (void)Str_FmtNbr_32(ver,  2,  2, ' ',  DEF_NO,  &val_buf[0]);

        ver = (CPU_FP32)OS_VERSION /   10;
       (void)Str_FmtNbr_32(ver,  0,  1, '\0', DEF_YES, &val_buf[6]);

#else
        ver = (CPU_FP32)OS_VERSION / 100;
       (void)Str_FmtNbr_32(ver,  2,  2, '\0', DEF_YES, &val_buf[0]);
#endif
#endif
```

```
    }  else if (Str_Cmp(p_tok, "OS_TIME"          ) == 0) {
        os_time_tick = (OS_TICK )OSTimeGet(&os_err);
#if (LIB_STR_CFG_FP_EN == DEF_ENABLED)
        os_time_sec  = (CPU_FP32)os_time_tick / OS_CFG_TICK_RATE_HZ;
       (void)Str_FmtNbr_32(os_time_sec, 7u,  3u, '\0', DEF_YES, &val_buf[0]);
#else
        os_time_sec  = (CPU_INT32U)os_time_tick / OS_CFG_TICK_RATE_HZ;
       (void)Str_FmtNbr_Int32U(os_time_sec, 7u, DEF_NBR_BASE_DEC, '\0', DEF_NO, DEF_YES,
&val_buf[0]);
       (void)Str_Cat(&val_buf[0], ".");
        os_time_len  =  Str_Len(&val_buf[0]);
        os_time_ms   = (CPU_INT32U)os_time_tick % OS_CFG_TICK_RATE_HZ;
        os_time_ms  *=  1000 / OS_CFG_TICK_RATE_HZ;
       (void)Str_FmtNbr_Int32U(os_time_ms, 3u, DEF_NBR_BASE_DEC, '0', DEF_NO, DEF_YES,
&val_buf[os_time_len]);
#endif

                                                /* -------- NETWORK PROTOCOL SUITE VALUES ------- */    (5)
    } else if (Str_Cmp(p_tok, "NET_VERSION") == 0) {
#if (LIB_VERSION >= 126u)
#if (NET_VERSION >  205u)
        ver =  NET_VERSION / 10000;
       (void)Str_FmtNbr_Int32U(ver,  2, DEF_NBR_BASE_DEC, ' ', DEF_NO, DEF_NO,  &val_buf[0]);
        val_buf[2] = '.';

        ver = (NET_VERSION /   100) % 100;
       (void)Str_FmtNbr_Int32U(ver,  2, DEF_NBR_BASE_DEC, '0', DEF_NO, DEF_NO,  &val_buf[3]);
        val_buf[5] = '.';

        ver = (NET_VERSION /     1) % 100;
       (void)Str_FmtNbr_Int32U(ver,  2, DEF_NBR_BASE_DEC, '0', DEF_NO, DEF_YES, &val_buf[6]);
        val_buf[8] = '\0';
#else
        ver =  NET_VERSION /   100;
       (void)Str_FmtNbr_Int32U(ver,  2, DEF_NBR_BASE_DEC, ' ', DEF_NO, DEF_NO,  &val_buf[0]);
        val_buf[2] = '.';

        ver = (NET_VERSION /     1) % 100;
       (void)Str_FmtNbr_Int32U(ver,  2, DEF_NBR_BASE_DEC, '0', DEF_NO, DEF_YES, &val_buf[3]);
        val_buf[5] = '\0';
#endif
```

```
#elif (LIB_STR_CFG_FP_EN == DEF_ENABLED)
#if   (NET_VERSION > 205u)
         ver = (CPU_FP32)NET_VERSION / 10000;
        (void)Str_FmtNbr_32(ver,  2,  2, ' ',  DEF_NO,  &val_buf[0]);

         ver = (CPU_FP32)NET_VERSION /   100;
        (void)Str_FmtNbr_32(ver,  0,  2, '\0', DEF_YES, &val_buf[6]);

#else
         ver = (CPU_FP32)NET_VERSION /   100;
        (void)Str_FmtNbr_32(ver,  2,  2, '\0', DEF_YES, &val_buf[0]);
#endif
#endif

                                            /* ------------ APPLICATION VALUES ------------ */      (6)
    } else if (Str_Cmp(p_tok, "TEMP_C") == 0) {
        (void)Str_FmtNbr_Int32S(AppTempSensorDegC, 3, DEF_NBR_BASE_DEC, '\0', DEF_NO, DEF_YES,
&val_buf[0]);

    } else if (Str_Cmp(p_tok, "TEMP_F") == 0) {
        (void)Str_FmtNbr_Int32S(AppTempSensorDegF, 3, DEF_NBR_BASE_DEC, '\0', DEF_NO, DEF_YES,
&val_buf[0]);
    }

    if ((Str_Cmp(p_tok, "TEMP_C") == 0) ||         /* Update temperature values.        */
         (Str_Cmp(p_tok, "TEMP_F") == 0)) {
         App_TempSensorUpdate();
    }

    return DEF_OK;
}
```

Listing 6-2 **HTTPs_ValReq ()**

L6-2(1) Initialize the storage location used to transfer the embedded target data to the HTTP server.

L6-2(2) Points the pointer used as the return argument to the location of the storage area for the values requested.

L6-2(3) These lines retrieve the µC/OS-III version number currently running on the embedded target and converts it into characters transferred to **&val_buf[].** Upon return from this function, the HTTP server will get the characters from this location and display them on the web page.

L6-2(4) The input parameter **p_tok** is used to determine which of the variables is requested by the HTTP server.

L6-2(5) These lines retrieve the µC/TCP-IP version number currently running on the embedded target and converts it into characters transferred to **&val_buf[]**.

L6-2(6) Based on selection for the temperature scale by **p_tok**, these lines retrieve the value of the temperature sensor on the YRDKRX62N board and converts it into characters transferred to **&val_buf[].**

The second function is **HTTPs_ValRx()**. It is a callback function that MUST be implemented in the application and SHOULD handle POST action for every name-value pair received. It is used to get data from the web page. The user enters information on the web page such as the on/off state of the LED. The HTTP server uses this function to get the user's input to the embedded target. Here is an example of HTML code where the name LED with a value of LED1 is used:

```
<form action="index.html" method="POST">
    <p>
        <input name="LED" type="hidden" value="LED1">
        < input type="submit" value="Toggle LED 1" class="bluebutton">
    </p>
</form>
```

Listing 6-3 shows the call back function **HTTPs_ValRx():**

```
CPU_BOOLEAN  HTTPs_ValRx (CPU_CHAR   *p_var,
                          CPU_CHAR   *p_val)
{
    CPU_INT16U    cmp_str;
    CPU_BOOLEAN   ret_val;


    ret_val = DEF_FAIL;

    cmp_str = Str_Cmp((CPU_CHAR *)p_var,                                              (1)
                      (CPU_CHAR *)HTML_LED_INPUT_NAME);
    if (cmp_str == 0) {
        cmp_str = Str_Cmp((CPU_CHAR *)p_val,                 /* Toggle LED 1.    */   (2)
                          (CPU_CHAR *)HTML_LED1_TOGGLE_INPUT_VALUE);
        if (cmp_str == 0) {
            LED_Toggle(LED1);
            ret_val = DEF_OK;
        }

        cmp_str = Str_Cmp((CPU_CHAR *)p_val,                 /* Toggle LED 2.    */   (3)
                          (CPU_CHAR *)HTML_LED2_TOGGLE_INPUT_VALUE);
        if (cmp_str == 0) {
            LED_Toggle(LED2);
            ret_val = DEF_OK;
        }
    }


    return (ret_val);
}
```

Listing 6-3 **HTTPs_ValRx()**

L6-3(1) This function is written to handle multiple inputs. The first argument **`*p_var`**, determines which type of variable is entered. In this case, we are checking for "LED".

L6-3(2) As a second step, we check which LED was clicked on the web page. The value of **`*p_val`**, it is either "LED1" or "LED2". When "LED1" is selected, it is turned ON or OFF by the **`LED_Toggle()`** function.

L6-3(3) When "LED2" is selected, it is turned ON or OFF by the **`LED_Toggle()`** function.

6-2 RUNNING THE APPLICATION

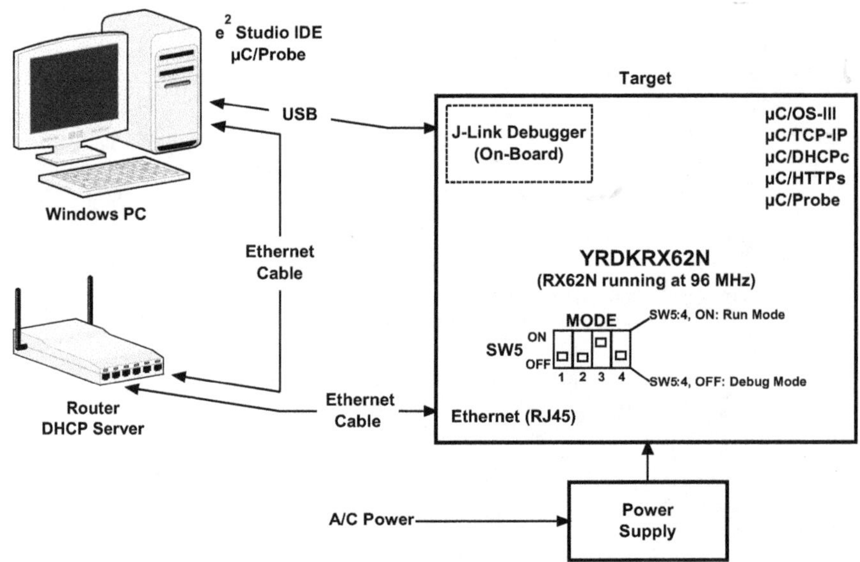

Figure 6-2 **Connecting a PC and the YRDKRX62N**

Once this code is running the LEDs at the bottom of the wheel on the board will be blinking. It is now possible for the PC connected to the same network as the board (see Listing 6-2) to use a web browser and to connect to the board, entering http://10.10.1.121 in the browser address bar or whatever IP address is assigned by the DHCP server and displayed on the LCD screen as shown in Figure 6-3.

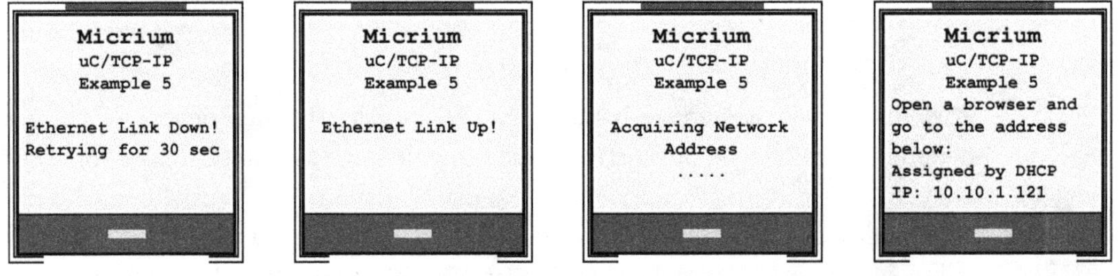

Figure 6-3 **Example #5 LCD screens: DHCP process**

Figure 6-4 shows the web page that is part of the HTTP server running on the target board. The µC/OS-III and the µC/TCP-IP version numbers of the code running on the board are extracted and displayed in the page.

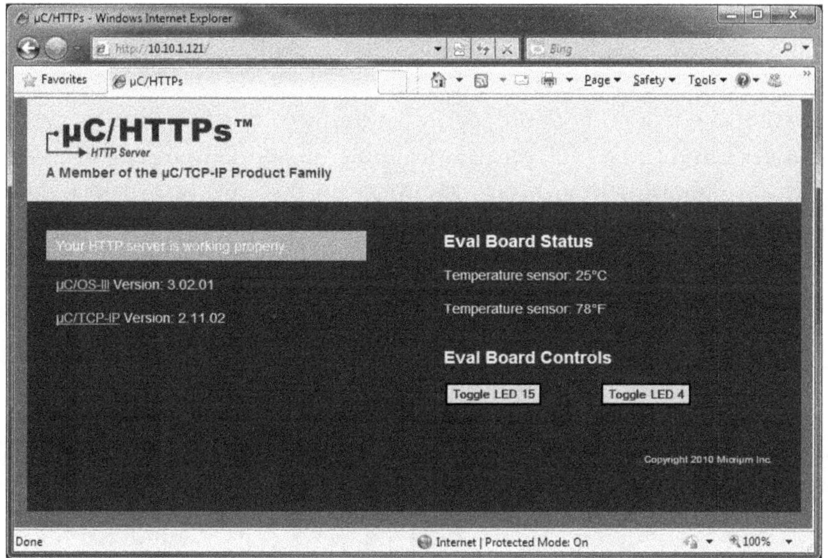

Figure 6-4 **Webpage on the target board web server**

As previously mentioned, the YRDKRX62N board has a temperature sensor and the code running reads this sensor and the value is used to populate the web page. The temperature value is displayed in Fahrenheit and Celsius degrees.

Finally, it is also possible for the web page to interact with the board. The two buttons on the page control the LEDs labeled LED15 and LED4 on the board. Clicking on the buttons, toggles the corresponding LED on the board.

While the project is running, use the µC/Probe workspace located in:

```
$\Micrium\Software\EvalBoards\Renesas\YRDKRX62N\GNURX-e2studio\
uC-TCP-IP-Book-Ex-Obj\uC-TCP-IP-Ex5\uC-TCP-IP-Ex5-Probe.wsp
```

Another interesting task is to use Wireshark. As there are new protocols in this example, the reader will be able to visualize the process to open, display, and use a web page.

6

6-3 SUMMARY

Combining the Ethernet driver and the complete TCP/IP stack, especially the TCP protocol and adding the application layer HTTP service code, this chapter quickly demonstrated how simple it can be to implement a web server once the TCP/IP is operational and working efficiently.

index.html code is provided to the reader as an example of what a web server can do. It is a simple demonstration of how to get data from the embedded target and display it on the web page; At the same time, the user enters data on the web page and transmit it to the embedded target.

There are a few things worth noting:

- HTTP is a very popular protocol and it allows simple embedded systems to offer a remote professional graphical user interface. The use of HTTP server in an embedded system relives the developer from having to develop a client as the HTTP client is a well-known browser (Internet Explorer, Safari, Firefox, Chrome, etc.).

- HTTP relies on TCP. Proper configuration and resource allocation needs to be performed to make sure the developer will be able to exploit protocol benefits.

- The µC/Probe workspace provided with this example project brings valuable data screens to help the user understand what is going on in the embedded system. It also provides enough information to view most of the internal µC/TCP-IP operations.

- While the HTTP server is running, Wireshark can be used to monitor network traffic and decode all of the protocols involved.

This chapter's example showed how to use an HTTP server. This application layer protocol adds a very nice set of features to a product giving it a 21st century look and feel. This code example is almost a summary of all that is necessary to make a TCP/IP stack run on an embedded target, from the Ethernet device driver to the application layer code, providing services to a user or a system.

Chapter

7

TCP/IP Sockets: Push Notifications to iOS devices

Devices running Apple's iOS system include the iPhone, iPod Touch and iPad. This chapter features an example of an embedded application running on the Renesas YRDKRX62N that sends notifications to an iOS device through the use of µC/TCP-IP sockets. In order to run this example you need an iOS device and the Renesas YRDKRX62N.

The following two sections make reference to an application that runs on a Mac OS X system known as *Growl* only to explain the technology behind this example. You do not need a Mac computer to run this example, but we strongly recommend reading the following two sections in order to understand the fundamental concepts behind this example.

7-1 GROWL: NOTIFICATION SYSTEM FOR MAC OS X

Growl is a notification system for Mac OS X. It allows Mac OS X-based applications that support Growl to display notifications with a unified user interface. Growl centralizes all your notifications in one place allowing you to control which notifications are shown and how they are displayed. You can have Growl show a bubble that fades in and out, or play a sound, or read the notification out loud, or even send an e-mail message. You can even have Growl ignore any notifications of specific types.

Some of the most popular applications running on Mac OS X that support Growl include *eBay Watcher*, which is a dashboard widget that floats around your desktop so you can watch your eBay auctions all at once.

Figure 7-1 shows one of the configuration screens from Growl where you can configure the pop-up notification's location over your desktop among other settings.

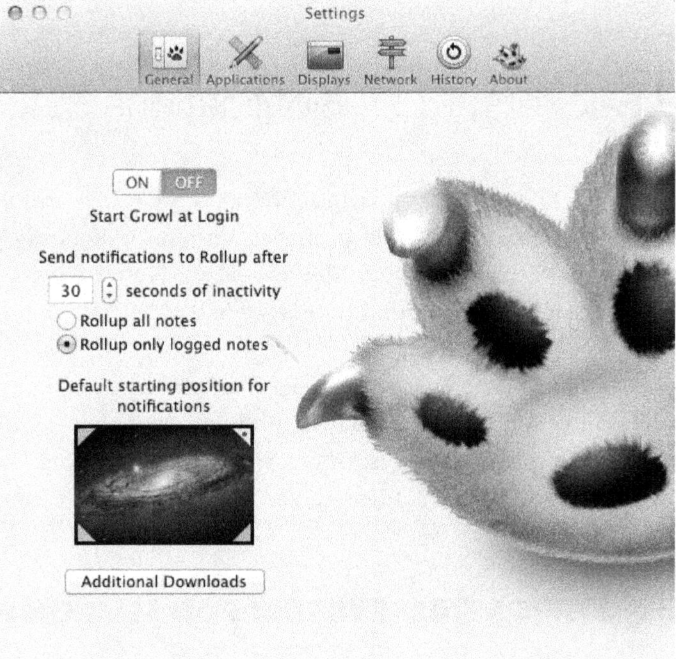

Figure 7-1 **Growl General Settings**

Figure 7-2 shows another configuration screen from Growl where you can enable and disable notifications in a per application basis.

Figure 7-2 **Growl Application Settings**

Figure 7-3 shows the configuration screen where you can configure the style for the notifications.

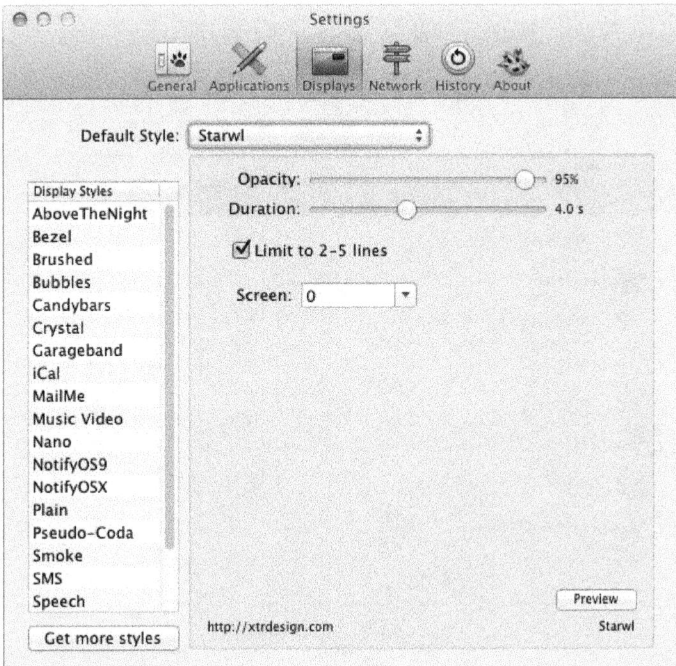

Figure 7-3 **Growl Displays Settings**

Figure 7-4 shows the network configuration screen. You can configure Growl to not only forward notifications over the network to any other computer, but also to listen for notifications from another computer.

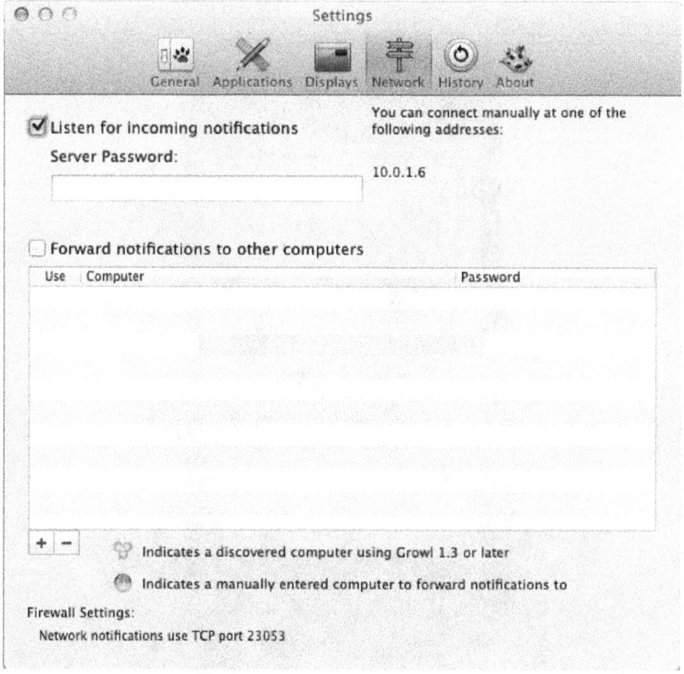

Figure 7-4 **Growl Network Settings**

More information on Growl can be found on the web at: www.growl.info.

7-2 PROWL: NOTIFICATION SYSTEM FOR iOS

Prowl is the Growl client for iOS. You can use the configuration screen shown in Figure 7-4 to forward notifications to your iOS device such as your iPhone as shown in Figure 7-5.

Figure 7-5 **Prowl Notification on an iPhone**

When a Growl notification pops up on your Mac computer, it can be forwarded to Prowl and displayed on your iOS device within seconds.

Figure 7-6 shows Prowl's configuration screen as seen from an iPhone. You can configure sounds and a schedule to specify quiet hours. At the same time, you can allow notifications with an emergency priority to break the quiet hours schedule.

Figure 7-6 **Prowl Configuration Screen on an iPhone**

Prowl is an application designed by Zachary West. More information can be found at: `www.prowlapp.com`

Figure 7-7 illustrates the typical scenario where you want to forward the notifications from your Mac OS X computer into your iOS device.

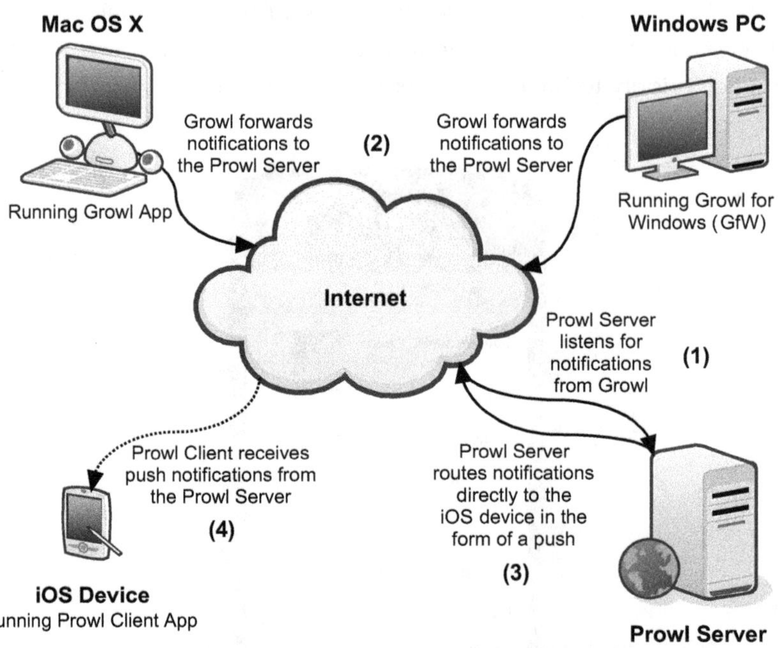

Figure 7-7 **Forwarding Growl Notifications from your Desktop to your iOS device**

F7-7(1) iOS devices include the iPhone, iPod Touch and the iPad. In order to setup your iOS device to receive push notifications, you first need to create an account in the Prowl server at **`www.prowlapp.com`** and register your iOS device with the server. The Prowl server stores in its database a unique id called *deviceToken* for each iOS device. This deviceToken is generated by the iOS device and it is managed by the *Apple Push Notification Service (APNS)*. The Prowl server simply waits for any incoming notifications from the Growl application running on your Mac OS X system.

F7-7(2) The Growl application running on a Mac OS X system is configured to forward notifications to the Prowl server using the Network Settings configuration screen shown in Figure 7-4. Push notifications are not designed for large data transfer, only for small alerts. There is also a Growl for Windows application for PC called *GfW.*

F7-7(3) The Prowl server routes notifications directly to the iOS device through a mechanism known as Apple Push Notification Service. Each push notification is addressed to a specific iOS device by using its unique deviceToken.

F7-7(4) The Prowl client application running on the iOS device receives the push notification from the Prowl server and displays the notification according to the user's schedule and display settings for such type of notification. It is worth mentioning that push notifications should not be used for critical alerts because the message will only be delivered if the iOS device has wifi or cellular connectivity.

The Prowl Server offers a very flexible API that allows developers to send notifications to the Prowl server not only from Growl but also from your own TCP/IP sockets application.

It is this API what enables TCP/IP socket applications such as the example presented in this chapter to push notifications from the Renesas Demonstration Kit YRDKRX62N to your iOS device using µC/TCP-IP sockets.

Figure 7-8 shows a modified block diagram for this new scenario.

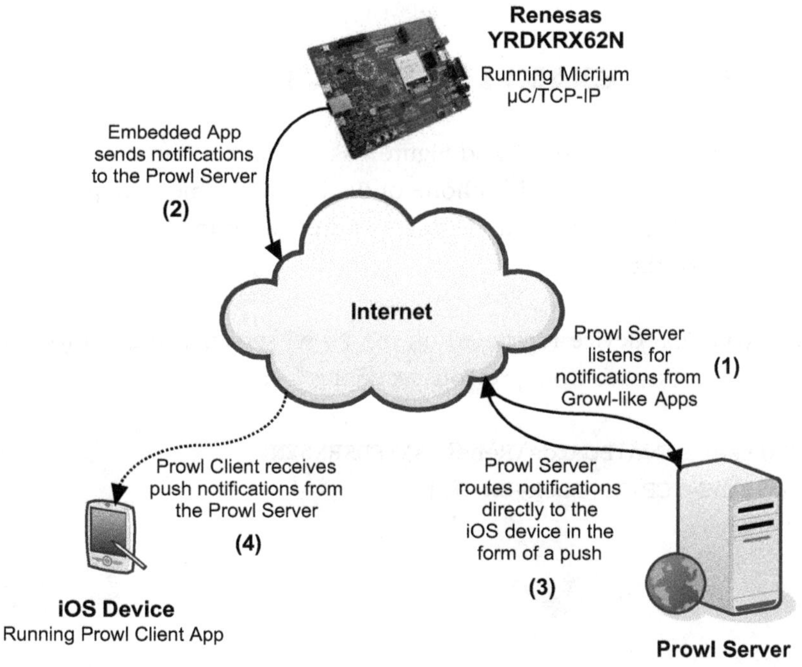

Figure 7-8 **Sending Growl Notifications from the RX62N to your iOS device**

F7-8(1) The iOS device is registered to the Prowl server exactly as described in F7-7(1). The Prowl server simply waits for any incoming notifications from any Growl application or in this case the embedded application running on the Renesas YRDKRX62N Demonstration Kit.

F7-8(2) The embedded application establishes a TCP/IP socket connection to the Prowl server using µC/TCP-IP sockets and delivers the notification in the form of an HTTP POST request.

F7-8(3) The Prowl server routes notifications directly to the iOS device through the Apple Push Notification Service. Each push notification is addressed to a specific iOS device by using its unique deviceToken.

F7-8(4) The Prowl client application running on the iOS device receives the push notification from the Prowl server and displays the notification according to the user's schedule and display settings for such type of notification.

7-3 RUNNING THE EXAMPLE PROJECT

As previously discussed in Figure 7-7 and Figure 7-8, in order to run this example you need an iOS device such as an iPod Touch, Iphone or iPad. You also need to purchase the Prowl application from the iTunes store and create a free account on the Prowl server at: `www.prowlapp.com/register.php`.

Once you have your iOS device registered on the Prowl server, you need to start e^2 Studio and open the same workspace from previous examples located at:

```
$\Micrium\Software\EvalBoards\Renesas\YRDKRX62N\
GNURX-e2studio\uC-TCP-IP-Book-Ex-Obj\
```

Select the item in the Project Explorer tree labeled as uC-TCP-IP-Ex6 to expand all items. Double click on the file **`app_cfg.h`** located under the **`scr/Lib/`** groups and replace the definitions listed below with the API Key, Provider Key and Application Name you configured at the Prowl server under your account.

```
#define APP_CFG_PROWL_SERVER_IP_ADDR      "209.20.72.170"
#define APP_CFG_PROWL_SERVER_PORT                  80
#define APP_CFG_PROWL_RX_BUF_SIZE                1024
#define APP_CFG_PROWL_TX_BUF_SIZE                 512
#define APP_CFG_PROWL_API_KEY             "eebb7f6ad8c44daeffa646183ec218f991c049cf"
#define APP_CFG_PROWL_PROVIDER_KEY        "d5534952c9926371af059219aee0f2024a459e5b"
#define APP_CFG_PROWL_APP_NAME            "Generic+Notifier"
```

Listing 7-1 **Configuring Prowl: app_cfg.h**

Select and right click the item in the Project Explorer tree labeled as uC-TCP-IP-Ex6 in order to build the project.

Just like previous examples, selecting the new file named **`uC-TCP-IP-Ex6.x`** under the **`Binaries`** folder and clicking on the Debug button downloads the code into the RX62N flash memory and starts a debug session.

Click F8 or the Resume button in the debug tool bar to start the application.

The LCD display onboard the YRDKRX62N should look like the ones illustrated in Figure 7-9 while the firmware application configures the IP address:

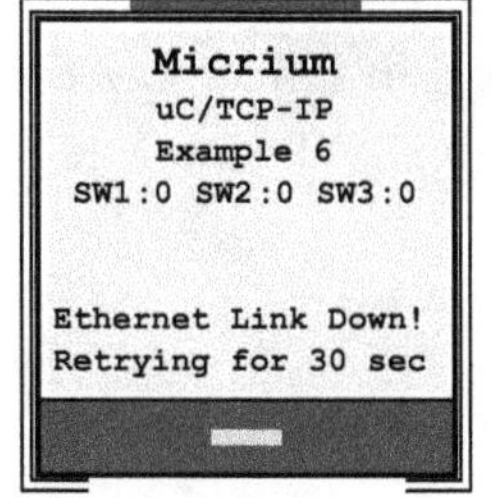

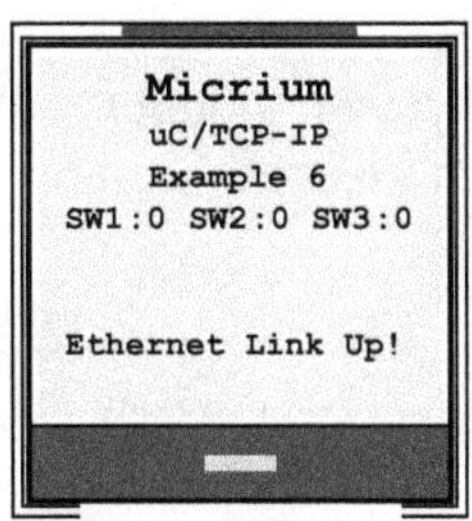

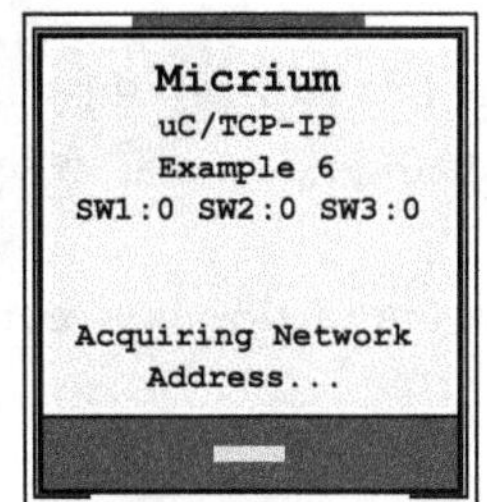

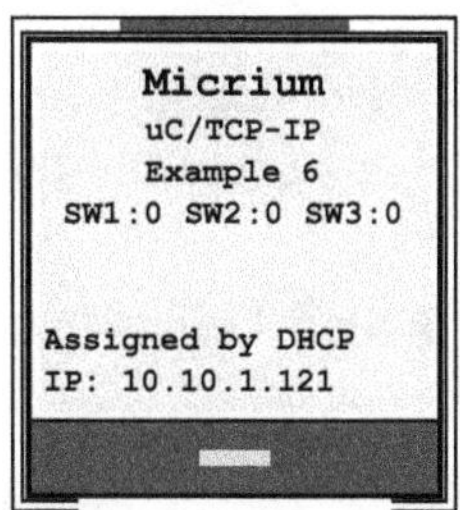

Figure 7-9 **Example #6 LCD screens: DHCP process**

The fourth line that reads **SW1:0 SW2:0 SW3:0** represents the state of the three push buttons onboard the YRDKRX62N labeled as SW1, SW2 and SW3. In order to send a push notification to an iOS device you need to press one of these 3 buttons. Figure 7-10 below illustrates the screens you should see when pressing SW1:

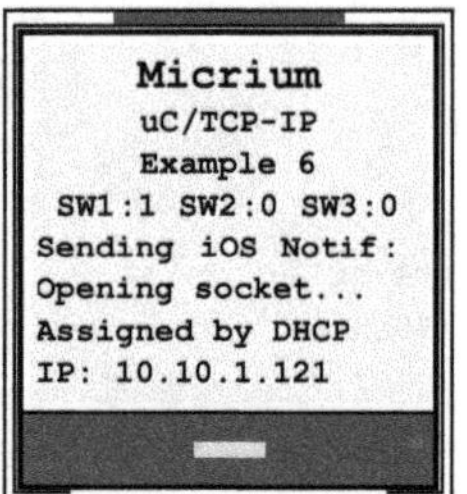

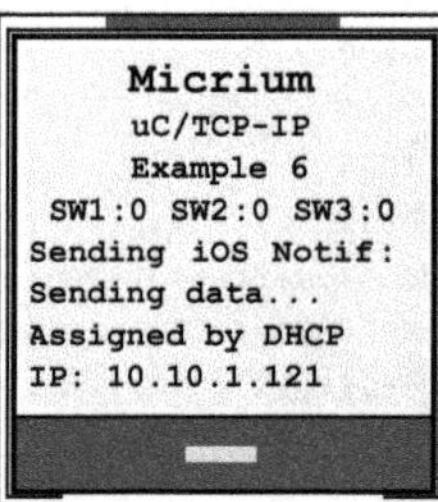

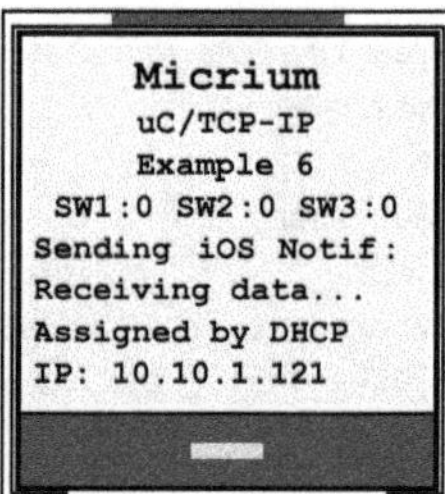

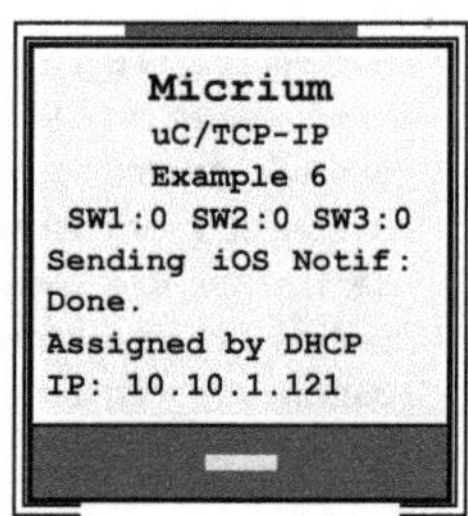

Figure 7-10 **Example #6 LCD screens: Sending iOS notification**

Any error messages are shown in the LCD screen but if everything is configured right you should get the notification in your iOS device immediately.

7-4 HOW THE CODE WORKS

This example is based on Example #2 that features a simple DHCP client. Two new tasks are included:

- User Interface Task **AppTaskUserIf()**: this task keeps reading the status of the push buttons and signals the notifier task in case one or more of the push buttons are pressed.
- Notifier Task **AppTaskNotifier()**: this task keeps pending on its built-in semaphore for a signal from the user interface task to send a push notification to an iOS device.

Figure 7-11 illustrates the interaction between these two tasks.

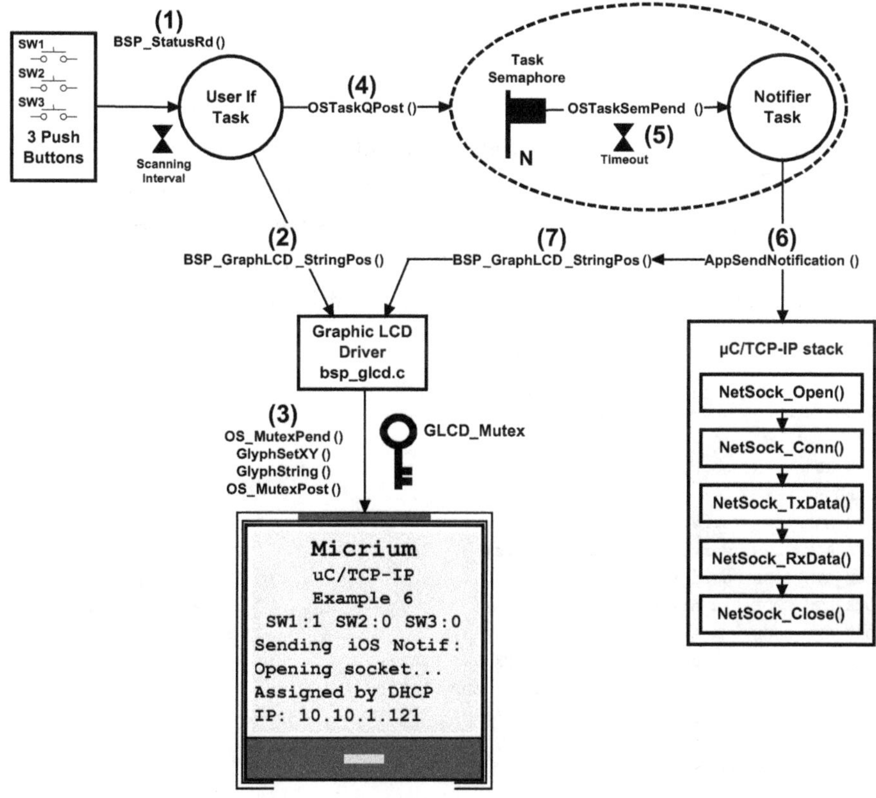

Figure 7-11 **Interaction between the User Interface and Notifier tasks**

F7-11(1) The user interface task implemented by **AppTaskUserIf()** in **app.c** keeps reading the status of the three push buttons.

F7-11(2) The status of the push buttons is represented by the string **SW1:1 SW2:0 SW3:0** where a 0 means Off and a 1 means On (pressed). The User Interface task keeps updating the LCD display with the current status of the push buttons by calling the function **BSP_GraphLCD_StringPos()**.

F7-11(3) Whenever the user presses one or more buttons, the User Interface task signals the Notifier's task built-in semaphore to let it know that a button has been pressed

F7-11(4) The Notifier Task implemented by **AppTaskNotifier()** in **app.c** keeps pending on its built-in semaphore for a signal from the User Interface task.

F7-11(5) Whenever the Notifier Task's semaphore gets signaled, the function **AppSendNotification()** is called in order to push a notification to the iOS device.

F7-11(6) The function **AppSendNotification()** calls a series of functions implemented by the µC/TCP-IP stack in order to establish a connection to the Prowl server and deliver the notification. The function displays the status of the delivery process by calling the function **BSP_GraphLCD_StringPos()** to print on the LCD display. The function **AppSendNotification()** is listed below.

```
static CPU_BOOLEAN AppSendNotification (CPU_CHAR *message)
{
    NET_SOCK_ID         sock;
    NET_IP_ADDR         server_ip_addr;
    NET_SOCK_ADDR_IP    server_sock_addr_ip;
    NET_SOCK_ADDR_LEN   server_sock_addr_ip_size;
    NET_SOCK_RTN_CODE   conn_rtn_code;
    NET_SOCK_RTN_CODE   rx_size;
    NET_SOCK_RTN_CODE   tx_size;
    CPU_CHAR            rx_buf[APP_CFG_PROWL_RX_BUF_SIZE];
    CPU_CHAR            tx_buf[APP_CFG_PROWL_TX_BUF_SIZE];
    NET_ERR             err;

    BSP_GraphLCD_ClrLine(5);
    BSP_GraphLCD_StringPos(5, 0, "Opening socket...");                      (1)
```

```
sock = NetSock_Open(NET_SOCK_ADDR_FAMILY_IP_V4,
                    NET_SOCK_TYPE_STREAM,
                    NET_SOCK_PROTOCOL_TCP,
                    &err);                                                  (2)
if (err != NET_SOCK_ERR_NONE) {
    return (DEF_FALSE);
}

server_ip_addr = NetASCII_Str_to_IP(APP_CFG_PROWL_SERVER_IP_ADDR, &err);   (3)
if (err != NET_ASCII_ERR_NONE) {
    NetSock_Close(sock, &err);                                              (4)
    return (DEF_FALSE);
}
server_sock_addr_ip_size = sizeof(server_sock_addr_ip);                     (5)
Mem_Clr((void *)&server_sock_addr_ip,
        (CPU_SIZE_T) server_sock_addr_ip_size);

server_sock_addr_ip.AddrFamily = NET_SOCK_ADDR_FAMILY_IP_V4;
server_sock_addr_ip.Addr       = NET_UTIL_HOST_TO_NET_32(server_ip_addr);
server_sock_addr_ip.Port       = NET_UTIL_HOST_TO_NET_16(APP_CFG_PROWL_SERVER_PORT);

BSP_GraphLCD_ClrLine(5);
BSP_GraphLCD_StringPos(5, 0, "Connecting...");

conn_rtn_code = NetSock_Conn((NET_SOCK_ID ) sock,
                             (NET_SOCK_ADDR *)&server_sock_addr_ip,
                             (NET_SOCK_ADDR_LEN) sizeof(server_sock_addr_ip),
                             (NET_ERR *)&err);                              (6)

if (err != NET_SOCK_ERR_NONE) {
    NetSock_Close(sock, &err);
    BSP_GraphLCD_ClrLine(5);
    BSP_GraphLCD_StringPos(5, 0, "Error.");
    return (DEF_FALSE);
}

BSP_GraphLCD_ClrLine(5);
BSP_GraphLCD_StringPos(5, 0, "Sending data...");

sprintf(&AppProwlEventName[0], "Button(s)+Pressed");                        (7)
sprintf(&AppProwlEventDesc[0], "Current+status+of+push+buttons:\n%s",
                               message);
```

```
                                        /* Compose the HTTP header.               */     (8)
sprintf(&tx_buf[0], "GET /publicapi/add?"                   \
                                        "apikey=%s&"        \
                                        "providerkey=%s&"   \
                                        "priority=0&"       \
                                        "application=%s&"   \
                                        "event=%s&"         \
                                        "description=%s "   \
                    "HTTP/1.1\r\n"      \
                    "Accept: */*\r\n"   \
                    "Accept-Language: en-US\r\n"  \
                    "User-Agent: Mozilla/4.0 "    \
                                "(compatible; MSIE 8.0; Windows NT 6.1; WOW64; "  \
                                 "Trident/4.0; SLCC2; .NET CLR 2.0.50727; "       \
                                 ".NET CLR 3.5.30729; .NET CLR 3.0.30729; "       \
                                 "Media Center PC 6.0; MDDS; .NET4.0C; "          \
                                 ".NET4.0E; MS-RTC LM 8)\r\n"                     \
                    "Accept-Encoding: gzip, deflate\r\n"  \
                    "Host: %s\r\n\r\n",
                    APP_CFG_PROWL_API_KEY,
                    APP_CFG_PROWL_PROVIDER_KEY,
                    APP_CFG_PROWL_APP_NAME,
                    AppProwlEventName,
                    AppProwlEventDesc,
                    APP_CFG_PROWL_SERVER_IP_ADDR);

                                    /* Transmit the data (send notification).     */     (9)
tx_size = NetSock_TxData(sock,
                         tx_buf,
                         APP_CFG_PROWL_TX_BUF_SIZE,
                         NET_SOCK_FLAG_NONE,
                         &err);

if (err != NET_SOCK_ERR_NONE) {
    NetSock_Close(sock, &err);
    BSP_GraphLCD_ClrLine(5);
    BSP_GraphLCD_StringPos(5, 0, "Error.");
    return (DEF_FALSE);
}

BSP_GraphLCD_ClrLine(5);
BSP_GraphLCD_StringPos(5, 0, "Receiving data...");
```

```
                                        /* Receive the response from the Prowl server. */    (10)
    rx_size = NetSock_RxData(sock,
                             rx_buf,
                             APP_CFG_PROWL_RX_BUF_SIZE,
                             NET_SOCK_FLAG_NONE,
                             &err);
    if (err != NET_SOCK_ERR_NONE) {
        NetSock_Close(sock, &err);
        return (DEF_FALSE);
    }

    NetSock_Close(sock, &err);                                                                (11)

    BSP_GraphLCD_ClrLine(5);
    BSP_GraphLCD_StringPos(5, 0, "Done.");

    return (DEF_TRUE);
}
```

Listing 7-2 **AppSendNotification()**

L7-2(1) Update the status line on the LCD display indicating each step of the process. In this case, the function **BSP_GraphLCD_StringPos()** is called to print "Opening socket..." on the LCD display. Any error messages will also be displayed in this status line.

L7-2(2) The function **NetSock_Open()** in declared in **net_sock.c** and it is called to create a TCP socket. If successful, the function returns a non-negative socket descriptor ID for the new socket connection.

L7-2(3) The function **NetASCII_Str_to_IP()** is declared in **net_ascii.c** and it is responsible of converting a string of an IPv4 address in dotted-decimal notation to an IPv4 address in host-order. In this case the IP address in question is the Prowl server's IP address defined by **APP_CFG_PROWL_SERVER_IP_ADDR**.

L7-2(4) The function **NetSock_Close()** is used to terminate communication and free up a socket. This function will be used whenever there is an error condition or at the end of the notification delivery process.

L7-2(5) **server_sock_addr_ip** is a data structure variable of type **NET_SOCK_ADDR_IP** used to hold the properties of the Prowl server's address such as Port number and the IP address itself. This line allocates memory for the variable and sets it up with the settings defined by **APP_CFG_PROWL_SERVER_IP_ADDR** and **APP_CFG_PROWL_SERVER_PORT**.

L7-2(6) **NetSock_Conn()** connects the new local socket defined by the descriptor **sock** to the remote Prowl server socket address defined by **server_sock_addr_ip**. Since the local socket was not previously bound to any local address and port, the local socket is bound to the default interface's default address and a random port number. When successful, a connected socket has access to both local (YRDKRX62N) and remote (Prowl server) socket addresses. This dedicated connection is maintained for the life of the connection until one or both sides close the connection.

L7-2(7) The Prowl server requires each notification to have a Name and Description. **AppProwlEventName[]** and **AppProwlEventDesc[]** hold such properties and they will be used later when composing the HTTP header.

L7-2(8) The HTTP header is documented by the Prowl Server API. It basically needs to post the API Key, Provider Key, Priority Level, Application Name and the Name and Description of the event. All the characters are copied to an application's transmission buffer called **tx_buf[]**.

L7-2(9) **NetSock_TxData()** copies the bytes from the application's transmission buffer **tx_buf[]** into the remote socket (Prowl server).

L7-2(10) **NetSockRxData()** copies any bytes received from the remote socket (Prowl server) into the application's reception buffer **rx_buf[]**.

L7-2(11) Terminate the connection and update the LCD display with the final status message.

7-5 SUMMARY

This example not only demonstrated how to use µC/TCP-IP sockets but also showed that adding the ability for a Renesas RX62N microcontroller to send push notifications to an iOS device can be easily accomplished. There are many applications where this type of technology could be put to use; security systems and sensor networks to mention a few.

For more details about programming TCP/IP sockets see Chapter 17, "Socket Programming" on page 355.

Chapter

8

Cloud Connectivity: Interfacing with Exosite's One Platform

This chapter presents an example of using μC/TCP-IP sockets to interface with Exosite's cloud-based *One Platform*.

Exosite's cloud-based One Platform is an online service that provides the infrastructure to collect, aggregate, transmit, analyze and display raw or filtered data coming from embedded systems such as sensors, machines and other devices connected to the internet. The data is presented to you on a web portal in the form of a dashboard that you can configure with popular widgets such as graphs, gauges, grids, switches, buttons, etc. You can also configure alarms and notifications based on thresholds and other data conditions.

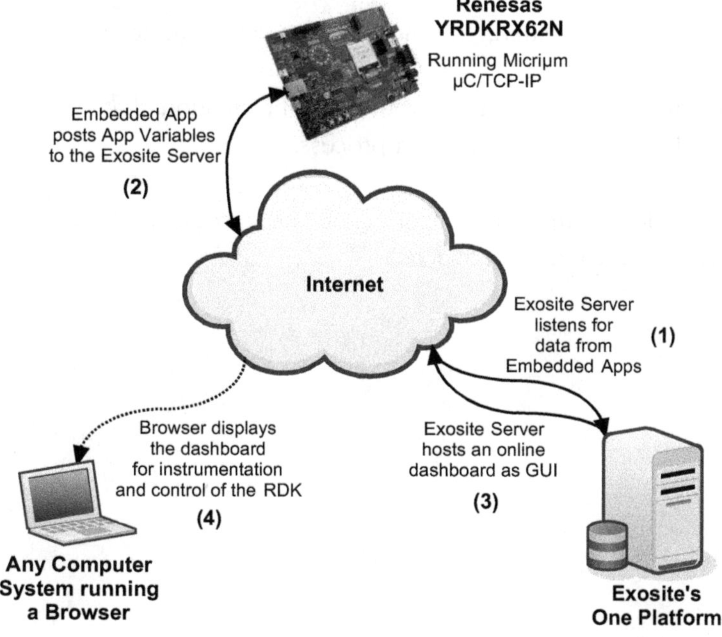

Figure 8-1 **Exosite's One Platform**

The basic service is free for evaluation and has no limitations other than the number of data sources, user access and storage capacity.

The example featured in this chapter will simulate a motor. You can adjust the speed with the potentiometer and the embedded application will keep posting data samples to Exosite's One Platform with real-time data such as motor speed. The example will show you how to create a portal account on the Exosite website and create a dashboard that displays the motor's speed in RPM. You will be able to configure e-mail alerts on over-speed conditions.

8-1 EXOSITE'S ONE PLATFORM CONFIGURATION

The following sections provide a brief guide tailored to get this specific example running. More information about Exosite's One Platform, Renesas hardware and Micrium software is available at `www.exosite.com/renesas`.

8-1-1 CREATING A PORTAL ACCOUNT

Accounts on Exosite Portals are free. Look for the Sign Up link in the upper right hand corner of the Exosite website at: `http://www.exosite.com`.

Once an account has been created, you must first activate your account before logging in.

You will receive an e-mail confirming your account creation that will contain a link to validate and complete the account creation process.

Click the link provided in the e-mail to activate the account and log-in at the following address: `https://portals.exosite.com`.

8-1-2 REGISTERING THE EMBEDDED DEVICE

Portals include a user interface to manage and visualize the devices (a client) sending data to the One Platform (server). Before a client can send data or receive data, it needs to be setup as a device in the Portal. Each device has a unique *CIK* (Client Interface Key) number that identifies it to the platform.

Adding a new device is simple and starts by going to the "Devices" page and clicking the "Add Device" button. A Device Setup popup window will guide you through the setup process by entering the device settings such as the device name, device type, device time zone, and provide a descriptive location value as shown in Figure 8-2.

Notice that the CIK is automatically generated (you are going to need this key when programming the embedded application).

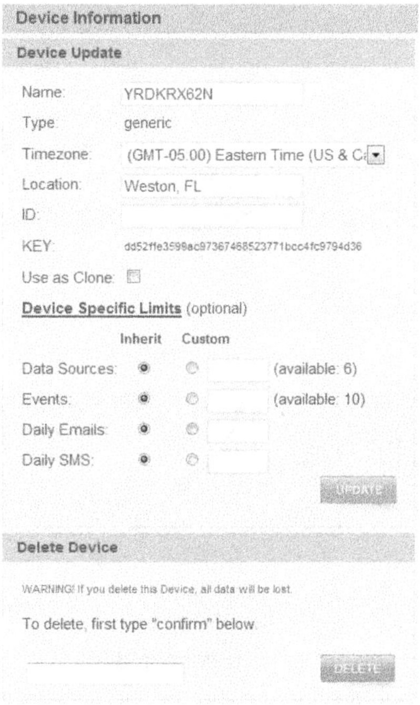

Figure 8-2 **Registering a new device**

8

8-1-3 CONFIGURING DATA SOURCES

Data received by the Exosite One Platform is represented inside of Portals as *Data Sources*. Each data source is unique so that it can be viewed and acted upon on its own for whatever an application or user requires. Data that is received is stored in a time-series based database, meaning the historical data points along with the time stamp of when each came in is available. You could think of each data source as a data stream, ready for on-demand processing.

Now that you have created a Device, the next step is to setup a Data Source for your device.

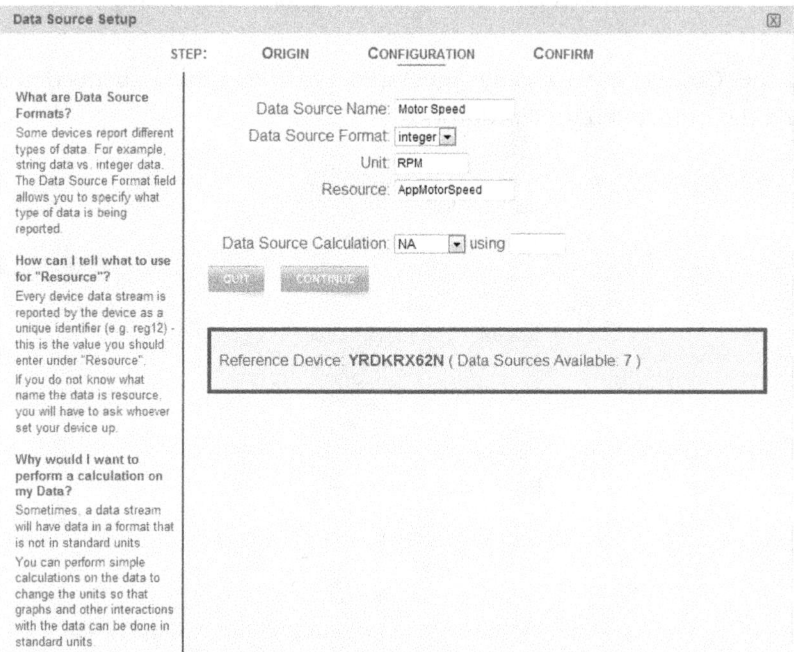

Figure 8-3 **Adding a new data source**

To add a new data source, click the Add Data Source button on the data source management page, in the upper right-hand corner. This will open a setup utility to walk you through adding a new data source.

Enter the data source settings as shown in Figure 8-3.

Now that you have created a Data Source, you can begin collecting and interacting with your data.

8-1-4 CREATING THE WEB-BASED DASHBOARD

A dashboard is a one-page web page that contains widgets containing different information from the Exosite One Platform. A widget could be a list of data sources and values, a graph showing three data sources, or a simple text dialog box to provide information about the specific dashboard. A dashboard is tied to a portal account and all devices, events, and data associated with that portal is available for visualization in the dashboard.

The first time you log into your account, a default dashboard is configured that looks like the one shown in Figure 8-4.

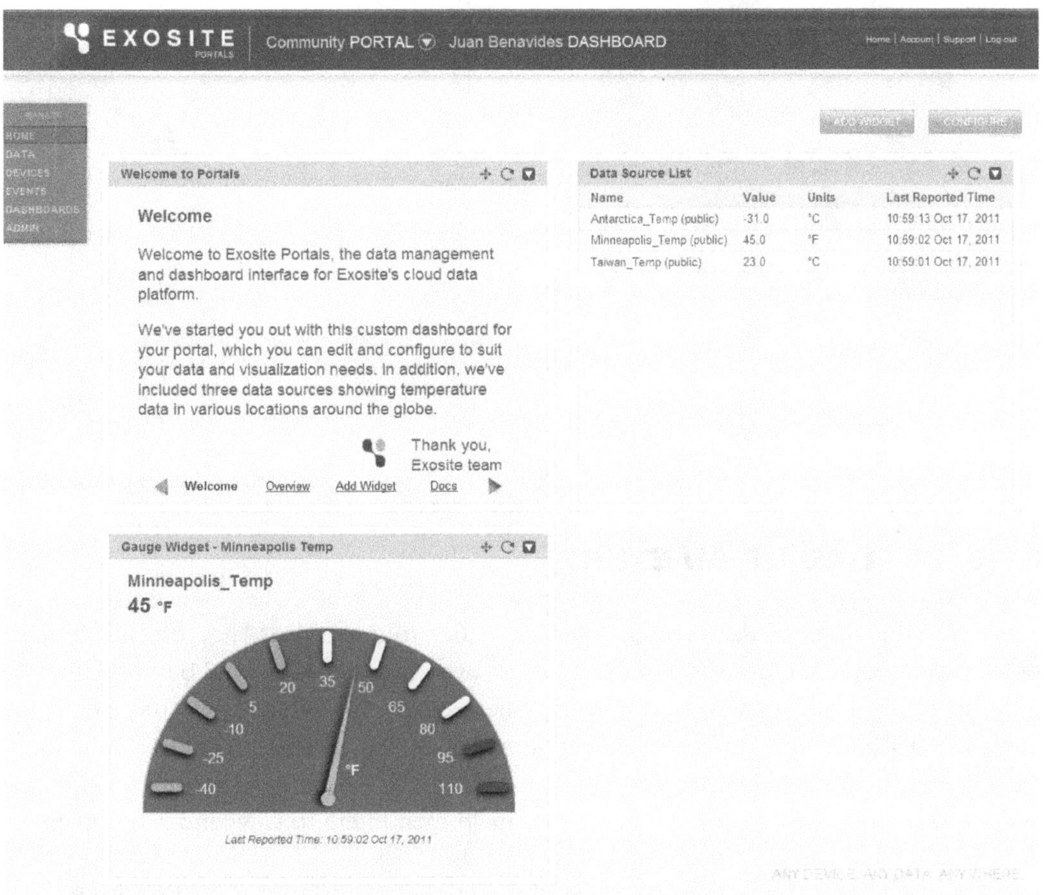

Figure 8-4 **Default Dashboard**

You can either delete the current widgets or edit the existent widgets by selecting one of the options from the menu that drops-down when you click on the button with the arrow facing down.

In order to run the example featured in this chapter you need to create a dashboard that looks like the one shown in Figure 8-5.

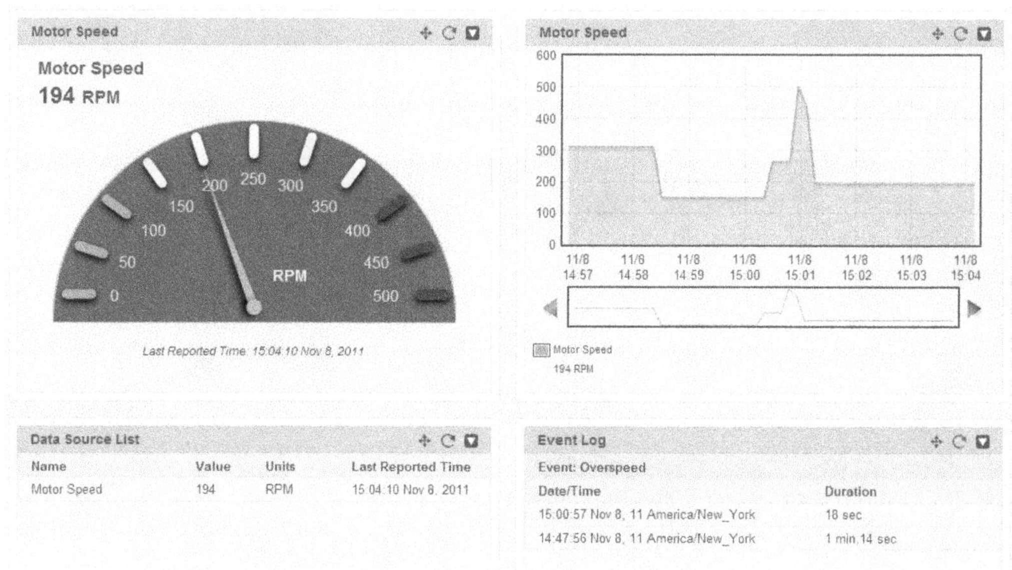

Figure 8-5 **Example Dashboard**

8-1-5 SETTING UP AN EVENT

Events are conditions of data sources that are either true or false. They essentially are a boolean data source themselves. For example, an over-speed event would be to check if the motor speed is above a value of 400 rpm. When above this value, it is 'True' and when below, it is 'False'. Events can tell users important states of a device or alert to a situation.

In order to create an event, select the "Events" main menu item to view and setup Events.

Enter the event settings as shown in Figure 8-6 and click the button "CONTINUE" and you should see this new event added to your list on the event page.

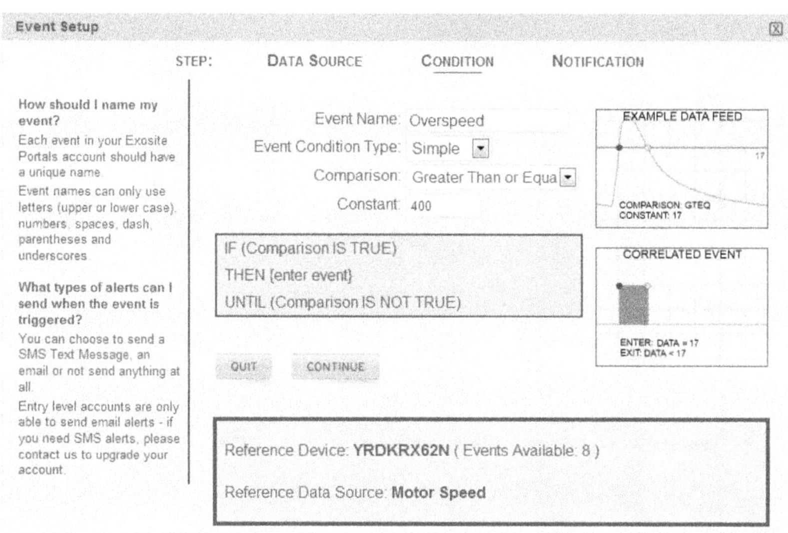

Figure 8-6 **Adding an Event**

Each incoming Event is stored as a piece of data, so in the future, you can look back and investigate event and alert history.

You may find a use for investigating Event trends, often as correlated with time or other data sources. For example, the motor speed threshold event as correlated with the motor temperature could be useful in determining safe operating conditions for a piece of equipment.

8-1-6 SETTING UP AN ALERT

Alerts are dispatches from the platform, triggered by an event. Within Portals a user can add new, edit, and check logs of alerts. These can be useful to be notified that an event condition has occurred. Multiple alerts can be created for an event, perhaps if notification needs to go to multiple individuals.

Alerts available to users in Portals include e-mail and SMS text messages. Other dispatch alerts are available for developers from the Platform using API functionality.

In order to create a new Alert, click the "Add Alert" button on the Events and Alerts page and a window as shown in should popup. Choose the event you want to alert on and click "CONTINUE".

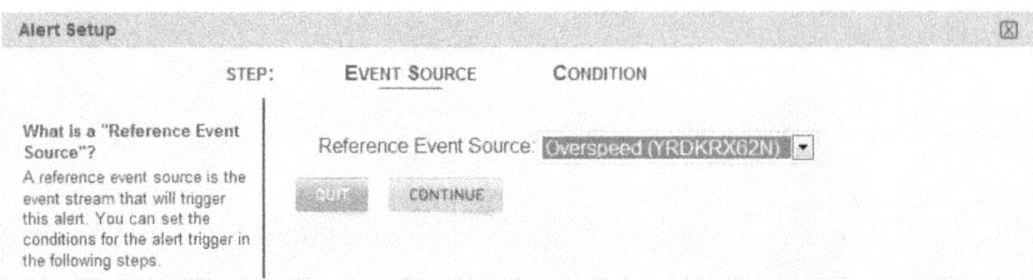

Figure 8-7 **Creating a new Alert**

Enter the alert settings as shown in Figure 8-8 and click "SUBMIT" when finished.

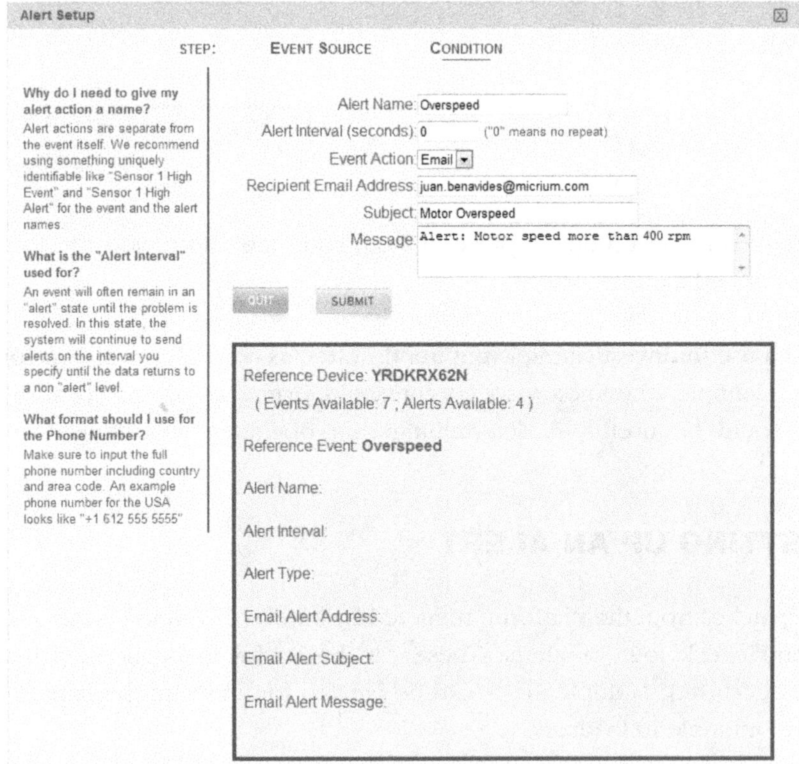

Figure 8-8 **Configuring a new Alert**

Whenever the incoming data meets the event criteria that the alert is based on, the alert will be generated. In this case, whenever the speed of the motor is faster than 400 rpm, the alert will be generated.

8-2 RUNNING THE EXAMPLE PROJECT

Assuming you have followed all the instructions from the previous four sections, section 8-1-1 "Creating a Portal Account" on page 970, section 8-1-2 "Registering the Embedded Device" on page 971, section 8-1-3 "Configuring Data Sources" on page 972 and section 8-1-4 "Creating the Web-Based Dashboard" on page 973, all that is left to do is configure the embedded system, download the code into the RX62N flash memory and run the embedded application.

Start e^2 Studio and open the workspace at:

`$\Micrium\Software\EvalBoards\Renesas\YRDKRX62N\GNURX-e2studio\uC-TCP-IP-Book-Ex-Obj\`

Select the item in the Project Explorer tree labeled as uC-TCP-IP-Ex7 to expand all items. Double click on the file **`app_cfg.h`** located under the **`scr/Lib/`** groups and replace the definitions listed below with the Client Identification Key (CIK) you configured the device at the Exosite website under your account.

```
#define APP_CFG_EXOSITE_SERVER_IP_ADDR    "173.255.209.28"
#define APP_CFG_EXOSITE_SERVER_PORT                     80
#define APP_CFG_EXOSITE_RX_BUF_SIZE                   1024
#define APP_CFG_EXOSITE_TX_BUF_SIZE                   1024
#define APP_CFG_EXOSITE_CIK               "dd52ffe3599ac97367468523771bcc4fc9794d36"
```

Listing 8-1 **Configuring the Exosite client device: app_cfg.h**

Select and right click the item in the Project Explorer tree labeled as uC-TCP-IP-Ex7 in order to build the project.

Just like previous examples, selecting the new file named **`uC-TCP-IP-Ex7.x`** under the **`Binaries`** folder and clicking on the Debug button downloads the code into the RX62N flash memory and starts a debug session.

Click F8 or the Resume button in the debug tool bar to start the application.

The LCD display onboard the YRDKRX62N should look like the ones illustrated in Figure 8-9 while the firmware application configures the IP address:

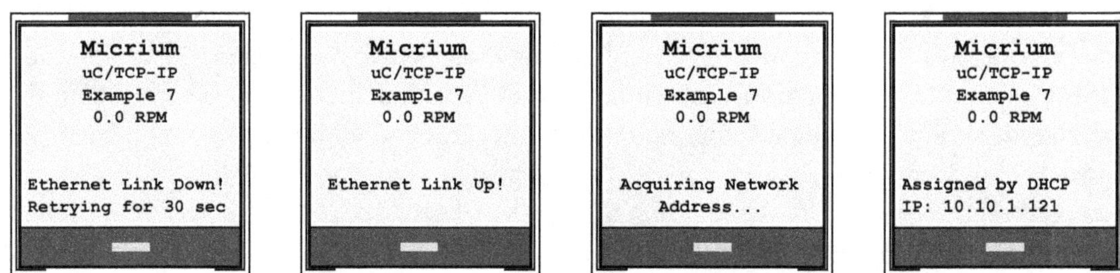

Figure 8-9 **Example #6 LCD screens: DHCP process**

The fourth line that reads `SW1:0 SW2:0 SW3:0` represents the state of the three push buttons onboard the YRDKRX62N labeled as SW1, SW2 and SW3. In order to send a push notification to an iOS device you need to press one of these three buttons. Figure 8-10 below illustrates the screens you should see when pressing SW1:

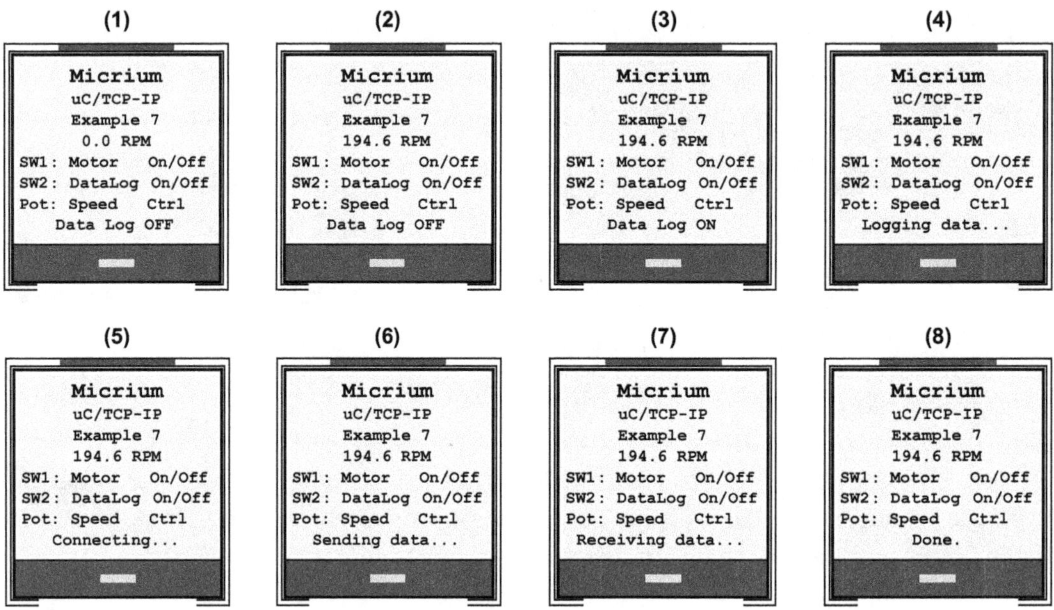

Figure 8-10 **Example #6 LCD screens: Sending iOS notification**

F8-10(1) Once the DHCP process configures the IP parameters of the YRDKRX62N as shown in Figure 8-9, the application is ready to run. The LCD display shows you the current motor speed in RPM and usage information such as: SW1, toggles On/Off the motor. SW2 toggles On/Off the data logging and the Potentiometer controls the speed.

F8-10(2) Pressing SW1 starts the motor, you can control the speed by turning the potentiometer. The range of speed is between 50 and 500 RPM.

F8-10(3) Pressing SW2 starts the data logging of the motor speed reading to the Exosite's One Platform. The last line on the LCD display indicates the state of the Data Logging.

F8-10(4) The application logs data every second and makes use of the last line on the LCD display to show the status of the logging process.

F8-10(5) The first step in the data logging process is to create a socket connection to the Exosite's One Platform.

F8-10(6) Once the connection is established, the application sends the data.

F8-10(7) The application waits for a response from the Exosite's One Platform.

F8-10(8) The application terminates the socket connection.

Any error messages are shown in the LCD screen but if everything is configured right you should be able to see the latest RPM reading in the dashboard hosted by the Exosite One Platform.

In order to find out which one is your dashboard's URL, login to your Exosite's account and select Dashboards from the left hand menu, you should see a list of your dashboards similar to the one in Figure 8-11. The URL is shown in the last column.

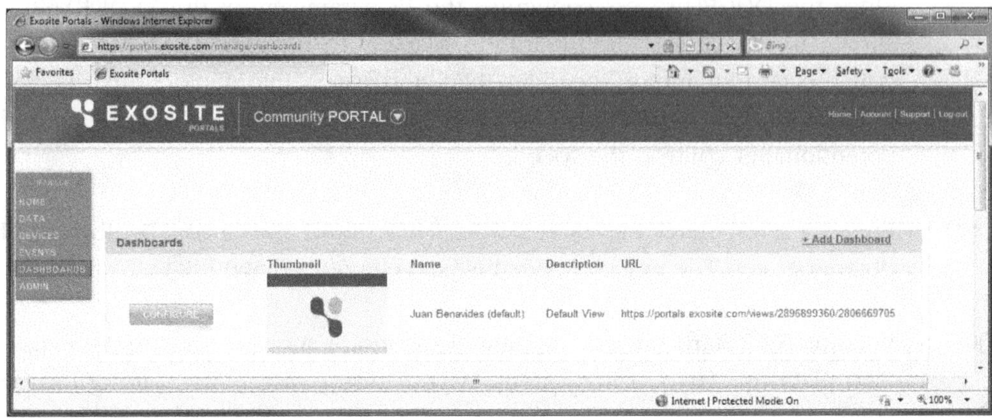

Figure 8-11 **Dashboard Public URL**

Figure 8-12 shows our dashboard that according to Figure 8-11 is at the public URL below: `https://portals.exosite.com/views/2896899360/2806669705`

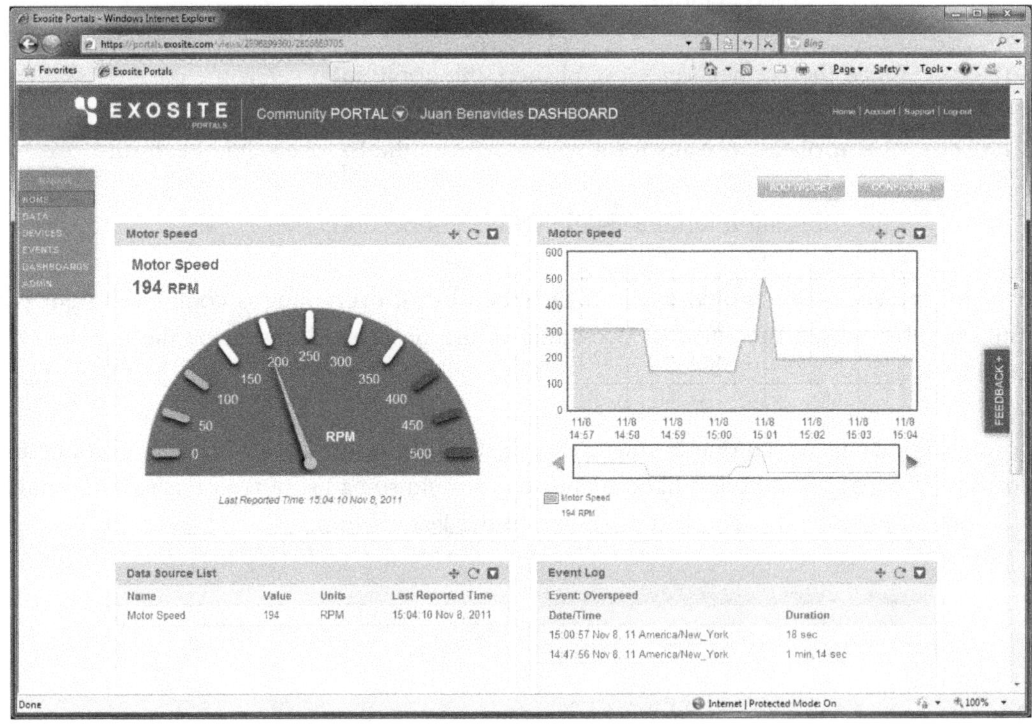

Figure 8-12 **Dashboard displaying run-time data**

8-3 HOW THE CODE WORKS

Exosite's API specifies how a device or piece of software can talk to the One Platform. Once the data is on the One Platform, the processing, analysis, visualization and alerting can begin.

Exosite can create custom API interfaces to match the communications protocol of existing products or the constraints of custom applications. There are four types of APIs readily available:

- HTTP
  - REST
  - JSON RPC
- UDP
- XMPP

The example featured in this book makes use of Micrium's µC/TCP-IP sockets to interface with Exosite's One Platform using their HTTP REST API.

This lightweight API uses a simple HTTP POST method as an easy and secure way to start sending your data to the cloud. It is perfect for client devices that don't have a lot of processing power or software functionality.

Data being sent from the Renesas YRDRX62N is sent as an HTTP POST request. An Exosite client identification key (CIK) is included as a header and the actual values to be sent are included in the body of the request. Multiple client resource values can be written in the body of a single POST request, each client resource is listed by its resource alias name, '=', and its value.

For example, whenever the embedded application running on the Renesas YRDKRX62N identified with a CIK of `dd52ffe3599ac97367468523771bcc4fc9794d36` wants to send data for the Motor Speed it would look like this:

```
POST /api:v1/stack/alias HTTP/1.1
Host: m2.exosite.com
X-Exosite-CIK: dd52ffe3599ac97367468523771bcc4fc9794d36
Content-Type: application/x-www-form-urlencoded; charset=utf-8
Content-Length: 12

AppSpeed=200
```

Listing 8-2 **HTTP POST Example**

The One Platform responds with one of the following codes:

Code	Response	Description
204	No Content	Successful Request, nothing will be returned
4XX	Client Error	There was an error with the request by the client
5XX	Server Error	There was an error with the request on the Server

Table 8-1 **HTTP POST Responses**

This example is based on Example #2 that features a simple DHCP client. Two new tasks are included:

- User Interface Task **AppTaskUserIf()**: this task keeps reading the status of the push buttons and signals the data logging task in case one or more of the push buttons are pressed.

- Data Logging Task **AppTaskDataLog()**: this task keeps pending on its built-in semaphore for a signal from the user interface task to log data to the Exosite's One Platform over TCP/IP.

Figure 8-13 illustrates the interaction between these two tasks.

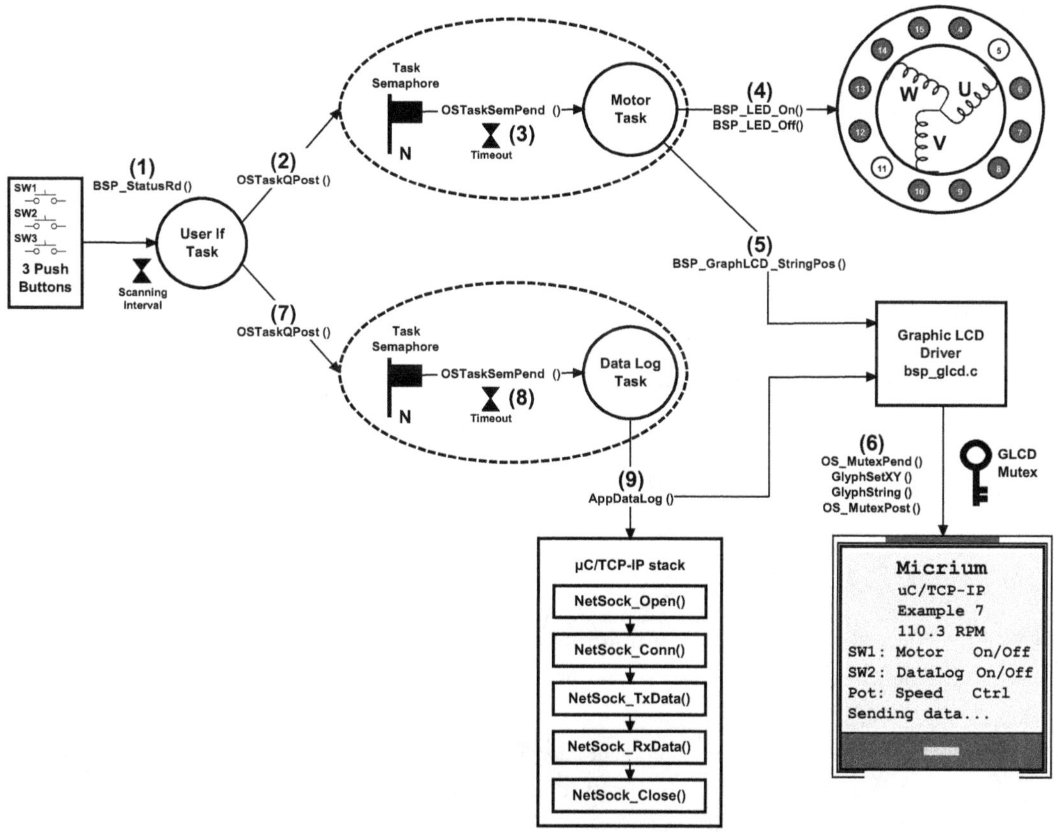

Figure 8-13 **Interaction between the User Interface and Data Logging tasks**

F8-13(1) The user interface task implemented by `AppTaskUserIf()` in `app.c` keeps reading the status of the 3 push buttons.

F8-13(2) Whenever the user presses the SW1 button, the application toggles between the On or Off state of the motor by posting a signal to the Motor Task's built-in semaphore.

F8-13(3) The Motor Task implemented by `AppTaskMotor()` in `app.c` keeps pending on its built-in semaphore for a signal from the User Interface task.

F8-13(4) The Motor Task is responsible for turning On and Off the LEDs by calling the functions **BSP_LED_On()** and **BSP_LED_Off()**. The Motor Task also keeps reading the position of the potentiometer with the purpose of determining the frequency of the LED sequence.

F8-13(5) The Motor Task displays the current speed of the motor on the LCD display by calling the function **BSP_GraphLCD_StringPos()**.

F8-13(6) The Graphic LCD driver implemented in **bsp_glcd.c c** makes use of a kernel object known as mutex, to control the access to the LCD, which is a shared resource. Any task calling the driver function to access the LCD display, needs to acquire the mutex, write to the LCD display and then release the mutex.

F8-13(7) Whenever the user presses the SW2 button the application toggles between the On or Off state of Data Logging by posting a signal to the Data Log Task's built-in semaphore.

F8-13(8) The Data Log Task implemented by **AppTaskDataLog()** in **app.c** keeps pending on its built-in semaphore for a signal from the User Interface task.

F8-13(9) The Data Logging Task logs the current speed to the Exosite's One Platform over TCP/IP by calling the function **AppDataLog()**.

The function **AppDataLog()** calls a series of functions implemented by the µC/TCP-IP stack in order to establish a connection to the Exosite server and send the data. The function displays the status of the delivery process by calling the function **BSP_GraphLCD_StringPos()** to print on the LCD display. The function **AppDataLog()** is listed .

```
static CPU_BOOLEAN AppDataLog (void)
{
    NET_SOCK_ID         sock;
    NET_IP_ADDR         server_ip_addr;
    NET_SOCK_ADDR_IP    server_sock_addr_ip;
    NET_SOCK_ADDR_LEN   server_sock_addr_ip_size;
    NET_SOCK_RTN_CODE   conn_rtn_code;
    NET_SOCK_RTN_CODE   rx_size;
    NET_SOCK_RTN_CODE   tx_size;
    CPU_CHAR            rx_buf[APP_CFG_PROWL_RX_BUF_SIZE];
    CPU_CHAR            tx_buf[APP_CFG_PROWL_TX_BUF_SIZE];
    CPU_INT08U          content_len;
    NET_ERR             err;
    OS_ERR              os_err;
    CPU_CHAR            message[32];

    BSP_GraphLCD_ClrLine(7);
    BSP_GraphLCD_StringPos(7, 1, "Opening socket...");                          (1)

    OSTimeDlyHMSM(0, 0, 1, 0,
                  OS_OPT_TIME_HMSM_STRICT,
                  &os_err);

    sock = NetSock_Open(NET_SOCK_ADDR_FAMILY_IP_V4,
                        NET_SOCK_TYPE_STREAM,
                        NET_SOCK_PROTOCOL_TCP,
                        &err);                                                  (2)
    if (err != NET_SOCK_ERR_NONE) {
        return (DEF_FALSE);
    }

    server_ip_addr = NetASCII_Str_to_IP(APP_CFG_EXOSITE_SERVER_IP_ADDR, &err);     (3)
    if (err != NET_ASCII_ERR_NONE) {
        NetSock_Close(sock, &err);                                              (4)
        return (DEF_FALSE);
    }

    server_sock_addr_ip_size = sizeof(server_sock_addr_ip);                     (5)
    Mem_Clr((void *)&server_sock_addr_ip,
            (CPU_SIZE_T) server_sock_addr_ip_size);

    server_sock_addr_ip.AddrFamily = NET_SOCK_ADDR_FAMILY_IP_V4;
    server_sock_addr_ip.Addr       = NET_UTIL_HOST_TO_NET_32(server_ip_addr);
    server_sock_addr_ip.Port       = NET_UTIL_HOST_TO_NET_16(APP_CFG_EXOSITE_SERVER_PORT);
```

8

```
BSP_GraphLCD_ClrLine(7);
BSP_GraphLCD_StringPos(7, 3, "Connecting...");

OSTimeDlyHMSM(0, 0, 1, 0,
              OS_OPT_TIME_HMSM_STRICT,
              &os_err);

conn_rtn_code = NetSock_Conn((NET_SOCK_ID ) sock,
                             (NET_SOCK_ADDR *)&server_sock_addr_ip,
                             (NET_SOCK_ADDR_LEN) sizeof(server_sock_addr_ip),
                             (NET_ERR *)&err);                              (6)

if (err != NET_SOCK_ERR_NONE) {
    NetSock_Close(sock, &err);
    sprintf(&rx_buf[0], "Error: %d", err);
    BSP_GraphLCD_ClrLine(7);
    BSP_GraphLCD_StringPos(7, 6, "Error.");
    OSTimeDlyHMSM(0, 0, 1, 0,
                  OS_OPT_TIME_HMSM_STRICT,
                  &err);
    return (DEF_FALSE);
}

BSP_GraphLCD_ClrLine(7);
BSP_GraphLCD_StringPos(7, 2, "Sending data...");

OSTimeDlyHMSM(0, 0, 1, 0,
              OS_OPT_TIME_HMSM_STRICT,
              &os_err);

sprintf(&message[0], "AppSpeed=%d", (CPU_INT16U)AppMotorSpeed);             (7)

content_len = strlen(message);

                                 /* Compose the HTTP header.          */   (8)
sprintf(&tx_buf[0], "POST /api:v1/stack/alias HTTP/1.1\r\n"  \
                    "Host: m2.exosite.com\r\n"
                    "X-Exosite-CIK: %s\r\n"    \
                    "Content-Type: application/x-www-form-urlencoded; charset=utf-8\r\n" \
                    "Content-Length: %d\r\n\r\n" \
                    "%s",
                    APP_CFG_EXOSITE_CIK,
                    content_len,
                    message);
```

```
                                  /* Transmit the data (send notification).      */    (9)
    tx_size = NetSock_TxData(sock,
                             tx_buf,
                             APP_CFG_EXOSITE_TX_BUF_SIZE,
                             NET_SOCK_FLAG_NONE,
                             &err);

    if (err != NET_SOCK_ERR_NONE) {
        NetSock_Close(sock, &err);
        BSP_GraphLCD_ClrLine(7);
        BSP_GraphLCD_StringPos(7, 6, "Error.");
        OSTimeDlyHMSM(0, 0, 1, 0,
                      OS_OPT_TIME_HMSM_STRICT,
                      &os_err);
        return (DEF_FALSE);
    }

    BSP_GraphLCD_ClrLine(7);
    BSP_GraphLCD_StringPos(7, 1, "Receiving data...");

    OSTimeDlyHMSM(0, 0, 1, 0,
                  OS_OPT_TIME_HMSM_STRICT,
                  &os_err);

                                  /* Receive the response from the Prowl server.  */   (10)
    rx_size = NetSock_RxData(sock,
                             rx_buf,
                             APP_CFG_EXOSITE_RX_BUF_SIZE,
                             NET_SOCK_FLAG_NONE,
                             &err);
    if (err != NET_SOCK_ERR_NONE) {
        NetSock_Close(sock, &err);
        return (DEF_FALSE);
    }

    NetSock_Close(sock, &err);                                                          (11)

    BSP_GraphLCD_ClrLine(7);
    BSP_GraphLCD_StringPos(7, 7, "Done.");

    return (DEF_TRUE);
}
```

Listing 8-3 **AppDataLog()**

L8-3(1) Update the status line on the LCD display indicating each step of the process. In this case, the function **BSP_GraphLCD_StringPos()** is called to print "Opening socket..." on the LCD display. Any error messages will also be displayed in this status line.

L8-3(2) The function **NetSock_Open()** in declared in **net_sock.c** and it is called to create a TCP socket. If successful, the function returns a non-negative socket descriptor ID for the new socket connection.

L8-3(3) The function **NetASCII_Str_to_IP()** is declared in **net_ascii.c** and it is responsible of converting a string of an IPv4 address in dotted-decimal notation to an IPv4 address in host-order. In this case the IP address in question is the Prowl server's IP address defined by **APP_CFG_EXOSITE_SERVER_IP_ADDR**.

L8-3(4) The function **NetSock_Close()** is used to terminate communication and free up a socket. This function will be used whenever there is an error condition or at the end of the data logging delivery process.

L8-3(5) **server_sock_addr_ip** is a data structure variable of type **NET_SOCK_ADDR_IP** used to hold the properties of the Prowl server's address such as Port number and the IP address itself. This line allocates memory for the variable and sets it up with the settings defined by **APP_CFG_EXOSITE_SERVER_IP_ADDR** and **APP_CFG_EXOSITE_SERVER_PORT**.

L8-3(6) **NetSock_Conn()** connects the new local socket defined by the descriptor **sock** to the remote Exosite server socket address defined by **server_sock_addr_ip**. Since the local socket was not previously bound to any local address and port, the local socket is bound to the default interface's default address and a random port number. When successful, a connected socket has access to both local (YRDKRX62N) and remote (Exosite server) socket addresses. This dedicated connection is maintained for the life of the connection until one or both sides close the connection.

L8-3(7) According to the API, the Exosite server requires each data log to have the name of the data source and the value. The string of characters **message[]** holds such properties and they will be used in the next step when composing the HTTP header.

L8-3(8) The HTTP header is documented by the Exosite Server API. It basically needs to post the CIK key and the Name and current value of the data source(s). All the characters are copied to an application's transmission buffer called `tx_buf[]`.

L8-3(9) `NetSock_TxData()` copies the bytes from the application's transmission buffer `tx_buf[]` into the remote socket (Exosite server).

L8-3(10) `NetSockRxData()` copies any bytes received from the remote socket (Exosite server) into the application's reception buffer `rx_buf[]`.

L8-3(11) Terminate the connection and update the LCD display with the final status message.

8-4 SUMMARY

Cloud connectivity for the Renesas YRDKRX62N is provided by Exosite. It gives your RDK a secure website dashboard at **https://renesas.exosite.com**. This online dashboard portal can be used to display data collected from your RDK, to send data to your RDK, and to connect & manage multiple RDK systems. Just like the rest of examples featured in this book, software source code for the RDK is provided as a download from the Micrium website so that you can extend it for your own connected device application.

Cloud connected devices send and receive data over the Internet using a wired or wireless data communications interface. On the YRDKRX62N, this includes the Ethernet interface and the RedPine WiFi interface (if available). Cloud-capable firmware is pre-programmed (and available for download & modification) that enables the RDK for cloud connectivity. Cloud connected devices are called "Clients".

Although the Internet is used as the medium for Client communication, cloud connectivity requires a cloud-based server platform that does things like: server-based authentication, storage, processing, routing of data, and application software functionality. Exosite's server technologies provide a redundant and distributed application framework that does this heavy lifting. It allows the RDK software to simply use an authentication key (a Client Interface Key - "CIK") and a data port name (an Alias - e.g. "AppSpeed") to interact with its own or other cloud-connected data. The server technologies that make this possible are called the "Data Platform" (Exosite's One Platform).

Real-world connected applications use the Data Platform in different ways, requiring configuration of the Data Platform that is beyond the scope of a single Client. This configuration is necessary for features such as ownership hierarchy, data permissions, public/private sharing, processing algorithms, event & alert conditions, Client provisioning, and data visualization. Data Platform Application Programming Interfaces (APIs) are used to configure these features on the Data Platform. These APIs are called "Platform APIs".

While automated systems interact with the Data Platform directly via the Platform APIs, human beings need a user interface. The online "Dashboard" user interface located at `https://renesas.exosite.com` is called the "Portals Website". Its secure browsing connection allows human users to configure the Data Platform and to visualize & manage connected RDK systems. Under the hood, the Portals uses the Platform APIs, and is just one example of a user interface that can be built on top of the Data Platform for connected applications.

The Renesas RX processor family is ideally suited to be the communications processor for many connected products. RX processors fill the gap between the more powerful SH family (processing horsepower, graphical user interfaces) and the simpler RL family (low power, no on-board cloud communications). This processor family has a good balance of flash, RAM, processing & peripherals to power products requiring industrial-grade processing and cloud connectivity.

It is easy to create a cloud connected product by using the production-ready reference designs provided by the RDK's hardware and software. All of the building blocks – from hardware schematics to cloud-capable firmware to data platform APIs – are all provided and functional out of the box. Just as you can purchase Renesas RX processors from your local distributor, you can also subscribe to Exosite's cloud services for your go-to-market product design.

Micrium's µC/TCP-IP stack provides support for interfacing with Exosite's One Platform's API. The µC/TCP-IP socket programming support includes two types of sockets: Datagram sockets and Stream sockets.

In addition to the BSD 4.x sockets application interface (API), the µC/TCP-IP stack gives the developer the opportunity to use Micrium's own socket functions with which to interact.

Although there is a great deal of similarity between the two APIs, the parameters of the two sets of functions differ slightly. The purpose of this cloud connectivity example is to give developers a first look at Micrium's functions by providing a concrete example of how to use the API.

For those interested in BSD socket programming, there are plenty of books, online references, and articles dedicated to this subject.

The example has been designed to be as simple as possible. Hence, only basic error checking is performed. When it comes to building real applications, those checks should be extended to deliver a product that is as robust as possible.

Appendix

Ethernet Driver

Chapter 2, "Introduction to Networking" on page 41 of Part I of this book showed that the internet protocol suite can be described as a set of layers. Each layer solves a set of requirements involving the transmission of data and provides a well defined service to upper layer protocols. The table below shows how the combination of Renesas electronics and Micrium software delivers the full implementation of each layer in Part II of this book.

Layer	Function	Implemented by
Layer 7, 6 and 5 Application	Interfaces with the API of Micrium's µC/TCP-IP stack.	Micrium's Examples with IP connectivity.
Layer 4 Transport	Isolates the three upper application layers from the complexities of layers 1 through 3 by providing the functions necessary to ensure the reliability of point-to-point data communications.	Micrium's µC/TCP-IP code at $\Micrium\Software\uC-TCP-IP-V2\Source\net_*.*
Layer 3 Network	Establishes, maintains and terminates network connections by handling the routing of packets from one piece of equipment to another.	Micrium's µC/TCP-IP code at $\Micrium\Software\uC-TCP-IP-V2\Source\net_*.*
Layer 2 Data Link	Handles the packaging of bits into frames and their transmission or reception over physical circuits. It is at this layer that most error detection and correction is performed.	Renesas' RX62N MCU integrated ethernet controller and Micrium's device driver code at $\Micrium\Software\uC-TCPIP-V2\Dev\Ether\RX-EtherC\net_dev_rx_etherc.*
Layer 1 Physical	Handles the transmission of bits over physical circuits. It is best described by its physical parameters such as the amount of signal voltage swing and the duration of voltages among others.	National Semiconductor DP83640 PHY and Micrium's driver code at $\Micrium\Software\uC-TCPIP-V2\Dev\Ether\PHY\DP83640\net_phy_dp83640.*

Table A-1 **TCP/IP model layers**

The details behind the examples are discussed in Chapters 8, 9, 10 and 11 and the source code is provided with the book.

Layers 3 and 4 are implemented by Micrium's µC/TCP-IP stack, which is discussed in great detail in Part I of this book.

Layer 2 is implemented by the Ethernet controller built-in the Renesas RX62N MCU.

Layer 1 is implemented by the Renesas Demonstration Kit YRDKRX62N and the onboard DP83640 PHY from National Semiconductor.

This appendix will cover the details behind the DMA-based µC/TCP-IP driver for the Renesas RX62N. It starts by describing some of the main features of the Ethernet Controller. The appendix proceeds at explaining a few details about the YRDKRX62N before describing the driver code.

For the examples provided with this book, the RX62N Ethernet driver is delivered in object code only. To access source code, a license must be obtained from Micrium (see **Appendix G, "µC/TCP-IP Licensing Policy" on page 795**).

Micrium provides a Network Device Driver API and data type naming conventions. By following these naming conventions, as well as standard Micrium conventions and software development patterns, the process of device driver debugging and testing is simplified, allowing developers to become familiar with device drivers authored by others.

It is important to develop a driver to be re-entrant, as µC/TCP-IP supports multiple interfaces of the same type. By avoiding global macros and variables (e.g., using the device data area, and defining macros within the driver **.c** file), driver developers ensure that projects containing multiple device driver files are able to compile.

Chapter 14, "Network Device Drivers" on page 299 provides the guidelines for the architecture of a Network Device Driver. Micrium also provides Network Driver templates that are located in the following directory:

```
$\Micrium\Software\uC-TCPIP-V2\Dev\Ether\Template
```

A-1 RX62N ON-CHIP ETHERNET CONTROLLER

The RX62N group has an on-chip Ethernet Controller (ETHERC) conforming to the Ethernet or IEEE802.3 MAC layer standard. The Renesas Demonstration Kit YRDKRX62N implements a physical-layer LSI (PHY-LSI) that enables the ETHERC to perform transmission and reception of Ethernet/IEEE802.3 frames. The ETHERC has one MAC layer interface port. The ETHERC is connected directly to the Ethernet DMA controller (EDMAC). The EDMAC controls most of the buffer management by using descriptors. This reduces the load on the CPU, thus enabling efficient data transmission and reception.

Figure A-1 shows a block diagram of the RX62N on-chip Ethernet Controller (ETHERC):

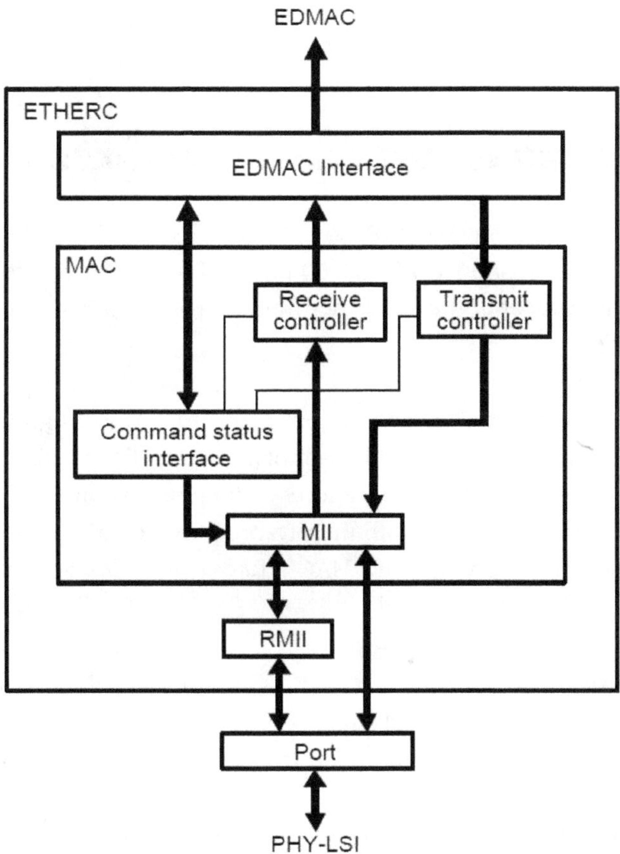

Figure A-1 **ETHERC Block Diagram**

A-1-1 ETHERNET CONTROLLER SPECIFICATIONS

- Compliance with flow control as defined in IEEE 802.3x standards
- Transmission and Reception of Ethernet/IEEE 802.3 frames
- Transfer rate at 10 or 100 Mbps
- Full- and half-duplex modes
- Conforms to MII (Media Independent Interface) or RMII (Reduced Media Independent Interface) as defined in IEEE 802.3u
- Detection of Magic PacketsTM* or output of a "wake-on-LAN" signal (WOL)

A-2 RENESAS DEMONSTRATION KIT YRDKRX62N

On board the YRDKRX62N demonstration kit, the RX62N on-chip Ethernet controller is connected to a National Semiconductor DP83640 physical receiver chip (PHY) enabling it to perform transmission and reception of Ethernet frames. The chip is configured in Reduced Pin-count mode (RMII).

The Ethernet PHY is configured at power-on reset for Auto-Negotiation, advertising 10Base-T and 100Base-TX in both full and half-duplex modes. Each unit is pre-programmed with a unique IEEE assigned MAC address ranging from 00:30:55:08:00:01 to 00:30:55:08:FF:FF. If there is a problem with the pre-programmed MAC address, the example code will default to 00:30:55:08:00:00. The MAC address programmed into the part at the factory is shown on the back of the board.

For the examples provided in this book, the YRDKRX62N along with the DP83640 implement the Ethernet Physical Layer for the Ethernet controller on the RX62N MCU.

For the purpose of Ethernet connectivity the YRDKRX62N demonstration kit offers a 10/100 Ethernet PHY with MII and RMII interface and it also provides the RJ45 Ethernet connector with integrated magnetics and LEDs.

The following sections provide the implementation of a driver for the RX62N integrated Ethernet controller based on the driver template in:

```
$\Micrium\Software\uC-TCPIP-V2\Dev\Ether\Template
```

Any changes from the template are identified.

A-3 DEVICE DRIVER CONVENTIONS

DEVICE DRIVER FILE NAMES

All Ethernet device drivers are named **net_dev_<controller>.c** and **.h**, where **<controller>** represents the name of the device. The names for the purposes of this book are **net_dev_rx_etherc.c** and **net_dev_rx_etherc.h** and are located in the following directory:

```
$\Micrium\Software\uC-TCP-IP-V2\Dev\Ether\RX-EtherC\
```

A-4 DMA-BASED DEVICE DRIVER MEMORY MAP FOR THE RX62N

The µC/TCP-IP device driver memory map comprises the RX62N Ethernet Controller module (ETHERC) memory map (device registers), the RX62N Ethernet DMA Controller module (EDMAC) memory map, and the different data structures allocated by the driver developer.

DMA-based device drivers such as the one presented in this book allocate memory from the µC/LIB memory module for descriptors, data buffers, pointers and other variables. By using the µC/LIB memory module instead of declaring arrays, the driver developer can easily align descriptors to any required boundary and benefit from the run-time flexibility of the device configuration structure.

Figure A-2 illustrates the memory map of the µC/TCP-IP device driver for the RX62N, and the following sections will make reference to this figure in order to explain the DMA process.

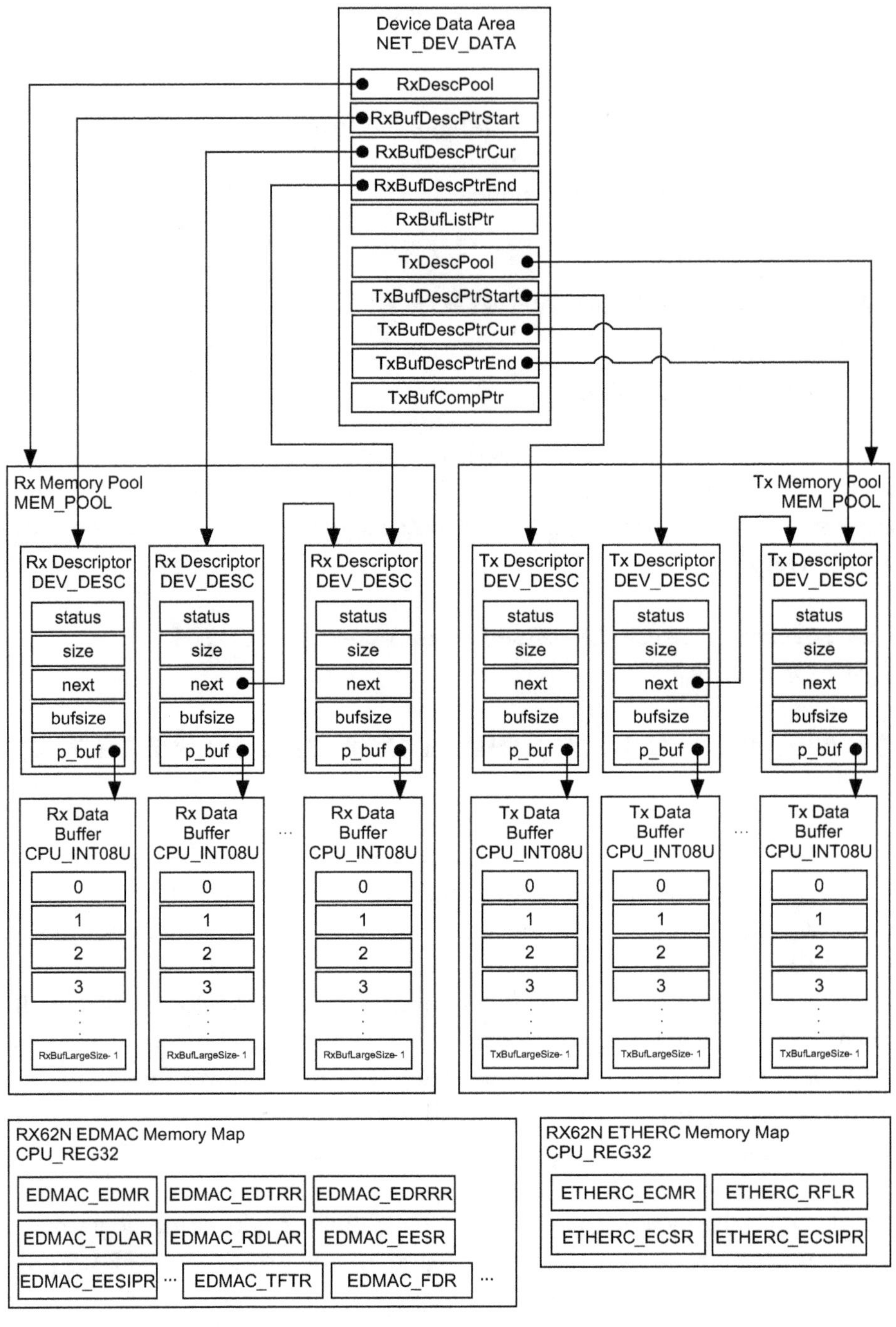

Figure A-2 **DMA-based Device Driver Memory Map for the RX62N**

A-4-1 DEVICE REGISTER STRUCTURE NAME

Each device driver contains a structure **NET_DEV** with typically one or more **CPU_REG32** data types, which represent each device register present in the device address space.

Some of the most important device registers are illustrated in Figure A-2 at the bottom of the figure and we will mention them in section A-4-2 "DMA" on page 1001 when we describe the DMA process.

Each structure member must be named in accordance with the documented register name provided within the device documentation. All register names within the **NET_DEV** structure are capitalized.

The device register definition structure must take into account appropriate register offsets and apply reserved space as required. The registers listed within the register definition structure must reflect the exact ordering and data sizes illustrated in the RX62N hardware manual.

The device register definition structure is mapped over the base address 000C0000h according to the EDMAC and ETHERC memory maps listed in the RX62N Hardware Manual from Renesas.

Reserved bits should be written with 0 and ignored on read to allow future extension. Unused registers read zero and a write has no effect.

An example of some of the first and last device registers defined in **net_dev_rx_etherc_reg.h** is provided in Listing A-1.

```
typedef  struct  net_dev {
    CPU_REG32  EDMAC_EDMR;           /* EDMAC Mode Register.                                  */
    CPU_REG32  RESERVED0[0x01];
    CPU_REG32  EDMAC_EDTRR;          /* EDMAC Transmit Request Register.                      */
    CPU_REG32  RESERVED1[0x01];
    CPU_REG32  EDMAC_EDRRR;          /* EDMAC Receive Request Register.                       */
    CPU_REG32  RESERVED2[0x01];
    CPU_REG32  EDMAC_TDLAR;          /* EDMAC Transmit Descriptor List Start Address Register. */
    CPU_REG32  RESERVED3[0x01];
    CPU_REG32  EDMAC_RDLAR;          /* EDMAC Receive Descriptor List Start Address Register.  */
    CPU_REG32  RESERVED4[0x01];
    CPU_REG32  EDMAC_EESR;           /* EDMAC/ETHERC Status Register.                         */
    CPU_REG32  RESERVED5[0x01];
    CPU_REG32  EDMAC_EESIPR;         /* EDMAC/ETHERC Status Interrupt Permission Register.    */
    CPU_REG32  RESERVED6[0x01];
    CPU_REG32  EDMAC_TRSCER;         /* Tx/Rx Status Copy Enable Register.                    */

    CPU_REG32  ETHERC_ECMR;          /* ETHERC Mode Register.                                 */
    CPU_REG32  RESERVED17[0x01];
    CPU_REG32  ETHERC_RFLR;          /* Receive Frame Length Register.                        */
    CPU_REG32  RESERVED18[0x01];
    CPU_REG32  ETHERC_ECSR;          /* ETHERC Status Register.                               */
    CPU_REG32  RESERVED19[0x01];
    CPU_REG32  ETHERC_ECSIPR;        /* ETHERC Interrupt Permission Register.                 */
    CPU_REG32  RESERVED20[0x01];
    CPU_REG32  ETHERC_PIR;           /* PHY Interface Register.                               */
    CPU_REG32  RESERVED21[0x01];
    CPU_REG32  ETHERC_PSR;           /* PHY Status Register.                                  */
.
.
.
    CPU_REG32  ETHERC_CEFCR;         /* CRC Error Frame Receive Counter Register.             */
    CPU_REG32  ETHERC_FRECR;         /* Frame Receive Error Counter Register.                 */
    CPU_REG32  ETHERC_TSFRCR;        /* Too-Short Frame Receive Counter Register.             */
    CPU_REG32  ETHERC_TLFRCR;        /* Too-Long Frame Receive Counter Register.              */
    CPU_REG32  ETHERC_RFCR;          /* Residual-Bit Frame Receive Counter Register.          */
    CPU_REG32  ETHERC_MAFCR;         /* Multicast Address Frame Receive Counter Register.     */
} NET_DEV;
```

Listing A-1 **Register Definitions in net_dev_rx_etherc_reg.h**

A-4-2 DMA

The 10/100-Mbps Ethernet MAC on the RX62N features a dedicated DMA controller responsible for updating the Transmit and Receive Buffer Descriptors every time a frame has been transmitted or received. DMA-based device drivers like the one described in this book contain one or more data types for the device descriptors. When possible, for devices with one descriptor format, the name of the descriptor data type should be **DEV_DESC**. Variations of this name may exist for devices with more than one type of descriptor. Listing A-2 shows an example of the Rx and Tx descriptors for the RX62N:

```
typedef  struct  dev_desc {
    CPU_REG32    status;                        /* DMA status register.            */
#if CPU_CFG_ENDIAN_TYPE == CPU_ENDIAN_TYPE_LITTLE
    CPU_REG16    size;                          /* DMA size                        */
    CPU_REG16    bufsize;                       /* DMA buffer size.                */
#else
    CPU_REG16    bufsize;                       /* DMA buffer size.                */
    CPU_REG16    size;                          /* DMA size                        */
#endif
    CPU_INT08U   *p_buf;                        /* DMA buffer pointer              */
    DEV_DESC     *next;                         /* DMA next descriptor pointer.    */
} DEV_DESC;
```

Listing A-2 **Descriptor Data Type Structure DEV_DESC defined in net_dev_rx_etherc_reg.h**

DMA device drivers will allocate memory for descriptors (when applicable) and a device data area. The data area structure typically includes error counters and variables used to track the state of the device as shown in Code Listing A-3:

```
typedef  struct  net_dev_data {
    DEV_DESC     *RxBufDescPtrCur;
    DEV_DESC     *RxBufDescPtrStart;
    DEV_DESC     *RxBufDescPtrEnd;
    DEV_DESC     *TxBufDescPtrCur;
    DEV_DESC     *TxBufDescPtrStart;
    DEV_DESC     *TxBufDescPtrEnd;
    void         *TxBufCompPtr;

    MEM_POOL      RxDescPool;
    MEM_POOL      TxDescPool;

    LIST         *RxReadyListPtr;
    LIST         *RxBufferListPtr;
    LIST         *RxFreeListPtr;
} NET_DEV_DATA;
```

Listing A-3 **Device Data Area Data Type Structure NET_DEV_DATA defined in net_dev_rx_etherc.c**

Figure A-2 on page 998 illustrates both the device data area and the two memory pools that contain the receive and transmit descriptors and data buffers.

The driver developer basically starts by allocating two memory pools large enough to store the receive and transmit descriptors and the receive and transmit data buffers; this is performed via calls to the µC/LIB memory module.

The number of descriptors and the size and number of data buffers become an optimization problem where you want to maximize performance by increasing the number of descriptors and the size and number of data buffers, but at the same time you want to keep your data footprint to the minimum. A minimum of two descriptors for the reception of Ethernet frames should be configured, because while the controller is transferring a recently received Ethernet frame, it must have an available descriptor in order to receive the next incoming Ethernet frame. See section 5-1 "µC/TCP-IP Example #4" on page 896 for more details about fine tuning µC/TCP-IP.

The next sections will describe the Reception and Transmission process with DMA.

DMA-BASED RECEPTION PROCESS

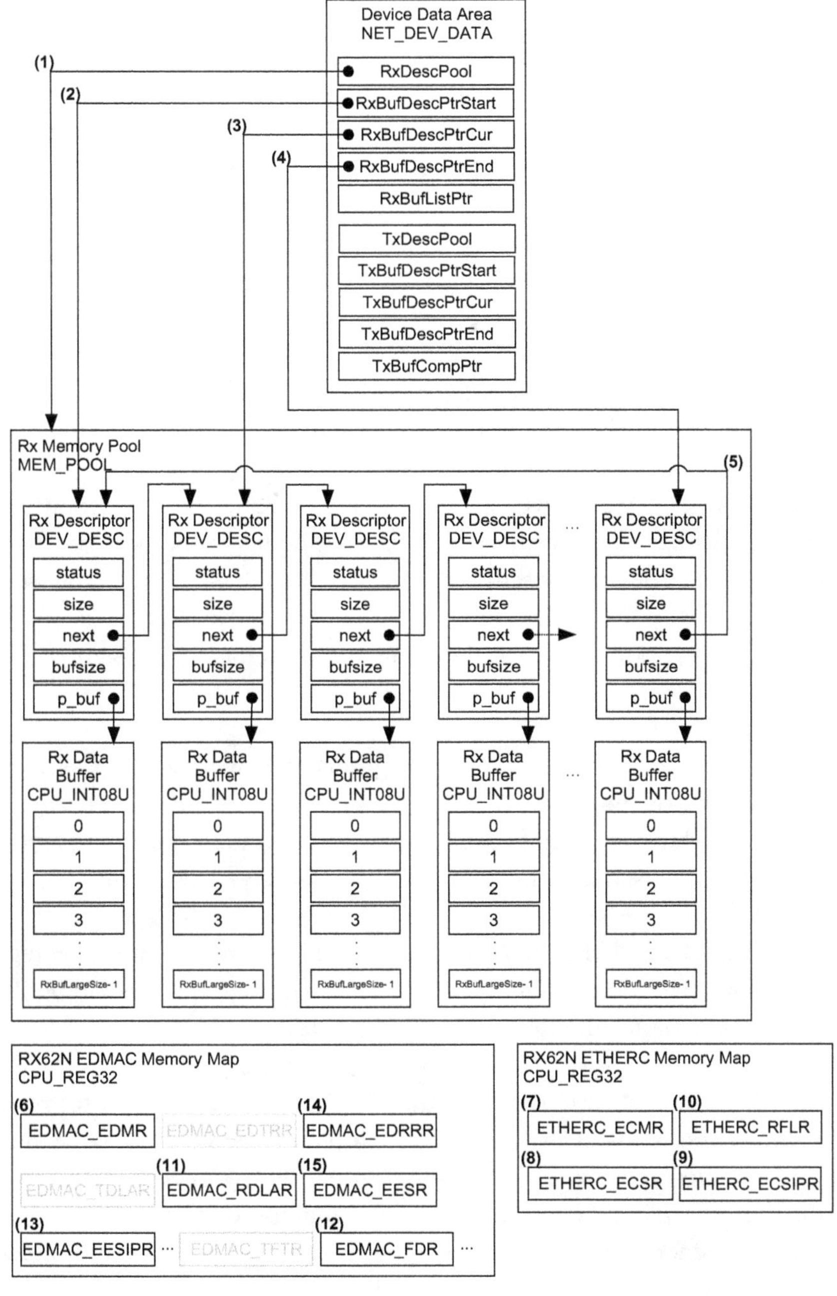

Figure A-3 **DMA-based Reception Process**

FA-3(1) The network device driver allocates a memory pool for all receive descriptors and receive data buffers based on the Network Device Driver configuration. For example, the number of receive DMA descriptors and the number of receive data buffers.

FA-3(2) The network device driver initializes the pointer **RxBufDescPtrStart**. This pointer keeps track of the first receive descriptor in the circular list.

FA-3(3) The network device driver initializes the pointer **RxBufDescPtrCur**. This pointer keeps track of the current descriptor expected to contain the next received frame.

FA-3(4) The network device driver initializes the pointer **RxBufDescPtrEnd**. This pointer keeps track of the last receive descriptor in the circular list.

FA-3(5) The network device driver allocates a list of descriptors by configuring each descriptor's **next** field with the address that points to the next descriptor in the circular list. The last descriptor's **next** field points back to the start of the circular list. At the same time, the network device driver configures each descriptor's **p_buf** field with the address that points to the start of the receive data buffer.

FA-3(6) The **EDMAC_EDMR** (EDMAC Mode Register) is a read/write user register that specifies the operating mode of the Ethernet DMA Controller. It controls many of the high level features of the EDMAC on the RX62N, including among others enabling and disabling the EDMAC and the Receive Descriptor Length.

FA-3(7) The **ETHERC_ECMR** (ETHERC Mode Register) is a read/write user register that configures the operating mode of the Ethernet Controller, including the Enable and Disable bit for the Reception process (**RE**).

FA-3(8) The **ETHERC_ECSR** (ETHERC Status Register) is a read/write register that indicates the status of the Ethernet Controller. Each state can be notified to the CPU by interrupts. When 1 is written to the **PSRTO**, **LCHNG**, **MPD**, and **ICD** bits, the corresponding flags can be cleared. Writing 0 does not affect the flags. For bits that generate interrupts, the interrupt can be enabled or disabled by the corresponding bit in the ETHERC interrupt permission register (**ETHERC_ECSIPR**). The interrupts generated due to **ETHERC_ECSR** are indicated in the ETHERC status register source bit (**ECI**) in ETHERC/EDMAC status register (**EDMAC_EESR**). At initialization, the driver needs to clear any pending interrupts.

FA-3(9) The **ETHERC_ECSIPR** (ETHERC Interrupt Permission Register) enables or disables the interrupt sources indicated by **ETHERC_ECSR**. Each bit can disable or enable interrupts corresponding to the bits in **ETHERC_ECSR**. Prior to operation and during initialization, all device interrupts should be disabled.

FA-3(10) The **ETHERC_RFLR** (ETHERC Receive Frame Length Register) specifies the maximum frame length (in bytes) that can be received by the RX62N.

FA-3(11) The **EDMAC_RDLAR** (EDMAC Receive Descriptor List Start Address Register) is a read/write register that specifies the start address of the receive descriptor list.

FA-3(12) The **EDMAC_FDR** (EDMAC FIFO Depth Register) is a read/write register that specifies the sizes of the transmit and receive FIFOs. In the case of the Reception process, the **RFD** bits specify the size of the Receive FIFO in a range between 256 and 2048 bytes

FA-3(13) The **EDMAC_EESIPR** (EDMAC/ETHERC Status Interrupt Permission Register) is a read/write register that enables interrupts corresponding to individual bits in the **EDMAC_EESR** register. An interrupt is enabled by writing 1 to the corresponding bit.

FA-3(14) The **EDMAC_EDRRR** (EDMAC Receive Request Register) is a read/write register that issues receive directives to the EDMAC. After writing 1 to the **RR** bit in this register, the EDMAC reads the receive descriptor. If the receive descriptor active bit is set to 1 (active), the EDMAC becomes ready for a receive request from the ETHERC. After data has been received for the receive buffer size, the EDMAC reads the next receive descriptor and becomes ready for frame reception. If the receive descriptor active bit of that receive descriptor is set to 0 (inactive), the EDMAC clears the **RR** bit and stops receive DMAC operation.

FA-3(15) The **EDMAC_EESR** (EDMAC/ETHERC Status Register) is a read/write register that shows communications status on the EDMAC and the ETHERC. The information in **EDMAC_EESR** register is reported in the form of interrupt sources. Individual bits are cleared by writing 1 (however, the **ECI** bit is a read-only bit that is not cleared by writing 1) and are not affected by writing 0. Each interrupt source can be masked by means of the corresponding bit in the ETHERC/EDMAC status interrupt permission register (**EDMAC_EESIPR**). Prior to operation and during initialization all pending interrupts should be cleared by the driver. After initialization and during normal operation the EDMAC generates a Frame Reception Interrupt (**FR**) that indicates that a frame has been received and the receive descriptor has been updated. The **FR** bit is set to 1 each time a frame is received. Writing a 1 to either field clears the interrupt. With each new received frame, the network device driver increments **RxBufDescPtrCur** by 1 and wraps around the descriptor list as necessary. When a frame is received, the EDMAC will generate a **FR** interrupt. The ISR handler must signal the network interface and the network interface will automatically call the receive function.

See section 14-9-1 “Reception with DMA” on page 327 for more details.

DMA-BASED TRANSMISSION PROCESS

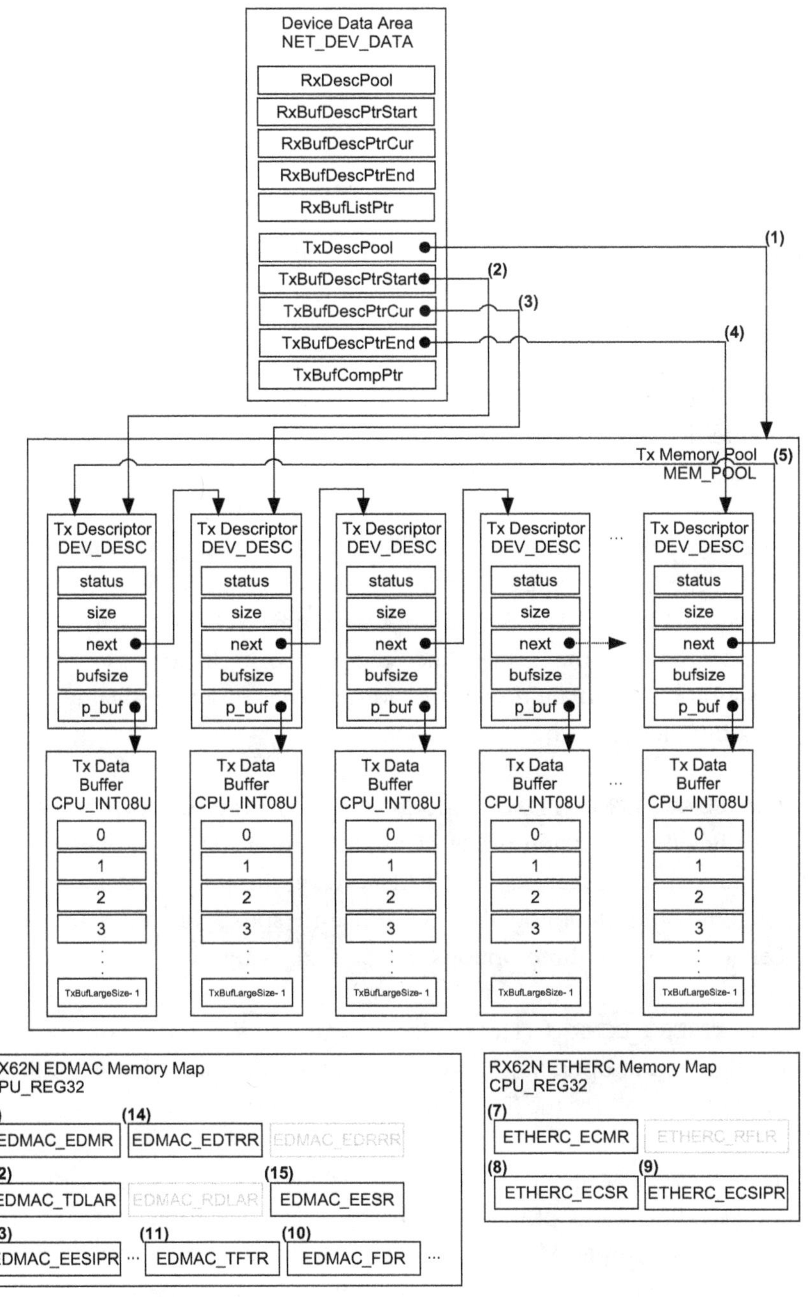

Figure A-4 **DMA-based Transmission Process**

FA-4(1) The network device driver allocates a memory pool for all transmit descriptors and transmit data buffers based on the Network Device Driver configuration. For example, the number of transmit DMA descriptors and the number of transmit data buffers.

FA-4(2) The network device driver initializes the pointer **TxBufDescPtrStart**. This pointer keeps track of the first transmit descriptor in the list.

FA-4(3) The network device driver initializes the pointer **TxBufDescPtrCur**. This pointer keeps track of the current descriptor expected to contain the next buffer to transmit.

FA-4(4) The network device driver initializes the pointer **TxBufDescPtrEnd**. This pointer may point to the last transmit descriptor in the list or it can also point to the last descriptor to transmit.

FA-4(5) The network device driver allocates a list of transmit descriptors by configuring each descriptor's **next** field with the address that points to the next descriptor in the circular list. The last descriptor's **next** field points back to the start of the circular list. At the same time, the network device driver configures each descriptor's **p_buf** field with the address that points to the start of the transmit data buffer.

FA-4(6) The **EDMAC_EDMR** (EDMAC Mode Register) is a read/write user register that specifies the operating mode of the Ethernet DMA Controller. It controls many of the high level features of the EDMAC on the RX62N, including among others enabling and disabling the EDMAC and specifying the Transmit Descriptor Length in one of three options: 16, 32 and 64 bytes.

FA-4(7) The **ETHERC_ECMR** (ETHERC Mode Register) is a read/write user register that configures the operating mode of the Ethernet Controller, including the Enable and Disable bit for the Transmission process (**TE**).

FA-4(8) The **ETHERC_ECSR** (ETHERC Status Register) is a read/write register that indicates the status of the Ethernet Controller. Each state can be notified to the CPU by interrupts. When 1 is written to the **PSRTO**, **LCHNG**, **MPD**, and **ICD** bits, the corresponding flags can be cleared. Writing 0 does not affect the flags. For bits that generate interrupts, the interrupt can be enabled or disabled by the corresponding bit in the ETHERC interrupt permission register

(**ETHERC_ECSIPR**). The interrupts generated due to **ETHERC_ECSR** are indicated in the ETHERC status register source bit (**ECI**) in ETHERC/EDMAC status register (**EDMAC_EESR**). At initialization, the driver needs to clear any pending interrupts.

FA-4(9) The **ETHERC_ECSIPR** (ETHERC Interrupt Permission Register) enables or disables the interrupt sources indicated by **ETHERC_ECSR**. Each bit can disable or enable interrupts corresponding to the bits in **ETHERC_ECSR**. Prior to operation and during initialization, all device interrupts should be disabled.

FA-4(10) The **EDMAC_FDR** (EDMAC FIFO Depth Register) is a read/write register that specifies the sizes of the transmit and receive FIFOs. In the case of the Transmission process, the **TFD** bits specify the size of the Transmit FIFO in a range between 256 and 2048 bytes.

FA-4(11) The **EDMAC_TFTR** (EDMAC Transmit FIFO Threshold Register) is a read/write register that specifies the transmit FIFO threshold at which the first transmission is started. The actual threshold is four times the set value. The ETHERC starts transmission when the amount of data in the transmit FIFO exceeds the number of bytes specified in **EDMAC_TFTR**, when the transmit FIFO is full, or when one frame of data write is performed. The transmit FIFO threshold must be set to a value smaller than the FIFO size specified by the FIFO depth register **EDMAC_FDR.**

FA-4(12) The **EDMAC_TDLAR** (EDMAC Transmit Descriptor List Start Address Register) is a read/write register that specifies the start address of the transmit descriptor list.

FA-4(13) The **EDMAC_EESIPR** (EDMAC/ETHERC Status Interrupt Permission Register) is a read/write register that enables interrupts corresponding to individual bits in the **EDMAC_EESR** register. An interrupt is enabled by writing 1 to the corresponding bit.

FA-4(14) The **EDMAC_EDTRR** (EDMAC Transmit Request Register) is a read/write register that issues transmit directives to the EDMAC. After having transmitted one frame, the EDMAC reads the next descriptor. If the transmit descriptor active bit in this descriptor is set (active), the EDMAC continues transmission. Otherwise, the EDMAC clears the **TR** bit and stops the transmit DMAC operation.

FA-4(15) The **EDMAC_EESR** (EDMAC/ETHERC Status Register) is a read/write register that shows communications status on the EDMAC and the ETHERC. The information in **EDMAC_EESR** register is reported in the form of interrupt sources. Individual bits are cleared by writing 1 (however, the **ECI** bit is a read-only bit that is not cleared by writing 1) and are not affected by writing 0. Each interrupt source can be masked by means of the corresponding bit in the ETHERC/EDMAC status interrupt permission register (**EDMAC_EESIPR**). Prior to operation and during initialization all pending interrupts should be cleared by the driver. After initialization and during normal operation, the EDMAC generates a Frame Transmit Complete Interrupt (**TC**) that indicates that all the data specified by the transmit descriptor has been transmitted from the ETHERC. The **TC** bit is set to 1, assuming the completion of transmission, when transmission of one frame is completed in single-frame/single-buffer operation or when the last data of a frame has been transmitted and the transmit descriptor active bit (**TD0.TACT**) of the next descriptor is not set in multi-buffer frame processing. After frame transmission, the EDMAC writes the transmission status back to the relevant descriptor. Writing a 1 to either field clears the interrupt. When the ISR handler receives a **TC** interrupt after the transmission completion, a list of descriptors for the completed transmit buffers is determined. Each completed transmit buffer address is passed to the Network Transmit De-allocation Task, where the correspondent buffer gets released if it is not referenced by any other part of the Network stack. The Network interface is also signaled for each one of the completed transmit buffers to allow the Network stack to continue transmission of subsequent packets. To complete the operation, the transmit descriptors are cleared to make room for subsequent transmissions.

See section 14-9-2 “Transmission with DMA” on page 331 for more details.

The following section describes in detail all the API functions that support the initialization of the DMA engine, allocation and initialization of the Device Data Area and Descriptors, ISRs and functions to interface with the PHY.

A-5 API

All device drivers contain an API structure named in accordance to the following rule: **NetDev_API_<controller>**, where controller represents the name of the device being abstracted by the driver, for example **NetDev_API_RX_EtherC**.

Device driver API structures are used by the application during the call to **NetIF_Add()**. This API structure allows higher layers to call specific device driver functions via function pointer instead of by name. This enables the network protocol suite to compile and operate with multiple device drivers.

Device driver function names may be arbitrarily chosen. However, it is recommended that device functions be named using the names provided below. All driver function prototypes should be located within the driver C source file (**net_dev_rx_etherc.c**) and be declared as static functions to prevent name clashes with other network protocol suite device drivers.

In most cases, the API structure provided below should suffice for most device drivers exactly as is, with the exception that the API structure's name *must* be unique and clearly identify the device being implemented. The API structure is also externally declared in the device driver header file (**net_dev_rx_etherc.h**) with the exact same name and type.

```
const  NET_DEV_API_ETHER  NetDev_API_RX_EtherC = { NetDev_Init,
                                                    NetDev_Start,
                                                    NetDev_Stop,
                                                    NetDev_Rx,
                                                    NetDev_Tx,
#if  (NET_VERSION >= 20600u)
                                                    NetDev_AddrMulticastAdd,
                                                    NetDev_AddrMulticastRemove,
#endif
                                                    NetDev_ISR_Handler,
                                                    NetDev_IO_Ctrl,

#if ((NET_VERSION <  20600u) && \
     (NET_VERSION >= 205u))
                                                    NetDev_AddrMulticastAdd,
                                                    NetDev_AddrMulticastRemove,
#endif
                                                    NetDev_MII_Rd,
                                                    NetDev_MII_Wr
                                                 };
```

Listing A-4 **RX62N Ethernet interface API**

It is the device driver developer's responsibility to ensure that all of the functions listed within the API are properly implemented, and that the order of the functions within the API structure is correct.

Device driver API function names are not unique amongst Micrium drivers. Name clashes between device drivers are avoided by never globally prototyping device driver functions and ensuring that all references to functions within the driver are obtained by pointers within the API structure. The developer may arbitrarily name the functions within the source file so long as the API structure is properly declared. The user application should never need to call API functions by name. Unless special care is taken, calling device driver functions by name may lead to unpredictable results due to reentrancy.

All functions that require device register access must obtain reference to the device hardware register space *prior* to attempting to access any registers. Register definitions should not be absolute and should use the provided base address within the device configuration structure, and the device register definition structure, to properly resolve register addresses during run-time.

DMA-based ethernet drivers such as the driver for the RX62N require three additional functions for initializing Rx and Tx descriptors, and for incrementing a pointer to the current Rx descriptor.

The functions common to DMA-based drivers are:

- `NetDev_RxDescInit()`
- `NetDev_RxDescPtrCurInc()`
- `NetDev_TxDescInit()`
- `NetDev_RxDescFreeAll()`

The API structure shown in Listing A-4 is defined in **`net_dev_rx_etherc.c`** and the following sections describe the API functions.

A-6 NetDev_Init()

The function `NetDev_Init()` is defined in `net_dev_rx_etherc.c`. The function initializes the Network Driver Layer and its prototype is shown below:

```
static  void  NetDev_Init (NET_IF   *pif,
                           NET_ERR  *perr)
{
                           /* Initializes the required clock sources.                    */
                           /* Initializes the external interrupt controller.             */
                           /* Initializes the external GPIO controller.                  */
                           /* Initializes the driver state variables.                    */
                           /* Allocates memory for device DMA descriptors.               */
                           /* Initializes the additional device registers in modes:      */
                           /* (R)MII mode / PHY bus type.                                */
                           /* Disables device interrupts.                                */
                           /* Disables device receiver and transmitter.                  */
                           /* Any other necessary device initialization.                 */
}
```

The arguments are:

- `pif`: Pointer to the interface requiring service.
- `perr`: Pointer to return error code.

A-7 NetDev_Start()

The function `NetDev_Start()` is defined in `net_dev_rx_etherc.c`. The function starts network interface hardware and its prototype is shown below:

```
static  void  NetDev_Start (NET_IF   *pif,
                            NET_ERR  *perr)
{
                            /* Initializes the transmit semaphore count.             */
                            /* Initializes the hardware address registers.           */
                            /* Initializes the receive and transmit descriptors.     */
                            /* Clears all pending interrupt sources.                 */
                            /* Enables the supported interrupts.                     */
                            /* Enables the transmitter and receiver.                 */
                            /* Starts / Enables DMA.                                 */
}
```

The arguments are:

- `pif`: Pointer to the interface requiring service.
- `perr`: Pointer to return error code.

A-8 NetDev_Stop()

The function **NetDev_Stop()** is defined in **net_dev_rx_etherc.c**. The function shuts down the network interface hardware and its prototype is shown below:

```
static  void  NetDev_Stop (NET_IF   *pif,
                           NET_ERR  *perr)
{
                           /* Disables the receiver and transmitter.                  */
                           /* Disables receive and transmit interrupts.               */
                           /* Clears pending interrupt requests.                      */
                           /* Flushes FIFOs, if applicable.                           */
                           /* Frees all receive descriptors (Returns ownership to hw). */
                           /* Deallocates all transmit buffers.                       */
}
```

The arguments are:

- **pif**: Pointer to the interface requiring service.
- **perr**: Pointer to return error code.

A-9 NetDev_Rx()

The function **NetDev_Rx()** is defined in **net_dev_rx_etherc.c**. The function returns a pointer to the received data to the caller:

```
static  void  NetDev_Rx (NET_IF       *pif,
                         CPU_INT08U  **p_data,
                         CPU_INT16U   *size,
                         NET_ERR      *perr)
{
                         /* Determine which receive descriptor caused the interrupt.     */
                         /* Obtain pointer in data area to replace existing data area.   */
                         /* Reconfigure descriptor with pointer to new data area.        */
                         /* Set return values. Pointer to received data area and size.   */
                         /* Update current receive descriptor pointer.                   */
                         /* Increment counters.                                          */
}
```

The arguments are:

- **pif**: Pointer to the interface requiring service.
- **p_data**: Pointer to pointer to received DMA data area. The received data area address should be returned to the stack by dereferencing p_data as *p_data = (address of receive data area).
- **size**: Pointer to size. The number of bytes received should be returned to the stack by dereferencing size as *size = (number of bytes).
- **perr**: Pointer to return error code.

A-10 NetDev_Tx()

The function `NetDev_Tx()` is defined in `net_dev_rx_etherc.c`. The function transmits the specified data and its prototype is shown below:

```
static  void  NetDev_Tx (NET_IF        *pif,
                         CPU_INT08U  **p_data,
                         CPU_INT16U   *size,
                         NET_ERR      *perr)
{
                         /* Check if the transmitter is ready.                          */
                         /* Configure the next transmit descriptor for pointer to data  */
                         /* and data size.                                              */
                         /* Issue the transmit command.                                 */
                         /* Increment pointer to next transmit descriptor.              */
}
```

The arguments are:

- **`pif`**: Pointer to the interface requiring service.
- **`p_data`**: Pointer to pointer to transmitted DMA data area. The transmitted data area address should be returned to the stack by dereferencing p_data as *p_data = (address of transmit data area).
- **`size`**: Pointer to size. The number of bytes transmitted should be returned to the stack by dereferencing size as *size = (number of bytes).
- **`perr`**: Pointer to return error code.

A-11 NetDev_RxDescFreeAll()

The function NetDev_RxDescFreeAll() is defined in net_dev_rx_etherc.c. The function returns the descriptor memory block and descriptor data area memory blocks back to their respective memory pools and its prototype is shown below:

```
static  void  NetDev_RxDescFreeAll (NET_IF    *pif,
                                    NET_ERR   *perr)
{
                                    /* Free Rx descriptor data areas.                 */
                                    /* Return data area to Rx data area pool.         */
                                    /* Free Rx descriptor memory block.               */
                                    /* Free Rx descriptor block to Rx descriptor pool. */
}
```

The arguments are:

- pif: Pointer to the interface requiring service.
- perr: Pointer to return error code.

A-12 NetDev_RxDescInit()

The function `NetDev_RxDescInit()` is defined in `net_dev_rx_etherc.c`. The function initializes the Rx descriptor list for the specified interface and its prototype is shown below:

```
static  void  NetDev_RxDescInit (NET_IF    *pif,
                                 NET_ERR   *perr)
{
                                 /* Obtain reference to the Rx descriptor(s) memory block.*/
                                 /* Initialize Rx descriptor pointers.                    */
                                 /* Obtain Rx descriptor data areas.                      */
                                 /* Initialize hardware registers by configuring the DMA  */
                                 /* engine with the Rx descriptor start address, by       */
                                 /* setting the maximum receive buffer size and by        */
                                 /* configuring the DMA descriptor ring start address.    */
}
```

The arguments are:

- `pif`: Pointer to the interface requiring service.
- `perr`: Pointer to return error code.

Memory allocation for the descriptors and receive buffers *must* be performed *before* calling this function. This ensures that multiple calls to this function do *not* allocate additional memory to the interface and that the Rx descriptors may be safely re-initialized by calling this function.

A-13 NetDev_RxDescPtrCurInc()

The function **NetDev_RxDescPtrCurInc()** is defined in **net_dev_rx_etherc.c**. The function increments the current descriptor pointer to the next receive descriptor and its prototype is shown below:

```
static  void  NetDev_RxDescPtrCurInc (NET_IF *pif)
{
                              /* Return ownership of current descriptor back to DMA.        */
                              /* Point to the next descriptor.                               */
}
```

The only argument is:

- **pif**: Pointer to the interface requiring service.

A-14 NetDev_TxDescInit()

The function **NetDev_TxDescInit()** is defined in **net_dev_rx_etherc.c**. The function initializes the Tx descriptor list for the specified interface and its prototype is shown below:

```
static  void  NetDev_TxDescInit (NET_IF   *pif,
                                 NET_ERR  *perr)
{
                                 /* Obtain reference to the Tx descriptor(s) memory block. */
                                 /* Initialize Tx descriptor pointers.                      */
                                 /* Obtain Tx descriptor data areas.                        */
                                 /* Initialize hardware registers.                          */
}
```

The arguments are:

- **pif**: Pointer to the interface requiring service.
- **perr**: Pointer to return error code.

A-15 NetDev_ISR_Handler()

As we previously discussed in section A-4-2 "DMA" on page 1001, the DMA engine is responsible for updating the Tx and Rx Buffer Descriptors every time a frame has been transmitted or received.

In the case of receptions, the EDMAC generates a Frame Reception Interrupt (**FR**) that indicates that a frame has been received and the receive descriptor has been updated. The **FR** bit is set to 1 each time a frame is received.

In the case of transmissions, the EDMAC generates a Frame Transmit Complete Interrupt (**TC**) that indicates that all the data specified by the transmit descriptor has been transmitted from the ETHERC. The **TC** bit is set to 1, assuming the completion of transmission, when transmission of one frame is completed in single-frame/single-buffer operation or when the last data of a frame has been transmitted and the transmit descriptor active bit (**TD0.TACT**) of the next descriptor is not set in multi-buffer frame processing. After frame transmission, the EDMAC writes the transmission status back to the relevant descriptor.

The function **NetDev_ISR_Handler()** handles such interrupts. The function is defined in **net_dev_rx_etherc.c** and its prototype is shown below:

```
static  void  NetDev_ISR_Handler (NET_IF            *pif,
                                  NET_DEV_ISR_TYPE   type)
{
                                  /* Handle Reception Interrupts.                     */
    if (EDMAC_EESR[FR]) {
                                  /* Signal the network interface (IF) receive task of a */
                                  /* received packet.                                 */
                                  /* Clear the interrupt.                             */
    }

                                  /* Handle Transmission Interrupts.                  */
    if (EDMAC_EESR[TC]) {
                                  /* Post each descriptor data area address to the    */
                                  /* transmit deallocation task.                      */
                                  /* Signal the network interface (IF) that the device  */
                                  /* transmit is ready.                               */
                                  /* Point to the next buffer descriptor and wrap around */
                                  /* the end of the descriptors list if necessary.    */
                                  /* Clear the interrupt.                             */
    }
}
```

The arguments are:

- **pif**: Pointer to the interface requiring service.

- **type**: Network Interface defined argument representing the type of ISR in progress. Codes for Rx, Tx, Overrun, Jabber, etc... are defined within net_if.h and are passed into this function by the corresponding Net BSP ISR handler function. The Net BSP ISR handler function may be called by a specific ISR vector and therefore know which ISR type code to pass. Otherwise, the Net BSP may pass NET_DEV_ISR_TYPE_UNKNOWN and the device driver MAY ignore the parameter when the ISR type can be deduced by reading an available interrupt status register.

The **NetDev_ISR_Handler()** function is called by name from the context of an ISR. This ISR handler must service and clear all necessary and enabled interrupt events for the device.

In the case of an interrupt occurring prior to Network Protocol Stack initialization, the device driver should ensure that the interrupt source is cleared in order to prevent the potential for an infinite interrupt loop during system initialization.

Many DMA devices generate only one interrupt event for several ready receive descriptors. In order to accommodate this, it is recommended that all DMA based drivers count the number of ready receive descriptors during the receive event and signal the receive task for ONLY newly received descriptors which have not yet been signaled for during the last receive interrupt event.

Many DMA devices generate only one interrupt event for several transmit complete descriptors. In this case, the driver MUST determine which descriptors have completed transmission and post each descriptor data area address to the transmit deallocation task.

A-16 NetDev_IO_Ctrl()

The `NetDev_IO_Ctrl()` function is defined in `net_dev_rx_etherc.c` and its prototype is shown below:

```
static  void  NetDev_IO_Ctrl (NET_IF       *pif,
                              CPU_INT08U    opt,
                              void         *p_data,
                              NET_ERR      *perr)
{
    .
    .
    .
}
```

The arguments are:

- `pif`: Pointer to the interface requiring service.
- `opt`: Option code representing desired function to perform.
- `data`: Pointer to optional data for either sending or receiving additional function arguments or return data.
- `perr`: Pointer to return error code.

The `NetDev_IO_Ctrl()` function provides a mechanism for the PHY driver to update the MAC link and duplex settings, as well as a method for the application and link state timer to obtain the current link status. Additional user specified driver functionality may be added, if necessary. Micrium provides an IO control function template since most of the code is re-usable.

This function's most important task is to execute the code within the `NET_IF_IO_CTRL_LINK_STATE_UPDATE` switch block. This particular IO control functionality is exercised whenever a link state change is detected either via interrupt or `NetTmr` task polling. Some MACs require software to set registers indicating the current PHY link speed and duplex. This information is used by the MAC to compute critical network access timing.

If link state update functionality is not properly implemented, erratic network behavior will likely result when operating at various combinations of link speed and duplex.

A-17 NetDev_AddrMultiCastAdd()

The **NetDev_AddrMultiCastAdd()** function is defined in **net_dev_rx_etherc.c** and its prototype is shown below:

```
static  void  NetDev_AddrMulticastAdd (NET_IF      *pif,
                                       CPU_INT08U  *paddr_hw,
                                       CPU_INT08U   addr_hw_len,
                                       NET_ERR     *perr)
{
    .
    .
    .
}
```

The arguments are:

- **pif**: Pointer to the interface requiring service.
- **paddr_hw**: Pointer to hardware address.
- **addr_hw_len**: Length of hardware address.
- **perr**: Pointer to return error code.

The **NetDev_AddrMultiCastAdd()** function configures the hardware address filtering to accept a specified hardware address.

The following code snippet may be added to **app.c** after network initialization to generate a call to **NetDev_AddrMulticastAdd()**:

```
NET_ERR      err;
NET_IP_ADDR  ip;
NET_IF_NBR   if_nbr;
…
if_nbr = 1;
ip = NetASCII_Str_to_IP("224.0.0.1", &err);
ip = NET_UTIL_HOST_TO_NET_32(ip);
NetIF_AddrMulticastAdd(if_nbr,
                       (CPU_INT08U *)&ip,
                       (CPU_SIZE_T  )sizeof(ip),
                        NET_PROTOCOL_TYPE_IP_V4,
                       &err);
```

The Ethernet device driver for the Renesas RX62N is capable of the following multicast address filtering techniques:

- Perfect filtering of ONE multicast address.
- Imperfect hash filtering of 64 multicast addresses.
- Promiscuous non-filtering. Disable filtering of all received frames.

This function for the RX62N implements the imperfect hash filtering of 64 multicast addresses mechanism.

A-18 NetDev_AddrMultiCastRemove()

The NetDev_AddrMultiCastRemove() function is defined in net_dev_rx_etherc.c and its prototype is shown below:

```
static  void  NetDev_AddrMulticastRemove (NET_IF       *pif,
                                          CPU_INT08U  *paddr_hw,
                                          CPU_INT08U   addr_hw_len,
                                          NET_ERR     *perr)
{
    .
    .
    .
}
```

The arguments are:

- pif: Pointer to the interface requiring service.
- paddr_hw: Pointer to hardware address.
- addr_hw_len: Length of hardware address.
- perr: Pointer to return error code.

The NetDev_AddrMultiCastRemove() function configures hardware address filtering to reject a specified hardware address. See NetDev_AddrMulticastAdd(). Once NetDev_AddrMulticastAdd() has been verified, the code used to compute the hash may be reproduced for NetDev_AddrMulticastRemove(). The only difference between the functions is that NetDev_AddrMulticastRemove() decrements the hash bit reference counters and clears the hash filter register bits.

A-19 NetDev_MII_Rd()

The `NetDev_MII_Rd()` function is defined in `net_dev_rx_etherc.c` and its prototype is shown below:

```
static  void  NetDev_MII_Rd (NET_IF       *pif,
                             CPU_INT08U    phy_addr,
                             CPU_INT08U    reg_addr,
                             CPU_INT16U   *p_data,
                             NET_ERR      *perr)
{
    .
    .
    .
}
```

The arguments are:

- **pif**: Pointer to the interface requiring service.
- **phy_addr**: (R)MII bus address of the PHY requiring service.
- **reg_addr**: PHY register number to read from.
- **p_data**: Pointer to variable to store returned register data.
- **perr**: Pointer to return error code.

The function **NetDev_MII_Rd()** is called by the PHY layer to configure physical layer device registers. This function may be copied from a template but will require changes to adapt it to your specific MAC device. The only recommendation for this function is to ensure that PHY operations are performed without a time-out and that an error is returned if a time-out occurs. A time-out may be implemented in the form of a simple loop that counts from 0 to **PHY_RD_TO**.

Should a timeout occur, software should return **NET_PHY_ERR_TIMEOUT_REG_RD**, otherwise **NET_PHY_ERR_NONE**.

A-20 NetDev_MII_Wr()

The `NetDev_MII_Wr()` function is defined in `net_dev_rx_etherc.c` and its prototype is shown below:

```
static  void  NetDev_MII_Wr (NET_IF       *pif,
                             CPU_INT08U    phy_addr,
                             CPU_INT08U    reg_addr,
                             CPU_INT16U    data,
                             NET_ERR      *perr)
{
    .
    .
    .
}
```

The arguments are:

- **`pif`**: Pointer to the interface requiring service.
- **`phy_addr`**: (R)MII bus address of the PHY requiring service.
- **`reg_addr`**: PHY register number to write to.
- **`data`**: Data to write to the specified PHY register.
- **`perr`**: Pointer to return error code.

The function `NetDev_MII_Wr()` is called by the PHY layer to configure physical layer device registers. This function may be copied from a template but will require changes to adapt it to your specific MAC device. The only recommendation for this function is to ensure that PHY operations are performed without a time-out and that an error is returned if a time-out occurs. A time-out may be implemented in the form of a simple loop that counts from 0 to `PHY_WR_TO`.

Should a time-out occur, software should return `NET_PHY_ERR_TIMEOUT_REG_WR`, otherwise `NET_PHY_ERR_NONE`.

Appendix

B

µC/OS-III and µC/TCP-IP Licensing Policy

B-1 µC/OS-III AND µC/TCP-IP LICENSING

This book includes µC/OS-III in source form for free short-term evaluation, for educational use or for peaceful research. We provide ALL the source code for your convenience and to help you experience µC/OS-III. The fact that the source is provided does NOT mean that you can use it commercially without paying a licensing fee. Knowledge of the source code may NOT be used to develop a similar product either. The book also includes µC/TCP-IP precompiled in linkable object form.

The reader can purchase the Renesas Demonstration Kit YRDKRX62N separately from Renesas and may use µC/OS-III and µC/TCP-IP with the YRDKRX62N. It is not necessary to purchase anything else, as long as the initial purchase is used for educational purposes. Once the code is used to create a commercial project/product for profit, however, it is necessary to purchase a license.

It is necessary to purchase this license when the decision to use µC/OS-III and/or µC/TCP-IP in a design is made, not when the design is ready to go to production.

If you are unsure about whether you need to obtain a license for your application, please contact Micrium and discuss the intended use with a sales representative.

B-2 µC/TCP-IP MAINTENANCE RENEWAL

Licensing µC/TCP-IP provides one year of limited technical support and maintenance and source code updates. Renew the maintenance agreement for continued support and source code updates. Contact sales@Micrium.com for additional information.

B-3 µC/TCP-IP SOURCE CODE UPDATES

If you are under maintenance, you will be automatically emailed when source code updates become available. You can then download your available updates from the Micrium FTP server. If you are no longer under maintenance, or forget your Micrium FTP username or password, please contact sales@Micrium.com.

B-4 µC/TCP-IP SUPPORT

Support is available for licensed customers. Please visit the customer support section in www.Micrium.com. If you are not a current user, please register to create your account. A web form will be offered to you to submit your support question,

Licensed customers can also use the following contact:

CONTACT MICRIUM

Micriµm
1290 Weston Road, Suite 306
Weston, FL 33326

+1 954 217 2036
+1 954 217 2037 (FAX)

E-Mail: sales@Micriµm.com
Website: www.Micriµm.com

Index

Numerics

A

B

C

D

E

O

P

Q

R

S

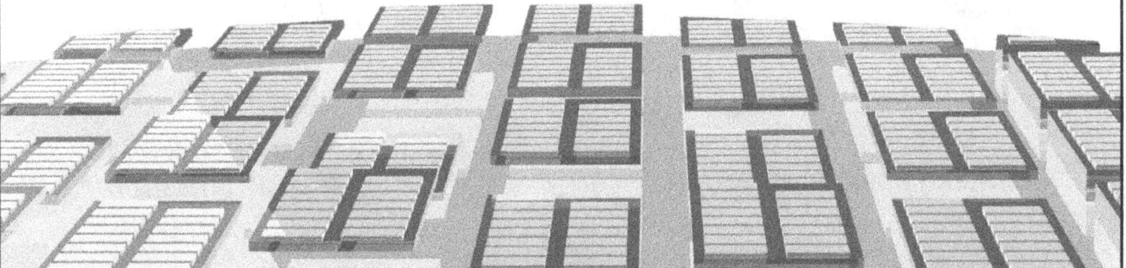

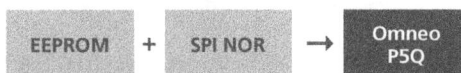

National Semiconductor 10/100 PHYTER®

DP83640

The IEEE 1588 Precision Time Protocol (PTP) is an important improvement to Ethernet systems that provides precise time synchronization for applications such as test and measurement, factory automation, and telecommunications. National Semiconductor's DP83640 Precision PHYTER transceiver is the industry's first to add the IEEE 1588 PTP functionality to a fully-featured, 10/100 Mbps Ethernet PHY.

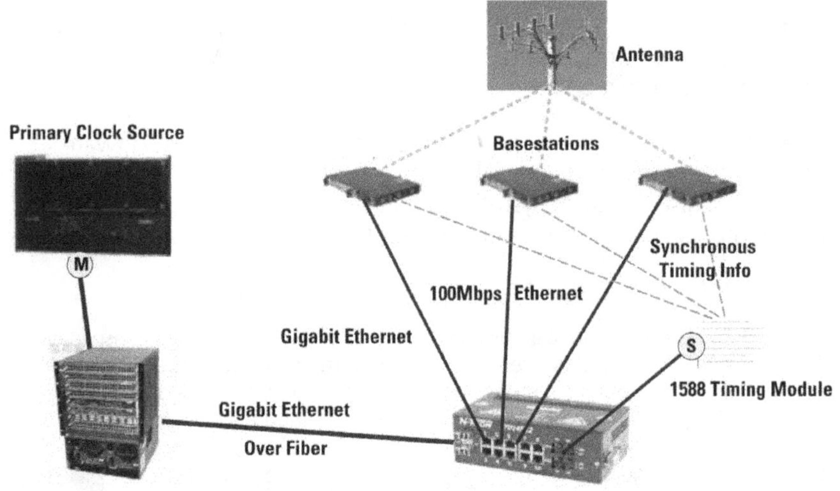

Wireless BTS Timing Sync Using IEEE 1588

High-Speed Industrial Ethernet

Product ID	Temp Range (°C)	Number of Ports	Interface	Typ Power (mW)	Package
DP83640*	-40 to 85	10/100 Single	MII/RMII	280	LQFP-48
DP83848I	-40 to 85	10/100 Single	MII/RMII/SNI	265	LQFP-48
DP83848VYB	-40 to 105	10/100 Single	MII/RMII/SNI	265	LQFP-48
DP83848J	-40 to 85	10/100 Single	MII/RMII	265	LLP-40
DP83849I	-40 to 85	10/100 Dual	MII/RMII	300/Port	TQFP-80

*IEEE 1588

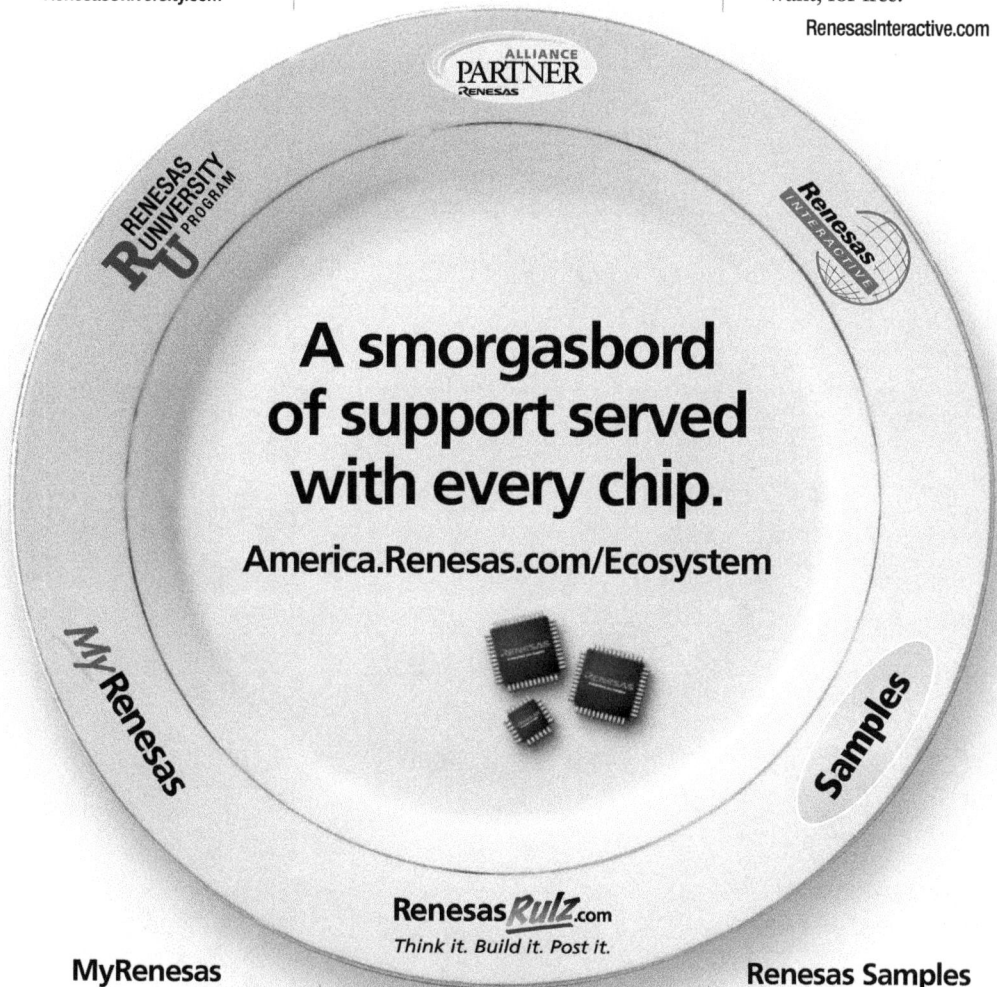

www.ingramcontent.com/pod-product-compliance
Lightning Source LLC
Chambersburg PA
CBHW070151240326
41458CB00126B/3018